Discovering the World of the Bible

Thomas Nelson Publishers
Nashville, Tennessee

Discovering the World of the Bible

LaMar C. Berrett

Published by special arrangement with the original publisher. Copyright © 1973 by Young House.

Library of Congress Catalog Card Number: 79-18338

ISBN: 0-8407-5182-6

Printed in the United States of America

To my wife, Darlene,
our nine children,
and all who love the Bible

Contents

List of Maps and Line Diagrams   8

Preface   9

Acknowledgements   11

How to Use   12

Abbreviations   14

Cyprus   15

Egypt   31

Greece   125

Iraq   163

Israel   205

Italy   379

Jordan   437

Lebanon   463

Syria   485

Turkey   505

Appendix and Index   561

   The Missionary Journeys of the Apostle Paul   562
   Chronological Chart   564
   Glossary of Unusual Terms   570
   Selected Readings   572
   Index   576

Maps and Line Diagrams

Cyprus   17
Nicosia   20
Egypt   33
Cairo   50
Egyptian Museum   56-57
Pyramids of Giza   63
Pyramids between Cairo and Dahshur
    67
Luxor and Karnak   80
Luxor Temple   81
Temenos of Amen, Karnak   82
Necropolis of Thebes   88
Tomb 33: Pentamenopet   91
Funerary Temple of Queen Hatshepsut
    93
Tomb of Tutankhamen   98
Tomb of Seti I   99
Tomb of Amenhotep II   101
Aswan Area   104
Sinai Peninsula   111
Greece   127
Athens   132
Acropolis, Athens   137
Agora, Athens   139
Delphi   142
Olympia   149
Corinth   156
Iraq   165
Baghdad   170
Babylon   188
Ur   198
Division of the Promised Land among
    the Tribes of Ancient Israel   206
Modern Israel   207
Jerusalem: Old City   220
Jerusalem: East of the Old City   238
Hezekiah's Tunnel (Photographed
    Map)   247

Jerusalem: South, West and North of
    the Old City   250
New Jerusalem   262
Israel: East of the Mount of Olives
    270
Israel: North from Jerusalem to
    Nablus   280
Israel: North from Nablus to the Sea
    of Galilee   290
Israel: Around the Sea of Galilee and
    North   307
Israel: West Coast from Joppa to
    Lebanon   328
Israel: West and Southwest of
    Jerusalem   338
Israel: South of Jerusalem   355
Masada   376
Italy   382
Rome   388
Roman Forum   395
Basilica of Saint Peter   406
Florence   432
Jordan   439
Amman   444
Jerash   448
Petra   459
Lebanon   464
Beirut   468
Baalbek   473
Syria   486
Damascus   488
Turkey   507
Istanbul   510
Ephesus   544
The Missionary Journey of the Apostle
    Paul   562
Chronological Chart   564

Preface

About A.D. 400 the church father Jerome, in the introduction to his commentary on the Book of Chronicles, wrote:

Just as those who have seen Athens understand Greek history better, and just as those who have seen Troy understand the words of the poet Vergil, thus one will comprehend the Holy Scriptures with a clearer understanding who has seen the land of Judah with his own eyes and has come to know the references to the ancient towns and places and their names, both the principal names and those which have changed [Yohanan Aharoni, The Land of the Bible: A Historical Geography *(Philadephia, 1967), p. xii].*

The Bible is the most popular book on the earth; and it is natural for its many readers to become so involved in the recorded sacred events that they wish to walk the paths of the prophets, see where the miracles were performed, and witness the scenes and culture of the biblical lands. People of all faiths desire to become acquainted with the portion of the earth that gave birth to three of the world's great religions: Judaism, Islam, and Christianity. For centuries pilgrims have been attracted to sacred biblical sites, and every day of the year some 2,000 new visitors come to Old Jerusalem, a city sacred to Christians, Moslems, and Jews. Here it is still possible, in the twentieth century, to observe patterns of living that are the same as they were in biblical times.

Although a number of biblical cities and sites have existed for thousands of years, others have long since crumbled, and are difficult to identify with any certainty. Yohanan Aharoni discusses this difficulty briefly:

In the final analysis the most certain identifications are still those dependent upon preservation of the ancient name, albeit with careful examination of written sources and archaeological data. Out of approximately 475 place names mentioned in the Bible only about 262 have been identified with any degree of certainty, i.e. 55 per cent. Of these 190 are based upon preservation of the name, viz. 40 per cent of the over-all total, of which 158 (33.3 per cent) are places still bearing the name, and 32 (6.7 per cent) where the name was found somewhere in the vicinity of the ancient site. Only 72 places (15 per cent of the over-all total) have been identified in situations where the ancient names is not to be found somewhere in the vicinity, of which only about half carry a degree of certainty, the remainder being more or less conjectural [The Land of the Bible, p. 117].

This book is an invitation to help you discover the world of the Bible.

Its contents will be valuable to students, teachers, missionaries, and anyone visiting these lands in person or vicariously through study.

I have noticed that local guides do not always know what the individual visitor wishes to see and may therefore bypass sites which to the tourist may be very significant. Guidebooks similarly cannot be all things to all people. This book is intended to fill some of the gaps.

The inclusion of the ten biblical countries in one book will save the traveler the expense of buying guidebooks in each country and major city. By orienting the reader to the places related to the Bible and including all significant scriptural references, I have endeavored to acquaint him with virtually all the known biblical sites, along with, of course, many points of interest apart from the Bible. I have also discussed the archaelogical documents of interest to students of the Bible.

And if by discovering the world of the Bible the reader develops a greater love of God and rededicates himself to an increased love of his fellowmen, the purpose of this book will be realized.

LaMar C. Berrett, Ed.D.

Acknowledgments

Because so many reference works, personal interviews, and experiences have been incorporated into this book, it would be impractical to give credit to all who have contributed to its contents. I acknowledge and am grateful to all who have studied and written about the world of the Bible. Without their valuable contributions this volume never could have been completed. For further, in-depth study of the countries of Bible lands, the reader is referred to the many interesting works listed under "Selected Readings," page 572.

Thanks also to Carole Wade, designer, and Arnold Logie, editor, who have helped to shape this work into a finished product.

Many of the photographs in this book came from my own collection. But special thanks should be given to several persons who allowed us to use their photos as well: Paul R. Cheesman, Stephen L. Fairbanks, Gustav Jeeninga, Carol Ann Larkin, Daniel H. Ludlow, Keith H. Meservy, H. Donl Peterson, Jerold L. Petty, Lawrence M. Stone, and Don O Thorpe.

Also, we acknowledge the permission of John C. Trever, author of *The Untold Story of Qumran* (Old Tappan, N.J.: Fleming H. Revell Company) to use the photo at the bottom of page 264.

How to Use

Throughout this book, the usual American units of measurement are used, including inches, feet, yards, and miles, accompanied occasionally by the corresponding metric figures. Temperatures are expressed in Fahrenheit degrees.

Both historical and modern sites important to every visitor are discussed in this volume. All cities are listed in a logical sequence of travel to avoid backtracking. Sites within cities are also listed in the same manner, so that the traveler will see the most possible in the time available.

City names in the text employ three type faces: (1) biblical names appear first, in bold capitals; (2) modern names are in bold upper- and lowercase letters; (3) variants, translations, and other explanatory matter are in italics. Hence for a city whose biblical name is *Beeroth*, translated as "wells," and whose modern name is *Bira*, with a variant name *el-Birch*, the head appears this way:

BEEROTH *("wells")*, **Bira,** *el-Birch*

Cities and sites of scriptural significance are followed by the pertinent scriptural references.

Points of interest within a city or things to see at a site—such as statues, paintings, or archaeological artifacts—are in smaller bold capitals in the text. The numbers of sites in the text correspond to the numbers of the same sites on the maps.

Throughout the book, square dots and boxes identify sites or references having to do with the King James Bible: square dot leaders introduce Bible references; square dots mark biblical sites on maps (except for capital cities, which are identified by stars); and square boxes enclose the number of biblical points of interest on maps and diagrams where numbered keys are used. All others use circles, including round dot leaders introducing references from the Apocrypha, the Koran, and such sources as Josephus and other ancient documents. Occasionally, for purposes of comparison, I have included a scripture reference elsewhere than in its appropriate section, preceded by *cf* ("compare").

Scripture references are arranged chronologically in their respective sections.

For greater ease in reading and in quickly extracting data from the text, I have shown even small numbers in figures rather than words where such a practice seems helpful for the reader.

Since most languages of the Middle East employ different characters, names have to be transliterated into English. Consequently, spellings frequently vary. Although they have been kept consistent enough in this volume to avoid confusion, different spellings occasionally have been allowed to remain, orienting the traveler to the similar variation he will encounter on road maps, street signs, and elsewhere. *Qiryat*, for example, could just as well be spelled *Kiryat*; the common Hebrew word *beit* ("house of"), which often begins place names, may also be spelled *bet* or *beth*; the Baldachin in Saint Peter's Basilica is also referred to by the Italian term *Baldacchino*.

For easy reference, a chronological chart, on pages 564–569, helps the student of the Scriptures to place major world empires, events, and people in their proper time periods and relationship to the Bible.

Finally, an index of place names gives the reader immediate access to references concerning any important site.

14

Abbreviations

Old Testament

Gen.	Genesis
Exod.	Exodus
Lev.	Leviticus
Num.	Numbers
Deut.	Deuteronomy
Josh.	Joshua
Judg.	Judges
Ruth	Ruth
1 Sam.	1 Samuel
2 Sam.	2 Samuel
1 Kings	1 Kings
2 Kings	2 Kings
1 Chron.	1 Chronicles
2 Chron.	2 Chronicles
Ezra	Ezra
Neh.	Nehemiah
Esther	Esther
Job	Job
Ps. (pl. Pss.)	Psalms
Prov.	Proverbs
Eccles.	Ecclesiastes
Song of Sol.	Song of Solomon
Isa.	Isaiah
Jer.	Jeremiah
Lam.	Lamentations
Ezek.	Ezekiel
Dan.	Daniel
Hos.	Hosea
Joel	Joel
Amos	Amos
Obad.	Obadiah
Jon.	Jonah
Mic.	Micah
Nah.	Nahum
Hab.	Habakkuk
Zeph.	Zephaniah
Hag.	Haggai
Zech.	Zechariah
Mal.	Malachi

New Testament

Matt.	Matthew
Mark	Mark
Luke	Luke
John	John
Acts	Acts
Rom.	Romans
1 Cor.	1 Corinthians
2 Cor.	2 Corinthians
Gal.	Galatians
Eph.	Ephesians
Phil.	Philippians
Col.	Colossians
1 Thess.	1 Thessalonians
2 Thess.	2 Thessalonians
1 Tim.	1 Timothy
2 Tim.	2 Timothy
Titus	Titus
Philem.	Philemon
Heb.	Hebrews
James	James
1 Pet.	1 Peter
2 Pet.	2 Peter
1 John	1 John
2 John	2 John
3 John	3 John
Jude	Jude
Rev.	Revelation

Apocrypha

1 Esd.	1 Esdras
2 Esd.	2 Esdras
Tob.	Tobit
Jth.	Judith
Rest of Esther	The Rest of Esther
Wisd. of Sol.	The Wisdom of Solomon
Ecclus.	Ecclesiasticus
Bar.	Baruch
Song of Three Children	The Song of the Three Holy Children
Sus.	Susanna
Bel and Dragon	Bel and the Dragon
Pr. of Man	Prayer of Manasses
1 Macc.	1 Maccabees
2 Macc.	2 Maccabees

Miscellaneous

ca.	about, approximately
cf	compare
b.	born
d.	died
esp.	especially

Cyprus

Cyprus, the first country governed by a Christian, is an island in the Mediterranean Sea, 60 miles west of Syria and 60 miles south of Turkey. It is 140 miles long and from 15 to 60 miles wide, with 3,572 square miles of land and 458 miles of coastline. It has been known by many different names, including Kypros, Makaria, Paphos, and Kittim (or Chittim).

HISTORY

Civilization on Cyprus dates from the sixth century B.C., and the island's recorded history goes back to the Egyptian occupation of 1450 B.C. After that, Cyprus was ruled in turn by the Assyrians, Persians, Ptolemies, Romans, Byzantines, English, Templars, Lusignans, and Venetians. In A.D. 1571 the Venetians lost it to the Turks, and for over three centuries the island was a Turkish province. Then in 1879 the British began an occupation that lasted until 1960, when Cyprus became an independent nation. The first president of the new republic was His Beatitude, Archbishop Makarios III.

When Cyprus received her independence, the Turks and Greeks (especially the former) felt they were not getting enough representation in the parliament. Turkey ruled the island long ago and wanted to rule it again. In 1963 war broke out between the Greeks and Turks. There were some skirmishes of ground troops, and planes sent from Turkey bombed Cypriot villages. The United Nations moved in to settle the problem and is still there. There is a "green-line" area where no Greeks are permitted, but the Greeks allow the Turks to move about freely.

- *Kittim (Chittim), the Hebrew name for Cyprus, is referred to in the Old Testament (Gen. 10:4; 1 Chron. 1:7; Isa. 23:1, 12; Jer. 2:10; Ezek. 27:6).*
- *Barnabas was a native of Cyprus (Acts 4:36).*
- *The gospel was carried here by Christians fleeing from Jerusalem after the martyrdom of Stephen (Acts 11:19).*

- *Cypriots preached to the Greeks at Antioch (Acts 11:20).*
- *Paul, Barnabas, and Mark began their first missionary journey here (Acts 13:4).*
- *Barnabas and Mark revisited here (Acts 15:39).*

RELIGION

Early settlers in Cyprus came from the Aegean Islands, bringing with them their relics of worship. Their gods were closely associated with Hellenic culture and mythology. The chief deity was the Paphian goddess Venus, named Aphrodite, goddess of love and beauty.

Christianity was introduced to the island by Christians fleeing from Jerusalem after the martyrdom of Stephen and was propagated there by a visit of Paul, Barnabas, and John Mark in A.D. 45. Greek Orthodox Catholicism has become very powerful in Cyprus. In 1960 about 77 percent of its population were Greeks belonging to the Greek Orthodox church, and 18 percent were Turks of the Moslem faith. The Cyprus church ranks fifth in the world of Greek Orthodoxy—after the Ecumenical Patriarchate of Constantinople and the patriarchates of Alexandria, Antioch, and Jerusalem. At the Council of Nicaea, in A.D. 325, Cyprus was represented with three bishops. The discovery of the remains of Saint Barnabas and a copy of Saint Matthew's gospel in Barnabas's own handwriting so impressed the emperor Zeno that in A.D. 478 he bestowed certain privileges on the archbishop of Cyprus: the archbishop was permitted to sign in red ink, wear a cape of imperial purple, and carry an imperial scepter.

CYPRUS TODAY

The population of Cyprus is between 600,000 and 700,000. The capital city of Nicosia has over 100,000 when the suburbs are included.

From the third millennium B.C. mining on Cyprus has been a part of the economy, and various empires have benefited from the Cyprus mines. The principal minerals mined now are copper, iron pyrites, asbestos, chromite, umber, and gypsum.

Products of special appeal to visitors are handmade lace, curtains and tablecloths, silks, basket work, pottery, and silverware. Sunshine is also considered an important commodity of Cyprus, with bathing, sailing, water-skiing, skin diving, and snow skiing as favorite sports.

Parents choose their children's mates, and a girl must have a dowry. When she marries, her father must provide such items as a house, furniture, and car for the bride and groom. If the family is poor, the girl quits school at age 12 and goes to work to help pay for her dowry. She must be a virgin when she enters marriage, because Mary, the mother of Jesus, was a virgin.

A Cyprus *pound* has 20 *shillings* or 1,000 *mils*.

Cyprus

MEDITERRANEAN SEA

MEDITERRANEAN SEA

Miles
0 5 10 20

Cape Andreas
Apostolos Andreas Monastery
Rizokarpaso
Yialousa
Akanthou
Kantara
Lefkoniko
Salamis
Monastery of Barnabas
Engomi
Alasia
Famagusta
Varosha
Kouklia
Sotira
Ayia Napa
Pergamos
Troulli
Kythrea
Tymbou
Nicosia
Larnaca
Salt Lake
Hala Sultan Tekke
Perivolia
Ayia Anna
Mazotos
Dheftera
Kapedhes
Monastery of Stavrovouni
Lefkara
Khirokitia
Lavia
Kyrenia
St. Hilarion Castle
Kormakiti
Cape Kormakiti
Syrianokhori
Argaki
Pendayia
Evrykhou
Kakopetria
Zoopiyi
Amathus
Platres
Perapedhi
Omodhos
Limassol
Kolossi Castle
Salt Lake
Akrotiri
Xeros
Pedhoulas
Episkopi
Curium
Kykko Monastery
Ayios Nikolaos
Kouklia
Petra tou Romiou
Kinousa
Polis
Droushia
Stroumbi
Ktima
Paphos
Cape Drepanum

CITIES AND SITES

Nicosia, *Ledra*

Nicosia, the capital and largest city of Cyprus, is the only large city inland. It has been the capital since the seventh century A.D., when the coastal towns were devastated by raiders. If the suburbs are included, the population is about 100,000. The main business avenue is Ledra Street.

POINTS OF INTEREST

1. The **OLD CITY WALLS**, 3 miles long, were built by the Venetians in A.D. 1567, when Cyprus was a possession of Venice. Three of the original gates remain: **PAPHOS GATE**, **FAMAGUSTA GATE**, and **KYRENIA GATE**. Old bastions serve now as playgrounds.

2. The **ARMENIAN CHURCH OF THE BLESSED VIRGIN MARY** was built in the fourteenth century in a Gothic style.

3. The **VENETIAN COLUMN**, in the middle of Atatürk Square, is a grey granite shaft about 20 feet high and 2 feet 4 inches in diameter. It is believed to have come from a temple at Salamis. Around its base are the coats of arms of Venetian families, and a lion once crowned its top.

4. The **TEKKE OF THE MEVLEVI DERVISHES**, near the Kyrenia Gate, was built in the seventeenth century as a house of Moslem worship. Called the "Dancing Dervishes" by Europeans, this cult has its present headquarters in Aleppo, Syria. In 1925 Kemal Atatürk suppressed all monastic orders of Turkey on the grounds of their reactionary attitude, and the only order of its kind in Cyprus was closed. The tekke is presently used as a museum for Turkish arts and crafts.

5. The **SELIMIYE MOSQUE**, located within the old city walls, was formerly the Catholic Cathedral of Saint Sophia. It was in this cathedral that kings of Cyprus were crowned. It was built between A.D. 1208 and 1267, in Gothic style, and resembles other medieval cathedrals. When the Turks captured Nicosia in 1570, however, they made the cathedral into a mosque by adding two very high minarets and a mihrab.

6. The **BEDESTAN**, on the south side of the Selimiye Mosque, is a fourteenth-century Gothic church. *Bedestan* is a Turkish word meaning "covered market," and the name goes back to the period of Turkish rule, when the church was used to sell textiles. It is often referred to as the "Church of Saint Nicholas of the English."

7. The **SULTAN'S LIBRARY**, at the east end of the Selimiye Mosque, houses beautifully decorated Arabic books.

8. The **MUSÉE LAPIDAIRE**, 50 yards east of the Sultan's Library, houses medieval tombstones, marble lintels, and carved stones.

9. The **WOMEN'S MARKET**, in the center of the Phaneromeni quarter, is most active on Fridays.

10.   The **BYZANTINE MUSEUM** displays mostly icons, of which it has a great many. It is located southwest of the Women's Market.

11.   The **ARCHBISHOPRIC AND SAINT JOHN'S CHURCH** was used as a monastery during the fifteenth century and is now the seat of the Greek Orthodox archbishop of Cyprus. The old Orthodox church supposedly contained a finger of Saint John the Baptist. Within the precincts of the old Archbishopric are the Cyprus **FOLK ART MUSEUM** and the **NATIONAL STRUGGLE MUSEUM**. The new **ARCHIEPISCOPAL PALACE** was built in 1956–60, in modern Byzantine style.

12.   The **U.S. EMBASSY** is directly north of the Hilton Hotel, within two blocks.

13.   The **PRESIDENTIAL PALACE** is located in a beautifully landscaped hillside area of southwest Nicosia.

14.   The **GOVERNMENT OFFICES** are located between the Presidential Palace and Paphos Gate.

15.   The **GENERAL HOSPITAL** is situated a short distance southwest of the Paphos Gate.

16.   The **CYPRUS MUSEUM** is one of the most interesting places to visit in Nicosia. Archaeological artifacts represent periods from the Neolithic to the Roman. In the first two rooms, vases and tools illustrate the Neolithic and Chalcolithic civilization of Cyprus (5800–2300 B.C.). Other rooms represent later civilizations. Perhaps the most impressive items would include the bronze **STATUE OF EMPEROR SEPTIMIUS SEVERUS** (room 6), the 300 B.C. marble **APHRODITE** from Soli (room 7), the limestone **HEAD FROM ARSOS** and **SLEEPING EROS** from Paphos (room 5), and the **FAIENCE RHYTON OF KITION** (room 9). The new gallery of **FUNERAL TOMBS** and **RELIEFS** shows the ancient burial customs of the Cypriots.

Engomi, *Alasia, Enkomi*

On the north bank of the Pedias River, 5½ miles northwest of Famagusta, 1½ miles southwest of Salamis, and 1 mile southwest of the Monastery of Saint Barnabas, are the ruins of Alasia, near the Greek village of Enkomi. Alasia was the capital city of Cyprus in the second millennium B.C. The ruins cover an area 1 mile square and date from 2700 to 1050 B.C. The city seems to have been destroyed by earthquake and other forces of nature by 1050 B.C. and was thus abandoned.

As early as 1896 the British excavated the area and found a number of tombs containing gold, ivory, and decorated pottery of the Mycenaean period. This was the richest cemetery in Cyprus.

Clay tablets, bronze statuettes, silver articles, stone buildings, and a gigantic town wall with stones that weigh more than sixty tons have been found in this ancient city of 10,000 to 15,000 people. There is also a bronze smelting house, dating back to the fourteenth century B.C.

Interestingly, when members of a family died they were buried, along with their valuables, underneath the floor of their house.

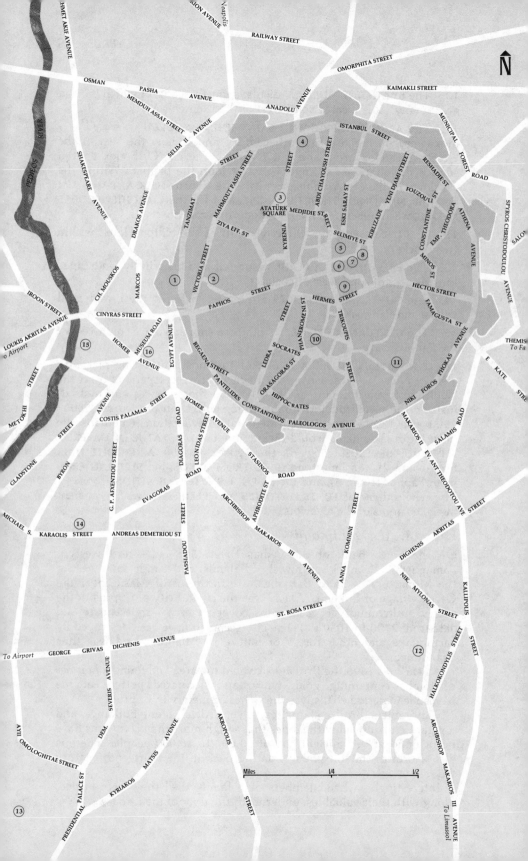

1. Old City Walls
2. Armenian Church of the Blessed Virgin Mary
3. Venetian Column
4. Tekke of the Mevlevi Dervishes
5. Selimiye Mosque
6. Bedestan
7. Sultan's Library
8. Musée Lapidaire
9. Women's Market
10. Byzantine Museum
11. Archbishopric and Saint John's Church
12. U.S. Embassy
13. Presidential Palace
14. Government Offices
15. General Hospital
16. Cyprus Museum

Monastery of the Apostle Barnabas

Since Barnabas was born at Cyprus and established the Church here, he is the patron saint of the island. He is considered the founder of the autocephalous Greek Orthodox church of Cyprus. Situated 1 mile west of Salamis, near Famagusta, the monastery was built at this location because the sepulcher containing Barnabas's remains and a copy of the Gospel of Matthew in Barnabas's own handwriting were found here in A.D. 478.

The clergy at Antioch disputed with the clergy of Cyprus over the question of whether the Cyprian bishopric was independent of the bishopric of Antioch. After the remains of Barnabas were discovered in A.D. 478, however, the emperor Zeno settled it once and for all. This event is illustrated in paintings on the walls of the monastery church. The scenes are as follows: (1) Barnabas appearing in a vision to Anthemios, Archbishop of Cyprus, indicating the resting place of his body; (2) Anthemios finding a chest in the sepulcher under a carob tree, as Barnabas had directed, the chest containing the remains of the apostle and a copy of Saint Matthew's Gospel in Saint Barnabas's own handwriting; (3) Anthemios presenting the gospel written by Saint Barnabas to the Byzantine emperor Zeno in Constantinople; (4) the emperor Zeno conferring the imperial privileges on Anthemios — that the church of Cyprus was independent, that the archbishop could sign in red ink like Byzantine emperors, and that he could wear a cape of imperial purple and carry an imperial scepter.

On the site marked by the monastery, Barnabas is supposed to have been stoned to death during Nero's reign. It is said that when John Mark heard that Barnabas's body was to be thrown into the sea he stole it, hid it in a cave, and buried it. The traditional burial place of Barnabas is about 100 yards east of the present monastery, near some eucalyptus trees. Holy water in the sepulcher is used by the faithful to treat skin diseases. The sepulcher is covered by a new mausoleum, built in A.D. 1953.

The monastery is kept alive by three monks who are blood brothers — Barnabas, Chariton, and Stephanos. Although their ages in 1971 were 74, 84, and 77 respectively, they are still excellent icon painters. Their father was a priest here also.

- *Joses, surnamed Barnabas, was from Cyprus (Acts 4:36).*
- *Paul and Barnabas brought relief money to Jerusalem from Antioch (Acts 11:27–30).*
- *Paul took Barnabas as his companion on his first missionary journey (Acts 13:2–3).*
- *Barnabas was called "Jupiter" (Acts 14:12).*
- *Paul and Barnabas preached in Antioch three years (Acts 15:30–40).*
- *Barnabas and Mark were missionary companions in Cyprus (Acts 15:39).*
- *Paul and Barnabas went up to Jerusalem (Gal. 2:1).*

SALAMIS, *Constantia, Kebres*

Salamis, the ancient capital of Cyprus, is about 6 miles north of the present city of Famagusta. It originally covered 2 square miles and is supposed to have been the birthplace of the apostle Barnabas. According to tradition, it was founded about 1185 B.C. by Teucer, a hero of the Trojan War, who named it after his homeland, the island of Salamis, off Piraeus, Greece.

Salamis was one of about ten city-states in Cyprus, each with its own king, and during the Hellenic and Roman periods it was the most populous and flourishing city on the island. It was famous for its copper mines, fruit, flax, wine, and honey.

The first king of Salamis in historical times was Evelthon (560–525 B.C.). A little over a century later, the city — and the whole isle — reached what is known as its golden era, during the reign of King Evagorus (410–374 B.C.). Evagorus supported commerce, letters, arts, and fleets. He encouraged many distinguished Athenians to immigrate to Salamis, including Polycrates, who established a school for rhetoric.

Salamis also had its times of trouble, however. Tradition indicates that Barnabas, allegedly a native of the city, was stoned to death here. Toward the end of Trajan's reign (A.D. 116), the Jews in Cyprus rose up in revolt and massacred 240,000 Greeks and Romans, whereupon Hadrian crushed the uprising with the utmost severity. This slaughter almost depopulated Salamis, and its destruction was afterward consummated by earthquakes in A.D. 332 and 342. For several centuries no Jew could enter the island; however, during the twentieth-century Zionist movement, Cyprus played an important role as a temporary stopping place for returning Jews.

After the earthquake destruction, the emperor Flavius Julius Constantius (A.D. 337–361), a son of Constantine the Great, rebuilt Salamis and named it Constantia. It became the metropolitan seat of the island. The city was sacked and burned in A.D. 647 by the invading Arabs, and it never again regained prominence. Its stones were transported to nearby Famagusta for construction. Salamis's fine harbor is now filled with silt, and much of the city is still unexcavated.

POINTS OF INTEREST

Many monuments have been uncovered, including the following:

The **GYMNASIUM**, or "Marble Forum," with its marble floors and columns, is perhaps the most important and beautiful monument in Salamis.

TWO ROMAN FORUMS have been excavated. The **STONE FORUM** is considered by archaeologists to be the greatest forum in the Roman Empire. It measures 700 by 200 feet. The **GRANITE FORUM** has columns of granite that were brought all the way from the Aswan quarries in upper Egypt.

The **BASILICA OF SAINT EPIPHANIUS** was built in A.D. 345.

The **ROMAN BATHS** are typical.

A **WATER TANK** stored water brought 35 miles by aqueduct from Kythrea. The water system could supply 120,000 people.

A **ROMAN THEATER** (second or third century B.C.) was excavated in 1960. Until then it had been covered with sand, debris, and shrubs. Only 18 of the original 50 tiers of seats remain. It held 20,000 spectators. On special occasions, theatrical groups present classical and Shakespearean plays at this theater.

■ *In the year A.D. 45, Barnabas and Saul, accompanied by John Mark, left Antioch in Syria on their first missionary journey and landed at Salamis. Here they preached in the synagogues (Acts 13:1-5).*

■ *They soon passed on through the whole island (Acts 13:6).*

■ *Paul did not return to Salamis, but Barnabas doubtless came here on his second missionary journey (Acts 15:39).*

Famagusta, *Mayosa, Ammochostos*

This ancient town, 40 miles from Nicosia, on the eastern seacoast of Cyprus, has 6,000 Turkish inhabitants.

As the visitor approaches Famagusta from the north, he will see what appear to be concentration camps with barbed wire fences. These camps were used for the Jews who were stopped by the British from entering Palestine after World War II. This was the setting for part of Leon Uris's book *Exodus*.

The real growth of Famagusta came in A.D. 1291, when Christian refugees (including wealthy merchants) fled here from Acre. It became a fabulously wealthy business center of the Mediterranean. By building 365 churches (according to tradition) perhaps the inhabitants expected to gain God's favor.

In A.D. 1489 the Venetians seized Cyprus and built the defensive walls, bastions, ramparts, and moats that still ring the town. Later, in A.D. 1571, earthquakes and a siege by the Turks against the Venetians left Famagusta desolate. Today the old city inside the walls is the Turkish quarter.

POINTS OF INTEREST

The **CITY WALLS** (A.D. 1489) are 50 feet high and 27 feet thick, with two gates: Sea Gate and Land Gate.

The **TOWER OF OTHELLO** was the citadel of Famagusta and the supposed setting of the original real-life tragedy on which Shakespeare's play *Othello* was based. Here Othello, Desdemona, and Iago become living characters. In fact, Shakespeare's plays are now presented in the Tower of Othello.

The **MOSQUE OF LALA MUSTAFA PASHA** was formerly the Cathedral of Saint Nicholas, a fourteenth-century Gothic church. It is now the principal mosque of the Turks.

The **VENETIAN PALACE** was the Royal Palace of the Lusignans, in which the kings of Cyprus lodged.

The **CHURCH OF SAINT PETER AND SAINT PAUL**, the **GREEK ORTHODOX CHURCH OF AYIOS GEORGHIOS XORINOS**, and the **ARMENIAN CHURCH OF SAINT MARY** all date from the fourteenth century.

Roman water tank, Salamis

Varosha

One mile south of Famagusta, the modern town of Varosha, with its beautiful beach and modern port, offers a striking contrast to old Famagusta. Varosha has a population of 30,000. Its annual Orange Day attracts thousands of visitors, and oranges are distributed gratis to all public restaurants for the visitors.

Larnaca, *Kition, Chittim, Kittim, Citium*

Larnaca is located on the southern coast of Cyprus, 26 miles southeast of Nicosia, and has a population of 20,000. It is built on the site of an ancient city-kingdom known as Kition, Chittim, Kittim, or Citium, and legend says it was founded by Kittim, described in Genesis as Noah's great-grandson. (See Gen. 10:1–5.)

Ancient Citium gave the world one of its most eminent thinkers, Zeno, the founder of the Stoic school of philosophy in Athens. Zeno was born in 331 B.C. The philosophy of the Cynics appealed to him, but between 325 and 300 B.C. he organized a school of his own. He later committed suicide, an act which his philosophy considered acceptable. The school of the Stoics flourished from 300 B.C. to A.D. 200 alongside the Epicureans. The Stoics had many gods, the Epicureans no gods. While the Epicureans sought pleasure to avoid pain, the Stoics felt that pleasure came through facing difficulties so that one could develop self-mastery. During the period of A.D. 100–200, Stoicism was the "philosophy of the masses" and was taught in the schools. Horace, Vergil, Hadrian, Cicero, Seneca, Epictetus, and Marcus Aurelius believed in Stoicism. Although Nero persecuted the Stoics as he did the Christians, when Hadrian became emperor he helped build Stoicism again.

Epictetus, born in A.D. 50, was a great advocate of Stoicism. Feeling that a philosopher was a healer of souls, he stressed morals more than intellect. His main teachings were the *fatherhood of God* and the *brotherhood of man.* He said, "If you do nothing else, do not sell your will cheap." He felt that the earth was created by intelligence, that there was design and unity in the universe, and that men by nature are fitted to share in the society of God because man is the son of God. He defined "freedom" as making one's own will consistent with God's. To Epictetus the role of knowledge was to prepare man to understand the universe and help him to achieve his right end. Self-mastery, he believed, would bring one in harmony with God. It is little wonder that Stoicism and teachers like Epictetus helped to pave the way for the acceptance of Christianity.

POINTS OF INTEREST

The **CHURCH OF SAINT LAZARUS** was built at Larnaca because, according to legend, after Saint Lazarus was raised from the dead by Christ he came to Cyprus and became the first bishop of the See of Citium. He died at Larnaca and was buried in the church named after him. The tomb in which his relics were placed was discovered in A.D. 890. His body was later stolen, but it was miraculously found in the Cathedral of Marseilles and is still preserved in a marble sarcophagus in the church, his second burial place.

The **FORT OF LARNACA** was erected by the Turks in A.D. 1625.

The **PIERIDES PRIVATE MUSEUM** consists of a collection of Cyprus pottery and the marble **BUST OF ZENO**, unveiled in 1921, which stands at the crossroad near the American Academy.

The **AYIA PHANEROMENI CHURCH**, halfway to the Salt Sea, is a rock cavern, where a holy icon is located. Tradition ascribes to the church various magical properties: to be healed, for instance, those who suffer from headache or malaria walk three times around it and leave a fragment of cloth or a piece of hair on the grill.

Besides the fine sandy beaches and palm-lined seafront at Larnaca, there is in the district the **LARNACA SALT LAKE**, 1½ miles southwest of the city. Between 20,000 and 50,000 tons of salt are harvested annually with man and donkey power. There is a legend that Lazarus left Bethany because he was threatened by the Jews (he was a living witness of Christ's powers), and he came to Larnaca. When a stingy old woman would not give him some grapes to eat, he cursed her field and it turned into a salt lake — hence the Salt Lake of Larnaca. Flamingos settle on the lake from December to March, and the lake and surrounding forests are very attractive.

By the Salt Lake is one of the most important monuments of the Islamic world, the **TEKKE** (shrine) **OF HALA SULTAN** (Umm Haram), said to be a foster aunt of the prophet Mohammed. At this spot she fell from her mule and died in A.D. 654 when she was with an Arab raiding expedition. This shrine ranks among the most sacred in the Mohammedan world after Mecca and Medina, and Moslems come here on sacred pilgrimages.

At **KITI**, 4 miles beyond the Salt Lake, is the **CHURCH OF OUR LADY THE ANGEL BUILT**, which houses a precious mosaic dating from the seventh century. The mosaic shows Mary and Jesus standing between Michael and Gabriel.

Monastery of Stavrovouni (*Mountain of the Cross*)

Built on the site of an ancient pagan temple, this monastery is situated on the top of a mountain, 2,260 feet above sea level, 23 miles west of Larnaca. It is said to be the oldest royal monastery in the world, allegedly founded by Saint Helena, mother of Constantine, in A.D. 327, when she stopped at Cyprus on her way back from Jerusalem. She claimed she had found the cross of Jesus and the cross of the penitent thief. According to tradition, she gave part of the holy cross to the monastery; hence its name, Mountain of the Cross. Visitors must be dressed modestly to enter the monastery: lipstick, short sleeves, and short pants are forbidden. The monks produce excellent honey, cheese, and grapes.

Khirokitia

This ancient Neolithic settlement is located approximately 20 miles southwest of Larnaca. Deriving its name from a nearby village, this ancient site dates back to the sixth millennium B.C. Circular houses in the shape of beehives were built with stones, and the remains of the dead were buried in a contracted position under the floors of their dwellings. Artifacts from this site may be seen in the Cyprus Museum at Nicosia.

Amathus

Five miles east of Limassol are the ruins of Old Limassol, named Amathus. It has never been systematically excavated, but many antiquities have been found here. A famous sarcophagus from Amathus is now housed in the Metropolitan Museum in New York City.

Limassol

The chief exporting city and second largest city of the island is Limassol, with a population of 50,000, located 54 miles from Nicosia, on the southern coast. Here the Greeks and Turks live together without the friction that exists in other cities. It is the center of the carob and wine industries of Cyprus. Other products of the area are raisins, citrus, asbestos, chrome, bricks, tiles, and a candy called *Turkish delight,* made from grapes. Limassol has beautiful beaches and many colorful festivals.

Historically, Limassol is known as the wedding site of Richard the Lion-Hearted and the Cypriot girl, Princess Berengaria of Navarre, in A.D. 1191. After the wedding she was crowned queen of England.

Here the Knights Templars and the Knights of Saint John of Jerusalem (Hospitalers) estalished their headquarters after the Arabs overran the Holy Land in A.D. 1291.

Kolossi Castle

During the fifteenth century the Hospitalers (Knights of Saint John of Jerusalem) built a square three-storied tower and castle as a part of a Crusader fortress. The tower is 75 feet high and the walls are 9 feet thick. The castle is 7 miles west of Limassol.

Curium

At Curium, near the village of Episkopi, 10 miles west of Limassol, are the remains of the **TEMPLE OF APOLLO HYLATES** (god of the woodlands), which dates from the seventh century B.C. and was the religious and political center of Curium. There are also ruins of **ROMAN BATHS, MOSAIC FLOORS,** a **THEATER,** and a **STADIUM.** Most of the ruins date back to the Roman period, from the first to the fifth century A.D. The site is very ancient, however, and Herodotus indicated that Curium was founded in 1200 B.C. by Greek immigrants from Argos. Excavators of the site have represented the University of Pennsylvania.

Across from the stadium is a site where, it is said, Christians were thrown over the cliff during the time of Roman persecution.

Petra tou Romiou

A group of white rocks protruding out of the Mediterranean Sea near the highway, 5½ miles east of Ktima, marks one of the traditional sites where Aphrodite (Venus) was supposed to have been born from the foam of the sea. The legend is found in the writings of Homer.

PAPHOS, Kouklia; Ktima, *New Paphos*

Ten miles east of Ktima (New Paphos), on the left bank of the Diarrizo River and about 1 mile from the sea, is the site of ancient Paphos. Today it is named Kouklia, after the nearby village. This is the traditional birthplace of Aphrodite, according to the writings of Homer, and was the chief religious center of Cyprus.

The TEMPLE OF APHRODITE (Venus) was built to overlook another traditional spot where Aphrodite, goddess of love and beauty, was born from the foam of the sea. Worship of Aphrodite seems to have been sensual in character, and pilgrimages were made to this site by people from all over the Greek world. British archaeologists excavated in 1888 and found stones of immense size. At first the ruins were believed to be of the Temple of Aphrodite itself, but it is now believed that the ruins uncovered are a part of the temple annex. They cover an area 400 feet by 230 feet.

Located on the west coast of Cyprus, 99 miles west of Nicosia and 10 miles west of Kouklia, is the city of Ktima, or New Paphos, often called Kato-Paphos (Lower Paphos). Apparently Old Paphos was destroyed by earthquakes toward the end of the twelfth century B.C., and New Paphos was built by King Agapenor of Tegea in Arcadia on his return from the Trojan War (1194–1184 B.C.). New Paphos became the administrative capital of the whole island in Ptolemaic and Roman days (294 B.C. to A.D. 395). After that period, however, Salamis became the capital of Cyprus.

New Paphos was the home of Cicero and Sergius Paulus, and tradition says that Paul's companion Tychicus was murdered here.

The population of the Ktima area is approximately 10,000.

POINTS OF INTEREST

The PAPHOS HARBOR was built in the time of Alexander the Great by Nikokles, the king of Paphos. This is the harbor where Paul the apostle embarked after doing missionary work in Cyprus. Here the Crusaders and pilgrims came on their way to the Holy Land, and here the worshipers of Aphrodite came to worship their goddess. This was the site of the first battle between the Cypriots and the Genoese invaders in the fifteenth century. The present fort at the harbor was built by the Turks in the sixteenth century.

The PAPHOS CASTLE was built in A.D. 1592 by Ahmet Pasha over an old castle destroyed by the Venetians. It is located on the seacoast.

FORTY COLUMNS is a name given to a Byzantine fortress of the port which surrendered to Richard the Lion-Hearted of England in A.D. 1191. It received its name from a number of broken granite pillars protruding from the debris.

SAINT PAUL'S PILLAR, a marble column, stands in an enclosure on the grounds of the thirteenth-century Greek Orthodox Church of Chrysopolitissa (Blessed Virgin Mary of the Golden City). According to tradition, when Paul visited Paphos with Barnabas he was tied to this stone and scourged "forty less one" — "forty less one" referring to a type of whip having thirty-nine strips tied together and not the number of lashes he received.

The **AYIA SOLOMONI CHURCH**, an ancient, rock-hewn, underground church, was dedicated to Saint Solomoni (Hannah), mother of seven children who were tortured to death for their faith in Jehovah during the persecution of the Jews in Palestine by Antiochus Epiphanes in 168 B.C. (2 Macc. 7).

The **ROCK OF DIGHENIS**, a granite column, is connected with a myth concerning Reghaena, queen of Cyprus, who failed to keep her promise to respond to Dighenis, her would-be lover. Dighenis threw a large rock at the queen's palace, and the queen in turn threw her spindle at Dighenis. She missed and the spindle turned into a granite column.

The **TOMBS OF THE KINGS**, the necropolis of New Paphos during the classical and Hellenistic periods (sixth to second century B.C.), lie 1½ miles west of Ktima. They consist of rock-hewn tombs, underground caves, and chambers with pillared courts and Doric capitals, which served as both tombs and hiding places for Christians during persecutions. In the tombs were found many treasures, such as statues and jewelry, some of which are now in the Metropolitan Museum in New York City. Sometimes when a king died, his servants and horses were killed, so that they would be able to help the king after his resurrection.

The **MOSAICS AT KATO-PAPHOS** are some of the most beautiful and well preserved in the ancient world. The scenes portrayed are based on characters from Greek mythology. Some believe this was the villa where the Roman proconsul lived (perhaps Dionysius or Sergius Paulus?).

The **EPISCOPAL PALACE**, with its Byzantine **MUSEUM**, is located in Ktima.

■ *Paul, Mark, and Barnabas visited here after passing through the whole island (approximately A.D. 45) (Acts 13:6).*
■ *Elymas (Bar-Jesus), a sorcerer, was smitten blind (Acts 13:6–11).*
■ *Sergius Paulus, the Roman governor— the first Gentile in the Church?— was converted as a result of the miracle of Elymas's blindness (Acts 13:7, 12). (Cyprus became the first country to be governed by a Christian.)*
■ *Paul sailed from here to Perga in Pamphylia, Asia Minor (Acts 13:13).*
■ *Barnabas and Mark returned to Cyprus, apparently to "visit our brethren in every city where we have preached," which would have included Paphos (Acts 15:36–39).*

Kykko Monastery

There are nineteen monasteries on Cyprus. Eleven are Greek Orthodox, four are Maronite, three are Latin, and one is Armenian.

The Monastery of Kykko is the largest and most famous on Cyprus. Named after the Kokkous trees, it is situated on a mountain 3,800 feet above sea level and 56 miles southwest of Nicosia. It was founded in A.D. 1100 during the reign of Emperor Alexius Comnenus, who donated to the monastery a picture of the Virgin Mary and Child that is believed to have been one of three icons painted by the apostle Luke. It is said that although fire has destroyed the monastery several times the icon has always escaped undamaged. It is now covered by silver plate and none of the original can be seen. This famous icon is important not only because it is believed that Luke was the painter but also because it is a "bringer of rain." Special prayers are given at the monastery to request rain during seasons of drought.

Near the icon are two relics: (1) a bronze arm, believed to be the withered arm of an infidel Negro who tried to light his cigarette at one of the lamps in front of the icon; (2) a "saw" of a swordfish, the gift of a sailor whom the Virgin of Kykko saved from drowning.

For centuries the monastery was very famous. Greek Orthodox pilgrims from all over the world visited it, and thus it became very wealthy.

Kyrenia

A small town of 3,500 people, Kyrenia is located on the Mediterranean Sea 16 miles north of Nicosia. It has a beautiful horseshoe-shaped harbor.

POINTS OF INTEREST

KYRENIA CASTLE, near the city, was built during the Byzantine era and rebuilt by the Lusignans in 1208 and the Venetians in the sixteenth century.

BELLAPAIS ABBEY, with its beautiful Gothic cloisters, is located 3 miles east of Kyrenia on the edge of a 50-foot cliff. It belonged to the Order of the Premontre, founded in A.D. 1120, near Laon, France.

SAINT HILARION CASTLE, overlooking Kyrenia, is a favorite site for visitors.

BUFFAVENTO CASTLE is situated a few miles southeast of Kyrenia. Some 35 miles east of Kyrenia is another castle, KANTARA.

Egypt

Egypt, also named Mizraim (Gen. 10:6, 13; 1 Chron. 1:8, 11), occupies the northeast corner of Africa. Of its 386,000 square miles, 97 percent is arid desert, swamp, or barren mountains. Egypt is 892 miles long and 758 miles wide.

HISTORY

From the dawn of prehistoric times the Nile River valley has been settled by man. Historical man in Egypt dates back to approximately 3200 B.C. When one compares the history of this 5,000-year-old civilization with the 200-year history of the United States of America, one begins to see a new concept of time.

The world's first "united nation" was formed when upper and lower Egypt became one in 3100 B.C. and formed the first of thirty dynasties of pharaohs. For 2,000 years Egypt enjoyed a magnificent civilization. A united government, a 365-day year, a system of writing for keeping records, a method of calculating, a firm belief in life after death, medical science, the science of astronomy, material wealth, sea trade, and knowledge of art and architecture were a part of the Egyptian genius that was to inspire the Greek, Roman, and western civilizations thereafter.

For 2,000 years the secrets of the Egyptians were hidden in the unreadable hieroglyphs. Only since the nineteenth century and the discovery and deciphering of the Rosetta Stone has man been able to understand the written records of this ancient civilization.

During the Eighteenth Dynasty (1567–1320 B.C.), under the rule of Thutmose III, Egypt expanded her borders to the Euphrates River and reached the zenith of her powerful years. But after Pharaoh Amenhotep IV, who changed his name to Akhenaten (Ikhnaton), Egypt was never the same. Following the reign of Ramses III (1195–1164 B.C.), the last of the great pharaohs, the grandeur ended. Wave after wave of invaders overran the country. In the seventh century B.C. the prophet Isaiah predicted that "the spirit of Egypt shall fail in the midst thereof. . . . And the Egyptians will I give over into the hand of a cruel lord" (Isa. 19:3-4). His prophecy was fulfilled many times — by the Assyrians, by the Persians, and finally in 332 B.C. by Alexander the Great, whose Ptolemaic period kindled a final flare of cultured glory. The library at Alexandria became the universal center of learning; all eyes turned toward the learning of Egypt. In the year 30 B.C., however, the glory ended when Cleopatra and Antony lifted the asp to their breasts and died. With their deaths, Egypt became a Roman province and lost her independent power in the ancient world.

OUTLINE OF EGYPT'S HISTORY

Early Dynastic Period *(3100-2686 B.C.). Dynasties I-II*

King Menes established the first capital at Memphis after upper and lower Egypt were united in 3100 B.C. This was the biblical Noph (Isa. 19:13; Jer. 2:16; 46:14, 19; Ezek. 30:13, 16).

Old Kingdom *(2686-2181 B.C.). Dynasties III-VI*

Djoser (Zoser), the outstanding pharaoh of the period, built the Step Pyramid, and King Snefru built the Bent Pyramid.

During the Fourth Dynasty the great pyramids of Cheops (Khufu), Chephren (Khafre), and Mycerinus (Menkure) were built.

First Intermediate Period *(2181-2060 B.C.)*
Dynasties VII-X

This was a period of decline. Princes ruled the provinces with frequent civil wars.

Middle Kingdom *(2060-1786 B.C.). Dynasties XI-XII*

This was the classical period, in which art and architecture flourished. The capital was moved to Thebes, the biblical No (Jer. 46:25; Ezek. 30:14-16; Nah. 3:8).

Second Intermediate Period *(1786-1567 B.C.)*
Dynasties XIII-XVII

The Hyksos from Asia, who controlled Egypt about 1674-1567 B.C., had their capital at Avaris in the Nile delta. They introduced horses and chariots into Egypt.

New Kingdom *(1567-1085 B.C.). Dynasties XVIII-XX*

After the Hyksos were driven from Egypt, this became the age of Egypt's supreme power, expansion, and wealth. It was a period of temple building at Luxor, Karnak, Abu-Simbel, Abydos, and Memphis.

In 1479 B.C. Thutmose III captured Palestine at Megiddo.

Famous pharaohs reigned: Hatshepsut, Amenhotep III, Amenhotep IV (Akhenaten, who married Nefertiti). (Greek authors render

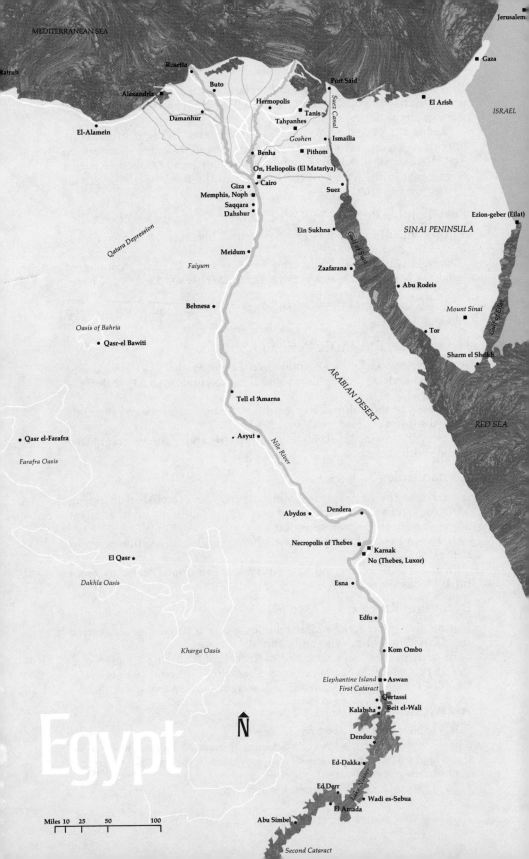

MEDITERRANEAN SEA

Matruh

Rosetta

Buto

Alexandria

Damanhur

El-Alamein

Hermopolis

Tanis

Tahpanhes

Goshen

Benha

Pithom

On, Heliopolis (El Matariya)

Giza

Cairo

Memphis, Noph

Saqqara

Dahshur

Qatara Depression

Faiyum

Meidum

Behnesa

Oasis of Bahria

Qasr-el Bawiti

Tell el 'Amarna

Qasr el-Farafra

Asyut

Nile River

Farafra Oasis

Abydos

Dendera

El Qasr

Necropolis of Thebes

Karnak

No (Thebes, Luxor)

Dakhla Oasis

Esna

Edfu

Kom Ombo

Kharga Oasis

Elephantine Island

Aswan

First Cataract

Qertassi

Kalabsha

Beit el-Wali

N̂

Egypt

Dendur

Ed-Dakka

Lake Nasser

Ed Derr

Wadi es-Sebua

El Amada

Abu Simbel

Second Cataract

Jerusalem

Gaza

Port Said

Suez Canal

El Arish

ISRAEL

Ismailia

Suez

Ezion-geber (Eilat)

SINAI PENINSULA

Ein Sukhna

Zaafarana

Gulf of Suez

Abu Rodeis

Mount Sinai

Gulf of Eilat

Tor

Sharm el Sheikh

ARABIAN DESERT

RED SEA

Miles 10   25   50   100

Amenhotep as *Amenophis*.) Other famous pharaohs of the period were Tutankhamen, Ramses I, and Ramses II. The children of Israel were in Egypt during this time.

During the period 1370–1352 B.C., Akhenaten believed in a revolutionary doctrine of monotheism and moved his headquarters to Tell el 'Amarna, in middle Egypt. During this period elaborate tombs were hewn in the Valley of the Kings, and the *Book of the Dead* was written on papyrus.

Post-Empire Period *(1085–341 B.C.)*. *Dynasties XXI–XXX*

Shishak ruled during the Twenty-second Dynasty (1 Kings 11:40; 14:25–26; 2 Chron. 12:2–9).

Necho, who ruled during the Twenty-sixth Dynasty, conquered Judah at Megiddo in 609 B.C. (2 Kings 23:29–30, 33–35; 2 Chron. 35:20–24; 36:4; Jer. 46:2).

The Persians ruled in Egypt from 525 to 398 B.C. and again between 378 and 341 B.C.

Greek Rule, Ptolemaic Period *(332–30 B.C.)*

Alexander the Great, who conquered Egypt at age 24, founded and built Alexandria. After his death, the Ptolemaic dynasty ruled for 300 years.

Egypt was the cultural hub of the old world, and the great minds flocked to Alexandria.

Cleopatra reigned (51–30 B.C.) until she and Antony committed suicide with the asp.

Roman Rule *(30 B.C.–A.D. 323)*

As early as the first century, Christianity was established in Egypt, with Alexandria as the center of activity. Tradition says that Saint Mark, the apostle, was responsible.

It was in Egypt that the monastic hermit style of Christianity originated.

In the middle of the fourth century A.D. the Coptic translations of the Bible were made.

Byzantine Rule *(A.D. 323–640)*

During this period, Egyptian temples were destroyed or converted into Christian monasteries and churches.

By 451, part of the Copts had decided to stop giving allegiance to the Pope, and they became known as the Orthodox Copts. The Uniate Catholic Copts, however, still recognize the papacy.

Arab Rule *(A.D. 640–1517)*

570. Mohammed was born at Mecca.

640. The second Moslem caliph, Omar I, invaded Egypt. The people of Egypt became Moslems, and Egyptian temples and Christian churches were converted into mosques.

1250–1390. The Bahri Mamelukes reigned.

1390–1517. The Circassian sultans reigned. This was a period of frequent revolts and disturbances.

Modern Period

1517–1798. Egypt was a Turkish province of the Ottoman Empire.

1798–1801. Napoleon conquered Egypt in 1798, but France was forced by the British to withdraw in 1801.

1801–1805. Egypt was under British control.

1805–1952. This was the dynasty of the Albanian Mohammed Ali and the last dynasty of Egypt.

1882–1936. The British occupied Egypt.

1952. King Farouk, the last of Mohammed Ali's dynasty, abdicated.

1953. Egypt became a republic after being ruled by foreign masters for 2,800 years.

1954–1970. Gamal Abdel Nasser, the president of Egypt, was the moving force behind the creation of the United Arab Republic in 1958. He died September 28, 1970.

1956. The Suez Canal was nationalized by Egypt.

1970. After the death of Nasser, the vice-president, Anwar El Sadat, became president of Egypt, and the Aswan High Dam was dedicated.

■ *Abraham went to Egypt because of famine (Gen. 12:10–20).*

■ *Hagar was an Egyptian who mothered Ishmael, Abraham's first-born (Gen. 16:1).*

■ *Ishmael married an Egyptian. The Ishmaelites were three-quarters Egyptian (Gen. 21:21).*

■ *Joseph was sold to Ishmaelites and carried to Egypt, where he was sold to an Egyptian officer, Potiphar, as a slave (Gen. 37:26–28, 36; 39:1–20). He was imprisoned (Gen. 39:21–41:40). He was exalted as a ruler (Gen. 41; Acts 7:9–10). He was reunited with his family (Gen. 42–45).*

■ *Jacob and his family came to Egypt when the famine struck them in Canaan. He spent the last 17 years of his life in Goshen, the southeast part of the Nile delta (Gen. 42–50).*

■ *The children of Israel were oppressed as slaves in Egypt, perhaps under Ramses II (Gen. 15:13; Exod. 1, 2; Acts 7:6).*

■ *Moses was born in Egypt during the oppression and was reared in the house of royalty (Exod. 2).*

■ *Moses accomplished the deliverance of Israel (Exod. 3–14).*

■ *Joseph's bones were carried out of Egypt (Gen. 50:25–26; Exod. 13:19: Josh. 24:32; Heb. 11:22).*

■ *Hadad fled to Egypt, married a sister of the queen of Egypt, and came back as the king of Edom and an enemy of Solomon (1 Kings 11:14–22).*

■ *Jeroboam fled to Egypt until Solomon died (1 Kings 11:26–40), and then Jeroboam returned and at Shechem he became king over ten tribes (1 Kings 12:1–25).*

■ *Shishak, king of Egypt, invaded and subdued Judah (1 Kings 14:25–26).*

- Zerah, king of Egypt, unsuccessfully invaded Judah (2 Chron. 14:9–15; 16:8).
- Hoshea, king of Israel, and Hezekiah, king of Judah, sought the help of the Ethiopian kings of Egypt against Assyria (2 Kings 17:4; 19:9).
- Necho, king of Egypt, slew Josiah (2 Kings 23:29–30; 2 Chron. 35:20–24).
- A remnant of the Jews fled to Egypt and settled (2 Kings 25:25–26; Jer. 42–44).
- Jeremiah was carried to Egypt, where he was located at Tahpanhes, 20 miles south of Tanis (Jer. 43:8).
- Jeremiah predicted woes against Egypt (Jer. 43:9–46:28), and tradition has Jeremiah beaten to death for uttering them.
- After being warned by an angel, Joseph took Jesus to Egypt to escape the death decree of Herod (Matt. 2:13–15, 19–21).
- Abraham went to Egypt because of famine (Josephus, Antiquities of the Jews, 1:8:1). (The Ras Shamra Tablets, dating to 1400 B.C., contain, among other things, the Keret Legend, which scholars see as evidence for the story of Abraham's journey to the south of Canaan. Genesis Aprocryphon, part of the Dead Sea Scrolls, also verifies the story.)
- Abraham taught the Egyptians astronomy (Josephus, Antiquities of the Jews, 1:8:2).

Egyptian Writing

HIEROGLYPHIC: sacred inscriptions of the pharaohs, consisting of small, carefully drawn figures or pictures

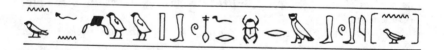

HIERATIC: the cursive form of hieroglyphs, usually found on papyrus and dating from 1300 B.C.

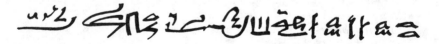

DEMOTIC: the popular writing of the Egyptians during the years 400–100 B.C.; a simplification of the hieratic

*Adapted from Kurt Schroeder, Guide to Egypt (Cairo, 1965), by permission.

COPTIC: a form of Egyptian writing which uses a Greek alphabet; spoken only by the Copts in the churches and monasteries

ⲁⲛⲑⲁ· ⲏⲁⲉⲍⲱⲁⲉⲛ ⲁⲛⲑⲁ·

ARABIC: used since the seventh century, and now the national language

تعتبر الجيزة من أهم أحياء القاهرة ؛ الفخمة على الشاطىء الغربي

Egyptian Alphabet

The ancient Egyptian alphabet consisted of the following 24 consonants. The vowels were not written.

	Sign	Conventional Reading		Sign	Conventional Reading
1		*a*	9		*n*
2		*i-j*	10		*r*
3		*ajin, a*	11		"soft *h*"
4		*w* or *u*	12		"hard *h*"
5		*b*	13		*kh*
6		*p*	14		"line *kh*"
7		*f*	15		*s (z)*
8		*m*	16		*s*

*Adapted from Kurt Schroeder, *Guide to Egypt* (Cairo, 1965), by permission.

17		*sh*	21		*t*
18		*k*	22		*th*
19		*k*	23		*d*
20		*g*	24		*dj* or *z*

Ancient Egyptian Signs

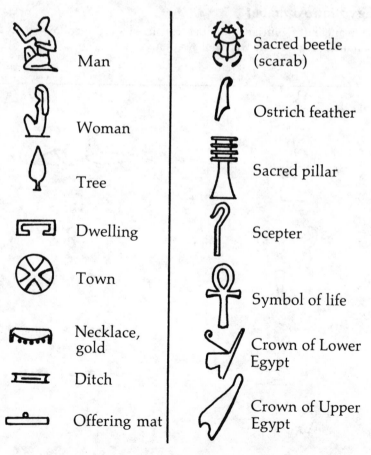

	Man		Sacred beetle (scarab)
	Woman		Ostrich feather
	Tree		Sacred pillar
	Dwelling		Scepter
	Town		Symbol of life
	Necklace, gold		Crown of Lower Egypt
	Ditch		Crown of Upper Egypt
	Offering mat		

*Adapted from Kurt Schroeder, *Guide to Egypt* (Cairo, 1965), by permission.

Eye

Plow

Lotus flower

Face

Writing utensils

Field

Soul, spirit

God

Heart

Double crown

Uraeus snake

Water

King of
Upper and
Lower Egypt

Sun-god Re

Winged Sun

Lord of both
lands

Cartouche

Papyrus symbol
of Lower Egypt

*Adapted from Kurt Schroeder, *Guide to Egypt* (Cairo, 1965), by permission.

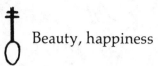 Beauty, happiness

 Son of the Sun (king's title)

The Most Important Kings' Cartouches

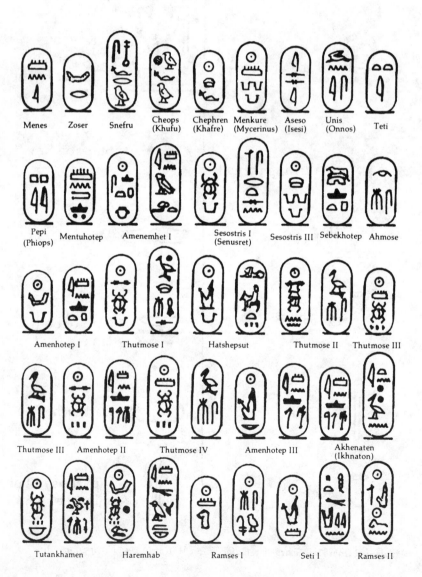

Menes   Zoser   Snefru   Cheops (Khufu)   Chephren (Khafre)   Menkure (Mycerinus)   Aseso (Isesi)   Unis (Onnos)   Teti

Pepi (Phiops)   Mentuhotep   Amenemhet I   Sesostris I (Senusret)   Sesostris III   Sebekhotep   Ahmose

Amenhotep I   Thutmose I   Hatshepsut   Thutmose II   Thutmose III

Thutmose III   Amenhotep II   Thutmose IV   Amenhotep III   Akhenaten (Ikhnaton)

Tutankhamen   Haremhab   Ramses I   Seti I   Ramses II

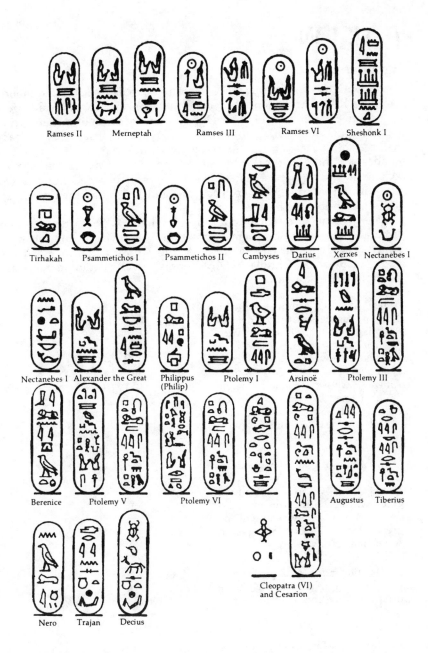

Ramses II Merneptah Ramses III Ramses VI Sheshonk I

Tirhakah Psammetichos I Psammetichos II Cambyses Darius Xerxes Nectanebes I

Nectanebes I Alexander the Great Philippus (Philip) Ptolemy I Arsinoë Ptolemy III

Berenice Ptolemy V Ptolemy VI Augustus Tiberius

Cleopatra (VI) and Cesarion

Nero Trajan Decius

*Adapted from Kurt Schroeder, *Guide to Egypt* (Cairo, 1965), by permission.

RELIGION

Egyptian Gods

The Egyptians showed reverence to many animals, the sun and moon, the Nile River, and man. The concept of an anthropomorphic god had come even before the First Dynasty, but because of ancient prior practices of worshiping animals, the Egyptians fused three ideas: nature, animal, and man. An example of this type of fusion is the goddess of love, Hathor, who might appear as a human or a cow. When she was given a human body, she still retained the element of a cow with horns over her head. The god Thoth had the head of an ibis, and Anubis the head of a jackal.

Each village and community usually had its local deities, and temples were built for them. Sometimes a universal god, such as Amen, became incarnate in the pharaoh, whose name included the god's name. *Amen*hotep (*Amen*ophis) and Tutankh*amen* are examples of this practice.

Amen (Amon, Amun) was the Theban universal god of all Egyptian gods. He is shown with plumes and sometimes with a sun-disc between the plumes, symbolizing celestial origin. Amen, whose name means "hidden one," is represented as a ram-headed deity; in the Roman period he was identified with Jupiter.

Mut, mother of gods, sky goddess, and wife of Amen, was represented as a vulture or painted green with a vulture's head and a double crown. She was one of the great triad of Thebes, along with Amen and Khons.

Khons, the moon god of Thebes, was the son of Amen and Mut, the three forming the Theban family triad.

Re (Ra, Re-Harakhte) was the sun-god, a form of the sun-god Horus. He is usually represented as a hawk with a solar disc over his head, or sometimes as a divine eye, ram, or man. He was the son of Nut, the sky goddess, and was venerated at Heliopolis.

Osiris was the judge of the dead and the god of vegetation (green human face). He carried a crook and flail, insignia of kingship. His wife was Isis.

Isis was the goddess of mothers and love. She was a daughter of Geb and Nut, the wife of Osiris, and mother of Horus. She is sometimes represented as a cow-headed being.

Horus, the sun-god, or god of the day, was the son of Osiris and Isis. He is portrayed as a winged sun-disc or as a falcon head with a double crown.

Anubis, as god of the heavens and god of the cemetery, supervised the passage of the soul to the judgment hall in Amenti, the region of the dead in the West. There the hearts of the dead were weighed against the feather of truth. He presided over the tombs and is portrayed as a jackal-headed god. He is called the son of Osiris.

Ptah was the local god of Memphis and the creator of all things. He is represented by the sacred bull, Apis.

Hathor, the goddess of love, joy, and sky, is portrayed as a woman wearing a headdress with horns and a red disc between the horns. At Deir el-Bahri she is portrayed as a cow nursing Pharaoh Amenhotep II. She is sometimes represented with cow's ears. She was regarded by the Greeks as Aphrodite.

Thoth was the moon god of Hermopolis and the god of writing. As the scribe of the gods, he measured time and invented numbers, and at the judgment he

recorded the results of the weighing of the heart. He is portrayed as a man with an ibis head or as a baboon.

Seshet was the goddess of writing.

Khnum, a ram head, was a god of Upper Egypt and husband of Anuket.

Sobk (Sebek) was a crocodile-headed god.

Maat was the goddess of truth and justice. Her symbol was the ostrich feather.

Atum, a god of Heliopolis, is represented by the form of a human, a snake, or a lion.

Sekhmet, the war goddess of Memphis and wife of Ptah, is usually shown with the head of a lion.

Seth, a god of Upper Egypt, was the god of the desert and storms and was portrayed as a human with the head of a large-eared (mulelike) animal. He was the brother of Osiris, whom he murdered.

Hapi was the god of the Nile River.

Nut, a sky goddess, or goddess of the lower heavens, was the wife of Geb and mother of Re. As goddess of the dawn she daily gave birth to the sun. She is shown sometimes with an elongated body and sometimes as a cow.

Shu, the god of air, is sometimes shown standing beneath Nut, as if supporting her with his outstretched arms.

Geb, the earth god, was the husband of Nut, the sky goddess. He is sometimes portrayed reclining beneath the arched body of Nut.

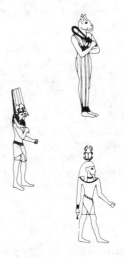

Bast (Bastet) was a cat-headed goddess of joy.

Mont (Month) was the Theban falcon-headed god of war.

Khepri (Khepre), the sun-god Re, is represented by the dung beetle (scarab, *Scarabeus sacer*).

Buto (Uazet, Wadjet) was the serpent goddess of the Delta. From earliest times to the present day the cobra serpent has been considered sacred. Three goddesses appear in serpent form: (1) Uazet, the Delta goddess of Buto; (2) Mert-Seger, the goddess of the Necropolis at Thebes; and (3) Rannut, the harvest goddess. Uraeus is the representation of the sacred serpent which appears on the headdress of rulers, often just over the forehead, as a symbol of sovereignty.

Nekhbet was the vulture goddess of Upper Egypt.

Mnevis, a sacred bull, was worshiped at Heliopolis.

Apis, the sacred bull of Ptah, was worshiped at Memphis and is considered by some to be the reincarnation of Osiris. When a new Apis was chosen, it had to have a white, square spot on its forehead, a figure of an eagle on its back, and a knot like a beetle under its tongue. Tombs of these sacred bulls (the Serapeum) are found at Saqqara. There seems to be a relationship between the god Apis and the golden calf made in the wilderness by the Israelites (Exod. 32).

Aten (Aton) was proclaimed the one and only god by Amenhotep IV at his new capital, Tell el Amarna. This monotheism was a revolutionary concept to the Egyptians. Aten is represented as the dazzling physical orb of the sun itself, and sun rays are directed out from the sun-disc. Amenhotep IV changed his name to Akhenaten (Ikhnaton).

Religious Life in Egypt

From earliest times the sun and the river were the two main Egyptian deities. The sun, like the river, was the giver of life. Re, the god of the sun, was the god of creation, the father of the pharaohs, and author of the cosmic order. Akhenaten worshiped one god, Aten, the source of all energy and power, a formless intelligence that permeated the universe. Another concept of deity was a divine triad of father, mother, and son.

The Egyptians were firm believers in a life after death, and they felt that the *Book of the Dead,* their guidebook for the deceased, contained the requirements for entrance into the realm of Osiris. They believed that man is accountable for his actions in this life and that he must stand judgment and testify that he is moral. Then his heart is weighed against a feather on a balance to see if he has proven his worthiness to have eternal life.

At Heliopolis a temple cult arose, with an organized priesthood of sun worshipers. The temple was the "house of God," and in addition to its holy place and outer court it had a holy of holies, in which was a symbol called the *benben,* a pyramid-shaped stone representing the sun-god. This was perhaps the forerunner of the pyramids. Only the priest could go into the holy of holies, where the bark and the golden cult image that represented the god were kept. Each day the god was fed, dressed, and adorned; even cosmetics were applied. The god appeared in public only on festivals, and was usually taken in a procession on the avenue of the sphinxes. False doors provided a way for the god to enter the temple. During the New Kingdom the god served as a divine oracle, as at Delphi in Greece. Sacrificing of animals and vegetables, as well as circumcising, is graphically portrayed on the walls of temple and tomb.

The Egyptians believed blessings would be bestowed upon them if they sacrificed to the gods. They also believed in a loving God, who stressed the joy of living on the earth, and in a life concerned with eternal values. In the creation story found in. the *Pyramid Texts*, *maat* (the divine order of nature) replaced chaos; order and law replaced disorder. It was the pharaoh's responsibility to maintain maat in all his doings. This meant honesty, respect, virtue, honor, moderation, self-restraint, humility, integrity, benevolence, and kindness.

The oldest religious documents are the *Pyramid Texts*, consisting of prayers and incantations written by the priests of Heliopolis. The *Coffin Texts* are a collection of spells used for the protection of Egyptians as they made their way to the realm of Osiris, and the *Book of the Dead*, written on papyrus, is nearly the same thing, only more elaborate. The *Book of Breathings* deals with the rituals of the temples and the tombs, which are designed with one main objective: eternal exaltation.

Egyptian temples generally have three different parts: a courtyard, a hypostyle hall, and a holy of holies. One cannot help but notice the likeness of Moses' tabernacle and Solomon's temple to that of the Egyptian temples. Moses' tabernacle had a courtyard, a holy place, and a holy of holies. Both Egyptians and Israelites allowed the priests only to go into certain parts of the temple (Exod. 25–27). Both had altars upon which animals were sacrificed. Both practiced circumcision. These similarities would cause one to believe the remark of the Egyptian guide at Luxor when he said, "There is nothing new under the sun." Surely there are eternal principles or concepts involved.

Embalming

Not all the secrets of Egyptian embalming are known, but apparently the following steps were taken to prepare the bodies of royalty for the afterlife. Most of the brain was drawn through the nostrils, and the part left was dissolved with aromatic lotions. The viscera were then removed through an incision in the side of the body, and the body washed out with palm wine. The lungs, stomach, liver, and intestines were embalmed and placed in separate urns, the heart was replaced in the body, and the abdomen was filled with crushed myrrh and cassia. The body was shaved and soaked in a bath of dry natron (a natural form of sodium carbonate), which absorbed all its remaining moisture. It was then washed, laid to dry on a funerary bed, and wrapped in linen. As prayers were recited, liquids were used to make the bandages stick together. This treatment would take up to seventy days for a person of royalty. Thus the body was prepared for eternity. After a complex funeral liturgy, it was placed in a coffin and was then ready for the return of the spirit.

In second-class embalming, for the less royal Egyptians, the viscera were not removed and embalmed separately, but were dissolved by means of cedar oil or oil of turpentine injected into the body cavity.

A third method, for the peasant class of people, consisted of simply desiccating the body without attempting to remove the internal organs. The corpse was then wrapped and buried.

EGYPT TODAY

Of Egypt's population of about 38 million, 95 percent live on the banks of the Nile River, the main street of the country. The Nile, the world's longest river (4,145 miles), is one of the few rivers that run north. Today modern pumping stations spill the waters of the Nile into a network of canals, from which the Egyptians, by ancient methods, lift the water onto their fields. *Shadufs* (water lifts), *saqiyas* (water wheels), and *tambours* (screws) may be seen frequently in the country.

The Nile delta, the richest farming area, measures 125 miles from north to south and 100 miles from east to west. The delta and river valley were annually flooded with a 25–50-foot wall of water and silt until the Aswan Dam was built to control the floodwaters.

The *fellaheen* are the common farmers of Egypt and are considered to be more or less "pure" Egyptian. They make up about 80 percent of the population. Over the centuries they have changed very little in religion, language, dress, and customs.

Another group of "pure" Egyptians are the three million *Copts*, or Coptic Christians — the tradesmen and artisans of Egypt. When the Arabs conquered Egypt, the Copts remained faithful to Christianity while most of the Egyptians were converted to Islam.

A third group of people are the *Bedouins*, the wandering shepherds, who number approximately 80,000.

Among the most used Arabic expressions are *salam aleikum* ("good day"), *ahlan wa sahlan* ("welcome"), *shukran* ("thank you"), *baksheesh* ("tip"), *bikam* ("how much"), *la* ("no"), *aywa* ("yes"), and *men fadlak* ("please").

Today the Egyptian *pound* is divided into 100 *piasters,* or 1,000 *milliemes*. There are many westernized stores with fixed prices, but merchants in the Khan Khalily bazaar are ready to bargain. Venders often quote prices double what they expect buyers to pay. Hotels and restaurants expect a 10-percent tip, but for small services 5–10 piasters is sufficient.

CITIES AND SITES

Cairo, *El Kahera, Masr*

One of the youngest cities in Egypt, Cairo was founded in A.D. 642 by the Moslems. Located on the east bank of the Nile, it was built because Memphis, the capital when they came into power, had an alien religion and was therefore objectionable to the Moslems. Cairo became the new capital of Egypt under the Fatimite caliphs about A.D. 970. When England controlled Egypt (1882–1922), the new part of the city was modernized. The old Cairo is oriental in design and has bazaars and crooked streets. The city boasts a population of about five million people.

POINTS OF INTEREST

1. The **AL QUBBA PALACE**, a couple of miles south and west of El Matariya, is one of the most important palaces that belonged to the Mohammed Ali dynasty. Named after the small town Qubba nearby, it was built by the khedive Ismail in 1863. Since 1955 it has been the official seat of the president of the Egyptian Republic. The buildings cover nearly 70 acres, and a garden covers 125 acres.

2. The **AIN SHAMS UNIVERSITY** is located between El Matariya and the railway station.

3. **MAIN RAILWAY STATION** and **RAMSES SQUARE**. The main railway station houses the **RAILWAY MUSEUM**, which has an interesting collection of old railway vehicles.

    Ramses Square has a large statue of Ramses.

4. **GEZIRA ISLAND**. The largest island of the Nile in Cairo (3 by ½ miles), and site of a battle between the Egyptians and Napoleon on July 21, 1798, is the **ISLAND OF GEZIRA**. On the north end of the island is **ZAMALIK**, the most beautiful residential quarters of Cairo. In the **GROTTO GARDEN** is an **AQUARIUM**, and the middle of the island is covered with a golf course, the **GEZIRA SPORTING CLUB** and the **NATIONAL CLUB**. The **TOWER OF CAIRO**, a revolving restaurant located on a needlelike structure, is the highest concrete structure in the orient — over 600 feet. It is built in the form of a lotus flower. The panoramic view from the restaurant is lovely. The **EXHIBITION GROUNDS**, **COTTON MUSEUM**, and **MUKHTAR MUSEUM**, with the works of the famous Egyptian sculptor Mohmoud Mukhtar, are all on the southern end of the island.

5. The **AGRICULTURAL MUSEUM** is located in the center of an area named *Madinet al Awqaf*, which is west of the Island of Gezira and southwest of an area named *Embaba*.

6. **CAIRO UNIVERSITY**, west of the Island of Roda, is the largest university in Egypt.

7. **ZOOLOGICAL GARDENS** and **BOTANICAL GARDENS**. Not far from the Nile River and west of the Island of Roda are the large **ZOOLOGI-**

BAHGAT

EL SABTIYA STREET

EL SABTIYA STREET

③

NAHDET MISR STREET

EL KHALIG EL MASRI STREET

EL GE

ISMAIL PASHA MUH STREET

ZAMALEK BRIDGE

26 JULY STREET

BULAQ EL GEDID STREET

BAB EL BAHR STREET

HASAN PASHA SABRI STREET

26 JULY BRIDGE

26 JULY STREET

EL GALA STREET

NAHDET MISR STREET

NAGIB EL RI HANI ST

EL GEISH STREET

Gezira Island

NILE CORNICHE

26 JULY STREET

SULEIMAN PASHA

26 JULY STREET

EL GUMHURIYA ST

EL MUSKI ST

④

NILE STREET

EL GEZIRA STREET

MAH BASYUNI

SHERIF PASHA STREET

ABD EL AZIZ ST

GOHAR

⑲

⑤

NAUWAL STREET

㉕

NIL ST

QASR EL

EL AZHAR STREET

⑳

WIZARET EL ZIRAA STREET

KASSAB STREET

EL TAHRIR ST

EL BUSTAN ST

HASAN

EL AKBAR ST

EL QALA STREET

⑱

SOLIMAN GOHAR ST

HASAN PASHA SABRI STREET

EL TAHRIR BRIDGE

FARID ST

㉑

DARB

⑥

EL TAHRIR STREET

GALA BRIDGE

㉒

EL SHEIKH RIHAN ST

GAMI ABDIN ST

EL QALA

EL AIMAN ST

EL DUKKI STREET

EL MISAHA STREET

㉔㉓

MAGLIS EL NUWAB ST

MOH BEY

EL MUIZZ STREET

RIVER NILE

NILE CORNICHE

EL AINI ST

KHAIRAT ST

EL MASRI STREET

EL HELMIYA STREET

SUQ EL SILAH ST

EL GIZA STREET

NILE STREET

MOH BEY

EZZ EL ARAB

EL KHALIG

BAB EL WAZIR ST

SARWAT STREET

Roda Island

HELWAN STREET

⑬

⑭

⑥

EL GAMIA STREET

UNIVERSITY (KRUPP) BRIDGE

EL QASR

EL SADD EL BARRANI STREET

TULUN STREET

DARB EL HOSR ST

⑫

⑦

GAMIAT EL QAHIRA STREET

EL GIZA STREET

NILE CORNICHE

EL MANYAL STREET

BAHARI EL OYUN STREET

EL ASHRAF ST

SALAH SALEM STREET

MURAD STREET

NILE STREET

EL ANWAR STREET

EL AHRAM STREET

⑧

EL GIZA BRIDGE

EL RODA ST

AMR EBN EL AS STREET

SID HASAN

⑯

EL MAHATTA STREET

⑨

⑩

Cairo

⑪

N

Miles   ½   1

1. Al Qubba Palace
2. Ain Shams University
3. Main Railway Station and Ramses Square
4. Gezira Island
5. Agricultural Museum
6. Cairo University
7. Zoological Gardens and Botanical Gardens
8. Giza
9. Roda Island and the Nilometer
10. Old Cairo
11. Coptic Museum, El-Moallaka Church, Saint Sergius's Church, Saint George's Church
12. Ibn Tulun Mosque, Beit el Kretelia, Anderson Museum
13. Sultan Hassan Mosque
14. Citadel, Alabaster Mosque, and Museums
15. Muqattam Hills, Bektashi Monastery, and Guyushi Mosque
16. Tombs of the Caliphs and Mamelukes
17. Al Hussein Mosque
18. Al-Azhar Mosque and Islamic University
19. Khan Khalily Bazaar
20. Museum of Islamic Art
21. Abin Palace Museum
22. American University
23. Geological Museum
24. American Embassy
25. Egyptian Museum

CAL GARDENS, covering an area of 52 acres. Housed there are 600 animals, 3,000 birds, 300 reptiles, and 150 kinds of fish.

The BOTANICAL GARDENS are also nearby, on the north.

8. GIZA. The residential area of Giza is located along the Nile just south of the Zoological Gardens.

9. RODA ISLAND and the NILOMETER. West of Old Cairo is RODA ISLAND, in the Nile River. On the southern tip of the island is the MENESTERLI GARDEN, and at the southern end of the garden is the old NILOMETER dating back to A.D. 716. This gauge measured the official level of the Nile River. Since taxes were computed in the olden days according to the height of the flood and its consequences to agricultural crops, the Nilometer was important. The modern Nilometer is located nearby.

■ *The Moslems claim that Moses was found by the pharaoh's daughter in the bulrushes on the island (Exod. 2:1-6).*

10. **OLD CAIRO.** On the right bank of the Nile, and south of the center of the city, is Old Cairo. It includes the old Roman **FORTRESS BABYLON**, the **COPTS' QUARTER**, and the first Arab settlement in Egypt: **AL-FUSTÂT** (A.D. 642). The **OLD CAIRO SYNAGOGUE** and **MOSQUE OF AMR** are nearby. In the Old Synagogue may be seen some of the most ancient manuscripts of parts of the Old Testament.

11. **COPTIC MUSEUM, EL-MOALLAKA CHURCH, SAINT SERGIUS'S CHURCH, SAINT GEORGE'S CHURCH.** The **COPTIC MUSEUM**, built in 1908 and located within the Fortress Babylon, houses the largest collection of Christian Coptic treasures in the world. Besides paintings, carvings, metalwork, early Christian vestments, and medieval glass and pottery, the library has a collection of Coptic manuscripts and religious works from the Coptic churches and monasteries in Egypt.

The **COPTIC CHURCH EL-MOALLAKA** (Holy Virgin's Church) is built on top of the gateway of the Fortress Babylon. It dates back to the fourth century A.D. and was the seat of the Coptic patriarchate. It has been rebuilt several times. According to legend, the Virgin Mary appeared here in A.D. 968.

SAINT SERGIUS'S COPTIC CHURCH (*Abu Serga*) dates back to the tenth century A.D. Joseph, Mary, and Jesus are said to have stayed here for thirty days during their flight into Egypt. Under the altar is a cave where the Holy Family is supposed to have lived. From here, according to tradition, the angel sent them back to Nazareth (Matt. 2:13–23).

SAINT GEORGE'S CHURCH (*Mary Gurguis*), which belongs to the Greek Orthodox Church, was built upon a bastion of the fortress of Babylon in the sixth century and houses a **BYZANTINE ICON MUSEUM**. A splendid view of the city may be obtained here.

12. **IBN TULUN MOSQUE, BEIT EL KRETELIA, ANDERSON MUSEUM.** The oldest Arab structure preserved in Cairo, the Ibn Tulun Mosque, was built by Ibn Tulun in A.D. 868. The minaret is unique because it has an exterior staircase. Next to this mosque is Beit el Kretelia, an annex of the Islamic Art Museum. It is a house furnished in the cosmopolitan Oriental spirit of the eighteenth century. The Anderson Museum is also located at Beit el Kretelia.

13. The **SULTAN HASSAN MOSQUE** is considered by many to be the most important piece of Arab architecture in Egypt. Built in A.D. 1356–63, it is 495 feet long.

14. **CITADEL, ALABASTER MOSQUE,** and **MUSEUMS.** On the southeast edge of the city is the **CITADEL**, a former fortress built in A.D. 1176. Of the early fortress, only the eastern outer wall remains. This was the site of the massacre of 480 Mamelukes in 1811 by order of Mohammed Ali.

The **MOSQUE OF SULTAN AL-NASIR** may be seen through the main gate on the left. Legend has it that the prison in which Joseph of old was confined (Gen. 39:21–41:40) was located on the site of the Citadel. Southwest of the Nasir Mosque is the **WELL OF JOSEPH**, said to have been dug by that same Joseph.

The **MOHAMMED ALI MOSQUE** (Alabaster Mosque) is located straight ahead after one enters the main gate. This mosque, the symbol of Cairo, was completed in 1857 under the supervision of a Turkish architect. As you enter the mosque, you can see **MOHAMMED ALI'S TOMB** on the right. The walls and pillars, made of alabaster from Beni Snel in Egypt, make this the most costly and beautiful mosque in the city.

The **MILITARY MUSEUM** is located in the old Palace of Hareen on the north end of the Citadel; **EL GAWHARA PALACE MUSEUM** is located on the south end. Also nearby is the **MUSTAFA KAMEL MUSEUM**.

15. **MUQATTAM HILLS, BEKTASHI MONASTERY,** and **GUYUSHI MOSQUE.** Behind the Citadel is a limestone range of hills, 660 feet high — the **MUQATTAM HILLS.** From the top of the hills the panoramic view is delightful. The road goes through the **LIMESTONE QUARRIES** from which the stone blocks for the pyramids were quarried.

Halfway up the mountain is the **BEKTASHI MONASTERY**, which belongs to a Moslem sect. The Janissaries were also members of this sect, and after the order was dissolved in Turkey in 1924, the monks fled to Egypt.

The **GUYUSHI MOSQUE**, one of the oldest mosques in Cairo, was built on top of the hills in A.D. 1085.

16. **TOMBS OF THE CALIPHS AND MAMELUKES.** At the foot of the Muqattam hills are numerous tombs of the Caliphs and Mamelukes. These huge mausoleums, dating back as far as the thirteenth century A.D., are designed with domes, minarets, chambers, halls, marble floors, and sarcophagi. Near the tombs are modern cemeteries. The largest of the tombs, the **MOSQUE OF SULTAN INAL**, covers an area measuring 346 by 187 feet.

17. The **AL HUSSEIN MOSQUE** houses sacred Islamic relics, such as pieces of Mohammed's clothes. Al Hussein was a grandchild of the prophet Mohammed.

18. **AL-AZHAR MOSQUE** and **ISLAMIC UNIVERSITY.** The six-minaret Al-Azhar Mosque, a part of the complex of the oldest and most notable Islamic university, dates from A.D. 972 and is called *The Splendid.* At first it was a place of worship only; however, from A.D. 988 it became a school of religion. The full period of study is from 15 to 22 years. Pupils begin their studies when they are 12–16 years of age, and a requirement for admission is to know the whole Koran by heart. Seven different degrees are offered, the highest being *Scholar.* Since most students are too poor to support themselves, the school and students are supported by endowments. Approximately 12,000 students are enrolled.

19. The **KHAN KHALILY BAZAAR**, established in 1292 by Prince Asraf Khalily, is now the popular shopping place for the tourist. Artisans are at work, and bargaining is in order.

20. **MUSEUM OF ISLAMIC ART.** Founded in 1880, this museum houses the world's largest collection of Islamic ceramics, carpets, textiles,

marble, weapons, inscriptions, furniture, and so forth. It is located in Ahmed Maher Square, in the same building that houses the **NATIONAL PUBLIC LIBRARY**.

21. The **ABIN PALACE MUSEUM** is in Al Gomhuriya Square. Built during the years 1863–73, this palace became the official royal residence for King Farouk and his predecessors from 1874 until 1952. It has 500 rooms, gorgeously decorated and furnished in Islamic Italian style.

22. The **AMERICAN UNIVERSITY** is situated southeast of El Tahrir Square.

23. The **GEOLOGICAL MUSEUM** is east of the American Embassy, near Tahrir Square at El Sheikh Rihan Street.

24. The **AMERICAN EMBASSY** is on El Zahra Street, southeast of the Hilton Hotel.

Egyptian Museum

25. The **EGYPTIAN MUSEUM**, on the north side of El Tahrir Square, near the Hilton Hotel, houses the world's most complete collection of Egyptian antiquities. The museum was built in the form of a rectangle in 1902. In the middle of the south side is the main entrance. If the visitor turns directly to the left after entering and makes the complete tour of the rectangle, while at the same time inspecting the side rooms of the main galleries, he will follow in chronological order the history of Egypt. It is interesting to the student of art to follow progressively the development of Egyptian art. Gallery 48, under the rotunda just inside the main entrance, has the most recent acquisitions.

OLD KINGDOM

OLD KINGDOM antiquities, dating from 2800 to 2200 B.C., are displayed to the left of the entrance, in galleries and rooms numbered 47, 46, 41, 42, 31, and 32. They contain statuettes, sarcophagi, stelae, false doors, and painted reliefs.

Room 47 contains three statues of **MENKURE** (Mycerinus) between the goddess Hathor and a local deity (nos. 180, 158, 149).

Room 42 houses a diorite statue of **KING KHAFRE** (Chephren) (no. 138), builder of the second of the three famous pyramids; a limestone statue of **PHARAOH ZOSER**, from the Third Dynasty (no. 6008); and a painted limestone statue of the **SQUATTING SCRIBE** from Saqqara with a roll of papyrus, dating from the Fifth Dynasty (no. 141).

In room 32 are two limestone statues of **PRINCE RA-HOTEP** and his wife, **NOFRET**, from the Fourth Dynasty. (The moustache is a rare feature in ancient Egypt.) Numbers 230–31 are statues of **KING PEPI I** and his son, **MER-EN-RA**. They are the oldest life-size metal statues of ancient Egyptian workmanship and date back to the Sixth Dynasty. In the gallery leading to the next room are large fragments of **INSCRIBED RED SANDSTONE** from Serbit el Khadem and Wadi Maghara in the Sinai Peninsula, about midway between the Suez and the

Monastery of Saint Catherine. They tell of Egyptian expeditions against desert Bedouins who were interrupting mining operations for malachite and turquoise.

MIDDLE KINGDOM

MIDDLE KINGDOM artifacts are housed in galleries and rooms numbering 26, 21, 22, and 16. Burial chambers, reliefs, and royal statues are just a few of the contents.

Item number 300, in room 22, is a **BURIAL CHAMBER** with a sarcophagus from Deir el-Bahri at Thebes, dating from the Eleventh Dynasty. A wooden statuette of **SENWOSRET I** from Lisht is also displayed.

NEW KINGDOM

NEW KINGDOM galleries and rooms are numbered 11, 12, 6, 7, and 8. Near the entrance is a statue of **THUTMOSE III**, who was the hero of the Battle of Megiddo of 1479 B.C. and who extended the borders of Egypt. Note the bas-relief horsebreakers. Before the date of this statue, no horses appeared on reliefs or paintings, as horses had not been known in Egypt until they were introduced by the Hyksos in the seventeenth century B.C.

Gallery 11 has a colored limestone **SPHINX OF QUEEN HATSHEPSUT** from Thebes (no. 6139) and a schist statue of **THUTMOSE III** (no. 400) from Karnak — both beautiful pieces of art.

In gallery 12 the famous **HATHOR COW** from Deir el-Bahri (Temple of Hatshepsut) is shown with Thutmose III standing under her head and feeding from her udder. Behind the cow is the chapel in which the holy cow once stood.

In the center of the north gallery, room 3 is totally devoted to **AMENHOTEP IV** (Akhenaten, Ikhnaton), who adopted a monotheistic religious belief and had the solar disc represent his god, Aten. This room shows a new art developed by Tell el 'Amarna artists, who sought to introduce grace and elegance in accordance with the aesthetics of that day. It is interesting to see their exaggeration of the king's deformities: his pointed skull, emaciated cheeks, protruding chin, almond-shaped eyes, swollen belly, and effeminate thighs. Amarna art is noted for its family-oriented and sentimental scenes. In case F is a huge stone statue of **AKHENATEN** (no. 472) and a very beautiful head of his wife, **QUEEN NEFERTITI** (no. 6206). Case C has a colored relief of Akhenaten and Nefertiti worshiping the sun-god Aten.

From room 3, visitors who, like the mummies, are "pressed for time" should go up the northwest stairs to view the **TUTANKHAMEN COLLECTION**.

Galleries 8, 9, 10, and 15 and room 14, on the northeast, have monuments from the Nineteenth and Twentieth Dynasties. The remainder of the rooms on the east are devoted to later periods, from the Twentieth Dynasty down to and including the Greek,

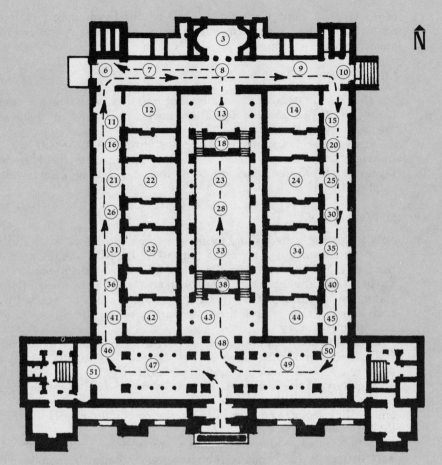

Egyptian Museum: First Floor

47, 46, 41, 42, 31, 32. Old Kingdom
26, 21, 22. Middle Kingdom
6, 7, 8, 9, 10, 15. New Kingdom
3. Akhenaten
25, 24. Late period
35, 34. Greco-Roman period
45, 44. Nubian collection
50, 49. Ptolemaic sarcophagi
43, 38, 33, 28, 23, 18. Atrium

*Adapted from Kurt Schroeder, *Guide to Egypt* (Cairo, 1965), by permission.

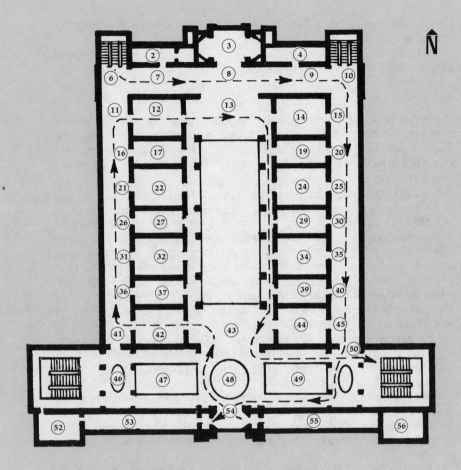

Egyptian Museum: Second Floor

6. Scarabs
2. Hetepheres
2A. Tanite kings
3. Ornaments
7, 8, 13, 9, 4, 10, 15, 20, 25, 30, 35, 40, 45. Tutankhamen
54, 55. Weapons
43, 42. Archaic period
41, 36, 26, 21, 16, 11. Coffins
32, 27, 22, 17, 12. Funerary pomp
13. Chariots and finds from tombs
14. Roman coffins and portraits
19. Deities and sacred animals
24, 29. Drawings and manuscripts
34. Tools, weapons, and musical instruments
49. Furniture

*Adapted from Kurt Schroeder, *Guide to Egypt* (Cairo, 1965), by permission.

Roman, Ptolemaic, and Byzantine periods. A copy of the **ROSETTA STONE** is included.

In Galleries 49 and 50 in the front of the museum are **GRANITE SARCOPHAGI** of the Ptolemaic period.

ATRIUM

The **ATRIUM, GALLERY 13,** and the **ISRAEL STONE**. The visitor should now proceed north through the **ATRIUM,** in the center of the building. The Atrium houses antiquities from various periods, including two **WOODEN BOATS** of the dead found at Dahshur and dating back to the Twelfth Dynasty.

GALLERY 13, on the north of the Atrium, houses war chariots and tomb artifacts. One of the most important Jewish and Christian antiquities located in Gallery 13 is the **ISRAEL STELA OF MERNEPTAH,** son of Ramses II. Called the "Israel Stone," this black granite stone was originally set up in 1490 B.C. by Amenhotep III, but was appropriated by Merneptah in 1224 B.C. and stood in his funerary temple at Thebes. It was discovered in western Luxor in 1896. It is 8 feet high, 4 feet wide, and 2 feet thick. Artwork decorates the top, and a text of Merneptah's hymns of victory, in Egyptian hieroglyphs, covers the rest of the stone. The relief above the inscription is divided into two almost identical scenes. In the center, the god Amen stands under the winged sun-disc, giving Merneptah the sickle-sword with his right hand and holding the scepter of the gods in his left. Mut is on the far left and Horus on the far right. In line 27 of the text, the word *Israel* appears in hieroglyphics. As this is the only mention of Israel in any Egyptian text, it helps to date the period. When the stone was set up in Merneptah's mortuary temple, a duplicate was carved on the great temple at Karnak. The latter now survives only in fragments, however.

The inscription of the stela is dated the third day of the third month of summer in the fifth year of the pharaoh's reign. The stone tells of the defeat of various peoples, including the Philistines. It says: "In Egypt there is great rejoicing; her cities shout for joy. . . . All men speak of Merneptah's conquests. . . . The devastated, the Hittites, are pacified. Canaan is conquered and all her wickedness. Ashkelon is captive, Gezer is fallen, Israel is ravaged and has no offspring. Palestine is widowed."

UPPER FLOOR

UPPER FLOOR. Gallery 6, at the head of the northwest stairway, has a collection of **SCARABS**.

On the left, room 2 houses the treasures from the tomb of **QUEEN HETEPHERES,** mother of Cheops (Khufu) (2700 B.C.), and room 2A houses the collection of the **TANITE KINGS**.

Galleries and rooms 7, 8, 13, 9, 4, 10, 15, 20, 25, 30, 35, 40, and 45 have the huge collection from the **TOMB OF TUTANKHAMEN.** After the death of Akhenaten and the brief reign of Smenkhkara,

Tutankhamen ("King Tut") became the pharaoh. He had been a follower of Akhenaten and monotheism, but when he came to the throne he moved to Thebes and apparently gave up his belief in monotheism. Discovered in 1922 by Howard Carter, King Tut's tomb shows the influence of both Amarna and Theban art, and its contents cover a quarter of the upper floor of the Egyptian Museum. The north gallery, with items from Tut's tomb, is the finest area in the whole museum.

Galleries 7, 8, and 9 have four **FUNERARY CHAMBERS** in huge glass cases. They are made of wood and covered with beautifully engraved gold leaf. The largest is 10 feet 10 inches by 16 feet 5 inches by 9 feet. Tutankhamen was buried in three gold mummiform coffins resting in a stone sarcophagus, which, in turn, lay in the four funerary chambers. A **MINIATURE BUILDING** — housing the **ALABASTER CANOPIC BOX**, which, in turn, housed four **CANOPIC URNS** — is adorned with a frieze of uraeus serpents, erect and crowned with the solar disc. Goddesses sculptured in high relief with arms outstretched seem to be guarding the building. The alabaster canopic box on a sledge is beautifully decorated with hieroglyphs and other art work. The four canopic urns have lids that portray Tutankhamen's head wearing the "nemset." These urns housed miniature coffins 15 inches long, in the shape of the innermost gold coffin of Tutankhamen. These miniature coffins were used to preserve the mummified viserca: stomach, intestines, lungs, and liver. Only the heart remained in King Tut's mummy.

Israel Stela of Merneptah

Tutankhamen's alabaster canopic box

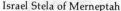

Two of the **MUMMIFORM SARCOPHAGI** of King Tutankhamen are located in the museum. The number 2 (middle) sarcophagus, in case 36, is inlaid in multicolored glass paste, and at the soles of his feet the goddess Isis, in gold bas-relief, mourns the death of the king. The number 1 (innermost) sarcophagus is in the number 29 case, and the

number 3 (outside) one is in the tomb at Thebes, with the body in it.
Case 33 contains the solid gold mask which covered the head of the
royal mummy. The stripes of the headdress are of blue glass. On the
forehead of King Tut are two goddesses: Wadjit of the North, a serpent goddess; and Nekhbet of the South, a vulture goddess. The
king's beard makes him similar to Osiris, as do the scepter and flail in
his hands on the mummiform coffins. Toward the east end of the
north gallery there are FUNERARY COUCHES.

Room 3 contains miscellaneous JEWELRY dating from the First
Dynasty to the Byzantine period.

Room 4 has the JEWELRY that came from TUTANKHAMEN'S TOMB.

The east galleries are filled with the Tutankhamen collection. Proceed through the gallery without entering the side rooms. Of particular interest is the famous THRONE in case 21, a PAINTED WOODEN
CHEST in case 20, ALABASTER VASES, BOOMERANGS, FANS, TRUMPETS,
COFFERS, BOATS, GAMES, and two WOODEN GUARDS of the tomb,
and so on. The throne in case 21 is carved in wood and decorated
with faience, glass paste, semiprecious stones, and silver. The
Amarna influence is clearer here than elsewhere. Note the solar disc.
The chair must have been made at Amarna, because a cartouche on
a side of the throne is inscribed with the name Tut-ankh-*Aten*,
"living image of Aten" — Tut's name before he left Amarna. When
he returned to Thebes he changed his name to Tut-ankh-*Amen*.

After visiting the east gallery, continue by going west through the
south gallery. Note the two WATER CLOCKS near the head of the
stairs.

Room 55 has an interesting set of PHOTOGRAPHS taken from the
air.

Room 54 displays WEAPONS.

Rooms 43 and 42 have archaic period funerary exhibits. In room
42 are the fragments of the famous PALERMO STONE and the slate
PALETTE OF KING NARMER, which dates back to 3100 B.C. It is 25
inches high and shows King Narmer celebrating a victory over
Lower Egypt. Narmer, in the solemn procession with no sandals,
is not unlike Moses removing his shoes at the burning bush (Exod.
3:1–5). Scholars occasionally attempt to belittle the Bible by pointing this
out. Those interested in art should notice the sense of order in the
horizontal bands. The Egyptian artist was faced with the fact that the
standing human figure, unlike that of an animal, does not have a single
main profile, but rather two competing profiles. For the sake of clarity he
had to combine these two views, and his method survived unchanged for
2,500 years. In the large figure of Narmer, the eye and shoulders are a
frontal view, but the head and eyes are in profile. This shows the
pharaoh in as complete a way as possible. The underlings (the two
animal trainers and four men carrying standards) do not have to have
their dignity preserved; hence they are shown in strict profile
throughout—except for their eyes.

Room 37 contains wooden SARCOPHAGI.

Room 32 has funerary objects of the OLD and MIDDLE KINGDOMS.

The rest of the rooms off the West Gallery have sarcophagi and funerary objects.

Crossing east through gallery 13, where the **CHARIOTS** are located, the visitor should go through the side rooms along the east corridor, beginning with number 14, which has Greco-Roman **COFFINS**. In the glass cases are shown complete **MUMMIES**. These artists broke with Egyptian tradition and painted the portraits in full face. Ancient Egyptians presented a profile, never a full face.

Room 19 is the room of the **DEITIES**.

Room 24, the **OSTRACON ROOM**, contains literary writings and drawings.

Room 29 is the **PAPYRUS ROOM**, with the soul-weighing scenes that are a part of the Book of the Dead. Examples of Egyptian writing from different periods are shown.

Room 34 shows the **MANNERS AND CUSTOMS** of daily life. In the last room is a collection of architectural models. Pyramids and their accompanying temples are shown in relief.

Those who desire to see the special **MUMMY ROOM** may do so for an extra fee. Those interested should inquire about it.

ON, *Heliopolis*, **El Matariya**

The site of this ancient city is in the northern suburbs of El Matariya, about 7 miles from the center of Cairo. From the Fifth Dynasty, this was the principal center of sun worship. The god was Re (Re-Harakhte), who replaced the older god Atum. The living manifestation of Re-Atum was the Mnevis bull.

Here was a great university, especially for the training of the priesthood. It is said that men like Plato, Pythagoras, Euclid, Solon, and Thales came here to learn from the priests of Heliopolis, that Manetho wrote his history of Egypt from the archives of the temple at On, and that Plato wrote his works here. Solon supposedly wrote his laws here. Strabo, the geographer, who was in Heliopolis twenty years before the birth of Christ, described the worship of the Mnevis bull at On and the Apis bull at Memphis.

Here possibly Joseph ruled as the prime minister of Egypt. Moses probably received his education here, becoming learned in all the wisdom of the Egyptians (Acts 7:22).

On has been almost deserted since the Roman period. The only remains of the city are parts of the **ENCLOSURE WALL** that surrounded the temple and an **OBELISK** of Aswan granite 68½ feet high, with hieroglyphics on all four sides. This is the oldest obelisk in all Egypt. On it is the cartouche of King Usertesen, who lived in 2760 B.C. The obelisk is known by some as the *Matariya Obelisk, Sesostris Obelisk*, or *Pharaoh's Needle*. The obelisks, connected with sun worship, represented the bright rays of the sun. Two other obelisks were once located here and were seen by the Israelites; one now stands in London and the other in Central Park in New York City. They were moved to Alexandria by Augustus Caesar in A.D. 23, and from there they were removed to their present locations.

- *Joseph married Asenath, daughter of Potipherah, the Egyptian priest of On (Gen. 41:45, 50; 46:20). As his wife's home, On was undoubtedly familiar to Joseph.*
- *Asenath bore Joseph two sons, Manasseh and Ephraim (Gen. 41: 50–52).*
- *Jeremiah called the area Beth-shemesh (City of the Sun) and said it would be destroyed (Jer. 43:13).*
- *Ezekiel spoke of the overthrow of On, called Aven (Ezek. 30:17).*
- *On is thought to be one of the five cities referred to by Isaiah (Isa. 19:18).*

EL MATARIYA *and the* Virgin's Tree

South of the Matariya Obelisk is the city of El Matariya, the traditional site of a resting place of Joseph, Mary, and Jesus when they fled to Egypt after Herod issued his edict to kill the babies in Bethlehem (Matt. 2:14). The VIRGIN'S TREE at Matariya stands in a garden on the right side of the main street, just before the Church of Our Lady of Matariya. It is a sycamore tree, planted in 1672 as a shoot of a fourteenth-century tree that stood in this same spot and supposedly gave shade to the Holy Family. The present tree looks dead. According to tradition, Mary washed Jesus' swaddling clothes in a spring 25 yards west of the tree. Many pilgrims still visit this site. The tree is believed by many to have supernatural qualities.

GOSHEN *("place of pasture"), the land of Ramses*

The home of the Israelites during their sojourn in Egypt, Goshen was located on the east side of the Nile River, from the Mediterranean Sea to the Red Sea. Goshen contained about 900 square miles of level and rich alluvial lands, and was called by Moses the "land of Rameses [Ramses]" (Gen. 47:11). It was the best of the land.

- *Joseph promised Goshen to his brethren (Gen. 45:10).*
- *Israel and his family entered Goshen and were met and instructed by Joseph (Gen. 46:28–34).*
- *At their request, the children of Israel were assigned Goshen for a home, where they prospered and multiplied (Gen. 47:1–12, 27).*
- *Jacob was carried from here to Canaan for burial (Gen. 50:1–14).*
- *The plagues did not come here as they did in the rest of Egypt (Exod. 8:22; 9:26).*
- *The children of Israel dwelt here 430 years (Exod. 12:40–41; Gal. 3:17).*
- *The Israelites went from Goshen to Succoth, where they were freed from Pharaoh (Exod. 12:37; Num. 33:3, 5).*

TANIS, *Ramses*

Tanis, identified as Ramses, was built as a store city by the Israelites while in Egypt, and was the starting point of the Exodus. After the Twentieth Dynasty, the royal necropolis was moved to Tanis from Thebes. The site is approximately 40 miles southwest of Port Said.

- *Ramses was the store city of the Israelites (Exod. 1:11).*
- *The Exodus began at Ramses (Exod. 12:37; Num. 33:3, 5).*

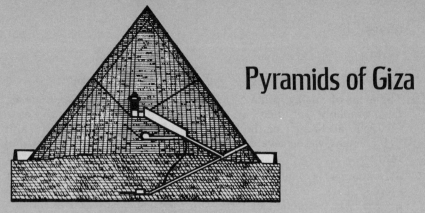

South-north longitudinal section of the Cheops pyramid

Pyramids of Giza

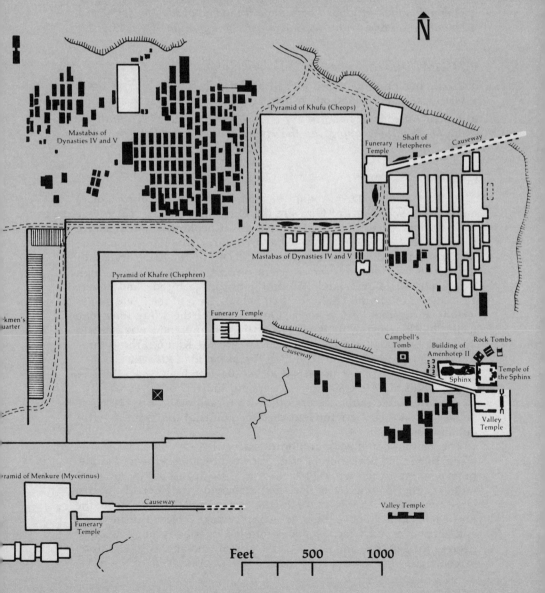

N

Mastabas of
Dynasties IV and V

Pyramid of Khufu (Cheops)

Funerary
Temple

Shaft of
Hetepheres

Causeway

Mastabas of Dynasties IV and V

Pyramid of Khafre (Chephren)

-kmen's
quarter

Funerary Temple

Causeway

Campbell's
Tomb

Building of
Amenhotep II

Rock Tombs

Sphinx

Temple of
the Sphinx

Valley
Temple

-ramid of Menkure (Mycerinus)

Causeway

Funerary
Temple

Valley Temple

Feet   500   1000

*Adapted from K. Lange and M. Hirmer, *Egypt: Architecture, Sculpture,
Painting,* 4th ed. (Hirmer Verlag München, 1968), by permission.

TAHPANHES ("the Negro"), Tahapanes, Tel Defneh

The name of this Egyptian city is the same as the Greek *Daphnae* and most probably identified with the modern Tell Defneh, which lies on the Pelusiac branch of the Nile about 20 miles southeast of Tanis. Tel Defneh was excavated by Petrie at the end of the nineteenth century.

■ *Tahpanhes is mentioned in the Old Testament (Jer. 2:16; 44:1; 46:14; Ezek. 30:18).*

■ *After the destruction of Jerusalem by Nebuchadnezzar in 587 B.C., many Jews fled to Tahpanhes (Jer. 43:7; also 2 Kings 25:26).*

■ *Jeremiah apparently lived here toward the end of his life (Jer. 43:8).*

■ *Jeremiah foretold many woes against the Egyptians (Jer. 43:9-13; 46:28).*

PITHOM ("narrow pass"), Tell er-Retabeh

This site has been identified as Tell er-Retabeh, and in biblical times it was located in the land of Goshen.

■ *Pithom was one of two "treasure cities" said to have been built for the pharaoh who oppressed the Hebrews (Exod. 1:11). (The other was Tanis.)*

Giza

The **PYRAMIDS OF GIZA**. About 7½ miles southwest of Tahrir Square and 6 miles southwest of Giza are the pyramids of Giza. They were built for and by Khufu (Cheops), Khafre (Chephren), and Menkure (Mycerinus). (*Cheops* and *Chephren* are the Greek names; *Mycerinus* is Latin.) The largest one, **CHEOPS**, is the lone survivor of the Seven Wonders of the Ancient World. It is 450 feet high (originally 481.4 feet) and 750 feet long on each side and covers 12-13 acres of ground (eight football fields). Each of the 2,300 stones weighs an average of 2½ tons. Only a few of the white limestone facing blocks remain. It is estimated that the pyramid was built in 20 years by 100,000 slaves as a burial site for Khufu. These three pyramids date from about 2700 B.C. The pyramid of **KHAFRE** is 447½ feet high; the pyramid of **MENKURE** is 204 feet high. Each builder respected his father by making his pyramid shorter.

The three large pyramids are offset from each other at a 45-degree angle, so that each faces the four cardinal points of the compass without any obstruction.

The visitor should walk around the Great Pyramid of Cheops if he wants to get an impression of size. Escorted by an experienced guide, he may climb to the top (571 feet on a 51-degree slope) in about 30 minutes, after paying a fee. He should also go inside one of the two large pyramids. The entrance to the pyramid of Cheops — on the north side, 55 feet above the base — is a passage 3 feet 11 inches high and about 3½ feet wide. It slopes into the interior at an angle of 26 degrees for 320 feet, and at the end is a small chamber with the stone sarcophagus. Loose boards uncovered on the south side of the pyra-

mid in 1954 proved to be a dismantled funerary boat of Pharaoh Khufu (Cheops), builder of the pyramid.

A **CAMEL RIDE** is a tourist attraction at the pyramid, and if time will allow, a ride into the desert is worthwhile. Around the pyramids are **MASTABAS** (tombs of the nobles) and **FUNERARY TEMPLES**. Of the 9 pyramids in the Giza area, 6 are small.

The **GREAT SPHINX**. Near the pyramids of Giza, the Great Sphinx has been staring across the desert for nearly 5,000 years. It is 240 feet long and 66 feet high. The face is 13 feet by 8 feet, and the ear is 4½ feet long. Carved out of the natural cliff, it has been covered by sand during much of its history. It represents the pharaoh Khafre (Chephren), who built the sphinx, or the god Horus, who guarded temples and tombs.

The head of an Egyptian sphinx might be a man or a beast; if a man, then the face usually represented the pharaoh of the time. Egyptian sphinxes with human heads and lion bodies symbolize power and intelligence. The other two types of sphinxes in Egypt are ram-headed and hawk-headed lions.

The body of the sphinx of Giza is a lion. Between the sphinx's legs is a stone, placed there by Thutmose IV, who cleared the sand from the sphinx in the 1400s B.C. It was also cleaned during Roman times and again in 1818, 1886, and 1925. In A.D. 1380 the face of the sphinx was damaged by an iconoclastic sheikh and later by the Mamelukes, who used it as a target.

The **VALLEY TEMPLE OF KHAFRE**, near the sphinx, is a granite temple with alabaster floors. This was a part of the temple complex that accompanied the pyramid of Khafre.

Temple of Queen Hatshepsut, Theban Necropolis

Pyramids of Giza

MEMPHIS, NOPH, *Mit-Rahina*

Fifteen miles up the Nile River south of Cairo, on the west bank, is the ancient capital of Egypt, Memphis. It was built by Menes, who first united the two kingdoms of Upper and Lower Egypt in 3100 B.C.

Memphis was the white-walled capital city of Egypt at the time of Abraham, Jacob, Joseph, and Moses. Moses was possibly reared there in the palace of the Pharaoh.

After Alexander the Great built Alexandria in the fourth century B.C., Memphis ceased to be the chief city. Following the Arab conquest, its population rapidly declined, and the temple was destroyed in the fourth century A.D. The old city has long been buried.

POINTS OF INTEREST

More than 200 sphinxes found in and around the city have been moved away, most of them to museums. However, one **ALABASTER SPHINX** is still here. Measuring 26 feet long by 13 feet 2 inches high and weighing 80 tons, it dates back to 1600 B.C.

A few minutes' walk southwest from the sphinx is a fine red granite **STATUE OF RAMSES II**, located in a mud room. The visitor must climb wooden steps to reach it.

A gigantic limestone **STATUE OF RAMSES II** is housed in a new building. It is 42 feet long and dates to the Nineteenth Dynasty — about 1250 B.C. About 550 yards north of the building lie the remains of the **TEMPLE OF PTAH**, where the huge statue once stood. The bull Apis was worshiped at Memphis as sacred to Ptah, the principal god of the city.

■ *Memphis (Noph) is mentioned repeatedly in the Old Testament (Isa. 19:13; Jer. 2:16; 44:1; 46:14, 19; Ezek. 30:13, 16; Hos. 9:6).*

Saqqara

Twenty-two miles south of Cairo and just west of Memphis is the modern village of Saqqara. Immediately west of the village is a complex of burial sites for more than twenty pharaohs and hundreds of nobles, dating back as far as the Third Dynasty (ca. 2686 B.C.). The oldest of all pyramids is here.

POINTS OF INTEREST

The **STEP PYRAMID OF ZOSER** (Djoser) is the oldest known pyramid and the oldest free-standing cut-stone structure in the world. It is the first of about 80 pyramids built on the west bank of the Nile and constructed over a span of 1,500 years. Built about 2778–2723 B.C., the Step Pyramid is 204 feet high, and the base measures 411 feet from west to east and 358 feet from north to south. A wall once surrounded the 37-acre complex. King Zoser is the first artist whose name is recorded in history. He was a genius in architecture, medicine, and other fields, and after his death he was deified. The Greeks equated him with Aesculapius (Asclepias), the patron-god of medicine.

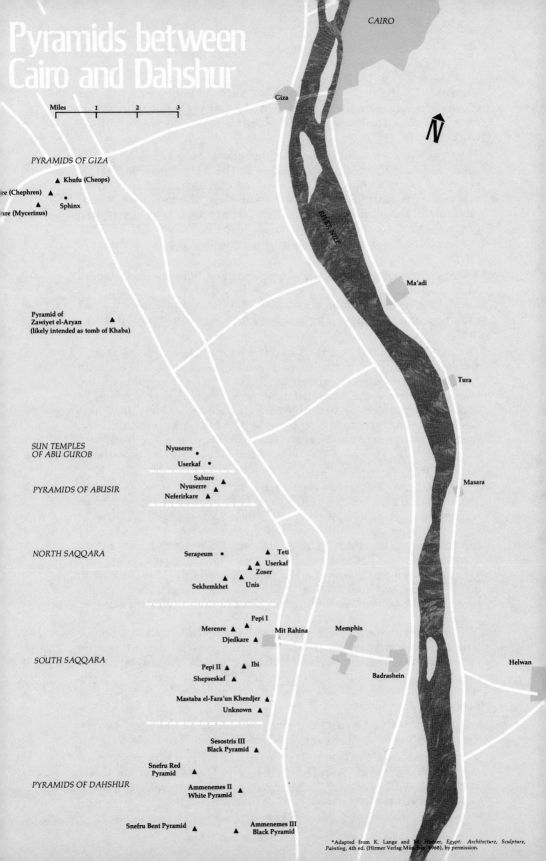

Pyramids between Cairo and Dahshur

CAIRO

Giza

Miles 1 2 3

N

PYRAMIDS OF GIZA

▲ Khufu (Cheops)
re (Chephren) ▲
ure (Mycerinus) ▲   ● Sphinx

RIVER NILE

Ma'adi

Pyramid of
Zawiyet el-Aryan ▲
(likely intended as tomb of Khaba)

Tura

SUN TEMPLES
OF ABU GUROB   Nyuserre ●
                      Userkaf ●

Masara

PYRAMIDS OF ABUSIR   Sahure ▲
                        Nyuserre ▲
                    Neferirkare ▲

NORTH SAQQARA   Serapeum ●   ▲ Teti
                              ▲ Userkaf
                           ▲ Zoser
                   ▲   ▲
              Sekhemkhet   Unis

                          Pepi I
                          ▲
          Merenre ▲   ▲   Mit Rahina   Memphis
              Djedkare ▲

SOUTH SAQQARA   Helwan
              Pepi II ▲   ▲ Ibi
          Shepseskaf ▲   Badrashein

          Mastaba el-Fara'un Khendjer ▲
                    Unknown ▲

                  Sesostris III
                  Black Pyramid ▲
          Snefru Red
          Pyramid ▲
PYRAMIDS OF DAHSHUR
              Ammenemes II ▲
              White Pyramid

      Snefru Bent Pyramid ▲   ▲ Ammenemes III
                                 Black Pyramid

*Adapted from K. Lange and M. Hirmer, *Egypt: Architecture, Sculpture, Painting*, 4th ed. (Hirmer Verlag München, 1968), by permission.

MUSEUM. By the Pyramid of Zoser is a museum housing a collection of alabaster vases from the Fifth Dynasty. Hieroglyphic inscriptions on some vases are known as the oldest religious documents in the world.

The PYRAMID OF UNIS (Onnos), dating back to 2450 B.C., is 385 yards southwest of the Step Pyramid of Zoser. The interior has the granite sarcophagus of the king and a roof of the burial chamber that tapers upward. The chamber walls are completely covered with hieroglyphics dealing with the hereafter. They consist of spells and prayers, and the entire collection of such spells, known as *The Book of the Dead*, has about 700 spells, found in the various pyramids of Egypt.

The MASTABA OF MERERUKA is situated northeast of the Step Pyramid. Mereruka was Grand Chamberlain of the Pharaoh. The tomb, 133 feet by 79 feet, was built about 2400–2200 B.C. and consists of 32 chambers and passages. The walls are covered with beautiful paintings.

The MASTABA OF TI, northeast of the Mariette House, is the largest and most beautiful of the private tombs at Saqqara. Ti was an "architectural overseer" about 2563–2429 B.C. The walls of the tomb, famous for their painted limestone relief of everyday life in ancient Egypt, have scenes of weaving, hunting, sculpturing, harvesting, boating, sacrificing, shipbuilding, fishing, papyrus gathering, flogging, ploughing, treading in the seed, eating, and the birth of a calf. Note the expression on the cow and calf in a scene that shows a calf being carried across the stream on the back of an Egyptian.

The SERAPEUM, 650 yards west of the Mastaba of Ti, is an underground burial site for the sacred Apis bulls that were worshiped at Memphis. The Apis bull, a manifestation of the god Ptah, was embalmed after death and buried with great ceremony in a special sarcophagus. This burial site is 35 feet underground and nearly 1,200 feet long. The main gallery is 660 feet long and houses 24 granite sarcophagi that average about 10 feet high, 13½ feet long, and 6½ feet wide. The lids are 3 feet thick. Each sarcophagus weighs about 60 tons, and the heavy granite pieces were transported from Aswan, 450 miles away.

The oldest tomb of the bulls dates back to 1600 B.C.; the one at Saqqara dates from 650 B.C. The Serapeum gets its name from the fact that Apis assimilated with Osiris after death and was then called *Osiris-Apis*, or *Oserapis*. In the Ptolemaic period, Oserapis was equated with the Greek god of the underworld, Serapis, and hence the name *Serapeum*.

■ *There seems to be a correspondence here to the children of Israel's golden calf episode under the direction of Aaron (Exod. 32).*

The MASTABA OF PTAH-HOTEP is located a short distance south of the Mariette House. Ptah-Hotep was a judge of the High Court during the Fifth Dynasty. The walls are covered with beautiful, well-preserved reliefs and paintings of daily life.

Above: Painting from the mastaba of Ti, Saqqara
Below: Sarcophagus of an Apis bull, Saqqara

Dahshur

About 5 miles south of Saqqara and 27 miles south of Cairo are the
five pyramids of Dahshur.

The **BENT PYRAMID** of King Snefru still has the original smooth stone that once covered all the pyramids. Snefru, an early Fourth Dynasty (2600 B.C.) king, was the father of Khufu (Cheops), the builder of the Great Pyramid at Giza. It is possible to climb this 325-foot Bent Pyramid with the help of a guide, but the climb is more difficult than climbing the Great Pyramid. The base is 620 feet wide. The Bent Pyramid is the predecessor of the first true pyramid, also built at Dahshur.

It has been suggested that perhaps the second pyramid, named the *Meidum Pyramid*, 35 miles south of Saqqara, was being converted from a step pyramid into a true pyramid at the same time that the Bent Pyramid was being built, but when the new sides collapsed into piles of rubble all the builders of the Bent Pyramid observed this disaster and decided to change the angle of their pyramid from 52 degrees to 43 1/3 degrees.

The **BLACK PYRAMID OF AMMENEMES III**, in the south end of Dahshur, is made of brick.

The **WHITE PYRAMID OF AMMENEMES II** is located in the center of Dahshur.

The **RED PYRAMID**, 325 feet high and 702 feet at the base, was built by Snefru. Its base is the same size as the pyramid of Khufu, but the pyramid is shorter because the angle of the sides is 43 1/3 degrees instead of 52 degrees.

The **BLACK PYRAMID OF SESOSTRIS III** is 100 feet high and 345 feet wide and is made of brick.

ALEXANDRIA

Alexander the Great established this city in 332 B.C. It is located on the Mediterranean coast near the mouth of the west branch of the Nile River and approximately 130 miles north of Cairo.

For centuries it was one of the most magnificent and renowned cities in the ancient world. It was the center of Hellenistic culture during the Ptolemaic dynasty (332 B.C.-30 B.C.). During Cleopatra's reign 50,000-100,000 Greeks, Egyptians, and Jews lived in the city. After the destruction of Jerusalem in Jeremiah's day, Jews fled to Alexandria in large numbers (Jer. 42:14). It was the largest town of the Roman Empire outside of Rome itself, and it boasted a library of 700,000 manuscripts.

Between 250 and 132 B.C. the Hebrew Scriptures were first translated into the Greek tongue in Alexandria. This volume was known as the *Septuagint* and is the only authorized version of the Old Testament in the Greek Orthodox church.

Alexandria became a center of Christianity very early. The apostle Paul seems to have refrained from going there because the gospel had already reached the city (Rom. 15:20). Eusebius says the apostle Mark brought Christianity to Egypt. During the second and third centuries Alexandria was the intellectual capital of Christendom. Here Clement and Origen taught in a theological school against the

Gnostic philosophy, and Athanasius defended the doctrine of the deity of Christ in the Nicene controversy.

The Jewish philosopher Philo lived in Alexandria. He was a contemporary of Jesus and took it upon himself to interpret the scriptures allegorically in order to make Jewish theology compatible with Greek philosophy. Philo's theory that mind or spirit was a product of the Deity led to his conception of the Deity as having complete absence of all qualities.

Philo was one of the many philosophers who helped to pave the way for a written definition of God that appeared later in Christian creeds. He indicated that God, being better than virtue, knowledge, good, and beauty, transcends all qualities. God is not in space, he said, because he contains it. He is without body, parts or passions: without feet, for whither should he walk who fills all things; without eyes, for why does he need eyes who made the light? He is invisible, for how can eyes that are too weak to gaze upon the sun be strong enough to gaze upon its maker? He is incomprehensible, says Philo. We know *that* he is, but we cannot know *what* he is.

When the Arabs made Cairo the capital of Egypt in A.D. 642, Alexandria began to decline. For nearly 1,000 years it had been the center of culture and commerce, but it soon became a fishing village. Mohammed Ali, however, saw the importance of Alexandria and gave the city the needed impetus to bring the population from 7,000 in 1805 to a million and a half in 1970. Today it is the second largest city in Egypt. With the exception of the Arab quarters and bazaars, the city is European in nature. It is a vital commercial center to Egypt and is the principal port of Egypt. Exports include cotton, grain, beans, sugar, and rice. White sandy beaches and a wonderful climate make Alexandria a major summer resort.

- *Alexandrians opposed Stephen (Acts 6:9).*
- *Alexandria was the birthplace of Apollos (Acts 18:24).*
- *Paul embarked on an Alexandrian ship when he left Myra and Malta (Acts 27:6; 28:11).*

POINTS OF INTEREST

Antiquities of the past are not prevalent in Alexandria, but the following are possible points to visit:

POMPEY'S PILLAR (*Amoud el Sawari*), a red Aswan rose granite column, dates from the Ptolemaic period and was erected in honor of Diocletian. It is southwest of the city, near the Arab cemetery. It is nearly 90 feet high, has a 9-foot diameter at the base, and tapers to 6½ feet at the top. A Corinthian capital graces the top. The column received its name from Pompey, whose tomb was believed to be on that spot. At this site the Serapeum, a temple to the god Serapis (god of the underworld), once stood during the Ptolemaic period.

CATACOMBS OF KOM EL SHUQAFA. A couple of blocks north of Pompey's Pillar are the Catacombs of Kom el Shuqafa, ancient burial

Sunset over the Nile

tombs dating from approximately A.D. 200–300. They are built on three levels and show decorations of Egyptian, Roman, and Greek influence. The lowest level, 100 feet below the surface and usually under water, is believed to be a sanctuary for the bull god Apis.

The **ANFOUSHY NECROPOLIS** (*Anfushi*), a second-century Greek burial site, is smaller and less important than the Catacombs of Kom el Shuqafa, but paintings on the walls, as well as the tombs themselves, make a visit worthwhile. It is located nearly 2 miles east of the Ras el Tin Palace.

The **RAS EL TIN PALACE**, at the West Harbor, is a palace to which King Farouk went into exile on July 26, 1952. The 300 rooms may now be viewed by the public.

AQUARIUM. Different forms of sea life from the Red Sea, the Mediterranean, and the Nile are on display at the Aquarium, in the western part of the city near Fort Qaitbai.

PHAROS (lighthouse) and **KAIT BEY FORT.** In 280 B.C. Ptolemy II built a huge lighthouse on the east end of Pharos Isand. It stood nearly 500 feet tall. It was adorned with marble columns, balustrades, and statues, and was known as one of the Seven Wonders of the World. From this first Pharos, the idea of a lighthouse spread throughout the world. An earthquake destroyed the lighthouse in the fourteenth century A.D., and Fort Kait Bey was built on the site. Pharos Island is connected to the mainland with fill.

The **ALEXANDRIA LIGHTHOUSE** is located near Fort Kait Bey.

MONTAZA PALACE, the royal summer palace, stands at the eastern end of the Corniche, and houses mementos of the last kings of the Mohammed Ali dynasty. The palace, flowers, and grounds are beautiful.

The GRECO-ROMAN MUSEUM was founded in 1891 and houses 40,000 items dating back to Greek and Roman periods, including a collection of 50,000 coins and Egyptian antiquities.

The CENTRAL MUSEUM FOR FINE ARTS is an art gallery featuring paintings by modern and other artists.

Rosetta, *Rashid*

Forty-five miles east of Alexandria, where the western branch of the Nile flows into the Mediterranean Sea, is the city of Rosetta. Northeast of Rosetta, at Fort Saint Julian, the Rosetta Stone was discovered by Bouchard, a French officer of the Engineers, in 1799. This black basalt stone slab was responsible for the breakthrough in the interpretation of Egyptian hieroglyphs. The stone is 3 feet 9 inches in length, 2 feet 4½ inches in width, and 11 inches in thickness. It is believed that originally the entire stone was 5-6 feet in height.

It has three inscriptions or versions of the same decree that was passed by the general council of Egyptian priests assembled at Memphis to celebrate the first commemoration of the coronation of Ptolemy V, Epiphanes, king of all Egypt. It is dated April 4, 196 B.C. Among other things in the decree are the benefits which Ptolemy V had conferred upon Egypt: remission of taxes; restoration of temple services; forgiveness of debts; endowments to temples; gifts of money and corn to temples; restoration of the temples of Apis and Mnevis Bulls and of other sacred animals. The inscription is written in two languages, Egyptian and Greek. The Egyptian is in two portions: (1) *hieroglyphic*, a type of picture writing; and (2) *demotic*, a cursive form of hieroglyphic writing, used in the Ptolemaic period (323 B.C.– 30 B.C.).

In 1822 a 32-year-old French scholar, Jean François Champollion, began to decipher the hieroglyphs. During the next ten years, until his death in 1832, he correctly deciphered the hieroglyphic forms of the names and titles of most of the Roman emperors, drew up a classified list of Egyptian hieroglyphs, and formulated a system of grammar and general decipherment that is the foundation upon which all later Egyptologists have worked. The Rosetta Stone is now housed in the British Museum.

UPPER EGYPT

Luxor, Egypt, is 416 miles south of Cairo and can be visited by car (two days' journey one way), train (8-11 hours), boat (several days), or plane (1-2 hours). On the way are several places of interest:

Deir Mawas, Tell el 'Amarna

At a point 190 miles south of Cairo are the ruins of Tell el 'Amarna, near the town of Deir Mawas, on the east bank.

Tell el 'Amarna was the residence of Pharaoh Amenhotep IV (Akhenaten), who lived about 1400–1360 B.C. When he was born the Egyptians believed in many gods — polytheism — with some gods more prominent than others. But Akhenaten launched a heretical revolt against the great god Amen and other gods and sought to impose upon Egypt a new god, Aten, and do away with other gods — a new monotheism. Aten was represented by a sun-disc with celestial rays penetrating the universe and bestowing life on all living things. Many modern scholars believe this is where Moses received his concept of one god. The name *Moses* is Egyptian, being a variation of the word for "child." *Thutmose* means "child of the god Thoth." There is no evidence of a direct connection between Moses' and Akhenaten's monotheism, but there were certainly Egyptian influences on Moses and the Israelites.

After ruling for five years at Thebes, Amenhotep IV changed his name to Akhenaten, carried out a reformation not only in religion but also in Egyptian art, and moved his capital from Thebes (Luxor) to Tell el 'Amarna, halfway between Thebes and Cairo. The 17-year reign of this "heretical pharaoh" (about 1375–1358 B.C.) is an interesting chapter in the history of Egypt. His statues exaggerate his physical imperfections: pot belly, stumpy legs, and camel legs. He cannot be mistaken.

Akhenaten's wife was the beautiful Nefertiti. The famous bust of Queen Nefertiti shows her in a royal headdress with a brightly painted face under a crown. *Nefer* means "good and beautiful."

Akhenaten fought against Amen Re and had the god's name erased from all Egyptian monuments. But forces were at work against Akhenaten. One of these forces was Queen Ty, Akhenaten's mother. When she came to Amarna, trouble brewed. Nefertiti, a strong believer in Aten, was banished to a separate part of the city and was stripped of her royal titles. Akhenaten took one of his daughters as his chief wife and made no further moves against Amen Re. The spirit of rebellion went out of Amarna, and five years later Akhenaten died.

Soon one of his young brothers, Tutankhaten, became pharaoh and changed the ending of his name to -*amen*. Young Tut went back to Thebes and Amen was restored for another 1,000 years.

Only a few traces remain of the **TEMPLE TO ATEN**. It was 2,409 feet long and 907 feet wide — evidently a huge complex. In a hillside there are 24 rock **TOMBS**, on whose walls remarkable intimate and familiar domestic scenes show a freedom of artistic expression that was hitherto unknown.

In addition to the bust of Nefertiti — a very important find — the Tell el 'Amarna Tablets (now located in the Berlin Museum, the British Museum, and other museums) are also very important. They are letters written on some 400 clay tablets in Akkadian cuneiform, and are part of the diplomatic correspondence between rulers and officials in Western Asia to the pharaohs Amenhotep III and Amenhotep IV (Akhenaten) about 1400–1360 B.C., before the Hebrew exodus. Those from Palestine and Syria include six from Abdiheba, governor of Jerusalem, who described Palestine as being gravely disturbed by "Habiru" invaders. The governor was seeking aid from the Pharaoh against the Habiru.

The question is, who were the Habiru? Were they Israelites? Some scholars feel that the letters tell of the Israelite invasion of Canaan and others believe that the Habiru are simply lawless gangs within Canaan. Part of letter no. 287 says: "Behold, this land of Jerusalem, neither my father nor my mother gave it to me . . . and the deed of the sons of Labaya who have given the land of the king to the Habiru . . . I fall at thy feet." Letters 47 and 48 are from Abdi-tirshi, the ruler of Hazor to the pharaoh of Egypt assuring him that he will guard the cities. Other letters are from Gezer, Ashkalon, Gaza, Joppa, Shechem, Lachish, Hebron, and Megiddo.

Asyut (Assiout), Lycopolis

This is the largest town in Upper Egypt, with about 100,000 people. It is 232 miles from Cairo and is the center of an important Coptic community. Here Plotinus, the Greek philosopher and founder of Neoplatonism, was born in 205 B.C. At age 20 he went to Alexandria to study philosophy under the great teachers there, and in 244 B.C. he settled in Rome. He developed his own philosophy and believed that material things represented evil. Men, he felt, should reject material things and purify their souls by communion with God. His ideas had an influence on early Christian thought.

Rock tombs in the area have been rifled by the natives and are not very impressive. The city is famous, however, for its beautiful silver shawls, carpetmaking, and ebony and ivory work.

Abydos, This, Thinis

Located 322 miles from Cairo and 7½ miles southwest of the el-Baliana railway station are the ruins of Abydos — some of the oldest in Egypt, dating from the First and Second Dynasties. TOMBS OF THE FIRST PHARAOHS (3100–2686 B.C.) are here. One of the pharaohs, Djer, was accompanied into death by 587 human victims.

The TEMPLES OF SETI I AND RAMSES II still stand. Osiris seems to have been the main god of these temples, but there are chapels to many other gods. Reliefs and colored paintings are well preserved, and many tombs of the New Kingdom are located at Abydos.

To celebrate the "resurrection" of Osiris, an annual "passion play" was held at Abydos. Osiris was symbolically buried, and then as stones were removed from the tomb the people shouted, "The Lord is risen!" In this rebirth of Osiris the Egyptians saw their own triumph over death.

Dendera, Ant

These ruins are located near Qena, 37 miles north of Luxor on the east bank of the Nile. A train takes one hour to reach Qena from

Luxor. A ferry must be taken to the west bank, and then the ruins can be found 3 miles from the Nile.

Dendera was a religious center for the worship of Hathor, goddess of love and joy, like the Roman Venus and the Greek Aphrodite. The TEMPLE dates from the first century B.C. but there are older ruins from as far back as the Fourth Dynasty. On the walls of the temple are many scenes, including some showing the Roman emperors Caligula, Tiberius, Nero, and Claudius, representing pharaohs worshiping the gods. On the south wall is a relief of Caesar and Cleopatra and their son. Six beautiful Hathor-columns form the facade of the temple, and 24 support the roof.

NO, *Thebes*, Luxor

The city of Luxor, 416 miles south of Cairo, bears the Egyptian name *Weset*, the biblical name *No*, and the Greek name *Thebes*. It is possible that ancient Thebes had a million inhabitants. In *The Iliad* Homer referred to "Thebes, city where rich are the houses in treasure, a hundred has she of gates . . ." — the richest and mightiest city in the world. It reached its glory about 1500 B.C., and names such as Tutankhamen, Hatshepsut, Amenhotep III, Akhenaten, and Ramses II are household words in Luxor. For hundreds of years temples, statues, obelisks, columns, and sphinxes were built to make this area the central place of worship of the Egyptians — a most important religious center of the god Amen, the first universal god in Egypt.

After 1000 B.C., however, Thebes was well on the way of decline. In 661 B.C. the city was sacked of what riches were left, and her wealth was carried off by Ashurbanipal (Nah. 3:8). But her temples, built to last through eternity, still remain.

The ancient city of Thebes consisted of three areas that are known today as *Luxor, Karnak*, and the *West Bank*.

■ Thebes *is mentioned as* No *in the scriptures (Jer. 46:25; Ezek. 30:14–16).*
■ *The fate of Thebes was that which Nahum predicted for the hated Assyrian city of Nineveh (Nah. 3:7–8).*
■ *Upper Egypt was called* Pathros *by Isaiah and Jeremiah (Isa. 11:11; Jer. 44:1).*

Modern Luxor

The narrow streets, open-fronted shops, primitive houses, street sweepers, donkeys, city smells, and the people of Luxor are a sight the Westerner will never forget. Carriages can be hired to take a traveler through the back alleys.

Temple of Luxor

On the edge of the Nile is the ancient temple of Luxor, built between 1400 and 1100 B.C. by the pharaohs Amenhotep III, Tutankhamen, Hatshepsut, and Ramses II. It was dedicated to the god Amen, his wife Mut, and their son, the moon god Khons. The temple complex is 857 feet long and 182 feet wide.

Obelisk of Ramses II, Luxor

In front of the pylons were six **STATUES OF RAMSES**. Only three remain now, and the two seated figures are 76 feet high. Only one of the rose-colored Aswan granite **OBELISKS** is still standing. The other was given to France in 1833 because of Champollion's work in deciphering the Rosetta Stone. It is now located in the Place de la Concorde in Paris.

The two obelisks were placed in front of the temple by Ramses II, who had a real flair for the superlative. He reigned for 66 years (ca. 1290–1224 B.C.), lived past the age of 90, sired more than 100 sons, had more than 50 daughters — many of whom he married — and bestrewed the Nile valley with countless monuments, obelisks, pylons, temples, and colossal statues commemorating his deeds. At Karnak he built the largest columned hall ever reared by man. Many believe that Ramses II was the king who "knew not Joseph" (Exod. 1:8) and put the children of Israel in bondage. As is attested by nine succeeding pharaohs bearing his name, no pharaoh of Egypt had greater influence than Ramses II.

Running north from the Luxor temple is the **AVENUE OF RAM-HEADED SPHINXES**. There were approximately 1,500 sphinxes lining the two-mile avenue between the Luxor and Karnak temples. During the great festival of Amen at Thebes a splendid procession moved along the avenue carrying the sacred bark of Amen. This was a 27-day religious festival, filled with the banging of tambourines, chanting of priests, and burning of incense. It is only recently that the avenue was excavated, but the temple itself was excavated beginning in 1884. Before that time the temple was buried under a hill of rubbish and native houses. It was discovered when a drainage shaft was being sunk from a house.

Entering the main entrance of the temple from the north, one comes to the **COURT OF RAMSES II**. On the southwest wall is a relief showing the Nile god Hapi tying together the lotus and papyrus plants, symbols of Upper and Lower Egypt. This was the uniting that took place in 3100 B.C., making Egypt the first united civilization. The female breasts on the male god Hapi symbolize the fertility and nourishment of the Nile.

The corridor decorated by Tutankhamen, the **COLONNADE OF HARMHAB**, is the next columned area, followed by the very beautiful **COURT OF AMENHOTEP III** (about 1411–1375 B.C.). The court is surrounded by 99 excellently preserved papyrus capital columns. This was the hypostyle hall of the temple, like the holy place in the temple of Solomon.

Other miscellaneous sanctuaries make up the temple complex, with beautiful bas-reliefs on the walls, outside and inside. Parts of the temple have been used by Christians and Moslems, and they remodeled and painted to suit their own needs.

Karnak

Nearly 2 miles north of the Luxor temple is the largest temple complex in the world. It covers 100 acres and took about 2,000 years to build (2133–100 B.C.). The temples are dedicated to Amen Re, Mut (wife of Amen Re), and Khons, their son (the divine triad). In fact, Karnak is a whole city of temples, the largest of which is the **TEMPLE OF AMEN**.

An **AVENUE OF SPHINXES**, constructed by Ramses in 1292 B.C., connects the Luxor and Karnak temples. There are several pylons or entrances to the various temples, but the following list of antiquities will begin at the largest of the pylons — those located on the west side of the complex.

The **PYLONS** forming the chief entrance are the largest at Karnak. They are 429 feet wide, 50 feet thick, and 144 feet high. Stairs ascend to the top, which offers an excellent view. These pylons were started in 304 B.C. and were never completed.

The **COURT** behind the pylons is the largest of all Egyptian temple courts — 340 by 277 feet. It dates back to 525–650 B.C. On the left as you enter the courtyard is the **TEMPLE OF SETI II** (1209 B.C.). The single **LOTUS-CAPITAL COLUMN** in the court was erected by the Ethiopian pharaoh Taharka in 688 B.C.

On the south side of the court is a small **TEMPLE OF AMEN**, built by Ramses III in 1198 B.C. It measures 172 feet in length. Large statues of Ramses III line the outer court of the temple. The three small chapels at the south end are to the gods Amen (middle), Mut (right), and Khons (left).

The **GREAT HYPOSTYLE HALL** is entered through a second set of pylons. This "Hall of Columns" is the largest columnar structure ever built by man. It consists of 134 sandstone columns arranged in 16 rows and covering an area of 56,000 square feet. The central avenue consists of 12 columns with open papyrus capitals. The columns are 69 feet tall and 33 feet in circumference, and 100 men could stand on top of each. The other columns, with closed papyrus-bud capitals, are 42½ feet tall and 27½ feet in circumference. All of the columns are made of stones stacked like pancakes, engraved, and originally painted.

The hypostyle hall was begun perhaps by Harmhab in 1350–1315 B.C. and finished by Ramses I about 1315 B.C. Reliefs were added as late as 1230 B.C. by Ramses II. The outside walls of the hall have beautiful **BATTLE SCENES**: the victories of Seti I over the Libyans on the north wall and the victories of Ramses II over the Hittites on the south wall. Karnak owes its special fame to this hall. From ancient times it was considered one of the Seven Wonders of the World. Because of its columns and aisles, the hall is a prototype of the later Christian basilicas. Each column matches the size of Trajan's Column in Rome.

The third set of **PYLONS OF AMENHOTEP III** (1411 B.C.) forms the entrance to an early temple dating back to 1580–1350 B.C. A 76-foot **OBELISK OF THUTMOSE I** is still standing in the court between the two pylons. There were originally four obelisks, dating from 1535 B.C.

Luxor and Karnak

N

Miles

2   1

Valley of the Kings
(Biban el Muluk)

El-Qorn

Deir el-Bahri

El-Asasif

Dra-abu el-Neggar

Amenhotep I

Thutmose III

Si-Ptah

Rameseum

Sheikh Abd el-Qurna

Thutmose IV

Deir el-Medina

Merneptah

Valley of the Queens
(Biban el Harim)

Qurnet Murai

Amenhotep III

Colossi of Memnon

Medinet Habu

Ramses III

Palace of
Amenhotep III

Thutmose III

Qurna

Seti I

Karnak

Luxor

RIVER NILE

*For the sake of clarity, only the names of the monarchs are shown alongside
their funerary temples.
**Adapted from K. Lange and M. Hirmer, Egypt: Architecture, Sculpture,
Painting, 4th ed. (Hirmer Verlag München, 1968) by permission.

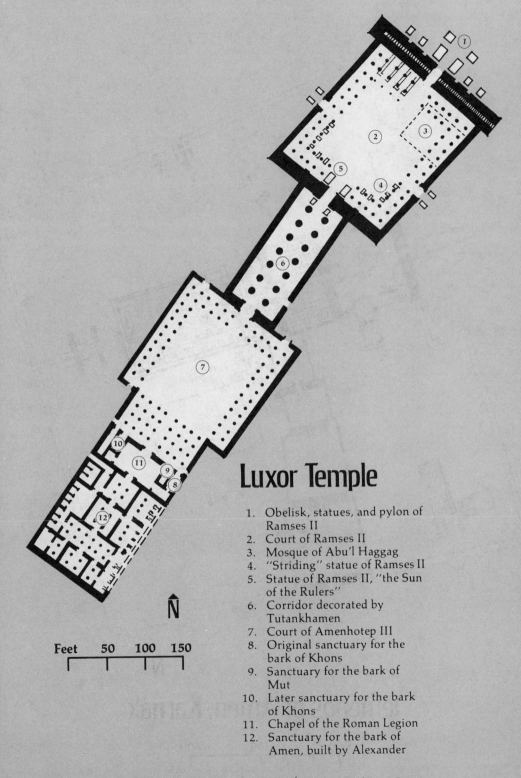

Luxor Temple

1. Obelisk, statues, and pylon of Ramses II
2. Court of Ramses II
3. Mosque of Abu'l Haggag
4. "Striding" statue of Ramses II
5. Statue of Ramses II, "the Sun of the Rulers"
6. Corridor decorated by Tutankhamen
7. Court of Amenhotep III
8. Original sanctuary for the bark of Khons
9. Sanctuary for the bark of Mut
10. Later sanctuary for the bark of Khons
11. Chapel of the Roman Legion
12. Sanctuary for the bark of Amen, built by Alexander

N̂

Feet 50 100 150

*Adapted from K. Lange and M. Hirmer, *Egypt: Architecture, Sculpture, Painting*, 4th ed. (Hirmer Verlag München, 1968), by permission.

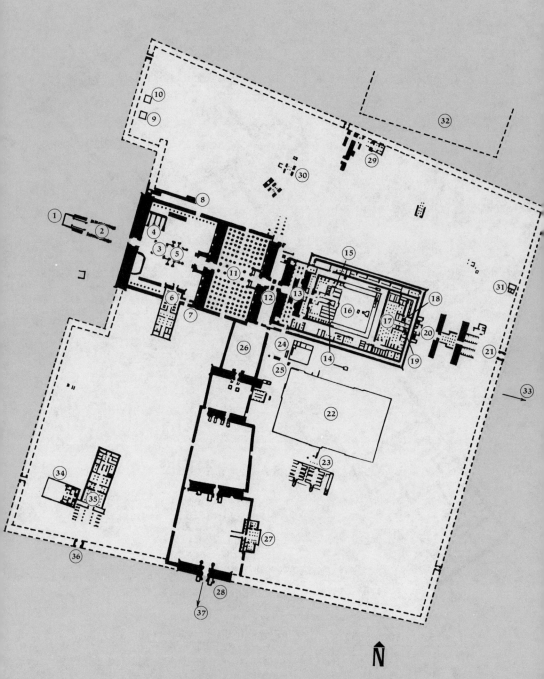

Ñ

Temenos of Amen, Karnak

Feet   300   600

1. Quay
2. Sphinx-lined dromos
3. The First Court
4. Way station of Seti II
5. Kiosk of Taharka
6. Way station of Ramses III
7. Triumphal inscription of Sheshonk I
8. Modern stairs to top of first pylon
9. Reconstructed chapel of Senusret I
10. Reconstructed alabaster chapel of Amenhotep I
11. The great hypostyle hall
12. Obelisk of Thutmose I
13. Hall of Thutmose I and obelisks of Hatshepsut
14. Sanctuary for the bark of Amen, built by Philip Arrhidaeus
15. Rooms of Hatshepsut
16. Middle Kingdom remains
17. Festival Hall of Thutmose III
18. Room with botanical pictures
19. Chapel of Alexander
20. The "Hearing Ear," a chapel for public prayers of Thutmose III, Ramses II, and later rulers
21. East gateway of Nekhtnebef
22. Temple lake
23. Fowl yard and storerooms
24. Top of fallen obelisk of Hatshepsut
25. Scarab-topped monument of Amenhotep III
26. Court of the cache
27. Festival Hall of Amenhotep II
28. Base of standing colossus of Amenhotep III
29. Temple of Ptah
30. Late chapels
31. Chapel dedicated to Osiris, "Ruler of Eternity"
32. Temenos of Montu, southern edge
33. Approximate position of temple of Akhenaten
34. Temple of Ipet
35. Temple of Khons
36. Gateway of Ptolemy III and Euergetes I
37. Avenue to the Temenos of Mut

*Adapted from K. Lange and M. Hirmer, *Egypt: Architecture, Sculpture, Painting,* 4th ed. (Hirmer Verlag München, 1968), by permission.

A fourth set of **PYLONS BUILT BY THUTMOSE I** is badly damaged. On the left, in a columned hall, is a polished red Aswan granite **OBELISK OF QUEEN HATSHEPSUT**. Standing 97 feet tall, it is the tallest obelisk still standing on Egyptian soil. It dates from 1485 B.C. A fragment of a companion obelisk lies near the sacred lake. Hatshepsut said she made two obelisks to the god Amen at Karnak. She had intended to make them of solid gold, but because this was not possible she gold-plated them. One can still discern near the corners the grooves in which Hatshepsut's craftsmen set the sheets of electrum (gold alloy).

Hatshepsut's successor, Thutmose III, suggested in his inscription that he made two obelisks entirely of gold alloy. They represented perhaps the vital rays of the sun-god Re. These were probably the two obelisks mentioned in the Louvre cylinder as weighing 1,250 talents (83,325 pounds) each, which stood in the sanctuary at Karnak, and which the priests of Thebes gave to Ashurbanipal to avert the sack of the city. When the Egyptian dynasties were on the decline, Greeks made fun of the sacred "tall pillars dedicated to god with a pyramid-shaped top" and dubbed them "obelisks," or "spits."

The **FIFTH SET OF PYLONS** leads to two small **ANTECHAMBERS BY THUTMOSE III**. From here the visitor passes through the last and smallest pylons into the **FIRST HALL OF ANNALS**, where two beautiful, highly polished **ROSE GRANITE SHAFTS** of Thutmose III show heraldic lotus and papyrus flowers, symbols of Upper and Lower Egypt. They are nearly 3,500 years old. Past the shafts is a two-roomed **GRANITE CHAPEL**, in which was kept the sacred bark (boat) of the god Amen. This room was the holy of holies of the temple and contained not only the bark but a closed shrine which was located on the bark. It contained a golden image of Amen. The image was considered not the god himself but a portrait of him. Once a year, on the fifteenth day of the second month, the "Luxor Festival" began. For this festive occasion the bark with the image was carried by the priests to the Nile and taken to the Temple of Luxor until a return journey.

The **SECOND HALL OF ANNALS** is located northeast of the **SANCTUARY**. The famous Annals of Thutmose III have, among other things, an account of the Egyptian battle at Megiddo in Israel.

The **FESTIVAL HALL OF THUTMOSE III** is next in line. It was built in 1500 B.C. over the site of an earlier temple dating back to 2000 B.C.

The last site on the east, within the walls, is the large **HALL OF STATE** with its 20 columns and 32 pillars in rows.

South and east of the Temple of Amen is the **SACRED LAKE**, dating back at least to 1292 B.C. Near its northwest corner is a large **GRANITE SCARAB OF AMENHOTEP III** and the **TOP OF A FALLEN OBELISK OF HATSHEPSUT**.

North of the Temple of Amen is the **TEMPLE OF PTAH**, and southwest of the Temple of Amen is the **TEMPLE OF KHONS**, built within the outer walls of the temple complex.

South of the temple complex is the **TEMPLE OF MUT**, a **SACRED LAKE**, and a small **TEMPLE OF RAMSES III**, all at the north end of the Avenue of Sphinxes. Mut's temple dates from 1411 B.C.

There is a huge adobe wall around the Karnak Temple complex. Our word *adobe* comes from the Egyptian word *tobe*, meaning "brick."

In 1954 there was found at Karnak a stone slab with 38 lines of hieroglyphics, telling of the expulsion of the Hyksos from Egypt.

Coptic Monastery

A 1½-hour ride north from Luxor brings one to the famous fifteenth-century Coptic Christian **MONASTERY OF DEIR EL SHAYEB,** or "the gray-haired saint." It contains three chapels plus rooms used for baptismal purposes. Coptic writing and crosses adorn the walls.

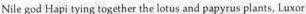
Nile god Hapi tying together the lotus and papyrus plants, Luxor

Above: Drying adobe bricks, Luxor
Below: Tomb 33, of Pentamenopet, with the temple of Queen Hatshepsut in the background, Valley of the Nobles

Pottery Factory

Near the Coptic Monastery is a pottery factory, where Egyptians fashion pots and jars by ancient methods of hand- and foot-wheel machines.

West Bank, *Necropolis of Thebes*

The Theban hills on the west bank of the Nile River are the location of the Necropolis — "city of the dead." Entire hillsides have networks of connecting tombs. It is like an immense anthill, where a person can travel freely without emerging above the ground. After a ferry boat ride across the Nile and a bus ride toward the west, the traveler usually visits the following sites:

The **COLOSSI OF MEMNON**, two 52½-foot-high sandstone seated figures, seem to be guarding the gigantic Necropolis. Originally, however, they guarded the mortuary temple of Pharaoh Amenhotep III (1411–1375 B.C.). In Hellenistic times the figures were thought to represent Memnon, who was slain by Achilles at Troy. The figure on the right used to emit a weird moan when the wind blew, and the noise was called "Memnon's voice."

The **TEMPLES OF MEDINET HABU** are located on the extreme south end of the Theban Necropolis. *Medinet* means "town" and refers to a Christian village that developed here in the fifth century A.D. There are four different constructions at Medinet Habu:

(1) the **MORTUARY PAVILION OF RAMSES III**;
(2) the **MORTUARY TEMPLE OF QUEEN AMENERTAIS**;
(3) the **MORTUARY TEMPLE OF RAMSES III**;
(4) the **MORTUARY TEMPLE OF THUTMOSE III.**

The **PAVILION OF RAMSES III** (1198 B.C.) is a castlelike fortress, built under the influence of Syrian architecture. It was intended to be the entrance to the great temple further back. As one passes through the gateway it is possible to see the grooves made by the chariots in the flagstones. The scenes on the sides of the entrance are the most deeply cut of any in Egypt, and the battle scenes on the walls are very beautiful. (It is interesting to note that Joseph also rode in a chariot. See Gen. 41:43.)

The **MORTUARY TEMPLE OF QUEEN AMENERTAIS** (700 B.C.) is a small temple on the west side of the court, between the pavilion and the mortuary temple of Ramses III. Queen Amenertais was the wife of the Ethiopian king Piankhi. Wall scenes show the queen making offerings to various deities.

The mortuary temples were built for the purpose of performing ceremonies in memory of the king or queen.

The **MORTUARY TEMPLE OF RAMSES III** is one of the best preserved and most impressive monuments in Thebes. Its pylons are almost perfect, and they are very beautiful, with scenes of Ramses III's victories. A perfect stairway in the right pylon leads to the top, and the visitor should not miss a view from this summit.

In the first court is a row of eight papyrus columns with open capitals. On the right is a row of pillars on which the statues of Osiris once stood. The deeply cut scenes on the walls show victories of Ramses III in Libya and Syria.

A causeway surrounded by colonnades and scenes leads through the second doorway into the second court. On the west is a terrace,

Necropolis of Thebes

Miles 1 ½ 1

N

Western Valley

Tomb of Aye

Tomb of Amenhotep III

Valley of the Kings
(Biban el Muluk)

Rest House

③ ⑥ ④ ⑤ ① ⑦ ②

Mountain Path to the Tombs of the Kings

Road to the Tombs of the Kings

Dra-abu el-Neggar

Terrace Temple of Hatshepsut

Tombs of Eleventh-Dynasty Nobles

Rest House

Deir el-Bahri

Pyramid Temple of Menhuhotep II

Causeway of Hatshepsut

El Asasif

Tomb 33: Pentamenopet

El Khokhah

Temple of Thutmose III

Temple of Si-Ptah

Davis House

Metropolitan House

Sheikh Abd el-Qurna
Tombs of the Nobles

⑨ ⑧

⑪ ⑫ ⑩

Rameseum

Temple of Amenhotep II

Temple of Thutmose IV

Rest House

Deir el-Medina

Mission Française

Deutsches Haus

Temple of Merneptah

Qurnet Murra

Valley of the Queens
(Biban el Harim)

Medinet Habu

Temple of Ramses III

TOMBS OF THE KINGS
1. Tutankhamen
2. Seti I
3. Amenhotep II
4. Ramses VI
5. Ramses III
6. Harmhab
7. Ramses I

TOMBS OF THE NOBLES
8. Nakht
9. Menna
10. Ramose
11. Sennufer
12. Rekhmere

then the hypostyle hall, which is now almost in ruins. It once had 24 pillars supporting the ceiling. Other chambers, chapels, and treasuries are located in the west end.

The **MORTUARY TEMPLE OF THUTMOSE III** (1557 B.C.) is located northwest of the pavilion of Ramses III. It was begun by Queen Hatshepsut and finished by Thutmose III. After Akhenaten's destruction, Harmhab and Seti I restored the temple.

VALLEY OF THE QUEENS (*Biban el Harim*). During the Seventeenth Dynasty the queens were buried in small tombs in the Valley of the Kings near the pharaohs' tombs. The wife of Amenhotep III was the first queen who had a large tomb of her own in the Valley of the Kings (1400 B.C.) When Ramses I buried his wife Seta in 1315 B.C. he chose a new valley, now known as the Valley of the Queens. From that date until 1090 B.C. the valley was used to bury queens and princes. It is located in the southern end of the Necropolis and close to the Theban Hills, and there are about 70 tombs here, of which 4 are recommended for visitors:

(1) **QUEEN NEFERTARI**, wife of Ramses II (no. 66);
(2) **QUEEN TITI**, wife of one of the Ramessides (no. 52);
(3) **PRINCE AMUNKHOPESHFU**, who died at the age of 12, son of Ramses III (no. 55);
(4) **PRINCE KHAEMWAS**, son of Ramses III (no. 44).

The **TEMPLE OF DEIR EL-MEDINA** was built by Ptolemy IV, called Ptolemy Philopator, in 210 B.C. and was dedicated to the goddesses Hathor and Maat. It is 1,000 yards directly west of the Rameseum, and has a delicate construction. After viewing the open court, the visitor sees 3 chapels. Above the entrance of the Hathor chapel are 7 Hathor heads, and in the right-hand chamber is a well-preserved scene of judgment, presided over by Osiris, god of the underworld. Horus and Anubis are seen weighing the heart against an ostrich feather, while the god Thoth writes down the sentence of the court. To the right is a monster of the underworld waiting to carry off the soul of the deceased should the judgment of the scales be unfavorable. Above are the 42 judges of the dead. During early Christian times, this temple was used as a monastery.

MORTUARY TEMPLE OF MERNEPTAH. Located southwest of the Rameseum is the Temple of Merneptah. It is not visited as a part of most guided tours, but is of interest because of the "Israel Stela" of Merneptah. (See the section on the Egyptian Museum, in Cairo, above.)

The **RAMESEUM** (the mortuary temple of Ramses II) was built by Ramses II (1298–1232 B.C.) and dedicated to the god Amen. (*Ramses* should be pronounced "Ra-mses," the prefix *Ra* being that of the god Amen-Re.) At one time the temple measured 890 feet in length, and although today it is a vast heap of ruins there is still much of interest to see here. The inner sides of the ruined pylons are war scenes of Ramses II against the Hittites.

In the first court there is a broken statue of Ramses that was once the **LARGEST STATUE IN ALL OF EGYPT**. It weighs over 1,000 tons and is 59 feet high. The index finger and ear are 3½ feet in length, and the shoulders are 23 feet wide. The statue was hewn from one piece of Aswan granite. Legend says that the Persian king Cambyses ordered the statue to be broken.

The second court has a fine sculptured black granite **HEAD OF RAMSES II**. In the second hypostyle hall parts of the roof remain, with finely decorated astrological figures. At the far end of this hall, on the right-hand wall, is a scene showing the three gods writing the king's name on the tree of life.

Ruins of other temples are located both north and south of the Rameseum.

TOMBS OF THE NOBLES at Sheikh Abd el-Gournah. Although these structures are called "tombs," the nobles who excavated them were not buried here. They were really "mortuary chapels," serving for the worship of the repose of the souls of the dead. About 75 of the known 120 preserved chapels are located in the vicinity of Sheikh Abd el-Gournah. The walls are covered with beautiful paintings depicting the daily manners and customs of the Egyptians 3,000 years ago. Most of the "tombs" date back to the Twenty-eighth Dynasty. In most cases a chapel contains a broad hall and then a passage leading to a niche, in which a statue of the dead was placed. The most interesting chapels are the following:

(1)   **NAKHT** (no. 52), overseer of the royal granaries. It has beautiful paintings of agricultural life and a famous scene of "The Dancers."
(2)   **MENNA** (no. 69), chief of the king's estates.
(3)   **SENNUFER** (no. 96), prince and chief overseer of the granaries. It has beautiful orchard scenes.
(4)   **RAMOSE** (no. 55), vizier of Egypt under Amenhotep and Akhenaten. This chapel has a well-known funeral scene, with mourning women.
(5)   **KHAEMHAT** (no. 57), superintendent of the granaries.

Also **USERHAT** (no. 56), **ENNE** (no. 81), **REKH-MERE** (no. 100), **NEFER-HOTEP** (no. 50), **AMENEMHAB** (no. 85), and **HARMHAB** (no. 78).

TOMB 33: PENTAMENOPET. Located at El Asasif, near the Arab village of Gournah and approximately one-half mile east of the Temple of Queen Hatshepsut, is perhaps the very largest "pit tomb" in the Necropolis. A painted sign at the entrance identifies it: "33 PENTAMENOPET XXVIth DYN." The nobleman Pentamenopet lived between 664 and 525 B.C. and was a contemporary of the third king of the dynasty, Necho (Neco, Nechoh) II, who ruled from 609 to 593 B.C.

Necho is a biblical figure. He marched into Palestine to assist Ashuruballit (2 Kings 23:29–30). He defeated Josiah of Judah, who had allied himself with Babylon at Megiddo. When Josiah was killed and his son Jehoahaz reigned in his stead, the prophet Jeremiah, a contemporary of Necho, lamented for Josiah. Necho deposed Jehoahaz and sent him to Egypt and made Jehoahaz's elder brother,

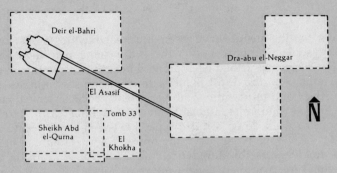

TOMB 33 AREA

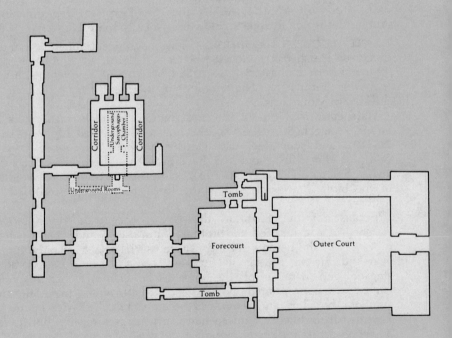

Tomb 33: Pentamenopet

Eliakim, king, changing the new monarch's name to *Johoiakim* (2 Kings 23:33–34; 2 Chron. 35:20–25; 36:1–4).

At the present time the "outer court" and "forecourt" are in ruins, and the entrance to the tomb is on the west side of the former "forecourt."

The walls on the inside have been blackened with smoke and damaged by souvenir hunters, but there are some paintings and figures still discernible. It had been painted beautifully like the other important tombs on the West Bank. Since it houses millions of dollars' worth of antiquities, the tomb is presently locked, sealed, and heavily guarded. Mummies are laid out on the floor, with barely enough room to walk down a narrow path between them. Statues, boxes, beds, jars, sarcophagi, and mummies fill the tomb. These antiquities are temporarily stored in tomb 33 because of its large size until they are placed in a new museum being built in Luxor. The tomb has no electric lights, and because of this, and the fact that the antiquities are so valuable and are scattered all over the floor of the tomb, it is little wonder that the Egyptian Department of Antiquities is not anxious to allow tourists into tomb 33.

TEMPLE OF QUEEN HATSHEPSUT. The magnificent funerary temple of Queen Hatshepsut is located at Deir el-Bahri, an Arabic title for "the northern monastery," so called because of a seventh-century monastery built here. The temple is at the base of majestic cliffs of the Libyan Mountains.

Hatshepsut was one of the most famous of all women rulers in Egypt. Some believe she was the queen who reared Moses (Exod. 2:5–10), and some feel that Hatshepsut may have lived several centuries after Moses and may have been the Queen of Sheba, who visited Solomon (1 Kings 10:1–13). With the exception of the women in the biblical account, she is the first great woman recorded in history.

Because of the Egyptian desire to concentrate royal blood, Hatshepsut had married her brother Thutmose II, and when he died in 1493 B.C. she became regent. Thutmose III was then only 10–12 years old. He was the son of Thutmose II by a harem girl, hence both stepson and nephew of the queen. To reinforce her regency, Hatshepsut appropriated male titles and attributes, including the symbolic beard of authority, and became "king." Twice before in Egypt's earlier history a queen had usurped the kingship, but it was a new departure for a female to pose and dress as a man.

Queen Hatshepsut was a very successful ruler. She fostered vast public works, restored old temples, and built new ones. She also exploited the copper mines of Sinai. She firmly dominated the nation.

Hatshepsut's nephew, stepson, and husband, Thutmose III, wanted the kingdom, but because he could not get it from his aunt, stepmother, and wife he became jealous and angry. Then, in the seventeenth year of her reign, the great queen died, and Thutmose III became king. His first act after Hatshepsut's death was to overthrow

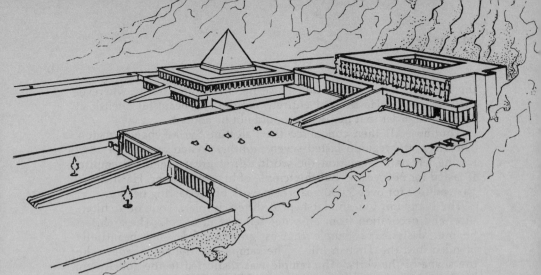

Temple of Queen Hatshepsut at Deir el-Bahri, as seen from the northeast.
In the background is the funerary temple of King Mentuhotep Nebhapetre.

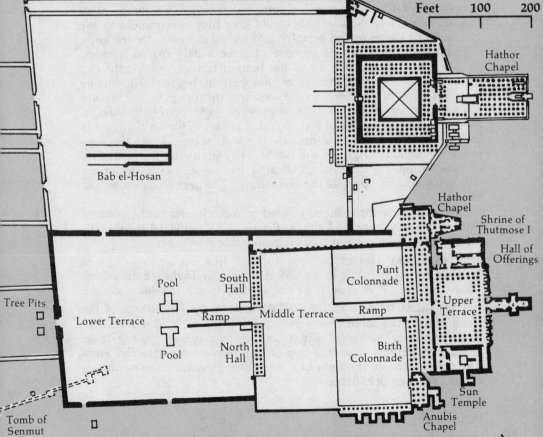

Feet   100   200

Hathor Chapel

Bab el-Hosan

Hathor Chapel

Shrine of Thutmose I

Hall of Offerings

Punt Colonnade

South Hall

Pool

Tree Pits

Lower Terrace

Ramp

Middle Terrace

Ramp

Upper Terrace

North Hall

Pool

Birth Colonnade

Sun Temple

Tomb of Senmut

Anubis Chapel

Funerary Temple of Queen Hatshepsut

*Adapted from K. Lange and M. Hirmer, *Egypt: Architecture, Sculpture, Painting,* 4th ed. (Hirmer Verlag München, 1968), by permission.

the statues in her temple and erase her name and image wherever they appeared. He bricked entirely around the beautiful obelisk at Karnak, in order that her works would not be adored.

Thutmose III then conquered the Palestine-Syria-Lebanon region. The siege at Megiddo lasted seven months. When he died in 1447 B.C. he left as his creation the world's first great organized empire. It lasted for 300 years. But the temple of his stepmother, Hatshepsut, has endured for over 3,000 years as a work of everlasting beauty.

The temple of Queen Hatshepsut differs in plan, style of architecture, and decoration from all other temples in Egypt. The architect Senmut designed a temple that is graceful, free, and beautifully blended into the Theban hills. The ramps and the colonnades echo the shape of the cliffs. The temple was dedicated to the god Amen, but it contained chapels for Anubis and Hathor. It was intended as a mortuary temple for the worship of Hatshepsut's soul after death. Royal funerary temples served the cult of the dead, and were as necessary for the dead man's resurrection as was his tomb. Here the offerings were made which would give him nourishment in the next world. The mortuary temples also served as homes for the gods.

Hatshepsut's temple is composed of three widely spaced terraces. At one time sphinxes led up to the bottom terrace, but hardly any traces remain of the sphinxes or the bottom terrace. An incline connects each of the terraces. Ascending the ramp to the second terrace, one comes upon a most impressive scene. On both sides of the ramp are colonnades of sixteen-sided pillars. That on the right is called the Birth Colonnade because the wall scenes depict the supposed miraculous origin of the queen. The preliminaries to the act of procreation are discreetly indicated by the figure of the queen sitting on a couch opposite the god Amen. The next scene shows the infant.

Colonnades, well-preserved colored scenes, chapels to the goddess Hathor, the sanctuary, and effaced figures of Queen Hatshepsut make a visit to this religious sanctuary a memorable experience.

The **MORTUARY TEMPLE OF MENTUHOTEP** lies just south of Queen Hatshepsut's temple. It is the oldest temple in Thebes, dating from 2060–1800 B.C. It is in such a ruinous state that it is seldom visited.

HIKING FROM DEIR EL-BAHRI TO THE VALLEY OF THE KINGS. From the mortuary temple of Queen Hatshepsut, it is a 30–40-minute hike to the Valley of the Kings. A path marks the way over the top of the Libyan Mountains, and it is a most impressive and beautiful view. The path begins on the right of Cook's Rest House, on the north side of the causeway of Hatshepsut.

Valley of the Kings

On the West Bank, over the tops of the cliffs behind the Temple of Queen Hatshepsut, is a valley in which over 60 royal tombs have been found. The valley is called the "Valley of the Kings," *Dra-abu el-Neggar*, *Biban el Muluk*, and the "Tombs of the Kings." It is probably the most impressive of all the sites in Thebes. It is dominated by the natural rock pyramid of the summit of El-Qorn.

The pharaohs and rulers who were buried in the Valley of the Kings reigned during the Eighteenth, Nineteenth, and Twentieth Dynasties — from 1580 to 1085 B.C. and during the time when the Israelites were in Egypt.

Most of the tombs follow a similar plan: three corridors in a line leading to the burial chamber. Some have small chambers on the sides of the first corridor, and some have rooms by the second and third corridors, used to store furniture, jewelry, and other items that were buried with the pharaoh. The walls are usually painted with scenes of pharaohs, gods, stars, hieroglyphs, and so forth, that generally have a religious theme. The most extensive tombs on the West Bank are more than 650 feet long. (Queen Hatshepsut's [no. 20] is 693 feet long.)

Only 17 of the known 64 tombs can be visited by the unprofessional tourist. Most of the tombs are either in ruins or are not accessible. The great majority of the tombs housed the bodies of kings, but among them is the tomb of Queen Tiy, wife of Amenhotep III and mother of Akhenaten. The principal tombs are described as follows:

TOMB OF TUTANKHAMEN (no. 62). On November 25, 1922, the first stone was removed from the wall enclosing the entrance of Tutankhamen's tomb, allowing archaeologist Howard Carter and his group a glimpse of the first royal sepulcher ever to be found intact in the Valley of the Kings. Carter had worked in the area for twenty years before he found this 3,265-year-old burial place, and even after he found it he spent almost six full years emptying the tomb and restoring on the spot every piece of the most complete set of burial objects known to man. Even though it appeared that grave robbers had been in part of the tomb twice, they had apparently taken only a few small gold objects and sixty percent of the jewels.

Lord Carnarvon supplied the money for the expedition. He saw the tomb, but died before he saw the mummy.

The first room of the tomb contained 170 different objects and pieces of furniture. Many of the latter were trunks filled with such materials as alabaster, ebony, gold, turquoise, and ivory, used as funerary objects. For two months the archaeologists worked on the materials in the first room (antechamber); then on February 17, 1923, they pulled down the wall to the burial chamber. After opening shrines, a stone sarcophagus, and mummiform coffins, they finally viewed the mummified body of Tutankhamen.

Although well protected from the elements, his body was in a bad state of deterioration. Besides the usual embalming materials, plus linen and 143 gold jewels distributed over his body, his head was covered by a solid gold mask and then he was sealed in a solid gold mummiform coffin weighing 2,448 pounds. On the headdress are small golden heads of Nekhbet, the vulture goddess of Upper Egypt, and Wadjet, the serpent goddess of Lower Egypt. The lines on the headdress are all the same gold color. The hands of the figure are folded on his breast, as in the representations of the god Osiris. The flail and the crook — emblems of royalty — are in his hands, and the beard is on his chin.

The innermost solid gold (91.85 percent pure gold) coffin was enclosed in a second mummiform coffin, made of Lebanon cedar wood covered with 22-carat gold leaf, with blue and red glass paste laid in a featherlike pattern. It was also made in the form of Osiris. The headdress has alternating blue glass paste lines on it. The footplate is covered with beautifully engraved gold foil, on which the goddess Isis is shown kneeling on the hieroglyph sign for "gold." It is similar to the footplate of the inner coffin.

A third mummiform coffin, made of Lebanon cedar wood and covered with 22-carat gold leaf, contained the other two. It also was made in the form of Osiris and has blue and red glass paste laid in the gold. This outside mummiform coffin is still in the original burial chamber and houses the mummified body of Tutankhamen.

The three coffins, totaling a weight of 3,030 pounds, were placed on a low lion-shaped bed of gold-gilt wood in a quartzite sarcophagus. This was in turn covered with four golden burial shrines — oak wood overlaid with gold, fitted together like Chinese boxes, one into another. The largest shrine — nearly filling the 13-by-21 foot room of the tomb — measured 10 feet 10 inches by 16 feet 5 inches by 9 feet and was made of gilt wood inlaid with blue lapis lazuli and glass paste. The shrines were separated by veils decorated with flowers, and each shrine was decorated with beautiful reliefs of flowers, gods, and hieroglyphic texts. The smallest shrine covered the sarcophagus and was inscribed with the names and titles of the king. Each corner was decorated with a beautiful high relief of a goddess protectively spreading her wings — not too much unlike the ark of the covenant carried through the wilderness by the Israelites (Exod. 25:10–22).

In the room called the "treasury" was found a shrine guarded by goddesses about 2½ feet high: Isis, Nephthys, Neith, and Serket. In the shrine was an alabaster chest in which were four canopic urns, each containing a miniature coffin 15 inches long and made in the same shape as the innermost gold coffin. These small coffins contained the mummified viscera of the king: liver, lungs, stomach, and intestines. Only the heart was left in Tutankhamen's body, which was facing the east.

It was a surprise to find two small anthropoid coffins in the treasury room. In them were smaller gold coffins, and in each was the mummy of a fetus preserved like a fully developed infant. One was a six-month and one a seven-month fetus. The smaller had a gold mask.

The paintings on the walls of the burial room are beautiful and well preserved. On a dark ochre background, under a band representing the sky of Egypt, tall human figures painted in bright colors — predominantly yellow, red, white, and black — occupied the full length of three of the walls.

Pharaoh Tutankhamen was not a famous leader in Egypt. He was

Tutankhamen's outer (third) sarcophagus, Valley of the Kings

9 years old when he came to the throne at the end of the Eighteenth Dynasty. He died in January, 1343 B.C. At the beginning of his reign he was at Tell el 'Amarna and his name was Tutankh*aten*, but he moved the capital back to Thebes and changed his name to Tutankh*amen*. Nebkheprure was his "first" or "coronation" name. He was married to Princess Ankheshamun, a daughter of Akhenaten. He died when he was 18 years old and was relatively unimportant. He became very important, however, when Howard Carter discovered his tomb, still intact, the first discovery of its kind. Inasmuch as his tomb is the smallest of the kings' tombs in the Valley of the Kings, one can imagine the huge store of treasures that would have been buried in the larger tombs of the more famous pharaohs.

Thus Tutankhamen, son of the god Amen, was prepared with his elaborate burial to rejoin the god who created him. Although not the most famous pharaoh in life, he has become one of the most famous in death.

TOMB OF SETI I (no. 17). This 700-foot-long tomb, with its passage-ways, halls, and staircases, is the largest and one of the best pre-served in the Valley of the Kings. The burial chamber is 150 feet below the entrance to the first staircase. It dates from the Nineteenth Dynasty (1313–1298 B.C.).

The tomb was discovered in 1817 by the Italian Giovanni Battista Belzoni, and in 1881 the mummy of Seti I was found in a "cachette" at Deir el-Bahri. It is now in the Egyptian Museum and is considered to be the most lifelike of all mummies of kings discovered to this date. The alabaster sarcophagus is in the Soane Museum in London. The paintings on the walls are well preserved high reliefs and show the sun-god, Isis, Nephthys, Hathor, Osiris, Egyptians, Asiatics, Negroes, Libyans, and others. They begin at the entrance and con-tinue throughout the tomb. Some of the paintings are unfinished. Burial chamber walls with text and pictures describe the voyage of the king as he traveled through the underworld, aided along the way by the sun-god. Signs of the zodiac decorate the ceiling of the burial chamber.

The **TOMB OF AMENHOTEP II** (no. 35) is, with little doubt, one of the most impressive and best preserved tombs in the Valley of the Kings. Amenhotep reigned in the Eighteenth Dynasty, about 1447–1420 B.C. Because of its unique construction, which includes a deep shaft in the corridor to mislead robbers, the tomb is sometimes called the "Tomb of Safety." When it was discovered in 1898 by M. Loret, there were still a number of mummies buried there, including the mummies of Amenhotep IV, Thutmose IV, and Seti II.

This is one of the most ancient of the tombs open to the public. The walls are painted with various scenes from the "Book of the Underworld," and the blue painted ceiling is decorated with yellow stars. The papyrus-yellow tint of the walls creates a unique atmo-sphere. At the lower level the body of Amenhotep II still lies in the sarcophagus, undisturbed for 3,300 years.

Paintings on the wall of Tutankhamen's tomb, Valley of the Kings

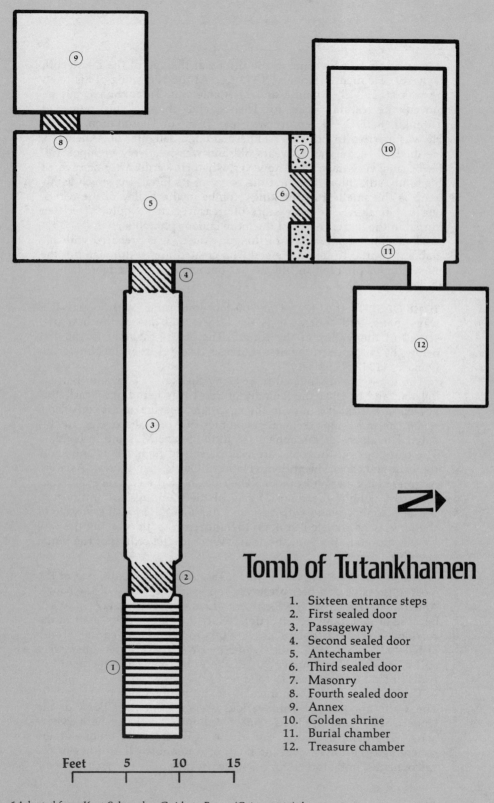

Tomb of Tutankhamen

1. Sixteen entrance steps
2. First sealed door
3. Passageway
4. Second sealed door
5. Antechamber
6. Third sealed door
7. Masonry
8. Fourth sealed door
9. Annex
10. Golden shrine
11. Burial chamber
12. Treasure chamber

Feet   5   10   15

*Adapted from Kurt Schroeder, *Guide to Egypt* (Cairo, 1965), by permission.

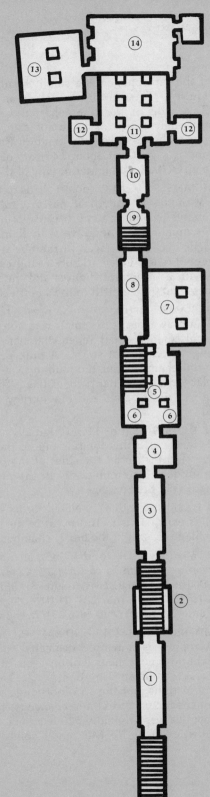

Tomb of Seti I

1. First corridor
2. Second corridor
3. Third corridor
4. Antechamber
5. Chamber
6. Walls portraying the sun's voyage through the underworld
7. Unfinished room, perhaps a decoy to deceive would-be robbers
8. Corridor
9. Corridor
10. Antechamber
11. First section of burial chamber, with 6 pillars
12. Side chambers
13. Sacrificial room
14. Sarcophagus

*Adapted from Kurt Schroeder, *Guide to Egypt* (Cairo, 1965), by permission.

Left of the sarcophagus is a small chamber where three mummies can be viewed. The one on the left is an elderly woman, possibly Queen Taa, wife of the pharaoh, but considered by some to be Hatshepsut, moved to this tomb for safety during the time of the great tomb robberies during the reign of Ramses X (1117–1114 B.C.). The second is a youth of about 14 years of age, possibly a son. The third is a girl, either a daughter or wife of the pharaoh.

TOMB OF RAMSES V AND VI (no. 9). This tomb was originally built for Ramses V of the Twentieth Dynasty (1160 B.C.), but when Ramses VI was unable to build a tomb because of his short reign, the priests placed his mummy in one grave with Ramses V. A broken granite sarcophagus may still be seen in the burial chamber. The freshness of the colored reliefs is remarkably well preserved. The decoration of the roof with astronomical figures and the huge arched body of the sky goddess Nut giving birth to the sun is extremely interesting.

TOMB OF RAMSES I (no. 16). Ramses I had a very short term as pharaoh, and as a result his tomb was not completed when he died. He was buried in a small inner chamber, which one reaches after descending two flights of stairs. A pink granite sarcophagus is still in the burial chamber, but the mummy was removed by priests to a hiding place at Deir el-Bahri for safety. The paintings on the wall, including pictures of gods and the journey of the sun-boat, are well preserved.

TOMB OF RAMSES III (no. 11). Originally commenced by Setnakht, father of Ramses III, this tomb is one of the largest in the Valley of the Kings. Ten niches on the sides of the first and second corridors are quite unique. The mummy is in the Egyptian Museum and the sarcophagus is in the Louvre.

TOMB OF HARMHAB (no. 57). Noted for its scenes of the underworld, this tomb is worth a visit. It was cut in the Nineteenth Dynasty, and the sarcophagus is still in the burial chamber.

OTHER TOMBS. Similar to the ones already described but of less importance are the tombs of RAMSES X (no. 6), RAMSES IV (no. 2), RAMSES IX (no. 6), MERNEPTAH (no. 8), SETNAKHT (no. 14), SETI II (no. 15), HATSHEPSUT (no. 20), THUTMOSE III (no. 34), THUTMOSE I (no. 38), and AMENHOTEP III (no. 23), in the western valley.

MORTUARY TEMPLE OF SETI I AND RAMSES II. On the northeast corner of the Acropolis is a temple dedicated to the god Amen. Seti I started to build it near the end of his reign (1290 B.C.) for him and his father, but it was finished by Ramses II. Most of the courts and the pylons are in ruins, but the 155-foot-long temple, with its 6 papyrus pillars, inner sanctuary, and miscellaneous chambers, still exists. The temple complex was originally 520 feet long. Reliefs of Ramses II and the three deities Amen-Re, Mut, and Khons decorate the walls.

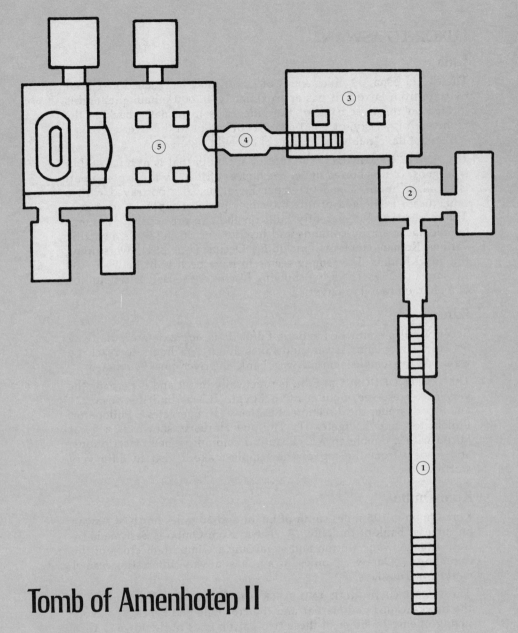

Tomb of Amenhotep II

1. Passageway
2. Bridge over pit
3. Room with 2 pillars
4. Stairs and passageway
5. Burial room

*Adapted from Kurt Schroeder, *Guide to Egypt* (Cairo, 1965), by permission.

LUXOR TO ASWAN

Esna

The city of Esna, 33 miles south of Luxor, may be reached in 1 hour by train from Luxor. It has approximately 40,000 inhabitants and is located on the west bank of the Nile. The town dates back to the Eighteenth Dynasty, or 1580 B.C. At this point in the river there is a 2,870-foot dam that helps to control the Nile waters.

The TEMPLE OF KHNUM is the ruin of antiquity that is of interest, but since most of it is buried under the houses of the city the exposed part is small. Khnum, a god of Upper Egypt, usually portrayed with a ram's head, is the god of this Ptolemaic period temple. A temple of Thutmose III was apparently built on the site previously. Khnum's temple has beautiful columns and inscriptions on the walls depicting various Roman emperors, including Decius (A.D. 251), worshiping the god Khnum. The temple seems to have been built between 180 B.C. and A.D. 250. The relief showing Decius is the last representation of a pharaoh found in Egypt.

Edfu

Seventy miles south of Luxor is Edfu. It is approximately halfway between Luxor and Aswan and takes about 2½ hours to reach by train. As the temple is on the west bank, the river must be crossed.

The TEMPLE OF HORUS at Edfu is practically intact and is perhaps the very best-preserved monument in Egypt. It was built between 237 and 57 B.C., under the direction of Ptolemy III, Euergetes I, Philopator, Philometor, and Euergetes II. The god Horus is shown as a great falcon with a double crown. Beautiful columns, reliefs, inscriptions, and a view from the top of the temple make a visit to Edfu very worthwhile.

Kom Ombo

Kom Ombo is 105 miles south of Luxor and 30 miles north of Aswan on the east bank of the Nile. A visit to Kom Ombo is best made by train from Aswan. Cotton and sugarcane are important crops of the community. Daraw, 3 miles away, has a very interesting camel market on Tuesdays.

The TEMPLE OF HARUAR AND SEBEK was dedicated to the worship of the hawk-headed god Haruar and the crocodile god Sebek. To avoid giving offense to either of these two patron gods of the town, a twin temple was constructed. The one on the left was for Haruar and the one on the right for Sebek. They were built during the Ptolemaic period, in the second century B.C. The columns, capitals, and low reliefs are very beautiful. In places there are sketches for reliefs which were never sculptured.

ASWAN AREA

Aswan, *Syene*

Aswan, at the First Cataract, is located 550 miles from Cairo and 136 miles south of Luxor. *Aswan* means "market." It is Egypt's southern-most winter resort and attracts many tourists. According to tradition, the first Egyptian pharaohs came from here, including the builders of the Pyramids of Giza. Because of the new Aswan Dam construction, the population swelled from 20,000 to 40,000 people during the 1960s.

The **ASWAN HIGH DAM**, *Sadd el Aali* was built by 30,000 Egyptian workers, the aid of Russian finances, and 2,000 technicians during the years 1960–71. The total cost was $800 million. It was begun January 9, 1960, by President Gamal Abdel Nasser detonating the first dynamite blast and was dedicated by President Anwar Sadat on Nasser's birthday, January 15, 1971 — nearly four months after Nasser's death.

Ranking as one of the largest and highest dams in the world, it is more than 2 miles long (11,811 feet), 364 feet high, and 3,215 feet thick at its base. A highway 131 feet wide crosses over the top. Fifty-five million cubic yards of rock fill were used in the construc-tion — enough to build seventeen Cheops pyramids — making it the world's tenth largest rock-fill dam. It backs up the waters of Lake Nasser, and instead of the 5,400 million tons of water that the old dam held, the new dam holds 165,000 million tons. Lake Nasser is 310 miles long, averages 6 miles in width, and is 500 feet deep in places.

The Nile Delta received its last full-scale flood in the summer of 1964, and with the new dam the annual flood has come to an end. A power station of 12 turbines capable of producing 10,000,000 kilowatt hours of electricity per year is an important part of the project. By 1970, all the electricity consumed in Cairo, 550 miles away, was being produced at the Aswan High Dam. A million new acres of agricultural land will be brought into production because of the new dam. Another million acres will be able to produce three crops instead of one. A whole new complex of industry is expected to locate in Aswan because of the abundance of water and power. A steel plant is projected to use the iron mined in the nearby desert.

Some feel, however, that although the dam will bring many benefits it will also be disastrous to the Egyptians, because of the blood fluke disease — *schistosomiasis* — spread by snails that invade the quiet, slow, warm waters now available in secondary and tertiary canals and ditches. Malaria will probably increase, farmers will have to use artificial fertilizers, the salt content and temperature of the Eastern Mediterranean may harm the fishing industry, and other negative factors would cause some to doubt the value of the Aswan High Dam.

The **OLD ASWAN DAM** was originally completed in 1902 but was heightened twice: once in 1912 and again in 1933. Located 4½

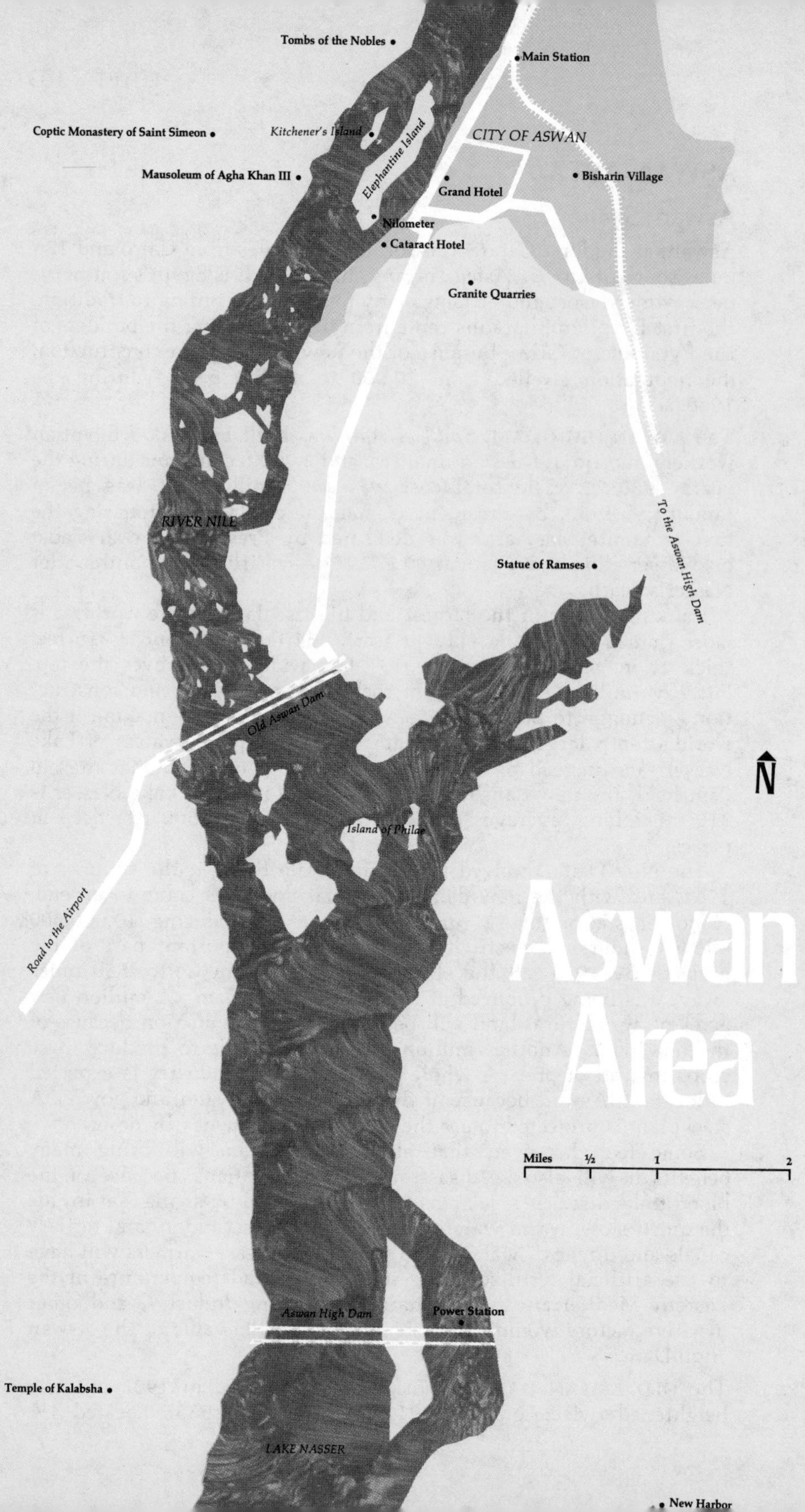

Tombs of the Nobles •

• Main Station

Coptic Monastery of Saint Simeon •   *Kitchener's Island*

CITY OF ASWAN

Elephantine Island

Mausoleum of Agha Khan III •   • Bisharin Village

• Grand Hotel

• Nilometer

• Cataract Hotel

• Granite Quarries

RIVER NILE

To the Aswan High Dam

• Statue of Ramses

Old Aswan Dam

N

Road to the Airport

Island of Philae

Aswan Area

Miles   ½   1   2

Aswan High Dam   • Power Station

Temple of Kalabsha •

LAKE NASSER

• New Harbor

miles north of the new dam, it marked the beginning of modern irrigation in Egypt. It is 7,062 feet long and for many years was the biggest valley dam in the world. It is 68 feet high, 100 feet thick at the base, and 36 feet wide at the top. It made a reservoir that covered over 11 square miles.

Granite Quarries

Twenty minutes south of Aswan are the world-famous granite quarries, whose granite can be seen in far-off Istanbul, Lebanon, Cyprus, Israel, and other countries. Here the granite was quarried for the pyramid passageways, obelisks, and sarcophagi. Still lying in the quarry is an unfinished obelisk, which was cracked before it could be excavated completely. It shows how the obelisks were carved out of the rock. It measures 137 feet long and 14 feet wide at the base and weighs approximately 1,170 tons. If it had been finished and used it would have been the tallest obelisk ever erected. A second quarry to the south has uncompleted blocks of granite that are interesting to see. From the heights there one may obtain a magnificent view.

Island and Temples of Philae

One may be rowed by boat from Shellal to the Island of Philae. Mostly submerged in the reservoir except from July to November, the island is located between the two dams at a point 2 miles south of the old Aswan Dam. The chief temple on the island was built to the goddess Isis, her husband Osiris, and son Horus during the period 600 B.C.–A.D. 138. The large pylons, sanctuaries, relief-covered walls, and other temples, arches, and ruins are very impressive. An international call has been made to save the temples of Philae.

ELEPHANTINE ISLAND, *El Gezira;* the Temple of Yahweh

Opposite the Cataract Hotel is the mile-and-a-half island called *El Gezira*, or Elephantine Island. A TEMPLE BUILT BY TRAJAN was erected on the ruins of the Temples of Thutmose III and IV and Ramses II. This and the TEMPLE OF KHNUM are not in a very good state of preservation. On the south end of the island are ancient and modern NILOMETERS to record the rise and fall of the Nile River. The ancient Nilometer has both Greek and demotic markings to indicate the water level. Near the Nilometer is a MUSEUM, housing artifacts found in the area. A MUMMY OF A SACRED RAM, representing the ram god Khnum, is on display. The southern end of the island also has traces of the former town of Elephantine, the "Door of the South."

A well-preserved papyrus document located in the Turin Museum and written about 1150 B.C. tells of the "Elephantine Scandal," wherein a priest of the Temple of Khnum was charged with thefts, bribery, sacrilege, and adultery. He was also charged with the misappropriation and sale of sacred Mnevis calves.

The famous *Elephantine Papyri* that were found there are partly

Kitchener's Island, *the Botanical Island*

From Elephantine Island a short boat ride takes one to this beautiful island formerly owned by Lord Kitchener. It has beautiful gardens, with trees from tropical regions, especially India.

Tombs of the Nobles

On the west bank, opposite the north end of Elephantine Island, are tombs cut into the face of the cliffs and dating from the Sixth to the Twelfth dynasties. Some of the reliefs are in bright colors. The most interesting tombs are those of PRINCE MEKHU (no. 25, Sixth Dynasty); PRINCE SERENPITU (no. 31, Twelfth Dynasty); PRINCE PEPI NEKHT (no. 35); PRINCE SERENPITWA (no. 36), the Governor of the South in the Twelfth Dynasty; SABNI (no. 26), the Ruler of the South; and HER KHOF.

Coptic Monastery of Saint Simeon, *Anba Somaan*

This monastery lies in the desert about 2 miles from the Nile River and near the Agha Khan Mausoleum. It was dedicated to Anba Hadra, a local saint of the fifth century. The monastery was built in the sixth century and abandoned in the tenth. The walls still have paintings of Jesus and the saints.

Bisharin Village

About 1 mile east of Aswan is this Bedouin village. The Bisharin are a Hamitic race, related to the Ethiopians. They are darkskinned, thin, and rugged, and their language and customs are different from those of other Nile Valley people. Men wear their hair in a thick fuzzy mop, and the women wrap theirs in numerous little oil-soaked plaits.

Mausoleum of Agha Khan III

This large mausoleum dominates a desert height on the Nile River, beyond Elephantine Island, at Aswan. Agha Khan III was the leader of the Ismaili Community, a sect of Islam. He spent two months of every year at Aswan, and when he died in 1959 his body was placed in the white marble tomb. He claimed direct descent from Fatima, daughter of Mohammed. His widow has a villa on the bank of the Nile near the tomb. His son, Ali Khan, married the American movie actress Rita Hayworth.

Temples of Lake Nasser

When it was decided to build the Aswan High Dam, the Egyptian government appealed to the United Nations to aid in the preservation of some of the monuments that were threatened with a watery tomb at the bottom of Lake Nasser. Twenty temples were relocated on higher ground, and some of the monuments were dismantled and taken to other nations.

The region around Lake Nasser is called Nubia, and the inhabitants have their own Nubian language. Nubia covers the desert and steppe-land between Aswan and Khartum, Sudan. During the Twelfth Dynasty Egypt conquered the Nubians and built temples and fortresses along the Nile. But by 1100 B.C. the Egyptian influence declined and the Ethiopians came to power.

The following temples are some of the more important ones that were saved for future generations to view:

The **TEMPLE OF KERTASSI** has been dismantled and rebuilt near the Aswan High Dam by the United Arab Republic.

The **TEMPLE OF BEIT-EL-WALI** has been moved to a site near the Aswan High Dam by the joint efforts of the Oriental Institute of Chicago and the Swiss Institute of Cairo. It was hewn out of solid rock under the direction of Ramses II in the thirteenth century B.C., and many beautiful reliefs adorn the walls.

The **TEMPLE OF KALABSHA** is one of the finest sandstone Nubian temples to be saved. It was 30 miles south of Aswan, but was removed to its present site near the Aswan High Dam in a superhuman task. The 13,000 blocks removed by the federal government of West Germany weighed a ton each. Next to the temple of Abu Simbel, this is the largest and finest temple in Nubia. It was erected during the reign of Augustus (27 B.C.–A.D. 14) in honor of the god Mandulis.

The **TEMPLES OF DENDUR, ELLESIYA, DEBRID,** and **TAFA** were given to the United States, Italy, Spain, and Holland respectively for their contribution in the salvage of the Nubian monuments.

The **TEMPLE OF DAKKA** has been removed to a site at Wadi es Sebua by the Academy of Sciences of Leningrad and the United Arab Republic. It was located originally on the west bank, 77 miles from Aswan.

The **TEMPLE OF WADI OF SEBUA** has been removed to higher ground near the site by the efforts of the United States, the United Arab Republic, and the French and Swiss Archaeological Institutes of Cairo. It was built by Ramses II and dedicated to the god Amen and the sun-god Re-Harakhte. The building has two rows of lion-sphinxes wearing the double crown. Scenes on the walls are similar to those on other temples. Many reliefs were painted over by Christians. Over the central statue of the Egyptian deities the early Christians placed a painting of Saint Peter with the key of heaven.

The **TEMPLE OF EL-DERR**, built by Ramses II, has been removed to a site at Amada.

The **TEMPLE OF EL-AMADA** was erected under the direction of Thutmose III and Amenhotep II (1500 B.C.). King Akhenaten defaced the reliefs, but King Seti restored them in the fourteenth century B.C. Early Christians whitewashed the reliefs, which helped to preserve them. The West German Institute of Cairo was given the responsibility of preserving the temple from the water of Lake Nasser, and it was rebuilt on higher ground near the site.

The **ROCK-TEMPLE OF ABU SIMBEL** is the most famous temple in Nubia and is 180 miles south of Aswan. It is carved out of solid sandstone rock and faces the east to let the light of the rising sun penetrate the innermost sanctuaries, "the heart of the Holiest of Holies." It was built by Ramses II between 1300 and 1233 B.C. and dedicated to the gods Amen-Re of Thebes and Harakhte of Heliopolis. On each side of the temple entrance are two colossal 66-foot-high statues of Ramses II. To the right and left of each statue are statues of other members of the royal family: Queen Tue, Ramses' mother, on the left of the second colossus; and Nefertari, his wife, on the right. The rock temple is 181 feet in length, and a large hypostyle hall has 8 huge 33-foot-high statues of the god Osiris. Reliefs on the walls show victory scenes.

When it was realized that the waters of Lake Nasser, behind the Aswan High Dam, would completely cover the Temple of Abu Simbel, the problem became an international concern. In 1959 UNESCO answered the United Arab Republic's appeal to save the Nubian monuments. The salvage project began in 1963 and cost $36,000,000. The United States offered to pay one-third of the cost.

In what has been one of the most interesting and expensive projects ever undertaken to preserve the beautiful art work of the Egyptians, Swedish engineers designed a plan to cut the statues and temples in sections and reassemble them in a natural setting on the plateau above. The project was completed in September 1968.

Visitors in Aswan may go to Abu Simbel by a hydrofoil boat in 5 hours and return the 180 miles to Aswan in the same day. Daily air service is also available.

The ROCK-TEMPLE OF HATHOR, north of the Great Temple of Abu Simbel, was also built by Ramses II and dedicated to the goddess Hathor and Ramses' wife, Nefertari. The facade is hewn to imitate a pylon. Two large statues represent the king and queen, with smaller statues of their children beside them. Mural reliefs decorate the walls.

THE RED SEA AREA (WEST SIDE)

The Red Sea is over 1,200 miles in length. It divides Africa and Arabia, and the two northern projections, the Gulf of Suez and the Gulf of Aqaba, embrace the Sinai Peninsula. The mean depth of the sea is 1,600 feet; it is 7,200 feet deep in the main basin.

- The Red Sea parted to save the Israelites. Baal-zephon is the traditional place, but the site is unknown (Exod. 14: 2, 9; Num. 33:7; Neh. 9:9; Ps. 106:7, 9, 22; Acts 7:36; Heb. 11:29).
- The same incident is mentioned in the Doctrine and Covenants (8:3).

Port Said, Bur Said

After Alexandria, Port Said is the most important port in Egypt. It is located at the entrance to the Suez Canal from the Mediterranean Sea and was founded in 1860 during the construction of the canal. Since its business is taking care of passing ships, it has been called "the town that never sleeps."

Ismailia, *Ismaileya*

This town is situated on the north shore of Lake Timsah and was the center of operations when the Suez Canal was being constructed.

Suez, *El Suweis*

Suez is a "canal town," 80 miles east of Cairo, at the south end of the Suez Canal and the north end of the Red Sea.

Ein Sukhna

This is the nearest beach to Cairo — 2½ hours by car. It is 35 miles south of Suez. It is one of the most beautiful white sandy beaches on the Red Sea, and all kinds of water sports can be enjoyed here.

Zaafarana

About 80 miles south of Suez, Zaafarana is the starting point to visit SAINT ANTHONY'S MONASTERY and SAINT PAUL'S MONASTERY. Both monasteries date from the fourth century A.D. and have ancient and rare manuscripts.

SINAI PENINSULA

This triangular tongue of land 175 miles wide and 250 miles long is located between deserts on the north and the two arms of the Red Sea — the Gulf of Aqaba on the east and the Gulf of Suez on the west. It is a rugged, little-watered desert with impressive mountain scenery. It has very little human population.

Sculptured stelae near turquoise mines of the Wadi Magharah date back to the First Dynasty (3100 B.C.). Most of them have been removed to the Cairo Museum. A TEMPLE OF HATHOR still exists near the mines at a place named Sarabit el Khadim.

Mount Sinai, in the south end of the peninsula, is composed of red and grey granite with gneiss, and schists of various kinds: hornblende and talcose, and chloritic overlying them. Later rocks, such as diorite and basalt, penetrate the rocks. Vegetation is confined to the valleys, especially near water springs.

It is difficult to imagine one or two million Israelites spending forty years of their lives in the wilderness of the Sinai Peninsula.

- *Abraham crossed the Sinai Peninsula (Gen. 12:10).*
- *Joseph, Jacob, and Jesus crossed the Sinai Peninsula to get to Egypt (Gen. 37:28; Gen. 46:1–7; Matt. 2:14).*
- *Moses fled to the Sinai Peninsula after killing the Egyptian (Exod. 2:11–15).*
- *The Midianites in Sinai were of the same people that sold Joseph into Egypt (Gen. 37:28, 36).*
- *Midian was a son of Abraham by Keturah (Gen. 25:1–2).*
- *After helping the daughters of Jethro at the well, Moses lived with Jethro (Reuel) in this area for the second forty years of his life (Exod. 2:15–3:1).*

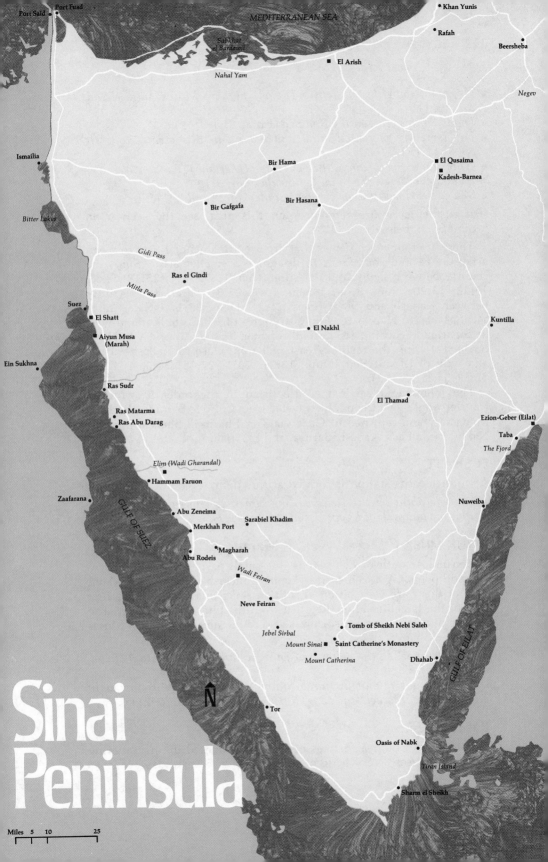

MEDITERRANEAN SEA

Port Said
Port Fuad
Khan Yunis
Rafah
Beersheba

Sabkhat
el Bardawil

El Arish

Nahal Yam

Negev

Ismailia

Bir Hama

El Qusaima
Kadesh-Barnea

Bir Gafgafa
Bir Hasana

Bitter Lakes

Gidi Pass

Ras el Gindi

Mitla Pass

Suez
El Shatt
Aiyun Musa
(Marah)

El Nakhl

Kuntilla

Ein Sukhna

Ras Sudr

Ras Matarma
Ras Abu Darag

El Thamad

Ezion-Geber (Eilat)
Taba
The Fjord

Elim (Wadi Gharandal)
Hammam Faruon

Zaafarana

GULF OF SUEZ

Abu Zeneima

Nuweiba

Merkhah Port

Sarabiel Khadim

Abu Rodeis
Magharah

Wadi Feiran

Neve Feiran

Tomb of Sheikh Nebi Saleh
Jebel Sirbal
Mount Sinai
Saint Catherine's Monastery
Mount Catherina
Dhahab

GULF OF EILAT

Ñ

Tor

Oasis of Nabk

Tiran Island

Sinai
Peninsula

Sharm el Sheikh

Miles 5 10 25

- *Zipporah, daughter of Jethro (Reuel) became Moses' wife (Exod. 2:21; 3:1).*
- *The Israelites crossed the Red Sea (Exod. 14:1–15:21).*
- *The Israelites were fed quail and manna in this area (Exod. 16; Num. 11:1–3, 31–32).*
- *Water came forth from a rock at Horeb (Meribah) (Exod. 17).*
- *Abraham crossed the Sinai Peninsula (Abr. 3:15).*
- *Moses received the priesthood under the hand of Jethro.*

(For further scripture references on this area, see the section on Mount Sinai, below.)

There are four place names that are used in a general way to mean a large area and sometimes to designate a smaller area: *Shur*, the country between Egypt and Palestine (Gen. 16:7; 20:1; 25:18; Exod. 15:22; 13:20; Num. 33:8; 1 Sam. 15:7; 27:8); *Paran*, the territory between Kadesh and Sinai (Gen. 21:21; Deut. 33:2; 1 Sam. 25:1; 1 Kings 11:18; Hab. 3:3); *Sin*, a dry strip of white chalky land west of Sinai and reaching to the Gulf of Suez (Exod. 16:1; 17:1; Num. 33:11–12); *Zin*, the territory east of Paran, close to Kadesh-Barnea and west of Mount Seir (Num. 13:21; 20:1; 27:14; 34:3, 4; Deut. 32:51; Josh. 15:1, 3).

The following place names are listed in the order in which a traveler would visit them if he traveled from Cairo to Saint Catherine's Monastery and returned to Gaza via Tor, Sharm el Sheikh, Eilat, El Nakhl, Mitla Pass, Kadesh-Barnea, and El Arish.

EL SHATT

A frontier corps station is located at this point 11 miles from Suez.

- *At some point on the Red Sea, the Israelites crossed when fleeing from the pharaoh of Egypt (Exod. 14:1–15:21).*

AIYUN MUSA *("Moses' Well")*, **Marah**

Eleven miles south of El Shatt is this small oasis with palm groves and still pools. A dozen springs supply brackish yet palatable water. Two of them are very bitter. Tradition links this site with the first stop of the Israelites after they fled from the pharaoh in Egypt. The largest and southernmost spring is said to be the spring which Moses sweetened.

- *Moses sweetened the water by casting a limb of a tree into it (Exod. 15:23–25).*
- *Tradition has it that at this location Moses' sister Miriam taught the women of Israel "the song of triumph" (Exod. 15:20–21).*

Ras Sudr, *Sidr*

Sultan Saladin built a fortress here that dominated the neighboring wadis and oases. Very little of the fortress remains today. It is 38 miles from Suez.

Hawara

On the slope of a ridge, a small thicket of stunted palms shading a spring of brackish water marks the site of Hawara.

ELIM, Wadi Gharandal

This is the traditional site of Israel's second camp after crossing the Red Sea (Exod. 15:27). It is located 63 miles from Suez. It had several fine springs and many palm trees.

Hammam Faruon

About 74 miles from Suez, at the foot of Jebel Hammam Faruon, there are several hot springs of sulphurous water. The Arabs believe the springs have healing qualities.

Abu Zeneima, *Abu Zenima*

This village is identified by some to be an Israelite encampment on the Red Sea. It is now a mining port and a village of the Sinai Mining Company, which extracts manganese from the neighboring Mount Om Bagma, 2,400 feet high. Ancient Egyptian inscriptions found at el-Maghra, on Gebal Habashi, indicate that the area was occupied as early as the First Dynasty, about 3100 B.C.

Sarabiel Khadim, *Sarabit el Khadim*

This is the site of ancient turquoise mines and inscriptions of crude Canaanite pictures, from which some of our alphabet may have evolved. They date from about 1500 B.C. Also in the area is the Egyptian TEMPLE OF HATHOR, dating back to the nineteenth century B.C. Stones with hieroglyphs eulogize the Egyptian kings and the goddess Hathor.

Magharah

Here were the oldest Egyptian copper mines that supplied the pre-dynastic cultures. Here also are STELAE commemorating the daring mining enterprises of Egypt and praising her pharaohs. There are also some early HEBREW CHARACTERS.

Abu Rodeis *and* Merkhah Port

Abu Rodeis has beautiful palm trees and is a center for Sinai's oil industry. It serves as a rest stop for tours to Mount Sinai.

Wadi el-Maktab *(Valley of Writings)*

The road winds between granite cliffs to the great valley where huge granite blocks are inscribed with Greek and Arabic writings and pictures of gazelles, camels, crosses, boats, stars, and so on. By taking the route via Wadi Feiran, one will bypass Wadi el-Maktab. Visitors may go to Sinai via Wadi Feiran and return via Wadi el-Maktab.

Wadi Feiran, Feiran Oasis *(biblical Paran and Rephidim?)*

The Wadi Feiran (Paran) is 81 miles long and is one of the longest, most beautiful, and most famous wadis in Sinai. It begins in the region of Jebel Musa, where it is called Wadi el Sheikh, and its mouth is located about 18 miles southeast of Abu Rodeis.

Because this wadi is one of the most important routes to Mount Sinai, pilgrims from the third century onwards have traveled this route and left inscriptions on the rocks that line the wadi.

POINTS OF INTEREST

HESSY EL KHATTATIN.   One of the first objects of special interest in the wadi is the Hessy el Khattatin — the miracle of water in Rephidim (Exod. 17:6). On the right bank, a large block of fallen granite stands at a sharp angle to the valley, surrounded with heaps of pebbles and small stones. Similar heaps are seen on the surrounding rocks, placed there by the Bedouins to remember a tradition concerning the site. According to the tradition, it was from this rock that water was supplied to the Israelites when Moses smote it with the rod. As the Israelites rested at this site they amused themselves by throwing pebbles upon the surrounding piece of rock. Arabs today believe that healing qualities are associated with the rock and the throwing of pebbles.

FEIRAN OASIS.   In the wadi, about 28 miles from its mouth, is the 3-mile-long, beautiful, palm-laden Feiran Oasis, about 2,000 feet above sea level. It is the Eden of Sinai. Thousands of date palms have attracted settlers to this site since ancient times. The Gabaly tribe of Bedouins, originally from Romania, inhabit the oasis, and the women wear beautiful, long, golden-colored veils that completely cover the face from the nose down. They are very timid when being photographed. The Sinai bishopric maintains a small farm and church at the oasis, with a monk in charge.

In the second century A.D. Claudius Ptolemaeus spoke of the town of Paran as an episcopal see and the central point of the monastic and anchorite fraternities of the peninsula. There are numerous old monasteries and hermits' cells on the rocky slopes and plateau of the Serbal Mountains surrounding the Feiran Oasis.

JEBEL EL TAHUNA.   On the right side of Wadi Feiran is Jebel el Tahuna (mountain of the mill), covered with tombs, monk cells, and chapels. Traditionally this is the mountain from which Moses viewed the battle with the Amalekites (Exod. 17:8–16).

MOUNT SERBAL.   To the south of Wadi Feiran is Mount Serbal, which rises 4,000 feet above the valley.

■ *Some regard Wadi Feiran as the site of Rephidim of the Bible, where Moses smote the rock and water came forth (Exod. 17:1–7; 19:2; Num. 33:14–15).*

■ *Some believe that Wadi Feiran is the biblical Paran, where the Israelites stayed during the Exodus (Num. 10:12; 12:16; 13:3, 26; Deut. 1:1; 33:2; 1 Sam. 25:1; 1 Kings 11:18).*

Wadi el Sheikh

From Feiran Oasis the road goes to the most important valley of the peninsula, Wadi el Sheikh, followed by Saint Catherine's Monastery, 30 miles away.

Tomb of Sheikh Nebi Saleh

This tomb, the Mecca of Sinai, is considered to be the most sacred in Sinai. It is 7 miles from Saint Catherine's Monastery and consists of a small, whitewashed chamber with a domed roof. Nebi Saleh, a companion of Mohammed during the seventh century, is buried in the building. He is extolled in the Koran as a venerable patriarch. Every May a great festival takes place at the tomb of Nebi Saleh, and is considered the national event of the year. Bedouins come gaily dressed from all parts of the peninsula. Sheep are sacrificed, camels compete in races, and a lively festival is held.

Saint Catherine's Monastery

In the sixth century A.D. the emperor Justinian built the fortress-monastery of Saint Catherine on the side of a mountain in Sinai to protect the life and property of the numerous monks living in the region. It is built like a miniature city. It has a fine Greek Orthodox Church of the Transfiguration, with beautiful sixteenth-century mosaics, a small moslem mosque (A.D. 1106), living quarters, a library, a bakery, and living quarters for pilgrims. The 33-49-foot-high walls are 279 feet by 312 feet in length. The monastery is 5,012 feet above sea level.

Legend tells of a godly maiden named Catherine, who lived in the city of Alexandria in the year A.D. 307. She was publicly accused by the emperor Maximinus of idolatry, and thus she was tortured and put to death. Angels brought her body to a peak near the monastery. The monks found her bones, transferred them to the monastery church, and hence the name.

In times past the only way to get into the monastery was by the use of a hoist that lifted the visitor 90 feet to an opening in the wall. The hoist is still used for heavy loads and supplies.

The monks in the monastery observe long periods of self-mortification. Prayers, light housekeeping duties, and small tasks make up their daily routine. Usually about a dozen monks live in the monastery, but in the past over a hundred monks have lived there at the same time.

Visitors to the monastery may climb 3,000 steps, built out of rock by monks as a penance, to the summit of the mountain, where tradition says Moses received the Ten Commandments.

Sinai Bedouins of the Jebelia tribe live near Saint Catherine's. They speak Arabic and claim they are descendants of Wallachian and Egyptian slaves who were settled there by Justinian in the sixth century A.D. to guard the monastery and act as servants to the monks.

POINTS OF INTEREST

The **BYZANTINE CHURCH OF THE TRANSFIGURATION** is richly adorned with icons. Legend says the church was built by Helena, mother of Constantine, in A.D. 342, as the Chapel of the Burning Bush, which burning bush was reputed to have been found here by early Byzantine monks. The traditional original site of the burning bush is found inside the Chapel of the Burning Bush, but the roots of the bush have been replanted outside the chapel and carefully nurtured. Not only do the monks believe they found the burning bush, but according to tradition they also located Mount Sinai, the spring of Moses, the path of Moses, the spot where Moses broke the tablets of stone, the site where the earth swallowed up Korah, the hill of Aaron, and the burial place of the golden calf.

Near the **CHARNEL HOUSE**, in the beautiful garden outside the monastery wall, is a small **BURIAL GROUND**, 15 feet square. After monks have been buried there for about one year, their bones are moved to the charnel house to be added to the heaps of skulls and bones that are already there.

The **SKELETON OF SAINT STEPHANOS**, the monastery sexton who died in A.D. 580, may be observed seated on a chair in the charnel house. Since he spent his life guarding the steps leading to the mountain of Moses, he was rewarded by having his skeleton seated in the charnel house, fully dressed in his habit.

A special treasure of the monastery is a copy of a **SCRIPT SIGNED BY MOHAMMED**. The story is told that a young camel driver sought refuge one night, and the monks realized that the driver was the prophet Mohammed. In return for their hospitality the prophet signed a scroll ordering his followers never to violate the monastery. The document was signed by the print of the prophet's hand. The original was taken by a Turkish sultan, but a facsimile is shown to visitors.

The monastery **LIBRARY**, one of the oldest and richest in the world, contains some 3,000 ancient works, including valuable Greek and Arabic manuscripts. One of them is the *Evangeliarium Theodosianum*, presented to the monastery by the emperor Theodosius III in A.D. 766. The lettering is in gold and it has pictures of seven saints. The famous *Codex Sinaiticus* was located here by Tischendorf in 1844. Parts of the Codex were in a wastebasket and were nearly used to start a fire. They proved to be one of the two oldest vellum manuscripts then known. Dating from about A.D. 340, the Codex contains all of the New Testament, the apocryphal New Testament books of the Shepherd of Hermes and the Epistle of Barnabas, plus parts of the Old Testament. The Codex came into the hands of the Russians, but the British Museum purchased it in 1933 for 100,000 pounds.

The library also houses many ancient and valuable icons; in fact, it is the most important collection of icons extant (over 2,000). In the eighth century, the issue of whether or not the veneration of icons constituted idolatry erupted into a civil war that shook Byzantium. Imperial decrees ordered the smashing of every holy image;

hence our word *iconoclast*, "icon smasher." The rising tide of Islam, however, had isolated Saint Catherine's from Constantinople, and the monastery's precious collection escaped destruction. A seventh-century icon of Peter holding the keys is one of the most beautiful icons in existence. The icon of the baptism of Jesus in the Jordan River shows Jesus immersed in the water.

In 1958 a team of experts under the direction of Dr. Kurt Weitzmann restored the art work at Saint Catherine's.

MOUNT SINAI ("cliffs"), Mount Horeb ("waste")

Christians, Jews, and Moslems have sought to identify the Mountain of God, where Moses received the Ten Commandments. And though there are still differences of opinion, research tends to strengthen the case for locating Mount Sinai in the south end of the peninsula.

The Mount Sinai range rises abruptly from the Wadi el-Sheikh and is composed of several high peaks in a mountain mass 2 miles long and 1 mile wide. The range runs from northwest to southeast, and Saint Catherine's Monastery is in the center of the northeast side.

RAS SUFSAFEH, the northernmost peak of the Mount Sinai range, is 6,830 feet high. It "dwells apart" from the mountain mass, and many feel that it was from this peak that Moses gave the law to the Israelites who were camped on the PLAIN OF RAHAH, northwest of the peak. This plain is about 2 miles long and ½ mile wide. The mountain peak is about 1,870 feet above the plain of Rahah, and is very difficult to climb.

JEBEL MUSA, or the MOUNT OF MOSES, is 7,363 feet above sea level. Since the sixth century A.D., this has been the traditional site where Moses received the Ten Commandments. On top of the peak is a small, recently built Christian church standing next to a mosque. A small grotto alongside the chapel is the traditional site where Moses received shelter while on the mount. Camels are provided for the visitor who desires to go to the top of the mountain. The camels go as far as ELIJAH'S CHAPEL, and steps lead from there to the summit. Just below the Chapel of Elijah and the splendid cypress trees, on the route of descent by stairs, is the arched gateway of Saint Stephanos, where he sat in the same attitude in which his skeleton now sits in the charnel house, quizzing the traveler as to his worthiness to ascend the mount. This trip to the top of Jebel Musa and back takes about half a day (5 or 6 hours).

Some have believed that JEBEL SERBAL is Mount Sinai. It is located northwest of Jebel Musa and is the most imposing peak in the chain. Although it is lower than the others (6,759 feet), it stands in solitary grandeur, and would seem an appropriate mountain to be identified with Mount Sinai.

In addition to those already named, JEBEL KATHERINA is the highest peak in this range — approximately 9,000 feet above sea level. Being the highest, it was identified as Mount Sinai as early as the fourth century B.C.

Those who believe the route of the Israelites was via Migdol and Baal-zephon, parallel to "the way of the Philistines," or on the old caravan route not too far from the seacoast, believe Mount Sinai to be Jebel el Halal, 25 miles west of Kadesh-Barnea, or possibly Jebel Libni, Jebel el Maghara, or another one in the area.

- *Mount Sinai was near Mount Seir (Deut. 33:2; Judg. 5:4-5).*
- *Near Mount Sinai Moses watched the flocks of Jethro and saw God in the burning bush (Exod. 3:1-4:17).*
- *Moses spent 40 days on Mount Sinai receiving the Ten Commandments as part of the Law, and then delivered the Law to the Israelites (Exod. 18-40; Leviticus and most of Deuteronomy).*
- *Jethro met Moses at Mount Sinai and suggested that judges be appointed (Exod. 18).*
- *Instructions for a tabernacle were received on the mount (Exod. 25-31).*
- *Here the golden calf was made and worshiped (Exod. 32).*
- *The children of Israel stripped themselves of ornaments, and Moses went outside the camp and interceded for them (Exod. 33:6-23).*
- *Moses went the second time to Mount Sinai to receive again what was written on the first tablets he had broken (Exod. 34; Deut. 10:2).*
- *Elijah was visited by the Lord on Mount Horeb, the mount of God (1 Kings 19:8-18).*

Tor, *el Tur ("mount")*

With a population of about 1,000, this is the largest settlement in southern Sinai. The people are mostly Moslem, but some of them are Greeks who own fishing boats. In the town are a hotel, a hospital, stores, and a quarantine station for pilgrims going to Mecca. The monastery and Greek Orthodox church here are attached to Saint Catherine's monastery. Two miles north of the town are hot springs, called in Arabic *Hammam Musa*, or the hot baths of Moses. It is believed the water has healing properties.

Sharm el Sheikh

On the extreme southeast corner of the Sinai Peninsula, where a small tongue of land splits the coast in two, lies Sharm el Sheikh, one of the beauty spots of the Red Sea coast. It was never inhabited until recent times, and in the near past it was used as a small military post for the Egyptians.

Tiran Island

Located 130 miles south of Eilat is an island 9 by 5 miles in size, with mountain ranges up to 1,600 feet high. Reefs between the island and the mainland leave only narrow, deep passages for shipping. It has thus become a very important military station. In the Israeli-Egyptian conflict the Egyptians set up their batteries of guns there to prevent Israeli shipping from passing through the straits. There is no water or vegetation on the island and no evidence that it was ever occupied by man in early times.

Oasis of Nabk, *Nabq*

About 20 miles north of Sharm el Sheikh, this abandoned oasis has small date palms and a well.

Dhahab

About 50 miles north of Sharm el Sheikh is Dhahab, an oasis inhabited by a sparse Bedouin population. There is a concentration of copper slag, indicating that ancient mines were once located in the area.

Nuweiba *and* Taba

These are identifiable points along the coast of the gulf of Aqaba. Nuweiba is approximately 45 miles south of Eilat and Taba is 5 miles south.

Island of the Coral, *Yi Haalmogim*

This small island, 9½ miles south of Eilat, has ruins of a Crusader fortress dating from the twelfth century.

EZION-GEBER, Eilat, *Elath*

Eilat is a port city and today vies with Tiberias as Israel's leading winter tourist resort. It has 15,000 inhabitants.

- *This was King Solomon's port (1 Kings 9:26–28).*
- *The children of Israel, under Moses' leadership, passed this way (Deut. 2:8).*
- *The Queen of Sheba must have landed here (1 Kings 10:1–13).*

Valley of Inscriptions

In the hills southwest of Eilat, at Ras el Nagb, near the "Pilgrim's Way" and the Sinai-Israel border, is the Valley of Inscriptions. On the walls of a canyon are inscriptions that include a seven-branched CANDELABRUM with an adjacent ram's horn — ancient Jewish emblems. Some Jewish Aramaic inscriptions are in Nabataean characters.

El Thamad

This is a point about 40 miles west of Eilat on the "Pilgrim's Way" (Darb el Haj). The Darb el Haj starts at Suez, goes east through Mitla Pass and the Gulf of Eilat, and to Mecca, in Arabia.

El Nakhl, *Qal 'at el Nakhl*

This FORTRESS is near the center of the Sinai Peninsula, on the "Pilgrim's Way," where a road comes to this point from the north and El Arish. It is midway between Eilat and Suez and is known as the "Fortress of Date-Palms." The main structure was built by Sultan

Selim I in the course of his conquest of Egypt in A.D. 1517. It was used as a hospice for Moslem pilgrims. The mosque of the fortress is in several stages of construction. East of the fortress is a sheikh's tomb, and around it are hundreds of Arab graves. It would seem that this site is not premedieval.

Ras el Gindi

Near the junction of three desert routes, about 15 miles north of Mitla Pass, is a FORTRESS built by Saladin in the twelfth century A.D. It is built on a summit of a 2,142-foot mountain. In some respects it is similar to Masada, near the shores of the Dead Sea. A 30-minute hike to the northwest corner of the preserved wall will bring the visitor to the main gate, with a Shield of David engraved in the arch over the gateway. A large mosque and a number of large buildings are in the fortress, in addition to an enormous roofed cistern and great underground cisterns.

Mitla Pass

About 25 miles east of Suez is Mitla Pass. Near the pass are the remains of ancient buildings that possibly belonged to an Amorite settlement and date to the Middle Bronze Age (Patriarchal Period). They are north of the road junction of Sudr el Haitan on the slopes of Ruweiset el Akheider, not far from the memorial of the former governor of Sinai, Colonel A. C. Parker.

Bir Hasana

This is a point in the Sinai Peninsula where the road from El Arish to El Nakhl crosses over the road that runs between Mitla Pass and El Qusaima.

KADESH-BARNEA, El Qusaima, *Ain el Qudeirat, near El Muweilah and Ain Qadeis*

Only in the El Qusaima area are there enough greenstuffs and water to sustain a body of people the size of Israel at the time of the Exodus. Here is the largest spring in North Sinai. This must be the wilderness of Zin and Kadesh-Barnea. It is 150 miles from Ramses in Egypt, 140 miles from Mount Sinai, on the "uttermost" border of Edom, on the south border of Canaan, in the wilderness of Zin (Num. 20:1, 16; 33:36–37; Deut. 1:2). Of all the sites visited during the travels of the Israelites in the Sinai Peninsula, this one has the most unanimous agreement among the scholars as to its location. The area is approximately 40 miles south and a little west of Beersheba.

Here the Israelites made their headquarters for 38 years, from the sending of the spies until they entered Canaan. Here was the springboard for the invasion of Canaan. Here Moses wrestled for the destiny of his people, and here his own destiny was decided. This area played a major role in the desert wanderings of the Israelites.

Ain el Qudeirat and Ain Qadeis are separated by 12 miles and seem to be the two main points identifying Kadesh-Barnea. *Kadesh* means "holy springs," and *Barnea* means "desert of wandering." There are a series of wells in the area. Remains of an ancient fort on a small tell were found in the neck of Wadi el Ain by Woolley and Lawrence and dated by Glueck to the early Hebrew monarchy. The tell is 200 by 120 feet in size. The Egyptians, like the Nabataeans of old, developed a small experimental farm here, and there is a very interesting communal olive press located in a vacant house at El Qusaima. It is very similar to those described in the Mishna, with two heavy stone rollers which move on a solid base about 7 feet in diameter. The rollers were turned by a camel or a pair of donkeys.

Most scholars believe Mount Hor, where Aaron died (Num. 33:38), was near Kadesh-Barnea and not near Petra in Jordan, as the Arab Moslems and Josephus believe. Some feel that the present Jebel el Madra, a limestone peak by Maale-Agrabim, is the peak Mount Hor. This is in the center of the Nahal Zin (Wadi Fikra). It was in the borders of Edom (Num. 20:23; 33:37) and was the first stopping place of Israel's wanderings after they left Kadesh-Barnea (Num. 20:22; 33:37).

Those who believe the Israelites came directly to the Kadesh-Barnea area via the Mediterranean seacoast believe that Mount Sinai was 25 miles west of Kadesh-Barnea — possibly Jebel el Halal.

- *Chedorlaomer and his confederates smote the Amorites and Amalekites here (Gen. 14:1-7).*
- *When Hagar fled from Sarah's wrath, she stopped at a well and an angel told her she would bear a son, Ishmael. The well was located between Kadesh and Bered (Gen. 16:6-14).*
- *Abraham dwelt between Kadesh and Shur after the destruction of Sodom and Gomorrah (Gen. 20:1).*
- *Here was the center of the wanderings of the tribes of Israel (Num. 20:1; Deut. 1:46).*
- *Spies were sent into the promised land from here, and here Israel sinned (Num. 13-14; 32:8; Deut. 9:23).*
- *Here Caleb gave a positive report on the land of Canaan (Num. 13:30; 14:6-9; Josh. 14:6-15).*
- *This was the scene of the rebellion of Korah, the murmuring of the people, and the budding of Aaron's rod (Num. 16-17).*
- *Here Miriam died. She had watched Moses in the ark of bulrushes (Exod. 2:4), had led the women in the song of victory at the Red Sea (Exod. 15:20), and had been both punished by leprosy and healed of it (Num. 12:1-15; 20:1; Deut. 24:8-9). (Some traditions have Moses buried here also.)*
- *Here Moses smote the rock and water came forth (Num. 20:11).*
- *Here Moses was told he could not enter the promised land (Num. 20:12; 27:14; Deut. 32:48-52).*
- *A delegation was sent from here to the king of Edom (Num. 20:14-21; Judg. 11:17).*
- *Here the final journey into the promised land began via Mount Hor (Num. 20:22).*
- *It was on the southern border of Judah (Josh. 15:3; Ezek. 47:19).*

■ *Jephthah sent a message from here to King Ammon (Judg. 11:12–28).*

■ *Kadesh was mentioned by David (Ps. 29:8).*

Above: Mount of Moses, Sinai

Below: Saint Catherine's Monastery, Mount Sinai

EL ARISH *("the booth")*

This is a town on the Mediterranean seacoast, 50 miles south of Gaza. Here the Wadi el Arish, called the "River of Egypt," flows into the Mediterranean. It is located on "the way of the land of the Philistines," or the "way of the sea." El Arish is known as the capital of Sinai. Its population is mostly Moslem, with a few Coptic Christians.

■ *Tradition indicates that when Jacob left Canaan and went to Egypt (Gen. 46:5–6) he built a booth and rested here.*

Greece

Greece is located on the southern tip of the Balkan Peninsula, in the eastern Mediterranean. It is bounded on the north by communist countries Albania, Yugoslavia, and Bulgaria, on the east by the Aegean Sea and Turkey, and on the west by the Ionian Sea. It comprises 51,182 square miles — slightly smaller than the state of Alabama — and about 1/5 of the country is made up of islands. Its population is around 9,000,000.

HISTORY

The apostle Paul visited Greece on his second missionary journey, in response to a night vision he had while in Troas (Acts 16:8-10), and visited Philippi, Amphipolis (Neochorion), Apollonia (Pollina), Thessalonica (Salonika), Beroea (Verroia), Athens, and Corinth. He later returned to Greece on a subsequent missionary journey.

Early Greek civilization embraces the years 1200-400 B.C., and the country has a written history from about 800 B.C., the year 776 B.C. being the year of the founding of the Olympic games and the starting point of Greek chronology. Although classical Greece dates from the fifth to the third century B.C., the country never really recovered from its defeat by the Spartans in the Peloponnesian War (431-404 B.C.).

The early Greeks were the foremost artists of their day, and Greek architecture has set the pattern for nearly every state capitol building in the United States, Southern States mansions, and columned buildings everywhere.

OUTLINE OF GREECE'S HISTORY

Bronze Age Greece *(4000-1200 B.C.)*

This was the period of the Minoan civilization on Crete and the Mycenaean civilization on the mainland. The Bronze Age on the mainland was called the *Helladic* civilization. The late Helladic Age, then, is the Mycenaean Age.

The Acropolis, Athens (Ewing Galloway)

The Dark Ages *(1200–700 B.C.)*

1200. The Dorians invaded Greece and destroyed the Mycenaean civilization. Sparta was settled by Dorians as a military camp.

1130. Iron came into general use for weapons and tools.

1100. Greeks began colonizing the Ionian coast of Asia Minor.

776. The first Olympic games were held.

750. Homer's epic poems, *The Iliad* and *The Odyssey*, were composed.

705. Greek architects began building in stone. The Greek alphabet developed.

Aristocratic Age *(750–507 B.C.)*

750–561. Athens became a republic. Greek law developed.
Greek territory expanded north and west to present Spain.
Solon initiated social reform in 594.
The philosophers Thales and Anaximander taught ca. 580.

Ca. 650. Large free-standing sculpture evolved. The use of coins began.

561–507. This was the age of the Athenian tyrants.
The mathematician Pythagoras lived ca. 530, the philosopher Herodotus ca. 500, and the philosopher Anaxagoras ca. 500–428.

Period of the Persian Wars *(499–479 B.C.)*

490. The Greeks stopped the first Persian invasion under Darius at the Battle of Marathon.

480. The Greeks defeated the Persian fleet under Xerxes at Salamis. The Persians destroyed the Acropolis in the same year, but Persia was defeated.

Golden Age of Athens, Age of Pericles *(479–431 B.C.)*

478–431. This was the period of the rise of the Athenian Empire and classical Greece. It was a time of democratic government and the beginning of Western civilization.
Rivalry between Sparta and Athens increased.
Polyclitus the sculptor lived in the fifth century.
Phidias designed the Parthenon sculptures. He was the greatest artist of the classical period.
Herodotus wrote the history of the Persian War, the first historical work of Western civilization.
Aeschylus and Sophocles wrote tragedies and Aristophanes wrote comedies.

Ca. 480–445. The sculptor Myron worked in Athens.

462–461. Pericles, the orator, brought democratic reforms to Athens (the first true democracy in history). He directed the building of the Parthenon.

Ca. 460. Hippocrates, the "father of medicine," was born at Kos.

Ca. 456. The Temple of Zeus at Olympia was completed.

447. Ictinus and Callicrates began to build the Parthenon.

YUGOSLAVIA

BULGARIA

ALBANIA

Orestias

Xanthi   Komotini

Philippi

Amphipolis   Neapolis (Kavalla)

Thessalonica (Thessalonike)
Berea (Veroia)

Kozani   Katerini

Limnos

AEGEAN SEA

Ioannina   Larissal

Troy

Karditsa   Volos

Troas
Assos

Preveza

Mitylene (Mytilini)   Pergamum (Bergama)

Lamia

TURKEY

Delphi   Levadia   Halkis

Itea   Thive

Chios

Gulf of Corinth

Patre   Egion   Eleusis   Dafni   Smyrna (Izmir)

IONIAN SEA   Megara   Athens

Corinth   Isthmia   Ephesus

Mycenae   Cenchrea   Andros   Samos

Argos   Epidaurus   Sounion

Tiryns   Navplion   Saronic Gulf   Miletus

Tripolis

Pergos   Olympia   Dilos

Megalopolis   Patmos

Sparta   Naxos   Cos (Coos)   Cnidus

Mistra

Githion   Milos   Rhodes (Rodo

MEDITERRANEAN SEA

Iraklion

Crete   Cnossos

Fair Havens

Claudia

N̂

Greece

Miles   25   50   100

Second Peloponnesian War *(431–404 B. C.)*

Sparta defeated Athens in the Peloponnesian War. Thucydides wrote an account of the war that ranks among the world's great literary works.

Socrates wrote and taught during this period, and Euripides wrote many fine dramas.

When Athens fell to Sparta in 404, its Golden Age ended.

Sparta's Supremacy over Athens *(404–371 B.C.)*

399. Socrates was tried and condemned to death and died by drinking the hemlock.

387. Plato started to teach in Athens.

Isocrates and Demosthenes won fame as orators during this period.

Hellenistic Age *(334–197 B.C)*

359–323. This was the period of the rise of the Macedonian Empire and the Hellenistic Age.

Ca. 350. The sculptor Praxiteles lived.

343. Aristotle became a tutor to Alexander of Macedonia.

338. Philip II of Macedonia defeated Athens and Greece became a part of the Macedonian Empire.

336. Philip II's son Alexander succeeded him.

334–323. Alexander conquered the Persian Empire, an area almost the size of the United States. He founded Greek cities everywhere, including Alexandria, Egypt. He died in Babylon in 323. Alexander affected the history of the world by spreading Greek civilization and language. Greek culture became a world culture.

197. The Romans conquered Macedonia and Greece for the first time.

Roman Rule *(147 B.C.–A.D. 529)*

147. Greece became a Roman province and the Hellenistic Age ended. Although the Romans fought three civil wars in Greece, there was a 300-year period of unbroken peace in Greece under Roman rule.

Byzantine Age *(A.D. 529–1453)*

The Byzantine Age was a second "golden age" that lasted for 1,000 years.

Ottoman Empire *(1453–1822)*

1453. The Ottoman Empire instituted Turkish rule in Greece, and Constantinople became the center of Greek culture.

Independence *(1822–present)*

1822. Greece declared its independence and defeated Turkey in 1829 (Greek War of Independence).

1830. Greece became a kingdom, and Otto I became the first king in 1832.

1924. Greece proclaimed itself a republic. Political upheaval followed.

1935. The country voted to become a kingdom again.

1941–44. Germany, Italy, and Bulgaria occupied neutral Greece during World War II.

1947–49. Civil war between communists and nationalists raged in Greece.

1958. Parliament approved an electoral reform law based on proportional representation.

1960. Cyprus received her independence from Britain after five years of fighting.

RELIGION

The Greek Orthodox church has 8,118,000 members in Greece. There are a few Moslems and a few Christians, about 15,000 of whom are Protestants.

To Greek Orthodox church members, "tradition" is older than the New Testament, and the teachings of Jesus according to tradition are equal in value to the scriptures of the New Testament. They believe in the Trinity, as the Roman Catholics do. Unlike the Roman Catholics, however, they do not have a supreme pontiff, but the authority lies in an ecumenical council, which settles questions of dogma, and so forth. The last ecumenical council for them was held at Nicaea in A.D. 787.

Greek Orthodox Catholics believe their church was founded by Jesus — to whom they trace their authority — and that it is the only true church. They recognize seven sacraments: baptism, confirmation, the eucharist, confession, ordination, marriage, and holy unction. They venerate sacred icons and relics as representations of the persons the items represent.

There are 13 autocephalous churches, with the Church of Constantinople as first in precedence and honor. The others in order of precedence are Alexandria, Antioch, Jerusalem, Cyprus, Russia, Greece, Georgia, Yugoslavia, Romania, Bulgaria, Poland, and Albania. In each place there is an archbishop, patriarch, exarch, or metropolitan that serves as the head of the church in that area.

The Patriarch of Constantinople (Istanbul), although not a supreme pontiff in the Roman sense, occupies a preeminent position among the heads of the Orthodox churches. He initiates all matters affecting dogma, ethics, and canon law, and convenes synods and ecumenical councils of the church. He is the unifying symbol who holds the whole structure of the Orthodox church together. His functions were determined by the second and fourth ecumenical councils. The fourth was held at Chalcedon in A.D. 450. Before the Treaty of Lausanne in 1923, the Patriarch of Constantinople had a flock of 4,000,000 souls; but since that date he has had only about 100,000.

GREECE TODAY

The summers in Greece are hot and dry, with some moderation of the temperature near the seacoast. The winters, however, are often characterized by temperatures of 40–50 degrees and a great deal of rain in much of the country.

Although the national origins of Greece's present-day inhabitants vary widely, most speak modern Greek.

Among the main industries of Greece are agriculture, fishing, mining, and textiles.

The unit of currency in Greece is the *drachma*, with 100 *leptae* in a drachma.

CITIES AND SITES

ATHENS

Athens is the capital city of Greece, with a metropolitan population of about 3,000,000. Over 90 percent of the people are members of the Eastern Greek Orthodox church. Complete religious freedom is recognized, but proselyting from and interference with the Greek Orthodox church is forbidden.

Athens' first name was *Cecropia*. According to tradition, Cecrops came out of Egypt and founded the city in 1556 B.C. and reigned as its first king. It was later named Athens, after the goddess Athena.

As the seat of Greek art, philosophy, and literature, Athens became the university city of the Roman world. Paul visited the city on his second missionary journey.

■ *Paul saw in Athens an altar dedicated "to the unknown god" during his second missionary journey. Taking this as his cue, he preached about the God of heaven (Acts 17:22–31).*

■ *Paul sent for Timothy (Timotheus) and Silas (Silvanus) to come to him in Athens, and he was left alone when Timothy was sent to Thessalonica (1 Thess. 3:1–2).*

POINTS OF INTEREST

The Acropolis

1. The **ACROPOLIS**, a steep hill 230 feet high, is located in the center of the city. It has been occupied since Neolithic times (3500 B.C.). In Mycenaean times (1600–1100 B.C.) the Acropolis was surrounded by a strong cyclopean wall. On the hilltop was the king's palace on the site of the Erechtheum.

The **PROPYLAEA** (437–432 B.C.) is the monumental entrance gate to the Acropolis. It is adorned with marble Doric and Ionic columns, and was built under the direction of Pericles. It served also as a public art gallery and public meeting place.

The **TEMPLE OF THE WINGLESS VICTORY** (Athena Nike) (437–425 B.C.) is located on the right of the Propylaea and is a masterpiece of Attic art. It is called "Wingless Victory" because the Athenians are believed to have cut off its wings so that victory should always remain in Athens. It once housed a wooden statue of the goddess.

ATHENA PROMACHOS. Between the Propylaea and the Parthenon is the base of a colossal statue, Athena Promachos, by Phidias. This bronze statue was so high that it could be seen from the sea.

The **PARTHENON** (447–438 B.C.) (Temple of the Virgins) was dedicated to the goddess Athena. It is built of Pentelic marble with no mortar, and its architects were Ictinus and Callicrates. Phidias designed the sculptural adornment under the direction of Pericles.

The Parthenon was built in the Doric style, with 8 fluted columns on its narrow sides and 17 on the long ones. It is 228 feet long, 100 feet wide, and 60 feet high. The sculptured bas-reliefs on the pediments are among the most perfect manifestations of Greek art. The eastern pediment showed the birth of Athena from the head of Zeus, and the western pediment showed the contest between Athena and Poseidon for possession of the city of Athens. On the upper external part of the main temple wall was the famous frieze showing the *Panathenaea*, the magnificent festival of the Athenians. The metopes portrayed conflicts between men and their enemies.

The temple entrance is on the eastern side. There are no decorations on the inside, but a solitary monumental statue of Athena (daughter of Zeus), 40 feet high, once stood in majesty. Phidias fashioned the statue of wood and covered it with gold and ivory — gold for clothing and ivory for flesh. During the Byzantine period the statue was taken to Constantinople and was later destroyed in a fire.

The magnificence of the architecture becomes apparent when it is realized that there is not a single straight line or absolute perpendicular in the entire building. Pericles' architects used curved lines to counteract optical illusion. Since the eye tends to make horizontal lines appear to dip at the center, the floor lines of the Parthenon follow a curve of a circle with a 3½-mile radius. If it did not, it would seem to sag.

Beams atop the Doric columns follow suit. The columns all tilt inward, and lines projected from the corner columns would converge 1½ miles up. The eye tends to make straight columns look concave, and therefore the Parthenon columns swell 2/5 of the way up in order to look straight; corner columns are slightly thicker. Metopes, carved slabs beneath the sculpture-rich pediments, or gables, vary in size to look square from below.

The Parthenon was a temple to Athena for nearly 900 years, a Christian church dedicated to the Virgin Mary for nearly 1,000 years, and for 200 years a Moslem mosque. In 1687, when the Venetian forces were besieging the Turks on the Acropolis, an explosion of a powder magazine destroyed the inside of the Parthenon. Restoration began in 1859.

1. Acropolis
2. Acropolis Museum
3. Theater of Dionysus
4. Odeum of Herod Atticus
5. Mars' Hill (Areopagus)
6. Pnyx Hill
7. Philopappus Hill
8. Prison of Socrates
9. Temple of Hephaestus
10. Agora
11. Stoa of Attalus
12. Roman Agora
13. Temple of Olympian Zeus
14. Hadrian's Arch
15. Stadium
16. National Archaeological Museum
17. Benaki Museum
18. Byzantine Museum
19. Museum of Greek Handicrafts
20. National Historical Museum
21. Museum of Keramikos
22. National Picture Gallery
23. Constitution Square
24. Tomb of the Unknown Soldier
25. Old Parliament Building
26. National Gardens
27. Zappeion
28. Royal Palace and Guards
29. Academy of Sciences
30. University of Athens
31. National Library
32. Byzantine Church of Saint Theodore
33. Byzantine Church of Kapnikarea
34. National Theater
35. Mount Lycabettus
36. Flea Market

A full-scale replica of the Parthenon is located in Nashville, Tennessee.

The **ERECHTHEUM**, on the north side of the Acropolis, was built in the Ionic order between 421 and 407 B.C., on the site of the ancient

Left: The Parthenon, showing the curvature of the base, Athens

Below: The Erechtheum, Athens, showing the caryatids on the right

Mycenaean palace. It was built to enclose the sacred sites of the fables concerning the beginnings of Athens. Legend has the contest between Athena and Poseidon take place there. Allegedly, Poseidon struck the rock with his trident, and seawater, symbolic of naval power, gushed forth, whereupon Athena struck with her spear and a fruiting olive tree grew up. The olive tree was considered to be more important; so Athena took the city under her protection.

The temple received its name from a mythical hero, King Erechtheus, who once lived on the site and was later identified as Poseidon. The eastern section was dedicated to Athena and the western section to Poseidon and Erechtheus. The six beautiful caryatids on the west end of the building are extremely fine pieces of sculpture. This temple, built on two levels, is very different from all other Greek temples.

2. The **ACROPOLIS MUSEUM** exhibits sculptures and other finds. The north side of the Acropolis has **CAVES** where the ancients worshiped old divinities.

3. **THEATER OF DIONYSUS.** On the south side of the Acropolis are two temples dedicated to Dionysus, dating back to the sixth century B.C. The Theater of Dionysus (fourth century B.C.), which was capable of holding 17,000 spectators, was used for the first performances of the tragedies of Aeschylus, Sophocles, and Euripides, and the comedies of Aristophanes. The first row of seats was reserved for priests, governors, and other dignitaries.

Above the theater is a cave containing the Byzantine **CHAPEL OF THE VIRGIN OF THE CAVE**. Just above the cave are two Corinthian columns.

To the east of the Theater of Dionysus is the **ODEUM OF PERICLES**, and west of the theater, on the hillside, was once the **ASKLEPEION OF ATHENS** (fifth century B.C.). In it were the temples of the gods Asclepias (Asklepios) and Hygea. Here the sick came to be healed.

The **STOA OF EUMENES** was built as a shelter for theater-goers by Eumenes, king of Pergamum (second century B.C.). It is located between the Theater of Dionysus and the Odeum of Herod Atticus.

4. The **ODEUM OF HEROD ATTICUS** (a theater) was built in A.D. 161 by Atticus. It is used now for summer festival concerts and holds 5,000 people.

West of the Acropolis

5. **MARS' HILL** (Areopagus, *Areios Pagos*). In Greek mythology, Ares is the god of war, the counterpart of the Roman god of war, Mars. The hill was called *Areopagus* because here the city court of Athens (Areopagus) met to decide matters concerning the city. The apostle Paul was brought here so the council might hear more of his doctrine, and here his famous address (Acts 17:19–34) was delivered. Dionysius and others believed, but the council mocked. Paul departed from them and went to Corinth.

6. **PNYX HILL** is located west of the Areopagus. On this, the town

assembly (the Athenian public) used to meet. Here was the first democratic government. The orators spoke from a platform hewn out of the rock, while upwards of 18,000 citizens could be accommodated. The "Sound and Light" production is presented here.

Above: Temple of Hephaestus, Athens
Below: Mars' Hill, Athens

7. The **PHILOPAPPUS HILL** (Hill of the Muses) and **MONUMENT** are located southwest of the Acropolis. The hill is covered with pine trees and adorned by a monument dedicated to a Syrian consul who blessed Athens. It dates from the second century A.D. In ancient times the hill was dedicated to the Muses (the nine goddesses presiding over arts and sciences) and called the Hill of the Muses.

8. The traditional **PRISON OF SOCRATES**, where he drank the hemlock, is located on the side of the Philopappus hill.

9. The **TEMPLE OF HEPHAESTUS** (Theseum) (450–440 B.C.), west of the Acropolis, is the best preserved ancient temple in Greece. Hephaestus was the god of fire and artisans, and from his forges came many marvels, among them the first mortal woman, Pandora, into whom the gods breathed life. Athens, a discerning city in matters of workmanship, held him in highest esteem.

The temple is commonly known as the *Theseum*, from its sculptures representing the exploits of the mythical hero Theseus, who

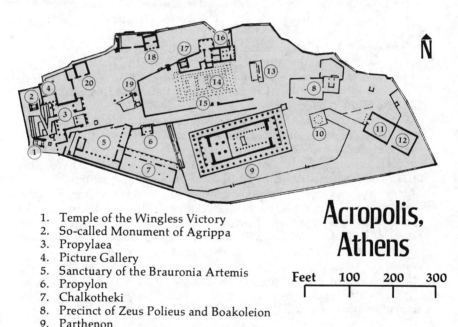

Acropolis, Athens

Feet   100   200   300

1. Temple of the Wingless Victory
2. So-called Monument of Agrippa
3. Propylaea
4. Picture Gallery
5. Sanctuary of the Brauronia Artemis
6. Propylon
7. Chalkotheki
8. Precinct of Zeus Polieus and Boakoleion
9. Parthenon
10. Temple of Roma
11. Heroon of Pandion
12. Service building
13. Great Altar of Athena
14. Old Temple of Athena
15. Propylon
16. Erechtheum
17. Pandroseum, Temple of Pandrosus, Sacred Olive Tree, and Cecropium
18. Dwelling of the Arrephori
19. Athena Promachos
20. Service building

cleared the roads into Athens of bandits and supposedly penetrated the Cretan labyrinth to kill the half-bull, half-human Minotaur. He became the king of Athens and ultimately united Attica into a single state.

The temple belongs to the Doric order, with 6 columns on the facades and 13 on the other sides. In the inner sanctuary were statues of Hephaestus and Athena.

10. The **AGORA** (marketplace) is located just east of the Temple of Hephaestus, on the northwest side of the Acropolis. The agora in all cities of Greece was an important center of government, intellect, and business. The Agora of Athens is famous because world-famous men graced her streets. Names such as Pericles, Praxiteles, Euripides, Sophocles, Socrates, Plato, and Aristotle have a familiar ring here. In one of the porticos Paul met daily with the Stoics and others to discuss Jesus and the resurrection (Acts 17:16-18).

The **ODEUM** was located to the west of the Stoa of Attalus. It served as the gymnasium, housed the schools of philosophy, and acted as a sort of university. This two-storied structure was destroyed in A.D. 267.

The **TEMPLE OF ARES** was located northwest of the Odeum and directly east of the Temple of Hephaestus. On the north side of the temple were the enclosure and the **ALTAR OF THE TWELVE GODS**, placed there in the time of Pisistratus. Only part of this can be seen because of the modern railway cut.

On the extreme west side of the Agora was the intellectual center of the city. Some of the most important buildings were there. Ranging from south to north, they are as follows: In the **THOLOS**, a circular building, leaders of the community were entertained. The **MITROON**, a sanctuary of the Mother of the Gods, is just north of the Tholos. It dates from the second century B.C., and it was here the city archives were housed. The **BOULEUTERION** (fifth century B.C.) was located just west of the Mitroon. Here the parliament of 500 assembled. In front of the Mitroon are the remains of the enclosure of the **NAMED HEROES**, where the bronze statues of the ten mythical heroes of Attica (Erechtheus, Cecrops, and others) stood on a long platform. Right behind the enclosure, to the east, stood the largest **ALTAR** in the Agora, dedicated to **ZEUS OF THE AGORA**. There are also other altars, buildings, and statues in the Agora.

11. The **STOA OF ATTALUS** (159-138 B.C.) has been reconstructed as a museum and was opened in 1956. The American Archaeological School began excavating there in 1931. This is the most important find at the Agora. It was originally built by Attalus II, king of Pergamum, in gratitude to the city of Athens, where he had studied as a youth. The Stoa has 2 floors, with 42 shops (21 on each floor) used for commercial purposes. There are 45 columns on the facade of each story. The street of the *Panathenaea* ran in front of the Stoa.

12. **ROMAN AGORA; TOWER OF THE WINDS** and the **CLOCK OF ANDRONICUS**; and **HADRIAN'S LIBRARY**. These are about 110 yards

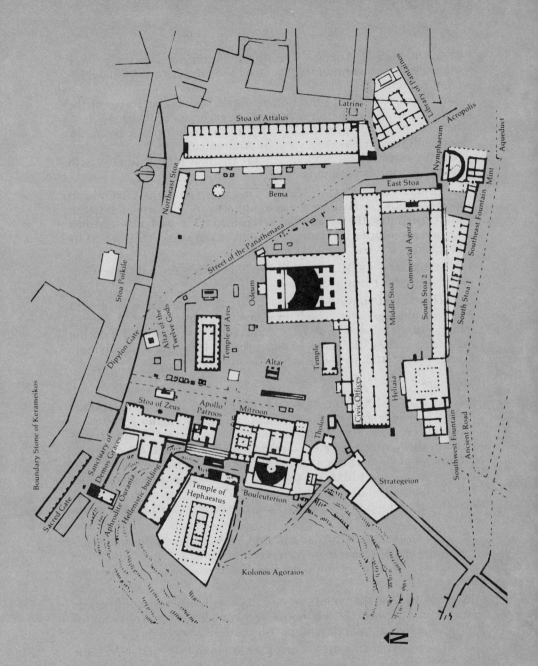

Stoa of Attalus

Latrine

Library of Pantainos

Acropolis

Aqueduct

Nymphaeum

Northeast Stoa

Bema

East Stoa

Mint

Street of the Panathenaea

Commercial Agora

Southeast Fountain

Stoa Poikile

Odeum

Middle Stoa

South Stoa 2

South Stoa 1

Dipylon Gate

Altar of the Twelve Gods

Temple of Ares

Altar

Temple

Heliaia

Civic Offices

Boundary Stone of Kerameikos

Stoa of Zeus

Apollo Patroos

Mitroon

Tholos

Southwest Fountain

Ancient Road

Strategeion

Sanctuary of Demos Graces

Aphrodite Ourania

Hellenistic building

Temple of Hephaestus

Bouleuterion

Sacred Gate

Kolonos Agoraios

N

Agora, Athens

Feet   100   200

east of the Stoa of Attalus. The Roman Agora consisted of a large rectangular court surrounded by stoas (colonnades), behind which were the shops.

On the eastern side of the Roman Agora stands the Tower of the Winds, an octagonal marble structure, on each face of which are bas-reliefs of the winds personified. Inside the building is a hydraulic clock, built in the first century B.C. by Andronicus.

On the north of the Roman Agora, Hadrian built a library with beautiful Corinthian columns.

13. **TEMPLE OF OLYMPIAN ZEUS.** This was the largest temple in ancient Greece. Today only the columns remain. Construction began under Pisistratus the tyrant (sixth century B.C.) and was finished after seven centuries by Hadrian (second century A.D.). Sixteen of its 104 columns survive. (One is prostrate.)

14. **HADRIAN'S ARCH** was built by the Athenians to show their gratitude to this friendly emperor.

15. The **STADIUM** was originally built by the orator Lycurgus in 330 B.C., but was later rebuilt in Pentelic marble by Herod Atticus in A.D. 140. It later fell into ruin, and Averoff reconstructed it on the old plan in 1894. It holds 60,000 people. Here the first Olympic Games of modern times were held in 1896.

Museums

16. **NATIONAL ARCHAEOLOGICAL MUSEUM.** The **MYCENAEAN EXHIBITS** include gold masks and gold cups from Vaphio (1500 B.C.). Objects from Troy are also preserved in the museum. Statues dating back to the sixth century B.C. are housed in the **HALL OF ARCHAIC WORKS**, and fifth-century classical statues — e.g., *Poseidon* (450 B.C.) — are in the **HALLS OF CLASSIC ART.** Sarcophagi, altars, bas-reliefs, vases, and the famous *Kouros* (Apollo), found in 1959 at Piraeus, are all a part of this splendid museum, located at 44 Patesia Road.

17. The **BENAKI MUSEUM** has ancient Greek art, Byzantine and post-Byzantine art, Mycenaean jewelry, textiles, ceramics, rugs, and other items. It is located on the corner of Vassilissis Sofias and Koubari streets.

18. The **BYZANTINE MUSEUM,** at 52 Vassilissis Sofias Street, is located in a Florentine-style house and contains a fine collection of early Christian, Byzantine, and post-Byzantine works of art.

19. The **MUSEUM OF GREEK HANDICRAFTS** is in the Turkish Mosque on Areos Street.

20. The **NATIONAL HISTORICAL MUSEUM,** on Stadium Street, has a collection of arms and uniforms.

21. The **MUSEUM OF KERAMIKOS** is located northwest of the Temple of Hephaestus.

22. The **NATIONAL PICTURE GALLERY** is on Rizari Street, northeast of the stadium.

Aramaic and partly Hebrew documents of the fifth century B.C. (oldest 495 B.C.). They are contemporary with Ezra, Malachi, and Nehemiah. Published by A. H. Sayce and A. E. Cowley between 1906 and 1911, they have become of great importance to the biblical period of Ezra and Nehemiah. From the papyri it was discovered that a Jewish military colony existed at Elephantine as early as 495 B.C.

The Jews built a temple to their god Yahweh (Yahu) on Elephantine Island. That a Jewish temple stood in Elephantine in the fifth century B.C. is surprising. The law of Deuteronomy, which Josiah had put in force in 621 B.C., prohibited any altar save one, which was located at Jerusalem. One of the prize pieces of papyri, however, was a letter from the Jews at Elephantine to Bagoas, governor of Judea, appealing for his aid in obtaining a restoration of the Temple of Yahweh, which had been destroyed in 410 B.C. at the instigation of the priests of Khnum, the ram-headed patron divinity at Elephantine. Calling Elephantine a "fortress," the letter describes how the temple was destroyed. It also indicates that "our fathers built this temple in the fortress of Elephantine in the days of the kings of Egypt and when Cambyses entered Egypt [525 B.C.], they found the temple already built."

Another document of importance is the so-called *Passover Papyrus,* a letter dated 419 B.C. ordering the Jews in the name of Darius II to celebrate the feast of "Unleavened Bread." Since the Temple of Khnum was right next to the Jewish temple, it was probably to avoid an offense to the worshipers of Khnum, the ram god, that the Jews had failed to sacrifice the Passover lamb. Papyri found more recently show that the Elephantine temple was probably restored.

The Jews who settled at Elephantine may have come there as a part of the Diaspora, after their captivity in Babylon under Nebuchadnezzar (586 B.C.). Many Jews were left in Palestine at that time (2 Kings 25:22), organized under the leadership of Gedaliah; but he was assassinated by Ishmael, who tried to organize a fresh revolt against Babylon (2 Kings 25:23-25). Dreading the almost certain consequences, many fled to Egypt against the wishes of Jeremiah (Jer. 42:14-22) and took the old prophet Jeremiah with them (2 Kings 25:26; Jer. 43:1-7). They settled in the city of Migdol — near the spot where the Israelites had crossed the Red Sea (Exod. 14:2; Num. 33:7) — Pathros (Upper Egypt) (Isa. 11:11; Jer. 44:1, 15; Ezek. 29:14; 30:14), Tahpanhes (20 miles southeast of Tanis), Memphis (Noph), and Elephantine. They soon cultivated the vices of the Egyptians, and Jeremiah attacked his fellow Jews in Egypt for their apostasy (Jer. 42:13-46:28; Lam. 5). According to tradition, Jeremiah was beaten to death for uttering the attacks.

Some feel the Elephantine Jewish colony was established under Pharaoh Amasis between 569 and 526 B.C. and disappeared from view after the Persian control of Egypt came to an end in 404 B.C.

Other Points of Interest in Athens

23. CONSTITUTION SQUARE
24. TOMB OF THE UNKNOWN SOLDIER
25. OLD PARLIAMENT BUILDING
26. NATIONAL GARDENS
27. ZAPPEION (Exhibition Hall)
28. ROYAL PALACE AND GUARDS
29. ACADEMY OF SCIENCES
30. UNIVERSITY OF ATHENS
31. NATIONAL LIBRARY
32. BYZANTINE CHURCH OF SAINT THEODORE
33. BYZANTINE CHURCH OF KAPNIKAREA
34. NATIONAL THEATER
35. MOUNT LYCABETTUS

Piraeus

Five miles southeast of Athens is Piraeus, the port of the city of Athens, where exports of Greek products are sent throughout the world. Seafood restaurants, two yacht basins, and an archaeological museum are of special interest.

Delphi, *Delfi ("dolphin")*

Delphi lies in the southern foothills of Mount Parnassus (8,069 feet), dominating the gorge and Gulf of Corinth below. The history of Delphi began when Zeus supposedly let loose two mighty eagles from opposite ends of the world. They met just above Delphi, and there Zeus set down a holy stone — *omphalos* — from heaven to make the "navel of the Earth." And so began the Delphic oracle, as divine powers of prophecy were taken from the vapors rising through a fissure from the center of the earth.

At first the goddess of Earth, Gaea, possessed the oracle. Her sanctuary was guarded over by her son, the serpent Python — the same Python who pursued Leto before she gave birth to Apollo and Artemis. Gaea passed the oracle to her daughter, Themis, who, according to legend, ruled until Apollo slew the serpent Python and took the oracle for himself. Apollo then left the sanctuary to cleanse himself of the murder of Python. His purification accomplished, he turned himself into a dolphin, hailed a ship on its way from Crete, appeared to the crew in the radiant form of a god, and took them to his sanctuary as his first priests. The sanctuary was named Delphi, from the Greek word *delphin*, meaning "dolphin."

Later, seafarers from Cnossos introduced the cult of Apollo Delphinius, which replaced that of Themis.

In time the mysterious prophecies of a pythoness exercised decisive influence in all matters of importance, and the sacred site of the oracle eventually became known far and wide. The duties of the

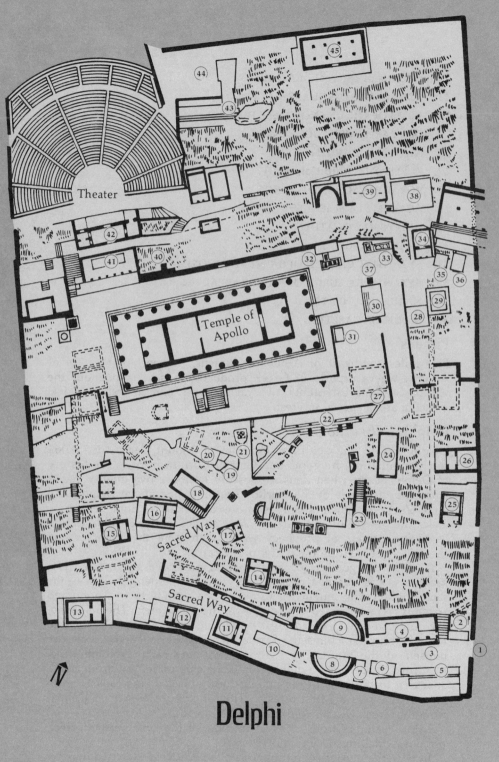

Theater

Temple of
Apollo

Sacred Way

Sacred Way

N

Delphi

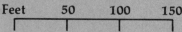

Feet   50   100   150

1. Main entrance
2. Bull of Kerkyra
3. Memorial Arcade
4. Spartan admirals
5. Votive offering of the Athenians of Marathon
6-9. Votive offerings of the Argives: (6) *The Seven Against Thebes;* (7) *The Trojan Horse;* (8) *The Epigons;* (9) *The Kings of Argos*
10. Base of the Tarentines
11-17. Treasure houses: (11) Sicyonian; (12) Siphnian; (13) Theban; (14) Aeolian; (15) Potidean; (16) Athenian; (17) Cnidian
18. Council house (Bouleuterion)
19. Sibylline rock
20. Gaia's shrine
21. Sphinx of Naxos
22. Hall of the Athenians
23. Steps
24. Treasure house of the Corinthians
25. Treasure house of the Cyrenes
26. Prytaneum (assembly hall for the *prytanes,* the chief officials)
27. Polygonal wall
28. Plataean tripod
29. Rhodian chariot
30. Altar of Chios
31. Pillar of Aemilius Paulus
32. Pillar of King Prusia
33. Tripods of the Deinomenides
34. Acanthian treasure house
35. Statue of King Attalus
36. Statue of King Eumenes
37. Pillar of King Eumenes
38. Shrine of Neoptolemos
39. Votive offering of Daochos
40. Site where the *Charioteer* was found
41. Votive offering of Krateros: *Alexander Hunting*
42. Proscenium (*skene*)
43. Hall and passageway
44. Spring of Kassotis
45. Cnidian assembly hall

high priestess of Apollo's temple were always performed by a woman — Pythia. Her prophetic utterances were sought by statesmen and commoners alike. In 336 B.C., Alexander the Great came to the oracle before he set out to conquer the world. The oracle said to him, "My son, thou art invincible."

Left: Tholos of the Sanctuary of Marmaria, Delphi

Below: Amphitheater and Temple of Apollo, Delphi

Pythia's prophecies were, on the whole, noncommittal and ambiguous, but occasionally strikingly accurate. The questions were put orally or in writing to a priest, who in turn passed them on to Pythia. Stunned by the fumes of the adytum, and chewing laurel leaves as she sat on her tripod over a fissure in the earth beside the navel of the earth, she fell into a trance. Her incoherent utterances (inspired by Apollo as his prophecies) were taken down, interpreted by learned priests, and then put into verse.

The *theopropes*, those who wished to consult the oracle, were required to perform various rites. They had to wash in the Castalian Spring and pay fees in the temple. Then the consultation began with the sacrifice of an animal. From the behavior of the beast (whether it trembled when sprinkled with cold water, for instance) attempts were made to gauge the attitude of deity. If the sacrificial signs were favorable, then the petitioners descended into the depths of the temple, where the voice of Pythia could be heard.

Even under the Romans Delphi continued to prosper, but in the first century B.C. barbarians invaded the sanctuary. Later, Nero carried off hundreds of statues. Slowly the sanctuary fell into decay. The abolishment of paganism by the Christian emperor Theodosius I in 393 finally ended its illustrious history. A Byzantine village was built over the ruins and Delphi became a memory. But the stories of Apollo's oracle continued to be told, and at last, in 1892, the village was moved and excavations were undertaken.

The Pythian games were held here in the stadium every four years between 582 B.C. and the fourth century A.D. They ranked second among the popular Greek festivals. Athletics, chariot racing, music, poetry, and drama were all part of the competition. The stadium seated 7,000 people and was built in the fifth century B.C.

POINTS OF INTEREST

The sacred site of Delphi consists mainly of a SANCTUARY, surrounded by a wall. There were about twenty TREASURE HOUSES (miniature replicas of temples, one for each state), a THEATER (fourth and second centuries B.C.), the TEMPLE OF APOLLO, the STADIUM, and others. The writings on the stone walls refer to codes of conduct, such as "know thyself" and "moderation in all things."

The ruins you see today are of the temple of Apollo built between 370 and 340 B.C. There were two previous temples: one built in 514–513 B.C. and destroyed by an earthquake in 373 B.C.; and the original temple, whose exact date of construction is unknown and which burned in 548 B.C.

The MUSEUM at Delphi contains fine exhibits of archaic and classical sculpture. The famous bronze CHARIOTEER, made in 479 B.C., is an extremely fine work. The museum also houses the pediments from Apollo's temple, statues of archaic Kouri youths CLEOBIS and BITON, sculptured by an Argive artist in 600 B.C. — a development from Egyptian art — the SPHINX OF NAXOS (Naxia) (sixth century B.C.), the cone-shaped OMPHALOS (navel) (fourth century B.C.), a

ROMAN SACRIFICIAL ALTAR (second century A.D.), APOLLO'S MUSICAL NOTES (second century A.D.), and many other exhibits.

On a small terrace nearby is the SANCTUARY OF MARMARIA. Its THOLOS is one of the marvels of Delphi. The Tholos is a little rotunda that once had 20 columns in a perfect circle. Now only three stand. A path goes from the sanctuary to the GYMNASIUM, where the contestants trained for the Pythian games (fourth century B.C.).

Olympia

This site dates back to 600 B.C. and earlier. It was a center for the worship of Zeus and scene of the Olympic games. Excavations have revealed the great Temple of Zeus, which contained the celebrated statue of the god by Phidias (ivory and gold over wood, 400 B.C.), which was one of the Seven Wonders of the World. It was moved to Constantinople and lost in a fire in A.D. 476. The Olympic games were held here every four years in honor of Zeus. They began in 776 B.C. and were discontinued by Emperor Theodosius I of Rome at the end of the fourth century A.D. Modern revival of the Olympic games began in 1896 at Athens.

Many archaeological items were found in Olympia, and a museum houses most of them. HERMES, by Praxiteles, is the only existing statue unreservedly assigned to an individual Greek artist. Today the figures on the GABLE ENDS of the temple of Zeus are generally preferred by specialists to those on the Parthenon.

Because the athletes performed in the nude, the Greek sculptors studied the figures in action and sculptured their statues in the nude.

Olympia was not a town; people came to the Olympic games and stayed in tents. The Olympian games were the greatest of the Panhellenic games. Others were held at Delphi (Pythian games), Corinth (Isthmian games), and Argos (Nemean games). Winners received garland, laurel, pine needle, or parsley wreaths respectively.

Sparta

About 1200 B.C. a Greek tribe, the Dorians, settled the area and formed the formidable Spartan state. It was a military state, destined to become well known because of its rigid militaristic training and inhuman discipline. An ancient THEATER (second century B.C.) is located on the southern side of Sparta's acropolis. Ruins of the TEMPLE OF ATHENA CHALKIOIKOS and the TEMPLE OF ARTEMIS ORTHIA (second century B.C.) may be seen, as well as a small MUSEUM. Modern Sparta was founded in 1834 on the ruins of an ancient town. It has a population of about 10,000 people.

Mistra

About 4 miles from Sparta is a haunted city of the dead, although during the later years of Byzantium it was a rich and famous place. It began its existence in A.D. 1249, and a castle was built by the Franks when they settled here after the collapse of the Byzantine Empire (1204). The city became an important political, military, and

Temple of Apollo, Delphi

artistic center, and monasteries, churches, palaces, walls, and a castle may still be seen.

Argos

Thirty-one miles from Corinth is the town of Argos, one of the most ancient towns in Greece. It enjoyed its greatest prosperity in the seventh century B.C. Renowned schools of sculpture and philosophy gave the school a high level of culture. The **THEATER OF ARGOS**, with its 20,000 seats, is perhaps the largest known theater of ancient Greece and is unique. The seats are not *built on* the rock but are *hewn from* it. In antiquity it had 90 rows of seats (today 83), compared with 55 at Epidaurus and 35 at Delphi. The **TEMPLE OF HERA** is of the Doric mode, similar to the Parthenon. There is a wonderful view from the temple. The ancient **FORT OF ARGOS, AGORA,** and **ROMAN ODEUM** are all worth seeing. Argos had the Panhellenic games — called here the Nemean games — every two years.

Navplion, *Nauplia*

Seven miles southeast of Argos is Navplion, the first capital of Free Greece (1829–34). Navplion is built around the feet of two fortresses, the gigantic Palamidi and Acronauplia, its beauty mirrored in the serene waters of a beautiful bay of the "Argolikos Kolpos."

According to tradition, Navplion's founder was Nauplios, born of Poseidon's illicit union with Amymone, the lovely daughter of the king of Argos. The **PALAMIDI FORTRESS**, a venetian stronghold, is located on top of the rocky hill back of the town. In its dungeons, Kolokotrones, the national hero, was guarded after being condemned to death. Two other fortresses, **ACRONAUPLIA** and **BOURTZI**, are here also. The later Venetian fort is now a hotel — in the harbor. Here are two historic churches: **SAINT SPYRIDON**, at whose entrance Capo d'Istria, the first governor of modern Greece, was assassinated in 1831; and **SAINT GEORGE**, with its fine frescoes, including a copy of Leonardo da Vinci's **LAST SUPPER**. It was built in Byzantine style in 1619.

Tiryns

The **WALLS** of the acropolis of Tiryns are impressive because of their size. Legend says the superhuman Cyclopes built them. The ancients regarded the walls as architectural miracles. The **PALACE**, more impressive than that at Mycenae, is built on the highest level of the acropolis. A most beautiful mosaic decorates the floor. Schliemann was one of the first archaeologists to excavate Tiryns.

Epidaurus

This site was originally a **SANATORIUM**, where thousands of physically or mentally sick people were treated. There were about 300 sanatoria throughout Greece, but the most renowned was that at Epidaurus. It was built under the direction of Epidaurus in the sixth century B.C. to honor Asclepias, god of healing. It functioned from

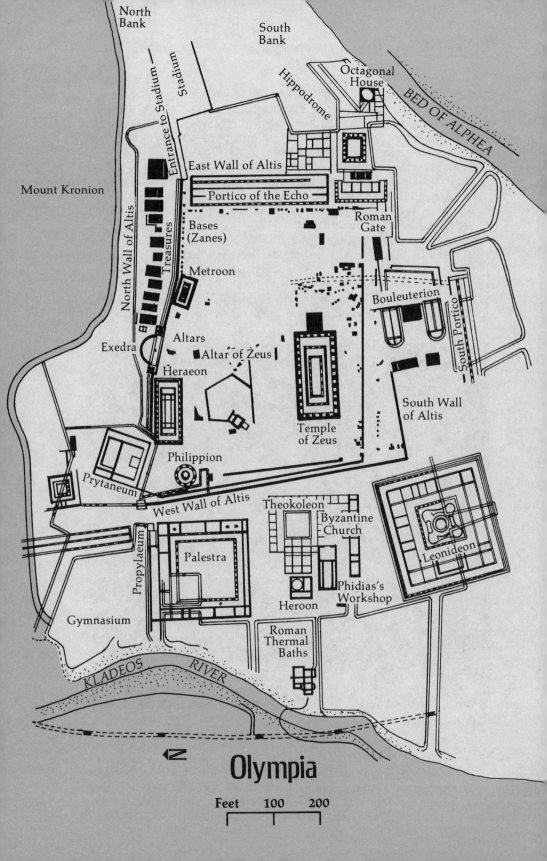

North Bank

South Bank

Octagonal House

BED OF ALPHEA

Hippodrome

Entrance to Stadium

Stadium

East Wall of Altis

Portico of the Echo

Roman Gate

Bases (Zanes)

Mount Kronion

North Wall of Altis

Treasures

Metroon

Bouleuterion

South Portico

Exedra

Altars

Altar of Zeus

Heraeon

Temple of Zeus

South Wall of Altis

Philippion

Prytaneum

West Wall of Altis

Theokoleon

Byzantine Church

Palestra

Leonideon

Propylaeum

Phidias's Workshop

Gymnasium

Heroon

Roman Thermal Baths

KLADEOS RIVER

N

Olympia

Feet   100   200

600 B.C. to A.D. 400. The **THEATER** is one of the largest and best-preserved in the world — the most beautiful of all Greek theaters. It seats 14,500 people, and its acoustics are famous. It was built in the fourth century B.C. under the direction of Polyclitus. Dramas are still presented here during the summer.

Epidaurus was excavated in 1881 after being covered by an earthquake. Besides the theater, there are a **GYMNASIUM**, a **STADIUM**, a **TEMPLE OF ASCLEPIAS**, and a **MUSEUM** that is wonderful!

Asclepias was to Epidaurus what Apollo was to Delphi. According to tradition, he lived about 1300 B.C., he was the son of Apollo, and he was a divinely inspired physician who even raised the dead (according to Xenophon). After his death he was deified. If tradition is correct, Hippocrates, father of medical science, was a seventeenth-generation direct descendant of Asclepias. The symbol of Asclepias was the serpent, and according to one tradition it was from this source that the medical profession adopted the same symbol.

Theater, Epidaurus

Mycenae

The Mycenaeans were descendants of the earliest Greek tribes who had entered the country soon after 2000 B.C. About 1600 B.C. they began to bury their dead in deep shaft graves and a little later in conical stone chambers known as beehive tombs. Nine tombs have been found — the most elaborate burial chambers outside of Egypt. The **BEEHIVE TOMB** (*Treasury of Atreus* or *Tomb of Agamemnon*) at Mycenae is one of the finest examples and dates back to 1300–1250 B.C. Two huge stones rest over the entrance. The inner one weighs 120 tons. The chamber is 90 feet high.

The **LION GATE** of Mycenae's acropolis is a work of art dating back to 1250 B.C. This gate, one of the most impressive remnants of massive ramparts, inspired awe in later Greeks, who regarded such work to be that of the Cyclopes, a mythical race of one-eyed giants. The lions on the gate function as guardians of the gate, like those on state capitol buildings. The bas-relief lions are regarded as the earliest example of this kind in ancient art.

The archaeological materials from this site are in the National Museum at Athens. They include a golden "mask of Agamemnon," a golden hilt of a sword, a golden cup, and hundreds of other gold articles. Also from this site wheat was found that was 3,000 years old — and it germinated!

According to tradition, Agamemnon was chosen as the military leader of the Greeks in the great expedition against Troy (Trojan War, 1180 B.C.). Legend attributed the cause of this war to the carrying off of the fair Helen, wife of Menelaus, king of Sparta, by the Trojan prince Paris. After the Trojan war, Agamemnon returned home victorious, bringing with him as a mistress Cassandra, daughter of the king of Troy. But on the day of his arrival at Mycenae he was murdered by the lovers Aegisthus and Clytemnestra.

The Dorians conquered Mycenae about 1150 B.C., and later, in 468 B.C., the neighboring Argives destroyed the town. The glory and bloom of Mycenae was over.

Mycenae had become legendary from Homer's epic, but until the last century, Homer's descriptions were believed to be the poet's imagination. Heinrich Schliemann (1822–90), however, believed in Homer and made it his life's work to prove the authenticity of his tales. Schliemann apprenticed as a grocer at 14, shipwrecked in the North Sea at 19, scratched out a living as a merchant's aide in Amsterdam, and there, in two years, taught himself seven tongues, including Russian. Sent to Saint Petersburg at 24, he launched his own firm and prospered on indigo. At 28 he trekked to the California Gold Rush, and while prospectors panned he bought and sold their finds, leaving nine months later with a fortune. When the Crimean War flared, his shrewd deals netted huge gains. He traveled the world, piled profit on profit, and learned nine more languages.

At age 46 he wrote the archbishop in Athens to find him a bride — a Greek. Back came photos, and he soon married. He and Sophia dug in Asia Minor and discovered Troy (1873), with its 8,700 pieces of gold bracelets, necklaces, rings, and other items. He then turned to Mycenae, and in 1876 he dug in the six deep shafts sunk under a stone-ringed terrace behind the Lion Gate. He found bones that had lain for 2,500 years. Gold literally covered the 19 bodies. Even a

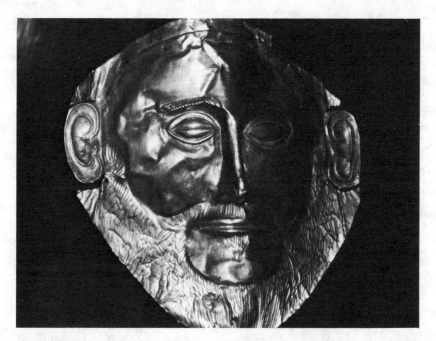

Above: Mask of Agamemnon, from Mycenae

Right: Lion Gate, Mycenae

baby wore a complete suit of gold foil. When Schliemann saw the gold mask of a bearded warrior he telegraphed the king of Greece and said, "I have gazed upon the face of Agamemnon." It is now known, however, that the gold mask predates by 300 years Homer's legendary king of Mycenae.

About 150 yards west of the Lion Gate is the NEW ENCLOSURE OF ROYAL TOMBS, dating from the seventeenth century B.C. Within these tombs was an abundant supply of gold, bronze, and ivory objects. The PALACE is located on top of the hill. The NORTH GATE and the SECRET AQUEDUCT are also worth seeing. This aqueduct consists of an underground tunnel which leads by means of 99 steps to an underground cistern about 40 feet deep. The 3,000-year-old cistern was fed with water from the Spring of Perseus, situated outside the acropolis.

CORINTH

Corinth is the capital of Corinthia on the Peloponnesus, 40 miles west of Athens. In the days of Paul it had a large population and was the most wealthy and important city in Greece. It was situated on a large isthmus between the mainland and the Peloponnesus, and was 1½ miles west of the present Corinthian canal. It had two main harbors: Cenchrea (Acts 18:18; Rom. 16:1), on the Saronic Gulf, an arm of the Aegean Sea; and Lechaeum, on the Gulf of Corinth, an arm of the Ionian Sea. Commanding the traffic of both the eastern and western seas, it was a city filled with sailors, merchants, adventurers, and refugees. The Christians considered Corinth a wicked city.

South of the present city rises the high rock, ACRO-CORINTHUS, the acropolis of Corinth, 1,500 feet above the city. Atop this was the Temple of Aphrodite, the goddess of love. Here the cult of Aphrodite flourished. The temple was served by more than 1,000 religious prostitutes, who lodged in luxurious quarters surrounding the shrine. Corinth was the most notorious seat of immorality in the Roman Empire. Calamity came, however, when earthquake, malaria, and harsh Turkish rule finally swept away everything except seven columns of one old DORIC TEMPLE OF APOLLO, one of the few objects above ground left today in the ancient city of wealth and immorality.

Many painters lived here and the Corinthian order of architecture originated here. In 146 B.C. Corinth was destroyed by fire and its treasures taken to Rome. A hundred years later, however, Julius Caesar restored it, and it became the most important commercial center in Greece. It was one of the richest cities in the world. The present town was rebuilt after an earthquake in 1928.

Excavations show that Corinth was inhabited as early as 5000 B.C., and building began here about 1000 B.C.

POINTS OF INTEREST

The TEMPLE OF APOLLO stands on the northwest side of the Agora. It was built in the middle of the sixth century B.C. The columns are peculiar in that they are not made of drums but are monoliths. Seven of the original 38 are standing upright.

The ODEUM (small theater) is located on the right side of the

approach to the museum. North of the Odeum is the large **THEATER**.

A **ROMAN VILLA** about a mile from the Theater housed the beautiful mosaics which now adorn the Museum.

The **AGORA** was lined with shops dating from the first century A.D. In front of the shops were 6 **ROMAN TEMPLES**.

The **TRIBUNE** (*Bema*), on the south side of the Agora, stands in the center of a group of approximately 30 shops. On this square platform the Roman generals used to address the people. This is where Paul the apostle appeared before Gallio, who turned him loose (Acts 18:12–17).

The **SOUTH STOA**, constructed in the fourth century B.C., was a very important building. A few columns still remain in position.

ROMAN GOVERNMENT BUILDINGS (first century A.D.) housed beautiful mosaic floors.

The **SACRED WELL**, behind the government buildings, dates from the fifth century B.C.

The **WELL OF PIRENE** is fronted by six arches. It has four underground stoas.

The **MUSEUM** at Corinth has preclassic exhibits and Mycenaean, Greek, and Roman objects. The medical section is especially interesting.

- *Paul founded the Church in Corinth during his second missionary journey. He spent 18 months here (Acts 18:1–18) and preached to Jews and Gentiles.*
- *Crispus, the chief ruler of the synagogue, and his house believed. The Jews opposed Paul; so he turned to the Gentiles (Matt. 10:14; Acts 13:46–52).*
- *Apollos exerted great influence in this area (Achaia) (Acts 18:24–28; 1 Cor. 1:12; 2 Cor. 3:1).*
- *Paul was brought to the judgment seat (Bema) by the Jews and appeared before Gallio, who turned him loose (Acts 18:12–17). Gallio was the brother of the stoic philosopher Seneca.*
- *Paul personally baptized a few persons (1 Cor. 1:14–16).*
- *Titus and Timothy were sent here (1 Cor. 4:17; 2 Cor. 7:13–15).*
- *It was from here that Paul apparently wrote 1 Thessalonians (Acts 17:15; 18:1, 5; 1 Thess. 1:1).*
- *Here Paul became acquainted with Aquila and Priscilla, with whom he lived and made tents and whom he later took with him to Ephesus. They had come to Corinth when Claudius expelled all Jews from Rome (Acts 18:2).*
- *Paul probably left Corinth to attend the celebration of the feast in Jerusalem (Acts 18:18–21). Little is known of the church after his departure.*

The Corinth Canal

In Paul's day there was no canal across the isthmus, although Nero, in 66 A.D., attempted to dig one, turning the first soil with a golden

Acropolis, Corinth

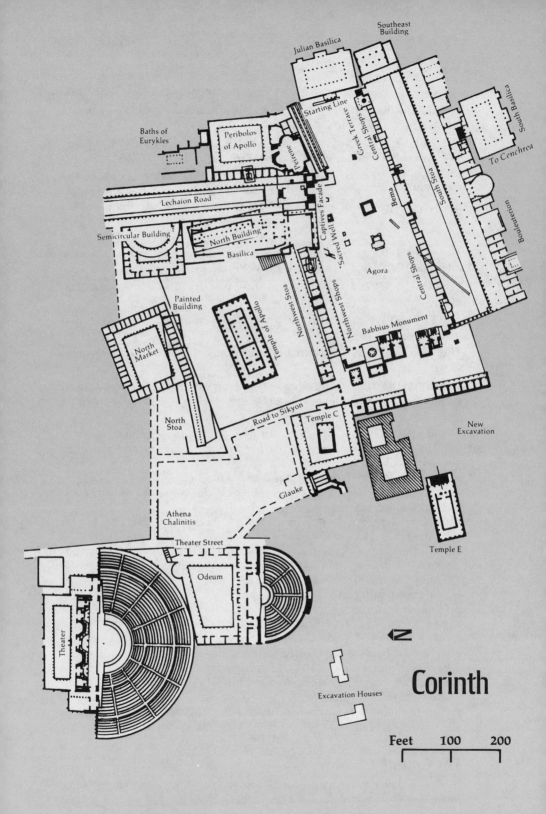

Baths of
Eurykles

Peribolos
of Apollo

Julian Basilica

Southeast
Building

Starting Line

Peirene

South Basilica

To Cenchrea

Lechaion Road

Greek Terrace

Central Shops

Bema

South Stoa

Bouleuterion

Semicircular Building

North Building

Basilica

Captives Facade

Sacred Well

Northwest Shops

Agora

Central Shops

Painted
Building

Northwest Stoa

Temple of Apollo

Babbius Monument

North
Market

North
Stoa

Road to Sikyon

Temple C

New
Excavation

Glauke

Athena
Chalinitis

Theater Street

Odeum

Temple E

Theater

N

Excavation Houses

Corinth

Feet   100   200

spade. It was a 200-mile journey around Cape Malea, with its treacherous and feared winds, and mariners found it more desirable to transfer their cargo across the 4-mile neck of land. Smaller boats were taken bodily out of the water and pulled across the isthmus on roller-like skid structures. The famous road over which the

Right: Corinth Canal
Below: Bema, Corinth

Corinthians conveyed ships is called the *Diolkos*. The present Corinth Canal was completed during the years 1881–93. It is 4½ miles long, 250 feet deep at its deepest, and 75 feet wide. The water is 25 feet deep.

Isthmia

At the time Paul was in Corinth, the Isthmian games were celebrated. They were like the Olympic games. They were staged in an arena and sports area 10 miles from Corinth. The TEMPLE OF POSEIDON was the most impressive building at Isthmia.

Perhaps Paul attended the games there, and perhaps he thought of the games at Isthmia when he wrote to Timothy and said, "I have fought a good fight, I have finished my course, I have kept the faith" (2 Tim. 4:7).

A unique STARTING GATE for the runners of a race is one of the most impressive things to see at ancient Isthmia.

CENCHREA

Ruins mark this harbor, from which Paul sailed to Ephesus (Acts 18:18).

Megara

Socrates spent time here teaching his pupils.

Eleusis

Now an important industrial center of 20,000 inhabitants, Eleusis was once a place of worship. The goddess was Demeter, and her daughter was Persephone.

It was here the *Eleusinian Mysteries* (famous secret rites of the Greeks) were held. The ruins of the TEMPLE OF ARTEMIS, the GREAT PROPYLAEA, and the TELESTERION (where the mysteries took place) are the most important ruins. They date from the fourth century B.C. The rich MUSEUM OF ELEUSIS contains most of the finds from the excavations.

Dafni

At Dafni is an excellent Byzantine monastery of the eleventh century, with mosaics and sarcophagi.

Sounion

This is one of the most enchanting places in the whole of Attica. It was inhabited as far back as 3000 B.C. The important places to visit are the SANCTUARY OF POSEIDON (a square surrounding Poseidon's temple), the TEMPLE OF POSEIDON (440 B.C.), and the TEMPLE OF SOUNION ATHENA. The most famous find at this site was the *Sounion Kouros*, a statue from the seventh century B.C., located in the Archaeological Museum.

NORTHERN GREECE

BEREA, *Beroea*, **Veroia**, *Verroia, Veria*

A town in the district of Macedonia called Emantia, Beroea was the headquarters of Pompey's infantry in the winter of 49–48 B.C. Sopater was a native of Beroea (Acts 20:4).

■ *Paul preached to a Jewish community there with much success (Acts 17:10–14; 20:1–5).*

THESSALONICA, **Thessalonike**, *Salonika*

Thessalonica, founded in 315 B.C., is the capital of Macedonia and the principal seaport of southeast Europe. With a population of 400,000, it is the second largest city in Greece. The city boasts many ANCIENT CHURCHES, which represent some of the best examples of the development of art and architecture, from the Roman to the Byzantine period.

■ *Paul founded the church here on his second missionary journey (Acts 17:1–9).*

■ *Mobs assaulted the house of Jason, where Paul was staying (Acts 17:5–9).*

■ *Paul's earliest epistle was apparently sent to Thessalonica from Corinth (Acts 17:15; 18:1, 5; 1 Thess. 1:1).*

■ *Aristarchus, who accompanied Paul on his third missionary journey through Asia Minor, was from here (Acts 19:29; 27:2) and was a Jew (Col. 4:10–11).*

AMPHIPOLIS (*"about the city"*), *Thrace*

This town is three miles from the mouth of the river Strymon, where the harbor of Eion was located.

■ *Paul and Silas passed through (Acts 17:1).*

PHILIPPI, *Crenides*

This was a city on the east coast of Macedonia. It was named after King Philip II of Macedonia. In 42 B.C. it was the scene of the battle between Antony and his enemies Brutus and Cassius. Antony won.

Paul and Silas came to Philippi on the second missionary journey. After the baptism of Lydia, the first Christian church in Europe was established here.

■ *Paul and Silas were beaten and imprisoned here (Acts 16:16–24). They were miraculously delivered, and the jailor was baptized (Acts 16:25–34).*

■ *Paul was here on his third missionary journey, as he returned to Jerusalem (Acts 20:2–6).*

■ *Paul's epistle to the Philippians was written from Rome when he was imprisoned (Phil. 1:7, 13–17).*

NEAPOLIS, **Kavalla**

This town, on the coast of Macedonia opposite Thasos, was about ten miles from Philippi.

■ *Neapolis was the harbor of Philippi where Paul landed after sailing from Troas (Acts 16:11-12).*

GREEK ISLANDS OF THE AEGEAN

MITYLENE, Mytilini, *Mytilene, Mitilini*

The chief town on the Island of Lesbos in the Aegean Sea gave its name to the whole island. It was one of the early Aeolian colonies and one of the earliest homes of Greek lyric poetry. It was the birthplace of Sappho and Alcaeus.

■ *Paul's ship spent the night here on his trip to Jerusalem after his third missionary journey (Acts 20:14-15).*

SAMOS

Samos is a large fertile island in the eastern Aegean. It has been a center of luxury, art, and science. Ruins of the famous SANCTUARY OF HERA and a MUSEUM are located here. It is the birthplace of Pythagoras, the famous mathematician after whom is named the Pythagorean theorem.

■ *Paul visited Samos (Acts 20:15).*

PATMOS, *Palmosa*

The bare, rocky northernmost Dodecanese island in the Aegean Sea, named Patmos, is 70 miles southwest of Ephesus, belongs to Greece, and is 8 miles long and 6 miles wide. *Skala* is the port, and *Chora* is the capital, with 1,000 inhabitants.

In the historical past, criminals were sent there to work in the mines. The apostle John was sent there by the emperor Domitian in A.D. 95. According to tradition, John came to Ephesus in A.D. 69-70, and after he was released from Patmos he returned to Ephesus. John was probably banished to hard labor on the island, with fetters, scanty clothing, insufficient food, sleep on the ground, and the lash of the overseer. Tradition says he spent 16 months on the island. During his banishment there, he received the visions recorded in the Book of Revelation (Rev. 1:9). The CAVE OF THE REVELATION is pointed out as being the place where he meditated and received these manifestations.

The MONASTERY OF SAINT JOHN was built in A.D. 1088, patterned after a Byzantine fortress. The RELICS OF OSIOS CHRISTODOULOS, founder of the monastery, are contained in a silver coffin in the chapel. The TREASURY and LIBRARY of the monastery are very important. The treasury has many jewels, gold, and other treasures. The library was founded in the eleventh century and has 800 old manuscripts. The ninth-century Codex of Plato was purchased from the library in 1814 and is now in the Bodleian Library.

■ *John was banished to the Isle of Patmos (Rev. 1:9).*

Dilos, *Delos*

Dilos is a small, rocky island in the Aegean Sea. It was the seat of a widespread worship of Apollo, who, with his sister Artemis, is said to have been born here. Here was the scene of a horrible massacre by Mithridates, king of Pontus, who slaughtered 80,000 Italians of the province of Asia in the first century B.C.

● *Dilos was mentioned in the letter of the Romans in favor of the Jews (1 Macc. 15:16–23).*

COOS, Cos, *Kos*

This island has a population of about 9,000. It is the next most beautiful Dodecanese island after Rhodes.

During the fourth century B.C. it had a population of 160,000 people and enjoyed prosperity, partly because of the famous sanctuary of Asclepias, god of medicine. The town was destroyed by an earthquake, but was reconstructed in 155 A.D. Again in the sixth century it was destroyed by earthquake and remained deserted for eight centuries.

The ASKLEPEION, the famous medical center, was a group of buildings set on a hillside in the form of an amphitheater. It had altars, houses, stoas, statues, and medicinal springs. One of the houses contained Hippocrates' famous school of medicine (460–377 B.C.). Cos was the home of Hippocrates, the great physician who is known as the "father of medicine." He lived here most of his life, but also practiced in Athens. The medical profession's oath is named after him: the "Hippocratic Oath." Hippocrates showed that disease had natural causes. He treated his patients with proper diet, fresh air, change in climate, and attention to habits and living conditions. His favorite medicine was honey. For pain he prescribed vinegar and honey. He set broken bones and practiced surgery as a last resort.

■ *Paul visited Coos (Acts 21:1).*

RHODES, Rodos

Because of its beauty and climate, this island is one of Europe's chief tourist attractions. It is the largest island in the Dodecanese. It lies 10 miles off the Turkish coast and has 65,000 inhabitants in 49 villages. (Rhodes was the daughter of Poseidon in Greek mythology.)

Settlers were there as early as 1400 B.C., and in its heyday Rhodes had 200,000 inhabitants. It was one of the most important and successful cities in ancient Greece.

In 302–290 B.C. the people of Rhodes built the giant *Colossus,* a bronze statue of their sun-god. It stood 150 feet high astride the entrance to one of the harbors. In 224 B.C. it fell into the sea and was later (657 A.D.) scrapped. It was considered one of the Seven Wonders of the World. From its name comes the word *colossal.*

Rhodes had fine schools of philosophy, rhetoric, and law. Cicero, Lucretius, Julius Caesar, Tiberius, Mark Antony, and others went to school there. It was also the home of Epimenides, the poet (600 B.C.).

The **ACROPOLIS, TEMPLES TO ZEUS, ATHENA,** and **APOLLO,** the **STADIUM,** and the **THEATER** are among the antiquities.

■ *Paul visited Rhodes on his way from Troas to Caesarea (Acts 21:1).*

CRETE

This island is 156 miles long and from 7 to 30 miles wide. It has mountains as high as 7,000 feet. It is the home of the Minoan civilization, the oldest in Europe (2800 B.C.) and the forerunner of the Mycenaean culture. Discoveries of this civilization were made first at Cnossos (Knossos). The civilization declined about 1400 B.C. There are now about 450,000 inhabitants on the island. Mount Ida (8,193 feet) is the birthplace of Zeus, according to legend.

CNOSSOS is the principal archaeological site in Crete. **PHAESTUS, AYIA TRIADA, MALIA,** and **GORTYS** are also important sites. Two **MUSEUMS** house finds from the island.

The apostle Paul spent some time here at Fair Havens on the south side of the island.

■ *Cretans were present at Pentecost (Acts 2:1, 11).*
■ *Paul was here for a while (Acts 27:7–13).*
■ *Paul left Titus in Crete (Titus 1:5).*

CLAUDA *(Cauda), Gavdos*

This is a small island 20–25 miles west of Crete, where Paul's ship was driven from Fair Havens. Here the ship was hauled in and undergirded and its sail slackened (Acts 27:16–17).

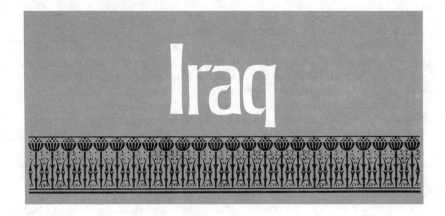

The Arab nation of Iraq has an area of 260,000 square miles and a population of nearly 9,000,000 people, more than 2,000,000 of whom live in the capital city of Baghdad, on the Tigris River. The valley of the Tigris and Euphrates rivers has been known through the centuries as "the cradle of civilization." It extends 600 miles from the Persian (Arab) Gulf to the highlands of Kurdistan in Turkey.

HISTORY

Some believe the Garden of Eden was located where the Tigris and Euphrates rivers meet, near Al Qurna, above the Shatt-al-Arab. Many believe that the descendants of Noah settled there after the Great Flood.

Although this ancient area of Mesopotamia is not rich in physical structure–type archaeological remains and has very little historical literature, thousands of tablets have been found, consisting of letters and records that give us a glimpse into the lives of the country's ancient peoples. These clay tablets have preserved the Assyrian and Babylonian languages in a wedged-shaped cuneiform writing called today *Akkadian*. The records cover a period of more than 2,000 years, and though the earliest documents date back to 2800 B.C., one of the "epics" gives an account of the creation. The *Behistun Inscriptions*, written from the Mount of Behistun by Darius, the first Persian ruler, in 538 B.C., are like the Rosetta Stone in importance. They are written in the Babylonian, Elamite, and Persian languages. Persian was the known language, from which linguists were able to decipher the unknown Babylonian language.

Present-day Iraq is geographically located where once were Shinar, Chaldea, Mesopotamia, Assyria, and Babylonia. The two main empires were Babylon, on the lower part of the Tigris and Euphrates rivers, and Assyria, on the upper part of the same rivers.

Iraq was not only the source of some of the earliest known civilizations but also the center of the Arabs' Golden Age, the period of the

Abbasid caliphate (A.D. 750–1258). This was an era of magnificence and splendor and an intellectual awakening that spread far beyond the borders of the Tigris and Euphrates. Arabic numbers, the decimal system, and algebra were given to the world from this great center of learning. Avicenna, a great medical doctor, wrote a medical text that was used throughout the Orient, Europe, and the Arab world. Trade and commerce were carried on with most large nations of the earth. Baghdad was the cosmopolitan and international center of the medieval world.

Modern Iraq was taken from Turkey in World War I and became a sovereign state at the end of the British mandate in 1932. Although oil had been discovered in 1867 by a Turkish governor, Midhat Pasha, and a petroleum refinery had been built at Baquba, north of Baghdad, it was not until 1927, when oil was discovered in the Kirkuk area, that the oil industry became very important. By 1934 the Iraq Petroleum Company was exporting crude oil through two pipelines, one leading to Tripoli and the other to Haifa.

In World War II, Iraq joined the Allied forces against the Axis powers, and between 1944 and 1946 Iraq took a major role in the formation of the Arab League.

When the Iraqi army overthrew the monarchy on July 14, 1958, Iraq became a republic, and Brigadier Abdul Karim Kassem became the first prime minister. Kassem launched many reform movements, but on February 8, 1963, Colonel Arif overthrew his regime and became president and appointed a new cabinet.

RELIGION

Most of Iraq's population is Moslem. There are, however, a relatively small number of people belonging to various Christian sects, mainly in the northern part of the country.

IRAQ TODAY

The lowland areas of Iraq are characterized by hot, dry summers and cooler, more humid winters. In the rolling, more elevated northeast, though, the temperatures are lower, with some snow in winter.

Iraq is mainly an agricultural country, producing large amounts of dates. Oil also plays a smaller, but significant, part in its economy.

The monetary unit in Iraq is the *dinar*, divided into 1,000 *fils*. The rate of exchange is 1,000 fils to $2.82.

CITIES AND SITES

HIDDEKEL, Tigris River

This river is more than 1,000 miles long and is one of the two main rivers of Iraq. Although narrower than the Euphrates, it carries more

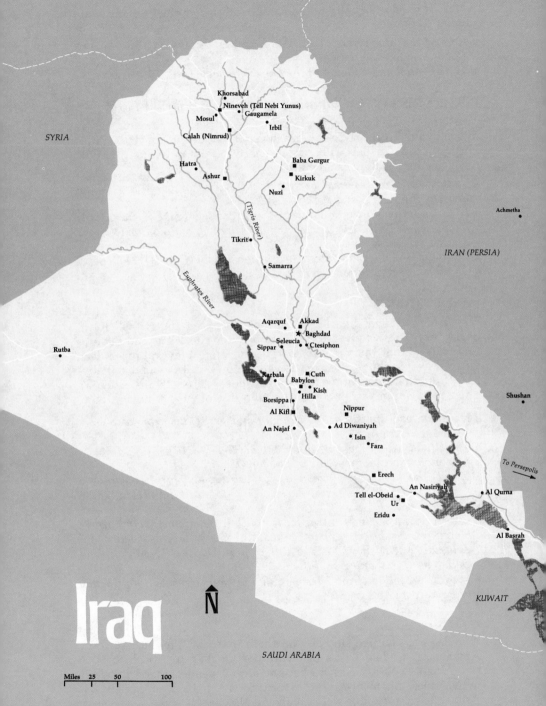

TURKEY

SYRIA

Khorsabad
Nineveh (Tell Nebi Yunus)
Mosul
Gaugamela
Calah (Nimrud)
Irbil

Hatra
Baba Gurgur
Ashur
Kirkuk
Nuzi

Achmetha

Tikrit
IRAN (PERSIA)

(Tigris River)

Samarra

Euphrates River

Aqarquf
Akkad
Rutba
Seleucia
Baghdad
Sippar
Ctesiphon
Shushan

Karbala
Cuth
Babylon
Kish
Hilla
Borsippa
Nippur
Al Kifl
Ad Diwaniyah
An Najaf
Isin
Fara

To Persepolis

Erech
An Nasiriyah
Tell el-Obeid
Al Qurna
Ur
Eridu

Al Basrah

KUWAIT

Iraq N̂

SAUDI ARABIA

Miles 25   50   100

water. It joins the Euphrates about 100 miles from the Persian (Arab) Gulf at Al Qurna.

- *One of the four rivers of the Garden of Eden was named Hiddekel (Gen. 2:14).*
- *Here Daniel had a vision of the angel Michael (Dan. 10:4).*

EUPHRATES RIVER *("bursting," "sweet"), Shatt el-Furat*

This large river, running the length of Iraq, rises in Armenia and is joined by the Tigris River at Qurnah City (Al Qurna), about 100 miles north of the Persian Gulf. It is nearly 1,700 miles long and is navigable for the first 1,000 miles.

- *Euphrates is represented as the name of one of the rivers in the Garden of Eden (Gen. 2:14).*
- *It formed the northern limit of the Promised Land (Gen. 15:18; Exod. 23:31; Deut. 1:7; 11:24) and the kingdom of Solomon (1 Kings 4:21).*
- *Jacob crossed the Euphrates when he left Laban (Gen. 31:21).*
- *The Book of Revelation refers to it (Rev. 9:14; 16:12).*

MESOPOTAMIA

The name *Mesopotamia*, which means "between the rivers" (Gen. 24:10; Acts 7:2), is given to the area between the Tigris and Euphrates rivers. From their mouth to a point where they approach each other above Baghdad the area is called Lower Mesopotamia (Babylon); from that point north it is called Upper Mesopotamia (Assyria). The city of Haran was in the northern portion of what is now Turkey.

- *Here Jehovah appeared to Abraham and gave him promises (Gen. 12:1–2, 6–7; 15:5, 18; 22:17; Acts 7:2).*
- *The city of Nahor was in Mesopotamia (Gen. 24:10).*
- *Mesopotamia was the home of Balaam (Deut. 23:4).*
- *It was the home of Laban, where Jacob resided for 14 years and worked for his wives, Leah, Rachel, Zilpah, and Bilhah (Gen. 28:1–31:21).*
- *Eleven of the twelve sons of Jacob (all but Benjamin) were born in Haran. Leah bore Reuben, Simeon, Levi, Judah, Issachar, and Zebulun; Rachel bore Joseph; Bilhah bore Dan and Naphtali; and Zilpah bore Gad and Asher (Gen. 29; 30).*
- *Jews or proselytes from Mesopotamia were in Jerusalem on the day of Pentecost (Acts 2:1–9).*

ASSYRIA

Assyria was located in the northern part of present-day Iraq. Archaeologists date traces of civilization in that area back to 5000 B.C. About 1800 B.C. Assyria became an independent nation under a native ruler, Shamshi-Adad (1813–1781 B.C.). Its first capital was Ashur; its later capitals were Calah and Nineveh.

Tiglath-pileser I, one of the great leaders of Assyria, reigned between 1115 and 1077 B.C. The empire became its strongest under Ashurnasirpal II, who captured rich Phoenician cities. During the years 858–824 B.C., Shalmaneser III conquered the sea routes of the Mediterranean and received tribute from Israel. He was followed by the rulers Shamshi-Adad V (824–811 B.C.), Tiglath-pileser III (744–727 B.C.), Shalmaneser V (726–722 B.C.), Sargon II (721–705 B.C.), Sennacherib (704–681 B.C.), Esarhaddon (ca. 680–669 B.C.), and Ashurbanipal (668–627 B.C.). The Assyrians had prosperity under Esarhaddon, but under Ashurbanipal the empire began to disintegrate.

Four other rulers controlled Assyria until the Medes under Cyaxares descended upon Assyria and took Ashur, the old capital, in 614 B.C.; Nineveh fell in 612 B.C. to a coalition composed of Medians, Babylonians, and Ummanmanda hordes. This brought an end to the great Assyrian Empire.

In 853 B.C. a coalition of small states, including followers of Ahab, resisted Shalmaneser III at Qarqar and Ahab's sparing of Benhadad (1 Kings 20:34) may have been due to this Assyrian threat. In 842 B.C. Jehu paid tribute to Shalmaneser III, and this is recorded on an Assyrian inscription found at Nimrud (Calah), called the *Black Obelisk of Shalmaneser.*

The first Assyrian king mentioned in the Old Testament is Tiglath-pileser III (or Pul) (2 Kings 15:19; 1 Chron. 5:26), who deported northern Israelites (2 Kings 15:29), and to whom Ahaz sent tribute (2 Kings 16:7–8; 2 Chron. 28:16), despite the warning of Isaiah (Isa. 7:3–10).

During the reigns of Shalmaneser V (726–722 B.C.) and Sargon II (721–705 B.C.), the Northern Kingdom of Israel was captured by the Assyrians and taken into captivity, "over the river," and its people became known in history as the "lost tribes of Israel."

- *The foundations of Assyria are mentioned in the Book of Genesis (Gen. 10:10–12).*
- *Israel paid tribute to Tiglath-pileser (2 Kings 15:17–22).*
- *Ahaz, king of Judah, acknowledged subordination to Tiglath-pileser (2 Kings 16:7–9; 2 Chron. 28:16), despite the warning of Isaiah (Isa. 7:3–10).*
- *Hoshea rebelled against Shalmaneser V, who besieged Samaria (2 Kings 17:3–6; 18:9).*
- *Shalmaneser V and Sargon conquered Samaria and carried Israel captive towards the north. They became the "lost ten tribes" (2 Kings 17:1–18; Isa. 20; Mic. 5:5–6; Ezra 4:2).*
- *The lost ten tribes will return (Isa. 51:9–11).*
- *Esarhaddon sent foreign peoples to occupy Samaria (Ezra 4:2), as did his successor, Asnapper (probably Ashurbanipal) (Ezra 4:10).*
- *Sennacherib invaded cities of Judah, and after receiving gifts from Hezekiah, king of Judah, he besieged Jerusalem. Sennacherib returned to Nineveh and was slain (2 Kings 18:13–19:37; Isa. 36–37). (The Taylor Prism is a non-biblical parallel account of this.)*

- *Hezekiah trusted in help from Egypt against Assyria (2 Kings 18:21; Isa. 30:1-7; 31:1-3; 36:4-6).*
- *Nahum and Zephaniah prophesied the destruction of Assyria and Nineveh (Nah. 1-3; Zeph. 2:13-15).*
- *Jonah preached to the people in Nineveh and they repented (Jon. 1-4).*
- *Jesus referred to Nineveh (Matt. 12:39-41).*
- Esarhaddon sent foreign peoples to occupy Samaria (1 Esd. 4:2; cf Ezra 4:2).

BABYLONIA

The story of Babylonia began with the settlement of the plain of Shinar by emigrants from the east (Genesis 11:1-2). The earliest identifiable inhabitants of the land were Sumerians, who developed and passed on to their successors a rich cultural heritage. Nimrod, a grandson of Ham, was a powerful figure who had a formative influence on the early history of the area (Gen. 10:6-10).

Babylonia's main historic periods were —

1. **EARLY CITY-STATE AND EARLY DYNASTIC PERIODS** (4000–2350 B.C.). When kingship descended from heaven after the Flood, says the Sumerian King List, it came first to Kish — one of many cities to hold power during this period. Ur's famous royal tombs with their rich contents date to this period (ca. 2500 B.C.). Sumerian language and culture dominated the Babylonian plain.

2. **SEMITIC EMPIRE** (2360–2180 B.C.). An empire founded by Sargon the Great extended from the Persian Gulf to the Mediterranean Sea. Akkadian, a Semitic language, became the dominant language.

3. **THIRD DYNASTY OF UR** (ca. 2060–1950 B.C.). Ur's political control of Mesopotamia brought peace and expansive mercantile activities to the whole region. Ur-Nammu constructed at Ur a great ziggurat, which in a restored state still stands today. Abraham's migration from Ur probably took place during this dynasty.

4. **FIRST DYNASTY OF BABYLON** (1830–1530 B.C.). Hammurabi and his famous code are part of what is important about this period. This is the classical age of Akkadian literature and science. A Hittite raid (ca. 1530 B.C.) destroyed Babylon, bringing this dynasty to an end, and a long dark period followed.

5. **NEO-BABYLONIAN EMPIRE** (626–539 B.C.). Nabopolassar, the Chaldean, assisted the Medes and other powers in overthrowing the dominant Assyrians. The fall of Nineveh in 612 B.C. made it possible for Babylonia to expand. Nebuchadnezzar (605–562 B.C.), the most famous of the Chaldean rulers, extended the empire to Egypt's borders, capturing Judea en route. On two separate occasions (597 and 587 B.C.) he carried many Jews into captivity in Babylon. The *Babylonian Chronicle* parallels the account of the captivity in 2 Kings 24:10-17 and 2 Chronicles 36. The captivity of Judah lasted until 538 B.C., when Cyrus the Persian conquered Babylon after Belshazzar

desecrated the sacred vessels taken from the temple in Jerusalem (Dan. 5). The Jews were released from bondage and the Babylonian Empire came to an end. The Persian kings retained Babylon as one of their royal cities, and so Cyrus (Ezra 5:13) and Artaxerxes (Neh. 13:6) are called kings of Babylon. The Persian Empire lasted 200 years; later, after the death of Alexander the Great (who died in Babylon on June 13, 323 B.C.), Babylonia became a part of the Seleucid Empire.

Toward the end of the second century B.C., the Parthians from Iran, led by King Evemere, deported many families, set temples and markets on fire, and controlled Babylon. Through the centuries cities fell into ruins, as God had prophesied (Isa. 13:19–22; 47; Jer. 50; 51), until the Arabs gave new life to the general area. Perhaps no city of prominence has suffered a more total extinction than the city of Babylon.

Babylon was the first of the Gentile world kingdoms represented by the image of Nebuchadnezzar's dream (Dan. 2:31–38). The Book of Revelation represents Babylon as the great harlot (Rev. 17; 18). Babylon is mentioned 250 times in the Bible and is often referred to in prophecies of Isaiah, Jeremiah, Daniel, and Habakkuk.

- *Babylon was begun by Nimrod (Gen. 10:10).*
- *Here the Tower of Babel was said to have been built (Gen. 11:1–9).*
- *Hezekiah, king of Judea, showed his treasures to Babylonia's ambassadors (2 Kings 20:12–18; 2 Chron. 32:27–31).*
- *Jeremiah declaimed against the folly of resisting Babylon (Jer. 20: 4–6; 25:8–14; 27:4–22; 32:1–5). He was arrested as a traitor (Jer. 37:11–21) and was offered a chance to go to Babylon, but he refused (Jer. 40:2–6).*
- *Under Nebuchadnezzar, the Babylonians carried Judah into captivity in Babylon. This happened in two different phases (2 Kings 24–25; 2 Chron. 36; Jer. 39; 52; Dan. 1:2; Matt. 1:11–12, 17; Acts 7:43).*
- *Daniel interpreted Nebuchadnezzar's dream and told him what would be in the latter days (Dan. 2).*
- *Shadrach, Meshach, and Abednego were delivered from the fiery furnace (Dan. 3).*
- *Daniel was saved from the lions (Dan. 6).*
- *Ezekiel was one of the prisoners taken to Babylon (Ezek. 1:1–2).*
- *When Zedekiah rebelled (2 Kings 24:20; 2 Chron. 36:13), the Babylonians came again. After a long siege they destroyed Jerusalem and took large numbers into captivity, and the kingdom of Judah came to an end (2 Kings 25:1–12; 2 Chron. 36:11–21).*
- *Babylon was spoken against by the prophets (Isa. 13; 14; 47; 21:1–10; 48:14, 20; Jer. 50–51).*
- *Cyrus allowed the Jews to return to their homes after 47 years in captivity (Ezra 1:2–4). The advent of Cyrus and the punishment of Babylon were constant themes of the later prophets of Israel (Isa. 8; 11; Jer. 1).*

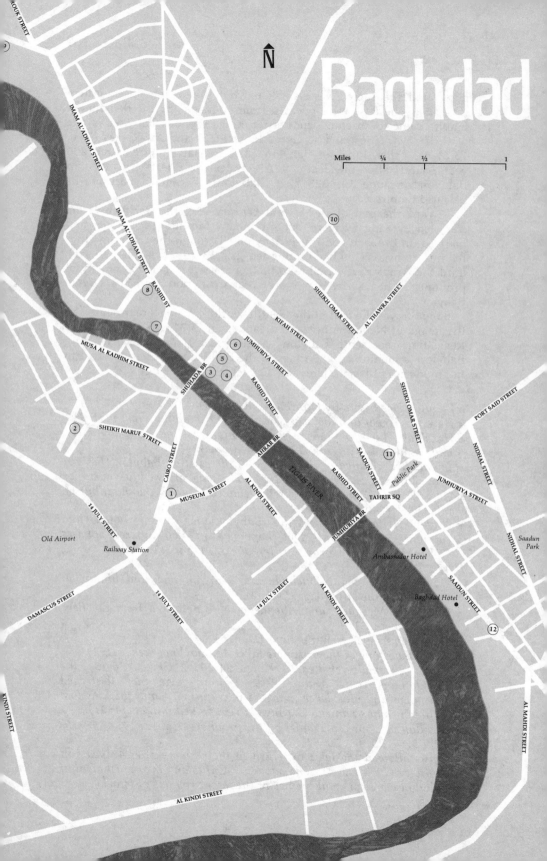

Baghdad

Miles   ¼   ½   1

Ñ

IMAM AL-ADHAM STREET

IMAM AL-ADHAM STREET

RASHID ST

MUSA AL KADHIM STREET

SHEIKH MARUF STREET

CAIRO STREET

SHUHADA BR

JUMHURIYA STREET

RASHID STREET

KIFAH STREET

SHEIKH OMAR STREET

AL THAWRA STREET

SHEIKH OMAR STREET

PORT SAID STREET

NIDHAL STREET

Public Park

SAADUN STREET

AHRAR BR

TIGRIS RIVER

RASHID STREET

TAHRIR SQ

JUMHURIYA STREET

NIDHAL STREET

Saadun Park

MUSEUM STREET

AL KINDI STREET

JUMHURIYA BR

14 JULY STREET

Old Airport

Railway Station

DAMASCUS STREET

14 JULY STREET

14 JULY STREET

AL KINDI STREET

Ambassador Hotel

SAADUN STREET

Baghdad Hotel

KINDI STREET

AL KINDI STREET

AL MAHDI STREET

(1) (2) (3) (4) (5) (6) (7) (8) (10) (11) (12)

1. Iraqi National Museum
2. Tomb of Sheikh Ma'ruf and Zobeidah's Tomb
3. College of Al Mustansiria
4. Islamic Museum
5. Copper Bazaar
6. Folkloric Museum
7. Abbasid Palace
8. War Museum
9. Kadhimain Mosque
10. Al Wastani Gate
11. Iraqi National Gallery
12. Tomb of the Unknown Soldier

■ *Babylon is referred to in the New Testament (Matt. 1:11-12, 17; Acts 7:43).*
■ *Babylon is sometimes a symbol for Rome (Rev. 14:8; 16:19; 17:5; 18:2, 10, 21; 1 Pet. 5:13).*
■ *It is also a symbol of evil (Rev. 17; 18).*

Baghdad

This twentieth-century capital city of Iraq is near the center of the country, on the Tigris River and 40 miles from the Euphrates. It is renowned for learning and famed for its silks and tiled buildings. The city was founded in A.D. 762 by Abbasid Caliph Mansur. The round city was surrounded by three lines of walls for purposes of fortification. It became the city of the *Arabian Nights* under Harun-al-Rashid in the tenth century. For many years the city was relatively unimportant, but since Iraq received her independence in 1932 and declared Baghdad as her capital, it has become increasingly more important. Its main street is *Rashid*, and the city center is a circle known as *South Gate*.

POINTS OF INTEREST

1. **IRAQI NATIONAL MUSEUM.** Beautiful pieces of art from various sites are housed in this very important museum, opened in 1966. This is the most important point of interest in Baghdad.

2. The **TOMB OF SHEIKH MA'RUF** and **ZOBEIDAH'S TOMB** are located west of the Iraqi National Museum.

3. **COLLEGE OF AL MUSTANSIRIA.** This is one of the world's old universities, dating back to A.D. 1233, and is the most important ancient monument in the city. It was founded by Caliph Al Moustasir, and became one of the most famous institutions of its sort in this country. It contained four law schools, representing the four orthodox sects. It had a large library, a hospital, kitchens, and baths. Since the fifteenth century the college has also been used for several other purposes.

4. **ISLAMIC MUSEUM.** Located on Bank Street, this museum is called *Khan Mirjan*. It exhibits copper, tiles, stuccos, pottery, and wood carvings from ancient times.

5. **COPPER BAZAAR.** On Rashid Street and its side alleys is the famous Copper Bazaar of Baghdad.

6. **FOLKLORIC MUSEUM.** Here are displayed Iraqi customs and dress to show the life of the native peoples of the country.

7. **ABBASID PALACE.** Tradition dates this palace to the thirteenth century and says it belonged to the Caliph Nasser (1180–1225), who made Baghdad the city of the *Arabian Nights*.

8. The **WAR MUSEUM** is northwest of Abbasid Palace.

9. **KADHIMAIN MOSQUE.** One of the most holy places for the Shiite Moslems is this large and beautiful mosque, 5 miles from downtown Baghdad. It has two golden domes and four richly decorated minarets. In the holy shrine are the venerated tombs of two of the twelve Shia Imams, Moussa Al Kadhim and his grandson, Mohammed Algawadi.

10. **AL WASTANI GATE.** This gate is one of the last standing gates in the northeast area of the city and now houses a museum of ancient arms.

11. **IRAQI NATIONAL GALLERY.** Contemporary paintings of Iraqi artists are housed here. It is also called the *Gulbenkian Museum* and is located near South Gate.

Other sites of interest to the tourist include the **TOMB OF THE UNKNOWN SOLDIER**, the **ALADDIN CAVE MARKET**, and the **KAILANI MUSEUM**.

TELL HARMAL. Six miles southeast of the city is an archaeological site which has produced clay tablets with mathematical problems inscribed on them indicating that schoolboys were learning about the hypotenuse of a right triangle 1,700 years before Euclid's time. The code of Eshnunna, the world's oldest book of law (2000 B.C.), and thousands of clay tablets were also found at Tell Harmal. It is believed that Hammurabi took his laws from the code of Eshnunna.

NORTH OF BAGHDAD

Akkad, *Agade, Akkud*

A city in the land of Shinar of Babylon (Gen. 10:10), this was the capital of Sargon I, who founded the first Semitic empire in the twenty-fourth century B.C. It gave its name to the whole of northern Babylonia and to the Semitic language (Akkadian) which became current in Babylonia and Assyria. Its site is unknown, but is believed to be in the area near Baghdad.

Aqarquf, Agergoof, *Dur-Kurigalzu, Qasr*

Fifteen miles west of Baghdad are the ruins of Aqarquf, a city founded by the Kassite king Kurigalzu II (1345–1324 B.C.). It was called Dur-Kurigalzu and is mentioned in contemporary texts from Nippur. A temple tower (ziggurat) marking the site is still about 185 feet high. It is modeled after the one at Ur. Ruins of several temples are also located here, and about ¼ mile northeast are the ruins of a palace.

Above: Kadhimain Mosque, Baghdad
Below: Ziggurat, Aqarquf

Samarra

Seventy miles north-northwest of Baghdad is the city of Samarra, with the ROWDHA AL ASKARIA MOSQUE and its beautiful gold dome, and the MOSQUE OF ALMAHIDI with its colored tile dome. Samarra became the capital when Caliph Al-Mutasin moved his capital there in A.D. 836. It was the capital for 56 years. On the northern outskirts of the city is the 185-foot-high MINARET IN SPIRAL, believed by some to be built like the Tower of Babel. The minaret and FRIDAY'S MOSQUE, located at its base, were both built about A.D. 830. Samarra gave its name to a widely distributed type of pottery dating from the fifth millennium B.C. The Roman emperor Julian was wounded and died nearby when retreating before the Persians in A.D. 363.

Tikrit

On the Tigris River some 30 miles north-northwest of Samarra is the town of Tikrit. This is the birthplace of Saladin, a Moslem leader who fought against Richard the Lion-Hearted in the Third Crusade. Tikrit was populated in the tenth century by Christians who possessed a large monastery.

ASHUR, *Assur, Ash Shargat, Qal'at Shergat*

Ashur was the capital city of Assyria, standing on the west bank of the Tigris River, about 70 miles north-northwest of Tikrit. It was founded at the beginning of the third millennium B.C. and was named after the national god, Ashur, who in turn gave his name to the country and empire of Assyria until the seventh century B.C. Though Ashurnasirpal II (884–859 B.C.) moved his capital to Calah, Ashur remained until its fall (614 B.C.) a city for which the Assyrians had great concern.

Ashur was captured by Hammurabi in the eighteenth century B.C. and was held in turn by Shalmaneser III (858–824 B.C.), Sargon II (721–705 B.C.), and Sennacherib (705–681 B.C.). When the Medes and Persians captured Ashur in 614 B.C., it was here that the victorious kings strengthened their alliance by giving a Persian princess in marriage to the crown prince Nebuchadnezzar II. For this princess, Nebuchadnezzar built the Hanging Gardens. Ashur was thoroughly excavated by the Deutsche Orient-Gesellschaft between 1903 and 1914. TEMPLES, an ACROPOLIS, PALACES, a ZIGGURAT, and GATEWAYS were uncovered, and it was found that people had lived there as early as 3000 B.C. The *Broken Prism* found at Ashur tells of Sargon's expeditions in Israel.

- *Ashur, rendered erroneously as* Assyria, *is mentioned in the Bible* (Gen. 2:14).
- *Commercial ties between Ashur and Tyre are also mentioned* (Ezek. 27:23).

Hatra, *Al Hadhr*

Thirty miles west of Ashur and 93 miles southwest of Mosul are the ancient, well-preserved, and beautiful ruins of Hatra, excavated and

Minaret in Spiral, Samarra

reconstructed under the direction of the Directorate-General of Antiquities and the field direction of the Inspector-General, Fuad Safar. In 1971, the excavation was under the direction of Wathig Salihi, a native of Iraq, who received his Ph.D. degree from Princeton University.

Parthians made up of Hellenized and Parthianized Arabs built the city between the second century B.C. and the third century A.D. It was a religious center for the worship of the sun-god Shamash and had a TEMPLE COMPLEX that covered an area of 360 acres. A large Roman-type temple was built before the second century B.C.

A huge wall with 160 towers and four gates surrounded the city of 60,000 inhabitants. The wall indicated perhaps one of the main purposes of the city — that of being a defensive city to control the caravan routes. In fact, there were two circular walls of great thickness.

The city was sacked in A.D. 116 and again in 198 by the Roman emperor Severus, but buildings built of Mosul marble have survived.

Among the beautiful Hatrene sculpture found at Hatra are Roman copies of Greek originals such as Apollo, Poseidon, Hermes, and the like.

CALAH ("firm"), NIMRUD, Kalhu

This ancient second capital city (after Ashur) of the Assyrians was founded by Ashurnasirpal II in 879 B.C. 24 miles south of the present-day Mosul, or ancient Nineveh, on the east bank of the Tigris River. It was the favorite residence of Assyrian kings for 150 years, and settlements existed there as early as the fourth millennium B.C. The city was probably destroyed about 614 B.C., just before the fall of Nineveh. The extensive ruins, covering an area five miles square, include palaces, temples, houses, and fortress walls. TWO GATES have been reconstructed, with huge winged bulls and lions and a frieze of colossal figures bearing gifts to Ashurnasirpal II. The *Annals of Ashurnasirpal II*, describing his conquests, are inscribed on the pavement slabs of the entrance to the temple. Ashurnasirpal II's temple has also been uncovered, and in a small temple near this palace was found a statue of him, the only extant perfect statue in the round of an Assyrian king. Among the gods of Nimrud, the following are mentioned: Ninurta, the protector or patron of Nimrud; Nabou, the Babylonian god of sciences and patron of scribes; and Tashmetoum, goddess (wife) of Nabou.

Shalmaneser III, king of Assyria during the years 858–824 B.C., set up in the main square of Nimrud a six-foot-high black limestone obelisk (victory monument), called today the *Black Obelisk of Shalmaneser* or *Jehu Stela* (841 B.C.) It was discovered by Sir Henry Layard at Nimrud in 1840. It tells of the Israelite king Jehu, son of Omri — who reigned when Elijah was preaching in Israel — and shows a picture of Jehu in bas-relief bowing before Shalmaneser and offering to him silver, gold, a gold beaker, golden goblets, pitchers of gold, lead, javelins, and staves for the hand of the king. This is the only known portrait of an Israelite king. The obelisk is in the British Museum and is one of the many external evidences corroborating biblical accounts.

Another external evidence found at Nimrud includes a relief show-

Above: Sawing stone, Hatra

Left: Bas-relief on the wall of Ashurnasirpal's palace, Nimrud

ing a ship of Tarshish that was part of the Phoenician fleet sailing from Ophir to Elath in the Gulf of Aqaba to bring gold and other valuables to Solomon. A relief also shows Phoenician merchants, servants of Hiram, bringing monkeys as royal gifts to Solomon. Both of

Right: Winged bull, forming the gateway to the palace of Ashurnasirpal II, Nimrud

Below: Ziggurat, Nimrud

these reliefs were located in the palace of Ashurnasirpal II at Nimrud.

CARVED IVORY PANELS with biblical-style CHERUBIM were used on furniture at Nimrud. They were very much like the figures in Solomon's temple.

A limestone relief titled *The Capture of Astartu* was found in the southwest palace at Nimrud. It related the account of the Assyrian forces invading Moab, Gilead, and Galilee under Pul (crowned under the name of Tukulti-apal-Esharra but more generally known as Tiglath-pileser III) between 743 and 738 B.C. The scriptures refer to this episode (2 Kings 15:19; 17:24).

A huge 10½-foot-high WINGED BULL with a human head guarded the gateway to Ashurnasirpal's palace. It had five legs so that observers from the side would always see four legs as the bull is in a walking position. From the front it looks as if the bull is standing. This ancient piece of sculpture is located in the British Museum.

The *Nimrud Building Inscription* tells of Sargon's expeditions in Israel.

- *Nimrod, the mighty hunter, is the traditional builder of Calah (Nimrud) (Gen. 10:8–12).*
- *Jehu was the king of Israel shown on the Black Obelisk of Shalmaneser (1 Kings 19:16–17; 2 Kings 9:13–14; 2 Chron. 22:7–9; 25:17).*
- *Phoenician sailors brought gold to Solomon from Ophir (1 Kings 9:26–28; 10:22–24; 2 Chron. 8:18; 9:10–11, 21–22).*
- *Cherubim are biblical symbols (Exod. 25:18–20; 1 Kings 7:23–29; 1 Sam. 4:4).*
- *Menahem of Israel sent tribute to Tiglath-pileser III (2 Kings 15:19).*

NINEVEH, *Ninua;* Tell Kouyoundjik *and* Tell Nebi Yunus *("tell of the prophet Jonah")*

On the banks of the Tigris River 225 miles north of Babylon is the great city of Nineveh, made famous to Bible students by the prophet Jonah's experiences there. It is located on the northern edge of the modern Mosul (Al Mawsil).

Sennacherib made Nineveh the capital city of the Assyrian Empire at the end of the eighth century B.C. By this time it was already 2,000 years old, and it was to be called by Jonah "an exceeding great city." It apparently took Jonah three days to cover its territory (Jonah 3: 3–4). Much of the city's importance came as a result of the cult of Ishtar of Nineveh, who already in the Amarna age was famous as far away as Egypt. Nineveh's political power was short-lived, however, and came to an end in 612 B.C. when it fell to the Medes. Within 300 years even its site was lost. It was discovered in the mid-nineteenth century. The extensive ruins with the long city walls and two large mounds, Kouyoundjik and Nebi Yunus, mark the site of the ancient capital city.

Between 1845 and 1851, a young Englishman, Austin Henry Layard, discovered the palaces of the Assyrian kings at their capitals of Nimrud and Nineveh (Kouyoundjik). At Nineveh two libraries of clay tablets, inscribed in the cuneiform writing, were found by Layard in the palace of Sennacherib and by Rassam in the palace of Ashurbanipal. These tablets were taken to the British Museum and were classified and arranged. In 1872, George Smith, an assistant in the Department of Antiquities, announced that he had discovered on one of the tablets a version of the story of the deluge which closely resembled that in Genesis. The story, however, was incomplete. Smith was sent to Nineveh, and there he discovered a missing portion. The still incomplete tablet found by Smith was later duplicated and compared with others found elsewhere. Although Smith had little formal training, he became a leading Assyriologist. He excavated again in Mesopotamia and died of fever on the way home. With the newly discovered tablets, called the *Gilgamesh Epic of the Creation and the Flood,* the rationalists could no longer maintain that the flood was nothing but a story concocted by Hebrew mythmakers. The tablets were a part of the Royal Library of Ashurbanipal (668–627 B.C.), which was the first systematically collected library in the ancient Middle East. There were 700 tablets in the library, with 25,000 cuneiform texts. Many are now in the British Museum.

The Assyrian Gilgamesh Epic was written on clay tablets between 1750 and 1400 B.C. — apparently before Moses wrote about the Creation and Flood in the Book of Genesis. It was known to the Babylonians in the eighteenth century B.C. and before that to the Sumerians. The *Epic of the Creation* tells of the creation of man in a god-ordered universe. Marduk, one of the city gods, became the god of heaven and earth. When compared with the biblical account in Genesis, it was found that both accounts start with "In the beginning"; both have a super celestial ocean of water out of which waters came; both have the number of days of the creation as seven; both have man created on the sixth day and the heavens on the fourth. There are significant differences between the accounts however: the Babylonian gods were mythological and polytheistic; man was created to be a servant to the gods, while the Bible gives man dignity.

The *Epic of the Flood* tells of Utnapishtim, the Babylonian Noah, and has many similarities to the biblical account: man existed before he came to the earth; the gods decided on the deluge (Gen. 6:7); the ark was to have a roof and vent (Gen. 6:16) and 6 decks or compartments (the Bible has an ark with 3 stories — Gen. 6:16); there were to be 10,800 baskets of pitch to make it watertight like the ark of Moses (Gen. 6:14); they were to load species of all creatures on board (Gen. 6:18–20); a terrific storm arose (Gen. 7:17–20); the mountains were covered (Gen. 7:19–20); the whole of mankind was returned unto clay (Gen. 6:17); the craft grounded on a mountain (Gen. 8:4); a dove was released on the seventh day (Gen. 8:10–12); sacrifices were made by Utnapishtim on the mountain, but instead of sending a rainbow, the gods smelled the sacrifice and "gathered like flies" and argued (Gen. 8:21); Utnapishtim and his wife became gods. There is no doubt a close relationship between the Gilgamesh Epic and the biblical account of the Creation and Flood.

The *Tablets of Tiglath-pileser III* (745–727 B.C.), found at Nineveh, tell of the tribute of Jehoahaz of Judah.

The *Royal Annals*, found at Nineveh (nos. 10 through 18), tell of Sargon's capture of Samaria in 721 B.C., as does 2 Kings 17:5. In fact, Sargon's expeditions in Israel are related over and over again in many inscriptions: *Nimrod Prism 4:25–41; Display Inscription; Khorsabad Pavement Inscription; Annals, 23–25; Broken Prism from Ashur; Nimrud Building Inscription; Annals Khorsabad; Broken Prism.*

The *Taylor Prism* of Sennacherib is a prism-shaped cuneiform record of antiquity found in Nineveh, and is important because it is a source outside of the Bible telling of the siege of Jerusalem by Sennacherib the Assyrian after Sargon had already captured the ten tribes of Israel and carried them north. Sennacherib's siege of Jerusalem took place between 705 and 681 B.C., and this account parallels the biblical accounts.

Although Hezekiah was anti-Assyrian, he paid tribute to Assyria (2 Kings 18:3–19:37; Isa. 36–37). Isaiah encouraged Hezekiah to withstand Assyria and not give in to her besieging, which encouragement Hezekiah apparently followed, and an angel smote the Assyrian army (2 Kings 19:35). The Taylor Prism says, "But as for Hezekiah, the Jew, who did not bow in submission to my yoke, forty-six of his strong walled towns . . . I besieged and conquered. . . . I made come out from them 200,150 people, . . . camels . . . and counted them as the spoils of war. He himself I shut up like a caged bird within Jerusalem, his royal city." It goes on to tell how Hezekiah later sent tributes to Sennacherib, and lists the ivory, ebony, gold, and silver gifts. The prism is located in the British Museum.

A bas-relief of *Sennacherib before Lachish* was located on a wall of the royal palace at Nineveh. It showed the king sitting on his throne in his camp outside the conquered city of Lachish, receiving his booty, about 700 B.C. Some prisoners were brutally impaled on stakes and some were flayed alive. These may have been Hezekiah's men — the Hebrews who influenced the city to resist — and are probably the earliest representations of Judeans. Lachish in ancient Judea was the Assyrian headquarters in subsequent campaigns, and from there Sennacherib sent his emissaries to parley with Hezekiah at Jerusalem (2 Kings 18:17). The large relief is now in the British Museum.

- *The city was founded originally by Asshur (Gen. 10:11).*
- *Sennacherib, founder of the newer city, met death in 681 B.C. after ruling 23 years. The account on the* Babylonian Chronicle *agrees in general with the Old Testament text in 2 Kings 19:36–37 and Isa. 37:37–38. Sennacherib was murdered by his sons.*
- *During the reign of Hezekiah, king of Judah, Sennacherib conquered much of Judah's territory, but his forces were destroyed by the angel of the Lord as they surrounded the city of Jerusalem (2 Kings 18:13–19:35; 2 Chron. 32:1–21; Isa. 35–39).*
- *Events at Lachish were recorded by the Taylor Prism, the bas-relief at Nineveh, and Isaiah (Isa. 36:2; 2 Kings 18).*

- *The Gilgamesh Epic account of the Creation and the Flood is similar to that in the Bible (Gen. 1–2; Gen. 6–8).*
- *The fall of Assyria and Nineveh to the Medes and Babylonians was fiercely hailed by Nahum and Zephaniah (Nah. 1:1; 2:8; 3:7; Zeph. 2:13–14).*
- *Jonah was sent on a mission to Nineveh to convert the city (Jon. 1–4).*
- *Jonah's mission to Nineveh was referred to by Matthew and Luke (Matt. 12:41; Luke 11:30, 32).*

Mosul, *Al Mawsil*

The largest city in northern Iraq is the modern Mosul, with a population of 200,000. It is the second largest city in the country, and is 225 miles north of Baghdad, on the west bank of the Tigris River. Situated at the foot of the Kurdistan mountains and at the head of the agricultural district of "the Plains," it is in a strategic location. The site of the ancient Assyrian capital of Nineveh is near the city of Mosul.

POINTS OF INTEREST

ARCHAEOLOGICAL MUSEUM. Artifacts from Nimrud and other archaeological sites are housed there.

The **GREAT MOSQUE OF MOSUL** (the Djami Mosque) has one remaining part, a minaret known as the **LEANING TOWER**, constructed by Nom Eddin (A.D. 1146–74). It stands near a twelfth-century church that was dedicated to Saint Paul and 40 martyrs.

The **MAUSOLEUM OF YAHIA** is topped with an octagonal pyramid.

The **PALACE OF BADR UD-DIN LULU** (Qara Serai), who ruled from A.D. 1234 to 1258, is located in Mosul.

Khorsabad, *Dur-Sharrukin (city of Sargon II)*

Twelve miles northeast of Nineveh is the site of the ancient capital of Assyria, founded by Sargon II (721–705 B.C.), who helped deport the ten tribes of Israel after the death of his father, Shalmaneser V, the son of Tiglath-pileser III. The *Nimrud Prism IV* gives the account of Sargon's expedition against and capture of Samaria. Sargon lived in Khorsabad for two years before his death. The *Khorsabad Pavement Inscription* and *Khorsabad Annals* found there tell of Sargon's expeditions in Israel. Excavators have worked at Tell Khorsabad since 1842, and findings include **SARGON'S PALACE**, the **PLAN OF THE CITY** and its citadel, **THE PAVEMENT INSCRIPTION, MONUMENTS,** and some **TABLETS,** among which the Assyrian "king list" is the most outstanding. Ten miles from Khorsabad is **JERWAN,** which is occupied by the Yezidi, worshipers of the devil, and is the site of the oldest aqueduct in the world of which there are still remains. It was built by Sennacherib to bring water 50 miles to Nineveh. At the Bavian Gorge, a couple of miles from Ain Sifui, 11 stelae contain descriptions of the building of the dam and water works and reliefs showing figures of Sennacherib and others.

Leaning Tower of the Great Mosque, Mosul

■ *Israel was taken over the river by Sargon II (2 Kings 17:3-6).*

Gaugamela, *Arbela, Arbailu, Karamless*

Between Mosul and Arbela is the ancient site of Gaugamela, one of the oldest sites yet unearthed. According to archaeologists, it was here that man turned from hunting and fishing to agriculture over 7,000 years ago. Many believe it is the oldest continuously inhabited city in the world. Damascus claims the same distinction. It was here that Alexander the Great defeated Darius III of Persia in a decisive battle of his Asian campaign. A small village is located here, with a complex of churches observing the Chaldean rites.

BABA GURGUR *and* KIRKUK

This is the traditional location of the fiery furnace into which Shadrach, Meshach, and Abednego were cast, and a mosque in Kirkuk is dedicated to the prophet Daniel. The city is 150 miles southeast of the present-day Mosul and 173 miles northeast of Baghdad. In 1927 oil was struck here, and Kirkuk, the large city of the area (100,000), became the center of the Iraq Petroleum Company. From here a 30-inch pipeline takes crude oil to a port on the Mediterranean in Syria, called Baniyas (Balanea). The pipeline also runs to Haifa in Israel, but it has been closed since 1948. The "eternal fire" of the "fiery furnace of Daniel" is kept burning by escaping gases. The name of Kirkuk was Arrapkha in antiquity.

■ *According to tradition, Shadrach, Meshach, and Abednego were delivered from the fiery furnace near this site (Dan. 3:20).*

Nuzi, Gasur, *Yorghan Tepe*

Nuzi is 10 miles southwest of Kirkuk, and the American School of Oriental Research found some 20,000 small clay tablets here, dating as far back as 2500 B.C. They tell of an ancient civilization in which installment buying was the custom. A map found here is the oldest ever found. The society of Nuzi gives the student of the Old Testament an insight into a society that was like that in which Abraham lived. There are many parallels between Nuzi and biblical customs.

SOUTH OF BAGHDAD

Seleucia

At a point about 16 miles south of Baghdad, on the western bank of the Tigris River, is a city founded as the capital of Mesopotamia in 312 B.C. by Seleucus I, surnamed Nicator — a general under Alexander the Great — and destroyed in A.D. 164. It was the political and cultural center of the Seleucid period and had a population of about 600,000. The Seleucids were a hybrid civilization, composed of Mesopotamian, Syrian, and Greek elements.

Ctesiphon, *Taq-Kisru, Salman-Pak*

About 17 miles south of Baghdad, on the east bank of the Tigris River, is the site of the Parthians' ancient winter capital (114 B.C.). Of importance here is the huge **SASSANIAN ARCH**, the widest single-span vault of unreinforced brickwork in the world. It was once a part of the facade of a palace and dates probably to Chosroes II, the Sassanid king who reigned from A.D. 590 to 628. Ctesiphon was sacked three times by Romans — Trajan in A.D. 116, Lucius Verus in A.D. 166, and Septimius Severus in A.D. 197 — but it did not surrender.

Sippar, *Abou Habba*

Eighteen miles southeast of Baghdad is this northernmost city of Babylonia. It is an important city of trade and had the sun god Samas (Shamash) as the local deity. More texts bearing on the Old and New Babylonian periods were found here than at any other site in Mesopotamia. Hammurabi established his famous code of laws in Sippar, apparently, but the stone bearing the code was taken from this site in a raid by Elamites in 1170 B.C. The code is now in the Louvre. (For further information on the Code of Hammurabi, see the section on Susa, below.)

Karbala

Karbala is about 60 miles southwest of Baghdad. It has a population of 65,000 and is second only to Mecca as a holy shrine to the Shiite sect of Islam. Under the golden domes of the Mosque of Husain rests the tomb of Husain, and non-Moslems are not allowed to enter the mosque. The Abbas Mosque marks the site of a battle that took place in A.D. 608 between Ali supporters, led by his son Husain, and the partisans of the Umayyads over the question of the rightful successors of Mohammed as the Caliph of Islam. Husain and his family were killed. Their martyrdom split Islam into two sects: the Sunnis, who believed the Caliphate should be an elective office, and the Shiites, who believed that the direct descendants of the prophet Mohammed had a right to the Caliphate.

CUTH, *Cuthah, Tell Ibrahim*

This city was located 40 miles south of Baghdad and 20 miles northeast of Babylon. Remains of the Temple of Nergal have been discovered.

■ *Sargon took colonists from Cuth to Samaria in 721 B.C., and the Jews called the Samaritans Cuthaeans (2 Kings 17:24, 30).*

BABYLON *("gate of God")*

The famous city of Babylon lies 57 miles due south of Baghdad and about 12 miles east of the present course of the Euphrates River. The nearest town is Al Hillah, 5 miles to the south. The word *Babel* means "gate of God," and *Babylon* is the Greek form of *Babel*. This is a capital city of the country that was earlier called *Shinar*, ancient *Sumer*, in Genesis. In later biblical books the area is called Chaldea. It is estimated that the ancient city of Babylon was 5 times larger than present-day London and located on both sides of the Euphrates River. A stone bridge connected the two parts of the city.

The Akkadians built a temple here to the goddess Ishtar as early as 2400 B.C., but it was not until several centuries later under Hammurabi (1792–1750 B.C., or perhaps two centuries earlier, according to some scholars), that the city rose to prominence. It reached the height of its glory under Nebuchadnezzar II (605–562 B.C.). Under Hammurabi Babylon flourished until the sixteenth century B.C., when the Hittites destroyed the city. The Kassites and later the Assyrians were conquerors until 612 B.C., when the Assyrian capital of Nineveh was destroyed and the Neo-Babylonian period began under Nebuchadnezzar. He built the palaces, canals, ziggurats, temples, and famous Hanging Gardens of Babylon, one of the Seven Wonders of the Ancient World. He married Anytas, a Median princess from the mountains, and to make her feel at home on the plains he erected a series of terraces and planted them with flowers, shrubs, and trees. They were watered with a unique watering system. It was such a magnificient city that Isaiah referred to it as "Babylon, the glory of kingdoms, the beauty of the Chaldees' excellency" (Isa. 13:19). The great dynasty of Neo-Babylon ended in 539 B.C., when Cyrus the Persian captured the city. The city declined until Alexander the Great conquered it in 331 B.C. and made Babylon the capital of his Asian empire. Alexander died in Babylon eight years later. Tradition says his tomb is located in the Archaeological Museum at Istanbul.

German archaeologists of the Deutsche Orient-Gesellschaft worked at the ancient ruins of Babylon during the years 1899–1940, and the ruins of the inner city were thoroughly excavated. A vast system of fortifications, streets, canals, palaces, and temples was discovered.

On the site, archaeologists found documents describing systematically the entire city. Several maps are preserved on clay tablets. The inner and outer walls were said by Herodotus to have been 13 miles long on one side, 300 feet high, and at least 80 feet thick. There were 25 gates on each side of the city.

The *Cyrus Cylinder* is one of the most famous documents ever found at Babylon. It is a baked clay cylinder about 9 inches long and written in cuneiform. Cyrus the Persian, king of Babylonia from 538 to 529 B.C., was responsible for setting the Jews free from their captivity under Nebuchadnezzar. This cylinder was prepared under Cyrus's direction and has on it a record called the *Nabonidus Chronicle*, telling of Cyrus's capture of Babylon without a battle, his return of prisoners to their own countries, and his restoration of treasures to the native temples. This external evidence helps to support the biblical accounts of the return of the Jews to Judea after their captivity. Cyrus indicated that his god Marduk called him to be the ruler, but Isaiah said that Yahweh elected Cyrus (Isa. 44:28; 45:1).

The *Babylonian Chronicle,* of the sixth century B.C., tells not only of the battle of Charchemish, but also of the capture of Jerusalem on March 16, 597 B.C., by Nebuchadnezzar, the appointment of Zedekiah as king, and the removal of Israelite prisoners, including Jehoiachin, to Babylonia. Jehoiachin and his family languished in prison in Babylon and died there. This is another archaeological evidence of the biblical accounts (2 Kings 24:10–18; 2 Chron. 36:9–11). The Chronicle and Old Testament accounts compare in many details. The Babylonian Chronicle is in the British Museum.

POINTS OF INTEREST

1. The **OUTER CITY WALL** is seen as the visitor approaches Babylon from the north. The road cuts through the wall. The wall was over 10 miles long and was actually composed of 3 walls. The inside one was made of crude adobe bricks, with towers. The outside one, of baked bricks, was wide enough to allow 2 chariots, drawn by 4 horses each, to pass each other on the top.

2. The **INNER CITY WALL,** built to enclose the most important and sacred part of the city, was about 4 miles long and had 8 gates, including the Ishtar Gate. Each gate was named after a god. The Inner City Wall was also composed of three walls: an inner wall *(Imgur-Enlil),* 21 feet wide, made of brick; an outer wall *(Nimid-Enlil),* half as wide

Ishtar Gate Reconstruction, Babylon

as the inner; and, outside this double wall and 65 feet away from it, another wall of burned bricks set in bitumen.

Outside the walls, a canal, fed by the Euphrates, provided still another barrier to the enemy.

3. A **GREEK THEATER** is located east of the main center of the city, between the Babylon Museum and the Hillah-Baghdad main road. It was probably built in the fourth century B.C. by Alexander the Great.

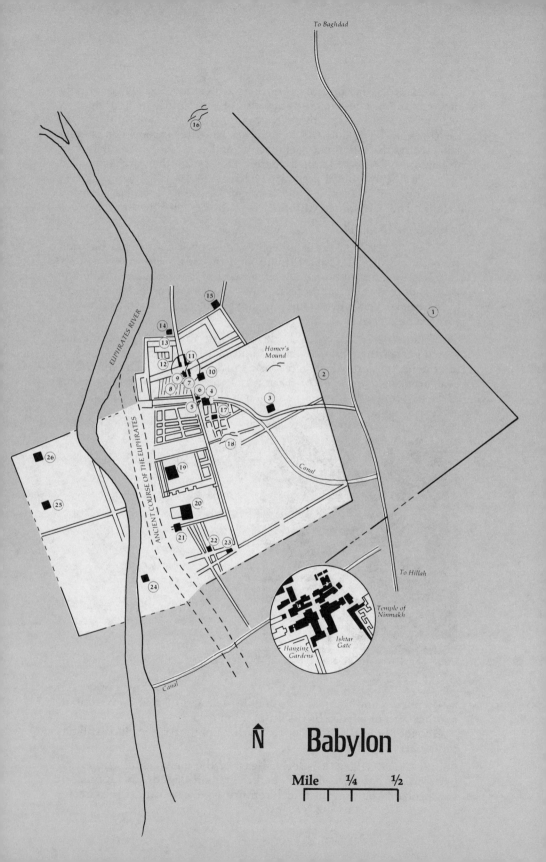

To Baghdad

16

EUPHRATES RIVER

15
14
13
12 11
9 7 10
8 6 4
5 17
18

Homer's
Mound

2

3

Canal

ANCIENT COURSE OF THE EUPHRATES

26

25

19

20

21

22 23

24

To Hillah

Temple of
Ninmakh

Hanging
Gardens

Ishtar
Gate

Canal

N̂   **Babylon**

Mile   ¼   ½

1. Outer City Wall
2. Inner City Wall
3. Greek theater
4. Hillah Rest House
5. Ishtar Gate Reconstruction
6. Babylon Museum
7. Procession Street
8. Southern Palace of Nebuchadnezzar
9. Hanging Gardens
10. Temple of Ninmakh
11. Ishtar Gate
12. Central Fortress
13. Northern Fortress
14. Lion of Babylon
15. Temple of the New Year Festival
16. Babel Mound and Summer Palace
17. Temple of Ishtar of Akkad
18. Mound of Merkes
19. Temple Tower of Babylon
20. Temple of Marduk
21. Tomb of Amran ibn-Ali
22. Temple of Gula
23. Temple of Ninurta
24. Temple of Shamash
25. Temple of Adad
26. Temple of Belit Nina

4. The **HILLAH REST HOUSE** provides sleeping facilities and meals for the visitor to Babylon. It is located by the Ishtar Gate Reconstruction.

5. The **ISHTAR GATE RECONSTRUCTION** stands at the modern entrance to ancient Babylon. It is half the original size, and the original bricks were employed in its construction.

Ishtar was one of the principal deities of Babylon.

North of the Ishtar Gate Reconstruction

6. The **BABYLON MUSEUM**, near the entrance and rest house, exhibits in chronological order large numbers of antiquities representing development processes of Iraq's ancient civilizations.

7. **PROCESSION STREET** is the Champs Elysées of Babylon. The ancient name of the street is *Ai-ibur-shabu* ("the enemy will never pass"). It is about 1 mile long and 30–60 feet wide and was paved with limestone slabs set in bitumen on top of bricks. Each slab bore the inscription: "Nebuchadnezzar, king of Babylon, son of Nabopolassar, king of Babylon, am I." This sacred street started north of the Ishtar Gate, went in a straight line south for about 1,000 yards, then turned west to the Euphrates River. It was lined with temples and palaces. Two hundred yards of the northern section of Procession Street was lined with walls decorated with 120 painted glazed brick

striding lions in bas-relief — 60 on each side. The lion was associated with the goddess Ishtar.

This street was used by Marduk, the local god, when the priests took the idol through the city on ceremonial occasions. The street's purpose was similar to that of the Avenue of Sphinxes in Luxor, Egypt.

8. The **SOUTHERN PALACE OF NEBUCHADNEZZAR** (Southern Fortress, City Palace) was perhaps the most important of Babylon's palaces. It was built by Nebuchadnezzar over a smaller palace built by Nabopolassar, his father, and it now covers an area 2,000 by 3,000 feet. It is on the left of Procession Street as the visitor goes north toward the Ishtar Gate. It is a typical Late Babylonian palace, with 5 courtyards side by side. The main court had a facade decorated with yellow, white, red, and blue glazed brick flowering creepers, lions, pseudocolumns, and trees. The throne room was about 50 by 95 feet in size. A niche (like a mihrab) was found here. The 18-foot-thick walls were decorated with enameled tiles. A construction of vaults in the northeast of the palace has been identified as the substructure of the famous Hanging Gardens. This palace has been excavated most thoroughly. On the western boundary of the citadel is a huge fortification which at one time was on the banks of the Euphrates River.

9. The **HANGING GARDENS**, in the northeast corner of Nebuchadnezzar's Southern Palace, were one of the Seven Wonders of the Ancient World. They were possibly roof gardens and perhaps were watered by a chain pump from deep wells below the garden.

10. The **TEMPLE OF NINMAKH** (Ninmah, E-Makh) adjoins the Ishtar Gate on the southeast. Ninmakh was the mother goddess or goddess of the underworld (the dead). The temple was built by Ashurbanipal (668–627 B.C.) and restored by Nebuchadnezzar II (605–562 B.C.) and by Marduk (561–560 B.C.).

Typical for this period, the temple is composed of a vestibule antechapel and a chapel shrine with a raised dais on which stood a statue of a goddess. It also had priests' living quarters, long corridors, a well in the courtyard, and an altar outside the temple, facing the doorway. There are many similarities between the temples in Babylon and those in Egypt.

11. The **ISHTAR GATE** provided entrance to the north side of the inner city of Babylon. The gate was built in three stages of construction, one above the other, by Nebuchadnezzar (605–562 B.C.). The first and lowest stage was 36 feet high and was decorated with 152 bas-relief bulls and dragons, in nonglazed brick, arranged in alternating rows. This is the only part of the original gate visible today, and it is in an excellent state of preservation. After this first stage was made, the level of the street was raised several yards and the reliefs were covered.

The second stage, built above the first, had bulls and dragons painted on the glazed brick but not in relief.

The third and most beautiful phase of construction was also decorated with bulls and dragons, but they were in relief, painted blue, and glazed. This part of the original gate is reconstructed in normal size in the Berlin Museum. A half-scale model is at Babylon. Although they are not all visible now, there were originally 575 dragons and bulls arranged in 13 rows on the gate, and the passage made by the gate was covered over. The mythical dragon-headed animal with a serpentlike tail, front feet shaped like a lion's, and hind feet like those of an eagle, was the emblem of Marduk, the local god. The bull symbolized Hadad (Adad), the storm god. The visitor can see bricks bearing old Babylonian inscriptions that mention the name of Nebuchadnezzar. North of the gate is a lookout post dating back to the days of Alexander the Great.

12.   The **CENTRAL FORTRESS** (Ancient Museum), west and a little north of the Ishtar Gate, was built for defense of the city. Because statues, stelae, and various trophies of war were kept here by Nabopolassar, it is sometimes thought of as an ancient museum. Some feel the Central and Northern fortresses are one complex.

13.   The **NORTHERN FORTRESS**, also on the northwest of the Ishtar Gate, was built for defense. It is also known as the Principal Palace and was built with bitumen and tiles by King Nebuchadnezzar.

14.   The **LION OF BABYLON**, near the north end of Procession Street, was sculptured out of black basalt. Nothing is known of its origin or significance, but it conveys such an impression of strength and majesty that it has become a symbol of the glorious past of Iraq. The lion is holding down a human figure, as if to say, "This will be your fate if you come against Babylon." The stone monument was found in the Northern Fortress, just opposite its present position.

15.   The **TEMPLE OF THE NEW YEAR FESTIVAL** was located northeast of the Ishtar Gate.

16.   The **BABEL MOUND AND SUMMER PALACE** are about 1¼ miles directly north of the Ishtar Gate at the Baghdad-Hillah main road. The palace was built by Nebuchadnezzar, who extended the town wall to enclose it. The palace is known as Babel and is located on the Babel Mound. Because it was already badly pillaged, archaeological excavators have done little at the site.

The palace rested on substructures, over 60 feet high, below the walls. In the back walls of some of its inner rooms archaeologists noticed vertical ventilation shafts of bricks, which led them to believe that Nebuchadnezzar came here in hot weather. Hence the name "Summer Palace."

South of the Ishtar Gate Reconstruction

17.   The **TEMPLE OF ISHTAR OF AKKAD** (Agade, Emeshdari) was south of the Ishtar Gate Reconstruction, on the east side of Procession Street. It consisted of a shrine and chambers.

18.   The **MOUND OF MERKES**, east of the Babylon ziggurat, consisted of shrines and residences.

19.   The **TEMPLE TOWER OF BABYLON** (ziggurat) was called by the

Babylonians *Etemenanki* ("house of the platform of heaven and earth"). It was located south of the Babylon Museum, adjacent to the present TOMB OF AMRAN IBN-ALI. We have some idea of what it looked like from the descriptions of the *Esagila Tablet* and Herodotus.

This 7-storied ziggurat, with a base 295 feet square and a height of 295 feet, was already old when Nebuchadnezzar had it rebuilt. It had been damaged by Sennacherib and rebuilt by Nabopolassar and Nebuchadnezzar. Many believe that this was the site of the original Tower of Babel (Gen 11:1–9).

The tower that Nebuchadnezzar built was the most important building at Babylon. Some even felt it marked the center of all space. It was built of mud adobe bricks in the center and an outside wall of baked bricks. The baked bricks have been removed from the site, and traces showing the foundation of its four walls are all that remain of this ziggurat. All of the adobe bricks have weathered back to mother earth.

The top level of the temple tower was the most sacred. It was constructed of blue glazed tiles and called the *Illumine Temple*, the house of the local Babylonian god, Marduk. Babylon was a religious center for all Babylonians who worshiped Marduk.

Instead of the splendid tower that once attracted Babylonian worshipers of Marduk, however, the visitor now sees a pond of water surrounded by growing reeds and weeds.

20. The TEMPLE OF MARDUK, the local god of Babylon and the supreme deity of the Babylonian pantheon since the reign of Hammurabi, is also known as *Esagila* ("house of the lofty head"). This sacred temple, one of over 1,000 temples in Babylon, stood just south of the Temple Tower of Babylon. It is now covered by an artificial hill, on which is located the tomb of Amran ibn-Ali. The temple consisted of a complex of large and lofty buildings with vast courtyards. The main chapel of this sanctuary measures 66 by 132 feet, and in the days of Nebuchadnezzar its walls and ceilings were overlaid with gold. Nebuchadnezzar's own account tells of the gold, silver, precious stones, and Lebanon cedar that he put in the temple. Golden images of Marduk stood in the sanctuary, with golden statues of winged creatures called *kerub* (cherub) guarding the entrance. Herodotus spoke of a "lower temple," in which was a golden image of Marduk sitting at a golden table with a golden footstool. The whole was said to weigh 3 tons. Outside the temple stood a golden altar and also a large altar for the sacrificing of full-grown animals.

As in other Babylonian temples and in Egyptian temples, the statue of the god stood in the center of an oblong chapel (holy of holies). An antechamber and main courtyard gave the temple three main areas, like the tabernacle of Moses and the temples of Solomon and Herod. Chambers around the courtyards were perhaps used for priests' quarters or storerooms.

21. The TOMB OF AMRAN IBN-ALI is on an artificial mound just south of the temple tower and on top of the Temple of Marduk area. Amran

was a Moslem believed to be a descendant of Mohammed. The tomb has three cupolas.

22. The **TEMPLE OF GULA**, often labeled *temple Z,* was located southeast of the tomb of Amran ibn-Ali.

23. The **TEMPLE OF NINURTA**, the god of war, is east of the Temple of Gula. It has also been called the *Temple of Ninib* or *E-Patutila.* This temple was built by Nabopolassar and restored by Nebuchadnezzar.

24. The **TEMPLE OF SHAMASH** was located west of the Temple of Ninurta and on the west side of the Euphrates River when the river ran through the middle of Babylon.

25. The **TEMPLE OF ADAD** was in the northwestern end of Babylon.

26. The **TEMPLE OF BELIT NINA** was also in the northwestern end of Babylon.

- *Babylon was begun by Nimrod (Gen. 10:10).*
- *Here the Tower of Babel was said to have been built (Gen. 11:1–9).*
- *It was famous for its manufacturing (Josh. 7:21), as a center of wisdom (Dan. 2:12; 4:6), and as a commercial center (Isa. 43:14; Ezek. 17:4).*
- *Hezekiah, king of Judea, showed his treasures to Babylonia's ambassadors (2 Kings 20:12–18; 2 Chron. 32:27–31).*
- *Jehoiachin was carried into captivity by Nebuchadnezzar; and Mattaniah, who changed his name to Zedekiah, became ruler by appointment of Nebuchadnezzar (2 Kings 24:15–17; Jer. 31:1).*
- *Daniel appeared before Nebuchadnezzar, was taught the learning and tongue of the Chaldeans, and was given the name Belteshazzar (Dan. 1:1–7).*
- *Daniel interpreted Nebuchadnezzar's dream and told him what would be in the latter days (Dan. 2).*
- *Gold and silver vessels from Solomon's temple at Jerusalem were used at a banquet by Belshazzar the king. During the banquet a hand wrote on the wall of the palace (Dan. 5:1–5).*
- *Daniel interpreted the handwriting on the wall (Dan. 5:25–29).*
- *Belshazzar, son of Nebuchadnezzar, was defeated and the handwriting on the wall was fulfilled when Darius overthrew Babylon (Dan. 5:30–31).*
- *Ezra told of the restoration of the Jews to Jerusalem after their captivity in Babylon (Ezra 1:1–11; 44:24–28; 45:12).*
- *Micah foretold the restoration under Cyrus (Mic. 5).*
- *Babylon is referred to in the New Testament (Matt. 1:11–12, 17; Acts 7:43).*
- *Babylon is sometimes a symbol for Rome (Rev. 14:8; 16:19; 17:5; 18:2, 10, 21; 1 Pet. 5:13).*
- *It is also a symbol of evil (Rev. 17; 18).*

Hilla

This city is a starting point to visit Babylon, Kish, Nippur, Isin, Shuruppak, Borsippa, or Al Kifl. It is 60 miles south of Baghdad and has a population of 55,000.

Kish, *Tell el Ohaimer*

Ten miles east of Babylon is the ancient city of Kish, a very old and famous town dating back to a period before Babylon. A SUMERIAN PALACE, a LIBRARY of clay tablets, and a complex of TEMPLES are located there.

Borsippa

This was an important ancient city 12 miles south of Babylon, dating from the Ur III period to the Arab period. Antiquities include an impressive TEMPLE TOWER, legal tablets, and a number of literary and astronomical texts dated from the Chaldean Dynasty on. Some believe that the ziggurat at Borsippa is possibly the original Tower of Babel.

AL KIFL *(Birs Nimroud)*

This is the traditional location of the TOMB OF EZEKIEL. He had been a member of a community of Jewish exiles who settled on the banks of the Chebar River, a tributary of the Euphrates. It is said that Ezekiel was murdered in Babylon and that he was buried on the banks of the Euphrates. According to tradition, his tomb was built by Jehoiachin.

■ *Ezekiel had a house in his place of exile and lost his wife by a sudden and unforeseen stroke (Ezek. 8:1; 24:15–18).*

An Najaf *and* Al Kufah

One of the holiest cities of the Shiite sect of Islam is Najaf, 33 miles southwest of Hilla. It has a population of 80,000. Here is located the tomb of Ali, son-in-law of the Prophet Mohammed, who, according to the Shiites, was the rightful heir to Mohammed as the Caliph. His tomb, in a mosque, is covered with gold, silver, and jewels — gifts of pilgrims. Non-Moslems are not allowed in the mosque. Under Ali, Al Kufah was the capital of the Moslem world.

Nippur, *Nibru*

The Sumerian god Enlil and his famous temple of Ekur at Nippur helped Nippur occupy a very important position in the history of Mesopotamia up to the middle of the second millennium B.C. From the early Sumerian period Nippur also served as a center for intellectual activities. Excavations since 1889 have brought to light many legal documents covering the history of the city up to the Parthian period. In one room 18 by 9 feet there were 730 tablets similar to those from the library of Ashurbanipal. They dated back to Artaxerxes (464–424 B.C.) and Darius (423–404 B.C.). The cache turned out to be the archives of a family of Babylonian businessmen, the Marashu family. There are a considerable number of Jewish names in the business transactions, proving that many Jews stayed in the area after the Exile. There are also ruins of a ziggurat, walls, and a temple. Some feel that the Tower of Babel may have been here.

The small town of Diwaniyah (10,000 population), 20 miles away, is the starting point to visit Nippur. There is a rest house at Diwaniyah.

Isin *(Ishan)*, **Bahriat**

Kings of the First Dynasty of Isin ruled here for more than 200 years (2017–1794 B.C.). It is about 18 miles south of Nippur.

Fara, *Shuruppak*

Fara is 12 miles southeast of Nippur on the old course of the Euphrates River. It is the *Shuruppak* of the Babylonian flood account. In 1902–3 a large collection of early Sumerian texts, seals, and seal impressions was excavated.

ERECH *("length," "size")*, *Uruk, Unug, Erekh, Warka*

Erech, 20 miles due east of As Samawah and 7 miles northeast of the Euphrates River, has a history paralleling that of Mesopotamia from its earliest to its latest phase. The site was occupied from the Neolithic period and became known as Uruk about 3400 B.C. Such famous men as Enmerkar, Gilgamesh, Tammuz, Lugalzagesi, and Utuhegal lived in Erech. The ruins are very impressive because of the number of temples located there. At Erech is the first ziggurat, or stepped pyramid. The original whitewash was still on the sides of this ziggurat, which led to its name, the **WHITE TEMPLE**. The **RED TEMPLE** is so named because of the dye color of the walls. In this temple was found crude pictographic script, representing the earliest stage of Babylonian writing — evidently the direct ancestor of cuneiform. Cylinder seals dating to the fourth millennium B.C. were found at Erech and are the oldest seals known. Diwaniyah, with a population of 10,000, is the starting point for excursions to Erech or Larsa. The rest house at Diwaniyah is 80 miles from Erech.

■ *Erech was a city of Shinar in Babylonia (Gen. 10:10).*
■ *Citizens from Erech were transferred to Samaria (Ezra 4:9–10).*

An Nasiriyah

On the east side of the Euphrates River, 236 miles south of Baghdad and 128 miles northwest of Basra, is the city of An Nasiriyah, with 40,000 people. It was built during the last century under the direction of Midhat Pasha As-Sadun. From this city, many archaeological sites may be visited, including Ur, Tell el-Obeid, and Eridu. It has a rest house for tourists.

UR *of the Chaldees ("light," "brightness")*, Tell el-Muqayyar

In 1854 J. E. Taylor, British Consul at Basra, Iraq, uncovered at Tell el-Muqayyar inscriptions identifying that mound site as the ruins of the ancient Sumerian city of Ur. Since then the site — 8 miles south of the Euphrates River, 55 miles southeast of As Samawah, and 10 miles south and west of An Nasiriyah — has generally been considered to be the home town of Abraham. Ur was located in an area known as *Sumer*, and both terms are used interchangeably (Isa. 48:20; Jer. 50:9–10; Ezek. 11:24).

According to some authorities, Ur was the capital of the earth's first great civilization. Here, traditionally, the Bible and history began. There were chariots here as far back as 3500 B.C. The wheel was in use 1,500 years before it was introduced to Egypt by the Hyksos. The Sumerians produced the sexagesimal system (numbering by sixties), which is still used in reckoning time and in the measurement of the circle. King Ur-Nammu, who founded the last great dynasty of Ur, is famous for having drawn up one of the oldest codes of laws known to man — 4,000 years ago. Hammurabi possibly borrowed from him. Sumer was conquered by Hammurabi about 1750 (or 1900?) B.C. when he came from Babylon.

Under Sargon I (ca. 2400 B.C.), Ur was united with Akkad. Around 2100 B.C. Ur-Nammu, king of Ur, defeated the king of Uruk and became the king of Sumer and Akkad. The kings who followed constituted the Third Ur Dynasty, the most glorious period of Sumerian history. (See the section on Babylonia, earlier in this chapter.) Later Ur became a part of the Babylonian Empire. It began to decline after the Kassite period, however, and by 400 B.C. it no longer existed.

Sir Charles Leonard Woolley excavated at Ur between 1922 and 1934 and found the famous ROYAL TOMBS, with their rich treasures of gold and silver. He also discovered mud and reed dwellings of a village of the "Ubaid" culture; an 8-foot-thick layer of clay deposited by a large flood, which Woolley at first felt was the Flood of Genesis; historical inscriptions; legal and administrative documents; and literary and archaic texts that date from archaic to Persian and Seleucid periods. The findings cover the entire span of Mesopotamian history.

Ur had a complex system of government, a system of commerce, town drains, streets, two-storied houses, a great temple tower (ziggurat), and other evidences of a highly developed civilization.

POINTS OF INTEREST

1. The TEMPLE TOWER OF UR-NAMMU, sometimes referred to as the *Red Ziggurat of Ur*, was the nucleus of a central sacred precinct dedicated to the moon god Nanna. This well-preserved ziggurat, or temple tower, was built by King Ur-Nammu (ca. 2000 B.C.), one of the greatest builders in the ancient Orient, who also built other ziggurats in Eridu, Erech, and Nippur. These are the earliest known stepped temple towers and are believed to be monumental renovations of older temple terraces.

Although massive, the Temple Tower of Ur-Nammu conveys a feeling of lightness, because of its nearly perfect proportions and its slightly curved lines. Although this curving device is thought by many to have been invented by the Greek architects who built the Parthenon 2,000 years later, it appears that architecture from this early period was a prototype for later structures.

The temple tower, 205 by 144 feet in size, has a mud brick core and an 8-foot-thick "skin" of reddish fired brick, set in bitumen, which has preserved it through the centuries while other ziggurats have crumbled away. It has been only partially reconstructed. On the northeastern side are three stairways: two follow the walls of the ziggurat and one extends out from the ziggurat at a right angle to it.

A Late Babylonian king, Nabonidus (Nabū-na'id), renovated the temple tower, so that the ruins now standing represent the work of both rulers.

In Babylonia it was customary to build a temple on top of the ziggurat, where an image or symbol of the particular god was located in a long chamber. The image was usually carved out of wood and ornamented with metals and precious stones, as Isaiah described (Isa. 44:12-20), and was displayed to the public at certain festivals.

Ziggurats may have been built as a type of ladder set up to heaven from earth like that of Jacob (Gen. 28:12) — a function similar to that of the Tower of Babel (Gen. 11:3-5). Some feel, though, that ziggurats are like altars. The temple complex at the bottom of the ziggurat had a temple library and rooms for temple equipment. Virgin women, called *Entu*, worked in the temple as they did in Rome. Offerings of incense, goats, oil, food, and drink were offered to the gods. The food was placed before the idol — a custom similar to that of the Egyptians.

2. **COURTYARD AREA** *(E-Yemen-Ni-Gur)* **OF UR-NAMMU.**

3. The **SHRINE OF THE GOD NANNA** is located on the north side of the temple tower.

4. The **COURT OF THE GOD NANNA**, northeast of the temple tower, dates back to the Kassite period.

5. The buildings labeled **E-NUN-MAH** — "the house of Nun-Mah," the moon god — are immediately southeast of the court of Nanna.

6. A **PASSAGEWAY** to the temple tower (ziggurat), the *E-Dub-Lal-Mah*, dates back to 2124 B.C. It is located southeast of the temple tower and was reconstructed as a chapel by the Kassites.

7. The **NINGAL SHRINE EGIPAR** (Gig-Par-Ku) of Bursin, a king of the Ur III period, is considered the most important building in the city, with its broad-roomed temple in the southeastern part.

8. **PALACE OF UR-NAMMU AND DUNGI** (E-Hursag).

9. Sixteen **ROYAL TOMBS** of the Third Dynasty of Ur (ca. 2000 B.C.) were excavated by C. Leonard Woolley for the British Museum and the University Museum of Philadelphia during the years 1922-34. The tombs were made of brick and had corbeled arches. They were a rich source of remains of Early Dynastic craftsmanship and produced fortunes of gold and silver. Buried with the royal persons were musicians, servants, soldiers, charioteers, chariots, and draft animals. Names of two persons of royalty are known from legends on seals found with the bodies: *Meskalamdu(g)* and *Akalamdu(g)*.

The **TEMENOS WALL** was built over the top of the Royal Tombs by the Babylonians at a later date.

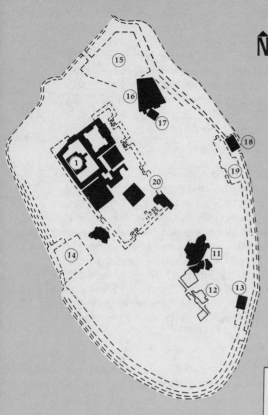

N̂

Ur

Feet   600

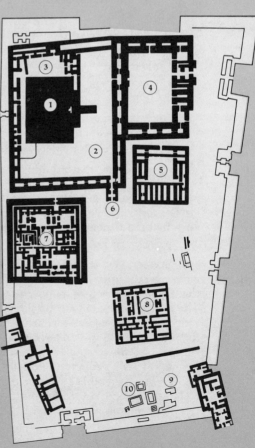

N̂

SACRED PRECINCT
OF NANNA —
THIRD DYNASTY

Feet   100   200   300

1. Temple Tower of Ur-Nammu
2. Courtyard area of Ur-Nammu
3. Shrine of the god Nanna
4. Court of the god Nanna
5. E-Nun-Mah
6. Passageway
7. Ningal Shrine Egipar (Gig-Par-Ku) of Bursin
8. Palace of Ur-Nammu and Dungi
9. Royal Tombs
10. Royal Cemetery
11. Dwelling quarters of the Ur III period and Isin and Larsa dynasties
12. Dwelling quarters of the Late Babylonian period
13. Temple of Enki
14. Western Harbor
15. Northern Harbor
16. Palace of the high priestess Bel-Shalti-Nanna
17. Harbor Temple of Nebuchadnezzar II and Nabonidus
18. Fortress
19. Dwelling quarters of the Ur III to Larsa period
20. Temenos Wall of Nebuchadnezzar

Many beautiful pieces of art were found in the Royal Tombs, including lyres with gold-covered bearded bulls' heads; a golden helmet of a prince, found in a sarcophagus beside the head of the alleged Prince Meskalamdu(g); fluted golden beakers; golden bowls, filled with food for the afterlife; funerary objects; and jewelry. The Iraqi Museum houses most of these objects.

One of the beautiful statues found in the Royal Tombs of Ur and dating back to 2700 B.C. is that of a he-goat, sometimes erroneously called "the ram caught in a thicket." It was probably a holder for an incense burner. The legs and face are made of gold, the belly of silver, the horns, eyes, and upper fleece of lapis, and the lower fleece of white shell on a wooden core. It is in the British Museum.

10. A ROYAL CEMETERY of the Early Dynastic period has remains of more than a thousand moderately equipped graves of ordinary citizens. They are located just west of the Royal Tombs and were also excavated by Woolley.

11. The DWELLING QUARTERS of a town dating back to the Ur III period (ca. 2000 B.C.) and the contemporaneous Isin and Larsa dynasties (ca. 2000–1600 B.C.) are located southeast of the temple tower. On a street called "Paternoster Row" is a traditional HOUSE OF ABRAHAM. In addition to houses, there are also small temples, schools, shops, and workshops.

12. DWELLING QUARTERS of the Late Babylonian period.

13. The TEMPLE OF ENKI dates back to the Ur III period.

14. WESTERN HARBOR.

Temple Tower of Ur-Nammu, Ur

15. **NORTHERN HARBOR.**

16. The **PALACE OF THE HIGH PRIESTESS BEL-SHALTI-NANNA** dates back to the time of King Nabonidus, of the Late Babylonian period.

17. **HARBOR TEMPLE** of Nebuchadnezzar II and Nabonidus.

18. **FORTRESS.**

19. **DWELLING QUARTERS** of the Ur III to Larsa period.

20. **TEMENOS WALL OF NEBUCHADNEZZAR.**

- *The Bible mentions Ur of the Chaldees (Gen. 11:28, 31; 15:7; Neh. 9:7; Acts 7:4).*
- *It was the home of Terah and his sons, Abram, Nahor, and Haran (Gen. 11:26).*
- *Haran, brother of Abram, died in Ur during a famine (Gen. 11:28).*
- *Abraham married Sarai in Ur (Gen. 11:29).*
- *Abraham left Ur to go to Haran after being warned by Jehovah (Gen. 11:31; 15:7; Neh. 9:7).*
- *Berodach-baladan came from Ur (2 Kings 20:12; Isa. 39:1)*

Tell el-Obeid (al-Ubaid)

About 4 miles north of Ur is the Tell el-Obeid, a prehistoric site dating back to 4000 B.C. and representing Babylonia's earliest civilization. It was excavated by Woolley and others.

Eridu, *Tell Abu Shahrain*

This ancient city is about 12 miles southwest of Ur and was once on the seashore or the shore of an inland lake. Its main god was Enki, the Sumerian counterpart of Ea, the water god. The Sumerian King List assigns to Eridu the oldest dynasty of Mesopotamia, and Eridu is

Dwelling quarters of the Ur III period and a traditional house of Abraham

reputed to be the most ancient city in the world (4000 B.C.). Many reed and mud huts found there may be the very first kind of construction in the lower Mesopotamia marshes. The temple unearthed there is the oldest religious structure known to man.

Merathaim

This is the region where the Tigris and Euphrates reach the ocean.

Al Basrah, *Basra; and Al Qurna*

The city of Basra is the only seaport of Iraq, and is located at the head of the Persian (Arab) Gulf 364 miles south of Baghdad. It was founded in the seventh century and now has a population of 100,000. Tradition has the Garden of Eden located at nearby Al Qurna, which is marked by the "tree of knowledge of good and evil," known as the "tree of Adam."

IRAN (PERSIA)

Along with the cities of Iraq, three cities in Iran are of particular interest to students of the Bible:

SHUSHAN ("lily"), *Susa, Susan, Susiana, Elam*

This was the capital city of the Elamite Empire (1100 B.C.), and was located on the Ulai (Karun) River approximately 80 miles north of the modern city of Ahvaz (Ahwaz). Excavators have been working on the mound for about 100 years and have found that it was occupied for more than 5,000 years. Susa was an administrative center for the Elamites, and all the known Elamite inscriptions of historical and literary content, in addition to Akkadian and Sumerian Ur III texts, legal texts, word lists, and school tablets, were found here. The school tablets show that Akkadian was taught to the students in Susa during that period.

The most important of all the finds at this site is the Codex Hammurabi, of which two or perhaps three copies, together with a number of Babylonian *kudurru-stones*, were once brought as spoils from Sippar to Susa by victorious Elamite kings. It was unearthed by Jacques de Morgan.

King Ur-Nammu, from whose code some believe Hammurabi borrowed, was Sumer's last great king.

Hammurabi became the king about 1750 B.C. and lived in Babylon. (Some date him as early as 1900 B.C., which may make him contemporary with Abraham.) With Hammurabi, Sumerian culture ended and Babylonia's began. We still benefit, however, from the Sumerian 60-second minute, the solar year, and a code of law.

The Code of Hammurabi was engraved on a black Diorite stela 8 feet high and made in the form of a boundary stone. On its face are 280-odd legal clauses, and it is the longest cuneiform inscription known. There is also a relief of Hammurabi receiving a scepter and ring from Shamash, the sun-god. The language is Akkadian. There are many resemblances between the Code of Hammurabi and the Hebrew code of the Old Testament, and many believe that Moses took the code as a precedent — a natural assumption in the absence of a belief in the eternal nature of the law of Moses as a law of God. Three of the Ten Commandments, numbers 7, 8, and 9 (concerning adultery, stealing, and bearing false witness), are very similar to laws within the Code of Hammurabi. However, there are also many omissions: commandments 1–6 and 10 are missing. The absence of number 6, "Thou shalt not kill," is especially noticeable. Other comparisons between the Law and the Code follow: both punish kidnapping, incest, and adultery by death; both have laws concerning false witness, slander, stealing, rape, slavery, and the rights of primogeniture; both have laws of "an eye for an eye"; both have similar laws concerning "concubines." The code is now in the Louvre.

Susa ruins include the PALACES OF CYRUS THE GREAT, the TOMB OF THE PROPHET DANIEL, ruins of the ZIGGURAT, plus the palace and temples of the Elamite kings in Chugha Zambil. Tradition says the tomb of the prophet Daniel lay in the bed of the Karun River, not far from Susa, and a mosque built on the bank of the river honors Daniel.

■ Shushan is mentioned in the Bible (Neh. 1:1; Esther 1:2).
■ The story of the Book of Esther took place here (Ezra 4:9; Neh. 1:1; Dan. 8:2; Esther 1:2, 5–9).
■ Chedorlaomer, king of Elam, took Lot captive (Gen. 14:1–12).

ACHMETHA ("place of horses"), Ecbatana, Hamadan

This city is the Achmetha of the Bible (Ezra 6:1–2), where Darius found the record of Cyrus's decree allowing the Jews to rebuild the temple in Jerusalem. This was the capital of Northern Media, and here Cyrus the Great held his court.

PERSEPOLIS ("city of Persia"), Istakhar, Parsa, Persai

Thirty miles east of Shiraz is the ancient Persian capital city of Persepolis, founded on a solid rock platform by Darius the Great (522–486 B.C.), after he had built his palace at Susa. Its towering columns, massive gates, and palaces are remnants of the "richest city under the sun." It was destroyed by Alexander the Great in A.D. 330, at the end of his great crusade.

The APADANA, approached by ornamental staircases, is beautifully carved. The PALACE OF DARIUS, with its HALL OF THE HUNDRED COLUMNS, and THE PALACE OF XERXES, with its WINGED-BULL DOORWAY, and the TREASURY show the beauty of the Persian artists. The PERSEPOLIS MUSEUM is built of original materials and typical architecture.

Three miles north of Persepolis, at the Necropolis of Naghshe Rostam ("Valley of the Tombs"), are the beautiful rock-hewn TOMBS OF DARIUS I, XERXES I, ARTAXERXES I, and DARIUS II. The PALACE,

HAREM, and TOMB OF CYRUS THE GREAT are located at Cyrus's ancient capital city of Pasargadae, 54 miles northeast of Persepolis.

- *Persepolis is mentioned in connection with the unsuccessful attempt of Antiochus Epiphanes to plunder its temples and palaces (2 Macc. 9:2).*

"And the Lord said to Abram . . . Lift up now thine eyes, and look from the place where thou art northward, and southward, and eastward, and westward: For all the land which thou seest, to thee will I give it, and to thy seed for ever" (Gen. 13:14–15).

This 4,000-year-old promise forms the basis and the essence of a spirit of return that has been an essential part of the Jewish spirit. Though dispersed throughout the earth, the Jews have never forgotten that the prophets of old foresaw not only a "dispersion" but also a "gathering." To Jews all over the world, the creation of a modern state for them is the answer to daily prayers for the past twenty centuries.

HISTORY

The modern state of Israel was brought into existence on May 15, 1948, with Dr. Chaim Weizmann as its first president and David Ben-Gurion as prime minister. Jerusalem was the capital. The new nation was born after about 2,000 years of foreign rule. It was bounded on the north by Lebanon, on the east by Syria and Jordan, and on the southwest by Egypt. During the six-day war of June 1967, Israel enlarged her land area from 8,000 to 26,000 square miles.

HISTORY OF THE HOLY LAND IN BRIEF

Pre-Biblical Period *(9000–2000 B.C.)*

The oldest known communities on the earth were in the Holy Land.

Biblical Period *(Beginning with Abraham, 2000 B.C.)*

In approximately 2000–1900 B.C., Abraham arrived in Canaan from Ur of Chaldea. When he arrived, Palestine was controlled by Amorites and Canaanites (local powers). Prior to Joshua's entry into the land, the Hyksos, Egyptians, and local dynastic leaders held control at

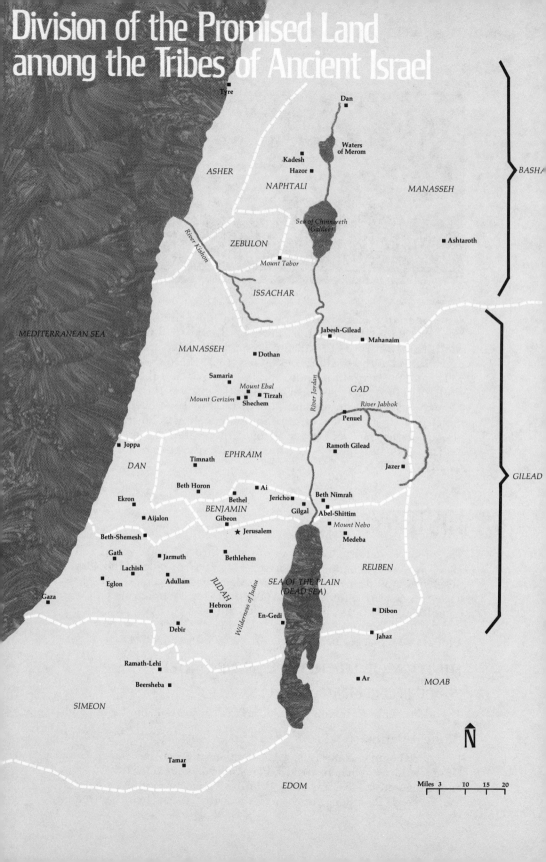

Division of the Promised Land among the Tribes of Ancient Israel

Tyre

Dan

Waters of Merom

ASHER

Kadesh
Hazor

NAPHTALI

BASHA

MANASSEH

Ashtaroth

River Kishon

Sea of Chinnereth
(Galilee)

ZEBULON

Mount Tabor

ISSACHAR

MEDITERRANEAN SEA

MANASSEH

Dothan

Jabesh-Gilead

Mahanaim

Samaria

Mount Ebal

Tirzah

Mount Gerizim Shechem

GAD

River Jabbok

River Jordan

Penuel

Joppa

Timnath

EPHRAIM

Ramoth Gilead

Jazer

DAN

Beth Horon

Ai

GILEAD

Ekron

Bethel

Jericho

Beth Nimrah

BENJAMIN

Aijalon

Gibeon

Gilgal

Abel-Shittim

Beth-Shemesh

★ Jerusalem

Mount Nebo

Gath

Jarmuth

Bethlehem

Medeba

Lachish

Adullam

REUBEN

Eglon

JUDAH

SEA OF THE PLAIN
(DEAD SEA)

Gaza

Hebron

Dibon

Debir

En-Gedi

Jahaz

Ramath-Lehi

Beersheba

Ar

MOAB

SIMEON

N̂

Tamar

EDOM

Miles 3   10   15   20

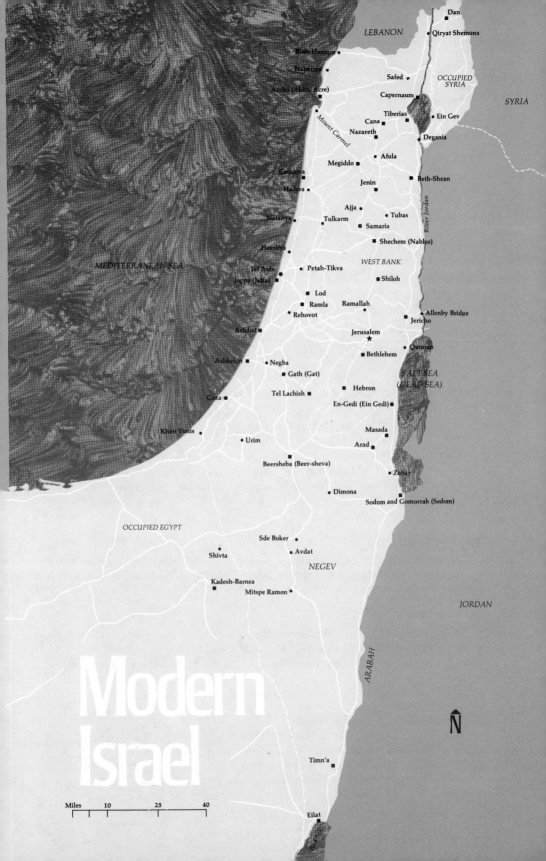

Dan

LEBANON
Qiryat Shemona

Rosh Haniqra
Nahariya
Safed
OCCUPIED SYRIA
SYRIA
Accho (Akko, Acre)
Capernaum
Tiberias
Ein Gev
Cana
Nazareth
Degania
Mount Carmel
Afula
Megiddo
Beth-Shean
Caesarea
Jenin
Hadera
Ajja
Tubas
Natanya
Tulkarm
Samaria
Herzliya
Shechem (Nablus)
MEDITERRANEAN SEA
WEST BANK
Tel Aviv
Petah-Tikva
Joppa (Jaffa)
Shiloh
Lod
Ramla
Ramallah
Rehovot
Allenby Bridge
Ashdod
Jericho
Jerusalem
Ashkelon
Negba
Bethlehem
Qumran
Gath (Gat)
Hebron
SALT SEA (DEAD SEA)
Gaza
Tel Lachish
En-Gedi (Ein Gedi)
Khan Yunis
Masada
Urim
Arad
Beersheba (Beer-sheva)
Zohar
Dimona
Sodom and Gomorrah (Sedom)
OCCUPIED EGYPT
Sde Boker
Avdat
Shivta
NEGEV
JORDAN
Kadesh-Barnea
Mitspe Ramon

ARABAH

Modern
Israel

Ñ

Timn'a

Miles   10   25   40

Eilat

River Jordan

various times. At the end of the thirteenth century, Joshua victorious-
ly led the Israelites into the Promised Land.

Ca. 1630. Jacob went to Egypt to be with Joseph.

Ca. 1250. Joshua entered the Promised Land.

Ca. 1200. The Philistines from Crete invaded Palestine. They
occupied much of Palestine by 1050 B.C.

1025. Saul was crowned the first king of Israel.

1004–965. David reigned as king of Israel.

965–922. Solomon reigned.

Ca. 920. Israel was divided into Israel and Judah.

721. The Assyrians captured Samaria and took Israel into captivity.
Israel became lost to history.

Babylonian Period *(605–562 B.C.)*

587. Nebuchadnezzar destroyed Jerusalem and took the tribe of Judah
into captivity in Babylon.

Persian Period *(549–332 B.C.)*

539. Cyrus, who conquered Babylon, allowed the Jews to return to
Jerusalem.

Greek Period *(332–167 B.C.)*

334. Alexander the Great conquered Palestine, and after his death
it was controlled by the Ptolemies of Egypt.

197. Palestine passed into the hands of the Seleucid Empire when
Antiochus III defeated the Egyptians at Caesarea Philippi (Paneas).

175. The Seleucid Antiochus IV (Antiochus Epiphanes) became
king. He abolished the worship of Jehovah. He desecrated the
temple by offering swine on the temple altar and installing a statue
of the Olympian Zeus.

Hasmonean Period *(167 B.C.–63 B.C.)*

Under the leadership of Mattathias, his sons, and other Jews, there
was a Jewish revolt against the Seleucids. The Jews had nearly 100
years of independence.

Roman Period *(63 B.C.–A.D. 330)*

63 B.C. Pompey conquered Palestine for Rome.

40 B.C. The Parthians surprised the Romans and took the land.

39 B.C. Herod the Great expelled the Parthians. Herod then reigned
until 4 B.C.

36–26 B.C. Pontius Pilate was the procurator of Judea.

4–1 B.C. Jesus was born.

A.D. 28–34. Jesus was crucified.

A.D. 66. This was the year of the first Jewish revolt under the Zealots.

A.D. 70. Jerusalem was destroyed by Titus, son of Vespasian.

A.D. 132–135. The Jews revolted a second time, under the leadership
of Bar Kokhba. Hadrian rebuilt Jerusalem as a Roman city, and
under penalty of death, no Jew was to approach the city. Hadrian

called it *Aelia Capitolina*. He also changed the name of the country from *Judea* to *Syria Palestina* — "Syria of the Philistines" — and hence the name, *Palestine* (Isa. 14:29, 31).

Byzantine Period *(Roman) (330-634)*

Constantinople, or Byzantium, as it was called, was made the capital of the eastern half of the Roman Empire. Christianity spread rapidly after Constantine's conversion.

Second Persian Period *(607-29)*

May 20, 614. Jerusalem was taken, and 33,877 people were slain by the Persians. Christian churches were destroyed and the work of 300 years' construction obliterated.

Arab Period *(634-1099)*

570. Mohammed was born in Mecca. At age 43 he received a series of revelations, which later became the *Koran*. He died in 632, after he had established the world religion of Islam and welded the Arab tribes together.

636. By this time all of Palestine was under Arab control, and Jerusalem became Islam's third sacred city, next to Mecca and Medina.

1009. Fatimid Caliph Hakim ordered the destruction of the Church of the Holy Sepulcher. In Asia Minor 30,000 Christian buildings are said to have been destroyed. These atrocities sparked the Crusades.

Crusader Period *(1099-1263)*

1098-99. These were the years of the First Crusade.

1099. Jerusalem was captured by the Crusaders, and the Latin Kingdom of Jerusalem was formed.

1187. Saladin, a Moslem prince from Egypt, gained control of Egypt, Syria, Mesopotamia, and Palestine. The Crusaders were routed at the Horns of Hittin in Galilee. The Christians later controlled Jerusalem for a short time in 1229 and 1241. Mongol tribes from central Asia also took Jerusalem, with a terrible slaughter, early in the thirteenth century.

Mameluke Period *(1263-1516)*

1263. The Mameluke Sultan Baybars of Egypt captured the remaining Crusader strongholds. The Mamelukes held the coastal cities intermittently for the next 250 years.

1400. Another Mongol invasion took place under Tamerlane.

Turkish Period *(1517-1917)*

1517. The Turkish Ottoman Empire conquered Palestine and held it for 400 years.

1799. Napoleon made an unsuccessful attempt to add Palestine to his French empire. He captured Joppa but failed at Acre.

1917. Jerusalem was taken by the Allies in World War I under General Allenby.

Modern Period *(1917-70)*

1878. Petah Tikvah was the first pioneering village.

1911. Degania, the first kibbutz, was founded.

1917. This was the year of the Balfour Declaration and liberation from Turkey by Great Britain.

1921. Nahalal, the first moshav, was founded.

1922. The British Mandate over Palestine was confirmed by the League of Nations.

1947. The United Nations adopted a Partition Plan, and Palestine was to be partitioned between Israel and Jordan by the United Nations.

May 14, 1948. The state of Israel was established, the British withdrew, and the Jewish-Arab war began.

July 18, 1948. This marked the end of the war officially. Palestine was partitioned between Israel and Jordan by the United Nations.

Feb. 16, 1949. Dr. Chaim Weizmann was elected president. David Ben-Gurion was the prime minister. (He was the prime minister again in 1955.)

1956. When Egypt nationalized the Suez Canal on July 26, 1956, Israel attacked and occupied nearly all of the Sinai Peninsula. Peace terms were made, and Israel withdrew to her 1949 armistice lines.

June 1963. Prime Minister David Ben-Gurion resigned and Levi Eshkol took his place. Eshkol died in 1969.

May 23, 1967. President Gamel Abdel Nasser of Egypt closed the Gulf of Aqaba to Israeli shipping, and a war began on June 5 between Israel and Egypt. Six days later, under the leadership of the defense minister, Moshe Dayan, it concluded with Israel occupying the entire Sinai Peninsula to the Suez Canal, the Golan Heights east of the Sea of Galilee, the west bank of the Jordan River, and all of Jerusalem. The Jews had access to the Western Wall (Wailing Wall) for the first time since 1948.

March 17, 1969. Golda Meir was installed as Israel's fourth premier, or prime minister.

POPULATION AND RELIGION

Since the beginning of the state of Israel the flow of immigration has been enormous. Jews have come from all over the world to what they consider to be their homeland. In 1948 there were 710,000 Jews in Israel, and 20 years later the population had reached a total of nearly 3,000,000, about 2,500,000 of whom were Jews, 325,000 were Moslems, 75,000 were Christian, and about 36,000 were Druzes and others. In June 1967 another million people became a part of Israel because of the "expansion" during the war, and by 1970 the population of Israel exceeded 4,000,000. Of the million that were added after the war, 960,000 were Moslems, 40,000 were Christians, and 5,000 were Druzes.

There are 26 cities and towns in Israel; 6 have mixed Arab and Jewish populations, and 2 are entirely Arab. There are 50 other urban centers, 700 Jewish villages, and 99 Arab and Druze villages. Although Tel Aviv has the largest population of any city, with 400,000, still Jerusalem is the capital, with her 275,000.

ISRAEL TODAY

Modern Israel has large airports, an airline, a merchant fleet, an efficient military organization, and rapidly expanding industry. She exports goods to many nations. Tourism is an essential part of her economy. Over 600,000 tourists visited Israel in 1971, and 36 percent of them were from the United States. The average length of stay of a tourist in Israel is one of the highest in the world — 15 days in 1969.

Even though Israel has had three major wars with her Arab neighbors (1948, 1956, and 1967) and has poured millions of dollars into defense, she has also spent millions on farming, education, and industry. The result has been a fulfilling of prophecy that the desert would blossom like a rose.

In Israel there are two seasons: winter, with its cold, rainy season, and summer, with its hot, dry season. The first rains start about October and end in April. Galilee has an average of 60 to 70 rainy days a year, and the Negev has between 10 and 20.

Spring comes to Israel in March, and the whole country is softly green and carpeted in wild flowers. The stony Judean hills are brilliant with red anemones, yellow daisies, mauve cyclamen, tiny cream-colored lupines, and almond blossoms, making the hills rich in color — all prepared for the spring festivals: Jewish Passover and Christian Easter.

The national language is Hebrew, but Israel's second language is English, which most youth can speak. A few Hebrew words from the tourist are warmly appreciated; the Israelis are accustomed to the tourists' mistakes.

Israeli currency is based on the pound, called the *lira* (plural *lirot*), divided into 100 *agorot* (singular *agora*).

Useful Everyday Expressions

hello — *shalom*
goodbye — *shalom*
thank you — *to-dah rah-bah*
please — *be-va-ka-sha*
yes — *ken*
no — *lo*

good morning — *bo-ker tov*
good evening — *erev tov*
bad — *rah*
good — *tov*
patience — *sav-la-noot*
good night — *lila tov*
excuse me — *slee-cha*
where is — *ay-fo*
money — *ke-sef*
bus — *auto-boos*
taxi — *taxi*
to the right — *yeh-meanah*
to the left — *smol-ah*
hotel — *ma-lon*
room — *che-der*
water — *my-im*
toilet — *bait key-say*
how much is it? — *ka-mah zeh oh-leh*
doctor — *row-feh*
café — *café*
waiter — *mel-tsar*
menu — *taf-reet*
ice cream — *glee-dah*
milk — *cha-lav*
mountain — *har*
Sunday — *yom ree-shon*
Monday — *yom shay-nee*
Tuesday — *yom shlee-shee*
Wednesday — *yom reh-vee-ee*
Thursday — *yom cha-mee shee*
Friday — *yom shee-shee*
Saturday — *sha-bot* (as in *hot*)

Map Reading in Israel

The following words often recur in the place names of Israel:

beit, beth, bet — house of, place of
be'er — well, cistern
ein — spring of
emek — valley
eretz — land of
gan — garden
gesher — bridge
migdal — tower
rehov — street
sha'ar — gate
ya'ar — forest
derech — road

givat — hill of
har — mountain
kerem — vineyard
kfar — village
kiriat — suburb of
ma'ayan — spring
meshek — farm
ramat — height of
s'deh — field of
tel, tell — hill, mound
shderot — boulevard
kvish — highway

Jerusalem and the Dome of the Rock, from the Mount of Olives

CITIES AND SITES

JERUSALEM

Jerusalem has also been known by the following terms: *Jebus; Salem; City of Peace; Urasalimu; Sion of God; Zion; City of David;* the *Holy City;* and *el-Kuds esh-Sherif* ("noble sanctuary").

At the time of Abraham it was called *Salem,* and before David's conquest it was an Amorite city called *Jebus.*

The first mention of Jerusalem in the scriptures is in Gen. 14:18: "And Melchizedek King of Salem brought forth bread and wine: and he was the priest of the most high God."

Although its name means "peace," there have probably been more wars fought at its gates than at any other city in the world. It is located "in the tops of the mountains" (Judean range), about 2,740 feet above sea level, 38 miles east of the Mediterranean and 14 miles west of the Dead Sea. The natural water supply is very poor, and conduits have brought water into the city from earliest times.

About 996 B.C. David took the city and made it his capital, and Solomon made it a beautiful city (965–922 B.C.), built a temple and palaces, strengthened the walls, and brought treasures into the city.

After the division of Israel, Jerusalem had both good and bad kings, and during the reign of Rehoboam (924 B.C.) it was raided and the treasures of the temple removed by Shishak of Egypt. It was strengthened by Uzziah, Jotham, and Hezekiah, but it was soon (701 B.C.) besieged by the Assyrians under Sennacherib and the people of Jerusalem were compelled to pay heavy tribute (2 Kings 18:3–16; 20:12–19; 19:35). The *Taylor Prism,* located now in the British Museum, tells of the tributes being given to Sennacherib of Assyria — especially by Hezekiah. In 609 B.C. Pharaoh Necho captured Jerusalem for Egypt.

The Babylonians, under Nebuchadnezzar, captured Jerusalem in 598 B.C. and destroyed it in 587 B.C. After 60 years of captivity, some of the Jews returned to Jerusalem in 538 B.C. and restored the walls and temple.

The *Babylonian Chronicle,* an archaeological find in Mesopotamia and a source independent from the Bible, tells about Nebuchadnezzar's capture of Jerusalem. The accounts in the Babylonian Chronicle and the Bible compare in detail (2 Kings 24:10–18; 2 Chron. 36). The Chronicle is now in the British Museum.

The *Jehoiakin Tablets* throw light on the treatment of Judah's king, Jehoiakin, while he was in captivity in Babylon. The tablets were found in Babylon.

The *Cyrus Cylinder* tells about Cyrus, the great Persian who restored the Jews to their homeland (538 B.C.), and of his life in Babylon. Isaiah felt Cyrus was anointed of the Lord (Isa. 45:1); Cyrus felt his god, Marduk, called him to be the ruler. Cyrus, said Isaiah, was elected by Yahweh (Isa. 44:28; 45:1–4). Concerning the liberation of the Jews, Cyrus said on his cylinder: "I gathered together all their inhabitants and restored to them their dwellings." Isaiah and Micah prophesied of the restoration by Cyrus (Isa. 44:24–28; 45:12–13; Mic. 5). The prophecies were fulfilled in the time of Zerubbabel (Ezra 1:1–11).

In 332 B.C. the Greeks, under Alexander the Great, captured Jerusalem. In 320 B.C. Ptolemy Soter captured it. In 302 B.C. it was annexed to Egypt. In 170 B.C. its walls were razed by Antiochus Epiphanes of Macedonia. Later the Maccabees fought the Greeks, and from 167 to 63 B.C. the Jews enjoyed independence under the Hasmonean kings. But finally the Romans came in 63 B.C. and besieged the city. In 37 B.C. Herod (half Idumaean) was appointed king of the Jews. He married a Jewess, among others. He was a great builder. He rebuilt Jerusalem with a palatial temple area more magnificent than Solomon's. He also built a palace and the city walls, including the Western Wall (Wailing Wall). Herod died in 4 B.C., and thus the city Herod built was the city that Jesus knew.

After the Jews unsuccessfully revolted in A.D. 66, the Romans under Titus destroyed the city in A.D. 70. This fulfilled Jesus' prophecy (Luke 19:41–44; 21:20–24) and was another part of the Jewish dispersion. Bar Kokhba's Jewish revolt (A.D. 135–37) returned Jerusalem to the Jews for 3 short years. The city was rebuilt and named *Aelia Capitolina* by Hadrian in 138. Roman temples were built on sacred sites, and Jews were forbidden to enter the city on penalty of death. Constantine converted Jerusalem into a Christian city. It was conquered by the Persians in 614 and by the Arab Moslems (Saracens) in 637, and remained under the latter's rule for almost 500 years. It fell into the hands of the Turks in 1076, suffered in the wars of the Christian Crusades that began in 1099, and finally, by 1517, it came under the control of the Turks and continued so for the next 400 years until it was taken by General Allenby of the British Army in 1917. It remained in the hands of the Arab Palestinians under the British Mandate until 1948, when it became the capital of the new state of Israel.

When the Jews captured Old Jerusalem in 1967, Moshe Dayan said on June 7, 1967, "We have returned to our holy places, never to part from them again." Jerusalem was united again, and the 70,000 Arabs from East Jerusalem were free to come and go as they desired. For the first time in 19 centuries the Old City was again under Jewish rule.

The city has been besieged many times and its walls built and rebuilt. It has been totally destroyed at least 5 times. The present city walls were built in 1542 during the Turkish reign of Sultan Suleiman, called "the Magnificent." In the walls there are 8 gates and 34 towers. The walls are 2½ miles in length and average 40 feet in height.

Before the recent wars, Jerusalem was divided into four quarters: Mohammedans in the east; Christians in the northwest; Armenians in the southwest; and Jews in the southeast.

Rubble has filled the streets so that one now walks several feet *above* where Jesus walked in some places.

Jerusalem is the most sacred city in the world, and the most important one in biblical history. Its role in history is out of proportion to its size and economic importance. It is sacred to Christian, Moslem, and Jew, and is the most Oriental of Israel's cities. On the streets you can see the black-bearded Hasidim (the Orthodox element in broad fur hats and black gowns), darker-skinned peoples from Morocco and Yemen, copper-faced Indians in saris, and hawk-nosed men from Iraq and Persia. It is truly a melting pot of nearly 300,000 people.

Yemin Moshe, the first modern Jewish suburb of Old Jerusalem, was founded outside the city walls in 1860. Sir Moses Montefiore led this movement.

- *Abraham paid tithes to Melchizedek here (Gen. 14:17-24).*
- *Joshua killed Jerusalem's king, who conspired against him (Josh. 10:1-27).*
- *The tribe of Judah conquered it (Judg. 1:1-8; 19:10, 11; 1 Chron. 11:4).*
- *The city was captured, strengthened, and beautified by David (2 Sam. 5:6-16; 1 Chron. 11:4-7).*
- *The ark was brought here and the city made the capital by David (2 Sam. 6:1-2; 1 Chron. 13-16; Ps. 24).*
- *David planned the temple (2 Sam. 7; 1 Chron. 17:22-27).*
- *The city was preserved from pestilence (2 Sam. 24).*
- *It was the scene of Solomon's building enterprises (1 Kings 6-9).*
- *It was sacked by Shishak and others (1 Kings 14:25-28; 2 Kings 14:13-14).*
- *It was strengthened by Uzziah (2 Chron. 26:9-15).*
- *It was saved from Assyria (2 Kings 18:13-20; Isa. 36-39; Ps. 46, 48).*
- *Jerusalem suffered from many wars (2 Kings 25; 2 Chron. 12, 25, 36; Jer. 39, 52).*
- *Jeremiah was a prophet in Jerusalem when Zedekiah was king of Judah (2 Kings 24:17, 18; 2 Chron. 36:15-16).*
- *King Zedekiah's sons were slain by the king of Babylon (2 Kings 25:7).*
- *Jerusalem was captured by Nebuchadnezzar in 598 B.C. and many of its inhabitants were taken to Babylon (2 Kings 24-25; 2 Chron. 36:15-21; Jer. 39:9-14).*
- *The word of the Lord is to come from Jerusalem (Isa. 2:3).*
- *Jerusalem was lamented by the exiles (Lam. 1-2; Pss. 130, 137).*
- *The return to Jerusalem was foretold (Isa. 35; 40; 43:1-21; 52).*
- *The walls of the city were rebuilt by Nehemiah (Neh. 2:4-20; 6:15-16; Pss. 126, 147).*
- *Jesus was here as a babe (Luke 2:22), at twelve years of age (Luke 2:41-52), and at the triumphal entry (Matt. 21:1-11).*
- *Jesus wept over it and foretold its doom (Matt. 23:37-24:51; Mark 13).*

- *Jesus was tried and crucified here (Matt. 27; Mark 15; Luke 23; John 19).*
- *The Holy Spirit descended here on the day of Pentecost (Acts 2).*

POINTS OF INTEREST

Within the Walls of Old Jerusalem

1. **TEMPLE SQUARE ON MOUNT MORIAH** *(Haram es-Sharif).* This is an area enclosed by walls measuring 913 by 1,515 by 1,586 by 1,050 feet on the sides and covering about 35 acres. Near the center of the area is the Dome of the Rock. This area was known early as the Hill of Zion, the dwelling place of God, and the exact position for the temple on Mount Moriah was indicated by God.

Solomon's temple was the first holy building here (950 B.C.). David collected the materials, but his son built the temple. The plan followed that of the tabernacle, and the ark of the covenant was placed in the temple. It was lavishly built and later burned to the ground by Nebuchadnezzar in 587 B.C. The Jews were taken captive to Babylon and the ark was lost.

After the return of the Jews from captivity, they rebuilt the temple in 516 B.C. It is called the second temple, or the temple of Zerubbabel. In comparison to Solomon's temple, the second temple was modest. In 168 B.C. Antiochus the Great desecrated the temple by stripping it of its sacred items and offering swine upon the altar. It was left desolate. Judas Maccabaeus cleansed it and restored it to use in 165 B.C.

Construction was begun on the temple of Herod about 20 B.C., to win for Herod popularity with the Jews and an eternal name for himself. He built up the walled area to 600 feet square, and the work was proceeding all during the Savior's life. It was not completely finished until A.D. 64, six years before its final destruction.

After the destruction of Herod's temple, the Romans built a temple to Jupiter on the site. Early Christians felt Mount Moriah had been cursed by God, and left it desolate, but when the Moslems captured Jerusalem in 639, the Mount became a sacred Moslem shrine. A mosque was built here first about 690, and when the Crusaders captured Jerusalem in 1099 they converted the mosque into a church. A century later, when the Crusaders were defeated by the Arabs, the Dome of the Rock again became a place sacred to the Moslems. The cross was replaced by the crescent, and although the mosque has undergone many changes it has been a Moslem shrine ever since.

- *It was here, according to tradition, that Abraham took his son, Isaac, to offer him as a sacrifice (Gen. 22:1-2).*
- *The threshing floor of Araunah the Jebusite was purchased by David to build an altar (2 Sam. 24:18-25).*
- *The exact position on Mount Moriah was indicated by God (2 Sam. 24:18-25; 1 Chron. 21:15, 18, 28; 22:1; 2 Chron. 3:1).*
- *David collected materials and his son Solomon built a temple (1 Chron. 22:14-15; 28:11-20).*

- *The temple of Solomon included the threshing floor site (2 Chron. 3:1).*
- *The temple of Solomon was burned by Nebuchadnezzar in 587 B.C. (2 Kings 25:8–9).*
- *When the Jews returned from captivity, they built the second temple. It was called the* temple of Zerubbabel *(Ezra 3:8–13; 4:23–24; 5:15; 6:15–18; Haggai).*
- *Herod started to build a temple for the Jews about 20 B.C. It was completed in A.D. 64 (John 2:20).*
- *Gabriel announced to Zacharias that Elisabeth would bear a son (Luke 1:1–25). That son was later known as John the Baptist.*
- *Jesus was circumcised and named (Luke 2:21–39).*
- *Jesus visited the temple at age 12 (Luke 2:41–50).*
- *Jesus carried out the first cleansing of the temple (John 2:12–25).*
- *Jesus healed the blind and the lame and taught the multitudes (John 8:20; Mark 12; Luke 19:47; John 8).*
- *Here it was that Jesus said, "He that is without sin among you, let him first cast a stone at her" (John 8:7).*
- *Jesus watched the widow cast in her mites (Mark 12:41–44).*
- *The second cleansing of the temple was done by Jesus (Matt. 21:12–16; Mark 11:15–18; Luke 19:45–48).*
- *Jesus taught the chief priests and elders concerning authority, the parable of the two sons, the parable of the wicked husbandman, the marriage of the king's son, rendering unto Caesar, the resurrection, marriage, the great commandment, and eight woes to the scribes and Pharisees (Matt. 21:23–23:29).*
- *Jesus foretold the destruction of the temple (Matt. 24; Mark 13; Luke 21:5–38).*
- *The veil of the temple was rent in twain from top to bottom when Jesus died (Matt. 27:51; Mark 15:38; Luke 23:45).*
- *Judas cast down pieces of silver (betrayal money) in the temple (Matt. 27:5).*
- *Peter healed the cripple at the temple and taught in the temple (Acts 3).*
- *Paul was seized in the temple and was eventually imprisoned in Rome (Acts 21:11–15).*
- *The temple is to be rebuilt (Zech. 8:7–9; Ezek. 40–48).*
- *Water is to come out from under the temple (Ezek. 47:1–2).*
- *The Lord will "suddenly come to his temple" (Mal. 3:1).*

2. **GATE OF THE TRIBES** (Sheep Gate, Jericho Gate). North of the Golden Gate is the Gate of the Tribes, which leads out of the temple site to the Lion's Gate.

- *A gate near Saint Stephen's Gate on the east side of the city was rebuilt by Nehemiah (Neh. 3:1, 32; 12:39).*

3. **THRESHING FLOOR.** Northwest of the Dome of the Rock, near the Mameluke Arch, is a threshing floor that is believed to have been owned by Araunah the Jebusite and purchased by David to build the altar.

■ *David bought the threshing floor from the Jebusite (2 Sam. 24:18–25; 1 Chron. 21:18–22:1; 2 Chron. 3:1).*

4.   **ARCADES.** Eight stairways lead to the raised platform of the Dome of the Rock, and at the head of the stairs are beautiful arcades. According to tradition, the souls of men will be weighed at the final judgment by scales that hang from the arcades.

5.   **DOME OF ASCENSION.** Northwest of the Dome of the Rock is a dome representing Mohammed's ascent into heaven. It dates back to 1200 and seems to be a copy of the Byzantine dome on the Mount of Olives which, according to tradition, marks the site of Jesus' ascension.

6.   **DOME OF THE ROCK.** This is a golden-domed octagonal-shaped mosque, built between A.D. 687 and 691 and decorated with brilliant blue, green, yellow, and white Persian tiles. The octagon is 180 feet in diameter, and each side measures 63 feet. The dome rises 108 feet from the ground, has a diameter of 78 feet, and is designed after the fourth-century shrine on the Mount of Olives which marks the site of the ascension of Jesus. It is covered with aluminum bronze alloy from Italy. The inside of the dome is decorated with stained glass windows and stones of marble. The columns within were taken from different Byzantine churches; hence their differences. Some still have Christian crosses on them. The Dome of the Rock is located on Mount Moriah, the site of Solomon's, Zerubbabel's, and Herod's temples (2 Chron. 3:1).

Many mistakenly refer to the Dome of the Rock as the Mosque of Omar. The truth is that Omar did not build the Dome. Another caliph, Abd-al-Malik, built it. However, the "true" Mosque of Omar is located in front of the Church of the Holy Sepulcher. When the Caliph Omar accepted the surrender of Jerusalem from the Christians in A.D. 638, the Patriarch of Jerusalem, Sophronius, showed Omar around the Church of the Holy Sepulcher. It was the hour of prayer, and the Patriarch suggested that Omar pray within the sacred walls. The great caliph refused, saying: "If I prayed inside the church, thou wouldst have lost it; the believers would have taken it from thee, saying, 'Omar prayed here.' " He stepped outside to make his prayer, and the true Mosque of Omar was built there. It stands to this day across the narrow street from the Church of the Holy Sepulcher. Omar did, however, build a wooden mosque on the temple square right after he captured Jerusalem. During the past 17 centuries the Dome of the Rock has been repaired many times, but it remains essentially the same as it was in 691. The Crusaders used the Dome of the Rock as a Christian church in 1099.

The Dome of the Rock is built over an immense rough-hewn rock about 40 by 52 feet, rising 7 feet above the level of the temple area. The rock is the summit of Mount Moriah. According to Jewish legend, the rock marks the center of the earth, and it was marked as such on maps. It formed the base of the Jewish altar of burnt offering. There is a hole in the rock through which blood would drain into a cave under the rock, called the "well of souls" because the souls of

Herod's Gate
83
EL HUNUD
37
Damascus Gate
79
SA'ADIEH
MU'ATHTHAIM ISSA ROAD
SHEIKH LULU
KISSAS
IBN EL-FARRAH
DAMASCUS GATE ROAD
AQABAT
AQABAT EL-MAWLAWIYEH
EL-BUSTAMI
MATHANA
ZAWI YAT
AQABAT DARWISH
EL OMARIYE
New Gate
76
EL-JABSHEH
EL KANAYES ROAD
AQABAT SHEIKH RIHAN
EL WAD
38
HAMRA
AQA SHADAD
SHEIKH HASSAN
SALAHIYA
BURJ LAQLAQ ROAD
19
BAB HUTTA ROAD
18
20
Stephen's Gate 17
EL-RUSUL ROAD
ES-SAYIDA
EL KHANQA
SUQ KHAN EZ-ZEIT
QANATER
VIA DOLOROSA
22
GHAWANIMA
AL-MUJAHIDEEN
21
2
23
ST FRANCIS
28
27
VIA DOLOROSA
24
BARQUQ RD
3
FRERES ROAD
26
25
GREEK ORTH PATR
30
29
AQABAT TAKIEH
ALA UDDIN
4
Golden Gate
DEMETRIUS
31
5
13
GREEK CATH PATR
ST GIRGES
KHAN EL-AQBAT
CHRISTIAN QUARTER ROAD
AQABAT EL SARAYA
BAB EL HADID
6
7
1
JAWALIDA
32
MURISTAN ROAD
SUQ EL-LAHHAMIN
SUQ EL-ATTARIN
EL-QIRAMI RD
KHALIDIYE
EL-WAD ROAD
9
8
Jaffa Gate
34
OMAR IBN EL-KHATTAB SQ
DAVID STREET
36
SUQ EL-KHAWAJAT
BAB EL-SILSILEH ROAD (STREET OF THE CHAIN)
33
ST MARK'S RD
SUQ EL-BAZAAR
TANUR
14
MARONITE C RD
SHONI HALACHOT
TIF'ERET YISRA'EL
MISGAV LADACH
10
11
ROAD
ASSYRIAN CONV
KARAITE
Excavations
12
ST JAMES
EL-ARMAN
QUARTER STREET (MUNADILEEN)
16
ARMENIAN ORTHODOX PATRIARCHATE ROAD
35
ARARAT
EL-MALEK
SUQ EL-HUSOR (HABAD STREET)
CHAYEI OLAM
CHAYEI OLAM
15
Dung Gate
BATEI MACHASSE STREET
N
ZION GATE SQUARE
BATEI MACHASSE
68
Zion Gate

Jerusalem
Old City

Miles   ¼   ½

1. Temple Square on Mount Moriah
2. Gate of the Tribes
3. Threshing Floor
4. Arcades
5. Dome of Ascension
6. Dome of the Rock
7. Dome of the Chain
8. Summer Pulpit
9. Sabil Quait Bey
10. Islamic Museum
11. Aksa Mosque
12. Solomon's Stables
13. Golden Gate
14. Western Wall (Wailing Wall)
15. Dung Gate
16. Jewish Quarter
17. Saint Stephen's Gate
18. Church of Saint Anne
19. Pool of Bethesda
20. Saint Anne Seminary
21. Pilate's Judgment Hall
22. Where Jesus received the cross
23. Where Jesus fell for the first time
24. Where Jesus met his mother
25. Where Simon was compelled to bear the cross
26. Where Saint Veronica wiped Jesus' face
27. Where Jesus fell the second time
28. Where Jesus consoled the women of Jerusalem
29. Where Jesus fell for the third time
30. Church of the Holy Sepulcher
31. Christian Quarter
32. Pool of Hezekiah
33. Citadel, David's Tower, and Herod's Palace
34. Jaffa Gate
35. Armenian Quarter
36. Bazaars
37. Spafford Children's Center
38. Moslem Quarter

the dead supposedly meet there every week. This cave is said to be the place where Elijah, Abraham, David, and Solomon prayed.

The Mohammedans hold this site as one of three most holy places — next to Mecca and Medina in importance. The Moslems believe that Mohammed went to heaven from this point on his winged steed, el Baruck (lightning). When he ascended, the rock began to rise with him, but an angel appeared and held the rock down. The fingerprints of the angel can be seen on the side of the rock. Footprints of Mohammed are also pointed out on the rock. A tall cupboard southeast of the rock is said to contain a few hairs from Mohammed's beard. The Moslems also believe Adam and Eve offered up sacrifices here and that Abraham took his son Ishmael (not Isaac) to offer him as a sacrifice on Mount Moriah. (Moslems keep Friday as their sabbath. They refrain from pork, alcohol, gambling, and making paintings or sculptures of human beings. They practice polygamy — up to four wives if they are rich. They pray five times a day and are monotheistic.)

■ *Abraham prepared to sacrifice his son Isaac (Gen. 22:1-22).*
■ *David bought the threshing floor of Araunah (2 Sam. 24:18-25; 1 Chron. 21).*
● *The submissiveness of Abraham's son when told he was to be sacrificed is poignantly told in the Koran (xxxvii:99-111).*

7. **DOME OF THE CHAIN.** On the east side of the Dome of the Rock is a small eighth-century treasury that resembles the Dome of the Rock. Arabs have stored their silver in the dome of this small structure over the years. Crusaders used it as a church and named it after Saint James. All 17 columns may be seen at once when viewed from any angle. It received its name from an iron chain suspended from its cupola.

8. **SUMMER PULPIT.** This structure was built by Burhan ed Din in 1456.

9. **SABIL QUAIT BEY.** This is a beautifully decorated Mameluke fountain provided by Sultan Quait Bey in 1487.

10. **ISLAMIC MUSEUM.** In the southwest corner of the temple square is a museum with Byzantine and Islamic antiquities.

11. **AKSA MOSQUE.** In the southwest corner of the temple block, over the area where Solomon built his palace, is the silver-domed Aksa Mosque. It is considered by many to have been built in honor of Saint Mary by Justinian in 536. The first mosque was built between 709 and 715 by Caliph Walid, son of Abd-al-Malik, who built the Dome of the Rock. It was built on the foundation of a Byzantine church and still follows the general lines of a basilica. It has been rebuilt many times and can presently hold 5,000 worshipers. In 1099 the Knights Templars used the mosque as their headquarters. In 1187 Saladin captured it for the Moslems.

The Aksa Mosque is used for group prayers, and the Dome of the Rock is used for individual worship. Just left of the door as you enter is the place where the Jordanian king Abdullah was murdered by the Mufti's men in 1951. Abdullah's grandson, Al-Hussein ibn Tabal, was with him. One of the bullets glanced off a medal of Al-Hussein, the future ruler of Jordan. In 1969, an Australian set fire to the mosque, which caused a stir among the Arabs.

El Aksa, mentioned in the Koran in a vision of the ascension of Mohammed, means the "distant place," with reference to its being removed from Mecca. This mosque is one of Islam's holiest shrines after Mecca and Medina.

Above: Dome of the Rock, Old Jerusalem

Left: Street scene, Old Jerusalem

The **EL KAS FOUNTAIN**, in front of the mosque, is used by Moslems for ritual washing.

12. **SOLOMON'S STABLES.** These are located under the southeast corner of the temple esplanade. When Herod the Great rebuilt the

temple area in Jerusalem, he made the temple area more expansive by building up the southeast corner of the temple grounds with a series of arches. A huge platform was built, resting on 88 pillars, 170 feet above the gorge of the Kidron. Holes in the pillars indicate that horses may have been kept here during Herod's or the Crusaders' time. Solomon had 4,000 stalls for horses and chariots. The stalls were also used by the Romans.

- *This corner of "Temple Square" is called the "pinnacle of the temple," where Satan tempted Jesus (Matt. 4:5; Luke 4:9).*

13. **GOLDEN GATE** (Eastern Gate, Gate of Mercy). This seventh-century Byzantine structure is located in the eastern wall of the temple complex. Legend has it that this will be the spot where the trumpet will sound and the dead will be raised. In the hope of postponing the day of judgment and the end of the world, therefore, the Turkish governor of Jerusalem blocked up the gate in 1530.

It is the only gate that leads directly into the temple area, and according to Jewish tradition, the Messiah will enter through this gate when he comes to Jerusalem. On the east side of the gate is a Moslem cemetery.

- *The gate is said to be built on the place where Jesus made his triumphal entry into Jerusalem (Matt. 21:8–11; Mark 11:8–11; Luke 19:35–38).*
- *This was the traditional route Jesus took to Gethsemane (Matt. 26:30, 36; Mark 14:26; Luke 22:39).*
- *Many Christians believe that at Jesus' second coming the gate will be opened (unblocked) and he will enter the city (Ezek. 44:1–3).*

14. **WESTERN WALL** (Wailing Wall, *Kotel Hama'aravi*). The Western Wall is a portion of the wall Herod built around the west side of his temple area and is the holiest shrine of the Jewish world. This part of the wall is 60 yards in length and 60 feet high. Many stones of the wall measure 30 feet by 3 feet by 5 feet. The wall is located by the western entrance to the temple area.

The wall received its name "Wailing" for at least two traditional reasons: (1) Early in the morning and late at night the wall is covered with drops of dew which legend says are tears that the wall sheds while weeping with Israel in her exile. Legend also has it that in the dead of night a white dove representing the presence of God appears and coos sadly with the mourners. Actually, a family of white doves lives in the holes of the wall. (2) The second reason is that the Jews come here to bewail the loss of their temple. Today the tears shed are tears of joy, for Israel has returned from exile and is once more able to pray at the wall. Before the six-day war of 1967, Jews were not able to visit the wall.

Jews may be seen praying at the wall at nearly any time; but Friday evening, the beginning of the Jewish Sabbath (*Shabbat*), is the time when crowds of Orthodox Jews gather to this sacred site and hold regular Shabbat services. Here one sees bits of paper (containing prayers) placed in the cracks of the walls. Torah scrolls, contained in

Golden Gate, east wall of Old Jerusalem

arks, are placed at regular intervals along the wall, and prayer shawls, phylacteries, and prayer books are available. At the north end of the wall is a large synagogue, used in the event of rain or an exceptionally hot day. Hassidim pray, "shokel," and sing at the wall, while small groups dance and sing.

Before the six-day war, the wall was hemmed in by houses or buildings and only a few could participate at it. Bulldozers of the Israeli government cleared the buildings away after the six-day war and now there is a large courtyard area that will take care of thousands of worshipers. Not only is this a place of holy worship, but here also the young recruits to the Israeli army take the oath.

Visitors at the wall have to be careful to observe Jewish customs: heads covered, no picture taking on the Shabbat, no pens or pencils in view, and so forth.

To the right of the Western Wall, on the southeast corner of the temple complex, the Israeli government has been conducting archaeological digging since 1968 under the direction of Professor Benjamin Mazar of the Hebrew University. The excavators have found items and buildings dating back to Herod's time and hope to find remains of the period of Solomon.

To the left of the Western Wall is **WILSON'S ARCH**, and under the arch the Jews gather to say their prayers. It is a section of a bridge, erected on arches, which connected the temple site with the upper city in the second temple period, or the beginning of the Christian period. It is named after a British officer who first explored the site about 1850. An excavation within the area, called Warren's Shaft, shows that the stones of Herod go down about 60 feet, or 14 layers below the present ground level to the original soil.

To the right of the Western Wall is **ROBINSON'S ARCH**. It projects from the wall. It was also a royal bridge used to get to the temple site from the upper city. It is named after Edward Robinson, an American scholar.

Herodian stairs (the **GRAND STAIRCASE**) used by pilgrims on their way to the second temple (Herod's) have recently been unearthed by archaeologists. They lead up to the two **HULDA GATES** cut into the southern wall of Herod's temple in the first century B.C. The steps are 80-100 meters (about 87-110 yards) long.

Entrance to the temple area may be made on the right side of the Western Wall through **MOORS GATE**. It is also called the Gate of the Maghrebians, as Moslems from North Africa (Maghreb) live near the gate.

■ *Perhaps this could be viewed as a "dress rehearsal" for the prediction of Jesus concerning weeping and wailing (Matt. 13:42).*

15. **DUNG GATE** (*Bab el Maghariba* ["gate of the Moors"]). South of the Wailing Wall is the Dung Gate, so named because past citizens of Jerusalem have dumped their garbage and refuse out of the city at this point.

■ *Nehemiah mentioned the gate (Neh. 2:13; 3:13-14; 12:31).*

Gethsemane

16. **JEWISH QUARTER.** Immediately west of the Wailing Wall and Dung Gate is the old Jewish Quarter, the center of Jewish life in the Holy City for 800 years, until 1948. The **SYNAGOGUE OF RAMBAN,** built on ancient ruins in A.D. 1267, is the most ancient synagogue in the old city. The **JOHANAN BEN ZAKKAI SYNAGOGUE** still stands, but other synagogues have been destroyed.

17. **SAINT STEPHEN'S GATE** (Lion's Gate, *Bab Sittna Miriam* ["Saint Mary's Gate"]). This gate is on the east side of the city. It was built with reliefs of lions on the gate's facade because of a dream of Sultan Suleiman. Through this gate the Israel army penetrated into the Old City on June 6, 1967. South of the entrance about one-half block is the **GATE OF THE TRIBES**, which opens into the temple area.

■ *This is near the place where Stephen was martyred, while Saul of Tarsus looked on (Acts 7:54–60).*
■ *Jesus spoke often of gates (Matt. 7:13–14).*

18. **CHURCH OF SAINT ANNE.** This church is one of the finest examples of Crusader construction in the Holy Land. It was built in 1100 on the site of a fifth-century Byzantine church, which had in turn been built over a cave believed to be the home of Joachim and Anne, parents of the Virgin Mary — hence the site of the "immaculate conception" (the doctrine that the Virgin Mary was kept free from original sin from the moment of her conception in Saint Anne's womb). At the right center of the church are steps leading down into the **GROTTO OF THE VIRGIN'S BIRTH.** At the end of the twelfth century the church was turned into a school of Islamic studies by Saladin. The "White Fathers," a Greek Orthodox missionary order, took possession of the site in 1878.

A **BIBLICAL MUSEUM** is located near Saint Anne's Church. It was built by the White Fathers and houses artifacts found in the area.

19. **POOL OF BETHESDA** ("house of mercy," *Beth-Zatha*). An extremely ancient pool, identified as the Pool of Bethesda, has been excavated near Saint Anne's Church by the White Fathers. Only a part of the pool has been excavated, which shows that the pool was built about 60 feet below the present ground level. The pool had porches on its sides, and according to Eusebius, was used to wash sheep before sacrificing them in the temple. A very large fifth-century Church of the Paralytic was built over the pool, but it was destroyed by the Persians in 614. The Crusaders built a chapel over the Byzantine ruins, and the apse and entrance are still visible above the remains of the excavated pool. Schick, Vincent, and Van der Vliet helped excavate the area.

■ *Jesus healed a lame man at the troubled waters of the pool of Bethesda (John 5:1–16).*

20. The **SAINT ANNE SEMINARY** is located just west of the Church of Saint Anne.

VIA DOLOROSA

The **VIA DOLOROSA** ("way of sorrow," Way of the Cross) is the

Western Wall, Old Jerusalem

traditional pathway Jesus took from Pilate's judgment hall to Calvary. Millions of pilgrims have walked this path. Each Friday at 3:00 P.M. a ceremony led by Franciscan priests is conducted along the Via Dolorosa, beginning at station number 1, and prayers are made at each of 14 **STATIONS OF THE CROSS** as originally pointed out by the Crusaders. Nine stations are based on the gospel accounts and five are based on traditions. Originally the Catholics had 36 stations. The Protestants have 7. Every Catholic who "makes" the Way of the Cross, either in Jerusalem or in his chapel at home, may receive indulgences for his efforts.

The 14 Catholic stations are as follows:

21. (1) **PILATE'S JUDGMENT HALL** (the Praetorium), where Jesus was condemned to death (Matt. 27:2–31). This is traditionally the site of Herod's great fortress, the Antonia, named after Mark Antony. Within the fortress Jesus was condemned, mocked, crowned, and given the cross to bear. The first station is now a Moslem boys' school, El Omariye, and the school stands on the ruins of the Antonia. The original staircase, known as the *Scala Santa* (the holy steps), where Pilate washed his hands, was transferred by Constantine's mother, Saint Helena, to Rome, where it is located in a church near San Giovanni in Laterano.

■ *Here was the tower of Hananeel in Nehemiah's day (Neh. 3:1; 12:39).*

22. (2) **WHERE JESUS RECEIVED THE CROSS**, at the foot of the Antonia. Located opposite the Praetorium is the Franciscan Bible School, with its **CHURCH OF THE FLAGELLATION** (Matt. 27:28–32). It stands on the traditional site where Jesus was scourged and a crown of thorns was placed on his head (John 19:1–2). A crown of thorns hangs over the sanctuary, and in the chapel an altar dedicated to Saint Paul commemorates his imprisonment in the Antonia (Acts 21–23).

The **"ECCE HOMO" ARCH**, over the Via Dolorosa, was built by Hadrian in the second century. The Latin phrase *ecce homo* means "behold the man," Pontius Pilate's declaration when he pointed to Jesus (John 19:5). Archaeological investigation has shown that the arch is a portion of a triple gateway leading to the Roman city of Aelia Capitolina. The **NOTRE DAME DE SION CONVENT DE L'ECCE HOMO** (Church of the Sisters of Zion) is located by the Gate (arch) of Ecce Homo, and tradition says it is built over the top of the "pavement" of Pilate's courtyard, where Jesus was condemned to death.

The **CHURCH OF CONDEMNATION** marks the traditional site where Pilate sentenced Jesus. Ancient plain and striated flagstones are visible on the floor of the chapel (John 19:13). They are remnants of the paved square within the Antonia Fortress called the **LITHOSTROTOS**. Symbols of games once played by Roman soldiers are still seen scratched in the surface of some of the flagstones. One of the games scratched on the floor is "Basilicus" which could have been used with Jesus as its object (Matt. 27:27–30; Mark 15:16–20). Christian tradition places the Praetorium on this square of "pavement." Large cisterns are located beneath the floor, and steps will take the visitor down into one of the cisterns.

The ECCE HOMO BASILICA, west of the striated flagstone, is called such because the northern section of Hadrian's triple triumphal gateway into Aelia Capitolina has been incorporated into the basilica, where it frames the main altar. The double guard rooms at the entrance to the Antonia are located northwest of the basilica. The sisters maintain a MUSEUM and have a picture of the "shroud of Jesus," which is of interest. A view from the roof of the convent is well worth the effort. The petite and friendly sisters will give you permission if you ask them.

Just west of the Sisters of Zion Convent is a GREEK ORTHODOX MONASTERY. In the basement may be seen remains of the road leading from the Antonia — the original Via Dolorosa. There are also caves here.

23. (3) WHERE JESUS FELL FOR THE FIRST TIME. Here the Polish Roman Catholic Biblical-Archaeological Museum and store now stand, on the corner as you turn left along El-Wad Street. From here the visitor walks about 75 feet to station number 4.

24. (4) WHERE JESUS MET HIS MOTHER. This is marked by an Armenian Catholic church, "Our Lady of the Spasm." The church is thought to stand on the site of the Byzantine church of Saint Sophia. In the crypt a sixth-century mosaic shows the outline of a pair of sandals that are said to be on the spot where Mary stood. About 75 feet from this point the visitor turns right. On the left-hand corner, station number 5 is located.

25. (5) WHERE SIMON THE CYRENIAN WAS COMPELLED TO BEAR THE CROSS OF JESUS. A small chapel, a nineteenth-century Franciscan oratory, is located here, and a stone in the wall of the chapel shows a light depression where, according to tradition, Jesus in his weariness rested his hand (Matt. 27:32; Mark 15:21; Luke 23:26). This station is located on the Via Dolorosa street. It is about 240 feet to station number 6.

26. (6) WHERE SAINT VERONICA WIPED JESUS' FACE. This is the house of the traditional Saint Veronica, who, after wiping the sweat and blood from Christ's forehead, is supposed to have found the imprint of Christ's facial features on the cloth. According to tradition, this was the woman who was cured by touching the hem of Jesus' garment. The site is served by the Little Sisters, a congregation of Greek Orthodox Catholics. Station number 7 is approximately 250 yards from station number 6.

27. (7) WHERE JESUS FELL THE SECOND TIME (up the large steps through the vaulted alley). This is located on the main market street (Suq Khan Ez-Zeit) opposite the junction with the Via Dolorosa. Two Franciscan chapels are attached to the station. One of the chapels has a red column of stone from Aelia Capitolina. This is the location of the Gate of Judgment, through which Jesus was led outside the city walls. Here a copy of the death sentence was fastened to one of the

columns of the portico. From here the visitor enters El-Khanqa Street to station number 8.

28. (8) **WHERE JESUS CONSOLED THE WOMEN OF JERUSALEM.** "Weep not for me, but weep for yourselves," Jesus said (Luke 23:27–32). The site is marked by the large Greek Orthodox Monastery of Saint Charalambos, about 100 yards up El-Khanqa Street.

29. (9) **WHERE JESUS FELL FOR THE THIRD TIME.** A Coptic monastery with a shaft of column built into the door marks the site. This site is located up an alley leading west from Suq Khan Ez-Zeit. A huge underground cistern lies within the convent. A circular cupola on a nearby terrace is the roof of Saint Helena's Chapel within the Church of the Holy Sepulcher. The Coptic Abyssinian monks and their ancient Ethiopian dialect are of interest.

30. (10-14) **CHURCH OF THE HOLY SEPULCHER.** Stations 10–14 are all inside the Church of the Holy Sepulcher. As you enter, bear to the right and go up the steps for stations 10–13. For details of stations 10–14, see the subsection "Church of the Holy Sepulcher," below.

Via Dolorosa

(10) **WHERE JESUS WAS STRIPPED OF HIS GARMENTS** and received gall to drink (Matt. 27:34; Mark 15:23–24; Luke 23:34; John 19:23). This site is located behind the Roman Catholic altar.

(11) **WHERE JESUS WAS NAILED TO THE CROSS** (Golgotha) (Matt. 27:35; Mark 15:25; Luke 23:33; John 19:18). The rock of Calvary, Catholic version, may be seen under a glass in the Greek Orthodox chapel, which is built right by the Catholic chapel.

(12) **WHERE JESUS WAS CRUCIFIED AND DIED ON THE CROSS** (Golgotha) (Matt. 27:50; Mark 15:25, 37; Luke 23:46; John 19:30). This location may be seen in the Greek Orthodox chapel under the altar, and a star marks the exact site. A split rock at the station was caused, according to tradition, by the earthquakes when Jesus was crucified.

(13) **WHERE JESUS WAS TAKEN DOWN FROM THE CROSS** and given over to Mary. The exact site, according to Catholic tradition, is under the Roman Catholic altar.

(14) **WHERE JESUS WAS LAID IN THE CHAMBER OF THE SEPULCHER** (tomb) and from there **RESURRECTED** (Matt. 27:57–61; 28:1–10; Mark 15:42–16:8; Luke 23:50–24:8; John 19:38–20:31).

CHURCH OF THE HOLY SEPULCHER

The **CHURCH OF THE HOLY SEPULCHER** (*Golgotha*, Catholic version) is the most sacred site on earth for a majority of Christians. The church is built over the traditional hill of Calvary and the tomb of Joseph of Arimathea (Catholic version). Several churches have been built on this site since Hadrian built a temple to Jupiter and Venus in A.D. 135. This he did hoping to wean the Christians from their veneration of sacred places. This temple remained until Constantine built a church in 335, which was destroyed in 614 by the Persians. Other churches were built on the site in the seventh and eleventh centuries and finally in the twelfth. The Crusaders' church of the twelfth century is still the basic outline of the present building.

Saladin defeated the Crusaders in 1187, and he allowed the Christians to use the shrine only if the key to the building remained in Moslem hands. It has been in the hands of the Arab Nuseibeh family since 1330. Various renovations and additions have been made over the years. In 1927 an earthquake left the building in a weak condition, and between 1936 and 1944 the British shored up the facade with ugly iron girders and tied up the interior with wood supports.

Since 1958 a "total restoration" has been in progress; but since the 6 communities cannot agree on "rights" and "renovations," the building is in a poor state of repair. Since reconstruction implies possession, it is difficult to get agreement on repair procedures. To have unity among those interested seems to be wishful thinking. The communities are classified as 3 "major" and 3 "minor" when it pertains to rights. Those who have major rights are the Roman, Greek Orthodox, and Armenian Orthodox Catholics. Those who have minor rights are Syrian (Jacobite), Coptic, and Abyssinian Catholics.

As you enter the building, the steps on the right lead to Latin and Greek chapels representing the tenth, eleventh, twelfth, and thirteenth stations of the Way of the Cross. They are built on the top of "Calvary," where tradition says Adam's skull was buried (*Golgotha*, "place of a skull") (Matt. 27:33; John 19:17).

The Latin Franciscan chapel on the right has stations 10, where Jesus was stripped of his garments, and 11, where Jesus was nailed to the cross. The Greek altar in the left chapel represents station 12,

where Jesus died on the cross. Between the columns which support the altar, a silver disc, with an opening in the center, covers the **SPOT WHERE THE CROSS OF JESUS STOOD**. It is possible to touch the rock of Golgotha through the hole in the center of the silver disc.

Station 13, which represents **JESUS' BODY BEING TAKEN FROM THE CROSS**, is marked by a wooden bust of the virgin Mary in a glass case. It is decorated with jewels and gold. Black discs on both sides of the altar mark the places where the **THIEVES' CROSSES STOOD**. On the right of the altar is shown the split in the rocks that were rent at the time of the crucifixion. It can also be seen in the **CHAPEL OF ADAM**, below which is housed an altar dedicated to Melchizedek. Legend has it that Adam was buried here, and that on the day of the Crucifixion the blood of the Redeemer fell upon that "first guilty head." This has given rise to the custom, mainly of the Greek Orthodox church, to represent, at the foot of the crucified, a skull and crossbones.

As the visitor leaves this chapel, to the left is the Greek sacristy, with many relics. The superior will allow people to visit the Greek treasury, which is kept in a room above "Calvary." The relics include "two big pieces of the **TRUE CROSS**," jewelled miters, vestments, and "the sword of Peter the Great of Russia."

Close to the entrance of the building is the **STONE OF UNCTION**, or "Stone of the Anointing," marking the spot where tradition indicates Jesus' body was prepared for burial.

The Holy Sepulcher, where Jesus was laid, is the fourteenth station of the Way of the Cross. This tomb, with a Muscovite cupola, is entered through a small Chapel of the Angel, which has a fragment of the **STONE UPON WHICH ANGELS SAT** after they had rolled it back from the entrance (Mark 16:6). The Holy Sepulcher has a marble slab raised above the floor, marking the **PLACE WHERE JESUS WAS BURIED**. According to tradition, the original stone slab is beneath the one that is displayed. Behind the edicule is a small Coptic chapel, where the rock of the Holy Sepulcher can be seen and touched. Behind the Holy Sepulcher is the chapel of the Syrian Jacobites in a dark chamber. A narrow opening leads to rock-hewn empty tomb shafts. This is a part of the traditional **TOMB OF JOSEPH OF ARIMATHEA**.

In the Greek cathedral, a large stone **CHALICE** on the Crusader floor is supposed to mark the **CENTER OF THE EARTH**. A flight of steps leads down to the **CHAPEL OF SAINT HELENA**, then on down to the Latin **CHAPEL OF THE FINDING OF THE CROSS**, where, according to tradition, the crosses of Jesus and the thieves were found by Saint Helena in 327 at the bottom of an unused cistern cut into Calvary. On the north side of the church is the **CHAPEL OF THE APPARITION**, commemorating Jesus' appearance to the Virgin. It contains a reddish **COLUMN OF THE FLAGELLATION**. Sword and spurs of the first Crusader king Godfrey of Bouillon are on display in the sacristy east of the chapel.

OTHER SITES IN OLD JERUSALEM

31. **CHRISTIAN QUARTER.** Surrounding the Church of the Holy Sepulcher, in the northwest section of the Old City of Jerusalem, is

the Christian Quarter. The Lutheran **REDEEMER'S CHURCH** was built in 1898 over the gateway and cloister of the Crusader Church of Saint Mary Latina. A magnificent view of the city may be had from the spire of the church. South of the Holy Sepulcher Church is an area known as *Muristan,* which means "hospice" in Arabic. Here thousands of pilgrims stayed during Crusader times. The **CHURCH OF SAINT JOHN THE BAPTIST** was built in the eleventh century. Excavations on the site have disclosed a reliquary which contains a fragment of the "true cross."

The **GREEK PATRIARCHATE** is a large building embracing Crusader churches. The visitor can walk along the roof of the Patriarchate to the cupola of the Holy Sepulcher Church, where, in Saint Thecla's chapel, there is a stone coffin which tradition says belonged to Mariamne, Herod's murdered wife. A nearby small ladder gives access to the galleries over the rotunda, where the edicule over the Holy Sepulcher can be seen.

The **MOSQUE OF OMAR** is built south of the entrance to the Church of the Holy Sepulcher. The minaret dates back to 1465 and commemorates Omar's prayer that he gave outside the entrance of the Church of the Holy Sepulcher. The **MOSQUE OF KHANQA** is north of the Church of the Holy Sepulcher. Many schools, monasteries, churches, and souvenir shops are located within the Christian Quarter.

32. **POOL OF HEZEKIAH.** Southeast of the Church of the Holy Sepulcher, in the Muristan quarter of the Old City, is the large, dry Pool of Hezekiah, or Bath of the Patriarchs. It can be seen by going through one of the shops on the west side of Christian Street, or on the north side of David Street.

33. **CITADEL, DAVID'S TOWER,** and **HEROD'S PALACE.** The **CITADEL** was built by Herod. It stands alongside Jaffa Gate and was the only part of the walls of Jerusalem to remain standing after Titus and the Roman army destroyed the city in A.D. 70. It has always been an important point for the various battles of Jerusalem and was a scene of fierce fighting during the Israeli-Arab conflict of 1948. The present citadel stands on Crusader foundations, but most of the citadel was built by Suleiman the Magnificent in 1540. Only part of the moat that surrounded the citadel is visible today.

The **TOWER OF DAVID** is the name given to the tower on the right of the Citadel's entrance. The interior of the tower has special exhibits. During the summer months a sound and light production titled "A Stone in David's Tower" is given at the tower.

HEROD'S PALACE was located south of the citadel where the police barracks now stands.

■ *Wise men from the east came to Jerusalem and asked Herod (the Great), "Where is he that is born King of the Jews?" (Matt. 2:1-2).*

■ *Pilate sent Jesus to Herod (Antipas) to be accused (Luke 23:7-12).*

34. **JAFFA GATE** (*Bab el Khalil* ["gate of the friend"]). The road from Jerusalem to Jaffa on the Mediterranean Sea starts here. It is also the

road to Hebron; and as it makes its way through the New Jerusalem it is the main thoroughfare. It was the first street built outside the old city walls (1870). The gate is located by the Citadel of David. General Allenby entered this gate in 1917 in his march through Palestine after defeating the Turks. After the six-day war in 1967 the Jaffa Gate was restored by funds collected from South African Jewry. An Arab inscription over the entrance reads "There is no God but Allah and Abraham is his friend."

35. **ARMENIAN QUARTER.** The **SAINT JAMES CATHEDRAL**, in the southwestern part of Old Jerusalem, is the most famous site in the Armenian Quarter. It is named after James the apostle, who, according to tradition, was flung from the pinnacle of the temple into the Kidron Valley and then stoned and buried. His bones were transferred to the church, and tradition says they are under the main altar.

The **ARMENIAN MUSEUM** has displays of the Patriarchate's priceless treasures.

The traditional site of the **HOUSE OF ANNAS**, the ex–high priest and father-in-law of the high priest Caiaphas in Jesus' day, is located in the southern portion of the Armenian Quarter. By the northeastern corner of the chapel is an olive tree to which, according to tradition, Jesus was tied while waiting to see Annas.

- *Jesus was compelled to appear before the high priest Caiaphas (John 18:13–14).*
- *Peter and John were brought before the council composed of Annas, Caiaphas, and other high priests (Acts 4:5–19).*

36. **BAZAARS.** Many small, narrow streets have their bazaars. For one you will always remember, turn down Suq el-Lahhamin (Butcher Street); it is to the left of the Holy Sepulcher, at the junction with Dabbage Road. Don't be alarmed at the begging of little children. The cry for "baksheesh" is a respectable pastime in the Moslem world. They help Allah by making it possible for Moslems to give alms. Don't be taken in by "official guides" along the way — who want "baksheesh" also.

The Arabs call a market a "souk" (*suq*). The three covered "souks" at the end of Bab el-Khan Zeit date from Crusader times.

37. **SPAFFORD CHILDREN'S CENTER.** Just inside the walls of Jerusalem, on a hill that originally extended north to include the hill designated by the Protestants as Golgotha, is a building used as a center to train young mothers in child care.

The Center is operated under the direction of two granddaughters of Horatio Gates Spafford. He brought his family from Illinois, USA, in 1881 after tragedy took the lives of four daughters at sea and a son died. They came to find peace and give themselves to God in the Holy Land.

When World War II was waging, Horatio's daughter, Bertha Spafford Vester, and her husband, with other members of the American colony, offered their services to both British and Turkish forces by operating a hospital and dishing out food rations. Bertha spent her long life in the charitable hospital service. She saw three wars in Jerusalem — her home.

In 1971 the hospital became a center of education and child care.

38. **MOSLEM QUARTER.** In the northeast section of Old Jerusalem is the Moslem Quarter.

Immediately East of the Old City

39. **MOUNT SCOPUS** ("to look over," *Har Hatsofim*). On the north end of the Mount of Olives and connected to it is Mount Scopus. (*Skopeo* is Greek and means "to watch.") It has played a decisive role in the many battles that have been fought for the Holy City since time immemorial. The Roman legions of Titus camped here in A.D. 70, the Crusaders in 1099, the British in 1917, and the Arabs in 1948 and 1967.

40. **BRITISH WAR CEMETERY.** This is the final resting place of soldiers who fell in the area during the battles of World War I. A Jewish section is on the left.

41. **FORMER HADASSAH HOSPITAL.** Near the cemetery are the buildings of the Hadassah Hospital before it was moved to its present location near Ein Karem. It was built in 1939 and was used as a medical school.

42. **HEBREW UNIVERSITY ON MOUNT SCOPUS.** The cornerstone of the Hebrew University was laid on Mount Scopus in 1918, and the university opened in 1925 with Lord Balfour present. The complex received a "demilitarized" status in 1948, and for 19 years it was controlled by the Jews. When access to Mount Scopus was so difficult, the Jews built a campus at Givat Ram in western Jerusalem. In 1968 foundation stones were again laid for a new university city on Mount Scopus. The faculty of law and science will be housed there first, and later the humanities and social sciences. The university on Scopus is to handle 10,000 students.

43. **TRUMAN RESEARCH CENTER.** Named after Harry S. Truman, president of the United States, this futuristic edifice was built as a study center for international scholars, scientists, and philosophers engaged in research to advance peace and prosperity among all nations. It houses a 350-seat auditorium, 2 seminar rooms, and a 50,000-volume library, including the complete library of philosopher Martin Buber.

44. **AMPHITHEATER.** North of the Truman Research Center is an amphitheater overlooking the Judean wilderness. It has a beautiful setting and good acoustics. It is used for lectures, concerts, recitals, and other such events.

45. **AUGUSTA VICTORIA HOSPITAL.** In 1910 a German hospice and sanatorium was opened and named after Kaiser Wilhelm's wife. It is built between Mount Scopus and the Mount of Olives. Its high, square tower is a landmark, but removed from its natural setting on

the Rhine. It served as a government house for the British until 1927, when it was badly damaged in an earthquake.

MOUNT OF OLIVES

46.   **MOUNT OF OLIVES** (Olivet).* The Mount of Olives, holy to three great faiths, is separated from Old Jerusalem by the Kidron Valley. It has four eminences extending from north to south:

47.   (1) The **NORTHERNMOST** is supposed to be the hill where the two **ANGELS ADDRESSED THE DISCIPLES** after the Ascension and said, "Ye men of Galilee, why stand ye gazing up into heaven?" (Acts 1:11). *Viri Galilaei* is the name given to a wooded compound on the hill which belongs to the Greeks. A modern chapel and a Byzantine chapel mark the site.

48.   (2) The **SECOND EMINENCE** is supposed to be the hill where **JESUS ASCENDED INTO HEAVEN** (Luke 24:50–53; Acts 1:9–12). (Acts 1:12 is at variance with Luke 24:50. Luke indicates Bethany is the site.) The **CHURCH OF THE ASCENSION** was built on this site before A.D. 387, and in 1187 the church was converted into a mosque. Only one small domed building remains of the original. Within this small octagonal building are, according to tradition, the **FOOTPRINTS LEFT BY JESUS** just before he ascended into heaven. This is a Christian shrine under Moslem control. The Moslems revere Jesus as a prophet and believe in the doctrine of the Ascension. Jesus, they believe, will raise Mohammed on resurrection day. A panoramic view of the area can be seen from the roof. The Church of the Ascension seems to have been the main inspiration for the architecture of the Dome of the Rock Mosque.

---

*Many Christians anticipate that the Mount of Olives will have a definite part in the final "wind-up" scenes of the last days: Armageddon, the two witnesses, the appearance of Jesus on the Mount of Olives, the "touching down" scene, and the beginning of the Messiah's reign. They believe that the Mount of Olives will cleave in the midst when Jesus comes (Zech. 14:4-5) and that all believers will come into the valley and the Jews will feel his wounds and accept him as their Messiah (Mal. 3:2).

Scattering of Israel Prophesied

Ca. 2000 B.C.   The covenant was made with Abraham (Gen. 12:1-3). It was also established with Isaac (Gen. 17:19-21; 26:2-5) and passed down through Jacob, Joseph, Moses, and Joshua (Gen. 25:23, 32:28; 35:9-12; Exod. 3:7-10; 23:30; Josh. 13:6; 15).

Ca. 1700 B.C.   Joseph was promised he would be a fruitful bough whose branches would run "over the wall" (Gen. 49:22).

Ca. 1500 B.C.   Israel was to be scattered among the heathen (Lev. 26:27-33; Deut. 4:27; 28:25, 36-37, 64).

Ca. 900 B.C.   Israel was to be scattered beyond the river (1 Kings 14:15).

Ca. 600-500 B.C.   Jeremiah, Ezekiel, Amos, and Zechariah all prophesied concerning the scattering (Jer. 7:15; 13:19; 15:1; 24:8-10; Ezek. 22:15; Amos 9:9; Zech. 10:9).

Ca. A.D. 34.   Luke spoke of the scattering (Luke 21:24).

Jerusalem
East of the Old City

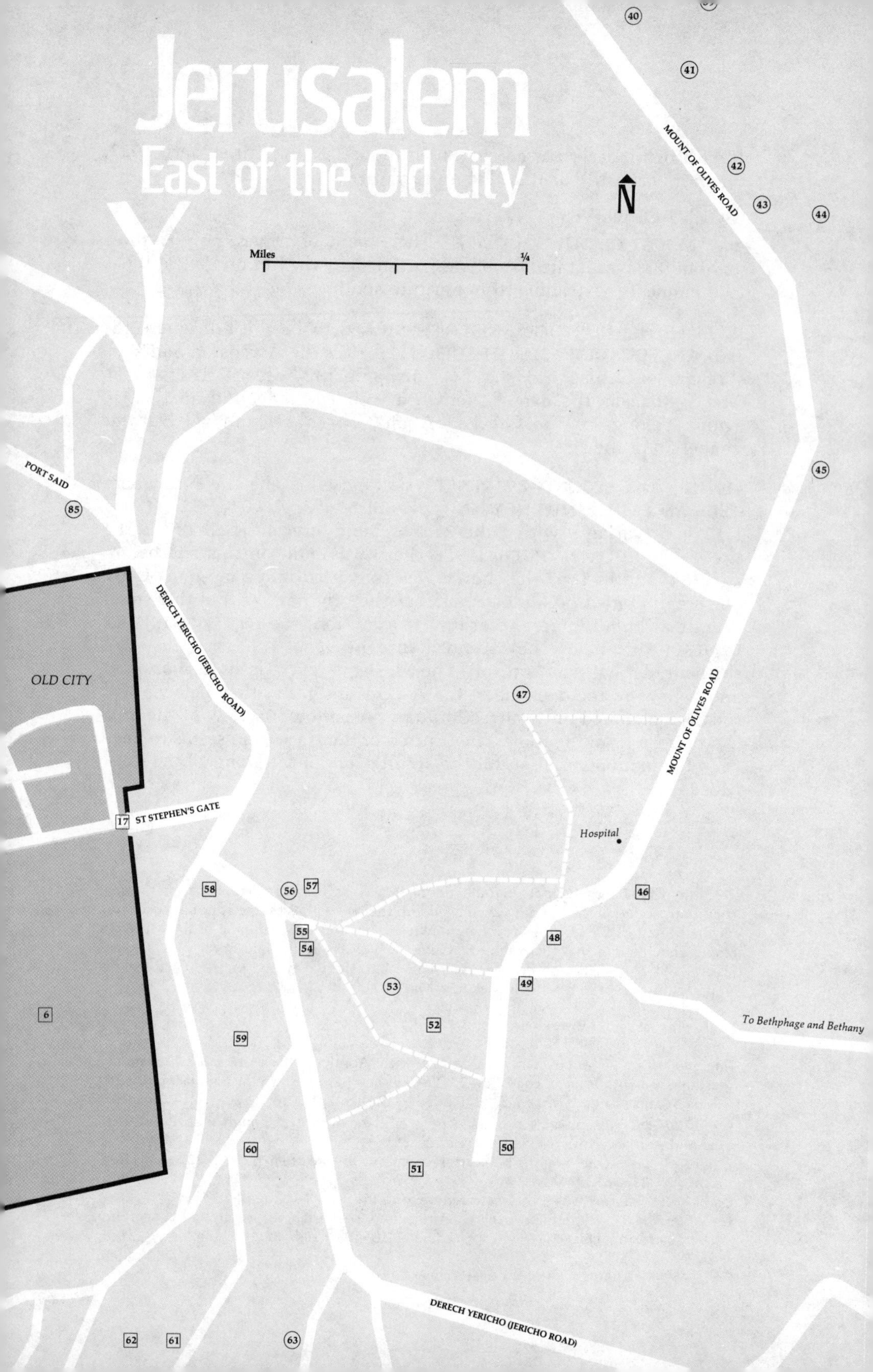

N̂

Miles

1/4

40

41

42

43

44

45

MOUNT OF OLIVES ROAD

MOUNT OF OLIVES ROAD

PORT SAID

85

OLD CITY

DERECH YERICHO (JERICHO ROAD)

17 ST STEPHEN'S GATE

47

Hospital

46

58

56 57

55
54

48

53

49

6

52

59

To Bethphage and Bethany

60

50

51

62   61

63

DERECH YERICHO (JERICHO ROAD)

39. Mount Scopus
40. British War Cemetery
41. Former Hadassah Hospital
42. Hebrew University on Mount Scopus
43. Truman Research Center
44. Amphitheater
45. Augusta Victoria Hospital
46. Mount of Olives
47. Hill where angels addressed the disciples after the Ascension
48. Hill where Jesus ascended into heaven
49. Church of the Pater Noster
50. Mount of Offense
51. Jewish cemetery
52. Dominus Flevit
53. Russian Orthodox Church of Mary Magdalene
54. Basilica of the Agony (Church of all Nations)
55. Gethsemane
56. Tomb of the Virgin Mary
57. Grotto of Gethsemane
58. Church of Saint Stephen
59. Kidron Valley
60. Absalom's Pillar, Tomb of Jehoshaphat, Grotto of Saint James, and Tomb of Zechariah
61. Gihon Spring
62. Hill Ophel
63. Royal Tomb of Shebna
64. Mount of Offense and Mount of Evil Counsel
65. Pool of Siloam and Hezekiah's Tunnel
66. Hinnom Valley
67. Potter's Field
    (For sites 64–67, see map on page 250.)

The **RUSSIAN COMPOUND** was built in the late nineteenth century. At the southeast corner of the church is a **STONE** where, according to tradition, the **VIRGIN MARY STOOD** at the time of the Ascension, which, according to the Russians, took place where the tower is. The **TOWER OF ASCENSION** has 6 stories and 214 steps, and is the most noticeable landmark on the Mount of Olives. The view from the tower is one of the most beautiful in Jerusalem and well worth the climb.

East of the main church is another **CHURCH WITH A MOSAIC** over a hollow, where, according to a document on the wall, the **HEAD OF JOHN THE BAPTIST WAS DISCOVERED** at the time of Constantine. A visit at 4:30 P.M. will make it possible to hear the nuns sing Vespers in the beautiful Russian chant.

Above: Mount of
Olives, with the Church
of All Nations and
Garden of Gethsemane
in the foreground

Left: Church of the
Ascension, Mount of
Olives

49. (3) On the **THIRD EMINENCE** the **CHURCH OF THE PATER NOSTER** ("our father") stands on the traditional spot where Jesus instructed his disciples on the Lord's Prayer (Matt. 6:9–15; Luke 11:1–4). (Since the instructions on the Lord's Prayer were given as a part of the Sermon on the Mount, this site is questionable.) The original church was built by Saint Helena in 333 and later destroyed by the Persians. Tiles along the walls of the cloister are inscribed with the Lord's Prayer in 44 languages.

The **CARMELITE CONVENT** and **BASILICA OF THE SACRED HEART** are on a hill adjoining the Church of the Pater Noster.

The **TOMB OF THE PROPHETS HAGGAI, MALACHI, AND ZECHARIAH** is located southwest of the Church of the Pater Noster. It contains 36 burial niches.

50. (4) The **SOUTHEAST EMINENCE** is called by some the **MOUNT OF OFFENSE** because it is supposed to be the "Mount of Corruption" on which Solomon erected the high places for the worship of strange gods (1 Kings 11:7). Some believe Solomon erected the high places on the mount south of the Jericho Road.

- *David fled over the Mount of Olives from Absalom (2 Sam. 15:30; 16:14).*
- *Jesus taught concerning the destruction of Jerusalem, his second coming, and the end of the world (Matt. 24–25; Mark 13).*

Gathering of Israel Prophesied

Ca. 1400 B.C. Moses knew of the gathering (Lev. 26:44–45; Deut. 30:1–5).

Ca. 800 B.C. Amos and Micah knew (Amos 9:14–15; Mic. 4:1–2).

Ca. 740–701 B.C. Isaiah and Nehemiah prophesied of the gathering (Neh. 1:8–9; Isa. 5:25–30; 11:11–12; 14:1; 35:4; 43:4–6; 54:7–8; 61:4).

Ca. 600 B.C. Jeremiah prophesied of the gathering (Jer. 3:12–18; 12:14–15; 16:14–16; 23:2–8; 30:3; 31:7–12; 32:37; 33:7–11; 50:4–5).

Ca. 575 B.C. Ezekiel knew (Ezek. 11:16–18; 20:34–42; 28:25–26; 34:11–16; 37:21–27).

Ca. A.D. 34. Matthew and John told of the gathering (Matt. 24:31; John 10:16).

Prophecies to Be Fulfilled
Before Jesus Comes to the Mount of Olives

(1) A new temple is to be rebuilt by believers (Zech. 8:7–9; Ezek. 40–47).

(2) Water is to come out from under the temple (Ezek. 47:1–2).

(3) The waters of the Dead Sea are to be healed (Ezek. 47:8–11).

(4) Gold and silver of nations are to be used (Jer. 32:41, 43–44; Zech. 14:14; Isa. 60:9–14).

(5) The promised land is to be fruitful again (Amos 9:14–15; Ezek. 36:33–36; Isa. 35:1–2, 6–7).

(6) Israel is to be attacked and delivered (Zech. 12:6–10; Isa. 54:15–17). "They shall rule over their oppressors" (Isa. 14:2).

(7) A king named David is to lead Israel (Ezek. 34:23–24; 37:21–25).

(8) The nations of the earth are to battle Judah and Judah is to be smitten (Zech. 14:2).

(9) The Savior is to appear to the descendants of Judah (Zech. 12:10).

(10) Two great world capitals are to be established in Zion and Jerusalem (Isa. 2:2–3).

(11) Two prophets are to be raised up to the Jewish nation in the last days, at the time of the restoration, and are to prophesy to the Jews after they are gathered and have built the city of Jerusalem in the land of their fathers (Rev. 11:3–12).

- *Jesus taught the parable of the ten virgins and the talents, and about the last judgment: "Inasmuch as ye have done it unto one of the least of these my brethren . . ." (Matt. 25).*
- *The Mount of Olives was the scene of Christ's triumphal entry (Luke 19:29-44).*
- *The fig tree was cursed (Matt. 21:17-22; Mark 11:12-14, 20-26).*
- *Here Jesus wept over Jerusalem (Matt. 27:37-39; Luke 19:37-44).*
- *This was the place of the ascension of Jesus and the appearance of the angels to the apostles (Matt. 28:16-20; Luke 24:50-53; Acts 1:4-12).*
- *At the Lord's coming the Mount of Olives will split in two (Zech. 14:4). Into the valley made by the split the Jews will flee and meet the Lord and his saints (Mal. 3:2; Zech. 14:3-9).*
- *The "touching-down scene" is mentioned in the New Testament (1 Thess. 4:16-18; Rev. 19:7).*

51. **JEWISH CEMETERY.** On the Mount of Olives is the largest and oldest Jewish cemetery in the world. It dates to biblical times. Many a Jew has made a pilgrimage to Jerusalem in order to live, die, and then be buried in this cemetery. Jews were anguished over the building of the Intercontinental Hotel on the eastern perimeters of the cemetery. They were shocked when the Jordanians used tombstones to pave army barracks. The Jews believe that the resurrection will take place here.

- *The final judgment and resurrection are expected to take place here (Ezek. 37:1-14).*
- *The Lord will stand upon the Mount of Olives (Zech. 14:4).*

OTHER CHURCHES ON THE MOUNT OF OLIVES:

52. **DOMINUS FLEVIT** ("the Lord wept"). This Franciscan church is the only church in the area with contemporary church lines. It is located down the path on which Jesus came to Jerusalem and honors the spot where, according to tradition, Jesus wept over Jerusalem (Matt. 23:37-39; Luke 19:37-44).

53. The **RUSSIAN ORTHODOX CHURCH OF MARY MAGDALENE** is marked by 7 striking onion-shaped spires in Slavic style. It was built in 1888 by the Czar of Russia, Alexander III, and is maintained by the White Russian nuns. It is located next to the **RUSSIAN ARCHAEO- LOGICAL MUSEUM.**

54. The **BASILICA OF THE AGONY (CHURCH OF ALL NATIONS)** adjoins the Garden of Gethsemane. This Roman Catholic basilica is a Byzantine-style chapel, built in 1924 on the site of a Crusader church. It houses the **ROCK OF AGONY**, where Jesus is supposed to have prayed. Six-teen nations contributed to the construction of the basilica, including the United States, whose seal is located in the southwest area of the ceiling. The facade pictures Jesus weeping over the fate of the Holy City.

Kidron Valley Area

55. **GETHSEMANE** ("wine and oil press"). The present Garden of Gethsemane is maintained by the Franciscans and contains eight ancient olive trees, which botanists claim may be 3,000 years old. Josephus tells us Titus cut down all the trees in the environs of Jerusalem in A.D. 70. Whether these are trees which somehow escaped destruction or whether they grew later from the roots of previous trees is difficult to say. The Church of All Nations, discussed above (site 54), stands here.

■ *Gethsemane was a garden across the Kidron from Jerusalem (John 18:1).*
■ *It lay across the Kidron from the Golden Gate (Luke 22:39).*
■ *Here Jesus took upon himself the sins of all mankind (Matt. 26: 36–56; Mark 14:32–49; Luke 22:39–53).*
■ *This was the place of Jesus' betrayal and arrest (Matt. 26:47–56; John 18:1–13).*

56. The **TOMB OF THE VIRGIN MARY** (Church of the Assumption of Mary) is a deep underground chamber that supposedly houses the tombs of Mary and Joseph. Forty-seven steps lead down into the darkened tomb. Some believe this is the place of Mary's ascension ("assumption") into heaven. This doctrine was defined as a Catholic article of faith on November 1, 1950. The Greek Orthodox church has possession of the shrine, which has suffered from floods three times since 1948. The church dates back to the Crusader period, but was built on a sanctuary site dating from the fifth century. Mary's tomb is located in the bottom to the right, and halfway up the staircase are two chapels: the one on the left contains the tomb of Joachim and Anne, Mary's parents; the one on the right is built over the tomb of Joseph, Mary's spouse. Beneath the church is a large cistern supported by 146 columns.

57. **GROTTO OF GETHSEMANE** (Cavern of Agony). A few steps east of the Church of the Assumption of Mary is a grotto maintained in its primitive form. Tradition has it that Jesus and his disciples prayed here. The grotto has belonged to the Franciscans since 1392.

■ *Traditionally, this is where Jesus prayed in the Garden of Gethsemane (Luke 22:41).*

58. **CHURCH OF SAINT STEPHEN.** The modern Greek Orthodox Church of Saint Stephen is located northwest of the Garden of Gethsemane. This is the traditional site where Stephen was stoned to death (Acts 8:58–59). Directly across the road to the north is an abstract iron memorial to Jewish paratroopers who fell here in June of 1967.

59. **KIDRON VALLEY** (Valley of Jehoshaphat). This is a wadi nearly 3 miles long lying between Jerusalem and the Mount of Olives. It is usually dry unless fed by rainfall. Opposite the temple area, the brook Kidron ("turbid") is 400 feet below the temple platform.

Further south, it runs between the villages of Silwan on the east and Ophel on the west.

From Israelite times, the valley has been a favorite burial site. Some call it the *Valley of Kings* because they believe David, Solomon, and other kings of Israel were buried here. The Moslems think it will be a place of judgment. Joel mentioned that judgments will take place in the Valley of Jehoshaphat (Joel 3:2, 12), and Moslems have a similar belief. Mohammed will sit on a pillow by the Dome of the Rock. A wire will be stretched from there to the Mount of Olives, where Jesus will be. All mankind will walk across the wire. The righteous will reach the other end safely, while the wicked drop off into the Valley of Jehoshaphat and perish.

60. **ABSALOM'S PILLAR, TOMB OF JEHOSHAPHAT, GROTTO OF SAINT JAMES, TOMB OF ZECHARIAH.** In the Kidron Valley, opposite the southern portion of the temple area, are four stone tombs. The first is a prominent stone pillar known as **ABSALOM'S PILLAR** (see 2 Sam. 18:18), or *Absalom's tomb*; but his body is probably not buried there because it is generally accepted that the stone structure was built during the period of the second temple (700 years after Absalom's death). To the left rear of Absalom's tomb is the **TOMB OF JEHO-SHAPHAT**. A beautiful frieze of acanthus leaves is carved over the entrance.

The **GROTTO OF SAINT JAMES** is a tomb hewn out of rock, to the right of the pillar of Absalom. According to tradition, the apostle

Olive tree, Garden of Gethsemane

James hid here at the time of Jesus' arrest. Hebrew tradition indicates this is the **TOMB OF THE PRIESTLY HOUSE OF HEZIR** (Neh. 10:20). Uzziah (Azariah) allegedly spent time here when he had leprosy (2 Kings 15:5).

To the right of Saint James Grotto is the first-century **TOMB OF THE ANCIENT PROPHET ZECHARIAH**. It has a top built like a pyramid, with three pillars carved on the side of the rock. Some believe this is the tomb of Zacharias, the father of John the Baptist, however.

It was customary for the Jews to whitewash their tombs each year, and it has been suggested that Jesus was referring to these very tombs in the Valley of Kidron when he accused the hypocritical Pharisees of being like whited sepulchers — beautiful on the outside but inside full of dead men's bones (Matt. 23:27).

- *Burying Israelites in the Kidron Valley was a custom (2 Kings 23:6; 2 Chron. 34:4).*
- *David fled over the Kidron from Absalom (2 Sam. 15:13-23).*
- *Josiah cast out the idols (2 Kings 23:4-14).*
- *Perhaps this was the scene of Ezekiel's vision of the dry bones (Ezek. 37:1-14).*
- *It is closely associated with the great day of judgment (Joel 3:2, 12).*
- *Jesus crossed the Kidron to Gethsemane (John 18:1).*
- *Many saints were resurrected and appeared in the Holy City (Matt. 27:52-53).*
- *Perhaps Jesus referred to the tombs in the Kidron Valley when he likened the Pharisees to whited sepulchers (Matt. 23:27).*

61. **GIHON SPRING** ("gushing spring," Fountain of the Virgin). This spring is located in the Kidron Valley on the west side of the road in the Arab village of Silwan. It was one of Jerusalem's earliest sources of water, and it supplies the water for Hezekiah's tunnel and the Pool of Siloam. It is called the Fountain of the Virgin because legend tells of Mary washing Jesus' clothes with water from this spring.

- *It was at this sacred spring that Solomon received his coronation (1 Kings 1:33, 38, 45).*
- *This was the spring that supplied water for Hezekiah's tunnel (2 Chron. 32:30).*

62. **HILL OPHEL** ("the high place"). The southern ridge of Mount Moriah extends from Mount Moriah to the Pool of Siloam. The City of David was located on this small ridge, and excavations have shown Jebusite and Solomonic walls. In the Kidron Valley, south of the Hill Ophel, are the green trees of the ancient **KINGS' GARDEN**.

63. **ROYAL TOMB OF SHEBNA** ("youthfulness"). In Silwan (the ancient Siloam), an Arab village on the eastern side of the Kidron Valley, is a rock-cut chamber tomb believed to have been built by Sheban-yahu, the royal steward of Hezekiah, king of Judah, who was rebuked by Isaiah for having built such an elaborate tomb in his lifetime. This tomb was discovered by a French archaeologist, Charles Clermont-Ganneau, in 1870. The text above the door, dating from the early seventh century B.C., was deciphered in 1953 by Professor N. Avigad, an Israeli scholar. It is the first known text of a Hebrew sepulchral inscription from the preexilic period.

- *Isaiah rebuked Shebna for building his elaborate tomb (Isa. 22: 15-19).*

64. **MOUNT OF OFFENSE** and **MOUNT OF EVIL COUNSEL**. East of the Pool of Siloam is the Arab village of Silwan. Behind the village rises

the traditional Mount of Offense, or Mount of Scandal — so called because Solomon erected on this mount altars to the pagan gods of his foreign wives. Some believe this site was on the Mount of Olives.

The Mount of Evil Counsel is south of the ancient city of David. A legend indicates that the high priest Caiaphas had a house there and conspired against Jesus. The Jewish village of Abu Tor and United Nations buildings are located on the mount.

- Solomon erected altars to pagan gods on the Mount of Offense (1 Kings 11:7-8).
- Tradition says that Judas hanged himself on the Mount of Evil Counsel (Matt. 27:5; Acts 1:18).

65. **POOL OF SILOAM** ("sending forth") and **HEZEKIAH'S TUNNEL** (Siloam Tunnel). Siloam's Pool is located on the south end of the Hill Ophel, site of the City of David, near the point where the Valley of Hinnom and Tyropoeon Valley (Cheese Maker's Valley) runs into the Kidron Valley. It was originally constructed by King Hezekiah as a reservoir at the southern end of the water tunnel. In the fifth century a church was built over the pool, but it was destroyed by the Persians in 614 and never rebuilt. A small modern mosque marks the site.

In the time of David, Jerusalem's main supply of water was the Gihon Spring, just outside the wall in the Kidron Valley. Lying just below the hill of Ophel, it was thus exposed to an attacking enemy. In 701 B.C. Sennacherib, king of Assyria, invaded Palestine and was soon to besiege Jerusalem (2 Kings 18:17-21). However, Isaiah prophesied that the king of Assyria would not come against the city or shoot an arrow against it (2 Kings 19:32-33). The *Taylor Prism*, found at Nineveh, tells of Sennacherib's invasion into Palestine and his failure to capture Jerusalem.

In order to protect the water supply from the invading Assyrians, Hezekiah had a 1,777-foot conduit (1,090 feet in a direct line) cut through the solid rock to carry the waters of Gihon Spring to the Pool of Siloam. The Gihon Spring was then covered over from the outside. It was probably completed just before Sennacherib besieged Jerusalem, but after Sargon had captured Samaria in 721 B.C.

Workmen began on each end and accomplished a remarkable engineering feat to meet in the middle within 4 feet of each other. The tunnel averages 6 feet high. In 1880 a boy discovered the *Siloam Inscription* 5 feet from the floor and 19 feet from the Siloam end of the tunnel. The inscription told of "the meeting of workmen." The stone is located in the Archaeological Museum at Istanbul. The inscription in early Hebrew script said: "The completing of the piercing through. While the stone cutters were swinging their axes, each toward his fellow, and while there were yet three cubits to be pierced through, there was heard the voice of a man . . . then ran the waters from the spring to the pool for twelve hundred cubits, and a hundred cubits was the height of the rock above the head of the stone cutters."

The Taylor Prism said that "considerable preparations" had been made by the Jews to "strengthen Jerusalem."

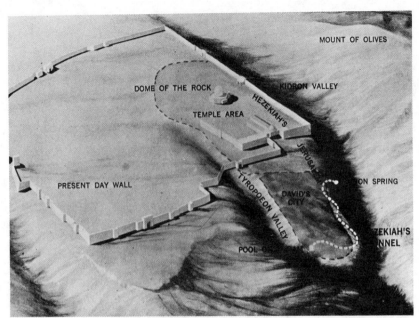

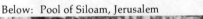

Above: Map of Hezekiah's Tunnel, Jerusalem
Below: Pool of Siloam, Jerusalem

- *Ophel is the hill where Jotham repaired the city wall (2 Chron. 27:3).*
- *Manasseh enclosed the hill in a high wall (2 Chron. 33:14).*
- *It is believed to be the same as the "pool of Siloah by the king's garden" (Neh. 3:15) and the "waters of Shiloah that go softly" (Isa. 8:6).*
- *Hezekiah's Tunnel is mentioned in the Old Testament (2 Kings 20:20; 2 Chron. 32:2-4, 30; Isa. 36-37; 22:11).*
- *Isaiah prophesied that the king of Assyria would not come against Jerusalem (2 Kings 19:32-33).*
- *The angel of God smote the Assyrian army (2 Kings 19:35).*
- *A tower fell at Siloam, killing 18 people (Luke 13:4).*
- *Jesus healed a blind man, who washed in this pool (John 9:7-11).*

66. **HINNOM VALLEY** (Valley of Slaughter, *Gehenna*, *Wadi er-Rababi*). The Hinnom Valley runs from the west at the southern foot of Mount Zion and joins the Kidron Valley. It formed part of the boundary between Judah and Benjamin. Here perpetual fires are said to have been kept burning to consume the rubbish of the city. It was a place of defilement, and the New Testament likens it to eternal punishment. A small bridge with an ornate drinking fountain erected by Suleiman the Magnificent (1520-66) traverses the Valley of Hinnom.

- *This was the boundary between Judah and Benjamin (Josh. 15:8; 18:16).*
- *It was the scene of Molech worship and pollution by Josiah (2 Kings 23:10; 2 Chron. 28:3; 33:6; Jer. 7:29-34).*
- *Here the kings Ahaz and Manasseh are said to have offered their sons to the god Molech (2 Chron. 28:3; 33:6; 2 Kings 23:10; Jer. 32:35).*
- *Gehenna was referred to as a type of "hell," a lake of fire, outer darkness, and so forth (Matt. 5:22, 29-30; 10:28; 18:9; 23:15; 33; Mark 9:43, 45, 47; Luke 12:5; James 3:6).*

67. **POTTER'S FIELD** (*Aceldama* ["the field of blood"]). On the southern side of the Valley of Hinnom, where it meets the Kidron Valley at the foot of the hill Ophel, is the Potter's Field, called *Aceldama* ("the field of blood"). This is the field of which Zechariah prophesied. It was purchased by the high priests with the 30 pieces of silver Judas threw down in the temple after he realized the enormity of his crime of betraying Jesus. The field was to be a place in which to bury strangers. The Greek Orthodox Convent of Saint Oniprius marks the site, which has many rock-hewn tombs full of the skulls and bones of pilgrims who have been buried here. Tombs are shown where, according to tradition, the apostles hid during Jesus' trial.

The high hill southeast of the Old City of Jerusalem, behind Potter's Field, is sometimes called the *Mount of Evil Counsel*. The United Nations headquarters are housed here in the government buildings of the British Mandate.

■ *Zechariah prophesied of this field (Zech. 11:12–13).*
■ *It was purchased by the high priests with Judas's 30 pieces of silver (Matt. 27:3–10; Acts 1:18–19).*

Immediately South, West, and North of the Old City

68. **ZION GATE** (*Bab en Nabi Daoud* ["gate of David the prophet"]). This is a city gate at the extreme south end of the Old City. Mount Zion and David's tomb are located outside the gate.

69. **MOUNT ZION** ("fortress"). Zion was the name of the citadel of the Jebusite city of Jerusalem, captured by David. Today, tradition (probably in error) says this was on the southwest hill of the city. Zion was also a title applied to the temple area. The present traditional site of Mount Zion is on a hill close to the southwest corner of the old walled city. In A.D. 340 a large basilica, called *Hagia Zion*, was built on the mount and it was probably from this building that the mount received its name. The basilica was destroyed by the Persians in 614. This area was once within the city wall, and is very sacred to the Jews because they believe David is buried here. On the slope of Mount Zion is a Protestant cemetery in which Sir Flinders Petrie, the noted archaeologist, is buried.

The **BASILICA OF THE DORMITION** is the most imposing building on the mount and is served by the Benedictine Fathers. This marks the spot (one of three traditional locations) where Mary, the mother of Jesus, died, or "fell into eternal sleep." Some Roman Catholics believe that it was from this spot that Mary was taken into heaven, body and spirit (the *Assumption*). In the crypt is a stone effigy of Saint Mary asleep on her deathbed. *Dormition Sanctae Mariae* is Latin for "the sleep of Saint Mary." In the chapel are beautiful mosaic pieces of art. The circular mosaic floor has symbols of the Trinity and representations of the apostles and the signs of the zodiac. One mosaic above an altar shows Mary as if she were the head of the Twelve Apostles.

North of the Dormition Church is a small Armenian chapel called the **HOUSE OF CAIAPHAS** because it marks the traditional site of Caiaphas's house.

The **AMERICAN INSTITUTE OF HOLY LAND STUDIES** is located on the southern slope of Mount Zion.

■ *The ark was carried from here to the temple (1 Kings 8:1; 2 Chron. 5:2).*
■ *"Out of Zion shall go forth the law" (Isa. 2:3).*
■ *Mount Zion was spoken of as Temple Hill (Isa. 8:18; Jer. 31:6; Mic. 4:7).*
■ *Zion was the name of the whole city (Ps. 102:21; Mic. 3:10–12).*
■ *Here Jesus was taken before Annas and Caiaphas (Matt. 26:3–5, 57–75; John 18:12–24).*
■ *Here Peter denied Jesus at the palace of Caiaphas (Matt. 26:59–75; Luke 22:54–62).*

Ñ
N

SHEIKH JARRAH

91

Jerusalem
South, West, and North
of the Old City

Miles ¼ ½

DERECH SHECHEM (NABLUS ROAD)

NAHLAT SHIMON

AMERICAN COLONY

WADI EL JOZ

To Mount of Olives

SHMUEL HANAVI

87

BEIT YISRAEL

G'MUL

REEM

SHMUEL HANAVI

DERECH SHECHEM (NABLUS ROAD)

ST GEORGE

YMCA

SALAH ED DIN (SALADIN) STREET

86

AZ-ZAHRA

NUR-ED-DIN

KHALID IBN-AL-WALID

BEIT ISRAEL

SHMUEL HANAVI MANDEL BAUM

88

PIKUD HAMERKAZ

ST GEORGE

85

EIN YA'AKOV

MEA SHEARIM

SHIFTEI YISRAEL

HAHOMA HASHELISHIT

DERECH SHECHEM (NABLUS ROAD)

HAROUN AL-RASHID

SULTAN SULEIMAN

DERECH YERICHO

VRAHAM MISLONIM

89

ADMON

IDO HANAVI

P.O.

80

84

82

83

SALANT

DEVORA HANEVIA

HANEVIIM

MORASHA

Arab Bus Station

Herod's Gate

Stephen's Gate

(JERICHO ROAD)

HAVATZELET

MONBAZ

HANEVIIM

HELENA HAMALKA

NATAN HA-AVI

HA'AYIN HET

HANEVIIM

SULTAN SULEIMAN

81

17

GRUZENBERG

SHIFTEI YISRAEL

ELISHA

Damascus Gate

78

79

CHES'JIN

YAFO (JAFFA)

YOH-NAN MIGUSH HALAV

HATIVAT HATZANHANIM (PARATROOPERS)

Golden Gate

13

SHLOMZION HAMALKA

KORESH

P.O.

LEDIDYA

77

SHMON BEN SHETTAH

HAMALKA

YAFO (JAFFA)

KORESH

76

New Gate

OLD CITY

BEN SIRA

SHLOMO HAMELECH

YA-NAI

AGRON

DAVID HAMELECH

MAMILLA

YAFO (JAFFA)

Joppa Gate

34

Dung Gate

15

61

HAEMEK

ELIYAHU SHAMA

62

ZAMEN-HOF

JULIANUS

WALLENBERG

AGRON

ELIOT

HESS

EMILE BOTTA

MISHKENOT SHA'ANANIM

HATIVAT YERUSHALAYIM

HAR ZION

Zion Gate

68

ABRAHAM LINCOLN

DAVID HAMELECH

YMCA

65

WASHINGTON

75

HATHANA

HAMIGDAL

HAR ZION

69

71

72

73

KEREN HAYESOD

MAPU

MISHKENOT SHA'ANANIM

70

MEN MOC SEFARIM

S ALEICHEM

DAVID HAMELECH

YEMIN MOSHE

74

SHAMA

HEVRON

HATIVAT YERUSHALAYIM

BOTINSKY

DRECH

VALLEY OF HINNOM

66

67

68. Zion Gate
69. Mount Zion
70. Upper Room of the Last Supper
71. Tomb of David
72. Chamber of Martyrs and Yeshiva of the Diaspora
73. Palace of Caiaphas and Saint Peter's in Gallicantu
74. Yemin Moshe
75. Herod's family tomb
76. New Gate
77. Notre Dame de France Monastery
78. Armenian Mosaic
79. Damascus Gate
80. Garden Tomb
81. Solomon's Temple Stone Quarries
82. Jeremiah's Grotto
83. Herod's Gate
84. Calvary (Golgotha)
85. Rockefeller Museum
86. Albright Institute of Archaeological Research
87. Tomb of the Kings
88. Mandelbaum Gate
89. Mea Shearim
90. Bukharian Quarter
91. Tomb of Simon the Just

70. **UPPER ROOM OF THE LAST SUPPER** (*Coenaculum* ["dining hall"], Cenacle). The upper story of David's building is the Hall of the Last Supper, or *Coenaculum* (Latin for "dining hall"), according to Christian tradition. It is a medieval Franciscan building dating back to 1335. The roof of the building offers a commanding view of the Old City.

- *This was the traditional site of the "last supper" (Matt. 26:17–30; Mark 14:12–25; Luke 22:7–30; John 13:1–30).*
- *According to tradition, the apostles met here after the Ascension (Acts 1:13–14).*
- *The upper room is believed by some to have been the place where 120 disciples were gathered when the Holy Spirit came upon them on the day of Pentecost (Acts 2:1–42).*

71. **TOMB OF DAVID** (1012–972 B.C.). The tomb or cenotaph of David, held sacred by Moslems and Christians and Jews, is made of stone and has silver crowns of the Torah on top of it. This site has been marked since about A.D. 1173, and is located on the first floor of the same building complex that houses the upper room of the Last Supper.

This is one of the most sacred of all sites to the Jews, second only to the Western Wall. A devout Jew will light a candle for you and say a few prayers if you desire. According to 1 Kings 2:10, it appears

David was buried at Bethlehem or the Hill of Ophel, south of the temple area.

72. **CHAMBER OF MARTYRS** (*Martef Hashoa*, Cellar of the Holocaust), **YESHIVA OF THE DIASPORA**. In the basement of a building by the tomb of David is a memorial to the 6,000,000 Jews slain by the Nazis in Germany during World War II.

On the floor above the Chamber of Martyrs is a very interesting English-speaking Yeshiva that welcomes all visitors of any religion. Here the visitor can see the traditional method of studying the Torah and Talmud.

73. **PALACE OF CAIAPHAS** ("depression"), **SAINT PETER'S IN GALLICANTU**. South of the Dung Gate, on the eastern slope of Mount Zion, is the traditional site of the palace of Caiaphas, the high priest at the time of Jesus' arrest and crucifixion. Jesus came here from Gethsemane. The Assumptionist Fathers built a church on the site in 1931. The site also has remains of a Byzantine monastery and a grotto where, according to tradition, Peter wept. The **STEPS** of the old street are shown, the **CELL DUNGEON** of Caiaphas where Jesus stayed, the **COURTYARD**, and the **SERVANTS' QUARTERS**. In Jesus' day the site was within the walls of Old Jerusalem.

- *This was the scene of Jesus' first trial (Matt. 26:57–63; Mark 14: 53–65; Luke 22:54, 63–71; John 18:12–14, 19–24).*
- *Here Peter denied the Lord three times (Matt. 26:34, 69–75; Mark 14:66–72; Luke 22:54–62; John 18:15–18, 25–27).*
- *The prison could have been the place where the apostles were imprisoned (Acts 4:3; 5:17–23).*

74. **YEMIN MOSHE**. This is the first "old-world quarter" to be built outside the walls of the Old City. It is now a quaint artists' quarter, across the valley from Mount Zion. At the entrance is the windmill constructed by Moses Montefiore in the nineteenth century, to provide the Jewish inhabitants with work. It is now a museum, housing the benefactor's original carriage. The long, one-story house, built in 1860, was the first dwelling constructed outside the walls of the Old City. It was financed by Judah Touro of New Orleans, and was one of the first efforts of American Jewry in Israel.

75. **HEROD'S FAMILY TOMB** (*Rehov David Hamelekh*). This family tomb, just east of the King David Hotel, was uncovered in 1892. It is believed that members of Herod's family were buried here, including Mariamne, whom he murdered. The mausoleum is built out of huge stone blocks in the form of a cross. Note the rolling stone used to block the door — the most beautiful in Israel. The beautiful stone sarcophagi found in the tomb are now at the Greek Patriarchate in the Old City. Herod is supposed to have been buried on a hilltop near Bethlehem or in Jericho (Josephus, *Wars of the Jews*, 1:23:8-9; *Antiquities of the Jews*, XVII:8:3-4).

Tomb of David, Jerusalem

76. The **NEW GATE**, opposite the Monastery of Notre Dame de France, was opened in 1889 in the time of the Turks by Sultan Abdul-Hamid and was thus known as the *Gate of the Sultan*. It was closed during the Jordanian occupation, 1948–67.

77. **NOTRE DAME DE FRANCE MONASTERY**. Opposite the New Gate is this monastery, founded in 1887 and managed by the Assumptionist Fathers.

78. **ARMENIAN MOSAIC**. On Prophets Street, just outside the Damascus Gate, is the oldest monument to an "unknown soldier" ever found. A beautiful mosaic with representations of birds, plants, and flowers was part of a fifth-century chapel above the tombs of Armenian soldiers who died in A.D. 451 while fighting the Persians.

79. **DAMASCUS GATE** (Shechem Gate, *Bab el Nasr* ["gate of victory"], *Bab el Amoud* ["gate of the pillar"]). The Damascus Gate is located on the northwest side of Old Jerusalem, where the highway starts toward Damascus, capital of Syria. The Jews call it *Shechem* or *Nablus* because the highway goes there also. This is the most beautiful and picturesque of the gates and is the main entrance to the city. It has always been considered the proper entry for crowned heads. It was built by Suleiman the Magnificent in 1537. Beneath the gate are remains of the ancient second-century wall and gate, recently discovered through excavations. The sixth-century Madeba Map of Jerusalem has a large pillar standing just outside the gate. This detail is preserved in the Arabic name for the gate.

80. **GARDEN TOMB** (Protestant Version). Immediately west of Golgotha and a short block north of the Damascus Gate on the Nablus road is the rock-cut Jewish tomb called the *Garden Tomb*, discovered by General Gordon of Khartoum. It had been occupied formerly by a church. Jewish tombs were often composed of two chambers: the first served as a vestibule, and in it the relatives congregated to mourn for the dead; in the second, on a couch cut into the rock, the corpse was laid. The entrance to the monument was closed by a round massive slab, like a millstone, which rolled in a groove.

- *Jesus was buried in a garden (Matt. 27:57–66; Mark 15:42–47; Luke 23:50–56; John 19:41–42).*
- *Jesus' tomb was guarded (Matt. 27:62–66).*
- *"Who shall roll us away the stone . . . ?" (Mark 16:3–4).*
- *Mary Magdalene saw the resurrected Christ in the garden (Mark 16:9; John 20:11–18).*
- *Peter and John raced to the garden (Luke 24:12; John 20:4).*
- *Jesus was resurrected (Matt. 28:1–15; Mark 16:1–11; Luke 24:1–12; John 20:1–18).*

81. **SOLOMON'S TEMPLE STONE QUARRIES** (Cave of Zedekiah). Just north of the Damascus Gate is a 7-foot fissure in the natural rock on

Left: Calvary
Below: Damascus Gate, Jerusalem

which the city wall is built. It is covered by a small iron gate. This fissure leads to an underground canyon — the famous quarries from which the stone was cut for the building of Solomon's temple. The huge cavern goes 214 yards into the heart of the mountain, below the buildings of the Old City. It branches off in several directions.

Members of the Masonic Lodge regard the first 3,600 overseers, who put the people to work on the stones for the temple, as the first Freemasons. Many blocks of the virgin stone have been shipped around the world for use as foundation stones in Masonic lodges.

- *Stone was used for the temple of Solomon (1 Kings 5:15; 6:7).*
- *Solomon's temple was described (2 Chron. 3).*
- *This was the possible hiding place of Zedekiah (according to legend) during the Babylonian siege under Nebuchadnezzar in 587 B.C. (2 Kings 25:1–5).*

82. JEREMIAH'S GROTTO (*Hazor Hamatara* ["court of the prison"]). This cavern, once a part of Solomon's quarries, is located behind the Arab bus station across from Solomon's quarries, at the end of a small lane.

- *According to tradition, Jeremiah wrote his* Lamentations *here (Jer. 38:6–13).*

83. HEROD'S GATE (Gate of Flowers). This gate, on the north side of the Old City, is located across from the post office, and is one of 8 gates in the Old City wall. It is believed that its name was given by medieval pilgrims who believed that the house of Herod Antipas, where Jesus was sent by Pilate, was nearby.

84. CALVARY (*Golgotha* ["skull"] in Protestant version, Gordon's Calvary). This is a knoll north of the Old City and over the top of Jeremiah's Grotto. It is presently used as a Moslem cemetery. Enter from Salah ed Din Street, at a point one-half block west of the post office. The entrance is marked with a crescent, indicating a Moslem cemetery, across the street from the Metropole Hotel. The knoll is also called *Gordon's Calvary*, after the English General Gordon, the hero of Khartoum.

- *Jesus was crucified (Matt. 27:32–56; Mark 15:21–41; Luke 23:26–46; John 19:16–37).*

85. ROCKEFELLER MUSEUM (Palestine Archaeological Museum). This excellent museum, built with a $2,000,000 fund from John D. Rockefeller in 1927, stands just north of the city wall near Herod's Gate. It contains one of the most extensive archaeological collections in this part of the world. Pottery, tools, and household effects are arranged by periods of time. The bones of a **MOUNT CARMEL MAN** claimed to date back 100,000 years are displayed. This museum has been a workshop to piece together the many manuscript fragments of the Dead Sea Scrolls. Note the following items of interest: a display of **LAMPS** used in different periods of time; a limestone **CANAANITE**

Sea of Galilee near Capernaum

ALTAR for burnt offerings, dating back to 1000 B.C. and found at Megiddo, used for incense of sin offering as described in Leviticus 4:7, 18–20, and 1 Kings 1:50 and 2:28 (note the horns on the corners); a COPPER SWORD from Megiddo, dating back as far as 3000–4000 B.C.; CANAANITE IDOLS of the Patriarchal period (Gen. 35:4; Josh. 24:23); reliefs from Sennacherib's palace at Nineveh (700 B.C.).

A fine library of over 35,000 volumes deals with the history, geography, and archaeology of the Holy Land.

86. **ALBRIGHT INSTITUTE OF ARCHAEOLOGICAL RESEARCH.** This is a branch of the American School of Oriental Research, a professional organization instituted to promote archaeological and related research in the world of the Bible. The school has a branch at Baghdad as well as Jerusalem. In 1968 it had 70 resident scholars in the area and 400 research technicians that worked with them. They did some work on the Dead Sea Scrolls in the past, and do a great deal of archaeological research. They were working at Megiddo and Ai in 1968 and at Gezer in 1971. The school is located on Salah ed Din (Saladin) Street northwest of the National Palace Hotel.

87. **TOMB OF THE KINGS.** Near the top of Saladin Street one may see a hollowed-out courtyard with small cave openings and 25 stone steps leading to a cistern that was used for ritual ablutions or preparation for burial. Inside one of the tombs, four carved sarcophagi were found. The family of Queen Helena of Mesopotamia, who was converted to Judaism around A.D. 50, was buried here. The tomb is misnamed. It is one of the most interesting burial tombs in Israel. Here the visitor can see one of the best-preserved examples of a rolling stone closing the entrance to a tomb. The sarcophagi from the tomb are located in the Louvre. A canal system brings water to the cisterns.

■ *The tomb of Joseph of Arimathea, where Jesus was buried, had a rolling stone (Matt. 27:60, 66; 28:2; Mark 15:46; 16:3–4; Luke 24:2, 12; John 20:1).*
■ *To enter, one had to "stoop down" (John 20:5, 11).*

88. **MANDELBAUM GATE** (Command Square). This was a gate that existed between Jordan and Israel during the period 1948–67. It was removed after the six-day war in 1967. It was named after Dr. S. Mandelbaum, whose house was bisected by the armistice line, and since 1967 has been named Command Square.

89. **MEA SHEARIM.** Around 1877 this area was built as the Orthodox Jews' religious quarter. Here they live as they did in the ghettos of Europe, with crowded but clean living quarters, schools, and synagogues. The Mea Shearim quarter was once protected by a wall with 100 gates. The name was taken from the account concerning Isaac in the Book of Genesis (Gen. 26:12).

Mea Shearim Street starts from Prophets Street and is one of the main streets in the area. It is the center of the mystical religious

Hassidic sect. Long beards, black gowns, beaver fur hats (shetrained), broad-brimmed hats, side curls (peot), and high black socks are worn here. The women wear bandannas over their shaved heads. These religious Russian and Polish Jews are fighting against the blasphemous modern life of Israel. They recognize no state of Israel before the coming of the Messiah. They clash with police in demonstrations protesting burial laws, the driving of cars on Saturday, and the use of swimming pools by men and women simultaneously. Signs in the area request women to dress modestly. The streets close on Friday evening and Saturday.

90. **BUKHARIAN QUARTER.** Jews from Bukhara (Central Asia, USSR) came to Jerusalem as early as 1862 and by 1895 had established their own quarters. The main Bukharian synagogue is called *Baba Tama*. The services in the synagogue are very Oriental in flavor and help make the Bukharian Quarter very interesting. The Bukharian Quarter lies northwest of Mea Shearim.

91. **TOMB OF SIMON THE JUST.** Northeast of the Sheikh Jarrah Mosque is a tomb that belonged to the high priest Simon (335–270 B.C.), one of the last members of the "Great Synod," which gathered the writings of the Old Testament.

New Jerusalem

In 1841 the Anglican Church, supported by the king of Prussia, founded a bishopric in Jerusalem. After 1860 a new Jerusalem began to come into existence outside of the old walls. The first important buildings outside the Old City were the Russian buildings. In 1881 a small colony of Americans was founded by Mr. Spafford and his wife, based upon the original communistic teaching of the Bible. In 1868 an attempt to found an ideal Christian community in Palestine was made by Germans from Wurtemberg, who revived the name of *Templar* and who had several flourishing colonies in Palestine in 1939.

By 1970 the new Jerusalem was a bustling city not too much unlike the larger cities in the Western world.

Jaffa Road is the city's main street, and where it crosses King George Street (Balfour Declaration) and Ben Yehuda Street (Father of Modern Hebrew) is the center of the city. Jaffa Road and Ben Yehuda Street offer the best in shopping — souvenirs, antiques, and so forth. The Mea Shearim market and the markets in Old Jerusalem are also good for shopping. In West Jerusalem there is little "bargaining," but in East Jerusalem the Oriental culture expects you to haggle over the price.

NEAR THE CENTER OF THE NEW CITY

92. **HALL OF HEROISM.** Just off Shiftei Yisrael Street, behind the Russian Compound Cathedral, is a small museum dedicated to the men involved in the underground resistance during the British Mandate. The museum is housed in a former British prison.

93. **RUSSIAN COMPOUND.** Located on Jaffa Road, the Russian Compound was once the world's largest hotel, accommodating 10,000 Russian pilgrims at one time. During the 1920s the Russians were the most numerous pilgrims to Israel. The green-domed cathedral stands on the highest ground of the compound, where the Assyrians camped when they besieged Jerusalem about 700 B.C. The Romans were also here in A.D. 70. The buildings of the compounds are now used by the Israeli government. By the cathedral is a pillar that is thought to have been quarried for Herod's temple.

94. **MAHANE YEHUDA.** This is a colorful open-air market that is especially lively on Fridays and before holidays. It is located west of the War of Independence Memorial, on the south side of Jaffa Street.

95. **HECHAL SHLOMO** ("Palace, or Temple, of Solomon"). This is the seat of Israel's chief rabbinate, the supreme religious center. It stands opposite Independence Park on King George Street. It has a synagogue with beautiful stained glass windows, a library, and the Abraham Wax Collection of Jewish religions and folk art. It has an excellent series of dioramas portraying certain biblical events. Jewish souvenirs can be purchased here.

96. **INDEPENDENCE PARK AND MAMILLA POOL.** This is the largest of all Jerusalem parks and is located on Agron Street and Mamilla Road, near the city center. A large reservoir, called Mamilla Pool, is believed to be a part of an ancient water system connected to Hezekiah's Pool in the Old City.

97. **YMCA BUILDING.** Built on King David Road in 1928 by James Jarvie of New Jersey, this building affords one of the best panoramic views of the city. The sixth-century Madeba Map of Jerusalem is reproduced in the vestibule.

98. **PRESIDENT'S RESIDENCE** (*Beit Hanassi*). In May 1972 the president of Israel moved into this new residence just southwest of the Academy of Sciences, on Hakeshet Street.

99. **JASON'S CAVE** (Alfasi Cave). On Alfasi road southwest of Hechal Shlomo, in a section of the city called Rehavia, is a second-century B.C. tomb with a pyramidal roof. Burial niches, etchings of a menorah, representations of a naval battle, and the name of Jason carved in the stone are of interest. Perhaps the tomb belonged to Jason, father of Antipater, a commissioner of Judas Maccabaeus in 161 B.C.

POINTS OF INTEREST IN OUTLYING NEW JERUSALEM

100. **MONASTERY OF THE CROSS.** Built originally by Georgian Monks in the eleventh century at Abu Tor, this monastery, according to legend, stands on the spot where once stood the tree from which the cross was made. The Greek Orthodox church maintains it now. It is called the **CHURCH OF EVIL COUNSEL.** It contains interesting catacombs, crypts, frescoes, and mosaics. Ancient legend says that the cypress trees in the court are shoots from the original trees planted by Lot, who settled here with his two daughters after fleeing from Sodom.

101. **KNESSET** (Parliament Building). This is a $7,000,000 structure of peach-colored stone on Jerusalem's "acropolis." It has a 24-foot-high Chagall mosaic in the reception hall, a synagogue, separate kitchens for milk and meat dishes, and exhibition rooms. The grill-work entrance way is the work of Israeli sculptor Polombo, who also designed the doors at Yad Vashem.

A large 16-foot-high bronze **MENORAH**, executed by sculptor B. Elkan and donated by Great Britain, stands in front of the building. Twenty-nine panels on the menorah depict highlights in Jewish history. Parliament meets Monday and Tuesday 4:00–9:00 P.M. and Wednesday at 11:00 A.M.

Israel is a republic with a president, who is elected for 5 years by a majority of the members of the Knesset (Parliament). The first president of Israel was Dr. Chaim Weizmann. The president is not head of the executive as in the United States; his powers resemble those of the British constitutional monarch.

The Knesset is a single house with 120 members. The members are elected by simple ballot, with proportional representation. Each party puts up a list of candidates, who then receive the number of seats proportional to the percentage they win of the total national vote. The *Mapai* (Labor Party) has been the largest single party, usually having about one-third of all the seats. David Ben-Gurion resigned in 1964 as the leader of this group, and Levi Eshkol succeeded him until 1967. Golda Meir took Eshkol's place. Other parties are the *Hernt, Liberal, Religious, Mapam, Achdut Avodah, Arabs,* and *Communists.*

102. The **NATIONAL MUSEUM** is a very large and beautiful museum that houses Israel's treasures. It opened in 1965 and contains the following four components:

(1) The **BETZELEL MUSEUM OF ART AND FOLKLORE** displays such items as Hanukkah lamps, Torah scrolls, costumes, jewelry from different Jewish communities, and paintings by Chagall, Rembrandt, Ruisdael, Picasso, and prominent Israeli artists.

(2) The **BRONFMAN ARCHAEOLOGICAL AND ANTIQUITIES MUSEUM** houses exhibits dating from the stone age to the Ottoman period. Of particular interest is a first-century bronze leopard from Avdat, sacrificial altars from Arad and Hazor, objects from caves identified with the Bar Kokhba revolt, and portions of the walls of the Jerusalem Cave. (See the "Jerusalem Cave" subsection in the division "West and Southwest of Jerusalem," later in this chapter.)

(3) The **BILLY ROSE ART GARDEN** is laid out in semicircular rock terraces and contains sculpture by Rodin, Daumier, Epstein, Lipschitz, and others. The garden was laid out by a Japanese landscape artist, Isamu Naguchi.

(4) The **SHRINE OF THE BOOK** is an onion-top-shaped building contoured to resemble the jar covers in which the Dead Sea Scrolls were discovered. It has 275,000 glazed bricks on the roof. It houses the Dead Sea Scrolls, scrolls found at Masada, and the Bar Kokhba letters.

Above: Knesset, New Jerusalem
Below: Library, Hebrew University, New Jerusalem

Like a huge jar lid, the architectural design of the Shrine of the Book is unique. The concern of the scrolls — and indeed the Qumran community to which they belonged — with the struggle of light against darkness, good against evil, knowledge

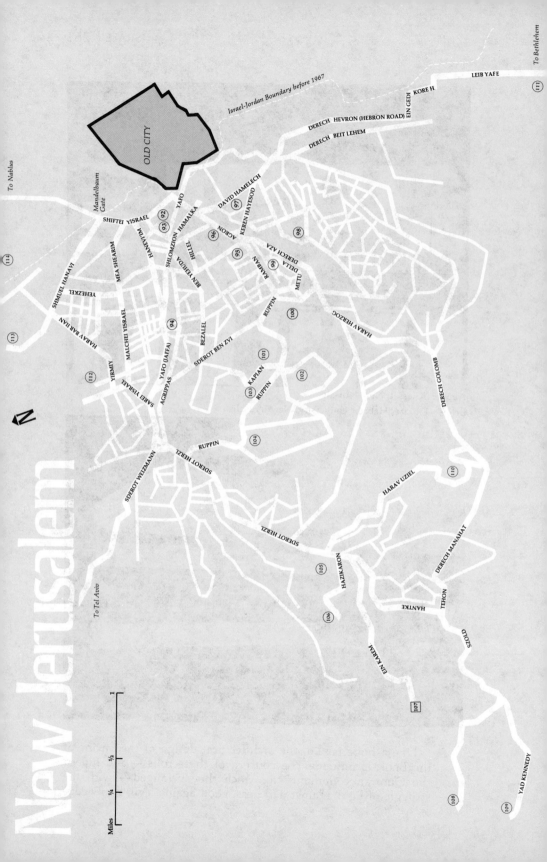

 92. Hall of Heroism
 93. Russian Compound
 94. Mahane Yehuda
 95. Hechal Shlomo
 96. Independence Park and Mamilla Pool
 97. YMCA building
 98. President's residence
 99. Jason's Cave
100. Monastery of the Cross
101. Knesset
102. National Museum
103. Kiriya
104. Hebrew University
105. Mount Herzl
106. Yad Vashem Memorial
107. Ein Karem
108. Hadassah Hospital
109. Kennedy Memorial
110. Model of Ancient Jerusalem
111. Ramat Rachel
112. Biblical Zoo
113. Sanhedrin Tombs
114. Ammunition Hill

against ignorance, finds architectural expression through the play of contrasts between the white dome and the nonfunctional rectilinear black wall. The black wall calls to mind by its color or shape the heavy burden which lay on Israel for more than 2,000 years.

Bronze gates open on a cavelike manuscript corridor leading to the SANCTUARY, which has a double parabolic dome, ribbed as by the hand of some giant potter. It swings upward from its 80-foot diameter to a 6-foot opening. The scroll of Isaiah, 24 feet long, girdles a jar-shaped fountain, and below the Isaiah scroll are simulated caves with scrolls. The building is buried like the Dead Sea Scrolls and is possibly one of the very few public buildings in the world planned to be essentially subterranean.

SMALLER MUSEUMS. In addition to the museums already noted, there are smaller museums worth visiting: The AGRICULTURAL MUSEUM, at the Ministry of Agriculture on Helena Hamalka Street; the NATURAL HISTORY MUSEUM, on Mohiliver Street; the MUSICAL INSTRUMENTS MUSEUM, in the Rubin Academy of Music, on Smolenskin Street; the TAXATION MUSEUM; the MUSEUM OF ISLAMIC ART, attached to the Meyer Center, near the president's residence and the Hechal Shlomo.

103. The KIRIYA. Northwest of the Knesset are three large buildings that contain important government offices: the Prime Minister's Office, Ministries of the Interior, Finance, State Archives, and others.

Above: Shrine of the Book and black wall, New Jerusalem
Below: Isaiah Scroll

104. **HEBREW UNIVERSITY.** This modern, clean university, dedicated in 1954, boasts a student body of 14,000. The campus is built around the National Jewish Library, the largest in the Middle East.

Bronze menorah, New Jerusalem

105. **MOUNT HERZL.** This is the burial site of jurist, dramatist, and journalist, Dr. Theodore Benjamin Herzl, who forecast the state of Israel 50 years before its birth and is known as the father of Zionism and the state of Israel. His black granite tomb stands on the summit of Mount Herzl, surrounded by gardens. Herzl's remains were interred here in 1949, 45 years after his death in Vienna. In the Herzl cemetery are buried Vladimar Jabotinsky, revisionist philosopher, and also Levi Eshkol, the late prime minister of Israel. The **HERZL MUSEUM** is located near the main entrance. On the northern slope of Mount Herzl is the **MILITARY CEMETERY**, where war casualties of 1948 are buried.

106. **YAD VASHEM MEMORIAL** ("Hill of the Remembrance"). Built in 1957 on the top of Mount Memorial is this beautiful memorial dedicated to the 6,000,000 Jews killed in Nazi Germany, at Bergen-Belsen, Auschwitz, Dachau, and so on. The archives in the memorial house contain the documentary evidence of the slaughter. From here the evidence was produced against Adolf Eichmann in 1961. The memorial stands a thousand yards west of Mount Herzl, and an eternal flame is housed in the **OHEL VIZKOR** ("tent, or hall, of remembrance") (Isa. 56:5), built of large unhewn boulders. Its mosaic floor is inscribed with the names of the 21 largest concentration and death camps. The 70-foot **PILLAR OF HEROISM** was erected in honor of the resistance fighters.

The **AVENUE OF THE RIGHTEOUS** leads to the memorial. The trees that line this avenue were all planted by and in honor of non-Jews who had risked their lives to help Jews escape from the Nazis.

107. **EIN KAREM** ("spring of the vineyard"). On the terraced slopes

of western Jerusalem is a quaint village noted as the **BIRTHPLACE OF JOHN THE BAPTIST**. There are a number of educational institutions in the village, as well as homes of many artists.

On the north side of the village is the Franciscan **CHURCH OF SAINT JOHN**, built over the traditional site of John the Baptist's birthplace. A small stairway left of the nave of the church leads into the grotto, where a hollow niche is pointed out as John's birthplace. A church was built on the site as early as the fifth century A.D. Behind the church is a seventeenth-century monastery.

The **SPRING OF THE VINEYARD** (*Ein Karem*) **MOSQUE** is south of the Church of Saint John and the main road through the village. The mosque is built over a rock, from which the spring emerges. The spring was called *Mary's Fountain* in Crusader times because it was associated with the visit of the Virgin Mary to Elisabeth (Luke 1: 26-40).

Southwest of the Spring of the Vineyard Mosque is the Franciscan **CHURCH OF THE VISITATION**. It may be reached by ascending the broad stone stairway outside the entrance gate of the Russian compound. The mosaic facade of the church portrays Mary's journey from Nazareth. The church was built in 1955 above the grotto that marks the traditional site of the visitation of the angel Gabriel to Elisabeth (Luke 1:26-40). In the lower church a cavity hollowed out of a large stone marks the traditional place of concealment where John the Baptist was hidden from Herod's soldiers.

According to one tradition, when Herod issued his edict to slay children under two years of age John was taken into the mountains, where he was raised on locusts and wild honey. When Zacharias refused to disclose the hiding place of his son, John, he was slain by Herod's order. The tradition identifies John's father as the Zacharias who was killed "between the temple and the altar" (Matt. 23:31-35).

- *Gabriel visited Zacharias in the temple (Luke 1:5-23).*
- *Gabriel visited Mary; then Mary came to Ein Karem to be with Elisabeth (Luke 1:26-40).*
- *Mary and Elisabeth spoke by the Holy Ghost (Luke 1:41-55).*
- *John was named, and Zacharias regained his speech (Luke 1:57-79).*
- *John baptized Jesus in the Jordan (Matt. 3:1-17; Mark 1:4-11).*
- *John was one of the greatest of prophets (Matt. 11:7-11).*

108. **HADASSAH HOSPITAL.** On the extreme west side of the city of Jerusalem is the largest medical center in the Middle East — a $30,000,000, 11-floor complex — opened in 1961. It has over 1,000 beds, medical, dental, and pharmacy schools, and laboratories. *Hadassah*, the Women's Zionist Organization of America, organized in 1912, sponsored this hospital. In the hospital's synagogue are Marc Chagall's world-famous monumental stained glass windows, depicting in abstract terms the Twelve Tribes of Israel.

109. **KENNEDY MEMORIAL.** On Mount Orah, near the village of Aminadav, is a 60-foot-high poured-concrete memorial, opened in May 1966 and shaped like the lower half of a tree trunk, symbolizing

the president whose life was cut short in his prime. It has an eternal fire burning and is encircled by 50 columns, each bearing the emblem of a state of the Union, plus the District of Columbia. The John F. Kennedy Peace Forest is planted to the southwest of the monument.

110. **MODEL OF ANCIENT JERUSALEM.** This model city of the Jerusalem of Herod's time (A.D. 66), near the Holyland Hotel, took 7 years to build. The scale is 1 to 50 (¼ inch equals 1 foot), and it occupies a quarter of an acre. The owner of the hotel had it built as a memorial to his son, who was killed in the war. Professor Michael Avi-Yonah of the Hebrew University made the plans. Original materials of marble, stone, wood, iron, and copper have been used in the model's construction.

111. **RAMAT RACHEL.** South of the Old City and west of the Government House area is the Kibbutz Ramat Rachel (hill of Rachel). It is the only kibbutz within the confines of Jerusalem. It is the city's southern bastion. Archaeologists have uncovered 7 levels of occupation, dating from the seventh century B.C. to the seventh century A.D. The Romans had a bath house and palace here, and the Byzantines built a church and monastery here in the fifth century A.D.

112. **BIBLICAL ZOO.** On Jeremiah Street, at the north side of the city, is the Biblical Zoo, containing birds and animals described in the Bible. It is one of the most unusual animal collections in the world. Nearly all of the 100 different animals and 30 birds mentioned in the Bible are housed here. Relevant biblical quotations and paraphrases are displayed with each animal: "Can the leopard change his spots?" (Jeremiah 13:23). They were collected by Professor Aaron Shulov of the Hebrew University's Biology Department, and the zoo was founded in 1939.

113. **SANHEDRIN TOMBS** (Tombs of the Judges). Near the end of Samuel Street, on the northern edge of Jerusalem, a road turns right to a public garden, called by the Christians the *Tombs of the Judges.* The judges of Israel's supreme court during the first and second century were buried in the Sanhedrin Tombs. There are over 21 tombs in the area, dating back to the first century of the Christian era. The richest and most monumental tomb is **NUMBER 14**, a 3-level catacomb carved out of rock. The entrance is decorated with relief carvings of pomegranates and acanthus leaves. There are 80 burial places in the tomb, and because of the large size it is believed by some to have been the burial place of the Sanhedrin. Some believe it was a very large family tomb.

■ *Jesus was arraigned before the Sanhedrin (John 11:47).*

114. **AMMUNITION HILL.** This hill was the main Jordanian outpost in the 1967 six-day war. It was in this area that the Maccabees made their way to deliver Jerusalem from the hands of the Greeks in 165 B.C. The Roman legions also had their main camp here when they battled Jerusalem in A.D. 70.

EAST OF THE MOUNT OF OLIVES

BETHPHAGE *("place of young figs")*, *Keft et-Tur*

On the eastern slopes of the Mount of Olives, between the summit and Bethany, is Bethphage, the traditional starting point of the Palm Sunday procession. A Franciscan convent chapel houses the very stone (traditionally) upon which Jesus mounted the donkey for his triumphal entry into Jerusalem. The paintings on the stone date back to the Crusader period and were restored by C. Vagarini in 1950. Tombs with rolling stones, cisterns, presses, and pottery found in the area indicate that this slope had a sizable population.

- *From here Jesus sent two disciples to bring a colt for him to ride in his triumphal entry into Jerusalem (Palm Sunday) (Matt. 21:1–11; Mark 11:1–11; Luke 19:29–40; Zech. 9:9).*

BETHANY *("house of dates, or figs")*, *Azereyeh, el-Azariye*

Bethany is 1.7 miles from Jerusalem, on the eastern slope of the Mount of Olives and on the road to Jericho. The **CHURCH OF SAINT LAZARUS**, run by the Franciscans, was built near the tomb of Saint Lazarus in 1953. The church has beautiful mosaics depicting the events that took place here. Behind the Church of Saint Lazarus is a sixteenth-century **MOSQUE**, standing by Lazarus' tomb. West of the mosque is a **GREEK ORTHODOX CHURCH** and the remains of a **CRU-SADER TOWER AND FORTIFICATION.**

- *This was the home of Mary, Martha, and Lazarus (John 11:1).*
- *Jesus often stayed here (especially during the Passion Week). This was his home in Judea (Matt. 21:17; Mark 11:11).*
- *Jesus taught Martha the better way (Luke 10:38–42).*
- *Jesus raised Lazarus from the dead (John 11:1–44).*
- *In the house of Simon the leper, Mary anointed Jesus for burial (Matt. 26:1–13; Mark 14:3–9; Luke 7:36–50; John 12:1–8).*
- *Jesus ascended into heaven from here (Luke 24:50–51).*

AI *("ruin," "the heap")*

From the Jericho-to-Jerusalem highway at a point near Adummim, the site of the city of Ai can be seen on top of a mountain 9 miles to the northwest.

- *Ai was connected with Abraham's journeys (Gen. 12:8, 13:3).*
- *It was the first city captured by the Israelites in Canaan after the fall of Jericho (Josh. 7; 8; 9:3).*
- *It was mentioned by Isaiah (Isa. 10:28).*
- *It was mentioned in the time of Ezra (Ezra 2:28; Neh. 7:32).*
- *Its captivity was prophesied (Jer. 49:3).*

ADUMMIM *("red places")*, *Maale Adummim, the Good Samaritan Inn, Khan Hathrour, Tal at ed-Damm ("the ascent of blood")*

About 12 miles east of Jerusalem, between Jerusalem and Jericho, is

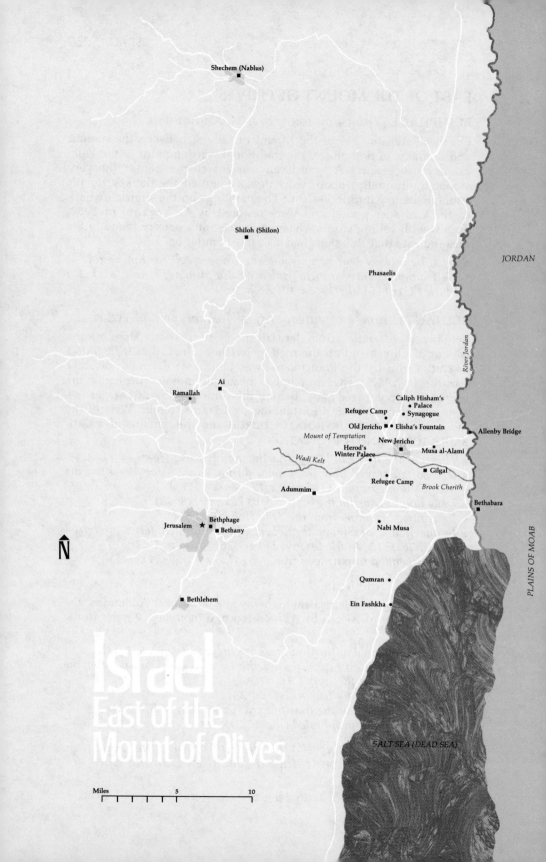

JORDAN

Shechem (Nablus)

Shiloh (Shilon)

Phasaelis

River Jordan

Ai
Ramallah

Caliph Hisham's
Palace
Refugee Camp
Synagogue
Old Jericho
Elisha's Fountain
Mount of Temptation
New Jericho
Allenby Bridge
Herod's
Winter Palace
Musa al-Alami
Wadi Kelt
Gilgal
Refugee Camp
Brook Cherith
Adummim
Bethabara

N̂

Bethphage
Jerusalem ★ Bethany
Nabi Musa

PLAINS OF MOAB

Bethlehem
Qumran
Ein Fashkha

Israel
East of the
Mount of Olives

SALT SEA (DEAD SEA)

Miles   5   10

the traditional site of the Samaritan's Inn mentioned in Jesus' story of the Good Samaritan. A Turkish police station was built here in 1903 and was destroyed in 1917. On a hill left of the highway stood a Crusader castle, built by the Templars. The ruins may still be seen.

■ *This was a boundary of the tribe of Judah, between Jericho and Jerusalem (Josh. 15:7; 18:17).*
■ *Tradition places the Good Samaritan inn here (Luke 10:34–35).*

WADI KELT, *Qilt*

About 2 miles east of Maale Adummim the road forks, and the road to the left follows the old Roman road through Wadi Kelt, a beautiful gorge in the desert, where stands the **GREEK MONASTERY OF SAINT GEORGE.**

There are also many caves here. Some believe — and it seems likely — that the Good Samaritan story took place in this area. At the mouth of the wadi are ruins of the New Testament Jericho.

Here Herod had his winter palace.

■ *A tradition also places the Good Samaritan inn here (Luke 10: 34–35).*

Nabi Musa, *Nebi Moussa*

About 18 miles from Jerusalem a road leads to the right where Arab tradition says Moses was buried. A mosque marks the site.

■ *Deuteronomy indicates Moses died in Moab and was buried there (Deut. 34:5–6).*

Refugee Camps

South and north of Jericho are the largest refugee camps built in Jordan at the time of the 1948 war. Thousands of Palestinian refugees lived here for nearly 20 years. In the six-day war of 1967, most of the refugees fled to Amman, Jordan, across the Jordan River from Jericho. A few refugees still live in the camps at Jericho.

Herod's Winter Palace

A luxurious palace was built by Herod the Great near the mouth of Wadi Kelt at a point west and a little north of the present refugee camp south of New Jericho. Ruins may still be seen. Mark Antony made a present of the New Testament Jericho to Cleopatra, who leased it to Herod the Great; the latter died here in 4 B.C. Nearby are the remains of a Herodian fortress. Some feel this area was the New Testament Jericho.

JERICHO ("fragrant"), *Tell es-Sultan*, "City of Palm Trees"

Five miles west of the Jordan River, 6 miles north of the Dead Sea, and 850 feet below sea level is the **NEW, TWENTIETH-CENTURY CITY OF JERICHO.** It is 17 miles northeast of Jerusalem.

OLD JERICHO is a mound 1,200 feet long and 50 feet high, support-ing 4 smaller mounds, the highest of which is 90 feet above the main mound. It is about 1½ miles northwest of the New Jericho. The mound was excavated by Kathleen Kenyon, and a stone tower was found that is estimated to be 8,000 years old — the oldest building on the earth. It is 35 feet in diameter.

The NEW TESTAMENT JERICHO is believed to have been at the mouth of Wadi Kelt, where Herod had his winter palace.

■ *Jericho was called "the City of Palm Trees" (Deut. 34:3; 2 Chron. 28:15).*
■ *Israel was numbered here (Num. 26:3, 63).*
■ *It was a walled city ruled by a king (Josh. 2:2–3).*
■ *Joshua's spies went to Jericho (Josh. 2:1–15).*
■ *The walls fell. It was captured and cursed by Joshua (Josh. 6:13–17, 26).*
■ *Achan sinned by keeping some of the spoils of the city (Josh. 7).*
■ *Its overthrow led other kings to try to make peace (Josh. 10:1–30).*
■ *It belonged to Benjamin and Manasseh (Josh. 16:1–7; 18:11–12).*
■ *It was rebuilt by Hiel the Bethelite (1 Kings 16:34), in spite of Joshua's curse (Josh. 6:26).*
■ *Elijah and Elisha and "the sons of the prophets" were at Jericho (2 Kings 2:4–18).*
■ *Here David's messengers suffered indignities (2 Sam. 10:1–5; 1 Chron. 19:1–5).*
■ *Elisha healed its waters (2 Kings 2:19–22).*
■ *Zedekiah was captured near here (2 Kings 25:5–7; Jer. 39:5–7; 52:8–11).*
■ *Israel returned captives and spoils of Judah by way of Jericho (2 Chron. 28:1–15).*
■ *Zacchaeus was converted here (Luke 19:1–27).*
■ *Great multitudes followed Jesus in Jericho (Matt. 20:29).*
■ *Jesus cured Bartimaeus and his companion (Matt. 20:29–34; Mark 10:46–52; Luke 18:35–43).*

MOUNT OF TEMPTATION, *Quarantana*

Just west of Jericho is the traditional Mount of Temptation, where immediately after his baptism Jesus went to be with God. He fasted 40 days and was tempted by the devil. The GREEK MONASTERY OF THE FORTY DAYS is on the Mount. The view from the top of the mount is beautiful.

■ *Jesus fasted and was tempted by Satan (Matt. 4:1–11; Mark 1:12–13; Luke 4:1–13).*

ELISHA'S FOUNTAIN, *Spring of the Sultan*

Elisha's Fountain is located across the street from the Old Jericho mound. Here, according to tradition, Elisha found polluted waters and threw salts in them to make them pure. The Arabs have a legend that barren women will become fruitful if they drink of the spring.

■ *Elisha healed its waters (2 Kings 2:19–22).*

Stone Tower, Jericho

Ancient Synagogue

Three-quarters of a mile northeast of Elisha's Fountain, a row of cypress trees leads to a house built over the floor of a synagogue that is 1,500 years old.

Caliph Hisham's Palace

This is about a mile northeast of Old Jericho. It was a winter resort for the Umayyad caliphs, whose capital was Damascus in Syria. Well preserved, it dates back to A.D. 724. A beautiful mosaic bath is worth seeing. This is a National Parks Authority site.

Phasaelis, *El Fasayil*

Twelve miles directly north of New Jericho are the remains of a town built by Herod and named after his brother Phasael.

Arab Development Society, Musa al-Alami

The Arab Development Society is about 7 miles north of the Dead Sea and 2½ miles east of New Jericho on the road to the Allenby Bridge. This is the "boys' town" of Jordan. It is a farm that was developed by a Jerusalem lawyer, Musa al-Alami, and charitable concerns such as the Ford Foundation.

Its charter was given in Jerusalem in 1945 as a purely charitable society, with the object of raising the social, economic, and educational standards of the Arab villages of Palestine. It aimed at establishing training centers for boys and girls. In 1949 the society received permission to launch a project in an area of 2,000 acres of dead and waste land lying between the River Jordan and Jericho. It soon became a boys' town — the first in the Middle East — for Arab children left homeless and orphaned by the Arab-Israeli War.

The first well water flowed onto the parched land in 1950. By 1953 1,000 acres had been reclaimed. The fields had 10,000 banana plants, 5,000 citrus trees, vineyards, and 16,000 pine saplings. Musa al-Alami had made the desert blossom like a rose. By then there were 65 whitewashed buildings with modern plumbing and electric power. Ten pump houses fed thousands of gallons of water along 9 miles of concrete aqueducts to the fields and orchards. From 8 to 11 crops of alfalfa are raised each year.

The Church of Jesus Christ of Latter-day Saints (LDS, "Mormon") helped to finance a large dairy on the farm. Louis B. Bigler and others from Utah, USA, helped to purchase cows and an expensive bull. In 1971 they had 200 cows, 100 of which they were milking. A milk processing plant makes delicious ice cream products.

Allenby Bridge

Five and one-half miles east of Jericho is the Allenby Bridge. It was near here that the children of Israel crossed the Jordan River and entered the Promised Land. The river stopped its flow and twelve stones were taken from the river bed.

■ *The children of Israel crossed the Jordan River near here (Josh. 3:14-4:13, 20-24; Ps. 114:3).*

BROOK CHERITH, Wadi Yabis

The old Roman road follows this brook.

■ *After announcing the drought, Elijah hid from Ahab at the brook Cherith and was fed by the ravens (1 Kings 17:1-7).*

ACHOR ("trouble"), el-Buquei'ah

■ *In this valley near Jericho Achan and his family were stoned and buried and his property destroyed (1451 B.C.) (Josh. 7:24, 26).*
■ *It was within the borders of Judah (Josh. 15:7).*
■ *The valley of Achor will be a place of pasture (Isa. 65:10).*
■ *It will be a door of hope (Hos. 2:15).*

GILGAL ("circle"), Riba, Khirbet el-Mefjer

One of the traditional locations of Gilgal is 3 miles southeast of Jericho. (Another possible site is about 19 miles north of Jerusalem. See other Gilgal, below.)

■ *Here Joshua set up twelve stones taken from the Jordan (Josh. 4:1-13, 20-24).*
■ *This was the Israelites' first camp after they crossed the Jordan, and here they were circumcised (Josh. 4:19-24; 5:2-10; 9:6; 10:7, 15; 14:6; 15:7; Deut. 11:30).*
■ *This is where the Israelites ate the Passover, manna ceased, and messengers of God came to Joshua (Josh. 5:10-15).*
■ *Israel camped here while besieging Jericho (Josh. 6).*
■ *Here the Gibeonites tricked Joshua (Josh. 9, 10).*
■ *Here Saul was crowned and rejected as a king (1 Sam. 11:14-15; 15).*
■ *Here Saul was denounced (1 Sam. 13:8-15).*
■ *Samuel preached here (1 Sam. 12).*
■ *Here was a place of sacrifices (1 Sam. 10:8; 13:8-10; 15:21).*
■ *Agag was slain here (1 Sam. 15).*
■ *People welcomed David as he returned from exile beyond the Jordan (2 Sam. 19:15).*
■ *Elisha and Elijah seem to have lived here (2 Kings 2:1).*
■ *Elisha purified the pottage (2 Kings 4:38-41).*
■ *Gilgal was referred to by prophets as a place of idolatry (Hos. 4:15; Mic. 6:56).*

RIVER JORDAN

The Jordan River is 200 miles long between the Sea of Galilee and the Dead Sea; yet the distance it covers is only 65 miles in a straight line. Its average width is 100 feet. It is the only river in the world that flows for most of its course below sea level.

■ *Lot chose the plains of the Jordan (Gen. 13:10-11).*
■ *Israel miraculously crossed it and gathered twelve stones from the river bottom ((Josh. 3:13-17; 4:1-9, 20-24; Ps. 114:3).*

Above: River Jordan, near where Jesus was baptized

Left: Caves near Qumran

- *Elijah divided its waters (2 Kings 2:6–8).*
- *Elisha divided its waters (2 Kings 2:14).*
- *Naaman was cured of leprosy by washing in it (2 Kings 5:10–14).*
- *Elisha made an axe head float (2 Kings 6:1–7).*

- *John baptized many here (Matt. 3:6).*
- *Jesus was baptized here (Matt. 3; Mark 1:4–11).*
- *Jesus won his first disciples here (John 1:25–51).*

SALT SEA, Dead Sea, *Sea of the Plain*, *Lake of Lot*

The Dead Sea is 47 by 10 miles in length and width. It is 1,278 feet deep and lies 1,292 feet below sea level. The water is 27 percent mineral. Chemicals extracted include potash, salts, bromine, gypsum, calcium chloride, and magnesium. Seven million tons of water are evaporated each day from the Dead Sea. On the northern shore are the buildings of the phosphate works that were used prior to 1948 but were destroyed in the war. Israel has built a large, modern plant at Sodom, on the southern end of the lake, that processes the various minerals.

- *In the Valley of Salt David smote 18,000 men of Edom (1 Chron. 18:12).*
- *Here Amaziah destroyed 10,000 Edomites (2 Kings 14:7; 2 Chron. 25:11).*
- *It is called by various names (Gen. 14:3; Num. 34:3, 12; Josh. 15:2, 5; 18:19; Deut. 3:17; Josh. 3:16).*

Qumran

The Dead Sea Scrolls, often considered the greatest archaeological find of the twentieth century, made Qumran famous. Many of the scrolls are now housed in the Shrine of the Book, at Jerusalem. Qumran, a National Parks Authority site, lies 13 miles north of Ein Gedi, 2 miles north of Ein Fashkha, and 10 miles south of Jericho. At the time of Jesus an ascetic group of Essenes lived here.

The scrolls they hid in the caves and the habits of the community have caused some to question the "uniqueness" of Jesus, speculating that Jesus probably and John the Baptist almost assuredly were Essenes. Most Christians do not share this view, however.

Muhammad adh-Dhib, a 15-year-old Bedouin, discovered cave number 1 in February or March of 1947. Archbishop Metropolitan Samuel of the Syrian Orthodox Church in Jerusalem purchased four of the scrolls from the Bethlehem antique dealer Kando, and Dr. Eleazar L. Sukenik purchased three. Sukenik purchased the scrolls on November 29, 1947, the very day the United Nations voted for the re-creation of the Jewish state after 2,000 years of nonexistence.

The seven main scrolls from cave number 1 were as follows: *Isaiah, Commentary on Habakkuk, Manual of Discipline, Genesis Apocryphon, War of the Sons of Light with the Sons of Darkness, Thanksgiving Psalms,* and an *Isaiah Fragment.* They date between 300 B.C. and A.D. 70.

POINTS OF INTEREST CONCERNING THE SCROLLS

(1) The GENESIS APOCRYPHON is another book about Abraham, and the original manuscript may have been written by Abraham.

Qumran and the Dead Sea

(2) ISAIAH seems to have been the most read and revered by the Essenes. It reads essentially the same as in the King James Version of the Old Testament; yet this scroll is 1,000 years older than any known Hebrew texts.

(3) THE WAR OF THE SONS OF LIGHT WITH THE SONS OF DARKNESS discusses military tactics.

(4) The BEATEN COPPER SCROLLS tell of buried treasures — $200,000,000 worth, according to some estimates.

(5) The TEMPLE SCROLL gives a detailed description of a temple, a command to build it, and instructions as to how. It differs from hitherto known ancient sources that were concerned with the first, second, and Herod temples (1 Kings 5-9; 2 Chron. 2-7; Ezek. 40-47).

(6) The APOCRYPHAL WRITINGS bear testimony of the coming of Christ and tell of Adam's baptism.

PARALLELS

The religious structure of the Qumran community has many parallels in the gospel as taught by Jesus and understood by many Christian churches today:

(1) ORGANIZATION: priesthood, three priests, twelve men as a council, overseers, bishops, teachers, and elders.

(2) ORDINANCES: baptism by immersion, baptism of the spirit, sacrament, temple covenants, and being just and true.

(3) DOCTRINES: love of God, a God with bodily parts, a Messiah, a premortal existence inferred, earth life as a probationary period, new

revelation, a new covenant, community of goods, sabbath observance, the last days, judgment, resurrection, and others.

(4) LOVE OF THE SCRIPTURES: the hiding of records, flight into the desert, peculiar literature, reading and writing of scriptures, metal used to write on, anticipation of the temple, a divine plan, the elect of God, typical New Testament expressions, denunciation of the Jews in Jerusalem, observance of the law of Moses, secrets, revelation, and inspired leadership.

Ein Fashkha, *En Eglaim*

Ein Fashkha is a freshwater spring a little south of Qumran. The Israelis flock to these springs to bathe off the salt after a swim in the nearby Dead Sea. It has been a favorite bathing site since the six-day war. Showers and dressing facilities are available to the bather.

NORTH FROM JERUSALEM TO NABLUS (SHECHEM)

BAHURIM *("low grounds")*, **Ras et-Tmim**

This site is 1 mile from Jerusalem and near the ancient road from Jerusalem to Jericho, northeast of the Mount of Olives.

- *It was located in Benjamin (2 Sam. 19:16).*
- *Shimei lived here (2 Sam. 16:5; 1 Kings 2:8).*
- *It was the home town of Azmaveth (2 Sam. 23:31).*
- *Jonathan and Ahimaaz hid in the well here (2 Sam. 17:18).*
- *Phaltiel, son of Laish, was ordered to relinquish Michal (2 Sam. 3:14‒16).*

NOB *("height")*, **Ras Umm et-Tala**

Two miles north of Jerusalem, near Anathoth, is the ancient site of Nob.

- *Here David received Goliath's sword from the priest Ahimelech (1 Sam. 21:1, 8‒9).*
- *David fled here from Saul (1 Sam. 21:1, 10).*
- *Saul took vengeance on its inhabitants and slew the priests (1 Sam. 22:6‒23).*

ANATHOTH *("answers," name related to the Canaanite goddess Anath)*, **Anata**, *Ras el-Kharrubeh*

This is a Levitical city in Benjamin, 3 miles northeast of Jerusalem.

- *It was the birthplace of Jeremiah (Jer. 29:27).*
- *It is mentioned many times in the Old Testament (Josh. 21:17‒18; 1 Kings 2:26; 1 Chron. 6:60; Ezra 2:23; Neh. 7:27; 11:31‒32; Isa. 10:30; Jer. 1:1; 11:21, 23; 29:27; 32:7‒9).*

GIBEAH *("hill Gabaah")*, **Shu'fat**, *Gibeath, Tell el-Ful*

Located 2 miles north of Jerusalem, Gibeah is a little east of the high road to Shechem. Four fortresses have been built here, one on an-

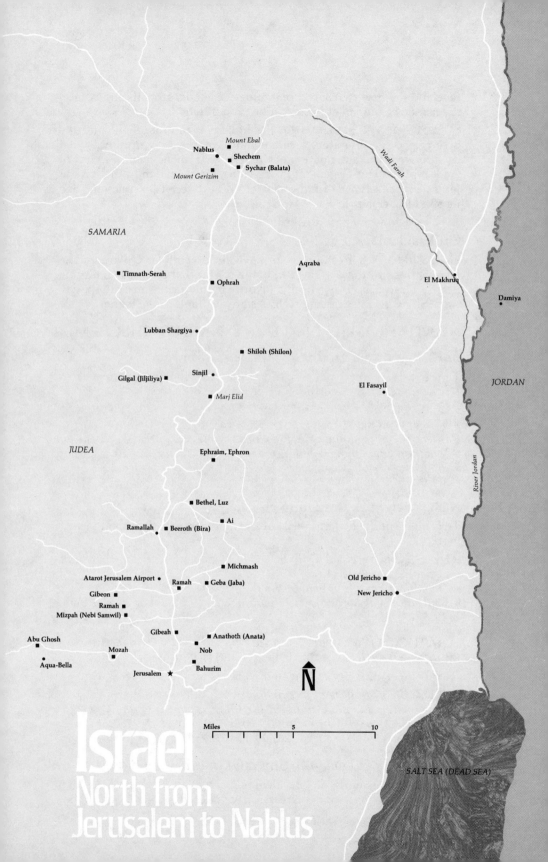

Mount Ebal

Nablus ■
Shechem ■
■ Sychar (Balata)
Mount Gerizim

SAMARIA

■ Timnath-Serah
■ Ophrah
Aqraba ●

El Makhruq ■

Damiya ●

Lubban Shargiya ●
■ Shiloh (Shilon)
Gilgal (Jiljiliya) ■   ● Sinjil
■ Marj Elid

El Fasayil ●

JORDAN

JUDEA
■ Ephraim, Ephron

■ Bethel, Luz
■ Ai
Ramallah ●   ■ Beeroth (Bira)

River Jordan

Wadi Farah

■ Michmash
Atarot Jerusalem Airport ●   Ramah ■   ■ Geba (Jaba)
Old Jericho ■
New Jericho ●
Gibeon ■
Ramah ■
Mizpah (Nebi Samwil) ■
Gibeah ■   ■ Anathoth (Anata)
Abu Ghosh ■
Mozah ■   Nob ■
Aqua-Bella ●
Jerusalem ★   Bahurim ■

N

Miles   5   10

Israel
North from
Jerusalem to Nablus

SALT SEA (DEAD SEA)

other. It was the capital of Saul, the first king of Israel. On the ruins of Saul's fortress, King Hussein of Jordan started to build a palace, but his construction was interrupted by the six-day war in 1967.

■ *Gibeah belonged to Benjamin (Josh. 18:28; 1 Sam. 13:2).*
■ *It was the scene of the destruction of most of the tribe of Benjamin (Judg. 20:12–48).*
■ *It was Saul's home town and his home after he was elected king (1 Sam. 10:26; 11:14; 13:16; 15:34; Isa. 10:29).*
■ *Here Saul summoned the people to war (1 Sam. 11:1–13; 13; 14).*
■ *It was the place of Saul's court (1 Sam. 14:2–3).*
■ *The bodies of seven sons of Saul were hung up in Gibeah (2 Sam. 21:6).*

MIZPAH *("watch tower")*, **Nebi Samwil** *("prophet Samuel")*, *Mizpeh, Tell en-Nasbeh*

Four miles directly northwest of Jerusalem, in the territory of Benjamin, is the ancient site of Mizpah. (There are some who believe the site is 7 miles northeast of Jerusalem.) It was a prominent religious center, particularly in the time of Samuel the prophet. Some believe Samuel is buried here. From the highway going north out of Jerusalem a high minaret may be seen in the distance to the west. This marks the site.

■ *It was in the territory of Benjamin (Josh. 18:21, 26).*
■ *Israel conferred here about the outrage of the Levite concubine (Judg. 20:1–3).*
■ *Samuel rededicated the people and attacked the Philistines (1 Sam. 7:3–14).*
■ *Saul was proclaimed the first king of Israel (1 Sam. 10:17–25).*
■ *Mizpah was fortified by King Asa (1 Kings 15:22; 2 Chron. 16:6).*
■ *Here Gedaliah reigned over the remnant left by Nebuchadnezzar (2 Kings 25:22–26; Jer. 40:5–16).*

RAMAH *("loftiness")*, *Ramathaim Zophim, Rentis (Area of Mizpah)*

This is a high place in the hill country of Ephraim. It can hardly be dissociated from the name of the high place Mizpah (Nebi Samwil). Its chief distinction is its connection with Samuel.

■ *It was the birthplace of Samuel (1 Sam. 1:18–20; 2:11).*
■ *The house of Elkanah and Hannah, Samuel's parents, was here (1 Sam. 1:19; 2:11).*
■ *Samuel lived here and judged Israel (1 Sam. 8:4).*
■ *Samuel anointed Saul the first king of Israel here (1 Sam. 10:1).*
■ *David fled from Saul and came here to seek safety with Samuel (1 Sam. 19:18).*
■ *Samuel died and was buried here (1 Sam. 25:1; 28:3).*

GIBEON *("hill")*, *el-Jib*

Approximately 5 miles directly northwest of Jerusalem, on the road leading west to Latrun, is Gibeon. Here an attempt was made to settle a quarrel between the armies of Ishbosheth, under Abner, and of David, under Joab, by having 12 men from each side fight. The plan failed because the 24 men killed each other at the pool.

Gibeon has a most spectacular **WATER SYSTEM**. Cut entirely from solid rock, it includes a pool 82 feet deep, 37 feet in diameter, and equipped with a circular stairway of 79 steps. Beyond the pool a tunnel, again carved from solid rock a distance of 167 feet, leads to a spring outside the ancient city. The unusual contest of arms probably took place beside this great pool.

When 5 kings of the Amorites fought against Gibeon, Joshua came to the rescue. Hailstones from heaven destroyed more of the enemy than the Israelites did. The sun and moon stood still so the Israelites could win the battle. The kings were slain by Joshua.

Gibeon was the only city that made peace with the Israelites in their conquest of Canaan, and its inhabitants were made servants to Israel (Josh. 11:19).

- *David defeated the Philistines here (1 Chron. 14:16; 2 Sam. 5:25).*
- *Gibeon was allotted to Benjamin and the Levites (Josh. 18:21, 25).*
- *Hailstones came, the sun and moon stood still for Joshua, and five kings were killed by Joshua (Josh. 10:1–27).*
- *At the pool of Gibeon 24 men killed each other when Abner defeated Joab (2 Sam. 2:12–28).*
- *Saul slew Gibeonites (2 Sam. 21:1–9).*
- *When David brought the ark of God back to Jerusalem, it seems that the tabernacle of the congregation was at Gibeon (2 Chron. 1:3–6).*
- *This was the place of Solomon's sacrifice and famous prayer and dream (1 Kings 3:4–15; 9:2; 2 Chron. 1:2–17).*
- *Here captives from Mizpah were freed (Jer. 41:11–18).*

RAMAH *("the height")*, **Er Ram**, *Arimathea*

Five miles north of Jerusalem, between Gibeah and Giba, is another Ramah. Near it are some remarkable ancient monuments, known locally as "the graves of the children of Israel," one of which was possibly the tomb of Rachel, according to ancient tradition.

- *The palm tree of Deborah was near here, between Ramah and Bethel (Judg. 4:5).*
- *Ramah was built up by Baasha, king of Israel, in a war against Judah (1 Kings 15:17; 2 Chron. 16:1).*
- *Building material was taken by Asa to build Giba and Mizpah (2 Chron. 16:6).*
- *The people of Ramah returned after captivity and settled here (Ezra 2:1, 26; Neh. 7:6, 30; 11:1–4, 32–33).*
- *Jeremiah was released from chains here (Jer. 40:1–4).*
- *It was the birthplace of Joseph of Arimathea, in whose tomb Jesus was buried (Matt. 27:57–60; Mark 15:42–45; Luke 23:50–51; John 19:38–42).*

GEBA *("hill")*, Jaba

Geba lies 6 miles north of Jerusalem, on the border of Benjamin's inheritance (Josh. 18:23–24).

- *It was a city of the Levites (Josh. 21:1, 17; 1 Chron. 6:60).*
- *Jonathan fought the Philistines here (1 Sam. 14:1–23).*
- *It was reoccupied by Judah after the 70-year exile in Babylon (Ezra 2:26; Neh. 11:1–4, 31–33).*

Atarot Jerusalem Airport

Five miles north of Jerusalem is the Atarot Jerusalem Airport (Kalandia).

MICHMASH, Mukhmas

This site is 7 miles north of Jerusalem, on the northeast of Ramah.

- *The contests between the courageous Jonathan and the Philistines took place here (1 Sam. 13–14; Isa. 10:28).*
- *It was resettled by the Jews as they returned from their captivity in Babylon (Ezra 2:1, 27; Neh. 7:6, 31).*

Ramallah *("the high place of God")*, Ram-Allah

Eight miles north of Jerusalem and 2,930 feet above sea level is the city of Ramallah. It is true to its name because it overlooks the entire area. The city has 50,000 people, of whom 95 percent are Christian Arabs. The city has a neat and clean appearance.

BEEROTH *("wells")*, Bira, el-Birch

Beeroth is 8 miles north of Jerusalem, by the town of Ramallah. This was the first stopping place for caravans going from Jerusalem to Galilee.

- *This is thought to be the place where Mary and Joseph first missed Jesus when he was still in the temple at age twelve (Luke 2:41–45).*

BETHEL *("house of God")*, LUZ, Beitin

Bethel is 11 miles north of Jerusalem and 2 miles (3 kilometers) east of the main road between Ramallah and Nablus. It was first called *Luz*. Tradition has the name *Bethel* refer to the stone set up by Jacob and anointed as a symbol of God's presence. After the division of the kingdom, Bethel became the Northern Kingdom's religious center. In 721 B.C. the Assyrians captured it, along with Samaria. Bethel was fortified during the Maccabean period, but was taken by Vespasian as the Romans approached Jerusalem. Very little remains of the city today. Ruins of what appears to be an ancient black stone synagogue mark the traditional site. The Arab village of Beitin is near the historical Bethel. According to tradition, the stone that Jacob set up as a pillar is the same stone that is now under the seat of the coronation chair in Westminster Abbey, in London.

- *Bethel was known as Luz (Gen. 28:19) and as Bethaven (Hos. 4:15).*

- *It was the place of Abraham's second altar of worship in Palestine (Gen. 12:7–8).*
- *Here Abraham and Lot separated (Gen. 13).*
- *Here Jacob had his dream of the ladder. He used the stone for a pillow and then set it up as a pillar and altar (Gen. 28:10–22).*
- *Jacob lived here (Gen. 35:1–15).*
- *Jacob revisited Bethel, and Deborah, Rebekah's nurse, died here (Gen. 35:1–8).*
- *Israel conquered Bethel, a royal city of the Canaanites (Judg. 1: 22–26).*
- *Samuel judged here (1 Sam. 7:16).*
- *Jeroboam set up a golden calf as a shrine (1 Kings 12:25–33).*
- *Jeroboam was warned by a prophet, who was thereafter led to disobedience by a prophet of Bethel and was destroyed (1 Kings 13).*
- *Because Amos foretold the death of the king and the captivity of Israel, he was forbidden by Jeroboam from prophesying in Bethel (Amos 7:10–17).*
- *Here was one of the "schools of the prophets," as they are often called (2 Kings 2:2–3).*
- *Elisha cursed the children, and bears tore them, according to the "bear story" (2 Kings 2:23–24).*
- *King Josiah overthrew idol worship (2 Kings 23).*
- *Bethel was the frequent subject of prophecy (Jer. 4:3–13; Amos 3:14; 4:4; 5:5; 7:10, 13).*
- *Amos was expelled from it (Amos 7:10).*

AI *("the ruined mound")*

Two to three miles southeast of Bethel is the traditional site of Ai. Excavations by Mme Marquet-Krause showed that a palace, a sanctuary, and fortifications existed here and some ruins date back to the third millennium B.C. A mile away is Hai, or Haiyan.

- *Ai was connected with Abraham's journeys (Gen. 12:8; 13:3).*
- *It was the first city captured by the Israelites in Canaan (Josh. 7; 8; 9:3).*
- *It was mentioned in the time of Ezra (Ezra 2:28).*
- *Its captivity was prophesied (Jer. 49:3).*
- *Perhaps this is the Aiath of Isaiah's description (Isa. 10:28) and the Aija mentioned in Nehemiah's account (Neh. 11:31).*

EPHRAIM *("doubly fruitful")*, EPHRON

Twelve miles north of Jerusalem and a few miles from Bethel is the traditional site of Ephraim. The exact site has not been determined.

- *It was near Abraham's sheep farm (2 Sam. 13:23).*
- *Abijah took Ephraim from Jeroboam (2 Chron. 13:19).*
- *Here Jesus retired after raising Lazarus from the dead (John 11:54).*

MARJ ELID *("valley of the feast,"* Valley of the Thieves)

This is a narrow valley running toward the northeast at a point about

10 miles north of Ramallah. The valley contains the ruins of an old Turkish Khan (Inn), and at the southern end is a crusader fort.

■ *Here the daughters of Shiloh were captured by the Benjaminites (Judg. 21:19).*

Sinjil

The site of the ancient crusader town of Saint Giles is located on the road that goes west to Gilgal.

GILGAL *("circle," "wheel")*, Jiljiliya

Approximately 19 miles north of Jerusalem and 3 miles west of the highway is a possible ancient site of Gilgal. (Another possible site is 3 miles southeast of Jericho. See other Gilgal, above.)

■ *Gilgal was visited by Elijah and Elisha (2 Kings 2:1; 4:38).*
■ *It is mentioned elsewhere in the Old Testament also (Deut. 11:30; Josh. 12:23).*

SHILOH, Shilon, *Seilun ("peaceful," "place of rest")*, Turmus-Aya

Shiloh was the first capital of Israel for 300 years before the conquest of Jerusalem. It was destroyed by the Philistines about 1050 B.C. A lintel with "horned altars" in bas-relief was found here. There are also remains of an ancient synagogue or mosque that are over a thousand years old. The VALLEY OF THE DANCERS is on the west of Shiloh.

■ *Here the tribes of Israel assembled after the conquest and received their allotment of territory (Josh. 18–22).*
■ *Shiloh was the home of the ark and tabernacle at the time of the judges (Josh. 18:1; Judg. 18:31).*
■ *Here the Benjaminites captured maidens for wives (Judg. 21:16–25).*
■ *Here Eli judged and Hannah prayed for a son (1 Sam. 1:1–10).*
■ *This was the scene of the wickedness of Eli's sons (1 Sam. 2:12–36).*
■ *Samuel grew up here in the service of the Lord under the high priest Eli (1 Sam. 3).*
■ *Here Eli died (1 Sam. 4).*
■ *Here Samuel judged Israel (1 Sam. 7:16–17).*
■ *Ahijah prophesied against Jeroboam (1 Kings 14:1–20).*
■ *The Assyrian king restored Jeremiah to liberty (Jer. 40:1–6).*
■ *Shiloh was used as an illustration and warning (Ps. 78:59–61; Jer. 7:12, 14; 26:6).*
■ *Samuel received his call here when still a child (1 Sam. 3).*

Lubban Shargiya

In the beautiful valley of Lebona is Lubban Shargiya, and less than a mile north of the city was the boundary line between Samaria on the north and Judea on the south in the days of the Savior. The line was also located 1½ miles north of Shiloh. As the traveler nears the valley of Lebona from the south, he can see two WATCHTOWERS built on the right side of the road to guard against intruders.

- *Watchtowers were built in biblical times (Isa. 5:2; Matt. 21:33).*
- *The parable of the wicked husbandmen mentions watchtowers (Matt. 21:33-44).*

OPHRAH *("hamlet")*, *et-Taiyibeh*

Ophrah lies 12 miles south of Shechem.

- *It was a town in Benjamin (Josh. 18:21, 23).*
- *An angel met Gideon here (Judg. 6:11).*
- *This was the scene of the activities of Gideon and Abimelech (Judg. 6:11; 9:5-7).*
- *It was the house and burying place of Gideon (Judg. 8:27-32).*
- *Here Abimelech slew 69 of his brethren (Judg. 9:1-5).*
- *Gideon built an altar here (Judg. 6:24).*

TIMNATH-SERAH, *Timnath*

Timnath-Serah is 6 miles north-northwest of Ophrah, where Joshua was buried.

- *This was Joshua's burial site (Josh. 19:50; 24:30).*

SYCHAR, **Balata**, *Balatah*, **Askar, Jacob's Well**

Jacob's Well is located at the fork of the road at Balata near Shechem, on the ground designated as "Jacob's parcel of ground," or the land that Jacob gave Joseph. Jews, Samaritans, Mohammedans, and Christians associate this well with Jacob. The well is 7½ feet in diameter, lined with rough masonry, and 80-90 feet deep to the water, which is very soft. The Greek Orthodox church owns the well and is building a chapel over it.

Some believe that Sychar was at Shechem. Others believe that Askar, about 1 mile northeast of Jacob's Well, was the ancient site of Sychar. Two hundred yards northeast of Jacob's well is JOSEPH'S TOMB, similar to Rachel's tomb. Here is the traditional spot where Joseph's bones were buried after being carried from Egypt.

- *This was the land that Jacob gave Joseph (Gen. 48:22).*
- *Here Joseph's bones were buried (Josh. 24:32; Gen. 48:22; Acts 7:16).*
- *Jesus talked to the Samaritan woman here (John 4:3-42).*
- *Others who went to Egypt were brought back here for burial (Acts 7:16).*

SHECHEM *("shoulder")*, **Nablus**, *Sechem, Neapolis, Tell Balatah*

Shechem, the first capital of the Northern Kingdom under Jeroboam, lies in a valley between Mount Gerizim and Mount Ebal, southeast of the present site of Nablus. The ancient tell is located just northwest of the traditional burial site of Joseph. Nablus is about the same size as Hebron, but is more modern. It is an Arab city and noted for its soap and pastry making. It is a much older site than Jerusalem and is mentioned 48 times in the Bible.

Nablus is presently the home of about 250 Samaritans, who live on the west side of the city. Here in the **SAMARITAN SYNAGOGUE** is the *Samaritan Pentateuch*, reputed by the Samaritans to be the oldest copy of the writings of Moses (3,605 years old) and written on parchment. Modern scholars date the document to A.D. 1100-1200, however. The Samaritans, remnants of the Ten Tribes, are those who stayed in Samaria when the Ten Tribes were carried north by the Assyrians (2 Kings 17:6, 23). They intermarried with non-Israelites (2 Kings 17:24) and were thus shunned by the Jews of Jesus' day. They claim, however, that their blood is pure to Aaron, and they marry within their own group. There are now approximately 400 Samaritans — 240 in Nablus and 160 at Holon — belonging to 5 large families.

Many Samaritans are very poor and live in houses near their synagogue. They wear white robes, they do not shave or cut their hair, and their hats are covered with red cloth. The Samaritan temple on Mount Gerizim was destroyed by John Hyrcanus in 126 B.C., but the Samaritans still celebrate the Passover feast every year on Mount Gerizim on the evening before the full moon of Nisan (April).

The creed of the Samaritans includes the following:

(1) God is one, incorporeal.
(2) Moses is the only prophet and the intercessor for man in the final judgment.
(3) The law of Moses is the only divine revelation.
(4) Mount Gerizim is the chosen place of God, the only center of worship, the "navel of the earth," and "the place where Adam offered sacrifices."
(5) On Judgment Day the righteous will be resurrected in paradise and the wicked will roast in eternal fire.
(6) Six thousand years after creation a Restorer will arise to ameliorate their fortunes. He will live 110 years.

- *This was the first place Abraham dwelt and built an altar in Canaan (Gen. 12:1-7).*
- *Jacob bought land and lived here after meeting Esau (Gen. 33: 16-20).*
- *Jacob's daughter was defiled (Gen. 34).*
- *Jacob hid strange gods here (Gen. 35:1-4).*
- *Joseph came here to seek his brethren, who were feeding their flocks. On this journey he was sold to the Ishmaelite traders (Gen. 37: 13-14).*
- *Near here Joseph's bones were buried in land purchased after he was carried from Egypt (Gen. 50:25; 33:18-19; Josh. 24:32).*
- *Blessings and cursings of Israel were pronounced here, and covenants were made (Deut. 11:26-30; 27; 28; Josh. 8:30-35).*
- *This was the scene of Joshua's final address and Israel's dedication to God: "We will serve the Lord" (Josh. 24:1-25, esp. 15).*
- *The pillar was a sacred stone erected by Joshua (Josh. 24:26).*
- *Abimelech, son of Gideon, set himself up as head over all Israel at*

Shechem. He slew 69 of his brothers and reigned 3½ years (Judg. 9).

- *The sacred oak of the pillar was here, beside which Abimelech was crowned (Judg. 9:6).*
- *Rehoboam was rejected, and the kingdom was divided (1 Kings 12:1-24).*
- *Jeroboam was elected and fortified it as his capital (1 Kings 12:25-33; 13-14).*
- *It was a city of refuge (Num. 35:11-32; Deut. 19:1-13; Josh. 20).*
- *The king of Assyria brought people from Babylon and placed them in cities of Samaria (2 Kings 17:24).*
- *The Samaritans hindered the building of the walls of Jerusalem (Neh. 2:19-20; 4:1-9; 6:1-14).*

MOUNT GERIZIM (*"waste places"*), Jebel et Tor (*Mount of Blessing*)

On the southwest of Nablus is Mount Gerizim, 2,848 feet above sea level and held sacred by the Samaritans. The Samaritans claim they have the **ALTARS BUILT BY ADAM AND NOAH** on the top of the mount. They claim that it was on this mountain that Abraham prepared to offer up his own son Isaac as a sacrifice.

At the beginning of the fourth century B.C. a Samaritan temple was built. It was destroyed by Hyrcanus in 126 B.C. In the walls of the Justinian Castle, built on the top in A.D. 583, are **TWELVE STONES** that the Samaritans say came from the bottom of the Jordan River as the Israelites crossed. The Samaritans spend a week of celebrating on the mount during the Passover. Sheep are slaughtered and roasted for the occasion.

A Samaritan and the Pentateuch, Nablus

- *This was known as the "Mount of Blessing" (Deut. 11:29–30; Josh. 8:33).*
- *Jotham spoke his parable to Shechem from Mount Gerizim (Judg. 9:7).*
- *At the Well of Jacob the Samaritan argued about worshiping "in this mountain" (John 4:20).*

MOUNT EBAL *("bare")*, *Jebel Eslamiyeh (Mount of Cursing)*

On the northeast of Nablus, directly across from Mount Gerizim, is Mount Ebal, 3,077 feet above sea level. Both Gerizim and Ebal mountains are important because it was here that Israel renewed her covenants with God. Joshua stationed half of the tribes on Ebal and half on Gerizim and the ark with the priests and Levites in the center. From Gerizim they shouted out the blessings of God that they would receive if they were faithful, and from Ebal they proclaimed the curses that would overtake them if they were disobedient to God. On the top of the mountain is a Moslem sanctuary said to contain the head of John the Baptist.

- *This was the "Mount of Cursing" (Deut. 11:29–30; 27:11–26; Joshua 8:30–34).*
- *Joshua built an altar and erected a monument bearing the law of Moses (Josh. 8:30).*

NORTH FROM NABLUS (SHECHEM) TO THE SEA OF GALILEE

TIRZAH *("delight")*, **Tell el Farah**

Four or five miles north of Shechem is the site of Tirzah. Its king was slain by Joshua. In Israelite times it superseded Shechem as the capital of the northern kingdom of Israel.

- *Its king was slain by Joshua (Josh. 12:1, 24).*
- *It was the capital of the Northern Kingdom under Jeroboam (1 Kings 14:17).*
- *Here Menahem matured his rebellion against Shallum (2 Kings 15:14).*

SAMARIA *("watch")*, *Sebaste, Sebastia*, **Sabastiya**

Forty-two miles north of Jerusalem, 9 miles north of Nablus, and on a hill 300 feet high are the extensive ruins of the ancient capital city of Samaria. Omri (876–869 B.C.), the sixth king of Israel, founded Samaria as Israel's capital city, and it was to the kings of Samaria that the ten tribes of Israel turned for leadership. The whole country took its name from the city, and the immediate area was occupied by the tribes of Ephraim and Manasseh.

Omri lived here 6 years, and when he died his son Ahab reigned in his place. Here Ahab built his ivory palace, which Amos spoke of and denounced. Samaria saw the wickedness of Jezebel, who induced Ahab to build a temple to Baal right in the capital city.

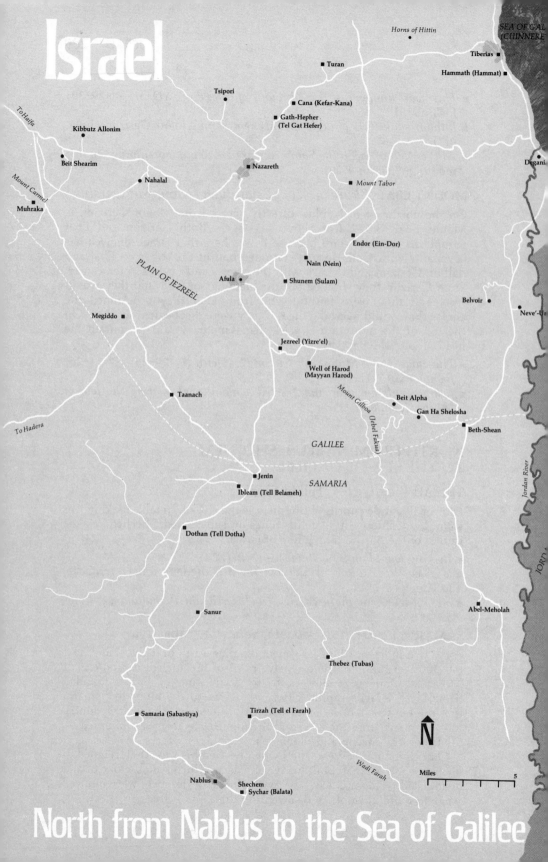

Israel

SEA OF GAL
(CHINNERE

Horns of Hittin

Tiberias

Turan

Hammath (Hammat)

Tsipori

Cana (Kefar-Kana)

Gath-Hepher
(Tel Gat Hefer)

Kibbutz Allonim

Degani

Beit Shearim

Nazareth

Mount Carmel

Nahalal

Mount Tabor

Muhraka

Endor (Ein-Dor)

Nain (Nein)

PLAIN OF JEZREEL

Afula

Shunem (Sulam)

Belvoir

Neve'-Ur

Megiddo

Jezreel (Yizre'el)

Well of Harod
(Mayyan Harod)

Taanach

Beit Alpha

Gan Ha Shelosha

To Hadera

GALILEE

Beth-Shean

Jenin

SAMARIA

Ibleam (Tell Belameh)

Jordan River

Dothan (Tell Dotha)

Abel-Meholah

Sanur

JORD

Thebez (Tubas)

Ň

Samaria (Sabastiya)

Tirzah (Tell el Farah)

Wadi Farah

Miles   5

Nablus

Shechem

Sychar (Balata)

North from Nablus to the Sea of Galilee

In addition to Omri and Ahab, Samaria was also the residence and burial place of 4 other kings of Israel: Jehu, Jehoahaz, Joash, and Jehoash. The prophets of Israel denounced the city for its transgressions and prophesied its doom.

Samaria was besieged by Shalmaneser IV in the seventh year of Hosea and taken by Sargon in 722-721 B.C. Its inhabitants, along with the Ten Tribes, were carried captive "over the river" and became lost to history. Some Israelites remained in the area, however, and intermarried with those who were brought from Babylon, Cuthah, Ava Hamah, and other places to take the place of the lost Israelites. Descendants from these mixed marriages were called Samaritans.

The *Black Obelisk of Shalmaneser III*, found in Nimrud and dated 859-824 B.C., contains the only known portrait of an Israelite king — Jehu. This Victory Monument shows Jehu, son of Omri, giving tribute to Shalmaneser III and tells about his capture.

The *Royal Annals*, found at Nineveh, are a part of several Mesopotamian documents that tell of Sargon's capture of Samaria in 721 B.C. Sargon told of taking 27,290 Israelites prisoner at Samaria (Annals 10-18).

In 331 B.C. Alexander the Great besieged Samaria, and it was later destroyed by John Hyrcanus in 120 B.C. It was rebuilt by Pompey and built again by Gabinius.

Herod the Great carried out very important building works here (35 B.C.), large portions of which remain. He built a promenade that covered the top of the hill, with huge granite columns in three rows. He is responsible for changing the name to *Sebaste* in honor of Caesar Augustus. Here he had his son and his wife, Mariamne, killed.

Excavations at Samaria under the direction of J. W. Crowfoot resulted in the discovery of finely carved ivory fragments from such an ivory building as Ahab's palace, which Amos denounced. The fragments included inlays of glass paste in ivory, representing floral motifs, and figured scenes that were apparently made by Phoenician artisans. They were probably a part of the furniture decorations in the royal palace. The ivory fragments are owned by the University Museum of Philadelphia, the Rockefeller Museum at Jerusalem, and the Palestine Exploration Fund of London. Harvard University began excavations at Samaria in 1908, financed by Jacob Schiff, a Jewish millionaire; and beginning in 1931 a joint expedition began excavating again. Ruins that have been uncovered include the PALACE OF OMRI AND AHAB, the TEMPLE OF AUGUSTUS, the ROMAN FORUM, the BASILICA, the HIPPODROME, the THEATER, the STREET OF COLUMNS, the GATEWAY, the WALLS, and the CHURCH OF SAINT JOHN THE BAPTIST, which dates from the Crusader period. Ostraca, ivories, and other remains and ruins make this one of the most important archaeological sites in Israel.

It is a National Parks Authority site.

SABASTIYA is the small village on the side of the hill at Samaria. Its name is a corruption of the Greek *Sebaste*. Local tradition holds that the prophets Elisha and Obadiah are buried at Samaria in a subterranean cave in the courtyard of a mosque. The minaret is built inside a Crusader cathedral, dating back to 1160. Some Christians believe that this is where John the Baptist was imprisoned and that his head is buried here. A church is named in his honor. A dungeon is pointed out as *the* dungeon in which John suffered imprisonment. (Machaerus in Jordan is also a traditional site for this event.)

- *Samaria was the capital, residence, and burial place of the kings of Israel, the Northern Kingdom (1 Kings 16:23-24, 28; 22:37; 2 Kings 6:24-30).*
- *Under the influence of Jezebel, Ahab made it a center of Baal worship (1 Kings 16:29-33).*
- *Amos denounced Ahab's house of ivory (Amos 6:1, 4; 1 Kings 22:39).*
- *Jezebel killed many prophets here (1 Kings 18:2, 4).*
- *Benhadad, king of Syria, twice besieged it and was unsuccessful (1 Kings 20; 2 Kings 6).*
- *Elijah destroyed the messengers of King Ahaziah and prophesied his death (2 Kings 1).*
- *Naaman, the Syrian leper, went to Samaria to be healed by Elisha (2 Kings 5).*
- *Elisha smote Benhadad's army with blindness and led some of them into Samaria (2 Kings 6, 7).*
- *Jehu killed Ahab's seventy sons and destroyed the idolatry (2 Kings 10).*
- *Samaria was captured and finally overthrown by Sargon (Shalmaneser's successor) and the Assyrians in 721 B.C. (2 Kings 17; 18:9-12).*
- *Many prophecies concerned its sin and doom (Isa. 8:4; 9:8-24; 10:9; 28; 36:19; Jer. 23:13; Ezek. 23:1-4; Hos. 7; 13:16; Amos 3:12; Mic. 1:6).*
- *Supposedly, this is where John's head was brought at the request of Salome (Matt. 14:1-12; Mark 6:17-29).*
- *Here Philip preached (Acts 8:5-25).*

SANUR

This is believed to have been the site of the biblical Judith's home.

- *Judith was the daughter of Merari, of the tribe of Simeon (Judith 8:1).*

THEBEZ *("seen afar")*, Tubas

In a fruitful valley 10 miles northeast of Nablus is Tubas, the site of the ancient city of Thebez.

- *In the reduction of this fortified city Abimelech met his death (Judg. 9:54; 2 Sam. 11:21).*

ABEL-MEHOLAH *("meadow of the dance")* (location uncertain, possibly Tell el-Maqlub or Tell Abu Sifri)

This is a city in Issachar, at the north of the Jordan Valley and 10 miles south of Beth-Shean. It is the birthplace of Elisha, a leading prophet of Israel after the death of Elijah. His prophetic career lasted more than 50 years during the reigns of Jehoram, Jehu, Jehoahaz, and Joash.

■ *This was the limit of Gideon's pursuit of the Midianites (Judg. 7:22).*
■ *It was the birthplace of Elisha (1 Kings 19:16; 4:12).*
■ *Elisha was the prophet who healed Naaman (2 Kings 5; Luke 4:27).*
■ *The people forsook the Lord and served Baal and Ashtoreth (1 Sam. 31:10; 1 Kings 11:5).*

DOTHAN *("double feast")*, *Dothian*, **Tell Dotha**

Dothan is about 14 miles north of Sabastiya (Samaria). It is a strategic military point at the entrance of a pass leading to the Valley and Plains of Esdraelon. At the end of the Dothan Valley is a "knocked out" Jordanian tank — a grim reminder of the six-day war.

■ *Joseph's brothers tended their flocks here and Joseph was sold to Ishmaelites to be carried to Egypt (Gen. 37:13–28).*
■ *Joseph's coat of many colors was rent by his brothers (Gen. 37:31–32).*
■ *It was the home of Elisha (2 Kings 6).*
■ *Here the Syrian army surrounded Elisha and his servant (2 Kings 6:13–23).*

IBLEAM *("place of victory")*, *Bileam*, **Tell Belameh**

This town of Asher was about 1 mile southwest of Jenin.

■ *It was given to Manasseh (Josh. 17:11).*
■ *Here the Canaanites successfully resisted the people of Manasseh (Josh. 17:12; Judg. 1:27).*
■ *As a Levitical city it was called Bileam (1 Chron. 6:70).*
■ *Near here Jehu killed King Ahaziah (2 Kings 9:27).*
■ *Zechariah, king of Israel, was killed here by Shallum (2 Kings 15:10).*

EN-GANNIM, **Jenin** *("fount of gardens")*

This is a typical oriental town, in a fertile region on the southern edge of the plain of Jezreel and 13 miles north of Dothan. It lies about a mile south of the Galilee-Samaria boundary line. On its western outskirts is a hill, which has a tower and a sacred tree. It is known as Khirbet Belame.

■ *It is mentioned in Joshua 15:34; 19:21; 21:29.*
■ *According to tradition, it was here that Jesus healed ten lepers (Luke 17:11–19).*

GALILEE *("the circle," home of Jesus)*

Galilee was the northern region of Palestine in the days of Jesus. The south boundary was the Carmel mountain range to the west and a line from Jenin to Beth-Shean on the east. Northward and to the northwest it was bounded by Syria and Phoenicia. The area was about 60 miles long and 30 miles wide.

When the Israelites conquered this area it was allotted to the tribes of Asher, Naphtali, Zebulon, and a part of Issachar. It was later conquered by the Assyrians, still later by Egypt, then by the Romans.

Under Rome, Herod the Great was ruler in 47 B.C. and was succeeded by his son Antipas as Tetrarch in 4 B.C. In the third century A.D., Galilee became the center of Rabbinic life. Remains of Jewish synagogues of this era are to be seen among the ruins of Galilean cities.

Galilee is important because Jesus spent most of his life here. Eleven of his disciples were Galileans, as also had been the prophets Jonah, Elisha, and possibly Hosea. A population of two or three million people may have lived in 204 towns of Galilee in Jesus' day. They were Aramaean, Phoenician, Greek, and Jewish.

Beginning in March, a vast blanket of green covers Galilee. One Galilee lover said, "In March, Galilee is so green it hurts your eyes." Here you can witness sleepy villages that characterize biblical days. Wells, jugs, veils, shepherds, donkeys, and robes take us back 2,000 years to Jesus' day. The Israelis have had to fight malaria and Arabs to settle the area, but it is now a beautiful paradise for the Israeli and Arab farmers.

- *There are many Old Testament references to this area (Josh. 20:7; Judg. 4:6-10; 1 Kings 9:11; 2 Kings 15:29, etc.).*
- *Jesus went into Galilee (Matt. 4:12-25).*
- *Jesus made his first preaching tour of Galilee; a leper was healed (Matt. 4:23-25; 8:2-4; Mark 1:35-45; Luke 4:42-44; 5:12-16).*
- *He made a second tour of Galilee (Luke 8:1-3; Matt. 11:2-30; Luke 7:18-35). He raised the widow's son at Nain from the dead (Luke 7:11-17).*
- *He made a third tour of Galilee; the Twelve were sent forth (Matt. 9:35-11:1; Mark 6:6-13; Luke 9:1-6).*
- *Jesus foretold his death (Matt. 17:22-23).*
- *Jesus took his final departure from here (Matt. 19:1; Mark 10:1; Luke 9:51).*
- *He appeared here after his resurrection (Matt. 28:16-20; Mark 16: 15-18).*

TAANACH ("battlement"), Ta'annek

This is a modern village of about 200 people located on the eastern half of the base of the Tell Ta'annek and 5 miles southeast of Megiddo. The tell was first excavated in 1899 and was one of the first sites of excavation in Palestine. The largest Akkadian tablet group ever found in Palestine was discovered here. A water system and one of the best preserved Palestinian buildings are at the site. A complete figurine mold, dating as far back as the eighth to eleventh century B.C., was also recently found.

- *This was a Canaanite town undefeated by Joshua (Judg. 1:27; Josh. 12:21).*
- *It was a famous battleground where Sisera gathered his forces to battle against Barak and Deborah (Judg. 5:19).*
- *There are other biblical references to the place (Josh. 17:11; 1 Chron. 7:29; Josh. 21:25; 1 Kings 4:12).*

PLAIN OF JEZREEL *("God sows"), Valley of Armageddon, Plain of Esdraelon, the Emek, Merj Ibn Amir*

This is the largest and most fertile valley in Israel and cuts in two the central ridge of mountains of Galilee in the north and Samaria in the south. It is a historic battleground, lying between Nazareth, Mount Carmel, Mount Gilboa, and Little Hermon — a triangle about 15 by 15 by 20 miles. This was a swamp land until, in the early 1920s, the Jewish National Fund launched its biggest land reclamation project. Israel's oldest and best-known settlements are here. One of the most famous is the giant moshav, Nahalal, where 75 families farm on "spokelike" farms that fan out from the city center.

Egyptians, Hittites, Israelites, Philistines, Assyrians, Syrians, Persians, Greeks, Romans, Crusaders, Turks, and the British under Allenby (1918) have marched and fought on these plains. The apostle John saw the gathering in the valley of Armageddon, in connection with the last great battle.

It was the location of King Ahab's winter palace.

- *It was named the* Valley of Jezreel *(Josh. 17:16).*
- *It was located in the area allotted to the tribe of Issachar (Gen. 49: 14–15).*
- *It was the scene of Deborah and Barak's strategy against Sisera (Judg. 4–5).*
- *It was the place of Gideon's victory (Judg. 7).*
- *Here Elijah ran before the chariot of Ahab (1 Kings 18:46).*
- *King Josiah was mortally wounded in battle (2 Chron. 35:20–24).*
- *King Saul and his son Jonathan died at Mount Gilboa near here in a clash with the Philistines (1 Sam. 31; 2 Sam. 1; 21:12–14).*
- *It will be the site of the last great battle of Armageddon (Zech. 12:10–11; Rev. 16:13–16).*
- *Great blessings are to come upon Israel on this very place — probably in the Millennium (Hos. 2:21–23).*

MEGIDDO, *Derekh Hayam, Tell el-Mutesellim ("hill of the governor")*

This was a royal city of the Canaanites, 22 miles north of Shechem on the southern edge of the plains of Jezreel, the most famous battlefield in the world. Thutmose III battled with Megiddo in 1478 B.C.; the walls of his temple at Thebes tell of his war plans. The mound, which was extensively excavated between 1925 and 1939 by the Oriental Institute of the University of Chicago, covers 13 acres and reveals 20 cities — each built on the ruins of the preceding one — dating from 4000 to 400 B.C. Its WATER SYSTEM dates back 2,800 years. A shaft 120 feet deep connects with a spring outside the city walls by a TUNNEL 215 feet long, which protected the city's water supply. Sunken GRAIN SILOS protected the grain. SOLOMON'S STABLES could house up to 450 horses. Exquisite IVORIES, a fragment of an EGYPTIAN STELA bearing the name *Shishak*, an elaborate CITY GATE, and the SEAL OF SHEVA are among the important discoveries at

Right: Canaanite altar with horns, found at Megiddo

Below: Megiddo, with a large Canaanite altar in the center

Megiddo. The Hebrew Seal of Sheva has the following words inscribed on it: *Eved Yravam*, which means "servant of Jeroboam." Although this seal is in a museum in Istanbul, most of the finds at Megiddo have been placed in the Rockefeller Museum in Jerusalem.

A most beautiful limestone **ALTAR WITH HORNS** like those used by the children of Israel is very interesting to Old Testament students (1 Kings 1:50). It is in the Rockefeller Museum in Jerusalem.

Megiddo is a National Parks Authority site.

- *Joshua killed the king and took the city (Josh. 12:7, 21).*
- *The city was possessed by Manasseh (Josh. 17:11; 1 Chron. 7:29).*
- *Sisera and his armies were defeated "by the waters of Megiddo" (Judg. 5:19-20).*
- *Solomon fortified the city as a "chariot city," and it served as one of his defense posts (1 Kings 9:15). Stables capable of taking care of 450 horses and 150 chariots have been excavated. Archaeologists have recently dated them to the time of King Ahab (874-853 B.C.). Solomon may have erected something similar on this spot a century earlier.*
- *Ahaziah, king of Israel, was slain here by Jehu (2 Kings 9:27).*
- *Josiah was killed in a battle with Pharaoh Necho and the Egyptian army at Megiddo in 610 B.C. (2 Chron. 35:20-24; 2 Kings 23:29-30).*
- *The last great battle of this age will be fought at Armageddon — in Hebrew Har Mageddon, "Mount of Megiddo" (Rev. 16:13-16; Ezek. 38-39; Zech. 14:2-3).*

MOUNT CARMEL *("fruit garden")*, **Muhraka**, *Jebel Mar Elyas*

This is a mountain range 13 miles long projecting into the Mediterranean Sea at Haifa. Its highest point is 1,810 feet above sea level. It is green the year round and has been venerated since antiquity. It was a sanctuary for the worship of Baal. The **CARMELITE MONASTERY OF SAINT ELIJAH** stands at Muhraka on the mount. A grotto is located here, where tradition indicates Elijah dwelt. Other buildings include a monument to French soldiers; a building to care for pilgrims; a lighthouse; a chapel at "the place of burning," where, tradition says, Elijah contested with the prophets of Baal; and another where the prophets are said to have been killed. A large statue of Elijah killing the prophets of Baal is located near the chapel. At the foot of Carmel is the **CAVE OF ELIJAH**, where, it is believed, the prophet took refuge in one of his flights from the anger of Ahab (1 Kings 19:8-13).

Mount Carmel is a National Parks Authority site.

- *An ancient altar to Jehovah stood here (1 Kings 18:30).*
- *Elijah's contest with the prophets of Baal was here (1 Kings 18: 19-40).*
- *The 3½-year drought was ended by Elijah's prayer (1 Kings 18: 41-45).*
- *It was visited by Elisha (2 Kings 2:25).*
- *From earliest times it was the site of altars, shrines, and caves where hermits found solitude (Amos 9:3).*
- *It was used as a symbol of beauty, fruitfulness, majesty, prosperity, and happiness (Isa. 35:2; Jer. 46:18; 50:19; 2 Chron. 26:10; Song of Sol. 7:5).*

Kibbutz Allonim

Three miles northeast of Beit Shearim is a beautiful farm area where a hard-working group of Jews have built a kibbutz with hothouses for roses, sorting and packing sheds for fruit, and a "merry-go-round" that is used for milking sheep. There are 600 people living here, 300 of whom are "members."

Beit Shearim ("house of gates")

About 12 miles east of Haifa are the Beit Shearim burial caves, which are reminiscent of the Sanhedrin Tombs in Jerusalem. In the second century A.D. Beit Shearim was the home of Israel's Supreme Court, the Sanhedrin, as well as the headquarters of the famous Rabbi Yehudi Ha'nassi, compiler of the Mishna. He was buried here.

SARCOPHAGI carved with rams' horns, eagles, human faces, gates, a star of David, ships, shells, lions' heads, or a menorah are beautiful. There were originally 200 sarcophagi here, but grave robbers looted them hundreds of years ago. On a tomb there is a COMBINATION SAILING SHIP AND STAR OF DAVID dating from the second or third century A.D.

The city of Beit Shearim was destroyed about A.D. 350, but artifacts remain. Israeli archaeologist B. Mazar started to dig here in 1936. Near the remains of an ancient synagogue — once the largest and most important in the area — is an interesting fourth-century OIL PRESS. A small MUSEUM is located here, and above the catacombs on the hillside the STATUE OF ALEXANDER ZEID stands near SHIEKH AVREKH, a tomb holy to the Moslems.

Beit Shearim is a National Parks Authority site.

Nahalal

Eight miles west of Nazareth is Nahalal, the first moshav in Israel, founded in 1920 and built in the form of a wheel with farms like spokes going out from the center. The houses are grouped around the center and the public buildings are in the center.

The moshav is an agricultural settlement where every settler lives separately with his family and tills a plot of land leased to him by the Jewish National Fund at a nominal rent. Each farmer works his farm with the help of his family and he is supposed to have only that amount of land that his family can manage. Purchases and sales are made on a cooperative basis. The moshav is the most common type of rural settlement in Israel.

- The name Nahalal comes from a biblical town of Zebulun, whose sons inherited the Valley of Jezreel (Josh. 19:10, 15; 21:34–35; Judges 1:30).

NAZARETH ("to blossom," "flower"), el-Nazirah (home town of Jesus), Kiryat-Natsrat

Nazareth lies in the hills of Galilee, 1,230 feet above sea level, about midway between the Sea of Galilee and the Mediterranean Sea. Today it houses Israel's largest Arab community (35,000), the majority being Christian. There are also about 25,000 Jews living in Upper Nazareth, the new 1957 suburb, named **KIRYAT-NATSRAT**. Nazareth is the headquarters of the Christian mission movement in Israel, with over 40 churches, convents, monasteries, orphanages, and private parochial schools.

This was the home of Joseph and Mary and for 30 years the scene of the Savior's life. Jesus' followers were called Nazarenes.

POINTS OF INTEREST

GREEK ORTHODOX CHURCH OF THE ANNUNCIATION (Gabriel's Church). This is Nazareth's oldest church. It was originally built in the days of Constantine, and the present church is over 300 years old. The Greek Orthodox members believe Gabriel appeared to Mary here. **MARY'S WELL**, near the church, gets its water from a spring within the church.

GROTTO OF THE ANNUNCIATION. Underneath the **LATIN CHURCH OF THE ANNUNCIATION** is a grotto that is held sacred as the site where the angel Gabriel appeared to Mary to tell her about her future son, Jesus. Two granite pillars, the **COLUMN OF GABRIEL** and the **COLUMN OF MARY**, mark the traditional place where the two persons stood. The Latin Church of the Annunciation is one of the largest Christian sanctuaries in the Middle East. It was built in the 1960s.

SAINT JOSEPH'S WORKSHOP. Under the **CHURCH OF SAINT JOSEPH** are two caves known through tradition as the carpenter shop and storage room of Joseph, husband of the Virgin Mary. This church is just north of the Latin Church of the Annunciation. Next to the Church of Saint Joseph there is a small museum.

OLD SYNAGOGUE. In the western part of the city, on Market Lane, is an ancient synagogue where, according to tradition, Jesus worshiped.

■ *Jesus went into the synagogue on the Sabbath day (Luke 4:16).*

MARY'S WELL, or the **VIRGIN FOUNTAIN**. This is the only spring-fed fountain in the city, and thus it is easy to believe that Mary would have drawn water here. It is located by the side of the road to Tiberias, and near the Greek Orthodox Church of the Annunciation, from where it gets its water.

MENSA CHRISTI. This is a small church belonging to the Franciscans. It contains a huge rock called in Latin *Mensa Christi* or the "table of Christ." Tradition indicates that Christ dined here with his disciples after the resurrection. The present church was built in 1861 and is located a small distance west of the old synagogue.

MOUNT OF PRECIPITATION. Known also as the "Leap of the Lord," this is a steep, forest-covered mount where Jesus was cast out of the city (Luke 4:28–30). It is southeast of the city.

TERRA SANCTA CONVENT. Of particular interest at this convent is a museum containing archaeological finds from the region of Nazareth.

- *At Nazareth the annunciation was made by Gabriel to Mary and Joseph (Isa. 7:14; Luke 1:26-38; Matt. 1:18-25).*
- *Joseph and Mary left to go to Bethlehem, where Jesus was to be born (Luke 2:1-7).*
- *Joseph, Mary, and Jesus returned to Nazareth from Egypt (Matt. 2:21-23).*
- *This was the home of Jesus' childhood and youth (Matt. 2:23; Luke 2:39, 51-52).*
- *Jesus left here when he was about thirty to go to the Jordan to be baptized (Mark 1:9).*
- *Here Jesus preached his first recorded sermon, he was rejected, and his life was threatened. The mountain from which the people sought to cast him is today called the* Mount of Precipitation *(Luke 4:16-30).*
- *Jesus was again rejected; he could perform few miracles because of the people's unbelief (Matt. 13:53-58; Mark 6:1-6).*
- *Nathanael mentioned Nazareth unfavorably, indicating it was rather an obscure village (John 1:46).*

Tsipori, *Sepphoris, Diocaesarea, Saffuriya*

Three miles northwest of Nazareth is the settlement of Tsipori. The name means "bird" and the town perches like a bird on top of a mount. During the first four centuries A.D., Tsipori was the largest and most important city of Galilee. It was a great spiritual center and the home of famous talmudic scholars. Rabbi Yehuda Hanassi compiled and edited the Mishna here. After his death in Tsipori he was buried at Beit Shearim. According to one tradition, Anna and Joachim, the parents of Mary, mother of Jesus, lived in Tsipori, and it was here that Mary herself was born. Ruins of a small eighteenth-century FORT, a Roman AMPHITHEATER, and a second-century BASILICA were discovered when the site was excavated by the University of Michigan in 1931.

About 3 miles northwest of Tsipori is a dam in the Valley of Beit Netofa. A conduit brings additional water to the reservoir from the Sea of Galilee.

GATH-HEPHER *("winepress of digging"),* Tel Gat Hefer, *Mashhad*

A village about 2 miles northeast of Nazareth, on a height north of the road that goes to Cana and Tiberias, is the traditional site of the burial place of Jonah. His tomb is shown here.

- *This was the birthplace of Jonah (2 Kings 14:25; see also the Book of Jonah).*

CANA *("place of reeds"),* Kefar-Kana, *Kafr Kannā, Khirbet Qana*

Cana is 4 miles northeast of Nazareth. It is believed that the CATHOLIC FRANCISCAN CHURCH is built over the site of Jesus' first miracle, the changing of water to wine. Stone waterpots, similar to those used in Christ's time, are shown. A GREEK ORTHODOX CHURCH with a red dome contains two stone basins, claimed to have been among the six water pots of the miracle. The SAINT NATHANAEL CHURCH of the Franciscans is built on the site of the traditional birthplace of Nathanael, a disciple of Jesus. It is located near the Catholic Franciscan Church.

Some believe the site of Cana is in southern Lebanon, southeast of Tyre.

■ *This was the home of Nathanael, of whom Jesus said, "Behold an Israelite indeed, in whom is no guile" (John 1:47; 21:2).*
■ *Cana was the scene of Jesus' first miracle — the changing of water into wine at the wedding feast (John 2:1-11).*
■ *Here Jesus healed — at a distance — the nobleman's son, who was in Capernaum (John 4:46-54).*

TURAN, Merj es-Sunbul ("meadow of the ears of corn")

Turan is an Arab village about 3½ miles northeast of Cana.

■ *According to tradition, the incident of Jesus' disciples plucking corn on the Sabbath took place in the Valley of Turan (Matt. 12:1; Luke 6:1).*

MOUNT TABOR ("mountain height," Mount of Transfiguration), et Tur

Mount Tabor is a cone-shaped, symmetrical mountain, 6 miles east of Nazareth on the northeast edge of the plain of Esdraelon. It is 1,843 feet above sea level. As most mountains and high places were scenes of heathen worship, Tabor is mentioned as the site of ensnaring rituals (Hos. 5:1).

Many ruins of cities are on and around Tabor. Antiochus founded a city here in 218 B.C. As early as the sixth century A.D., three churches had been built here in memory of the three tabernacles that Peter proposed at the time of the Transfiguration, which tradition says occurred here. Franciscan and Greek Orthodox monasteries are located here now, plus the BASILICA OF THE TRANSFIGURATION and the GREEK CHURCH OF SAINT ELIAS (Elijah). The traditional CAVE OF MELCHIZEDEK, where Abraham visited Melchizedek, is near the entrance to the monastery courtyard and the Greek church.

In the Jewish revolt of A.D. 66, Josephus held the top of Tabor as a stronghold (before he defected to the Romans). A wall he built can still be seen. A beautiful view of the valley can be obtained from here. At the foot of the mountain is the Arab village of DABURIYYA, on the site of the ancient town of Dovrat.

■ *Mount Tabor was a boundary between Issachar and Zebulun (Josh. 19:22-23).*
■ *Here Deborah and Barak gathered to defeat Sisera in the Valley of Jezreel (Judg. 4:6-17).*
■ *The brothers of Gideon were slain here (Judg. 8:18-21).*

- *It was referred to by the prophets (Jer. 46:18; Hos. 5:1; Ps. 89:12).*
- *Tradition says the transfiguration of Jesus took place here, where Jesus found a spot secluded enough to answer the description, "an high mountain apart by themselves" (Matt. 17:1; Mark 9:2; Luke 9:28). (Many believe this described Mount Hermon, however.)*
- *Tradition says the Greek Church of Saint Elias (Elijah) was built beside the cave where Melchizedek welcomed Abraham (Gen. 14:18-20).*

ENDOR ("fountain of Dor"), **Ein-Dor**, *H. Safsafot*

Close to Nain and Shunem on the north side of the Valley of Jezreel (Esdraelon) and 3½ miles south of Mount Tabor is the site of Endor. The ancient Endor and the modern Kibbutz Endor are about 2 miles apart.

- *This was the home of the witch Saul visited on the eve of his battle with the Philistines (1 Sam. 28:7-25).*
- *Here the fugitives of Sisera's army perished (Ps. 83:9-10).*

NAIN ("pleasant"), **Nein**, *Na'im Nēn*

Nain is an Arabic town on the northwest slope of a mountain known as *Little Hermon*, or *Hill of Moreh*, and 4 miles northeast of Afula.

- *The widow's son was raised by Jesus from the dead (Luke 7:11-17).*

SHUNEM ("uneven"), **Sulam**, *Solem*

Located 7 miles south-southeast of Nazareth, 2 miles from Nain, and 7 miles south of Mount Tabor is the ancient site of Shunem.

- *The border of Issachar reached to Shunem (Josh. 19:17-18).*
- *Here the Philistines gathered their forces prior to the battle with Saul, whose armies were at Mount Gilboa (1 Sam. 28:4).*
- *It was the birthplace of Abishag, wife of David in his old age (1 Kings 1:1-4).*
- *Here Elisha stayed and here he raised the Shunammite's son to life (2 Kings 4:8-37).*

Afula

This modern city of 20,000 people, 8 miles south of Nazareth, is the market center of the Jezreel Valley. It was founded in 1925 by the American Zionist Commonwealth and named after the word *Ofel*, a biblical tower.

- *Elisha was in the area (2 Kings 5:24).*

JEZREEL ("God sows"), **Yizre'el**, *Zarin*

Twelve miles south of Nazareth, 4 miles south of Afula, and across the plain of Jezreel, is Kibbutz Jezreel, founded in 1949. Nearby is the village of ZARIN, at the site of ancient Jezreel. Here Ahab, king of Samaria, had a palace during the ninth century and Jezebel founded an institution for the worship of Baal.

Latin Church of the Annunciation, Nazareth

- *Elijah ran from Carmel to Jezreel (1 Kings 18:42, 46).*
- *Here Ahab built one of his palaces (1 Kings 21:1).*
- *It was the place of Naboth's vineyard and cruel murder and the tragic meeting of Ahab and Elijah (1 Kings 21).*
- *Jezebel was eaten by the dogs here, and the dogs licked Ahab's blood (1 Kings 21:17-25; 22:37-38; 2 Kings 9:30-37).*
- *Jehu was anointed king and slew Joram and Jezebel (2 Kings 9).*

MOUNT GILBOA *("bubbling fountain")*, **Jebel Fakua**

A hilly district east of the plain of Jezreel, about 10 miles long and 1,696 feet above sea level, is known as Mount Gilboa.

- *It was the place of the last battles and death of Saul and his sons, Jonathan, Abinadab, and Melchishua (1 Sam. 28:4; 31:1-6; 2 Sam. 1:5-10; 1 Chron. 10:1-6).*
- *The death of Saul and Jonathan made David lament, and he prayed that no dew would ever fall on Mount Gilboa (2 Sam. 1:19-27).*

WELL OF HAROD, *("terror," "trembling")*, **Maayan Harod**, **Ein Harod**, *Gidona, Aid Jalud*

This spring is located north of Mount Gilboa, near Gidona, and 8 miles southeast of Afula. This is a National Parks Authority site.

- *Gideon gathered here to fight against Midian (Judg. 7:1).*
- *The Midianites were delivered into the hands of the 300 who lapped the water (Judg. 7:4-7).*
- *Perhaps Saul encamped here (1 Sam. 29:1).*

Beit Alpha, *near Kibbutz Hefzibah*

The best preserved mosaic floor of an ancient synagogue in Israel is found on the grounds of Kibbutz Beit Alpha, at the foot of Mount Gilboa in the Valley of Jezreel. It is one of the most beautiful relics in Israel. The kibbutz was founded in 1922 by pioneers from Poland and Galatia. During their swamp-draining operations in 1928 they found the sixth-century A.D. ruins of a synagogue with an elaborate mosaic floor. The excavation was supervised by the late Prof. E. L. Sukenik, who held the chair in archaeology at the Hebrew University.

The floor is divided into three panels: (1) Abraham's would-be sacrifice of Isaac; (2) a zodiac wheel; and (3) a group of religious ornaments, such as the ark of the law and the candelabra.

An Aramaic inscription refers to the emperor Justinus (Justin I) and indicates that the mosaic was laid down during his reign (A.D. 518-27). It is the only dated inscription found in the synagogues of Palestine. This is a National Parks Authority site.

- *The beautiful mosaic at Beit Alpha shows Abraham ready to offer up his son Isaac as a sacrifice (Gen. 22:3-13).*

Gan Ha Shelosha *("garden of the three")*, *Gan Hashlosha*, *el-Sakhne ("the warm" [water])*

In the Valley of Jezreel, about a mile south-southeast of Beth Alpha, is a glorious natural swimming pool set amid the green lawns and trees of Gan Ha Shelosha. It is named in memory of three young settlers who were killed by Arabs in 1938. Gentle waterfalls and pleasant surroundings make this a popular and refreshing picnic spot. This is a National Parks Authority site.

BETH-SHEAN ("house of security"), Beit-Shean, Tell Bet-Shean, Beisan, Scythopolis, Nyssa, Tell el-Husn

This modern city of 15,000 people lies 15 miles south of the Sea of Galilee at a point where the Valley of Jezreel meets the Valley of the Jordan. It was established in 1949. The ancient city was inhabited in 3000 B.C., and the tell contains 18 levels of settlements. Six temples have been unearthed. The University of Pennsylvania excavated it in 1921–23. Relics are now in the Rockefeller Museum and the University of Pennsylvania Museum. Some of the relics include —

(1) The STELA OF SETI I, pharaoh of Egypt in 1318 B.C. This stone has many hieroglyphs and Egyptian pictures. It tells of the Egyptians and their battle at Beth-Shean. (Rockefeller Museum, Jerusalem)

(2) The STELA OF THE GODDESS ASHTORETH. It is Egyptian also, and it speaks of the Temple of Ashtoreth, which is mentioned in the account of Saul's death (1 Sam. 31:10). (Pennsylvania Museum, Philadelphia)

(3) The STELA TO MEKAL, LORD OF BETH-SHEAN (1500 B.C.). It has Egyptian hieroglyphs that tell of the king giving offerings to Mekal, god of Beth-Shean. (Rockefeller Museum, Jerusalem)

The BETH-SHEAN MUSEUM has an interesting collection from the area. The ROMAN AMPHITHEATER (A.D. 200) seats 5,000 and resembles the one at Caesarea. It is the best preserved Roman theater in Israel.

This is a National Parks Authority site.

- Beth-Shean was a part of Manasseh's inheritance (Josh. 17:11).
- Because of the chariots of iron, Manasseh could never subdue it (Judg. 1:27).
- Beth-Shean is located at the foot of Mount Gilboa, where Saul and Jonathan were slain. When their bodies were found, the Philistines fastened them to the wall of Beth-Shean, but valiant Israelites gave the bodies a proper burial (1 Sam. 31:8–13; 2 Sam. 21:12–14).

Neve'-Ur ("abode of Ur")

This city, near the Jordan River about 7 miles north of Beth-Shean, takes its name from Ur of the Chaldees in Iraq, birthplace of Abraham. The founders of Neve'-Ur came from Baghdad, the capital of Iraq. Interestingly enough, the empty pipeline that once carried oil from Kirkuk, Iraq, to Haifa is located near Neve'-Ur.

Belvoir ("good view"), Kochav Hayarden

About 8 miles northeast of Ein Harod and 9 miles south of Degania are the remains of a twelfth-century French Crusader fortress. Its location on a hill gives it a sweeping view of the Jordan Valley and

Mountains of Gilead. It may be approached from the Jordan River valley. This is a National Parks Authority site.

AROUND THE SEA OF GALILEE AND NORTH

SEA OF GALILEE, CHINNERETH, GENNESARET, TIBERIAS, Kinneret, *Gennesar, Behr Tabariyeh*

The Sea of Galilee is 13-14 by 7-8 miles in size, 130-57 feet deep, 686 feet below sea level, and 32 miles in circumference. In the King James Version of the Bible the name is spelled *Chinnereth* (Num. 34:11; Josh. 12:3; 13:27). The modern name, *Kinneret*, means "harp," and the sea is shaped like a harp. In New Testament times it was known as *Gennesaret* (Luke 5:1). It was named *Tiberias* after Herod Antipas built the city of Tiberias and made it his capital (John 6:1, 23; 21:1). It was also known as the *Sea of Galilee* (Matt. 4:18; 15:29; Mark 1:16; 7:31; John 6:1). Several cities were located on its northwest shoreline, including Tiberias, Magdala, Tabgha, Bethsaida, Capernaum, and Chorazin.

The sea is abundant in fish: carp, sardine, mullet, catfish, and combfish — the same fish caught by the disciples of Jesus. The combfish is interesting because the eggs of the fish are hatched in its mouth and the small fish stay there until they are old enough to take care of themselves. Today the fish are caught in nets, the same as in the days of old. The modern diesel-powered boats are equipped with sonar devices for hunting out schools of fish.

Owing to the height of the mountains surrounding the lake, different temperatures give rise to sudden and violent storms.

- *The tribe of Gad settled on its shores (Deut. 3:17; Josh. 13:27).*
- *Jesus called Peter, Andrew, James, and other apostles (Matt. 4:18-22; 10; Mark 1:16-20; 2:13-14; Luke 5:1-11).*
- *Jesus healed a leper (Matt. 8:1-4).*
- *Jesus spoke to the multitudes from Peter's boat (Mark 3:7-12; Luke 5:1-3).*
- *Galilee yielded two catches of fish in response to Jesus' command (Luke 5:4-11; John 21:6-8).*
- *Jesus stilled the storm (Matt. 8:23-27; Mark 4:35-41; Luke 8:22-25).*
- *Jesus walked on the stormy water (Matt. 14:22-33; Mark 6:45-52; John 6:16-21).*
- *Jesus taught the "parable of the sower" and other parables on the sea (Matt. 13:1-52; Mark 4:1-34; Luke 8:4-18).*
- *Jesus taught about the Sabbath day (Mark 2:23-28).*
- *Jesus healed the multitudes (Matt. 15:29-31; Mark 1:29-45).*
- *The Twelve Apostles were ordained in the hills near the Sea of Galilee (Mark 3:13-19).*
- *Jesus appeared here after the resurrection (Mark 14:28; 16:7; John 21:1-23).*

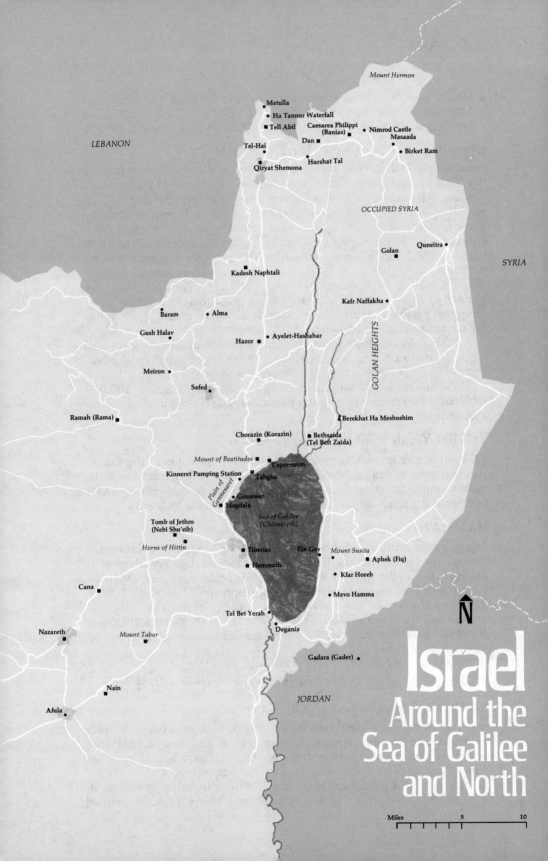

LEBANON

Mount Hermon

Metulla
Ha Tannur Waterfall
Tell Abil
Caesarea Philippi (Banias)
Nimrod Castle
Masaada
Tel-Hai
Dan
Birket Ram
Qiryat Shemona
Hurshat Tal

OCCUPIED SYRIA

Golan
Quneitra

SYRIA

Kadesh Naphtali

Kafr Naffakha

Baram
Alma
Gush Halav
Hazor
Ayelet-Hashahar

GOLAN HEIGHTS

Meiron
Safed

Ramah (Rama)

Berekhat Ha Meshushim

Chorazin (Korazin)
Bethsaida (Tel Beit Zaida)

Mount of Beatitudes
Capernaum
Kinneret Pumping Station
Tabgha
Plain of Gennesaret
Ginnosar
Magdala

Sea of Galilee (Chinnereth)

Tomb of Jethro (Nebi Shu'eib)

Horns of Hittin

Tiberias
Ein Gev
Mount Susita
Aphek (Fiq)
Hammath
Kfar Horeb

Cana

Mevo Hamma

Tel Bet Yerah

Nazareth
Degania

Mount Tabor

Gadara (Gader)

Nain

JORDAN

Afula

N

Israel
Around the
Sea of Galilee
and North

Miles   5   10

■ *Devils cast from the Gadarene demoniac entered the bodies of 2,000 swine, who ran down a steep place and into the Sea of Galilee on the eastern shore (Matt. 8:28–34; Mark 5:1–21; Luke 8:26–40).*

Degania, *"The Mother of the Kibbutzim"*

Israel's first kibbutz was founded in 1909 on the southern shores of the Sea of Galilee by Russian pioneers — including David Ben-Gurion. The father of Moshe Dayan also lived here, but left to help establish Nahalal. The name *Degania* is taken from the Hebrew *Dagan*, meaning "corn." There are two Deganias, "A" and "B." Degania "A" has a Syrian tank at the gate — a souvenir of the 1948 battles. Degania "B" was settled by the younger Degania settlers next door to Degania "A." Degania has an excellent natural history museum called **BEIT GORDON**. The book, *Pioneers in Israel*, by Shmuel Dayan (father of Moshe) gives a graphic description of early struggles of the kibbutz. Degania served as an example for other Jewish pioneering experiments.

A kibbutz is a collective type of farm, wherein all members live and work on national land leased to them at a nominal rent by the National Fund. There is no privately owned land on the kibbutz.

There are about 230 kibbutzim in Israel and approximately 100,000 kibbutzniks (members). About 4 percent of Israel's population live on kibbutzim.

Tell Bet Yerah *("house of the moon")*

This tell is 6½ miles south of Tiberias, on the grounds of the Ohalo regional school, near Kibbutz Kinneret. Ruins dating from the third millennium B.C., a second-century **SYNAGOGUE**, a fourth-century **BATH HOUSE**, and a sixth-century **BYZANTINE CHURCH** may be seen.

HAMMATH *("hot spring")*, **Hammat**, *Hammata*

About a mile south of Tiberias is the site of the biblical city Hammath, famous for its hot baths. Recent archaeological digs reveal what is believed to be the ancient city. A fourth-century A.D. **SYNAGOGUE** found here has a very beautiful and well-preserved **MOSAIC FLOOR**, depicting the ark of the covenant set between menorahs. Animals and figures are a part of another one. The **TOMB OF RABBI MEIR BAAL-HANESS**, near the hot springs, is considered one of the holiest sanctuaries in Israel.

Hammath is a National Parks Authority site.

■ *This was one of the fortified cities of Naphtali (Josh. 19:35).*

TIBERIAS, *Tveriah, Tabariyeh, Teveriya*

Tiberias lies on the west side of the Sea of Galilee, about 10 miles south of Capernaum. It was built or rebuilt and named by Herod Antipas (A.D. 26) in honor of the emperor, and here Herod built the finest synagogue in Galilee. It was the capital of Galilee under Agrippa I and the Roman procurators. After the fall of Jerusalem in A.D. 70, the Jews settled here and sometime before A.D. 220 codified

Sea of Galilee

and wrote down their traditional civil and ritual laws, with the title of *Mishna*, under the direction of Rabbi Yehuda Ha' Nassi.

The *Jerusalem Talmud* was compiled in this town in A.D. 400, and the vowel and punctuation grammar was introduced into the Hebrew language by the learned men in Tiberias. (The Jerusalem Talmud was rather overshadowed by the *Babylonian Talmud*, completed a century later in the academies in Mesopotamia.) Many illustrious Jewish sages are buried at Tiberias, including the intellectual giant of medieval Jewry, Maimonides (the "Ramban"), who died in Egypt in A.D. 1204. **MAIMONIDES' TOMB** is reached from the end of Hagalil Road. Other tombs of famous rabbis are nearby.

In Christian times Tiberias was the seat of a bishop. It fell to the Moslems in A.D. 637. A **JEWISH SCHOOL** of rabbinical theology has been here for a long time. An important **CRUSADER AND TURKISH FORTRESS** is located near the Sea of Galilee in Tiberias.

The modern city is located about 2 miles north of the ancient city. **HOT WELLS**, or springs, have made the city a health resort. They are probably the earliest known thermal baths in the world, having been used for the past 2,500 years. Josephus, Pliny, and other historians have mentioned them.

Public **BEACHES** for swimming are found north and south of the city. Ferries transport people to Ein Gev daily. A boating excursion along the coast to Capernaum is exciting.

Other places of interest include the following: the **MUSEUM OF ANTIQUITIES**, the **TOMB OF RABBI MEIR BAAL-HANESS**, the **TOMBS OF**

THE SAGES, the TOMB OF RABBI AKIVA, the CRUSADER WALLS, and the WALLS OF HEROD ANTIPAS.

Tiberias, with a population of 25,000, is the only city of any size on the lake now. It is Israel's leading winter resort. The city was destroyed by an earthquake in 1837 but is now a modern Jewish city.

Although Jesus was in the general area, we have no statement of a particular visit to the city itself.

- *It was one of the cities given to Naphtali (Josh. 19:35).*
- *It gave its name to the lake (John 6:1; 21:1).*
- *It is referred to (John 6:23).*

HORNS OF HITTIN

A strangely shaped ridge 7½ miles west of Tiberias and southwest of Arbel is called the Horns of Hittin. The hill is shaped like two animal horns. After the Moslems had captured nearly all of Palestine, it was here that the Crusaders suffered their final and decisive defeat at the hands of Saladin in 1187. The nearby VALLEY OF ARBEL is where the Messiah of Israel will be revealed, according to Jewish tradition.

- *Some believe the Sermon on the Mount was given here (Matt. 5-7).*

TOMB OF JETHRO, *Shu'eib ("pre-eminence"),* **Nebi Shu'eib**

On the edge of the Arbel Valley and at the foot of the Horns of Hittin, overlooking Tiberias, is a tomb of Shu'eib (Jethro, father-in-law of Moses). This is the sacred shrine of Druzes.

Most of the Druzes live in and around Shefaram, a Druze village with men who wear curling moustaches, baggy white trousers, and headgear that is higher than the usual loose Arab *kaffiyehs*. The Druzes speak Arabic but belong to an exclusive religious sect that broke away from Islam over 1,000 years ago. Their tenets are secret.

- *Jethro was the father-in-law of Moses (Exod. 3:1; 4:18; 18:1).*
- *He visited Moses at Sinai (Exod. 18).*
- *Hobab, Jethro's son, was a guide to the Israelites (Num. 10:29-32).*

MAGDALA *("tower of greatness"), Migdal, Dalmanutha, Magadan, Tarichaea*

Located 4 miles north of Tiberias, Magdala was one of the sites which Josephus fortified when he was governor of Galilee — before his defection to the Romans. When the city fell to Titus in the struggle of the Jews against the Romans, 6,700 Jews were killed; 6,000 of the strongest were sent to Nero to dig the Corinthian canal and 30,400 were auctioned off as slaves.

- *This was the home of Mary Magdalene (Luke 8:2; Mark 16:9).*
- *Jesus came here after feeding the 4,000 (Matt. 15:39; Mark 8:10).*
- *The Pharisees and Sadducees sought a sign and Jesus told them of the sign of the prophet Jonas (Matt. 15:39-16:4; Mark 8:11-21).*

PLAIN OF GENNESARET

This is a very fertile plain on the northwest shore of the Sea of Galilee, 3 miles by 1 mile in size, just north of Magdala.

■ *Many diseased were healed by touching the hem of Jesus' garment (Matt. 14:34-36; Mark 6:53-56).*

Ginnosar

This is a kibbutz with a large GUEST HOUSE and BEACH, on the west side of the Sea of Galilee about 4 miles north of Tiberias.

Kinneret Pumping Station, *Eshed Kinnrot; and* Minya

Nestled behind a hill on the northwest shore of the Sea of Galilee, 5½ miles north of Tiberias, is a large pumping station that pumps water out of the sea into a huge pipe 10 feet in diameter. It is piped through the Valley of Beit-Netofa to the Yarkon waterworks and from there to the Negev.

On the sea near here is MINYA, a seventh-century ruin of a palace and mosque.

■ *Palestine is to become fruitful again and the deseret to blossom as the rose (Amos 9:14-15; Ezek. 36:33-36; Isa. 35:1-2, 6-7).*

TABGHA, *Tabigha, Heptapegon ("seven springs")*

Tabgha is 2 miles southwest of Capernaum and 7½ miles north of Tiberias. The CHURCH OF THE MULTIPLICATION stands on the site where tradition says Jesus fed the five thousand. (The feeding of the five thousand, however, according to Luke 9:10, was near Bethsaida, to the northeast.) The church has one of the best preserved mosaic tile floors in all of Israel, and dates back to the fourth century A.D. A newer church has been built over the floor of the old Byzantine church, and near the church is the BENEDICTINE MONASTERY.

The CHURCH OF THE ROCK, SAINT PETER'S CHURCH (Chapel of the Primacy), is located on the seashore. Here, some believe, Peter received the keys of the kingdom from Jesus. The church was erected in 1943 by the Franciscans on ancient ruins.

Across the road northeast of the Church of the Multiplication are the ruins of an ANCIENT CHURCH. About a block east of the ruins, on the same side of the road, is the CAVE OF JOB, and on the south side of the road in the area are springs of water.

■ *The name* Tabgha *is not in the Bible.*
■ *Jesus fed 5,000 and 4,000 near Bethsaida (Luke 9:10-17; John 6:1-14).*
■ *Tradition indicates that Saint Peter's Church is located where Jesus met with his apostles after the resurrection and told Peter to "feed my sheep" (John 21:15-17).*

CAPERNAUM, *Kefar Nahum ("town of Nahum"), Tell Hum*

This famous city of New Testament times was located about 2½ miles from where the Jordan enters the Sea of Galilee and 10 miles from the modern Tiberias. It was a customs station and place of residence of the high Roman officer. The commander of some Roman soldiers stationed here built a synagogue for the Jews. When Jesus finally withdrew from Nazareth he went to Capernaum, and this became the center of his activity for 18–20 months. More of Christ's miracles were performed here than in any other city.

Capernaum possibly had a population of 10,000.

Excavations at Capernaum have yielded ruins of **ONE OF THE FINEST LIMESTONE SYNAGOGUES** in the Holy Land. Although some think it might have been the one built by the kindly centurion, experts believe it was built in the second century A.D. A **FRANCISCAN MONASTERY** is near the synagogue. In the courtyard are **STONE IMPLEMENTS** of ancient inhabitants — flour mills and an oil press. Carved in stone are the **ARK OF THE COVENANT**, the **SHIELD**, or **STAR, OF DAVID** (6 points), a **FIVE-POINTED STAR**, a **CANDELABRUM**, and other designs.

- *Jesus made it his home, "his own city" (Matt. 4:13–17; 9:1; Luke 4:31; John 2:12; Mark 1:21).*
- *Here Jesus called Peter, Andrew, James, John, and Matthew and attended Matthew's farewell feast (Matt. 4:13, 18–22; 9:9–13; Mark 2:13–22; Luke 5:27–39).*
- *Peter lived here (Matt. 8:5, 14; Mark 1:21, 29; Luke 4:31, 38).*
- *Jesus taught here in the synagogue (Mark 1:21; Luke 4:31–33).*
- *Jesus delivered a man of an unclean spirit; he also healed Peter's mother-in-law and many others (Matt. 8:14–17; Mark 1:21–34; Luke 4:31–41).*
- *He healed the centurion's servant (Matt. 8:5–13; Luke 7:1–10).*
- *The palsied man was healed when he was let down through the roof (Matt. 9:1–8; Mark 2:1–12; Luke 5:17–26).*
- *Jesus raised Jairus's daughter from the dead (Matt. 9:18–26; Mark 5:22–43; Luke 8:40–56).*
- *Jesus healed the woman who had "an issue of blood" (Matt. 9:20–22; Mark 5:25–34; Luke 8:43–48).*
- *The blind and dumb demoniac was healed (Matt. 9:27–35; 12:22–45; Mark 3:22–30; Luke 11:14–26).*
- *The nobleman's son was healed by Jesus (John 4:46–54).*
- *Jesus healed the withered hand (Matt. 12:9–14; Mark 3:1–6; Luke 6:6–11).*
- *Great multitudes were brought to Jesus and were healed (Matt. 8:16–17; 9:36–38).*
- *Jesus gave a number of discourses here, including an outstanding one on the "bread of life" (Matt. 13; 15:1–20; 18:15–35; Mark 2:23–28; 7:1–23; 9:33–50; Luke 6:1–5; John 6:22–71).*
- *Jesus pronounced a curse upon the city (Matt. 11:23–24; Luke 10:15).*
- *Peter caught a fish with a coin in its mouth (Matt. 17:24–27).*
- *Jesus taught that we must be as little children to be saved (Matt. 18:1–6; Mark 9:33–37; Luke 9:46–48).*
- *Jesus taught here in the synagogue (Mark 1:21; 3:1; Luke 4:33–38).*

Above: Old synagogue, Capernaum
Below: Candelabrum on the stonework of the old synagogue, Capernaum

BETHSAIDA *("place of nets")*, **Tel Beit Zaida**

On the east side of the Jordan River, about 1½ miles north of the point where the Jordan enters the Sea of Galilee, is Tel Beit Zaida, believed to have been the biblical Bethsaida.

Olive press,
Capernaum

- *Bethsaida was the birthplace of Peter, Andrew, and Philip (John 1:44; 12:21-22).*
- *The feeding of the 5,000 was near here (Matt. 14:13-21; Mark 6:31-44; Luke 9:10-17; John 6:1-14).*
- *The feeding of the 4,000 was near here (Matt. 15:32-38; Mark 8:1-9).*
- *The blind man was healed after Jesus led him out of the town (Mark 8:22-26).*
- *Jesus pronounced a curse on the city (Matt. 11:21-22; Luke 10:13). (The three cities of Bethsaida, Capernaum, and Chorazin were cursed, and none exist today. Tiberias was not cursed, and it still exists.)*

MOUNT OF BEATITUDES

The traditional Mount of Beatitudes is located to the north of the Plain of Gennesaret. It is now the site of an Italian convent and hospice that was a project of Mussolini in 1937.

- *The Sermon on the Mount was delivered here (Matt. 5, 6, 7; Luke 6:12-49).*

CHORAZIN, Korazin, Khorazin, Kerazeh

This biblical site lies 3 miles north of Capernaum. It was a Jewish town of the Talmudic era and is represented only by some ruins of an old third- or fourth-century A.D. synagogue. Four miles south-west of Chorazin is the gorge of **WADI AMUD**, where in 1925 a Paleo-

Above: Star of David, Capernaum
Below: Ark of the covenant, Capernaum

lithic skull was found in one of the caves. The skull has been designated as "Galilee Man."

■ *A curse was pronounced upon Chorazin by Jesus (Matt. 11:21–22;
Luke 10:13–14).*

Hexagonal pool,
Berekhat Ha Meshushim

Berekhat Ha Meshushim, *Hexagonal Pools*

Hidden within the valleys of the Golan Heights, 6½ miles northeast of Capernaum, the misnamed **HEXAGONAL POOLS** at Berekhat Ha Meshushim are most unusual natural swimming pools. They are surrounded by columns of lava pentagons, the result of an ancient volcanic eruption. The cool, refreshing stream running through the valley and through the pools makes a beautiful wonder of nature.

Safed, *Safad, Zefat, Tsefat*

Near Mount Jermak, Israel's loftiest mountain range (3,962 feet), is Safed, Israel's highest town (2,790 feet). This was a Jewish strong-hold in the war against the Romans and later was the site of a Crusader fort until A.D. 1266. It was the Mameluke capital of Galilee. This is where the Sefardic Jews came when they were perse-cuted in Spain. These Jewish intellectuals launched into a complex and quite mystical interpretation of the Old Testament called *Cabala*. Safed became a city of many **SYNAGOGUES** and **UNIVERSITIES**. Now it has become a resort town. Many painters, sculptors, and ceramicists have settled here, and a visit to the **ARTIST'S COLONY** is worthwhile. A **CITADEL** at the top of a hill was built by the Crusaders in the twelfth century. A **MUSEUM** houses sculpture and art.

This city, Jerusalem, Hebron, and Tiberias are the four cities held sacred to the Jews. Safed is the capital of Cabalistic mysticism. The first Hebrew book by Yom Too was printed here in A.D. 1578. In 1738 an earthquake demolished the entire city, and 4,000 persons, mostly Jews, were buried in the ruins.

In 1948 there were 10,000 Arabs and 2,200 Jews in Safed, but when war broke out the Arabs fled.

■ *Many believe this was the city Jesus referred to when he said that "a city that is set on an hill cannot be hid"* (Matt. 5:14).

Meiron, *Meron*

This is a settlement of orthodox Jews, established in 1949 and located high in the Galilean mountains. Among the famous tombs in the city is that of HILLEL the Elder, the famous scholar of the Torah. A second-century Talmudist, Shimon Bar Yochai, defied the Romans and wrote the *Zohar*, the "Book of Splendor," while hiding in a cave here. This is the Bible of the Cabalist sect. In Meiron the members of the sect have a rock they call "Messiah's Chair." They believe that when the Messiah arrives, he will sit there while Elijah blows the trumpet to announce his coming. Many ancient synagogues may also be found here.

Lag Beomer holiday occurs on the eighteenth of the month of Iyar, 26 days after Passover (*Pessah*). On the eve of the celebration a great pilgrimage is made from Safed to Meiron. Thousands come to Safed and from thence to Meiron on the afternoon preceding the celebration, to dance and sing during the festival known as *Hilulu de Rashbi.*

RAMAH (*"high"*), Rama

This village of Christian-Druze people is located about 6 miles southwest of Meiron. There are several other Ramahs in Israel.

■ *It was a city captured by Joshua and allocated to the tribe of Naphtali (Josh. 19:32, 36).*

Gush Halav, *Jish, Gishala*

Located 2½ miles north of Meron is the home of Yohanan of Gishala, commander in the Jewish war against Rome. It was the last Jewish fortress to fall before Vespasian. The tombs of the sages Avtalion and Shemaya are situated here.

Baram

The ancient synagogue of Baram is located in the mountains of Galilee 5 miles directly north of Meron and less than a mile from the Lebanese border. It is the best preserved and one of the earliest synagogues in Israel. It dates back to the end of the second or beginning of the third century A.D., after Galilee became the center of Jewish life. An ornamental lintel has a sculptured garland set between symbols of victory. Baram is the legendary burial site of Queen Esther.

Baram is a National Parks Authority site.

HAZOR (*"enclosed"*), Tell Hazor, *Hatzor, Tell-el-Qedah*

Tell is an Arabic word meaning an artificial mound created by successive layers of habitations superimposed one upon the other, usually implying great antiquity. Hazor is not a natural hill. It is 14 miles due north of the Sea of Galilee, and archaeologists have identified 21 occupational levels on this 25-acre site, covering a 3,000-year period extending to the second century B.C. Its first inhabitants dwelt here 4,500 years ago. It was once the largest city in the country, with a population of 40,000 people. It was one of few Palestinian cities of antiquity noted in prebiblical literary documents from Egypt, Palestine, and Mesopotamia. The documents indicate it was a major center of commerce in the Fertile Crescent. It was captured by pharaohs Thutmose III, Amenhotep II, and Seti I.

Although the tell was identified as Hazor as early as 1928, it was in 1955–58 that Professor Yigael Yadin and a team of archaeologists from the Hebrew University excavated Hazor. Nine of the 21 levels were of the Bronze or Canaanite period. During the last 5 of these the occupation also extended to an area of about 150 acres to the north of the tell, known as "Lower City." Canaanite houses in the southwest corner of the lower city belonged to the thirteenth century B.C., and showed signs of violent destruction and abandonment. This now fits excellently with the tradition of its capture by Joshua, dated by many scholars to the late thirteenth century B.C. The level below this corresponded to the fourteenth century B.C. — the period of the Amarna letters. Two of the letters were written by the ruler of Hazor, Abdi-tirshi.

During the summer of 1969, further excavation at Hazor produced the "prize discovery": the UNDERGROUND WATER SYSTEM from the Israelite period — the largest of its type and more than twice the size of the one at Megiddo. It dates back to the time of Ahab (732 B.C.). (The water tunnels at Megiddo and Gibeon, as well as Hezekiah's tunnel, were made in the eighth or ninth century B.C.) The Tell Hazor tunnel is 82 feet long, 13 feet high, and 13 feet wide.

The archaeologists found the STANDARD OF THE SNAKE GODDESS (a bronze relief of an image of the goddess with a snake in each of her hands) recalling the brass serpent of Moses (Num. 21:8; 2 Kings 18:4). A bone HANDLE OF A MIRROR OR SCEPTER has a carving of a winged angel or deity guarding a "tree of life." It dates from the eighth or ninth century B.C. A STELA showing two hands raised to an emblem of deity (a sun-disc within a crescent) was found in the holy of holies of a fourteenth-century Canaanite temple.

Hazor is a National Parks Authority site and has a beautiful, new, modern MUSEUM, located at the entrance of KIBBUTZ AYELET HASHACHAR, one of Israel's most beautiful kibbutzim.

- *Joshua fought with Jabin, king of Hazor, and other kings who had united. Joshua took the city and burned it to the ground (Josh. 11:1–14). It had 40,000 people at the time.*
- *The Israelites fell into the hands of another, later Jabin, who controlled Israel from Hazor for 20 years and was noted for his 900 iron chariots. The captain of his army was Sisera. Under the inspiration of Deborah, Barak and the Israelites won a great victory over Sisera in the Esdraelon Valley (Judg. 4).*
- *Solomon rebuilt Hazor along with Megiddo and Gezer (1 Kings 9:15).*
- *The city was captured in 732 B.C. by Tiglath-pileser III, king of Assyria (2 Kings 15:29).*
- *A bone handle was found here, showing a young date palm as the*

Above: Mount of Beatitudes
Below: Sun stone, Chorazin

Tree of Life, protected by a four-winged Seraph and cherubim and a flaming sword (cf Gen. 3:24).

Ayelet-Hashahar *("morning star")*

Immediately northeast of the Tell of Hazor is a collective settlement that was established originally by young people from Russia in 1915 as a pioneering kibbutz in Upper Galilee. It was shelled and bombed intensively by Syrian forces and suffered many casualties. It has a beautiful guest house.

Alma

Five miles northwest of Hazor is a small village where a third-century inscription was found with these words: "Peace upon this place and upon all the places of his people, Israel."

Lake Hula *(Hulah) Area, Mei-merom*

As early as 1883, young Polish Jews settled in the Hula Lake and swamp area. The Einan waterworks pump water to the heights of Galilee. In 1957 the drainage of the swampland was completed and the size of Lake Hula was greatly reduced.

KADESH NAPHTALI, *Kedesh ("holiness"), Tell Quades, Ramot Naftali*

This ancient Canaanite fortress became a Levitical city of refuge. It was the home of Barak. Heber, whose wife Jael killed Sisera, lived nearby. It is also the location of Joshua's tomb. Kadesh was an important city in Israel, and its name appears in hieroglyphs on the walls of the temple in Karnak, Egypt. The date of the hieroglyphs is 1310 B.C., the time of Seti I.

- *It was a city of Naphtali (Judges 4:6).*
- *It was the home of Barak, who mustered the tribes of Israel and routed the Canaanites along the Kishon River (Judg. 4:6).*
- *It was captured by Tiglath-pileser (2 Kings 15:29).*

Qiryat Shemona *("city of eight"), Kiryat Shmona*

This town of 20,000 people is the urban center of upper Galilee. Because it is near the Upper Galilee and Golan Heights areas, it is a center for tourism. It was settled about 20 years ago and named after 8 who fell in defense of nearby Tell Hai in 1920.

Tell Hai *("hill of life")*

A museum of the Hagana underground movement is located 1½ miles north of Qiryat Shemona. Joseph Trumpeldor, founder of the Jewish pioneer (Hehaluts) movement in Russia, is buried in a grave marked by a large lion of Judah statue. An inscription on the statue reads: "It is good to die for our country."

Sea of Galilee, near Capernaum, with the Plain of Gennesaret and Horns of Hittin in the background

ABEL ("fresh grassy meadows"), Beth-maacha, Abel-Maim, Tell Abil

Three miles east of Beth-rehol, west of Dan, and north of Lake Hula is the site of the biblical Abel.

■ Here the rebel Sheba was pursued and killed by Joab (2 Sam. 20:10, 14–15).

Ha Tannur Waterfall

Located near the main highway and 1 mile north of Tell Abil is a beautiful waterfall of the Iyon River. A 5-minute hike on a footpath brings the visitor to the base of the falls.

Metulla ("overlooking")

The village of Metulla, founded in 1896, is the northernmost Israeli settlement. It is on the Lebanese border and has many small hotels and restaurants. The broad valley called by the Bible *Iyon* stretches north into Lebanon from Metulla. A beautiful view of the Hula valley is also obtained from Metulla.

Hurshat Tal ("dew grove")

Just east of the settlement of Ha Gosherim is a pleasant camping site with ancient oak trees and natural springs. It is maintained by the National Parks Authority.

DAN ("judge"), Laish, Leshem, Tell-el-Qadi

Dan marked the northern limit of the land of Israel. It is 4 miles west of Banias and identified with a tell (mound) 40 to 80 feet high. The largest of all the springs that make up the source of the Jordan River rises from the west side of the mound. Here the Danites captured Laish, which they rebuilt and called Dan (Judg. 18). They established a sanctuary and ritual that persisted as long as the house of God was in Shiloh. The priesthood of this idolatrous shrine continued in the family of Jonathan until the conquest of Tiglath-pileser.

Two miles west of Dan is KIBBUTZ HA GOSHERIM, a well-known tourist stop with a guest house and swimming pool.

■ Here Abraham rescued Lot from Chedorlaomer (Gen. 14:13–16).
■ Jeroboam set up a golden calf here, as the Egyptians did (1 Kings 12:26–33).
■ Dan was subdued by Benhadad, king of Syria (1 Kings 15:20; 2 Chron. 16:4).
■ It was regained by Jeroboam (2 Kings 14:25).
■ The city was conquered and its inhabitants were carried captive to Assyria by Tiglath-pileser (2 Kings 15:29).
■ The expression "from Dan even to Beersheba" is used in the Old Testament to indicate the northern and southern limits of the country (Judg. 20:1; Sam. 3:20).
■ The name Leshem was changed to Dan, the name of the leader of the tribe of Dan (Josh. 19:47).

Deir monastery at Petra

CAESAREA PHILIPPI, **Banias**, *Baniyas, Paneas, Neronica, Neroneus*

Caesarea Philippi is located at the base of Mount Hermon, northeast of the Sea of Galilee. The Greek name was *Paneas*, probably named after Pan, the Greek god of forests, meadows, flocks, and herds. It was rebuilt by Philip the tetrarch and named in honor of Augustus and Philip to distinguish it from Caesarea on the coast. In 20 B.C. Herod the Great erected a temple here to the god Pan. The site was later called *Neronica* by Agrippa II. The Hermon River branch of the Jordan River rises just north of the town. Legend says the Jordan River has two sources, Jor and Dan; hence *JorDan*.

- *It was the northern limit of the Lord's journeys on his second tour to the north (Matt. 16:13; Mark 8:27).*
- *Peter's confession of Jesus' divinity, Jesus' prediction of his (Jesus') death, and possibly the transfiguration took place here (Matt. 16:13-20; Mark 8:27-9:10; Luke 9:18-36).*

Nimrod Castle *(Fortress) at Kalaat Namrud, Kalat Nimrud, Qalaat Nemrod*

About 1 mile northeast of Banias is a former stronghold of the Assassins. It was conquered first by the Crusaders and then by the Mamelukes. The castle-fortress is one of the best preserved. The visitor can have an excellent view of the Upper Jordan Valley from this point. Near here is Israel's skiing area.

Masaada

This small Druze village is located about halfway between Banias and Birket Ram. Threshing floors here are like those of Jesus' day.

Bringing in the harvest

Left: A Druze threshing
wheat, near Masaada
Below: Winnowing wheat

Birket Ram *("height pool")*

At Birket Ram, about 5 miles east of Banias, there is a small village
by a lake. The lake is in an old crater.

MOUNT HERMON ("prominent," "sanctuary"), Sirion, Senir, Jebel-esh-Sheikh

Mount Hermon marks the southern terminus of the Anti-Lebanon range. It is 16–20 miles long from north to south and 9,200 feet high. Snow lies on the peak yearlong.

- Israel conquered all of the Amorite territory to Hermon (Deut. 3:7–9).
- This was the northern limit of the territory of the Ten Tribes of Israel (Deut. 4:47–48; Josh. 11:1–3; 12:1–5; 13:5).
- Half of the tribe of Manasseh dwelt here (1 Chron. 5:23).
- The dew of Hermon was a symbol of religious blessing (Ps. 133:3).
- The transfiguration took place on a "high mountain" (Matt. 17:1–9; Mark 9:2–9; Luke 9:28–36).
- The lunatic was healed (Matt. 17:14–21; Mark 9:14–29; Luke 9:37–43).

GOLAN ("circle"), Jolan, Golan Heights

The tableland east and northeast of the Sea of Galilee is named Golan. At the end of World War I this area was given to Syria. In Old Testament times it was a part of the inheritance of Manasseh. It had a dense population in the second and third centuries A.D., and Golan was one of its principal cities. Josephus mentioned Golan as a city and Gaulanitis as a district (Antiquities of the Jews, XIII:15:3; XVII:8:1). The exact site of the city of Golan is uncertain, but it is perhaps modern Sahen el Jolan, 17 miles east of the Sea of Galilee.

The Syrian bombardment of Ein-Gev from the Golan Heights precipitated the six-day war of June 1967. Israel served notice on Syria that she must be prepared to face the consequences and Syria appealed to Egypt and Iraq. Egypt cried for war, turned out the United Nations at Gaza and the Straits of Tiran, and soon the war was on. Taking the Golan Heights was very difficult and cost 115 Israeli lives. The Jews made the cities ruinous heaps (Isa. 14, 17).

- Moses assigned Golan to the tribe of Manasseh (Deut. 4:41–43; Josh. 20:8).
- It was assigned to the sons of Gershon (Josh. 21:27; 1 Chron. 6:71).

Quneitra, Qnaitra, Kuneitra, El Kuneitra

This is a ghost town from which 30,000 Syrians fled the Israeli army in 1967. Before, it was the Syrian army headquarters. It is about 40 miles from Damascus, Syria's capital. The city is in ruins, and near the town a new Jewish kibbutz, MEROM-GOLAN, was formed in 1967. In 1968 another village of EIN-ZEVAN was founded west of Merom-Golan. A number of other Jewish communities have been established on the Golan Heights since the 1967 war.

APHEK ("fortress"), Fiq

This town on the Golan Heights, 4 miles directly east of Ein Gev on the Sea of Galilee, is possibly the location of one of the four Apheks of the Bible.

■ Here Ahab defeated Benhadad (1 Kings 20:26–30; 2 Kings 13:17).

Mevo Hamma

This new Israeli community, 2 miles south of Kfar Horeb, is built where once the Syrian guns shot down on Kibbutz Ha'on and Kibbutz Ein Gev. Syrian bunkers are located on the edge of the heights and a beautiful panoramic view of the Sea of Galilee can be seen from here.

Ein Gev

This kibbutz, founded in 1937 by German and Czechoslovakian pioneers, boasts a 5,000-seat AMPHITHEATER, where a musical festival attracts large crowds during Passover time. Visitors can purchase a favorite dish called "Saint Peter's fish" at a cafe right on the shore of the Sea of Galilee, and also feed the fish there. The settlers of Ein Gev were the first Jewish fishermen of modern times.

Ein Gev has been a perennial target for Syrians with itchy trigger fingers; the Jews built concrete shelters and slit trenches long ago.

Between Ein Gev and Tiberias there is a regular ferry service across the Sea of Galilee, which is 5½ miles wide at that point.

Near El Kursio, about 4 miles north of Ein Gev, an ancient synagogue has recently been excavated.

Susita, Sussita, Hippos

Immediately east of Ein Gev is Mount Susita, so named because it resembles the back of a horse (Hebrew Sus). On the top of the mount are ruins of a Greek Decapolis city and a later Roman fortress.

GADARA, Gader, Gergesa, Jedur, Hammet Geder

This was a city of the Decapolis (league of 10 cities east of the Sea of Galilee), on the Yarmuk River 6 miles southeast of the Sea of Galilee. Its territory may have extended to the sea. (See the section on Gadara, in chapter 7, "Jordan").

■ Jesus healed the demoniac and the demons entered into and destroyed the swine (Matt. 8:28–34; Mark 5:1–20; Luke 8:26–39).

WEST COAST FROM JOPPA TO LEBANON

JOPPA ("height," "beauty"), Jaffa, Yafo

Joppa is immediately south of the modern Tel Aviv and is a part of "greater" Tel Aviv. It has a population of 60,000. It is to Tel Aviv what Old Jerusalem is to New Jerusalem. It is 30 miles south of

Caesarea and 35 miles northwest of Jerusalem. It has a recorded history of 3,500 years. Under Solomon, Jaffa became Jerusalem's seaport. Under the Romans, 8,000 Jews were killed here. Crusader Richard the Lion-Hearted built a citadel here, but Saladin's brother took it away from him and slaughtered 20,000 Christians in the process. It was razed by Napoleon in 1799 and rebuilt by the Turks.

The first Zionist pioneers of the nineteenth century entered the Promised Land through Jaffa harbor, but the harbor is scarcely used today.

On top of a hill near the seashore is the **MONASTERY OF SAINT PETER**, marking the traditional site of Peter's vision of the great sheet; and nearby is a small **MOSQUE** in a little alley close to the lighthouse, built on the traditional site of the **HOUSE OF SIMON THE TANNER**. The **JOPPA MUSEUM** houses archaeological findings.

- *Cedars were brought to Joppa en route to Jerusalem for the temples of Solomon and Zerubbabel (2 Chron. 2:16; also Ezra 3:7).*
- *Jonah embarked from here for Tarshish (Jonah 1:3).*
- *Peter raised Tabitha, or Dorcas, to life (Acts 9:36–43).*
- *Here Peter had his vision of the great sheet, and Cornelius was converted (Acts 9:43–10:48).*
- *Joppa was the home of Simon the tanner (Acts 10:5–6, 32).*
- *Peter told the church at Jerusalem his experiences (Acts 11:5–21).*

Tel Aviv (*"old-new land," "hill of spring"*)

This is the first city in the world to be built, populated, and administered entirely by Jews in modern times. It is the largest completely Jewish city in the world. Although founded in 1909 on the sand hills, it is now a thoroughly modern city and Israel's largest, with a population of 400,000. It is located immediately north of Joppa. Its new hotels on the beach are making it into the "Middle Eastern Miami Beach," and to an idealistic mapam kibbutznik, the mere mention of its name conjures up an image of Gomorrah in its worst depravity.

Tel Aviv is the commercial, industrial, and cultural heart of the country. Crowds throng the streets and beaches, and it seems that the young city reflects the exuberance of youth. Tel Aviv and its neighbor are combined and called *Tell Aviv-Yafo.*

POINTS OF INTEREST

CITY HALL is a beautiful 12-story building in the "Kings of Israel Square" (*Kikar Malkhai Israel*). A view from the top is desirable.

MIGDAL SHALOM is Tel Aviv's tallest building and is in the heart of the financial district. It houses exhibits and has an observatory.

KIKAR DIZENGOFF is like Times Square or Piccadilly Circus. Saturday nights are especially lively.

TEL AVIV UNIVERSITY is in the Ramat Aviv area. It has humanities, science, medicine, business administration, and other faculties.

CARMEL MARKET is Tel Aviv's largest open-air market and has a colorful Oriental flavor. It is located on Rehov Allenby, on the corner of Rehov Nahlat Benyamin.

The FLEA MARKET (*Shuk Hapishpishim*) is located in Yafo, near Kikar Hagana. There are antiques and odd objects here for "bargaining."

The ZOO is located at 76 Rehov Keren Kayemet.

EXPEDITION GARDENS is the site of the biannual Tel Aviv International Fair and Special Exhibits.

The TEL AVIV MUSEUM has paintings and sculptures by Israeli and international artists. It is located in the home of Meir Dizengoff, founder and first mayor of Tel Aviv. It was in this home that the State of Israel was declared into existence on May 14, 1948.

BET HAGANA is a museum that shows the development of Israel's defense forces and the War of Independence. It is located at 23 Sderot Rothschild.

At MUSEUM CENTER — *Ramat Aviv* — there are museums of glass, money, ceramics, science, ethnography, and folklore.

The MUSEUM OF ANTIQUITIES of Tel Aviv-Yafo houses archaeological finds and records illustrating the history of Tel Aviv-Yafo.

OTHER MUSEUMS include the MUSEUM OF THE HISTORY OF TEL AVIV, the ALPHABET MUSEUM, MAN AND HIS WORK, the TCHERNICHOVSKY MUSEUM, the JABOTINSKY MUSEUM, the PERMANENT INDUSTRIAL EXHIBITION, SHALOM ALEICHEM HOUSE, the ISRAEL EXPORT INSTITUTE, and THE ISRAEL COMPANY FOR FAIRS AND EXHIBITIONS.

TELL KASSILE, *Tell Qasila*

On the northern outskirts of Tel Aviv is the site of an ancient fortress that guarded Yarkon port during the days of Solomon. Tradition indicates that the "cedars of Lebanon" were brought by sea to this point and hauled overland to Jerusalem for Solomon's temple. Others believe the cedars were brought to the port of Joppa.

■ *Hiram, king of Tyre, sent cedar trees to David and Solomon (2 Sam. 5:11; 2 Chron. 2:3–16).*

Petah-Tikva (*"door of hope"*), *Petah Tiqwa*

Five miles east of Tel Aviv is the oldest Jewish agricultural settlement in Israel, founded in 1878 by Jews from Jerusalem.

APHEK, ANTIPATRIS (*"belonging to Antipater"*)

Two miles northeast of Petah-Tikva is the site of ancient Antipatris. It was built about 35 B.C. by Herod in memory of his father, Antipater, on the ruins of Aphek. It guarded the main highway to Jerusalem before the highway entered the hills. A thousand years after the Philistines defeated the Hebrews, Herod built a square fortress here. The remains visible today are from the days of the Crusaders. Near Antipatris is BOSH-HA-AYIN, whose spring water is pumped to the thirsty desert.

LEBANON

MEDITERRANEAN SEA

Rosh Haniqra
Tell Achzib
Montfort
Nahariya
Shavei Zion
Yehiam
Lohamei-Hagetaot
Kafr Yasif
Ramah
Safed
Accho
Cabul (Kabul)
Yodefat
Sea of Galilee
(Chinnereth)
Tell Shiqmona
Haifa
Shefaram
Tiberias
Atlit
Nazareth
Dor
Afula
Megiddo
Caesarea
Beth Shean
En-Gannim (Jenin)
Hadera
JORDAN
Kefar Vitkin
Kibbutz Há Ogen
Natanya
Tulkarm
Jordan River
Plain of Sharon
Shechem (Nablus)
N
Tell Arshaf
Kefar Sava
Herzliya
Aphek (Antipatris)
Tell Kassile
Tel Aviv
Petah-Tikva
Joppa (Jaffa)

Israel
West Coast from Joppa to Lebanon

Miles   5   10

Lod
To Jerusalem
Ramla

- *Here the Philistines captured the ark of the covenant, which had been brought from Shiloh to the battle (1 Sam. 4:1-11).*
- *Here Paul stayed overnight as the soldiers took him from Jerusalem to Caesarea (Acts 23:23, 31).*

PLAIN OF SHARON

This is a strip of comparatively level land between the mountains and the Mediterranean Sea, from 8 to 12 miles wide and 30 miles long (from Mount Carmel to Joppa). It is fertile and beautiful like the "rose of Sharon."

- *David's herds were pastured here (1 Chron. 27:25, 29).*
- *Its excellence was spoken of by Isaiah (Isa. 35:2; 65:10).*

Herzliya

About 4 miles north of Tel Aviv is Herzliya, a city of 37,000 inhabitants. Excellent bathing beaches and hotels make it a holiday resort.

Tell Arshaf, *Rishpon, Apollonia, Arsur*

On the seacoast 1 mile north of Herzliya are ruins of a city known as *Arshaf* in Canaanite times and *Rishpon* in the days of Omri. It was renamed *Apollonia* in the Hellenistic period and later annexed by Alexander Yannai. Near the Crusader castle of Arsur, Richard the Lion-hearted defeated Saladin in 1191.

Natanya

This beautiful, clean coastal city is known as the "pearl of Sharon," even though one of the main industries of the city is the cutting of diamonds. The city was founded in 1929, and because of its beautiful BEACHES it soon became a popular resort city. During World War II it was the chief rest and recreation center for battle-weary soldiers of the Allied forces in the Middle East. The diamond industry was started by Belgian refugees during World War II. Today the export of polished diamonds grosses some $120,000,000 a year. Citrus groves and tourists help make the livelihood of 60,000 inhabitants.

Kibbutz Há Ogen

Five miles northeast of Natanya is a beautiful kibbutz that operates a plastic factory. The Jews here are very cordial and will show visitors through the factory.

Kefar Vitkin, *in* EMEK HEFER

About 3 miles north of Natanya, on the north part of the Plains of Sharon and near the seacoast, is Kefar Vitkin, whose farmers were the pioneers of Emek Hefer in 1930.

- *Emek Hefer is the Valley of Hefer (Hepher) mentioned as one of Solomon's twelve districts that provided victuals for his household (1 Kings 4:7, 10).*

Hadera *("green")*

This is a citrus belt city of 30,000 population, 25 miles north of Tel Aviv, near the Mediterranean seacoast. It was founded in 1891 at the beginning of modern Zionism.

CAESAREA

This was a seaport on the Mediterranean about 30 miles north of Joppa and about 70 miles northwest of Jerusalem, built by Herod the Great in 22 B.C. as his summer palace on the site of ancient Strato's Tower. It was the capital of the Roman government in Palestine for about 500 years. It was named in honor of Caesar Augustus (Luke 2:1) and had lavish palaces, public buildings, a theater, a hippodrome, and an amphitheater. It also had a spacious system of SEWERS under the city.

The HARBOR Herod built was considered a great feat. It was always free from the waves of the sea. The mighty breakwater was constructed by letting down huge stones into twenty fathoms of water. A WALL and TOWERS, a promenade, and dwellings for mariners were also provided.

Caesarea became the home of the Roman procurators, including Pontius Pilate. Herod Agrippa I died here, being "eaten of worms." He was smitten by the angel of the Lord (Acts 12:19–23).

Terrible cruelties were practiced against the Jews under Felix and Florus. Here Vespasian was hailed emperor by his soldiers, and Titus celebrated the birthday of his brother, Domitian, by setting 2,500 Jews to fight with beasts in the amphitheater. Riots between Gentiles and Jews in Caesarea precipitated the final war against the latter. The great Jewish war was begun here by the Jews in A.D. 66, and coins "Judaea Capta" were minted here after their defeat. Rabbi Akiva was martyred here by the Romans after Bar Kokhba's abortive rising, and many a Jew or Christian was thrown to the lions here following the revolt.

In the third century A.D. the Christian scholar Origen established the School of Caesarea. Eusebius was bishop of Caesarea from A.D. 313 to 340. In 548 a massacre of the Christians was organized and carried out by the Jews and Samaritans. The city passed into Moslem hands in 638. In the time of the Crusades it fell to the Christians and then again to the Moslems. It was the scene of a Moslem massacre of many Christians in 1101. It was overthrown by Sultan Baybars I in 1265 but was later regained by the Turks.

Excavations have uncovered along the seashore the great second-century AQUEDUCT that brought water to the city from the Mount Carmel Springs, some 12 miles away.

At Caesarea the first ARCHAEOLOGICAL EVIDENCE OF PONTIUS PILATE has been unearthed. It is an inscription bearing the names of Emperor Tiberius and Pontius Pilate, the Roman procurator of Judea who ruled between A.D. 26 and 36. The original stone is in the Israel National Museum, and a replica is located on the site.

A famous glass bowl supposedly used by Jesus at the Last Supper

Crusader fortress, Caesarea

was recovered here when the Frank Crusaders reconquered Caesarea. It is now in Genoa, Italy, and is known as the *sacro cantina*. It corresponds to the legendary "Holy Grail."

At a glance you will see vestiges of three civilizations here: the steps leading to Saint Louis's **CRUSADER FORTRESS**, the crumbled **ROMAN COLUMNS** jutting out of the sea, and a **MINARET** from the nineteenth-century **TURKISH OCCUPATION**.

The present ruins include the **WALLS** of the ancient city (the original wall was nearly 3 miles long on the landward side), and within them those of a much smaller town of the twelfth century, whose walls were rebuilt in the thirteenth. There remain also some of the ruins of the **CATHEDRAL**, which appear to be on the site of the **TEMPLE** raised by Herod to Augustus. A **ROMAN HIPPODROME** over 1,000 feet long was built to accommodate 20,000 people. On the south side of the medieval town are ruins apparently of a large **THEATER** close to the shore. Large quantities of building stones have been carried to other towns and used for new building projects.

Caesarea is a National Parks Authority site and has a beautiful golf course, the first in Israel.

■ *Philip preached here, lived here, and had four daughters who prophesied (Acts 8:40; 21:8–9).*

- *Peter came here and preached to Cornelius, who was baptized (Acts 10).*
- *Paul visited here three times, and Agabus warned him not to go to Jerusalem (Acts 9:30; 18:22; 21:8–16; 25:3–6).*
- *Peter came here after his deliverance from prison (Acts 12:19).*
- *Paul spent two years in prison here (Acts 23:22–26:32). Note his addresses to Felix, Festus, and Agrippa. Agrippa replied, "Almost thou persuadest me to be a Christian" (Acts 26:28).*

DOR ("circle"), Dora, Tantura, el-Burj

A mound near Zikhron Ya'aqou, 8 miles north of Caesarea, has been identified as the biblical city of Dor, with its harbor and remains of a fortress and a Byzantine church. King David captured it from the Philistines and King Solomon gave it to his son-in-law, making it the center of one of the 12 regions responsible for providing the royal household with food for 1 month a year. In Roman times it was called Dora. Dor, in antiquity, was one of the centers for producing the dye known as "Tyrian purple," or "royal purple," for it was so expensive that it was confined to emperors and nobles. The color was actually a purplish red and was extracted from a tiny sac found in a mollusc which abounded along the coast. It was not until the nineteenth century that the Tyrian purple could be matched. The Jews were famous for dyeing cloth during Roman times.

- *The king of Dor was killed in battle with Joshua (Josh. 11:2, 8; 12:7, 23).*
- *The city was administered by Ben-abinadab for Solomon (1 Kings 4:7, 11).*

Atlit, Athlit, Chateau de Pelerin

On the Mediterranean seacoast about 9 miles south of Haifa is the ancient Phoenician port of Atlit. The Crusader fortress Chateau de Pelerin at this site was built in 1217 and destroyed by the Baybars in 1291.

Tell Shiqmona, Sycaminium

On the tip of Cape Carmel, just south of the city of Haifa, was a Jewish settlement and seat of the sages in the Mishna period. There was also a Crusader fort here.

Carmel Caves

It is believed that 100,000 years ago *Homo carmelensis*, intermediate between the Neanderthal man and the modern species of man, lived in the caves of Mount Carmel.

Haifa

Haifa was destroyed by Moslem conquerors in the seventh century, conquered by Crusaders in 1100, and destroyed in 1761 by Taher el Amar. Haifa is Israel's shipbuilding center and third largest city (225,000). It is one of the most beautifully situated cities in the world, in a setting similar to that of San Francisco. Mount Carmel juts into the Mediterranean Sea at this point. Israel's only underground subway, the **CARMELIT** (a mile long), is located here. Little existed here until 1933, when the British built a modern harbor, the main port in Israel. Now the city has the nation's largest heavy industries.

In 1898, Theodor Herzl, father of Zionism, prophesied a future large city at Haifa, and thus it has become.

Thousands have come "home" to the promised land through the Port of Haifa. This modern city has been a "sight of heaven" for the homeless refugees.

POINTS OF INTEREST

The **DAGON GRAIN SILO** and **ARCHAEOLOGICAL MUSEUM** display both ancient and modern methods of grain storage. The excellent museum has grains over 4,000 years old.

Other places of interest include the **MUNICIPAL MUSEUM OF ANCIENT AND MODERN ART**, the **CHAGELL ARTISTS' HOUSE**, the **JAPANESE ART MUSEUM**, the **ETHNOLOGICAL MUSEUM**, the **MUSEUM OF PREHISTORY**, the **MARITIME MUSEUM**, the **ILLEGAL IMMIGRATION AND NAVAL MUSEUM**, the **CARMELITE MONASTERY**, and the campus of the **TECHNION**, Israel's Institute of Technology.

The **BAHA'I SHRINE, GARDENS**, and **ARCHIVES BUILDING** mark the world center of the Baha'i faith. This complex is one of Haifa's most impressive attractions. The Baha'i faith began in Persia in the mid-nineteenth century, and its leaders were exiled to Palestine. They claim 3,000,000 followers.

Baha'is believe in the brotherhood of all men, a common world

Accho and the Mosque of El Jezaar

language, and the unity of all religions. They believe all prophets
were sent by God to preach the same message. The most recent of the
prophets was Baha'ullah (1817–92). He was exiled by Moslem and
Turkish authorities to Acre, where he wrote his doctrines and died in
the Baha'i House, just outside Acre. In the Haifa Persian Gardens,
the huge domed temple entombs the remains of El Bab (Mirza Ali
Muhammed), the Baha'ullah's herald, who suffered a martyr's death.

The **CARMELITE MONASTERY** on the Cape of Carmel served as a
hospital to Napoleon's army as they laid siege to the Turkish Acre in
1799. **ELIJAH'S CAVE** is a very sacred Jewish, Moslem, and Christian
site. According to tradition, Elijah hid here when he fled from King
Ahab, and Jesus, Mary, and Joseph sought shelter here when they
returned from Egypt. The site of the cave is marked by the Carmelite
CHURCH OF STELLA MARIS.

■ *According to tradition, Elijah sought shelter in a cave as he fled
from Ahab, perhaps on his way to Zarephath (1 Kings 17:10).*
■ *Tradition says the Holy Family sought shelter in Elijah's Cave
after returning from Egypt (Matt. 2:20–21).*

Shefaram

This was the seat of the Sanhedrin around A.D. 150. It is 12 miles east
of Haifa.

CABUL, Kabul *("dry," "sandy")*

Nine miles southeast of Akko was the border city of Asher and
Galilee. This is the area transferred to King Hiram by Solomon. It
was the first town to be conquered by the Romans during the Jewish
revolt of A.D. 66.

■ *It is mentioned in the Old Testament (Josh. 19:27).*
■ *This was the name given by Hiram to twenty cities of Galilee
(1 Kings 9:11–13).*

Yodefat, *Jotapata,* Yotapata

About 8 miles northwest of Cana are the ruins of a fortress known as
Jotapata. (See map: "West Coast from Joppa to Lebanon.") It was
in this fortress that the Jews held out against the Romans in A.D. 66
and where the Jewish historian Josephus surrendered to the Romans.

ACCHO, Akko, Acre, *Acco, Ptolemais, Tell el Fukhkhar*

Akko is a 4,000-year-old Canaanite and Phoenician port city that
commanded the approach from the sea and land to the rich Plain of
Jezreel. It is 9 miles north of Haifa and 12 miles south of Lebanon
and has a population of 20,000. The Egyptians Thutmose III, Seti I,
and Ramses II are among the conquerors of Acre. The Assyrians
Sennacherib, Esarhaddon, Ashurbanipal, and several of the Ptolemies
engaged in its conquest or defense. It played a part in the history of
the Maccabees, and Queen Cleopatra of Egypt held it for a time. Here
Herod the Great entertained Caesar. When Alexander the Great conquered Palestine, the Greeks changed the name of Acre to Ptolemais,

and this was the name of the city when it was visited by Paul. After the fall of Jerusalem, Acre was the Crusader capital for 100 years (1187–1287). It was the last place held by the Crusaders in Palestine, and was taken by the Saracens in 1291. Acre has had 17 recorded sieges, and in 1798 it became famous when the Turkish soldiers at Acre withstood Napoleon's famous siege. The city is famous for the remains of **CRUSADER CONSTRUCTION**.

The ancient site of Acre is believed to have been located on a mound, Tell el-Fukhkhar, 2 miles east of the sea. The present site dates back to the fourth century B.C.

During the Middle Ages Jewish pilgrims, including Maimonides, the Jewish philosopher, landed at Acre on their way to the holy sites.

A **CITADEL** built by the Turks and used as the central prison by the British during the Mandate houses the **ENGLISH HANGING ROOM**, where members of the Israeli underground forces were put to death. On the second floor is a room where Baha'ullah, founder of the Baha'i sect, was imprisoned by the Turks in 1868. Part of the citadel has been turned into a museum of the national struggle for liberation: the **CITADEL MUSEUM OF HEROISM**. The citadel is also used as a mental hospital.

The **MOSQUE OF EL JEZAAR** is claimed by some to be the largest and most splendid mosque in Israel. It was built in 1781 on the ruins of a Saint John's Knights monastery church.

The **KHAN EL UMDAN** was built in 1785 as a caravansary and is open to visitors. The **BURJ ES-SULTAN** is a well-preserved **CRUSADER FORTRESS**. The **CITY WALLS** are preserved in the neighborhood of the Knights' Hall and it is possible to walk on top of the walls. The **CRYPT OF SAINT JOHN**, near the Mosque of El Jezaar, is of special interest, as is the **MUSEUM**.

The **BAHA'I HOUSE**, 1 mile north of Acre, is where the Baha'i sect's leader, Baha'ullah, was placed by the Turks in nominal freedom after he had spent 24 years in the Acre jail. His remains are entombed in the main house. Lovely green grounds surround the building. Some Baha'i followers were imprisoned in the Crusader Prison at Akko.

On the north of Acre is a handsome **AQUEDUCT** built in 1780 by Pasha Ahmad Jezaar over one the Romans left. It originally supplied Acre with water from Galilee Springs.

- *The city was assigned to the tribe of Asher but never conquered (Josh. 19:24–31; Judg. 1:31).*
- *It was called Accho (Judg. 1:31).*
- *Paul stopped here briefly on his final trip to Jerusalem (Acts 21:7).*

Kafr Yasif

This traditional home town of the famous Jewish historian, Flavius Josephus, is located 5 miles northeast of Acre.

Lohamei-Hagetaot

Three miles north of Acco is a kibbutz founded in 1949 by Jews from Poland and Lithuania. Because of the active part they took in the revolt of the Jewish ghettos during World War II, the MUSEUM OF THE HOLOCAUST, with displays of doomed ghettos and Nazi extermination camps, has been built at the kibbutz.

Shavei Zion

Four miles north of Acre, at Shavei Zion, are relics of an early Christian church, with cross ornaments in floor mosaics.

Nahariya ("river")

Lying on both sides of the stream Gaaton, 5 miles south of the Lebanon-Israel border, is a city of 21,000 inhabitants, founded in 1934 by German Jews fleeing the Hitler regime. It was the first settlement in western Galilee. It has beautiful promenades and beaches. The remains of a Canaanite temple, 3,500 years old, were uncovered next to the beach. Molds for statues of the goddess Asherah of the Sea (Astarte, Ashtoreth) were found. The Gaaton Brook, flanked by stately eucalyptus trees, divides the main boulevard of this beautiful city.

TELL ACHZIB, Ekdippa, Ez-Zib

About 2 miles north of Nahariya is Tell Achzib. This is the site of an important Phoenician port which became a part of the inheritance of the tribe of Asher.

- It was a city of Asher (Josh. 19:29–31).
- The natives could not be dislodged (Judg. 1:31).

Rosh Haniqra, Ladder of Tyre

Six miles north of Nahariya, on the shores of the Mediterranean Sea and within a mile of the Lebanon border, is Rosh Haniqra, "Cape of the Grotto." The cliff of Rosh Haniqra is the southernmost point of a range of hills running along the Mediterranean seashore; they are called the LADDER OF TYRE. A legend indicates that Abraham said in effect, "This is the place" for the promised land. Rosh Haniqra has been a passageway for the armies of Alexander the Great, for the Crusaders, and for the Allies in 1914 and 1941. Waves have carved labyrinthine grottos out of the rocky cliff and a cable car takes the visitor down to the white grottos.

Yehiam, Kibbutz Yehiam, Crusader Fort Judin

A Crusader castle, built by Teutonic knights of the Order of Templars, is located by Kibbutz Yehiam, 8 miles east of Nahariya. It was restored in the eighteenth century by the local emir. It is a good example of an Ottoman ruler's feudal residence. The fortress fell to the Moslem Mamelukes in 1291, when the Crusader rule came to an end in the Holy Land.

This is a National Parks Authority site.

Montfort

Located 12 miles east-southeast of Nahariya is the castle of the Teutonic knights, Montfort. It was built in 1226 by the Crusaders and was the seat of the Teutonic knights. It was destroyed by Sultan Baybars in 1271. The ruins were excavated by the Metropolitan Museum of Art of New York in 1926.

WEST AND SOUTHWEST OF JERUSALEM

MOZAH, *Moza*, **Motsa**

The village of Motsa lies 4½ miles west of Jerusalem. The brook of Sorek comes in from the north. Beyond it, on a high ridge, is a large building topped with a minaret, the traditional tomb of Samuel the prophet (Nebi Samwil).

■ *It was a town of Benjamin (Josh. 18:21, 26).*

Aqua-Bella *("beautiful water")*

About 1 mile south and east of Abu Gosh are the ruins of a twelfth-century Crusader monastery named Aqua-Bella. This is a National Parks Authority site.

KIRJATH-JEARIM, *Emmaus*, **Abu Ghosh**, *Abu Gosh, Kiryat-Yearim, Kulonieh*

This is an Arab village 9 miles west of Jerusalem, in the mountainous terrain. The CRUSADER CHURCH is one of the finest remains of Crusader times and dates back to 1142. It was built on Roman fortress foundations over the top of a spring and called Fontenoid. The site of Abinadab's house is marked by a huge statue of Mary carrying the baby Jesus in her arms. A French MONASTERY OF THE ARK was built here in 1924. It is called OUR LADY OF THE ARK OF THE COVENANT and is served by the Sisters of Saint Joseph. An old church here has a lovely mosaic floor. A beautiful view of Jerusalem can be obtained here, and as pilgrims come from the west they get their first glimpse of the Holy City.

■ *Here Abinadab lived and kept the ark of the covenant for twenty years (1 Sam. 7:1-2; 2 Sam. 6:1-16; 1 Chron. 15:25-29).*
■ *David took the ark from here to Jerusalem (2 Sam. 6).*
■ *The Crusaders believed this was Emmaus (Luke 24:13).*

BETH HORON *("place of hollows")*, *Beit Ur el-Foqa, Beit Ur et Tahta*

Because of its important position guarding the approach to the Jerusalem Corridor, Beth Horon was the scene of many battles.

■ *Solomon fortified Beth Horon (2 Chron. 8:5; 1 Kings 9:17).*
■ *It was located on the frontier between Benjamin and Ephraim (Josh. 16:3-5; 18:11, 13).*
● *Here Judas Maccabaeus defeated the Syrians (1 Macc. 3:13-24).*

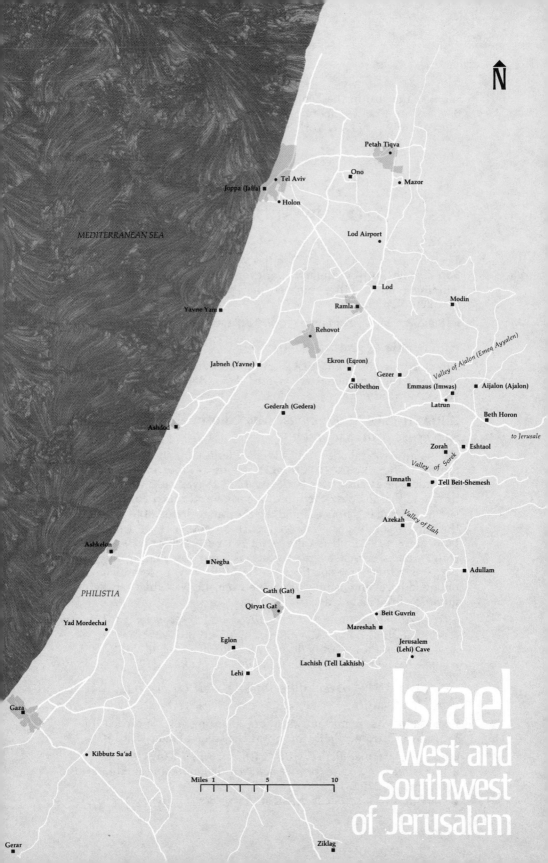

N

Petah Tiqva

Ono

Mazor

Joppa (Jaffa) ■ ■ Tel Aviv
■ Holon

MEDITERRANEAN SEA

Lod Airport

Lod

Yavne Yam ■

Ramla ■

Modin ■

Rehovot

Ekron (Eqron) ■

Gezer ■

Valley of Ajalon (Emeq Ayyalen)

Jabneh (Yavne) ■

Gibbethon ■

Emmaus (Imwas) ■

Aijalon (Ajalon) ■

Latrun ■

Gederah (Gedera) ■

Beth Horon ■

Ashdod ■

to Jerusale

Zorah ■   Eshtaol ■

Valley of Sorek

Timnath ■   ■ Tell Beit-Shemesh

Ashkelon ■

Azekah ■   *Valley of Elah*

Negba ■

Adullam ■

PHILISTIA

Gath (Gat) ■

Qiryat Gat ■

Beit Guvrin ■

Yad Mordechai ■

Mareshah ■

Eglon ■

Jerusalem
(Lehi) Cave ■

Lachish (Tell Lakhish) ■

Lehi ■

Gaza

Kibbutz Sa'ad ■

Miles 1   5   10

Israel
West and
Southwest
of Jerusalem

Gerar ■

Ziklag ■

VALLEY OF AJALON, AIJALON, Emeq Ayyalen, *Ayalon*

This valley is about 2½ miles northeast of Latrun. It has served as a battleground for the Israelites, Philistines, Maccabees, Romans, Arabs, Crusaders, British, and Jews.

- *Here Joshua defeated the Amorites; great hailstones killed many, and the sun stood still while the battle was won (Josh. 10:6–27).*
- *In this valley Saul won a victory over the Philistines (1 Sam. 14:31).*
- *This was an important pass mentioned with Gibeon (Josh. 10:12).*

AIJALON, Ajalon (*"place of deer"*), Yalo, Elon-beth-hanam

This was an ancient city of Israel located in the Valley of Ajalon 20 miles southeast of Tel Aviv and 14 miles west of Jerusalem. It is mentioned in the Tell el 'Amarna letters and was occupied as early as 2000 B.C.

- *The tribes of Joseph subdued it (Judg. 1:35).*
- *It later became an Ephraimite city of refuge (1 Chron. 6:67, 69).*
- *Beriah and Shama, who defeated the men of Gath, came from here (1 Chron. 8:13).*
- *It was fortified by Rehoboam (2 Chron. 11:5, 10).*
- *It was captured by the Philistines in the time of Ahaz (2 Chron. 28:16, 18).*

EMMAUS, Imwas, *Ammaous, Nicopolis, Amwas*

One mile northeast of Latrun and about 15 miles west of Jerusalem is a traditional site of Jesus' appearance to two travelers on the evening of the resurrection. The name comes from *Hamma*, which means "warm well," and there are several warm wells in the area. Next to a new monastery are the ruins of a Byzantine Crusader church.

- *Jesus appeared to two disciples (Luke 24:13–35).*
- *This was the scene of an engagement between Judas Maccabaeus and Gorgias (1 Macc. 3:40, 57; 4:3–27).*
- *It was fortified by Bacchides (1 Macc. 9:50).*

Latrun

Latrun is about 15 miles east of Ramla on the Jerusalem Road. It is a strategic fortress captured by the Israelis in the 1948 war with a loss of over 1,000 soldiers. This fortress guarded the entrance to the Jerusalem Corridor. A trappist monastery is the only other structure that now stands in Latrun. When traveling through the Jerusalem Corridor, one should note the overturned tanks and trucks that are now **WAR MEMORIALS** in honor of the men who lost their lives to open the corridor. On the Jerusalem Road note that the mountains are covered with pine trees and Saint John trees (carob, bread, or locust). These are part of a gigantic reclamation project, in which 90,000,000 trees had been planted by 1970. Note the **TABOR OAKS** in the middle of the freeway. They are among the oldest trees in Israel. The Turks destroyed most of the trees in Israel, but because of a mosque at this location they preserved these trees.

- *Reforestation is felt to be in fulfillment of Ezekiel's prophecy (Ezek. 36:8).*

GEZER *("a precipice")*, **Tell Gezer**

Gezer was a Canaanite stronghold which withstood Joshua's on-slaught. Later it was one of Solomon's fortified cities, along with Megiddo and Hazor.

In 1908 at Tell Gezer, 20 miles west-northwest of Jerusalem and 2 miles south of the main road, the British Palestine Exploration Fund, headed by R. A. S. Macalister, discovered a small 4½-by-2¾-inch inscribed limestone tablet now called the *Gezer Calendar*. It is dated to the tenth century B.C. and is the most ancient inscription in early Hebrew writing — dating back to the time of Saul or David. The inscription is an agriculture calendar telling what crops were harvested during certain months. The Gezer Calendar is located in a museum at Istanbul.

Standing at a Canaanite high place at Gezer are CULT PILLARS, representing pagan deities. A great WATER TUNNEL at Gezer dates back to about 1500 B.C. The late Nelson Glueck, president of Hebrew College in Jerusalem, has done archaeological work at the site, and more recently William Dever has been directing the archaeological work here. A relief was found at Nimrod showing Gezer being besieged by Assyrian troops about 732 B.C.

- *Joshua defeated Horam, king of Gezer, but failed to capture the city itself (Josh. 10:33).*
- *An Egyptian pharaoh gave the city as a dowry for his daughter, one of King Solomon's wives (1 Kings 9:16).*
- *Solomon rebuilt the city as one of his fortified chariot cities, like Meggido and Hazor (1 Kings 9:15-19).*
- *Cult pillars were perhaps the graven images spoken of by Micah (Micah 5:13).*
- *Gezer was occupied, cleansed, and fortified by Simon the Maccabaean in 142 B.C. (1 Macc. 13:43-48).*

EKRON *("naturalization")*, **Eqron**, *Akir*, *Khirbet el-Muqanna*

This was the most northerly of 5 principal Philistine cities — located 15 miles southeast of Joppa. The Philistines brought the captured ark of the covenant to Ekron, and from here it was sent back. Ekron was destroyed in 711 B.C. by the Assyrians.

- *When Joshua was old, Ekron still remained to be subdued (Josh. 13:3); it was allotted to Judah (Josh. 15:11-12, 21, 45-46) and then to Dan (Josh. 19:40-43).*
- *It was prominent in connection with Philistine suffering on account of the ark (1 Sam. 5-6).*
- *Israel pursued the Philistines to Ekron after David killed Goliath (1 Sam. 17:52).*
- *Beelzebub was worshiped here (2 Kings 1).*

- *It was denounced by the prophets (Jer. 25:15–17, 20; Amos 1:8; Zeph. 2:4; Zech. 9:5–7).*

GIBBETHON *("mound")*, **Tell Malot**, *Tell el-Melat*

This was a town that belonged to Dan. It is a mile southeast of Ekron.

- *It was located in territory of Dan (Josh. 19:40, 44).*
- *It was appointed as a Levitical city (Josh. 21:20, 23).*
- *While Nadab was besieging the city he was assassinated by Baasha (1 Kings 15:25–27).*
- *Omri was besieging it when Zimri assassinated Elah (1 Kings 16: 15–16).*

MODIN, *Modim*

This was the place of origin of the Maccabees, with whom 18 tombs cut into the rocks are associated. It is near Aphek and 6 miles east of Lod. Each year at Hanukkah, the Feast of Lights, a torch is kindled at this spot and carried by relay runners to Mount Herzl, Jerusalem, where it is used to light a great menorah symbolizing that which was relit by Judas Maccabaeus in the temple in 165 B.C.

- *The Maccabees lived at Modin (1 Macc. 2).*

RAMLA *("sand")*

This "newest" of the old cities of Israel lies 2 miles southwest of Lod and 10 miles southeast of Tel Aviv. It has a population of 30,000 people, most of whom are new Jewish immigrants. A clock-faced tower marks the **HOSPICE OF SAINT NICODEMUS AND SAINT JOSEPH OF ARIMATHEA** on the main street, Herzl Avenue. The Crusaders believed that Joseph of Arimathea lived here, and it is also believed that Napoleon "slept here" when he attempted in vain to conquer Palestine from the Turks. The **POOL OF SAINT HELENA**, near the police station and Main Street, is an eighth-century reservoir or underground cistern. It was built by the legendary caliph Harun al-Rashid of *A Thousand and One Nights* fame and is named after Saint Helena, mother of Constantine. Visitors can ride a gondola on its waters. The **GREAT MOSQUE** in Ramla is one of Israel's best examples of Crusader architecture. The **WHITE TOWER** was built in the fourteenth century as a minaret of the white mosque which had been built earlier. A view from its top is desirable.

- *Tradition says this was Joseph of Arimathea's home (John 19:38).*

LOD *("fissure")*, *Lydda, Diospolis*

Eleven miles southeast of Joppa is the city of Lod, twin of Ramla. According to tradition, Lod was a fortified town in the days of Joshua and was rebuilt by descendants of the tribe of Benjamin. The Greeks changed the name to Lydda. In A.D. 70 the Romans burned the town.

During the second and third centuries Lod was famous as a seat of Jewish learning and housed an academy.

Lod is the legendary city of Saint George, who, according to tradition, was buried here in A.D. 303 after he was martyred by the Romans for tearing down the anti-Christian edicts of the Roman emperor. The **SAINT GEORGE CHURCH** is named in his honor, and after his death the name of the city was changed to *Georgeospolis*.

Lod is the location of Israel's largest **AIRPORT**. (The airport is actually 3 miles north of the city.) This airport is the home of El-Al Airlines and is 32 miles from Jerusalem.

- *It was founded by Shemed, a Benjaminite (1 Chron. 8:1, 12; Neh. 11:31–35).*
- *Some natives settled here after their captivity in Babylon (Ezra 2:1, 33; Neh. 7:6, 37).*
- *Peter healed Aeneas (Acts 9:32–35).*

Mazor

Ten miles east of the seacoast and Tel Aviv is this Roman mausoleum of the second or third century A.D.

ONO *("strong")*

This was an ancient fortified town built by the "sons of Elpaal." It was located about 5 miles east of the seacoast, at Tel Aviv.

- *It was a Benjaminite city (1 Chron. 8:1, 12).*
- *Nehemiah was invited to a conference here (Neh. 6:2).*
- *It was reoccupied after the exile (Neh. 7:6, 37; 11:35).*

Note: From this point the biblical sites and places of interest are listed in an order from the Valley of Sorek south to Lehi, west to Gaza, and north to Joppa.

VALLEY OF SOREK *("vineyard")*, *Nahal Kesloh, Wadi es-Sarar*

This was a valley, or wadi, in which Delilah lived, and is 14 miles west of Jerusalem.

- *It was near Eshtaol and Zorah (Judg. 13:25; 14:1–2).*
- *Here Samson and his parents lived and here he met and succumbed to the enticements of Delilah (Judg. 16:4–21).*

ESHTAOL *("hollow way")*, *Eshwa*

This was a lowland city of Judah, 13 miles west of Jerusalem and 2½ miles south of the main road from Jerusalem to Tel Aviv. It was inherited by the tribe of Dan in biblical days and was reestablished in 1949.

- *It was a city of the lowland of Judah (Josh. 15:21, 33).*
- *It was near here that Samson was buried (Judg. 16:30–31).*
- *It was the home of some of the Danites who attacked Laish (Judg. 18:2, 11, 27).*

ZORAH *("prominent," "wasp")*, *Sarah*

This was a town on the top of a high hill on the north side of the

Valley of Sorek, 14 miles southwest of Jerusalem and just west of Eshtaol.

- *It was allotted to Judah (Josh. 15:21, 33).*
- *It was the birthplace of Samson (Judg. 13:2, 25).*
- *Samson was buried between Zorah and Eshtaol (Judg. 16:31).*
- *Zorah was fortified by Rehoboam (2 Chron. 11:5, 10).*
- *It was repopulated after the exile (Neh. 11:29).*

BETH-SHEMESH *("temple of the sun"), Ain Shems,* Tell Beit-Shemesh

This was a Canaanite town dedicated to the worship of the sun-god. Later it was a town of Judah called *Ir-Shemesh* and allotted to the children of Aaron. It was located on the south slope of the Wadi-es-Sarar (Vale of Sorek), 15 miles west of Jerusalem. Excavations by the British Palestine Exploration Fund (1911–12) and Haverford College in Pennsylvania (1928–33) have shown evidence of occupation from 3000 B.C. until its destruction by Nebuchadnezzar in the fourth century B.C. Casemate walls of the early iron age probably indicate David's fortifications against the Philistines.

- *The ark was returned here from the Philistines by the men of Ekron (1 Sam. 6:7–21).*
- *Amaziah of Judah was defeated and captured by Jehoash, king of Israel (2 Kings 14:11–14; 2 Chron. 25:17–24).*
- *It was one of the cities of Judah taken by the Philistines in the time of Ahaz (2 Chron. 28:16, 18).*

TIMNATH, Khirbet Timna, *Khirbet Tibneh*

This was a city on the northern frontier of the tribe of Judah, between Beth-shemesh and Ekron to the west, or 2 miles southwest of Beth-shemesh.

- *Its location is given in the Bible (Josh. 15:10).*
- *Here Samson celebrated his marriage, which seems to have been the beginning of his downfall (Judg. 14:1–15:6).*
- *The town was held by the Hebrews in the reign of Uzziah but was lost to the Philistines by Ahaz (2 Chron. 28:16, 18).*

AZEKAH *("breach"),* Kefar-Zekharia, *Tell Zakariyeh*

This was a city in the lowland of Judah, overlooking the Valley of Elah. It stood on the high hill opposite Kefar-Zekharia. With the exception of Lachish, it was the last stronghold to be captured by Nebuchadnezzar before the downfall of Jerusalem in 587 B.C. In the Lachish letter number 4, reference is apparently made to the cessation of fire signals from Azekah, presumably an indication of its fall while Lachish still held out.

- *It was located in Judah, overlooking the Valley of Elah (Josh. 15:21, 35; 1 Sam. 17:1–3).*
- *Joshua defeated Canaanite kings here (Josh. 10:5, 10).*
- *It was fortified by Rehoboam (2 Chron. 11:5, 9).*

VALLEY OF ELAH ("oak trees"), Wadi es-Sant

This is a valley in the Shephelah, the scene of the battle between David and Goliath. It lies 20 miles west and a little south of Jerusalem and just south of Azekah (between Kefar-Zekharia and Azekah). The valley gets its name from elah trees in the area. The stream bed stretches eastward toward Bethlehem. It is dry except in the winter.

■ *Here David killed Goliath (1 Sam. 17; 21:9).*

ADULLAM ("resting place"), Tell esh-Sheikh-Madhkur

This was a city in the Shephelah assigned to Judah (Josh. 15:35). It was 16 miles southwest of Jerusalem and 4½ miles southeast of Elah.

■ *Judah's friend, Hirah, came from here (Gen. 38:1, 12, 20).*
■ *It was formerly a Canaanite city (Josh. 12:8, 15).*
■ *Rehoboam fortified it (2 Chron. 11:5, 7).*
■ *The children of Israel returned to it after the Exile (Neh. 11:30).*
■ *The cave of Adullam, where David hid, must have been in an adjoining valley (1 Sam. 22:1; 2 Sam. 23:13).*
■ *Micah predicted that the glory of Israel would seek refuge here (Mic. 1:15).*

Beit Guvrin, "Bell Caves," Eleutheropolis, Gibelin, Beit Jibril

One mile north of Tell Mareshah, ½ mile south of the modern settlement of Beit Guvrin, and 7 miles east of Qiryat Gat was a large important Roman town. Emperor Septimius Severus visited Beit Guvrin and granted the inhabitants special privileges. Its name was changed to *Eleutheropolis* ("city of liberty"). The Crusaders named the city Gibelin, and in the Middle Ages it was called *Beit Jibril* ("house of Gabriel"). Third-century JEWISH RUINS, beautiful MOSAICS, and CRUSADER RUINS have been found. The mosaics are in the Israel National Museum.

In the area are hundreds of interesting CAVES dating back to the Roman and Byzantine periods. The purpose of the man-made caves is questionable. Some believe they were for burials. They are shaped like a bell or beehive and have round holes at the top. Chisel marks and Christian crosses are plainly seen on the walls. It is believed that clay was taken from these caves to build the walls around Ashkelon.

MARESHAH ("possession"), Tell Maresha, Marissa, Tell es-Sandahannah, Marasha

This ancient biblical site is located 1 mile south of Beit Guvrin, 3½ miles northeast of Tell Lachish, and 7 miles east of Qiryat Gat. It was excavated by Bliss, and pottery found here dated back to 800 B.C. It served as a base for Seleucid operations against Judas Maccabaeus and his family. (See 1 Macc. 5:66, in which *Maresha* should be read for *Samaria*.) It was finally destroyed by the Parthians in

Above: Valley of Elah
Below: Bell cave, Beit Guvrin

40 B.C. Caves in the area have paintings that date from the third
century B.C. A very interesting columbarium called *es-Suk* in Arabic
is located on the western side of the hill Mareshah. Two burial
caves are located in the valley east of Mareshah. Cave number 1 is

painted and has 44 burial places cut in the rock. Greek inscriptions on the walls are notes of a maiden addressed to her lover.

- This was a town in the lowland of Judah fortified by Rehoboam (Josh. 15:21, 44; 2 Chron. 11:5, 8).
- Asa conquered a million Ethiopians (2 Chron. 14:9–13).
- Micah prophesied: "Yet will I bring an heir unto thee" (Mic. 1:15).

LACHISH ("height"), Tell Lakhish, Lakhish, Tell ed-Duweir

This ancient Hyksos city, the biblical city of Lachish, lies 20 miles inland from Ashkelon and 6 miles southeast of Qiryat Gat. After Joshua conquered the city it became a city of Judah on the border of Philistia (Josh. 15:21, 39). It was important because it guarded the approaches to the Judean hills and Jerusalem to the north and Egypt to the south. Today it is merely a tell. The town of Lachish is referred to several times in the Tell el 'Amarna letters.

In 701 B.C. the Assyrian king Sennacherib personally led an attack against Lachish and conquered it on his way to besiege Jerusalem during Hezekiah's reign. During the siege of Lachish Sennacherib sent his emissaries to parley with Hezekiah at Jerusalem. A bas-relief on the wall of Sennacherib's palace at Nineveh carefully depicted his method of conquering Lachish. The bas-relief, portraying archers, spearmen, slingers, chariots, and horsemen, is now housed in the British Museum.

The Taylor Prism, found at Nineveh, also tells of Sennacherib's sieges of 46 walled cities of Palestine in this campaign.

The tell was excavated between 1832 and 1838, then later in 1935 by an American archaeologist, John L. Starkey. Near the entrance he found objects from the Assyrian assault, such as iron arrowheads, scale armour, and an Assyrian helmet with a crest of bronze. He also found some inscribed potsherds (18 ostraca) known as the Lachish Letters (590 B.C.) — epistles exchanged between the cities of Lachish and Azekah as they were being besieged by Nebuchadnezzar in 586 B.C. The letters corroborate the Bible story. Lachish was one of the last cities to hold out against Nebuchadnezzar but was finally defeated and destroyed.

Starkey was killed by Arab robbers on his way to Jerusalem shortly after his discoveries, and the digging on this site has not been resumed.

The Lachish Letters were written during Jeremiah's time. The ostraca provide the earliest external Israelite witness for the full form of the tetragrammaton, YHWH (Yahweh).

- Joshua completely destroyed the inhabitants of Lachish (Josh. 10:31–33).
- Rehoboam strengthened its defenses about 921 B.C. (2 Chron. 11:5–12).
- The Judean king Amaziah was murdered here (2 Kings 14:17, 19).
- The Assyrian king Sennacherib attacked Lachish and sent emissaries to parley with Hezekiah (2 Kings 18:13–17).
- The reconstructed city was one of the last Judean cities to hold out

Tell Lakhish

against Babylonia, but it was destroyed by Nebuchadnezzar in 586
B.C. (Jer. 34:7; cf Lachish Letters).
■ *Lachish was resettled by Jews after the captivity in Babylon (Neh.*
11:30).
■ *Micah denounced Lachish as "the beginning of the sin to the*
daughter of Zion" (Mic. 1:13).

Jerusalem Cave, *Khirbet Beit Lei (Bayt Layy)*

Near Amazia, on the western slope of the Judean range of mountains, 22
miles southwest of Jerusalem, 10 miles west of Hebron, 5 miles east of
Tell Lachish, on the eastern slope of the hill of Khirbet Beit Lei, is an
ancient rock-cut burial cave called the Jerusalem Cave. It is located on
what was the border between Judah and the Philistines.

The cave was uncovered in 1961 during road construction operations. Excavations were carried out in June of 1961 under the direction of Dr. Joseph Naveh of the Israel Department of Antiquities.

The cave is named the *Jerusalem Cave* because it had the earliest
mention of Jerusalem in a Hebrew inscription.

In the soft limestone cave were three chambers, two of which had
three benches in each. On the benches were found human bones
and jewelry. The entrance to the cave was blocked by large stones.

Of particular interest in the cave are the drawings on the walls:
three human figures, two ships, circles, and Hebrew inscriptions.
One of the figures is of a man apparently holding a lyre, and the other
man is shown raising his hands as though in prayer. One of the
Hebrew inscriptions reads as follows, according to Dr. Naveh:

Yahveh (is) the God of the whole earth; the mountains of Judah
belong to him, to the God of Jerusalem.

Frank Cross, Jr., has interpreted the Hebrew letters a little differ-
ently. It is especially important to note that it is written in the first
person:

*I am Yahweh thy God: I will accept the cities of Judah and will
redeem Jerusalem.*

The other two inscriptions read:

Exalt us, O merciful God!
Deliver us, Lord!

The form or style of this burial cave dates back to the pre-
Babylonian exile period in Jewish history, and through archaeology,
paleography, and history it has been determined that the sixth
century B.C. is the date of the drawings and writings on the walls.

Frank Cross, Jr., feels that the Hebrew inscriptions are not funerary
in nature but were placed here by chance visitors, refugees, or travelers who took shelter in the cave. One inscription is a petition for
deliverance, another is a plea to be spared from guilt or punishment,
and the third is in the form of a prophetic oracle in which Yahweh
speaks in the first person in poetic form.

The Israel Department of Antiquity preserved the portions of the
walls of the cave that contain the inscriptions, and they are presently
exhibited in the National Museum in Jerusalem.

GATH (*"wine press"*), **Gat**, *Tell es Safret* (?)

This ancient city of the Philistine Pentapolis (5 cities) is believed to
have been a little over a mile northeast of the city of Qiryat Gat, in
the mouth of the Valley of Elah, but there is disagreement over its
location. Recent diggings reveal traces of settlements dating back
to 3000 B.C. Its final destruction dates from 721 B.C., when Sargon
invaded Palestine.

■ *Here Anakim took refuge (Josh. 11:22).*
■ *The ark was brought here from Ashdod (1 Sam. 5:8).*
■ *It was the home of Goliath (1 Sam. 17:4; 2 Sam. 21:19).*
■ *David took refuge here when persecuted by Saul (1 Sam. 21:10).*
■ *It was captured by David (1 Chron. 18:1).*
■ *It was rebuilt by Rehoboam (2 Chron. 11:5-12).*
■ *It was destroyed by Uzziah (2 Chron. 26:1-6).*
■ *It was captured by Hazael of Damascus, Syria (2 Kings 12:17).*
■ *It was referred to by Amos and Micah (Amos 6:2; Mic. 1:10).*

EGLON (*"circle"*), **Khirbet Egla**, *Tell Hessi (Hasi)*

This conical mound 5 miles southwest of Gath on the bank of Nahal
Shikma — Sycamore Brook — was probably the Eglon of biblical
days. It was an important fortified city.

In 1892 the British Palestine Exploration Fund excavated the hill.
This was the first archaeological research to be done outside the
limits of Jerusalem in Palestine. Clay tablets with cuneiform writing
dating back to 1450 B.C. were found at Eglon.

- *It is mentioned in connection with Joshua's campaigns (Josh. 10:3-5; 12:12).*
- *King Debir of Eglon joined forces with five other kings against the Gibeonites (Josh. 10:3).*

LEHI *("jawbone"), Ramath-Lehi*

This was a place in Philistia about 32 miles southwest of Jerusalem and 6½ miles west-southwest of Tell Lachish, where Samson slew 1,000 Philistines with the jawbone of an ass.

- *Samson slew the Philistines with the jawbone (Judg. 15:14-17).*

ZIKLAG, Ziglag *("winding"), Tell Tsiglag, Khirbet Zuheilikah*

This site is about 35 miles southwest of Jerusalem, about 13 miles directly south of Tell Lachish, and ½ mile west of Kibbutz Bira.

- *It was given by Achish, the Philistine king, to David for a residence (1 Sam. 27:6-12; 1 Chron. 12:1, 20).*
- *It was raided by the Amalekites, on whom David took vengeance (1 Sam. 30:14-26).*
- *The messenger that announced the death of Saul was slain here (2 Sam. 1:1-16; 4:10).*
- *It is mentioned in a list of the postexiles (Neh. 11:28).*

Urim *("lights")*

About 8 miles southwest of the Gilat crossroads, on the main road between Gaza and Beersheba, is Urim, a communal settlement founded in 1948. Many Jewish pioneers of this settlement are from the United States.

- *The scriptures mention the Urim along with the Thummim as being in the high priest's breastplate and giving an oracular response (Exod. 28:30; Lev. 8:8; Num. 27:21; Deut. 33:8; 1 Sam. 28:6; Ezra 2:63; Neh. 7:65).*

BETH-PHELET, Tel Sharuhen, *Saruhen, Tell Fara*

Five miles southwest of Urim and 12 miles southeast of Khan Yunis is the site of the ancient Sharuhen, a town in the area of the tribe of Simeon. In ancient Egyptian records this city is named as the scene of a great victory of the Egyptians over the Hyksos. Flinders Petrie excavated here in 1930 and felt it was the ancient biblical site of Beth-Phelet. This conclusion is questioned, however. Carvings on ivory found at the site date back to 1200 B.C.

- *It was a town of Judah (Joshua 15:21, 27; Neh. 11:25-26).*

Rafa, *Rafah*

Five miles southwest of Khan Yunis is Rafa, the starting-point for the Assyrian conquest of Egypt by Esarhaddon in 671 B.C. It was here that Cleopatra married Mark Antony.

Khan Yunis

This town, 15 miles southwest of Gaza, dates back to a Mameluke settlement but was built on foundations of an older settlement.

GERAR *("circle")*, **Tell Gamma**, *Umm-Jerar, Tell el-Jemmel*

Tell Gerar is believed to be located 8 miles south of Gaza (Gen. 10:19). Part of Tell el-Jemmel was excavated by Flinders Petrie. There is some question as to the exact location of the site.

The brook Besor cuts through Tell Gerar, making a steep cliff on the northeast side.

- *Here Abraham met the king of Gerar, Abimelech (Gen. 20).*
- *It was here that Abraham reported that his wife was his sister (Gen. 20).*
- *Here Isaac reported that his wife, Rebekah, was his sister (Gen. 26:6–16).*
- *Here wells were dug by Abraham and reopened by Isaac (Gen. 26:17–22).*
- *Part of David's army remained at the brook Besor while he attacked the Amalekites (1 Sam. 30: 9–10).*

Kibbutz Sa'ad

This is a religion-centered kibbutz, with a new synagogue, a beautiful lawn, and flowers. It is 4 miles southeast of Gaza, on the road to Beersheba.

PHILISTIA *("migration")*

This southern coastal region of Palestine was occupied by the Philistines, who were non-Semitic.

- *During the time of Eli the Philistines conquered the Israelites and captured the ark (1 Sam. 4).*
- *A plague forced them to return the ark (1 Sam. 6).*
- *Here the Philistines worked iron (1 Sam. 13:19).*
- *Sargon marched against Philistia and captured Ashdod (Isa. 20:1).*
- *Later Hezekiah smote the Philistines (2 Kings 18:8).*

GAZA *("the strong place")*, *Ghezzeh, Azzah*

Gaza, an Arab town, is probably the oldest and most important of the 5 principal Philistine cities. It is 40 miles south of Joppa and is the last important city on the seacoast as the traveler goes south toward Cairo. It was controlled by Egypt, Assyria, and then Alexander the Great, who captured it in 332 B.C. and killed all of its men and sold the women and children into slavery. It has been the scene of the martyrdom of many Christians. During World War I it was the main base of the Turks. The British lost about 10,000 men in capturing the city. In the six-day war of 1967 it was the scene of much bloodshed before the Israeli fighters gained control of the city.

- *It was a prominent city of Canaan in early times (Gen. 10:19).*
- *Joshua reached but did not conquer it (Josh. 10:41; 11:22).*

- *It was given to Judah and captured by them (Josh. 15:47; Judg. 1:18).*
- *The Bible tells of Samson's exploits here. He took the city gates to Hebron — 40 miles away. He was imprisoned in Gaza, was blinded, and met his death here (Judg. 16).*
- *The Philistines presented a trespass offering to Jehovah (1 Sam. 6:17).*
- *Hezekiah defeated the Philistines at Gaza (2 Kings 18:8).*
- *It was occupied by Pharaoh Necho (Jer. 47:1).*
- *It was prophesied against (Amos 1:7; Zeph. 2:4).*
- *Philip went toward Gaza. On the way he met and baptized the Ethiopian eunuch (Acts 8:26–27).*

Yad Mordechai

About 7½ miles south of Ashkelon is Yad Mordechai, a kibbutz established in 1943 and known for its resistance to Egyptian armored divisions in 1948. A reconstructed BATTLEFIELD, with tanks and men, is very realistic. A beautiful, modern MUSEUM is worth visiting.

This is a National Parks Authority site.

ASHKELON *("holm oak"), Khirbet Asqalan*

One of the oldest known Canaanite cities in the world (2000 B.C.) became the Philistine city of Ashkelon, the only Philistine city built on the coast with a harbor. The Tell el 'Amarna letters (fourteenth century B.C.) mention Ashkelon as a rich but rebellious city. Pharaoh Ramses II recorded the capture of this city on a thirteenth-century B.C. bas-relief at Karnak, in upper Egypt. The carved picture shows Egyptian soldiers storming the fortified city with the help of ladders, while the bearded Ashkelonite defenders man the walls.

Under Roman rule many beautiful buildings were constructed in Ashkelon. It was the seat of the worship of the Syrian goddess Derketo, who, like Dagon, was in the form of a fish. Herod the Great was born here and embellished the city. The Crusaders fought many battles here, until it was taken by Baldwin III in 1153. It was finally destroyed in 1270, and it never recovered.

Some scholars of Greek legend claim that Ashkelon, and not Crete, may have been the original home of Aphrodite, goddess of love. An ancient burial cave in Ashkelon has beautiful PAINTINGS on the ceiling. The WALL around the city protrudes through the sands, and remnants of the ancient HARBOR may be seen along the beach. There is also a SCULPTURE PARK here, with bits of columns and other archaeological finds. The British Palestine Exploration Fund excavated here in 1920–21, but much remains to be done.

Ashkelon is a resort town now and a National Parks Authority site. Opposite Ashkelon is Israel's main OIL FIELD, at HELETZ. The first oil discovery was made in 1955, and oil wells can now be seen among the orange trees. They produce about 10 percent of the country's oil consumption.

- *Ashkelon was captured by Judah (Josh. 13:3; Judg. 1:18).*

- *Here Samson slew 30 men (Judg. 14:19).*
- *The ark was returned with a trespass offering (1 Sam. 6:17).*
- *"Publish it not in the streets of Ashkelon" (2 Sam. 1:20).*
- *The prophets spoke against it (Amos 1:8; Zeph. 2:4, 7; Jer. 25:20; 47:6–7).*

Negba

Negba is a kibbutz 7 miles east of Ashkelon, founded in 1939. At that time it was the southernmost Jewish colony. During the 1948 war the Jews in this kibbutz were completely surrounded by Egyptian forces, and were about to be overwhelmed; but they held out and were never taken. It was somewhat miraculous. Note the BRITISH POLICE POST, the EGYPTIAN TANK, BARBED WIRE, and WATER TANK for evidence of the heavy fighting.

Negba is a symbol to modern Israel like Masada, the Jews' last stand against the Romans in A.D. 72. It gives courage to the Jews as they withstand their enemy forces.

ASHDOD *("fortress," "castle"), Azotus, Esdud*

This was an ancient Hyksos town and later a Philistine city, about 3 miles south of the present new city of the same name. The old city was a center of worship of the god Dagon, and a temple was erected in his honor. The new city, established in 1957, is being developed into Israel's largest seaport. The largest industry in the city is the Leyland bus factory.

- *Anakim prevented Joshua from taking it (Josh. 11:22).*
- *It was allotted to Judah but was not taken (Josh. 13:1–3; 15: 46–47).*
- *It was the chief seat of the worship of Dagon — where the ark was carried by the Philistines when they defeated Israel (1 Sam. 5).*
- *It was possessed by Judah in the time of Uzziah (2 Chron. 26:6–7).*
- *It was captured by Sargon, king of Assyria (Isa. 20:1).*
- *Jews intermarried with its inhabitants, arousing Nehemiah's indignation (Neh. 13:23–24).*
- *It was prophesied against (Amos 1:8; Zeph. 2:4).*
- *Philip came here after baptizing the eunuch (Acts 8:26–40).*

GEDERAH *("sheepfold"),* Gedera

This Zionist settlement, 7 miles northeast of Ashdod, was begun in 1884 by Russian students. The founders were persistent in conquering brackish water, isolation, hostility, poor housing, and poor food.

- *It was a town of Judah in the lowlands (Josh. 15:21–63).*

JABNEH, Yavne, *Yabneel, Yavniel, Kerem Yavne, Yavneh*

Four miles southwest of Rehovot is the site of Yavne. When the temple was destroyed in A.D. 70, Rabbi Johanan ben Zakkai asked Titus to give Yavne as a safe place for himself and his fellow sages. This request was granted, and a great school of learning was established here, called *Kerem Yavne*. It was here that the sages estab-

Sabra Cactus in Lower Galilee

lished the canon (authorized version) of the Old Testament. The Mishna was also begun here and finally completed in Galilee. Tradition maintains that Johanan's school was on top of a hill where today a mosque has been built on the remains of a Crusader castle. To the west of the village is an ancient mausoleum capped with two domes. Jews have believed this to be the TOMB OF GAMALIEL.

■ *Uzziah fought the Philistines here (2 Chron. 26:6).*
■ *Gamaliel was a member of the Sanhedrin (Acts 5:34–40).*
■ *Paul studied under Gamaliel (Acts 22:3).*

Rehovot

This city, 13 miles south of Tel Aviv, was founded by Polish Jews in 1890. Its chief pride is the WEIZMANN INSTITUTE OF SCIENCE, Israel's foremost scientific establishment. It contains 50 acres of beautiful, futuristic buildings and green gardens. It was dedicated in 1949 in honor of Israel's first president, Dr. Chaim Weizmann, a distinguished chemist who did vital research for the Allies in World War I. He died in 1952 and is buried in a beautiful garden at the Institute. About 500 students and 400 scientists do research at the Institute in such areas as nuclear physics, electronics, biophysics, chemistry, plant genetics, and mathematics.

The WIX CENTRAL LIBRARY houses 100,000 books and subscribes to more than 1,750 scientific journals from all over the world.

YAVNE YAM *(Yavne on the Sea)*, JAMNIA, *Yamnia*

This was the ancient Greek port of Jamnia, where Judas Maccabaeus fought and vanquished the Greeks in 156 B.C. It was a Jewish spiritual center erected with Vespasian's permission by Johanan ben Zakkai after the fall of Jerusalem. It was also a Crusader stronghold. All that is left are crumbling pieces of masonry sticking out of the water, remains of a harbor and ancient walls.

● *Here Judas Maccabaeus fought the Greeks (2 Macc. 12:9).*

Holon

About 2 miles southeast of Joppa is the Jewish city of Holon, established in 1935. A Samaritan colony originally from Nablus is located now at Holon.

SOUTH OF JERUSALEM

VALLEY OF REPHAIM *("strong")*, Emeq Refaim

Running west out of south Jerusalem is the Valley of Rephaim. This was the scene of one of David's great victories over the Philistines.

■ *David battled the Philistines here (2 Sam. 5:17–25).*

Ramat-Rahel *("Rachel's heights")*, *Ramat Rachel*

Ramat-Rahel, in the southeastern part of Jerusalem, is Israel's only kibbutz within the municipal bounds of a city. It was founded in

1925. Many battles were fought here in the War of Liberation. Excavations near Ramat-Rahel have uncovered ancient ruins, and an excellent view of the surrounding country may be seen from the kibbutz. (See also site no. 111, in the section on Jerusalem, above.)

CHURCH OF ELIJAH, *"My God is Yah" (Jehovah),* *Mar Elias Monastery*

About 2 or 3 miles south of Jerusalem is a Greek Orthodox sixth- and eleventh-century monastery, built where, according to tradition, Elijah rested when he fled from the wicked Jezebel. It is inhabited by a few Greek Orthodox monks.

■ *Elijah rested here when he fled from Jezebel (1 Kings 19:1–4).*

RACHEL'S TOMB

One mile north of Bethlehem is a 23-foot-square tomb where, according to tradition, Rachel, wife of Jacob and mother of Joseph, is buried. She died on her way to Bethlehem while giving birth to her last son, Benjamin. This is a sacred place to Jews, Moslems, and Christians. Men and women in the area frequently visit the tomb, weep, and pray. Women often pray for fertility and successful child-birth. The tomb dates back to the fifteenth century. Near the tomb are first-century remains of a Roman aqueduct.

■ *Jacob went from Beersheba to Haran, where he worked twenty years, seven of them for Rachel (Gen. 29; 31:38).*
■ *This was Rachel's burial place (Gen. 35:10–20; 48:7; 1 Sam. 10:2).*

BETHLEHEM *("house of bread," "place of food")* *Ephrathah, Ephrath, Beit Lahm*

Bethlehem is located on the hills 6 miles south of Jerusalem, 2,350 feet above sea level. Constantine built a church over the cave stable which is pointed out as being the scene of Christ's birth, and since that time many convents, monasteries, churches, and shrines have been built in the area.

It was from Bethlehem that Elimelech and Naomi went to Moab with their two sons at the time of the famine (Ruth 1:1). After the death of her husband and sons, Naomi, with Ruth, her daughter-in-law, returned to Bethlehem (Ruth 1:19–22), and Ruth's marriage to Boaz is a fitting climax to the lovely story. She became the great-grandmother of David, king of Israel (Ruth 4:17, 1 Sam. 17:12). Thus Bethlehem is the original home of the Davidic family, and for this reason Joseph came here to pay taxes.

POINTS OF INTEREST

The **CHURCH OF THE NATIVITY**, in Manger Square, is the oldest church in Christendom. It was built over the cave where it is believed Jesus was born. It was originally constructed by Constantine about A.D. 326 after his mother, Helena, determined the site. The present

N

MEDITERRANEAN SEA

Israel
South of
Jerusalem

Miles   5   10   15   20   25

Tel Aviv

■ Ashdod

Beit Shemesh ■

Valley of Rephaim

★ Jerusalem
■ Ramat-Rahel

Rachel's Tomb ■
■ Bethlehem
■ Qumran

Solomon's Pools ■
Herodion ■

■ Ashkelon
• Negba

Qiryat Gat ■

Bell Caves •
Valley of Berachah
Spring of Philip •
Tekoa •

Yad Mordechai ■
Tel Lachish ■

Beth-Zur (Beit Zur) ■
Seir •
Halhul ■

Valley of Eshcol

Hebron ■

■ Gaza
Adoraim (Dura) ■

SALT SEA
(DEAD SEA)

Saad •

Ziph ■

En-Gedi (Ein Gedi) ■

Gerar (Tell Gamma) ■

Dahahiriya •
Maon ■

Eshtemoa (Es Sammui) ■

Masada ■

JORDAN

• Urim
Beth-Phelet (Tell Sharuhen) •

Arad (Tell Arad) ■

Beersheba (Beer-sheva) ■

Ein Bokek •

Zohar •

Flour Cave •

Dimonah (Dimona) •

Sodom and Gomorrah (Sedom) ■
(Lot's Wife)
Salt Works •

Oron •

• Nitsana
• Shivta
Sde Boker •

ARABAH (ARAVA)

Tell Avdat •

NEGEV

Mitspe Ramon •

large church was built originally during the reign of Justinian (527–65) but was completely altered by the Crusaders. It is owned jointly by the Greek, Roman, and Armenian churches. The doorway to the church is so low you have to bend to enter it. Legend has it that the doorway was made that small to prevent the unbelievers from riding into the church on horseback.

Below the church is the **GROTTO OF THE NATIVITY**, the birthplace of Jesus. In this cave Joseph and Mary sought shelter when there was no room for them in the inn. Marking the traditional birthplace is a silver star inscribed in Latin: "Here of the Virgin Mary, Christ was born." The star has 14 points, representing the 14 stations of the cross. It was placed by the Roman church in 1717 and removed by the Greeks in 1847. The removal of the star, along with its subsequent restoration by the Turkish government in 1853, was one of the contributing factors of the Crimean War. Across from the Grotto is a small **CHAPEL OF THE MANGER**, where, according to tradition, Mary placed the baby Jesus in a manger. Boards of the manger are, according to tradition, located in the Basilica of Santa Maria Maggiore in Rome. There are some bones in the **CAVE OF THE INNOCENT CHILDREN** that are supposed to be bones of babies killed by the order of King Herod. There is also a **ROOM WHERE JEROME WORKED ON THE LATIN VULGATE BIBLE**. Flanking the basilica of the Church of the Nativity is the **CHURCH OF SAINT CATHERINE**.

About a block east and a little south of the Church of the Nativity is the Franciscan **CHURCH OF THE MILK GROTTO**. According to tradition, it was here that Mary, while nursing Jesus, dropped some milk on a stone. This promptly turned the rocks of the cavern chalky white. Visits are made here by nursing mothers who believe this will help their lactation. Round cakes made from the powdered stone are sold as souvenirs. In the grotto is a most beautiful carving of **JESUS' FLIGHT INTO EGYPT**.

KING DAVID'S WELLS are located on a hill to the north of the Church of the Nativity on King David Street. Traditionally, this was where David wanted a drink while fighting the Philistines (2 Sam. 23).

Near Bet Sahur, a village east of Bethlehem, is the **FIELD OF THE SHEPHERDS**, and nearby is the **GROTTO OF THE SHEPHERDS**, a subterranean chapel. Tradition indicates that this is where the shepherds were visited by the angels (Luke 2:8–14).

Bethlehem is one of the more prosperous cities; the soil is productive, and there are small manufacturing concerns producing furniture, olivewood statues, mother-of-pearl beads, and ornaments. The colorful **MARKET** is located a block west of Manger Square.

- *Bethlehem was the home and burial place of Ibzan, the judge (Judg. 12:8–10).*
- *Micah hired a Levite from Bethlehem as priest (Judg. 17:7–13).*
- *The Levite concubine who was abused at Gibeah was from Bethlehem (Judg. 19).*
- *The story of Ruth and Boaz centers here (Book of Ruth).*

Above: Bethlehem
and Shepherds' Field

Right: Street scene,
Bethlehem

- *It was the place of David's birth and his anointing as king of Israel in Saul's place (1 Sam. 16:1-14; 17:12).*
- *David was a herdsman here (1 Sam. 17:15; 34-37).*
- *David went from here to Saul's army and slew Goliath (1 Sam. 17:12-58).*

Church of the Nativity, Bethlehem

- *It was claimed that David came here when he fled from Saul (1 Sam. 20:6, 28).*
- *David obtained water from the well by the gate (2 Sam. 23:14–17; 1 Chron. 11:15–19).*
- *Bethlehem became insignificant after David; it was fortified by Rehoboam (2 Chron. 11:5–6).*
- *Micah foretold Christ's birth at Bethlehem (Mic. 5:2; Matt. 2:4–6; John 7:42).*
- *Matthew and Luke told of Jesus' birth (Matt. 1:18–25; Luke 2: 1–7).*
- *Here the shepherds visited the infant Jesus (Luke 2:8–20).*
- *The wise men also visited and worshiped (Matt. 2:1–12).*
- *The angel appeared to Joseph, he fled with Mary and Jesus to Egypt, and Herod had the children killed (Matt. 2:13–23; Jer. 31:15; 40:1).*

Mar Saba

Eight miles east of Bethlehem is Mar Saba, founded by Saint Sabas in A.D. 483. This was the center of Palestinian monasticism.

The Herodion

Three or four miles southeast of Bethlehem is an incredible fortified palace built by Herod the Great at the end of the first century B.C. At its foot were palaces, terraced gardens, and pools, and 200 white marble steps led to the citadel on top. During the Roman and Jewish

Arab boy, near
Bethlehem

wars of A.D. 66–70 and 132–35, the fortress played an important part. Josephus described these wars. During the Byzantine period Christian monks inhabited the site. Some believe that Herod died in Jericho but was buried here — not far from where he ordered the slaying of the infants.

This is a National Parks Authority site.

- *Herod was the king of Judea when Jesus was born (Matt. 2:3).*
- *Herod ordered all babies under two years of age to be slain (Matt. 2:16).*

TEKOA *("firm," "settlement"),* **Tell Tequ'a**

This ancient village, 2,800 feet above sea level and 10–12 miles south of Jerusalem, overlooks the desolate hills on the east toward the Dead Sea. Extensive ruins are still here. Amos, the prophet who lived here, was a "herdman, and gatherer of sycamore fruit [a small fig]" (Amos 7:14). None of these trees are found in the area now. Josephus wrote that the tomb of Amos was located here. Some Arab Bedouins live at Tekoa in caves.

- *This was one of the fortified cities of Rehoboam (2 Chron. 11:6).*
- *From here came the "wise woman" brought by Joab to make a reconciliation between David and Absalom after Absalom had slain his brother, Ammon, because of the latter's wrong to Tamar, their sister (2 Sam. 14:1–24).*

■ *It was the native city and burial place of Amos, the herdsman prophet (Amos 1:1; 7:14).*

SOLOMON'S POOLS

Eight miles south of Jerusalem and 2 miles south of Bethlehem are 3 large rock-built reservoirs, near a small Turkish fortress dating back to A.D. 1540. Water is supplied by springs. In the past, water ran by gravity to Jerusalem and Bethlehem via conduit from these reservoirs. They are probably misnamed, since two of them were built by Herod or Pontius Pilate and the third pool was built in the fifteenth century. About a mile beyond the pools is the **MONASTERY OF HORTUS CONCLUSUS**.

■ *Solomon's pools are mentioned (Eccles. 2:4–6).*

VALLEY OF BERACHAH *("blessing")*, **Berakha**

About 7 miles southwest of Bethlehem is the Valley of Berakha.

■ *King Jehoshaphat and the children of Israel went forth to meet the enemy here. The Lord destroyed the enemy, and in the Valley of Berachah Israel blessed the Lord (2 Chron. 20:26).*

BETH-ZUR *("house of the rock")*, **Beit Zur**, *Khirbet et-Tubeiqah*

Close by the Spring of Philip, on the mountainside west of the spring, are the ruins of Beth-Zur, an important city of Judah. Here Maccabaeus defeated Antiochus's army decisively in 165 B.C.

■ *It was a city in Judah (Josh. 15:1, 58).*
■ *It was fortified by Rehoboam (2 Chron. 11:5, 7).*
● *Simon fought against and ruled over it (1 Macc. 11:65; 14:7).*

SPRING OF PHILIP, **Ein-Dirwa**

On the road to Hebron, near Beit-Zur and near a house and Mohammedan "praying place," are traces of an ancient church and two rock tomb chambers. A spring provides water for the villagers and perhaps provided water for Philip's baptism of the eunuch.

■ *This is traditionally where Philip baptized the eunuch (Acts 8:26–40).*

HALHUL *("full of hollows")*

Three miles north of Hebron and less than a mile east of the main highway between Hebron and Bethlehem is Halhul, the ancient site of a Canaanite town of that name. It is the highest village in the country. In the Middle Ages the sacred tombs of Gad the seer and Nathan the prophet were shown in the village. Now it is said that the tomb is that of the prophet Jonah.

■ *It was a city of Judah (Josh. 15:1, 58).*

SEIR, Siir, *Siair*

According to tradition, this small village is where the tomb of Esau is located. The village is 2 miles east of Halhul.

■ *This is where Esau settled permanently (Gen. 35:29; 36:6; Deut. 2:4–5; Josh. 24:4).*

VALLEY OF ESHCOL *("cluster of grapes"),* Eshkol

Located 2½ miles north of Hebron is the Valley of Eshkol, from whence Moses' spies returned carrying clusters of grapes. This event portrayed in picture has become the official tourist emblem of Israel. The valley still produces grapes in abundance.

■ *The spies brought back grapes, pomegranates, and figs from the brook Eshcol (Num. 13:22–24).*

HEBRON *("ford," "company"),* Kiriath-Arba, El Khalil *("the friend"),* Kirjath-Arba, Ramad el-Khalin

Hebron, David's capital for seven years, is 20 miles south of Jerusalem and 30 miles north of Beersheba, 3,042 feet above sea level. It was named after Arba, the father of Anak (Josh. 15:13–15; 21:11). The ancient town stood a mile northwest of the present city, where a large oak called the OAK OF MAMRE has purportedly been standing since the twelfth century. Nearby is a cistern called the BATH OF SARAH, and also a RUSSIAN MONASTERY. There are 38 springs in the area, and northeast of the city is ABRAHAM'S WELL, where Abraham pitched his tent. This site is designated today as *Mambre.*

The POOL OF SOLOMON is supposed to be one of the authentic sites in Hebron.

The TOMB OF THE PATRIARCHS is the CAVE OF MACHPELAH, located beneath a huge mosque dating back to Herod's time. Cenotaphs in the mosque commemorate those who are buried below. The cenotaphs are supposed to be directly over the actual tombs in the cave. (A *cenotaph* is an empty tomb in honor of a person buried elsewhere.) A limited view of the cave may be had through a small opening under a small dome supported by four pillars and located near the cenotaphs of Isaac and Rebecca. No one is allowed to enter the cave. The cenotaphs are elaborately decorated with gold-embroidered velvet. The locations of the cenotaphs are as follows: ISAAC and REBEKAH are in the large room on the south, Isaac to the west and Rebekah to the east; ABRAHAM and SARAH are just north of the open courtyard, with Abraham on the west; JACOB and LEAH are in rooms farthest north, with Jacob on the west; JOSEPH'S CENOTAPH is in a room to the west, just before the tombs of Jacob and Leah. Some believe that ADAM and EVE are also buried in the Cave of Machpelah. One legend has Adam being created out of the dust of Hebron. In the western portion of the courtyard is a long hall called the WOMEN'S MOSQUE. In the corner near Abraham's cenotaph is a small window, inside which is a stone that tradition indicates has the impression of Adam's foot on it.

Above: Mosque over the Tomb of the Patriarchs, Hebron
Below: A familiar street scene in Israel

To the Jews, Abraham was the first Jew, and thus Hebron is one of the four sacred cities of the Jews. The others are Jerusalem, Tiberias, and Safed. Three parcels of ground, Hebron and the sites of the Jerusalem temple and the tomb of Joseph, are claimed by the Jews because the property was purchased by their ancestors.

Hebron was burned by Titus during the first Jewish revolt and has passed through several conquerors' hands over the years. In modern times, Hebron was a center of Jewish learning until the riots and massacres of 1929 and 1939. Since then it has been entirely Arab.

The city is quaint, with its interesting shops in the marketplaces, its veiled women, and its dirty streets. A stop in Hebron is worthwhile. Hebron is famous for its handblown glass and leather products. If you see a Moslem wearing a white band around the base of his fez, you will know he has been to Mecca.

During the years 1964–67 members of an American expedition excavated in Hebron under the direction of Dr. Philip C. Hammond of the University of Utah. They dug on the slope just west of the Mosque of Abraham and recovered 160,000 pieces of ceramic materials. They found a 36-foot-thick wall built in 1728 B.C. and a house dating back to a period of time before the pyramids of Egypt were built (3500 B.C.). According to Dr. Hammond, Hebron is the oldest continuously occupied unwalled city in the world, although portions of it were walled at one time. Hundreds of different levels of major human occupation have been uncovered, dating back to the beginning of agriculture for man.

Hebron is mentioned 69 times in the Old Testament, from Genesis to Jeremiah.

- *The place was named* Hebron *(Josh. 14:15; 20:7).*
- *Abraham built an altar here after he and Lot separated (Gen. 13:18).*
- *From here Abraham went to rescue Lot (Gen. 14:13–24).*
- *Here Ishmael was born (Gen. 16). The Arabs believe Ishmael, father of all Arabs, is also buried here.*
- *Abraham entertained three heavenly messengers and made intercession for Sodom and Gomorrah (Gen. 17:1; 18:16–38).*
- *Abraham, Isaac, and Jacob dwelt here (Gen. 35:27; 37:1).*
- *Abraham, Sarah, Isaac, Rebekah, Jacob, and Leah were buried in Machpelah (Gen. 23; 25:7–11; 49:29–31; 50:13).*
- *Isaac and Jacob spent much time here (Gen. 35–37).*
- *Joseph left Hebron to go to Dothan in search of his brothers (Gen. 37:3–19).*
- *Jacob and his sons went from here to Egypt (Gen. 46:1).*
- *Moses' spies visited it and gathered grapes, pomegranates, and figs. This was where Anak and the giants lived (Num. 13:22–33).*
- *Hoham, its king, was overcome by Joshua (Josh. 10: 3–27).*
- *Hebron was taken by Joshua and given to Caleb (Josh. 10:36–37; 14:6–15; 15:14–19).*
- *It was made a Levite city of Judah (Josh. 15:54; 20:7; 21:13).*
- *It was a city of refuge (Josh. 20:7).*
- *David was anointed the first king of Judah, then of all Israel, and Hebron became the first capital of David (2 Sam. 2:1–4, 10–11; 5:1–5; 1 Kings 2:11).*
- *Abner was slain by Joab (2 Sam. 3:6–39).*
- *David slew the murderers of Ishbosheth (2 Sam. 4:5–12).*

- *Absalom organized his revolt against his father, David, and made Hebron his headquarters (2 Sam. 15:7–12).*
- *It was fortified by Rehoboam (2 Chron. 11:5–12).*
- *It was colonized by Jews returning from Babylon (Neh. 11:25).*

NEGEV, *Negeb ("the dry land")*

The Negev is an ill-defined tract of country south of Hebron, extending 70 miles to the desert. It is bounded on the east by the Dead Sea and Arabah (Arava), while on the west it fades into the maritime plain. The area was settled by the Nabataeans in the early Christian period and again in Byzantine times, when it was a frontier area. There are many traces of Nabataean methods of obtaining water for their crops: channeling of hillsides, building cisterns for collection and storage of water, damming of wadis, and terracing of slopes against erosion of soil. The state of Israel is developing the Negev into a farming area, with water piped in from the north. Today it is the home of about 13,000 Bedouins. They are divided into tribes, and each tribe is governed by a sheikh and has its own grazing territory. Once a week the Bedouins go to Beersheba to market their animals and produce. The Bedouins live as the patriarchs of Israel did over 3,000 years ago. They are very hospitable.

Ein Gedi, David's hideout in the northeast corner of the Negev

- *This was an arid area in Palestine (Deut. 1:7, 34:3; Josh. 15:19; Judg. 1:15).*
- *It was the scene of Abraham's wanderings (Gen. 12:9, 13:1).*
- *Here Hagar was succored by an angel (Gen. 16:7, 14).*
- *Isaac (Gen. 24:62) and Jacob (Gen. 37:1; 46:5) both dwelt here.*
- *Its dry winds were dreaded (Isa. 21:1).*
- *It was filled with many wild beasts (Isa. 30:6).*

ADORAIM, Dura *("circle"), Adora*

Four miles southwest of Hebron is the village of Dura, where some believe Noah was buried.

- *Genesis records the story of Noah and the flood (Gen. 5:29–8:22) and the death of Noah (Gen. 9:29).*
- *The city was fortified by Rehoboam (2 Chron. 11:9).*
- *It was called by the Maccabees Adora (1 Macc. 13:20).*

ZIPH *("refining place")*

Ziph is 4 miles southeast of Hebron. David spent some time here while fleeing from Saul and escaped while Ziphites tried to betray him into Saul's hands.

- *David fled from Saul (1 Sam. 23, 26).*

MAON *("habitation"), Biyehuda, Tell Main, Wilderness of Maon*

Seven miles southeast of Hebron was the biblical city of Maon. It was the home of Abigail, the wife of Nabal, who later became David's wife.

- *Nabal dwelt in the wilderness of Maon (1 Sam. 25:2).*
- *David sojourned in this area while in hiding (1 Sam. 23:24–26; 25:2–7).*

ESHTEMOA, Es Sammui, *Eshtamoah, Samu, Samua*

This town, 7 miles south of Hebron, was a city in Judah assigned to the Levites.

- *It was a town of Judah (Josh. 15:50; 21:14; 1 Sam. 30:28; 1 Chron. 6:57).*

BEERSHEBA *("well of the seven," "well of the oath"),* Beer-sheva, *Tell es Seba, Shibah*

Beersheba is 35 miles west of the south end of the Dead Sea and 50 miles south of Jerusalem. It marked the southern border of Judah (Josh. 15:28; Judg. 20:1; 1 Sam. 3:20) and was the southern limit of the cultivated land. Seven ancient wells existed here to provide water, and one of them is reported to have been the WELL OF ABRAHAM. Beersheba is 950 feet above sea level. Excavations reveal that people lived in underground villages as far back as 6,000 years ago.

In 1917, during the First World War, Beersheba was the first town captured from the Turks by General Allenby. When Israel captured it from the Egyptians in 1948 it had 3,000 people. Today, because of Israel's efforts, it has 30,000 Jewish inhabitants and is the capital of the Negev. It is the Dodge City of Israel.

Visitors to Beersheba should remember that Thursday is **MARKET DAY**. On this day Bedouins gather to the market and buy and sell camels, donkeys, sheep, vegetables, jewelry, and other items. This takes place in a newly constructed marketplace (1966). The marketeering goes on between 5:00 and 11:00 A.M.

A **MUNICIPAL MOSQUE**, a **MUSEUM**, and the **ARID ZONE RESEARCH CENTER** are also of interest in Beersheba. The **RAILWAY STATION** is worth visiting. It was along the Beersheba line running to Egypt that Lawrence of Arabia blew up the trains.

In 1969 the Israeli government put up housing for the Bedouins and called the site *Tell Sheva* ("hill of seven"), after the nearby mound, which some scholars believe was the ancient site of Beersheba in the days of Abraham. The **TELL** has recently been excavated.

- *An angel spoke to Hagar (Gen. 21:14–21).*
- *Abraham and Abimelech, the Philistine king, made a covenant concerning Abraham's well (Gen. 21:22–34).*
- *Abraham lived here (Gen. 22:19).*
- *Isaac and Abimelech made a covenant (Gen. 26:26–33).*
- *God appeared to Isaac (Gen. 26:23–25) and to Jacob (Gen. 46:1–7).*
- *A well was dug by Isaac (Gen. 26:32–33).*
- *Jacob fled from Esau toward Haran (Gen. 28:10).*
- *Jacob offered sacrifices to God as he journeyed to Egypt to live with Joseph (Gen. 46:1–5).*
- *Samuel's two unworthy sons were judges here (1 Sam. 8:1–3).*
- *An angel appeared to Elijah here and served him food (1 Kings 19:1–8).*
- *It was the birthplace of Zibiah, the mother of king Joash (2 Kings 12:1; 2 Chron. 24:1).*

Tell Beersheba

Camel market, Beersheba

- *The proverbial expression "from Dan to Beersheba" describes the length of Palestine (2 Sam. 17:11; 1 Chron. 21:2; 2 Chron. 30:5; 2 Kings 23:8).*
- *Some Jews lived here after the captivity (Neh. 11:27, 30).*
- *Amos classified it with Gilgal and Bethel and prophesied its destruction because of idolatry (Amos 5:5; 8:14).*

Dimonah, *Dimona*

About 22 miles southeast of Beersheba is the new urban settlement Dimona, founded in 1955 and named after a town of Judah. An estimated 400 Negroes live among the white Jews here. There is no claim that this is the site of the ancient Dimonah.

- *Dimonah was a city in the south of Judah (Josh. 15:21–22).*

Sde Boker *("field of the rancher")*, *Sede Boqer*

Sde Boker is the famous Ben-Gurion Kibbutz, where Israel's first prime minister, David Ben-Gurion, a wise, genteel, hospitable person, lived. He became an example to his people by moving onto this kibbutz in the middle of the desert.

Sde Boker was established by 16 young men and 3 young women in 1952. It was a daring exploit, and during the first year one of the girls, a university graduate from Jerusalem, was murdered by Arab marauders while out with the sheep. There are now about 100 persons living at the kibbutz. David Ben-Gurion and his wife, Paula, joined the group in 1954 after Mr. Ben-Gurion served 3 terms as prime minister (1948–53). He later served as minister of defense and then prime minister again.

The **SDE BOKER INSTITUTE FOR DESERT RESEARCH** is 1½ miles

David Ben-Gurion

south of the kibbutz. This first "desert" university in the world is the fulfillment of Ben-Gurion's dream. Its dormitories accommodate 100 students.

Ein Avdat

Two or three miles south of Sde Boker are the springs and beautiful pools of Wadi Ein Avdat. The natural water pools and canyon make swimming and hiking a favorite pastime for visitors in the area. This is a National Parks Authority site.

Tell Avdat, *Abda*

Avdat is an ancient tell 15 miles south of Sde Boker. It is surrounded by green fields that were once farmed by the Nabataeans. Ruins of the numerous Nabataean, Roman, and Byzantine settlements lie on the top and sides of the tell. They date from the first to the seventh century A.D. The Nabataeans used Avdat as an important station for caravans carrying precious cargos from Arabia to the Mediterranean seacoast. The Nabataeans lived east of the Byzantine ruins that remain on the tell. They preserved water by (1) digging holes or caves, (2) clearing triangular areas to divert the water, (3) building dams, and (4) building canals and channels.

In A.D. 105 the emperor Trajan captured Avdat and made it a Roman province. There are still some Roman ruins outside the walls.

In 1959 students of the Institute of Desert Research began using Nabataean methods of preserving water by the "runoff" water system in order to raise crops in fields near Tell Avdat. A great deal of agricultural experimentation has been done here.

The ruins include a WINE PRESS, SAINT THEODORIUS'S CHURCH, a BYZANTINE MONASTERY, a POTTERY HOUSE, CAVES, HOUSES, a BATH HOUSE, and an eighth-century BAPTISMAL FONT.

This is a National Parks Authority site.

Shivta, *Subeita*

About 13 miles west-northwest of Sde Boker and 28 miles southwest of Beersheba are the ruins of Shivta, one of the best-preserved ruins of the Byzantines in the Negev. It dates back to the fifth or sixth century and was excavated by the British Colt archaeological expedition in 1934.

Among the most important ruins are the NORTH CHURCH, the SOUTH CHURCH, the CENTER CHURCH, the MUNICIPALITY HOUSE, DWELLING HOUSES, RESERVOIRS, WINE-PRESSES, WORKSHOPS, a BAKERY OVEN, and a POTTERY KILN. The South Church has a BAPTISTRY with a stone font that suggests baptism by immersion.

This is a National Parks Authority site.

Nitsana

Located 46 miles southwest of Beersheba and 18 miles west-southwest of Shivta are the ruins of an ancient Nabataean city. The city is near a major crossroad. One highway leads west to El-Arish, on the Mediterranean Sea, and one leads south to the Suez Canal.

Mitspé-Ramon, *Makhtesh-Ramon, Wadi Ruman*

About 14 miles southwest of Avdat is a great oblong depression in the earth's crust, about 20 miles long and 5 miles wide. It is a barren volcanic-type geological formation, from which rare fossils dating back to the Triassic period have been found. The fossil of the Tanystropheus, with a lizard-like body over 16 feet long, was found here, along with other strange fossils.

BROOK OF PARAN (*"full of caverns"*), *Wadi Jirafi*

About 22 miles south of Mitspé-Ramon and 5 miles north of Tsomet Tsihor is the dry bed of the Brook of Paran, which begins in the central part of Sinai where Israel camped while being led by Moses. It is the longest watercourse that drains the southern Negev.

■ *Spies were sent into Canaan from the wilderness of Paran (Num. 13:1–3).*

ARABAH, Arava

The *Arava* is the name given by the Hebrews to the whole of the great depression (rift zone) that goes from Mount Hermon to the Gulf of Aqaba. The right arm of the Red Sea is an extension of the same rift. In modern times the Arava is the valley area between the Dead Sea and the Red Sea. It is about 10–20 miles wide and about 110 miles long. According to tradition, the Israelites traversed the Arava when they went to Kadesh-Barnea, and again when they returned to the south in their detour past Edom (Num. 20:21; 21:4; Deut. 2:8).

The lower part of the Arava was an important trade route, and copper was mined there.

- *It is spoken of in the Scriptures (Deut. 3:17; 4:49; 11:30; Josh. 8:14; 1 Sam. 23:24; 2 Kings 25:4; Jer. 39:4; Ezek. 47:8).*
- *It is sometimes translated "wilderness," or "desert," or "steppe" (Job 24:5; 39:6; Isa. 33:9; 35:1, 6; Jer. 2:6).*

Beer-Menuha; *and* SELAH, SELA, Petra *("rock")*

A workers' camp is located at Beer-Menuha, at the forks of the road. Directly east of this point, in the tops of the mountains of Edom, is Sela of the Bible (Petra of the Greeks). The traditional tomb of Aaron on Mount Hor, the highest peak, can be seen on a clear day. It is marked by a mosque.

- *Amaziah of Jerusalem, king of Israel, took Selah by war (2 Kings 14:1, 7).*
- *The Bible tells of the death of Aaron (Num. 20:28–29).*

TIMN'A *("restraining"), Copper Mines and Smelters*

Timn'a is 16 miles north of Eilat. At this site there is a large, new copper-mining plant that has been set up since 1948. Copper was mined here anciently, and now the mine is being worked after 2,000 years.

Dr. Nelson Glueck, an American archaeologist, found the mines, furnaces, slag heaps, and the ruins of the enclosure Solomon built to keep his slave labor from escaping. The ruins date back to the tenth and ninth centuries B.C. Prof. Beno Rothenberg, of the Hebrew University, and other experts believe that the so-called "King Solomon's Mines" were in operation centuries before Solomon's time, and that the mines were inactive during his reign. The ancient copper mines are 2 miles northwest from the modern mining and smelting operation. Near the mines the visitor may see 5 russet-colored projections of rock, called SOLOMON'S PILLARS.

- *This area would have been on the Israelites' route as they journeyed to Canaan (Num. 33:35; Deut. 2:8).*

EZION-GEBER, ELATH, Eilat, *Elat, Berenice, Tell el-Kheleifeh*

To Israelis, Eilat is the end of their world — a 4-hour drive from Beersheba. Eilat is a port city, settled in 1950 on the Israel, or west, side of the head of the Gulf of Aqaba, an arm of the Red Sea. Aqaba is a Jordanian port on the opposite side, and off to the right, beyond the storage tanks, is Saudi Arabia. The biblical Elath was a little north of the modern Eilat.

Today Eilat vies with Tiberias as Israel's leading winter tourist resort. It boasts fine BEACHES and 360 days of sun each year. It has 15,000 inhabitants. It is a combination port, military installation, and vacation land. There are also GRANITE QUARRIES in the area. The QUEEN OF SHEBA HOTEL is about a mile away from the Jordanian border. GLASS-BOTTOMED BOATS give the tourist a look at the wonderful marine world, including beautiful corals that thrive below the

Above: Solomon's Pillars, near Timn'a
Below: "Lot's Wife," Sodom

surface of the Red Sea. There is also a small **MARITIME MUSEUM** in the city. Jewelry made of copper stones can be purchased in Eilat. Two big desalination plants make it possible to drink the sea water. The temperature gets up to 120 degrees here, but the dry air is not oppressive. Before the six-day war, Israel's Red Sea shoreline was only 6 miles long and was a strategic port for Israel's back door.

The *Ezion-geber* of the Bible is a mound that lies less than a mile east of the Jordan-Israel border, directly east of Eilat. It was excavated by Nelson Glueck. Remains of a copper smelting and refining plant were found here.

- *This was a stopping place during the Israelites' wanderings in the wilderness (Num. 33:35; Deut. 2:8).*
- *This was King Solomon's port (1 Kings 9:26-28; 2 Chron. 8:17). Copper and salt were shipped to Africa and gold and spices brought to Israel in return.*
- *Phoenician sailors brought gold to Solomon from Ophir (1 Kings 9:26-28; 10:22-24; 2 Chron. 8:17; 9:10-11, 21-22).*
- *Solomon had a "navy of Tharshish" (1 Kings 10:22).*
- *The Queen of Sheba must have landed here (1 Kings 10:1-13).*
- *Elath was later built up again by Uzziah, king of Judah, in the eighth century B.C. (2 Kings 14:22).*
- *Ships of Jehoshaphat were broken at Ezion-geber (1 Kings 22:49).*
- *The Israelites crossed the Red Sea (Exod. 14).*

SODOM (*"place of lime"*) and GOMORRAH (*"fissure," "submersion"*), **Sedom**, *Sedem, Sdom*

South of the Dead Sea was the Valley of Siddim (Gen. 14:10), where once stood the cities of Sodom and Gomorrah, believed to be now entirely submerged in water. The area now has a potash and bromide business that is part of a $50,000,000 expansion. North of the chemical plant about 3 miles, above one of the many salt caves in the area, is a natural stone outcropping that supposedly (with much imagination) has the form of a woman. It is known as **LOT'S WIFE**.

- *Five wicked cities were in the valley: Sodom, Gomorrah, Admah, Bela (Zoar), and Zeboiim (Gen. 10:19; 13:10; 14:2-11).*
- *They were destroyed (except for Bela), but Lot was saved (Gen. 19; Deut. 29:23; Isa. 13:19; Jer. 50:40; Matt. 10:15; 2 Pet. 2:6; Jude 7).*
- *Lot's wife turned into a pillar of salt (Gen. 19:26; Luke 17:32).*
- *They were used as a warning by Moses (Deut. 29:23; 32:32); by Isaiah (1:1-10; 13:19); by Jeremiah (23:14; 49:18; 50:40); by Amos (4:11); by Zephaniah (2:9); by Jesus (Matt. 10:15; 11:24); by Paul (Rom. 9:29); by Peter (2 Pet. 2:6); and by Jude (4, 7).*
- *They were cited as types, or symbols (Rev. 11:8).*

Peratsim Canyon *and* Flour Cave

About 1/7 of a mile north of the Mifale Sdom Salt Works is a road running northwest into the desert. At a point 3½ miles from the main road is Peratsim Canyon, which is carved in the beautiful white clay. A hike down the shallow canyon about 1/3 of a mile will place the visitor at the opening of a cave known as *Flour Cave* because of its white flour appearance. The cave is approximately 300 feet long and very dark inside. Israeli youth enjoy hiking through this marvel of nature.

Ein Zohar

This is a hot mineral spring near the Dead Sea and just north of the road between Sodom and Arad.

Citadel of Zohar *("nobility," "distinction")*

The remains of the second- or third-century Roman fortress of Zohar are located about 2 miles west of the Dead Sea along Wadi Zohar, a dry riverbed, and near the road from Arad to Nevé-Zohar, on the shore of the Dead Sea. In ancient times it was on the "Road of the Salt" and was used to defend the road.

ARAD *("a court")*, Tell Arad

In the early 1960s a new city of Arad was built by the Israelis in the Negev, 5 miles east of the ancient city and about 17 miles south of Hebron. Here are underground reservoirs of natural gas.

On the mound, Tell Arad, there has been found a sanctuary built according to the layout of the Holy of Holies in King Solomon's temple in Jerusalem, as described in the Bible.

The Hebrew University and Department of Antiquities excavated the 5,000-year-old Tell Arad from 1962 to 1967, and a number of ostraca were uncovered.

On the south side of the road, between Arad and the road connecting Hebron with Beersheba, is a government-operated SCHOOL FOR BEDOUIN CHILDREN that is very interesting to visit.

- As the Israelites penetrated into the Promised Land from the south, the men of Arad took some of the children of Israel prisoners, whereupon Israel vowed to destroy the city and Joshua killed the king (Num. 21:1-2; 33:40; Josh. 12:14; Judg. 1:16).
- In its vicinity the Kenites settled (Judg. 1:16).
- King Solomon had a fortress here.
- Shishak I of Egypt captured Arad.

Ein-Bokek

At Ein-Bokek, about 3½ miles north of Nevé-Zohar, there is a health resort featuring mineral water from the hot springs of Hamei-Zohar. Above the resort are the ruins of the Bokek Fort, built to guard the sweet-water spring.

MASADA, Metsada *("fortress")*

About 2½ miles from the western shore of the Dead Sea and 15 miles north of Sodom, in the wilderness of Judah, is a rock fortress ½ mile long, 220 yards wide, and nearly 2,000 feet above the level of the Dead Sea. It is located opposite the white peninsula of Halashon ("the tongue"), which projects into the Dead Sea from the Jordan shore.

Herod the Great (37 B.C.-4 B.C.) built his winter palaces here. Around his fortress he built a WALL 18 feet high and 38 TOWERS 75 feet high. When Rome marched on the Jews in A.D. 66, a band of

Jewish patriots, Zealots, led by Menachen Ben Yehuda of Galilee, fled to Masada and captured it from a Roman garrison. The Romans had captured Jerusalem, and Masada was one of the last strongholds to resist the Romans. This small band of Jewish patriots was a "thorn in the flesh" of the Romans. Under the leadership of Flavius Silva, the Romans built a 3-mile wall around Masada; and after a 3-year siege and the construction of an earthen ramp, the Romans broke into the fortress and found that all had killed each other and themselves, except 2 women and 5 children. On that April 15, A.D. 73, 960 persons perished.

Eleazar gave a long oration to the Jews to help prepare them for the mass "murder-suicide." This speech is recorded by Josephus in his *Wars of the Jews*, VII:8:6–7.

Among the important finds are the ROMAN WALL, the WATER SYSTEM with giant cisterns (the largest held 80,000 gallons of water), PALACES, ROMAN BATHS, STOREROOMS, COINS, POTS, SWIMMING POOLS, BAPTISMAL FONTS, JEWISH SYNAGOGUE (the oldest in the world), a BYZANTINE CHURCH, and fourteen SCROLLS, including *Deuteronomy, Ezekiel, Leviticus, Psalms*, and nonbiblical texts: *Sabbath Sacrifices, Book of Jubilees*, and *Ecclesiasticus*. These scrolls are especially important because of the exact dating and the important scroll *Songs of the Sabbath Sacrifices*, which is identical to a Qumran scroll.

Yigael Yadin was the archaeologist responsible for the excavation of Masada in 1963.

Masada has become a shrine and symbol to the new nation of Israel. "Masada shall not fall again!" is the oath of the cadets who graduate from Israel's military academy. Nearly every school child has climbed Masada. It is a national tradition. Masada represents (1) the stand of a few against the many, (2) the weak against the strong (like David and Goliath), (3) religious and spiritual freedom, and (4) men of different sects and beliefs living together. They were united in a struggle for freedom. Some were Essenes, some were Zealots, and some are not identified.

Ascent to the top of Masada is possible by gondola or by foot up the 2-mile-long serpentine path or by the shorter ramp path. A road from Arad leads to the foot of the ramp path. This is a National Parks Authority site.

■ *Some picture Masada as the "stronghold" where David's followers joined him (2 Sam. 24:23; 1 Chron. 12:1–16).*

EN-GEDI *("spring of the kid")*, **Ein Gedi**, *Hazazon-tamar ("pruning of the palm")*, *Tell el-Jurn*

Ein Gedi has been an oasis in the desert for thousands of years, with immense fountains of water emerging from underground springs. It is on the west shore of the Dead Sea, about midway in Ein David Gorge. It is 10½ miles north of Masada and has a kibbutz nearby which was settled in 1949 and named Ein Gedi. Here is Israel's only waterfall that runs year-round. The water drops nearly 300 feet. You

Above: Masada
Below: Storehouses, Masada

can quickly put on your bathing suit in the dense thicket and swim in beautiful natural swimming pools. There are many caves in the area.

There have been inhabitants at Ein Gedi since pre-Israel times.

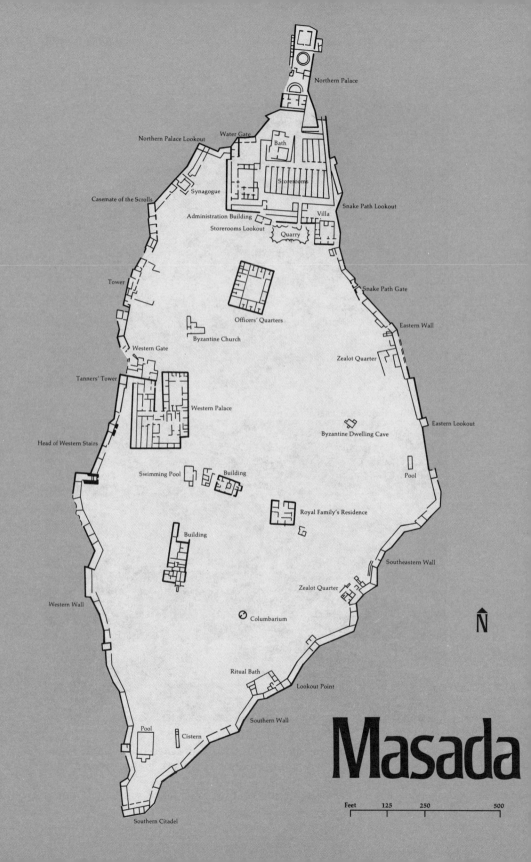

Northern Palace

Northern Palace Lookout

Water Gate

Bath

Storerooms

Synagogue

Casemate of the Scrolls

Administration Building

Snake Path Lookout

Villa

Storerooms Lookout

Quarry

Tower

Officers' Quarters

Snake Path Gate

Eastern Wall

Byzantine Church

Western Gate

Zealot Quarter

Tanners' Tower

Western Palace

Byzantine Dwelling Cave

Eastern Lookout

Head of Western Stairs

Swimming Pool

Building

Pool

Royal Family's Residence

Building

Southeastern Wall

Zealot Quarter

Western Wall

Columbarium

N̂

Ritual Bath

Lookout Point

Pool

Cistern

Southern Wall

Masada

Southern Citadel

Feet   125   250   500

North of here the Dead Sea scrolls were found, and near here the Bar-Kokhba Scrolls were found by Yigael Yadin.

Perhaps the springs of Ein Gedi may help fulfill the prophecy of Ezekiel (47:1, 10) that the waters of the Dead Sea will be healed and that fish will abound there.

- *It was occupied by Amorites (Gen. 14:7).*
- *It was in the territory of Judah (Josh. 15:20, 62).*
- *Here David took refuge and cut off Saul's shirt (1 Sam. 23:29–24:22).*
- *Here Jehoshaphat defeated his enemies (2 Chron. 20).*
- *It was a fruitful area (Song of Sol. 1:14).*
- *The Acacia tree, from which the ark of the covenant, table, staves, etc. were built, grows in this area, as well as in other desert areas (Exod. 25:5, 10, 13, 23, 28).*

Old synagogue, Masada

Italy is the familiar boot-shaped peninsula extending from the Alps into the Mediterranean Sea. It is 750 miles long and 80–135 miles wide, and is almost 1½ times the size of the state of Utah. Its population is over 50,000,000, about 99 percent of whom are Roman Catholics. The monetary unit is the *lira*, which is divided into *centesini*.

Italy is important to students of the scriptures because of the influence the Roman conquerors had upon Bible lands and Christians. An edict of Rome, for instance, sent Joseph and Mary from Nazareth to Bethlehem and Jesus was born as prophesied (Mic. 5:2; Luke 2:1–7).

Jesus' ministry came during the 300 years that Judea was controlled by Rome, and he suffered death by crucifixion, a Roman form of punishment (Isa. 53; Ps. 22; Matt. 27:31–36; Mark 15:22–25; Luke 23:33; John 19:15–18).

The closing years of Paul's ministry were spent here, and it is believed he suffered martyrdom here (Acts 28:14–31). Catholic tradition has Peter crucified in Rome.

CITIES AND SITES

ROME, *the Eternal City (whose Greek name,* rōmē, *means "power")* *

Rome is located mainly on the left bank of the Tiber River, about 15 miles from the Mediterranean Sea. The traditional date of its founding is 753 B.C., and it grew to be the capital of the Roman Empire and center of the western Catholic church. It is still the capital of Italy.

According to legend, Rome was planned by the gods, who, after

*Because of its importance in history, Rome has here received the more detailed treatment usually accorded the country as a whole in the introductory sections of the other chapters of this book.

Theater, Pompeii, Italy

the fall of Troy, ordered the defeated Aeneas, a son of Venus, to lead his fellow Etruscan refugees to a promised land in the west. The Trojans came to Italy and founded Lavinium 16 miles southeast of the location of present-day Rome.

In the eighth century B.C. the Latin princess Rhea Silvia, sworn to chastity as a vestal virgin, is said to have given birth to twin sons fathered by the god Mars. As punishment for the violation of her oath, her uncle, King Amulius, imprisoned her and ordered the infants, Romulus and Remus, to be abandoned to die on the banks of the flooding Tiber. The boys were found by a she-wolf, who nursed them until a shepherd discovered them and took them into his home. When they reached manhood, they resolved to build a new city on the Tiber, and Romulus traced the boundaries of Rome with his plow. Romulus became Rome's first king.

The seven hills of Rome, the highest of which is 174 feet, were inhabited by three different nations, but were included in one city and surrounded by a wall by Servius Tullius in 578 B.C.

In 509 B.C. Rome became a republic, and in 389 B.C. it was captured, sacked, and burned by the Gauls. It was hastily rebuilt, but the streets were narrow, irregular, and crooked. In many respects Rome remained a very inferior city until the reign of Nero in A.D. 54-68.

The Roman Empire was the result of a long period of political, social, and constitutional growth. For 700 years class struggled against class. Little by little the common people asserted their rights and secured a measure of political, social, and legal justice; but they could not maintain a balanced justice, and so both the aristocracy and the democracy needed guidance and a controlling power. This was the signal for the founding of the empire which some have called the grandest political achievement of the ages. It gained control of practically the whole known world, and by uniting the many small principalities into one great empire it contributed very greatly to the ease with which the gospel could spread during the time of Christ and his apostles.

Rome's career spanned 1,000 years. Her genius was her ability to nourish and embellish the intellectual and cultural achievements of the Greek world and spread them across Europe. Roman architecture, art, literature, and religion all show the influence of Greece, yet bear the stamp of Roman power and assurance. Horace's statement is true: "Captive Greece took Rome captive." As the tourist visits cities of the Roman world he will note the triumphal arch, aqueduct, theater, basilica, forum, and baths. The same structures may be seen in many countries; whomever Rome conquered she also built.

During the reign of Nero (A.D. 54-68) the city of Rome was almost entirely destroyed by a great fire, and Nero set about to rebuild it. He restored those parts of the city that had been destroyed, made new streets that were wide and straight, and erected massive buildings of stone.

In Paul's day Rome was the greatest city in the world, with a population of over 1,000,000. When Paul wrote the letter to the

Romans, probably from Corinth in the spring of A.D. 58, he had evidently never been there but had planned to go. In his letter Paul discussed the doctrine of justification by faith.

Later (about A.D. 61), Paul arrived at Rome as a prisoner and was there in his first imprisonment for two or more years. A few of his experiences there are given us. During this time he wrote the books of Ephesians, Philippians, Colossians, Hebrews, and Philemon; and either at this time or more probably at a later imprisonment there about A.D. 67 or 68 he wrote 2 Timothy. Aquila and Priscilla, with whom Paul had such pleasant association, came from Rome.

The emperors that followed Nero continued to increase and embellish the city, but during the reign of Commodus (A.D. 180–92) a great part of it was again destroyed by fire. The period between this time and the fall of the western empire (A.D. 476) saw the rise of many prominent rulers, among whom was Constantine, who succeeded in making Christianity a state religion by the Edict of Milan in 313, which established toleration and restored the property of the Church.

During the fifth century great calamities befell Rome with the ravages of the northern barbarians. In the sixth century she was besieged by the Goths under Totila. During the seventh and eighth centuries famine, earthquakes, a pestilence, and five tremendous inundations of the Tiber desolated the city and drove the inhabitants from a great portion of the ancient site.

Then, about A.D. 800, the Romans appear to have remembered their former institutions. They organized a corporation, which received advice rather than commands from the Pope — who had assumed the title of *Lord* — and the history of Rome soon became merged in the history of the pontiffs. The Rome of the Middle Ages was the scene of vicissitude, turmoil, and destruction.

Today Rome boasts of 3,000,000 residents. Actually it is the seat of two governments, for Vatican City, comprising no more than 110 acres and known as the "state within a city," is the capital of Roman Catholicism.

- *Both Jews and Gentiles belonged to the church in Rome (Rom. 1:6-13; 7:1).*
- *The church in Rome was regarded as a Gentile church (Rom. 1:5-7, 13, 15).*
- *Aquila and Priscilla lived in Rome (Acts 18:2).*
- *Paul planned to go there (Acts 19:21; Rom. 1:13; Acts 23:11).*
- *Paul was a prisoner in Rome for two years (Acts 27-28).*
- *Paul wrote the following letters while in Rome: Ephesians, Philippians, Colossians, 2 Timothy, Hebrews, and Philemon.*
- *Peter most likely preached in Rome and wrote 1 Peter there (1 Peter 5:13).*

Italy

AUSTRIA

SWITZERLAND

Bozen

Torino

Milan

Verona

Venice

Triest

YUGOSLAVIA

ANCE

Genoa

Reggio

Bologna

Ravenna

Pisa

Florence

Volterra

Siena

Ancona

Perugia

Orvieto

Pescara

Rome

Tivoli

Anzio

Appii Forum

Monte Cassino

Foggia

Caserta

Naples

Puteoli (Pozzuoli)

Pompeii

Bari

Salerno

Brindisi

Capri

Taranto

Sardenia

Corsica

Gulf of Taranto

Cagliari

Crotone

MEDITERRANEAN SEA

Palermo

Messina

Rhegium (Reggio)

Sicily

Catania

Syracuse (Siracusa)

Miles   25   50   100

Melita (Malta)

Inset (Gulf of Naples detail)

Caserta

Solfatara

Naples

Mount Vesuvius

Pozzuoli

Herculaneum

Pompeii

Salerno

Gulf of Naples

Sorrento

Positano

Capri

Amalfi

ROMAN HISTORY IN BRIEF

The Monarchy (*ca. 753–509 B.C.*)

753. Rome, according to tradition, was founded by Romulus and Remus.
616–509. Rome was ruled by Etruscan kings. A temple to Jupiter was built on the Capitoline, and the Circus Maximus was built.

Early Republic (*509–264 B.C.*)

Rome was a Republic. Its borders extended over the Mediterranean, and the Latin language predominated.
The Appian Way was built during this period.

Rise to Mediterranean Leadership as a Republic (*264–133 B.C.*)

264. The first Punic ("purple," "Phoenician") war was fought against the Carthaginians. The Romans were victorious.
218–201. The second Punic War was fought. Hannibal attacked through Spain, but Rome won.
146. The third Punic War resulted in the destruction of Carthage. Roman power was firmly established.

Revolution and Rise of One-Man Rule (*133–31 B.C.*)

133. Tiberius Gracchus was elected tribune.
82–79. Sulla (Sylla) was dictator to Rome.
73–71. Spartacus led a slave revolt that ended in disaster for the rebels.
63. Cicero became consul.
60. The first triumvirate consisted of Pompey, Julius Caesar, and Crassus.
49–48. In this period of civil wars, Caesar defeated Pompey.
44. Dictator Julius Caesar was assassinated. Mark Antony took command.

The Settlement of Augustus (*31 B.C.–A.D. 14*)

31. Antony and Cleopatra were defeated at Actium by Octavian. Mark Antony had lost his heart to Cleopatra and now his fleet to Octavian. After this defeat at Actium, the lovers took their lives in Egypt — Cleopatra with an asp. Octavian secured the death of Cleopatra's 17-year-old son Cesarion, who was a political rival, and under Octavian Rome consolidated its empire.
27 B.C.–A.D. 14. After Octavian Augustus (Caesar Augustus) had defeated Mark Antony, he became the first Roman emperor, for 41 years of a golden age. (*Augustus* means "the revered.") Through dictatorial powers Octavian Augustus erected beautiful buildings in Rome, including the Pantheon, and restored 82 Roman temples. The initials *S.P.Q.R.* stand for *Senatus Populusque Romanus,* symbolizing the senate and people who voted him dictator for life, thus yielding the ancient authority of the Republic. The months of July and August are named after Julius Caesar and Augustus.

After Octavian's death there were 15 years of chaos.

31 B.C. -A.D. 476. These years marked the beginning and end of the Roman Empire.

The Early Empire (*A.D. 14–192*)

14–37. This was the reign of Tiberius, the ruler in the days of Jesus. Tiberius was murdered by suffocation.

4 B.C.–A.D. 65. This was the period of Seneca and the "Golden Age."

37–41. Caligula reigned, addressing himself as "god." He was cruel, capricious, and mad. He was assassinated in A.D. 41.

41–54. Claudius, a paralytic, reigned. He was a sensible ruler but was finally poisoned.

54–68. These years marked the reign of Nero, who became emperor at age 16. (Nero was so evil he even poisoned his own mother.) Paul the apostle was imprisoned.

64. Rome burned, and Nero accused the Christians.

65. The playwright and philosopher Seneca died.

68–69. Galba, Otho, and Vitellius reigned. Galba was murdered, Otho committed suicide, and Vitellius was defeated in battle and killed.

69–79. Vespasian, a wise ruler, reigned.

79. Mount Vesuvius erupted and buried Pompeii and Herculaneum. The Colosseum was dedicated.

79–81. This was the reign of Titus, son of Vespasian. (Titus had conquered Jerusalem in A.D. 70.)

82. The Arch of Titus was dedicated.

81–96. Domitian reigned, terrorizing Rome for 15 years. He was assassinated.

96–98. This was the reign of Nerva, the first of five good leaders.

98–117. Trajan reigned, extending the empire to its largest limits.

117–38. This was the reign of Hadrian, who built the famous wall in England, villa at Tivoli, and temple to Venus and Roma at Rome.

138–61. Antoninus Pius reigned. These were majestic days for Rome.

161–80. These years marked the reign of Marcus Aurelius, the last of five good leaders. A sense of unity and reconciliation of peoples developed.

180–92. The reign of Commodus, a despot, marked the beginning of the decline and fall of Rome.

Collapse of the Empire (*192–284*)

193–211. The reign of Septimius Severus was fairly good.

211–17. Caracalla reigned and was assassinated.

235–84. In the chaotic five decades from the death of Alexander Severus in 235 to the advent of Diocletian, some 20 emperors and usurpers ruled. With the exception of two, all of these rulers met violent deaths.

The Late Empire (284–395)

284–305. This was the reign of Diocletian, the last of the emperors who persecuted the Christians.

312. Constantine the Great defeated Maxentius at the battle of Milvian Bridge.
Christianity was given equal rights with other religions in A.D. 313 by the Edict of Milan.

312–24. Constantine ruled as emperor of the West.

315. The Arch of Constantine was built.

324. After defeating Licinius, the emperor of the East, Constantine became the sole ruler of the Roman Empire.

330. The seat of the empire was moved to Byzantium (Constantinople, Istanbul) by Constantine. Constantine ruled until 337.

361–63. Julian the Apostate tried to revive paganism.

364. The Roman Empire was divided, with Rome as the capital of the western empire.

340–430. Ambrose and Jerome, theologians, and Augustine, philosopher, lived.

379. Theodosius proclaimed Christianity the state religion. The Church then became able to execute heretics and wield the power of Rome.

382. Saint Jerome went to Rome to begin work on a new version of the Bible.

The Collapse of the West (395–476), **but Perpetuation of Rome in the East** (395–1564)

395. The Roman Empire was permanently divided into eastern and western halves.

413–26. Saint Augustine's work *The City of God* established the Christian ideals of perfection.

476. Romulus Augustulus, the last emperor after a thousand years of dominion, was deposed.

536–93. Goths and Greeks fought over the city of Rome and devastated it.

590–604. Gregory the Great was enthroned and assumed the title of Sovereign Pontiff.

754. The temporal power of the papacy began.

774. Charlemagne conquered Lombardy and annexed it to the dominions of the Pope.

800. Charlemagne, who reunited most of western Europe under a single reign, was crowned in Saint Peter's by Pope Leo III. Charlemagne called his realm the *Holy Roman Empire.*

1073–75. In the investiture dispute, Pope Gregory VII struggled with the emperors for supremacy.

1084. The Normans devastated the city of Rome.

1309. Clement V moved the seat of the Holy See to Avignon until 1377. Rome's population was reduced to less than 20,000.

1377. Gregory XI returned to Rome, where he resided in the Vatican Palace.

1447. Pope Nicholas V commenced a new basilica of Saint Peter.

1510–11. Martin Luther visited Rome.

1513–21. Leo X was Pope. These were golden days of Rome. The arts flourished.

1572. Gregory XIII dropped 10 days out of 1582 — October 5 became October 15 — thereby instituting the Gregorian calendar.

1626. The new Saint Peter's Basilica was completed.

1798. The French under Napoleon established a republic for a short time. The temporal power of the popes was abolished.

1814. Napoleon fell. Rome and the papal states were restored to the popes.

1870. Rome became the capital of Italy.

1929. The Lateran treaty established the "City of the Vatican" under the sovereignty of the Pope.

1946. The monarchy was abolished and Italy became a republic.

POINTS OF INTEREST

Subheads divide these points of interest in Rome into four separate tours. Sites 67 to 89, below, are not necessarily listed in the order in which one would encounter them. Those the tourist wishes to visit, however, can be incorporated into the other tours at his convenience.

Ancient Central Rome and the Forum

1. **PALAZZO VENEZIA** (Venice Palace). Located on the Piazza Venezia, this palace was built in 1455 for Cardinal Pietro Barbo, who became Pope in 1464 under the name of Paul II. Many popes lived here, and Charles VIII, king of France, lived here in 1494. It is a typical example of the first period of Renaissance architecture and of the change from castle to palace. Benito Mussolini lived here and delivered speeches from the balcony during the Fascist regime. **VENEZIA SQUARE** in front of the palace marks the center of Rome. A **MUSEUM** is housed in the palace.

2. **MONUMENT TO VICTOR EMMANUEL II**, first king of Italy. This huge monument was erected to the principle of Italian independence. Designed by Count Giuseppe Sacconi, it took 26 years to build (1885–1911). It was completed for the fiftieth anniversary of the kingdom of Italy. A Venetian sculptor, Chiaradia, worked for 20 years on the equestrian statue of the king. (Emmanuel II himself is buried in the Pantheon.) Under the statue of Roma is the **TOMB OF THE UN-KNOWN SOLDIER** (1921). Inside the monument is the **MUSEUM OF THE RISORGIMENTO**. The monument faces north-northeast, and the Via del Corso, going north-northeast from the monument, parallels the Tiber River to the Milvian Bridge.

3. **FORUM AND COLUMN OF TRAJAN** (A.D. 114). The emperor Trajan ruled from A.D. 53 to 117. He was born in Spain and became an excellent Roman general and ruler, administering many public works and welfare programs. To mark his triumph in the Dacian War (A.D. 105) he built a forum that surpassed all others in size and splendor.

It included the TEMPLE OF TRAJAN and many important buildings. The greatest monument of the Dacian War is the noble column that still stands. It consists of 19 hollow blocks of marble, measures 97 feet high and 12 feet in diameter, and has an internal spiral staircase with 185 steps. The helicoidal band, or frieze (3–4 feet wide and 650 feet long), of 2,500 human figures gives us a view of the arms, arts, costumes, military tactics, and so on of the Romans and Dacians. The ashes of Trajan were placed in a golden urn at the foot of the column and his statue on top of it. In the sixteenth century Trajan's statue was replaced by a STATUE OF SAINT PETER. The whole forum was considered one of the marvels of the world. The eastern hemicycle can still be seen. It had a double tier of public offices and shops.

4. IMPERIAL FORUMS: JULIUS CAESAR (ca. 46 B.C.), AUGUSTUS (25 B.C.), NERVA (A.D. 98). By the end of the second century A.D., no fewer than 6 emperors had created a series of "new" forums.

The FORUM OF JULIUS CAESAR, marked by a bronze statue of Caesar in the excavated ruins, was built with the spoils of his Gallic Wars (48 B.C.), when he defeated Pompey. The Temple of Venus Genitrix was built and later rebuilt by Trajan.

The FORUM OF AUGUSTUS followed. Augustus was the first Roman emperor (27 B.C.–A.D. 14). He built his forum and the TEMPLE OF MARS ULTOR (the Avenger) in its center to mark his victory in battle with Brutus and Cassius at Philippi in 42 B.C. He thus avenged the murder of his great-uncle, Julius Caesar. A 100-foot wall was built around the area to protect it.

The FORUM OF NERVA — Nerva was the first of a series of 5 good emperors — was built in A.D. 96–98. The Temple of Minerva stood in this forum.

5. CHURCH OF SANTA MARIA D'ARACOELI. (See church no. 9 in the section on the 25 churches of Rome, below.)

6. The CAPITOL is located on the CAMPIDOGLIO, one of seven hills. On the hill stands the thirteenth-century SENATORIAL PALACE, the residence of the mayor of Rome.

On the hill is also a bronze equestrian second-century STATUE OF MARCUS AURELIUS, who wrote that "men exist for the sake of one another" (A.D. 161–80). Because the Christians thought the rider was Constantine, this statue has escaped metal-hungry generations.

The PALAZZO DEI CONSERVATORI and the CAPITOLINE MUSEUM (see "Art Galleries and Museums" nos. 2 and 3, below) were designed by Michelangelo. The TABULARIUM, erected in 78 B.C. on the site where the palace now stands, housed the bronze tablets of law. It is one of the few remains of the Republican era. A glorious view of the most celebrated spot in ancient Rome (the Forum) may be had from the tabularium.

The TEMPLE OF JUPITER CAPITOLINUS once occupied a prominent spot on the Campidoglio. Note the TARPEIAN ROCK, past the remains of the Temple of Jupiter, where traitors of Rome were sentenced to death.

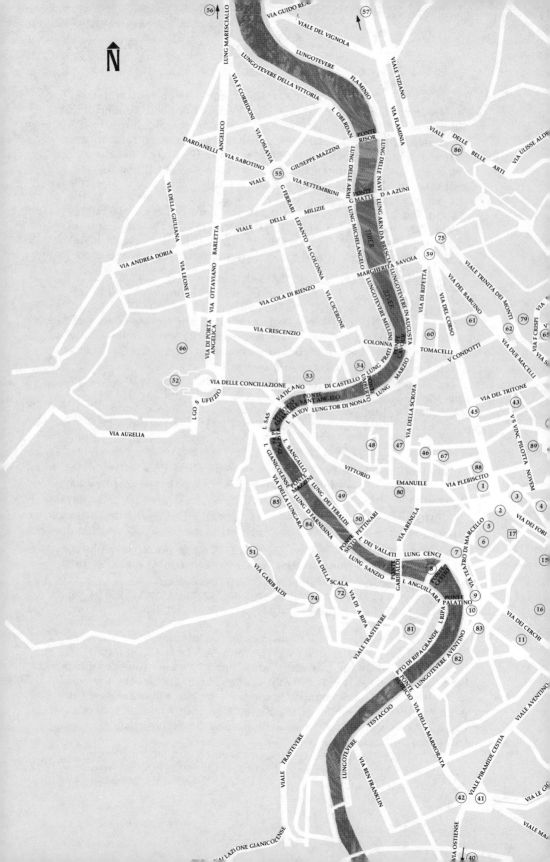

Rome

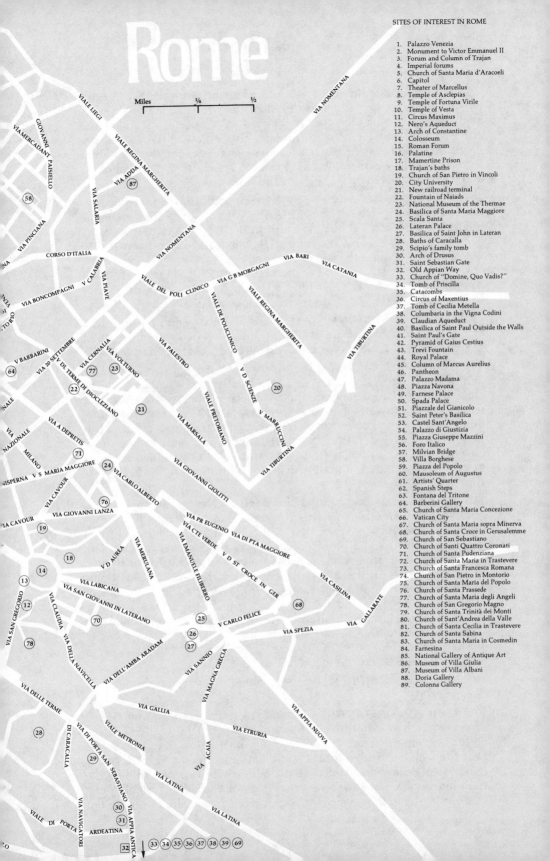

Miles ¾ ½

VIALE LIEGI

GIOVANNI PAISIELLO

VIA MERCADANTE

VIA ADDA

VIALE REGINA MARGHERITA

VIA SALARIA

58

VIA PINCIANA

CORSO D'ITALIA

87

VIA NOMENTANA

VIA BONCOMPAGNI

V CALABRIA

VIA PIAVE

VIALE DEL POLI CLINICO

VIA G B MORGAGNI

VIA BARI

VIA CATANIA

VIALE DE POLICLINICO

VIALE REGINA MARGHERITA

VIA TIBURTINA

V BARBARINI

V 20 SETTEMBRE

VIA CERNALIA

VIA VOLTURNO

VIA PALESTRO

V D SCIENZE

20

64

V D DL TERME DI DIOCLEZIANO

77

23

V D SCIENZE

22

21

VIALE PRETORIANO

V MARRUCCINI

VIA MARSALA

VIA TIBURTINA

VIA NAZIONALE

VIA A DEPRETIS

71

VIA GIOVANNI GIOLITTI

NISPERNA

V S MARIA MAGGIORE

24

VIA CARLO ALBERTO

VIA CAVOUR

76

VIA GIOVANNI LANZA

VIA PR EUGENIO

VIA DI PTA MAGGIORE

VIA CAVOUR

19

VIA CTE VERDE

V D ST CROCE IN GER

18

V D AUREA

VIA MERULANA

VIA EMANUELE FILIBERTO

14

VIA LABICANA

13

VIA SAN GREGORIO

VIA SAN GIOVANNI IN LATERANO

12

VIA CLAUDIA

70

25

V CARLO FELICE

VIA CASILINA

68

VIA GALLARATE

78

VIA DELLA NAVICELLA

26

27

VIA SPEZIA

VIA DELL'AMBA ARADAM

VIA SANNIO

VIA MAGNA GRECIA

VIA DELLE TERME

VIA APPIA NUOVA

VIA GALLIA

VIA ETRURIA

28

DI CARACALLA

VIA DI PORTA SAN SEBASTIANO

VIALE METRONIA

VIA ACAIA

VIA LATINA

29

VIA LATINA

VIALE DI PORTA

VIA NAVICATORI

ARDEATINA

30

31

VIA APPIA ANTICA

32

33 34 35 36 37 38 39 69

VIA NOMENTANA

SITES OF INTEREST IN ROME

1. Palazzo Venezia
2. Monument to Victor Emmanuel II
3. Forum and Column of Trajan
4. Imperial forums
5. Church of Santa Maria d'Aracoeli
6. Capitol
7. Theater of Marcellus
8. Temple of Asclepias
9. Temple of Fortuna Virile
10. Temple of Vesta
11. Circus Maximus
12. Nero's Aqueduct
13. Arch of Constantine
14. Colosseum
15. Roman Forum
16. Palatine
17. Mamertine Prison
18. Trajan's baths
19. Church of San Pietro in Vincoli
20. City University
21. New railroad terminal
22. Fountain of Naiads
23. National Museum of the Thermae
24. Basilica of Santa Maria Maggiore
25. Scala Santa
26. Lateran Palace
27. Basilica of Saint John in Lateran
28. Baths of Caracalla
29. Scipio's family tomb
30. Arch of Drusus
31. Saint Sebastian Gate
32. Old Appian Way
33. Church of "Domine, Quo Vadis?"
34. Tomb of Priscilla
35. Catacombs
36. Circus of Maxentius
37. Tomb of Cecilia Metella
38. Columbaria in the Vigna Codini
39. Claudian Aqueduct
40. Basilica of Saint Paul Outside the Walls
41. Saint Paul's Gate
42. Pyramid of Gaius Cestius
43. Trevi Fountain
44. Royal Palace
45. Column of Marcus Aurelius
46. Pantheon
47. Palazzo Madama
48. Piazza Navona
49. Farnese Palace
50. Spada Palace
51. Piazzale del Gianicolo
52. Saint Peter's Basilica
53. Castel Sant'Angelo
54. Palazzo di Giustizia
55. Piazza Giuseppe Mazzini
56. Foro Italico
57. Milvian Bridge
58. Villa Borghese
59. Piazza del Popolo
60. Mausoleum of Augustus
61. Artists' Quarter
62. Spanish Steps
63. Fontana del Tritone
64. Barberini Gallery
65. Church of Santa Maria Concezione
66. Vatican City
67. Church of Santa Maria sopra Minerva
68. Church of Santa Croce in Gerusalemme
69. Church of San Sebastiano
70. Church of Santi Quattro Coronati
71. Church of Santa Pudenziana
72. Church of Santa Maria in Trastevere
73. Church of Santa Francesca Romana
74. Church of San Pietro in Montorio
75. Church of Santa Maria del Popolo
76. Church of Santa Prassede
77. Church of Santa Maria degli Angeli
78. Church of San Gregorio Magno
79. Church of Santa Trinità dei Monti
80. Church of Sant'Andrea della Valle
81. Church of Santa Cecilia in Trastevere
82. Church of Santa Sabina
83. Church of Santa Maria in Cosmedin
84. Farnesina
85. National Gallery of Antique Art
86. Museum of Villa Giulia
87. Museum of Villa Albani
88. Doria Gallery
89. Colonna Gallery

7. **THEATER OF MARCELLUS** (13 B.C.). This huge theater was begun by Julius Caesar and finished by Augustus, who named it after his nephew, the son of Octavia. It seated 12,000 spectators and is the only ancient theater left in Rome. The **PORTICO OCTAVIA** (by Augustus) adjoins the theater as a place of shelter for the spectators in unfavorable weather. It has a double arcade with 270 columns, and enclosed the temples of Jupiter and Juno.

8. The **TEMPLE OF ASCLEPIAS**, the Greek god of medicine, stood on the Island in the Tiber (*Isola Tiberina*). It was once the center for pilgrimages of sick people. The **CHURCH OF SAINT BARTHOLOMEW** is built on the site. The ancient **PONTE FABRICIO** (62 B.C.) and **PONTE CESTIO** (46 B.C.) unite the island to the city.

On the other side can be seen the **SYNAGOGUE**, built in 1904 in Assyro-Babylonian style. Behind it is the Ghetto, where the Jews were segregated for years and where the lower classes of Jews still live.

9. **TEMPLE OF FORTUNA VIRILE** (first to third century B.C.). This temple was erected by Servius Tullius and converted into a Christian church in A.D. 872. It was originally dedicated to Mater Matuta.

10. The **TEMPLE OF VESTA**(*Santa Maria del Sole*, Round Temple), dating from the first century B.C., was built entirely of marble. The entablature and roof have disappeared. The columns are nearly 30 feet high. Southwest of here is the **FLEA MARKET**, across the Ponte Sublicio at Plazza Portese and along the Tiber from this point. Near here is the **ARCH OF THE GOLDSMITHS**, built in honor of Septimius Severus, and the **CHURCH OF SANTA MARIA IN COSMEDIN**, with the **BOCCA DELLA VERITÀ**, a marble disc representing a human face. (See church no. 25, below.)

11. **CIRCUS MAXIMUS**. During the reign of Nero, this huge circus was built by Tarquinius Priscus to seat 250,000 spectators. Chariot teams ran around the *spina*, the backbone of the oval track, for 7 laps (2½ miles), and a bronze dolphin was flipped over on each lap. Clubs sponsored drivers and gambled their fortunes. Romans loved a day at the races. It was also a place for the martyrdom of Christians.

The Great Fire that swept Rome in A.D. 64 started in the shops of the circus, and the wind quickly swept the fire over the Palatine, where it burned through the city for six days. Nero blamed the Christians for the fire.

The Palatine Hill is behind the circus, and on the southeast corner of the Palatine **SEPTIMIUS SEVERUS** built his **PALACE**.

12. **NERO'S AQUEDUCT** (ca. A.D. 64). These ruins are on the Via San Gregorio.

13. **ARCH OF CONSTANTINE** (A.D. 312–15). This last and most well preserved arch was built by the senate and people at one end of the Forum to commemorate the victory of Constantine over Maxentius near the Milvian Bridge in 312. The battle started at Saxa Rubra, 9 miles from Rome, and ended at the Milvian Bridge. In this battle, tradition says, Constantine saw the "sign of Christ": ☧ (called the *labarum*). The arch, however, does not refer specifically to the sign of

the cross or event of the vision. The arch was built of marble taken from the arches of Trajan and Marcus Aurelius and from other monuments. Medallions depicting sacrifices being made to Apollo and Mars show Constantine as something other than a converted "Christian." He was later baptized, however, and has subsequently been canonized by the Roman Catholic church.

14. **COLOSSEUM** (Flavian Amphitheater) (A.D. 80). This immense amphitheater was begun by Vespasian in A.D. 72 and finished by his son Titus 8 years later. Jewish prisoners were employed in its construction. When Titus opened the amphitheater in A.D. 80, he passed out slaves as door prizes to lucky ticket holders. The structure was probably called the *Colosseum* because the "Colossus" of Nero (Nero's Golden House) was in its vicinity.

Here, over a period of 400 years, 50,000 Romans would seat themselves and witness bloody scenes of Christians being eaten by lions, gladiators fighting to the death, animals pitted against men to fight to the death — sometimes 5,000 to 9,000 wild animals were used in one day — and naval battles to the death with the arena filled with water. The biggest naval battle was Claudius's gala of A.D. 52, in which two fleets and 10,000 men turned the lake red with blood.

The elliptical Colosseum is 150 feet high, 615 feet long, and 510 feet wide. It covers 6 acres, and its circumference is 1/3 of a mile. On the outside there were three rows of arches, columns, and statuary.

In case of rain, the Colosseum was covered with an immense velarium (or awning) which was fixed by two squads of sailors.

The Colosseum was used as a quarry for a time, but restored in part in the eighteenth century. The poets wrote of the marvel that has endured 1,900 years: "While stands the Colosseum, Rome shall stand."

15. **ROMAN FORUM** (ca. 500 B.C.). This is an ancient meeting place, marketplace, and religious and political center, lying in a valley that runs from west-northwest to east-southeast between the Capitoline and Palatine hills. Here, according to legend, the Romans and Sabines fought after the rape of the Sabine women. Peace was established, and the valley between the Palatine and the Quirinal was chosen by the two tribes as a common ground for a market and meeting place. That is the meaning of the word *forum*. Here the destinies of the nations were discussed by leaders of the Roman Republic (509 B.C.) and later by the leaders of the Roman Empire. From here all roads fanned out; here Romulus was said to be buried; here was the senate, where Cicero spoke and Caesar was murdered. Here such terms as "equality before the law" and "government for the good of the governed" were nourished and given to the world for future governments of free men. The Forum's monumental architecture was copied wherever Rome ruled, and cities from England to Egypt were centered on similar structures. Buildings, monuments, arches, statues, and temples remained intact until the sixth century A.D., but have since been ruined by war, earthquake, nature, and

vandals. The Forum was excavated in the nineteenth century.

Principal monuments of the Forum include the following (looking from northwest to southeast):

(1) **TABULARIUM** (78 B.C.). The Senatorial Palace was built on this site. The Tabularium took its name from the bronze tablets kept there, containing peace treaties and other public documents.

(2) The **TEMPLE OF VESPASIAN** (ca. A.D. 95), in the center, was built in honor of the deified emperor and his son Titus. The 3 columns and entablature are of the best Roman period. Note the umbilical connection — white stone on a brick column 4 feet high.

(3) The **TEMPLE OF SATURN** (the Roman harvest god), on the right, dates from 497 B.C. It has 8 granite columns and is one of the oldest sanctuaries in the Forum. The columns now standing were reconstructed in the fourth century A.D. The *Saturnalia,* or dedication feast of this temple, was a 7-day festival from December 17 to 24. Many families offered young pigs as sacrifices. All schools and businesses observed this holiday and presents were exchanged. Many believe that the modern Christmas festival was derived from the Saturnalia.

(4) **VIA SACRA** is the street running through the Forum, beginning on the right.

(5) The **ARCH OF SEPTIMIUS SEVERUS** (A.D. 203), on the left, was erected in honor of the emperor and his two sons, Caracalla and Geta. It was originally surmounted by a bronze chariot in which the emperor was seated between his sons. Reliefs commemorate victories over the Parthians.

(6) The **CURIA**, or Senate House (47 B.C.), on the left, was erected by Julius Caesar as a council chamber for the senate. It was restored in 1933.

(7) The **ROSTRA**, in the center, was a speakers' platform, where it is believed Mark Antony appealed to the Romans for vengeance on Caesar's murderers, while the dead Caesar lay at his feet. Caesar was assassinated in Pompey's Theater (Curia), but his body was brought to the Rostra on an ivory catafalque (a framework holding a coffin). Shakespeare has inspired generations with the words he attributed to Mark Antony: "Friends, Romans, countrymen, lend me your ears. I come to bury Caesar, not to praise him. The evil that men do lives after them, the good is oft interred with their bones. So let it be with Caesar." The mob went wild, threw torches into the bier, and kept it burning all night. The black stone altar of the ruined Temple of the Divine Julius marks the spot. Fifteen years of chaos followed Caesar's murder. Cicero was slain also, and his head and hands were nailed to the Rostra.

(8) The **COLUMN OF PHOCAS** (A.D. 608), in the center, is the last monument in the Forum. The gilded statue of the emperor Phocas stood on its top.

(9) The **BASILICA JULIA** (46 B.C.), on the right, was built by Caesar

Roman Forum

and contained four law courts and other chambers. In this basilica the principles of Roman law were first formulated.

(10) **BASILICA AEMILIA** (left).

(11) **TEMPLE OF JULIUS CAESAR** (center).

(12) **TEMPLE OF VESTA** (round, center).

(13) **TEMPLE OF CASTOR AND POLLUX** (484 B.C.), on the right. The existing three columns and frieze were restored by Trajan or Hadrian.

(14) **SANTA MARIA ANTIQUA** (right).

(15) **TEMPLE OF AUGUSTUS** (right).

(16) **HOUSE OF THE VESTAL VIRGINS** (ca. 31 B.C.). This was a luxurious palace. The vestals were priestesses of the goddess Vesta and were selected from among the daughters of patrician families when they were between 6 and 10 years of age. They were honored by all Romans. Their duty was to watch the sacred fire in the temple and guard the Palladium. At age 35 they were released.

(17) The **TEMPLE OF ANTONINUS AND FAUSTINA** (A.D. 141), on the left, was erected by Antoninus Pius in honor of his deified wife, Faustina. When Antoninus died, the senate inscribed his name on the temple and he was worshiped also. The 50-foot columns are made of costly cipolius marble. The interior of the temple was converted into the Church of San Lorenzo in the twelfth century.

(18) The **TEMPLE OF ROMULUS** (A.D. 309), the round building on the left, was built by Maxentius in memory of his son, whom he deified and named after the founder of the city.

(19) **TEMPLE OF VENUS AND ROMA**, by Hadrian (A.D. 117–138).

(20) The **BASILICA OF MAXENTIUS** (Constantine), dating from about A.D. 315, on the left, is the largest building in the Forum. The building had a central nave and two aisles. It was begun by Maxentius in A.D. 306 and was finished by Constantine. Michelangelo studied this basilica for his plans of Saint Peter's Basilica.

(21) **ARCH OF TITUS** (A.D. 81) (center). The senate erected this arch after the death of Titus to commemorate his triumphs in Palestine in A.D. 70. It is faced with Pentelic marble.

When a Roman garrison was massacred at Jerusalem in A.D. 66 and the Jews revolted beyond the walls of the city, Rome responded with a large army led by Vespasian. His son Titus finally led the armies to complete the retaliation. Blood flowed freely in the streets of Jerusalem when ten thousand of those that were caught were slain (according to Josephus), and the temple was burned. Not one stone was left standing on another as Jesus had prophesied (Matt. 24:2).

On one side of the arch in bas-relief is a beautiful representation of a triumphal procession carrying Jewish spoils, including the table of shewbread and the seven-branched golden candelabra.

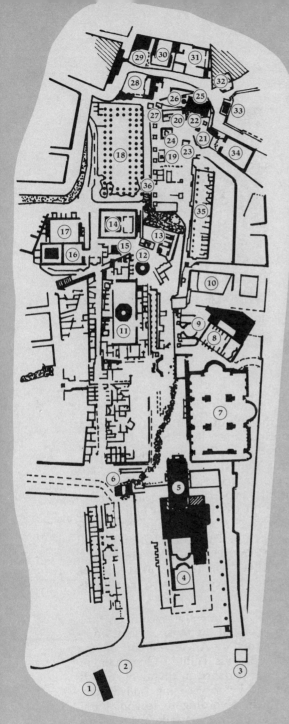

1. Arch of Constantine
2. Meta Sudans
3. Colossus of Nero
4. Temple of Venus and Roma
5. Santa Francesca Romana
6. Arch of Titus
7. Basilica of Maxentius
8. Saints Cosmos and Damianus
9. Temple of Romulus
10. Temple of Antoninus and Faustina
11. House of the Vestal Virgins
12. Temple of Vesta
13. Temple of Julius Caesar
14. Temple of Castor and Pollux
15. Fountain of Juturna
16. Santa Maria Antiqua
17. Temple of Augustus
18. Basilica Julia
19. Lacus Curtius
20. Rostra
21. Comitium
22. Lapis Niger (black stone)
23. Anaglypha of Trajan
24. Column of Phocas
25. Arch of Septimius Severus
26. Umbilicus Urbis
27. Miliarium Aureum
28. Temple of Saturn
29. Portico of the Twelve Gods
30. Temple of Vespasian
31. Temple of Concordia
32. Mamertine Prison
33. Church of Saints Martina and Luca
34. Curia
35. Basilica Aemilia
36. Sacra Via

Roman Forum

Feet   300   600

Arch of Titus, Rome

16.   The **PALATINE** (800 B.C.) was the site of the first city of Rome. During the Republic, many important men lived here: Gracchus, Cicero, Mark Antony, Claudius (father of Tiberius), and Octavius (father of Augustus). The emperor Augustus built his palace here. Caligula, Severus, and other emperors, such as Nero and Domitian, built more and more buildings until the imperial palace reached down to the Forum and even to where later the Colosseum was built. Ruins of the imperial palace may still be seen. A walk on the Palatine is worthwhile. Entering through the Arch of Titus, turn left and climb the stairs on the right. The **VILLA FARNESE, DOMUS TIBERIONA, SCALAE CACI, HOUSE OF LIVIA, PALACE OF FLAVII, STADIUM OF DOMITIAN**, and **BATHS OF SEVERUS** may be seen, and also the **CIRCUS MAXIMUS**.

17.   **MAMERTINE PRISON** (*San Pietro in Carcere*) (seventh century B.C.). It is believed that this prison is one of the most ancient structures in Rome. It was carved out of rock by Ancus Marcius on the Capitoline Hill and later enlarged by Servius Tullius. One chamber is located above the other. Many have perished in this dungeon. It is believed by some that both Paul and Peter were imprisoned here. Beneath the floor is a fountain which, according to legend, burst forth miraculously to enable Peter to baptize his jailors, Processus and Martinianus.

18.   **TRAJAN'S BATHS** are built on the site of Nero's Domus Aurea (Gilded House), about 2 blocks northeast of the Colosseum. These were the first great Roman baths built in Rome.

19.   The **CHURCH OF SAN PIETRO IN VINCOLI** (Saint Peter in Chains)

is located approximately 3 blocks north of the Colosseum on the Via Annabaldi. (See church no. 2, below.)

Southeast Rome, the Catacombs, Saint Paul's

20. CITY UNIVERSITY. The University of Rome transferred here in 1941.

21. NEW RAILROAD TERMINAL (1950).

22. FOUNTAIN OF NAIADS (*delle Terme*). This fountain is noted for its powerful jets. Rutelli (1902) is responsible for the four bronze groups of naiads and sea monsters. It is located in the Piazza dell' Esedra (Exedra Square, now Republican Square).

23. NATIONAL MUSEUM OF THE THERMAE (Baths of Diocletian). The Baths of Diocletian (A.D. 306) were the largest of all Roman baths and could hold 3,000 bathers. The water heating system consisted of underground fires stoked by slaves. The air was carried through floor and wall ducts. Central heating was a Roman invention. In 33 B.C. Rome had 170 baths, and later a thousand. In the second century (A.D. 117–38) Hadrian banned mixed bathing and separate hours were set for the sexes. (See also "Art Galleries and Museums" no. 4, below.)

24. BASILICA OF SANTA MARIA MAGGIORE (Mary Major). (See church no. 5, below.)

25. SCALA SANTA (Holy Staircase). (See church no. 2, below.)

26. LATERAN PALACE. (See church no. 2, below.)

27. BASILICA OF SAINT JOHN IN LATERAN. (See church no. 2, below.)

28. The BATHS OF CARACALLA (A.D. 212) were begun by Caracalla and completed by Alexander Severus. They had marble walls, mosaic floors, granite columns, and bronze doors, and accommodated 1,600 bathers at a time. Massages, perfumes, a gymnasium, libraries, art galleries, and shops made the place very luxurious. The habits of luxury and idleness that were accentuated by the magnificent baths of the emperors were among the causes of the decline of the Roman Empire. The baths are now used for open-air operas.

29. SCIPIO'S FAMILY TOMB is in the Scipio Park on Via Sebastiano.

30. The ARCH OF DRUSUS (second century A.D.) was probably used to carry the aqueduct for the baths of Caracalla. Each facade had four pillars of African marble. Drusus, son of Livia, took command of the legions against the free tribes of the eastern Alps.

31. SAINT SEBASTIAN GATE (*Porta San Sebastiano*) (A.D. 279) was formerly Port Appia in the Aurelian Wall.

32. OLD APPIAN WAY (*Regine Viarum*) (312 B.C.). This is known as the first "Roman road." It was built by Appius Claudius. Roman tombs, catacombs, and beautiful cypress trees line the way for many miles. This is the road over which Paul walked as he came to Rome. The APPII FORUM is a station 40 miles from Rome. Here Paul was met by the Christians who encouraged him.

- *Paul walked this way to Rome (Acts 28:14–16).*
- *Paul met Christians at Appii Forum on the way to Rome (Acts 28:15).*

33. CHURCH OF "DOMINE, QUO VADIS?" According to legend, Peter had a vision of Christ here. After the fire that burned Rome, Nero persecuted the Christians, and Saint Peter was asked to leave Rome to escape the persecution. Not far from Porta Appia he met a traveler going towards Rome. Peter knew the man (Christ) and said to him: "Domine, quo vadis?" (Master, where goest thou?). Jesus replied, "I am going to Rome to be crucified again." The vision vanished, but the divine footprints remained on a paving stone. This is the legend recorded by Origen (A.D. 254).

34. TOMB OF PRISCILLA. In front of the chapel of Quo Vadis is the circular ruin of the tomb of Priscilla, one of the few identifiable tombs on the Appian Way. Priscilla was the wife of Abascantius, a favorite freed-man of Domitian. Statius (A.D. 45–96), the best poet of those days, wrote a letter of condolence and spoke of the tomb.

35. The **CATACOMBS** (first to fourth century A.D.) consist of a vast labyrinth of subterranean galleries (underground cemeteries), where the early Christians buried their dead, held their worship services, and hid from their enemies. There were at least 25 large ones and 20 smaller ones, which together measure an estimated total of 11 miles. They were situated along the main highways from the first to the third milestone outside the city. Two or three bodies were wrapped in linen and placed in each of the columbarium-like niches. Hermetically sealed slabs closed the niches. Bones of the Christians have been carried off into many nations to be used as relics. Paintings of fish, doves, peacocks, anchors, and so on adorn the walls.

The most frequently visited catacombs are those of **SAINT CALIXTUS** and **SAINT SEBASTIAN** on the Via Appia. It is believed that during the persecutions of the third century the bodies of Peter and Paul were hidden in the catacombs of Saint Sebastian.

Other catacombs are **DOMITILLA** on Via delle Sette Chiese, **SAINT AGNES** on Via Nomentana, and **PRISCILLA** on Via Salaria. The Basilica of Saint Sebastian (according to tradition) has a stone bearing the print of Jesus' foot in the first chapel, on the right. This footprint allegedly appeared when Peter asked Jesus, "Domine, quo vadis?"

36. CIRCUS OF MAXENTIUS. On the northeast side of the Old Appian Way and near the Tomb of Cecilia Metella is the Circus of Maxentius, which dates back to the third century A.D. It is the best preserved circus in Rome.

37. The **TOMB OF CECILIA METELLA**, wife of Licinius Crassus, dates from the reign of Augustus (first century A.D). It is round and measures 70 feet in diameter. In the thirteenth century it was converted into a fortress, and the battlemented walls were used to make a stronghold for the family. It is located on the Old Appian Way.

38. The **COLUMBARIA IN THE VIGNA CODINI** (first century A.D.)

contain cinerary **URNS** chiefly of persons attached to the family of the Caesars. This is one of the numerous sepulchers of imperial Rome (prior to Constantine). It is the burial place of the middle class. The niches in the rock, resembling pigeon holes, contained the urns for the ashes of the dead. On the top of Masada, in Israel, Roman columbaria with the niches can be found. The **TOMBS OF PANCRATTI AND VALERII** are excellent examples of the tombs along the Old Appian Way.

39. The **CLAUDIAN AQUEDUCT** may be seen in the Roman country. It was built by Claudius in A.D. 52.

40. **BASILICA OF SAINT PAUL OUTSIDE THE WALLS.** (See church no. 4, below.)

41. **SAINT PAUL'S GATE** (*Porta San Paolo*, formerly *Porta Ostia*) was built by Aurelianus and rebuilt by Honorius. The Aurelian wall was built in A.D. 270–75 as a protection against the barbarians.

42. **PYRAMID OF GAIUS CESTIUS** (43 B.C.). Gaius Cestius was a praetor, or tribune. This structure is located at Porta Ostiense. In medieval times it was known as the tomb of Romulus. It is 117 feet high and covered with white marble slabs. At the foot of the pyramid is an **OLD PROTESTANT CEMETERY**, with the graves of John Keats (1821), Severn (1879), Shelley (1822), J. A. Symonds, and A. Humboldt.

Northwest Rome, the Pantheon, Saint Peter's

43. The **TREVI FOUNTAIN** (1732–51) was ordered by Pope Clement XII and built by Nicolo Salvia. It became famous by the legend of "three coins in the fountain": "If you toss a coin into the fountain you will return to Rome." The fountain is the facade of a large palace.

44. The **ROYAL PALACE** (*Palazzo del Quirnale*) was begun in 1574 to be used as a summer palace for the Pope. It has been the residence of the kings of Italy since 1870 and is now the residence of the president of the republic. It is built on the ruins of Constantine's baths.

45. The **COLUMN OF MARCUS AURELIUS** (A.D. 176), in the heart of the city in the Piazza Colonna, commemorates Marcus Aurelius's victories over the Germanic tribes. In 1589 the **STATUE OF SAINT PAUL** replaced the bronze statues of the emperor Marcus Aurelius, which had disappeared. The column is 138 feet high. This column is an imitation of the Column of Trajan. The reliefs on the spiral band are inferior to those of Trajan's column, however.

46. The **PANTHEON** (27 B.C.–A.D. 123) is a large, round temple dedicated to the gods of the seven planets. It is one of the few ancient Roman buildings that are well preserved. It was preserved from decay through its dedication to Christian worship. The portico (porch) was probably built by Agrippa in 27 B.C., and Hadrian rebuilt the building in A.D. 123. The diameter of the rotunda — the largest

Trevi Fountain, Rome

and most daring of antiquity — is 143 feet. It has been a model for a thousand capitols and shrines around the world. It rises 143 feet to form a perfect hemisphere. The window at the top is 30 feet wide. The 16 Corinthian columns in front are 46 feet high, and each is hewn from a single stone. It is a classic example of Roman architecture. The Romans borrowed Greek architecture when they copied Doric, Ionic, and Corinthian columns; they borrowed the arch of the Etruscans. But they tried to outdo the Greeks with great feats of engineering. They were "boastful builders." They were among the very first to use concrete to achieve grandeur, and the dome of the Pantheon is an example of such use of concrete.

For beauty's sake, the cement was usually veneered with brick, tile, pebble, marble, stucco, or plaster. The Pantheon, the pride of the city, was covered with gilded bronze so that its gleam could be seen all over Rome. The temple's bronze fittings were melted down to cast the baldachin of Saint Peter's. It was consecrated as a Christian church, Saint Mary of the Martyrs, by Pope Boniface IV in 609.

The ancient bronze doors remain. On the inside are the chapels of the ancient gods, now occupied by saints. Many bodies of martyrs were removed from the catacombs to be buried here. The Pantheon also contains the tombs of two kings of Italy — Victor Emmanuel II (1878) and Humbert I (1900) — plus artists Raphael and Peruzzi.

The **OBELISK OF MINERVA**, in front of the Pantheon, originally stood in front of the Temple of Isis. It was put here by Alexander VII in 1667. It is mounted on the back of an elephant designed by Bernini.

47. **PALAZZO MADAMA** (Senate of the Italian Republic).

48. **PIAZZA NAVONA**. This is a splendid piazza, built where once stood the Stadium of Domitian. The celebrated **FOUNTAIN OF THE RIVERS**, by Bernini (A.D. 1651), is located here. An obelisk from the

Circus of Maxentius rises in the middle of four statues representing the Nile, Ganges, Danube, and Rio de la Plata — symbols of the universality of the Church. The FOUNTAIN OF NEPTUNE is by della Bitta and Zappala. The FOUNTAIN OF THE MOOR is by Mari. The CHURCH OF SAINT AGNES IN AGONE (see church no. 12, below) faces the monument. It is said that before her martyrdom Saint Agnes was denuded and her hair miraculously covered her body.

49. **FARNESE PALACE**, in Farnese Square, is one of the most beautiful in Rome. It was built in the early 1500s under the direction of Michelangelo. Stones from the Colosseum and the Theater of Marcellus were used in its construction. It is presently serving as the residence of the French embassy.

50. The **SPADA PALACE** was built about 1550 under the papacy of Paul III. It is now the meeting place of the Italian Council of State.

51. **PIAZZALE DEL GIANICOLO** (Janiculum Hill). On this hill, at the foot of the lighthouse, is the most famous magnificent view of the city. Nearby is the monument of Giuseppe Garibaldi (1895), who took part in the defense of Rome against the French. He assisted in overthrowing the kingdom of Naples and uniting the country of Italy under Victor Emmanuel II.

BASILICA OF SAINT PETER

52. The famous **BASILICA OF SAINT PETER** is the largest church in the world and dates back to 1612. The facade (1612) is 372 feet wide and 133 feet high. It has 8 columns of travertine 93 feet high and 8 feet in diameter. It is surmounted by a balustrade with 19-foot statues of the Savior and the apostles. The dome is 138 feet in diameter and 435 feet high. The nave of the basilica is 691 feet long (over two football fields in length) and 90 feet wide. The bronze ball on the top is 8 feet in diameter and can hold 16 persons.

For 176 years (1450–1626) the great Renaissance masters Rossellino, Alberti, Bramante, Raphael, Michelangelo, della Porta, Maderna, and others exerted their genius while more than 40 popes lavished their treasures in this imposing church.

The basilica stands on the site of the circus of Nero, where thousands of Christians suffered martyrdom. According to tradition, Peter was executed in the middle of the circus at the foot of the 320-ton (132 feet high with the base) Egyptian red granite obelisk, which Caligula brought to Rome from Heliopolis, Egypt, in the first century A.D. and Nero put in the Circus Maximus. It now stands in the center of the piazza, in front of the basilica. Close to the circus existed a cemetery where martyred Christians were buried; and thus Peter was buried there. In A.D. 90, the bishop Anacletus erected a small oratory over Peter's grave. Later, at the request of Pope Sylvester I, the emperor Constantine destroyed the old circus and over its northern foundations built the first Saint Peter's Basilica (A.D 319), which was half as large as the present one. It lasted 1,100 years until the present one was started in 1450. The present one took 176 years to build, and when it was dedicated in 1626 its cost was $50,000,000.

The PIAZZA in front of the basilica has the form of an ellipse measuring 645 feet wide at its greatest breadth. A quadruple colonnade of 284 columns, designed by Bernini (1656–67), encloses the area. The columns are surmounted by 140 statues of saints, each 12 feet in height. The 85-foot Egyptian obelisk was moved from the circus to its present site in 1586, with great pomp and ceremony. Between the obelisk and the fountains, stones on the paving indicate the point from which each wing of the colonnade seems to have only one range of columns instead of four.

A walking tour of the basilica would include the following items in sequence:

(1) The LOGGIA DELLA BENEDIZIONE is located over the central entrance. In it the new popes used to be crowned, and from here the pontiff prays for the people at Easter. The bas-relief beneath, by Buonvicino, represents Christ giving the keys of the kingdom to Peter.

(2) The PORTICO is 233 feet long and 44 feet wide. The ceiling is decorated with stucco and gold. At the two ends are STATUES OF CONSTANTINE AND CHARLEMAGNE by Cornacchini. The CENTRAL ENTRANCE BRONZE DOORS belonged to Constantine's basilica and were made by Filarete in 1445. The large panels represent Jesus, Mary, Paul, and Peter. The bottom two panels represent the beheading of Paul and the crucifixion of Peter by Nero.

(3) The CENTRAL NAVE has a pavement of marble. The round SLAB OF PORPHYRY marked with a cross and located just inside the central doors indicates the spot where Charlemagne and 43 other medieval emperors were formerly crowned. In the pavement METAL LETTERS indicate the respective lengths of other Catholic churches. The interior is paneled with beautiful marbles. With some exceptions, all of the pictures are in mosaic. The original paintings, from which these are copied, are in museums. There are 45 altars, 390 statues in marble, bronze, and stucco, and 748 columns in the church.

(4) Cambio's BRONZE STATUE OF SAINT PETER, on the right side of the nave near the high altar, dates from A.D. 445. Roman Catholics' kisses have polished and worn its right toes and foot.

(5) The HIGH ALTAR stands beneath the dome and under the BALDACCHINO ("canopy"), by Bernini (1633). The canopy is made entirely of bronze. Some plates covering the pronaos of the Pantheon were melted to help supply the bronze. The Baldacchino is 95 feet high and weighs 700 tons. Beneath it, the high altar stands directly above the primitive oratory erected by Anacletus in A.D. 90 over the grave of Saint Peter.

The CONFESSIO is located immediately in front of the high altar. Marble steps lead down to the gilded bronze doors closing the ORATORY, which contains the bronze sarcophagus of Saint Peter, surmounted by a golden cross. A statue of Pius VI by

Basilica of Saint Peter, Rome

Canova kneels facing the shrine. Pius is buried here also. He died in France in 1799 as a prisoner of Napoleon.

(6) **FOUR COLOSSAL 16-FOOT STATUES** stand in the niches of the huge pilasters (each 234 feet in circumference). The upper recesses are used as shrines for the greatest relics. The statues are of **SAINT LONGINUS** (northeast), by Mochi, with the lance that pierced the side of Jesus in the recess; **SAINT HELENA** (northwest), by Bolgi, with a fragment of the true cross in the recess; **SAINT VERONICA** (southwest), by Bernini, with the *sudarium*, or veil, which bears the impression of the Savior's features; **SAINT ANDREW** (southeast), by Duquesnoy, with the head of Saint Andrew in the recesses. These relics are exhibited to the people from the balconies of Saint Veronica and Saint Helena in days of high festivals.

Return now to the northeast corner — right front as you enter — of the basilica, where the tour will take you west through the **RIGHT AISLE**.

(7) **PIETÀ**, by Michelangelo (1499). This masterpiece was executed by Michelangelo when he was 24 years old. It is regarded as the finest existing group of devotional sculpture. Every line in the Virgin speaks of life, and every line in Jesus speaks of death. It is the only work ever signed by the master, whose name may be seen on the band crossing the breast of the Virgin. This statue was on display at the New York World's Fair.

(8) The **COLONNA SANTA** (*Vitinea*), to the right of the *Pietà* was once a spiral column which stood in the confessio of the old basilica. It is said that the column was brought from the temple at Jerusalem and was the one Christ leaned against when discoursing with the doctors.

(9) As you proceed down the right aisle you pass the **TOMB OF LEO XII**; the **CHAPEL OF THE CRUCIFIX**; the **CENOTAPH OF QUEEN CHRISTINA** of Sweden; the **ALTAR OF SAINT SEBASTIAN**; the **TOMB OF INNOCENT XII**, with figures of Charity and Justice; the **TOMB OF THE COUNTESS MATILDA OF TUSCANY** (d. 1115), by Bernini, the sarcophagus showing Gregory VII granting absolution to the emperor Henry IV; **BRAMANTE'S TABERNACLE**; the **TOMBS OF GREGORY XIII** (rectifier of the calendar) and **GREGORY XIV**; the mosaic of **SAINT JEROME**; the **GREGORIAN CHAPEL**; the **TOMB OF GREGORY XVI**, with figures of Wisdom and Prudence; the **MADONNA DEL SOCCORSO**; the **TOMB OF BENEDICT XIV** (d. 1758), with figures of Science and Charity; the **MASS OF SAINT BASIL** (a painting) on the left.

A turn to the right leads you past **SAINT WENCESLAUS' ALTAR** to mosaics of **SAINTS PROCESSUS** and **MARTINIANUS** in the center. Then past **SAINT ERASMUS' MARTYRDOM** in mosaic, a turn again toward the west takes you past the statue of **SAN BRUNO** on the left and the monument to **CLEMENT XIII** on the right. This statue of Clement XIII is the best work of Canova (1795). On the left is the figure representing **RELIGION**, and on the right a figure representing **DEATH**. On the left is the **ALTAR OF NAVICELLA**. Walk past the **CHAPEL OF SAINT MICHAEL** and **MICHAEL IN MOSAIC**, past the mosaic of **SANTA PETRONILLA** and the **TOMB OF CLEMENT X** on the right and the mosaic of **TABITHA'S RESURRECTION** on the left, past the **TOMB OF URBAN VIII** (1644) — by Bernini — to the **CATHEDRA OF SAINT PETER** at the extreme west end of the basilica.

(10) **CATHEDRA OF SAINT PETER**. Executed in 1667 in gilt bronze, by Bernini, the cathedra encloses the ancient **EPISCOPAL WOODEN CHAIR USED BY THE APOSTLE PETER**. It is supported by four colossal figures of the Fathers of the Church: Ambrose, Augustine, Athanasius, and Chrysostom. The traditional cathedra also consists of a table-type structure believed to have been used by Saint Peter and his successors at religious ceremonials.

(11) Moving now down the left aisle of the basilica, we pass the **TOMB OF POPE PAUL III** (1549), by Giacomo della Porta — a pupil of Michelangelo — with the figures of Justice on the left and Prudence on the right. This sculpture is said to be the finest in Saint Peter's.

Turning south, one passes on the right the **TOMB OF ALEXANDER VIII** (1691) and on the left mosaics of **SAINT PETER** and **SAINT JOHN** by Mancini. In the **CHAPEL DELLA COLONNA** may be seen the marble relief of the **RETREAT OF ATTILA**, by Algardi, and the altar of the **MADONNA DELLA COLONNA** on the south wall. The **TOMB OF ALEXANDER VII** (1667), by Bernini, is seen next with the figures of Charity and Truth. The painting on slate of the **PUNISHMENT OF SIMON MAGUS**, by Vanni, is seen on the left.

Around the corner to the south is the mosaic of **SAINT THOMAS**, by Camuccini, and in the center is the mosaic of **SAINT PETER'S CRUCIFIXION**, after Reni. Another mosaic of **SAINT VALERIA AND SAINT MARTIAL**, the **TOMB OF PIUS VIII** with statues of Christ, Peter, and Paul, and then the mosaic of **ANANIAS AND SAPPHIRA'S DEATH** are seen before the **CLEMENTINE CHAPEL**. The **MASS OF SAINT GREGORY THE GREAT** and the **TOMB OF PIUS VII** are next, followed by a mosaic after Raphael entitled **TRANSFIGURATION**. The **TOMB OF LEO XI** is on the right and the **TOMB OF INNOCENT XI** (d. 1689) is on the left, with figures of Religion and Justice.

(12) The mosaic **IMMACULATE CONCEPTION**, by Bianchi, is located in the center of the **CHOIR CHAPEL** (*Cappella del Coro*).

(13) As you leave the Choir Chapel, you see on the left the **TOMB OF INNOCENT VIII** (d. 1492), with a bronze work over the sarcophagus. The enthroned figure of the Pope is holding a lance representing the one that pierced the side of Jesus and which is preserved in the basilica. On the right is the **MONUMENT OF PIUS X** (d. 1914).

Moving east along the left aisle, we pass the mosaic **PRESENTATION OF THE VIRGIN**, by Romanelli, the monument of

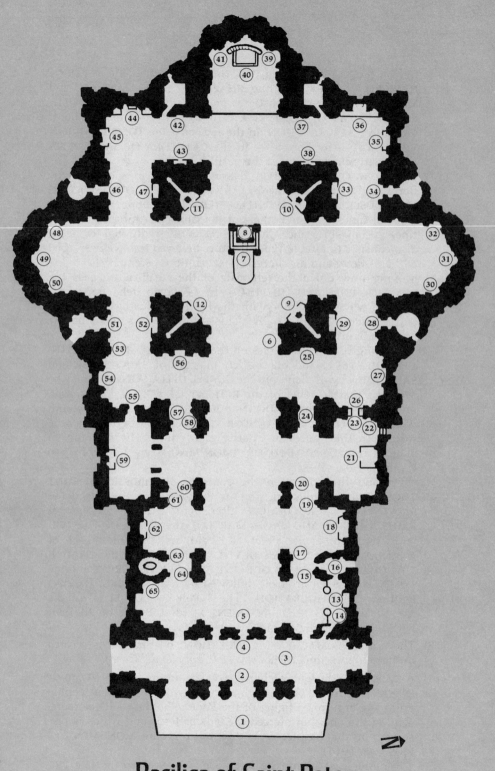

Basilica of Saint Peter

1. Facade by Maderna
2. Mosaic by Giotto
3. Portico by Maderna
4. Bronze doors, with bas-relief by Bernini above
5. Slab of porphyry, marking coronation site
6. Bronze statue of Saint Peter
7. Confessio
8. Baldacchino and high altar
9. Statue of Saint Longinus
10. Statue of Saint Helena
11. Statue of Saint Veronica
12. Statue of Saint Andrew
13. Michelangelo's *Pietà*
14. Colonna Santa
15. Tomb of Leo XII
16. Chapel of the Crucifix
17. Cenotaph of Queen Christina
18. Altar of Saint Sebastian and monuments to Pius XI and Pius XII
19. Tomb of Innocent XII
20. Tomb of Countess Matilda of Tuscany
21. Bramante's tabernacle
22. Doorway leading to the Scala Regia
23. Doorway leading to the organs
24. Tombs of Gregory XIII and Gregory XIV
25. Mosaic of Saint Jerome
26. Gregorian Chapel and Tomb of Gregory XVI
27. Madonna del Soccorso
28. Tomb of Benedict XIV
29. Mass of Saint Basil
30. Saint Wenceslaus' Altar
31. Mosaics of Saints Processus and Martinianus
32. *Saint Erasmus' Martyrdom*

33. Statue of San Bruno and Altar of the Navicella
34. Monument to Clement XIII
35. Chapel of Saint Michael
36. Mosaic of Santa Petronilla
37. Tomb of Clement X
38. *Tabitha's Resurrection*
39. Tomb of Urban VIII
40. Cathedra of Saint Peter
41. Tomb of Paul III
42. Tomb of Alexander VIII
43. Mosaics of Saint Peter and Saint John
44. Saint Leo's Altar
45. Chapel della Colonna
46. Tomb of Alexander VII
47. Altar to Saints Peter and Paul
48. Mosaic of Saint Thomas
49. Saint Peter's Crucifixion
50. Mosaic of Saints Valeria and Martial
51. Tomb of Pius VIII
52. *Ananias and Sapphira's Death*
53. Clementine Chapel
54. Mass of Saint Gregory the Great
55. Tomb of Pius VII
56. *Transfiguration*
57. Tomb of Leo XI
58. Tomb of Innocent XI
59. Choir chapel
60. Tomb of Innocent VIII
61. Monument of Pius X
62. *Presentation of the Virgin,* Urn of Pius X, and monuments to Benedict XV and John XXIII
63. Monument of Maria Clementine Sobiesky
64. Tomb of the Stuarts
65. Baptistry

MARIA CLEMENTINE SOBIESKY, the TOMB OF THE STUARTS, and lastly the BAPTISTRY. The font of the baptistry is said to be the upturned lid of the porphyry sarcophagus which contained the ashes of Hadrian in the Castle of Sant'Angelo, and in which Otho II was subsequently buried.

(14) TO THE DOME. The doorway beneath the monument of Maria Clementine Sobiesky in the left aisle gives access to the dome. An elevator or stairs may be taken to the roof. Another flight of stairs will take you 308 feet above the roof into the top of the dome. At a point 240 feet from the ground you may enter the inside of the dome and get a breathtaking view of the interior of the church and dome. From the top of the dome one can see Rome and its surroundings as if from a helicopter. It is a *must* on the tourist's list. A perpendicular iron ladder ascends to the bronze ball. The ball holds 16 persons.

(15) BENEATH THE PAVEMENT. In the construction of the new basilica, a 13-foot space was left between the pavement of the new and old basilicas to preserve the structure from dampness. This space constitutes the VATICAN GROTTOS, wherein are deposited the majority of the tombs and fragments of sculpture, frescoes, and mosaics that were formerly housed in the old Basilica of Saint Peter. The SACRED CRYPT, approached from an opening in the southeast pilaster, under the statue of Saint Andrew, is the only portion remaining of the old basilica. The bones of Peter are supposedly buried on this level directly beneath the high altar. Studies under the direction of Professor Guarducci, of the University of Rome, are said to have identified the remains of Peter. This discovery was published in March 1965. Pope Paul VI made a statement on June 26, 1969, that the bones had been convincingly identified. However, Graydon F. Snyder, of the Bethany Theological Seminary, disagrees, saying that "where they [the bones] are now may never be known" (*The Biblical Archaeologist*, 32, no. 1 [Feb. 1969]:24). The bones were found in a niche hollowed out of the so-called Red Wall, near which Saint Peter was buried after his martyrdom by Nero in A.D. 64 or 67.

53. CASTEL SANT'ANGELO (Hadrian's Mausoleum). (See also "Art Galleries and Museums" no. 6, below.)

Hadrian's Mausoleum was erected in A.D. 136 as a tomb for himself and the succeeding Caesars of his family. Originally it was covered with white marble and surmounted by statues. As an example of Roman architecture, it was second only to the Colosseum. It served as a fortress in the fifth century and was a place of refuge for the Pope when Rome was invaded. Passages connect the tomb with the Vatican. In A.D. 590, Pope Gregory the Great, leading a procession to pray for an end to the plague in Rome, allegedly saw a vision of the archangel Michael sheathing his sword. This, they believed, meant the plague would end. On top of the tomb a large statue of

Michael commemorates the event. The castle served as a state prison and held such people as Arnaldo da Brescia.

The **BRIDGE OF SANT'ANGELO**, *(Ponte Umberto)*, facing the castle, was built by the emperor Hadrian to serve as a monumental approach to the mausoleum. In 1675 the colossal statues of angels holding "instruments of the passion" were sculptured for the bridge by Bernini's students.

The castle remains in the possession of the popes. It is now a **MUSEUM**, and the fourth floor (papal floor) has beautiful frescoes by artists of the Raphael school. The fifth floor offers a panoramic view of the city.

54. **PALAZZO DI GIUSTIZIA** (Palace of Justice).

55. **PIAZZA GIUSEPPE MAZZINI.**

56. **FORO ITALICO** (former *Foro Mussolini*). This consists of a group of stadiums and buildings for sports. Note the 55-foot obelisk made from a single block of Carrara marble.

57. **MILVIAN BRIDGE** *(Ponte Milvio)* over the **TIBER RIVER** *(Tevere)*. The emperor Diocletian was the first Roman emperor to abdicate. He stepped down of his own volition in A.D. 305 after 21 years. He intended to have two Caesars succeed him as Augusti and in time turn the government over to their own appointed Caesars, but it took less than a year for this arrangement to break down. Soldiers once more tried to dictate succession, and by 311 there were four rival Augusti.

One of those desiring the office was Constantine. He marched on Rome to battle it out with a rival claimant, Maxentius. Eusebius, the biographer, said that Constantine had a vision as he went to battle at the Milvian Bridge. He supposedly saw a cross or the letters *chi* and *rho*, the first two in Christ's name, in the sky and the inscription *Hoc signo vince* ("In this sign conquer"). Constantine ordered the Christian labarum (☧) emblazoned on his soldiers' standards, helmets, and shields. Maxentius lost the battle and his life; the west and the Christians won Constantine. When he became the sole emperor of the west in 312, he was known as the first Christian emperor, and Christianity became the state religion. This was the wedding of Church and state, and the document permitting freedom to Christianity in A.D. 313 is known as the *Edict of Milan*.

Constantine died in 337, and it was not until the following year that Eusebius, his biographer, told the story of the supposed conversion. After the conversion, Roman funds went into church coffers and bishops became servants of the state. Imperial regulations and church regulations were united. The decline of Rome was hastened when Constantine decided to move the capital to Byzantium and rename the city Constantinople. It was to be a replica of Rome, even to the seven hills. There Roman emperors continued to rule for another 1,100 years.

Constantine was finally baptized a Christian on his deathbed, in 337.

58. **VILLA BORGHESE** (seventeenth century). This is Rome's largest and finest park. It was once the summer residence of the Borghese family. On its highest point is the **BORGHESE MUSEUM AND GALLERY.** Famous art pieces include the following sculptures: **PAULINA BORGHESE** (Sister of Napoleon I), by Canova; **DAVID AND HIS SLING, APOLLO AND DAPHNE,** and the **RAPE OF PERSEPHONE,** all by Bernini. The gallery contains one of the finest collections of paintings in Rome. The most renowned painting is Titian's **SACRED AND PROFANE LOVE** (1515). Others include the **MADONNA AND CHILD,** by Lorenzo di Credi; **THE ENTOMBMENT,** by Raphael; **VENUS,** by Franciabigio; **SAINT JEROME,** by Barocci; **DANAË WITH CUPIDS,** by Correggio; and **THE THREE AGES,** by Sassoferrato.

The **NATIONAL MUSEUM OF MODERN ART** and the **ZOO** are also located in the villa. From **MOUNT PINCIO,** a scenographic panorama of Rome can be admired. (See also "Art Galleries and Museums" nos. 1 and 8, below.)

59. **PIAZZA DEL POPOLO** (Square of the People). This is a masterpiece of town planning by G. Valadier. The Church of Santa Maria del Popolo and the twin churches of Santa Maria in Monte Santo and Santa Maria dei Miracoli face the square. On the center of the square

Milvian Bridge, Rome

is the second obelisk of the city, brought to Rome by Augustus. It dates back to Ramses II and the thirteenth century B.C.

60. The **MAUSOLEUM OF AUGUSTUS** is located in the center of the Piazza Augusto.

61. **ARTISTS' QUARTER** (*Via del Babuino*).

62. The **SPANISH STEPS** (*Piazza di Spagna*) are perhaps the most magnificent flight of steps in the world. They were a gift from France in 1725 to pave the muddy slope to the French church. They begin in the Spanish Square, where the residence of the Spanish embassy to the Holy See is located. The 137 steps of the grand staircase, designed by De Sanctis (1725), lead to the terrace of the French **CHURCH OF SANTA TRINITÀ DEI MONTI**. (See church no. 21, below.) The house where Keats died in 1821 stands on the right at the foot of the steps. It is now a museum in memory of Keats and Shelley. At the foot of the steps there is a quaint, boat-shaped **FOUNTAIN** called the **BARCACCIA**, by Pietro Bernini. To the south stands the **COLUMN OF THE IMMACULATE CONCEPTION**, erected to commemorate the dogma of the Immaculate Conception of the Holy Virgin.

63. **FONTANA DEL TRITONE**, by Bernini. Located in the Piazza Barberini, these are perhaps the most original fountains in Rome. Four dolphins form a base for the basin and a Triton blows a stream of water into the air from his conch.

64. **BARBERINI GALLERY**. In the Palazzo Barberini is the Gallery of Barberini. It contains among other pictures the famous **FORNARINA** by Raphael.

65. **CHURCH OF SANTA MARIA CONCEZIONE**. (See church no. 7, below.)

The Vatican

66. **VATICAN CITY**. This unique city is an independent sovereign center of the Roman Catholic church. It covers 109 acres and has a population of about 1,000. It contains more art treasures than any empire. It has its own railroad station, post office, mosaic factory, and radio station. The Vatican has been the papal residence since 1377.

VATICAN PALACE

The **VATICAN PALACE** became the residence of the popes after 1377. Before this date they had resided at the Lateran Palace. The Sistine Chapel was added in 1473, and the Belvedere in the garden was erected in 1490. With the addition of the Vatican museums, it is the largest palace in the world. It has 11,000 halls, chapels, rooms, and apartments.

MUSEUMS

The most ancient public museums — and the most splendid — in the world are housed in the Vatican. They include the **COLLECTIONS**

OF ANTIQUITIES, the LIBRARY, the BORGIA APARTMENT, RAPHAEL'S STANZE, the SISTINE CHAPEL, and the PICTURE GALLERY.

COLLECTIONS OF ANTIQUITIES. The MUSEUM OF PIUS CLEMENTINE contains sculptures. The ETRUSCAN and EGYPTIAN MUSEUMS are small but good. The majority of the Egyptian works were found in Hadrian's Villa at Tivoli. The CHIARAMONTE MUSEUM contains a collection of 800 pagan and Christian inscriptions, busts, statues, sarcophagi, and bas-reliefs. The MUSEUM OF CHRISTIAN ANTIQUITIES contains objects from the catacombs dating from the first five centuries.

The VATICAN LIBRARY is a huge hall 50 feet wide and 200 feet long. The ceiling is painted with frescoes. The library contains about 500,000 printed volumes, 60,000 ancient manuscripts, and 7,000 incunabula. The CODEX VATICANUS, HOMILIES OF GREGORY THE GREAT, the DIVINE COMEDY of Dante, and the CORRESPONDENCE OF HENRY VIII AND ANNE BOLEYN are a part of the collection.

The BORGIA APARTMENT is a series of 6 rooms with frescoes and stuccos dating from A.D. 492–95. These rooms were occupied by Pope Alexander VI (Borgia) and his family. Here he lived in fabulous luxury for 11 years.

The STANZE OF RAPHAEL consists of one large room and four smaller halls corresponding to the Borgia apartments immediately below them. Raphael was 25 years of age in 1508 when he began to paint the four medallions representing figures symbolic of the moral powers — Theology, Philosophy, Poetry, and Justice — on the ceiling of the Stanza della Segnatura. Pope Julius (1503) loved this work so much that he assigned Raphael the task of decorating the walls of the four rooms with frescoes. Raphael died in 1520 and his pupils finished most of the work. Frescoes include the MASS OF BOLSENA, LIBERATION OF PETER FROM PRISON, MIRACULOUS EXPULSION OF HELIODORUS FROM THE TEMPLE, and ATTILA REPULSED FROM ROME BY POPE LEO I.

An 18-foot scene of the VICTORY OF CONSTANTINE over Maxentius at the Milvian Bridge over the Tiber River shows Constantine winning in "the name of Christ." One large room, the Sala di Constantino, illustrates the victory of Christianity through the instrumentality of Constantine and the establishment of the Church. A large fresco represents Constantine addressing his soldiers regarding the appearance of the cross he purportedly beheld as he went into the battle with Maxentius. He then used the ensign "sign of the cross" (☧), or *labarum*, on his shields, belt buckles, and so forth, and the motto was "In this sign conquer."

CONSTANTINE'S DONATION OF ROME TO POPE SYLVESTER is a painting of the Old Saint Peter's. The emperor is shown kneeling at the feet of the Pope and offering him a golden statuette of an armed soldier. On this donation was based the power of the Pope to bestow the crown of the empire. Charlemagne and all succeeding emperors received their crowns by virtue of this gift.

Above: Sistine Chapel, Rome
Below: Government Palace, Vatican City

One large wall fresco depicts the **BAPTISM OF CONSTANTINE**.

The **CHAPEL OF NICCOLO V** has frescoes depicting the martyrdom of Saint Lawrence and Saint Stephen. The frescoes were done by Beato Angelico.

The **LOGGIAS OF RAPHAEL** consist of a long gallery decorated in 1517–19 from designs by Raphael or under his direction. A series of 48 beautiful scenes on the ceiling is known as **RAPHAEL'S BIBLE**.

SISTINE CHAPEL (seat of the conclave for the election of the popes). The magnificent Sistine Chapel was built in 1473 by Giovanni dei Dolci, under Sixtus IV. Thus its name *Sistine*. Several Florentine painters were responsible for the fresco paintings in the upper long walls in 1482. Michelangelo was employed to paint the ceiling in 1508, and he completed it in 1512. Twenty-two years later, when he was nearly 60 years of age, Michelangelo was asked by Clement VII to paint the altar wall with the famous **LAST JUDGMENT**. This took Michelangelo 8 years to complete and was finished in 1541.

The **MARBLE SCREENS** *(iconostases)* — that divide the room into two parts like Solomon's temple — and the **SINGING GALLERY** are the work of Mino da Fiesole. The **ALTAR**, where only the Pope officiates, is inlaid with mother-of-pearl.

The 6 frescoes on each side wall, painted about 1483 by and under the direction of Botticelli, illustrate episodes from the lives of Christ and Moses. The Old Testament scenes on the left wall face corresponding scenes of fulfillment from the New Testament. The pairs of opposite scenes are as follows: (1) the **CIRCUMCISION OF MOSES' SONS** and the **BAPTISM OF JESUS**, (2) the **LEADING INTO THE WILDERNESS** and the **CLEANSING OF THE LEPER AND TEMPTATION OF CHRIST**; (3) the **ISRAELITES' DEPARTURE FROM EGYPT** and the **CALLING OF THE FIRST DISCIPLES**; (4) the **GIVING OF THE LAW** and the **SERMON ON THE MOUNT**; (5) the **PUNISHMENT OF KORAH, DATHAN, AND ABIRAM** and **CHRIST GIVING THE KEYS TO SAINT PETER**; (6) the **PROMULGATION OF THE LAW AND DEATH OF MOSES** and the **LAST SUPPER**.

The **CEILING** of the Sistine Chapel is considered Michelangelo's masterpiece and the most powerful piece of painting in existence. The combination of architect, sculptor, and painter was required to produce this masterpiece. Michelangelo was not satisfied with the work of other painters; so he painted them himself in a period of 3½ years (1508–12).

Over 200 figures are shown in the various scenes. The center pictures on the ceiling are as follows: (1) the **SEPARATION OF LIGHT FROM DARKNESS**; (2) the **CREATION OF SUN AND MOON**; (3) the **SEPARATION OF EARTH FROM WATERS**; (4) the **CREATION OF MAN**; (5) the **CREATION OF EVE**; (6) the **FALL OF MAN**; (7) the **SACRIFICE OF NOAH**; (8) the **DELUGE**; (9) the **DRUNKENNESS OF NOAH**.

On the sides of the center section are the paintings of various prophets and sibyls, the biggest figures in the painting. The striking figures of the youths in the empty spaces of the framework are some of the master's most beautiful creations.

The **LAST JUDGMENT** scene, behind the altar, measures 66 feet in height and 33 feet in width. It is the largest and most comprehensive painting in the world. This painting took Michelangelo 8½ years to

Above: Rome and Saint Peter's Basilica, from Castel Sant'Angelo

Below: Bridges over the Tiber, from Castel Sant'Angelo

paint, making a total of 12 years that he spent painting the Sistine Chapel.

The *Last Judgment* is a stunning apocalyptical vision (perhaps based somewhat on Dante's *Inferno*) divided into four groupings:

(1) On the top, groups of **ANGELS** bear the instruments of the passion.

(2) In the center top, below the angels, **CHRIST** appears as the judge, with the Virgin Mary on his right and the saints and martyrs on his left. They are holding up the symbols of instruments of their martyrdom: Peter and the keys, Saint Lawrence and the gridiron, Saint Bartholomew with his skin and a knife, Saint Blasius with the rake, Saint Catherine with the wheel, Saint Sebastian with the arrows, and other saints with their crosses.

(3) In the center the **SEVEN ANGELS OF THE APOCALYPSE** sound their trumpets to awaken the dead, while other angels show the damned the books of judgment. The condemned ones are delivered to the fury of the demons, each figure typifying one of the seven capital sins.

(4) In the lowest part, the **DEAD** emerge from their graves and shake off their shrouds. Michelangelo portrayed himself in the garb of a monk on the extreme left bottom corner. Charon, with his boat in hell ready to ferry souls across the River Styx, is striking down the rebellious with his oar. On the extreme right bottom is the judge Minos, whose face is a portrait of Biagio da Cesena, master of ceremonies to Paul III. Cesena had censured the picture on account of the nudity of the figures, and Michelangelo obtained revenge by painting him among those condemned, with the ears of an ass and a serpent wound around his body. Later, Pope Pius IV had Daniele da Volterra cover the most prominent pictures with draperies.

Smoke from candles and torches blackened the walls over the years, but they have recently been restored from their blackened condition.

OTHER GALLERIES. The **SALA REGIA** was built as a hall to give audience to ambassadors. The ceilings and walls are decorated with rich frescoes, one of which is the **CRUCIFIXION OF SAINT PETER.**

The **SALA DELL'IMMACOLATA** has paintings dedicated to the dogma of the Immaculate Conception of the Virgin Mary.

The **GALLERIA GEOGRAFICA** (Gallery of Maps), dating back to 1585, measures 164 yards in length. It is so named because of the enormous maps of the Italian provinces painted on the walls.

The **GALLERIA DEI CANDELABRI** gets its name from 8 very tall marble candelabra.

The **SALA DELLA BIGA** has many beautiful pieces of sculpture, such as a copy of the **DISCOBOLUS OF MYRON, BIGA, THE TWO-HORSE CHARIOT,** and **APHRODITE** after Praxiteles.

The **PINACOTECA,** or **GALLERY OF PICTURES,** is composed of the pictures of the world's master painters. Raphael's last great work, **THE TRANSFIGURATION,** is a part of the collection, as is Leonardo da Vinci's **SAINT JEROME.** Nine tapestries of Raphael hang in this gallery. They were originally to be hung on the lower part of the walls of the Sistine Chapel and were hung there in 1519. Twice they were carried off by conquerors of Rome, but they found their way back. The subjects of the principal scenes of the tapestries were chosen from the lives of the apostles Peter and Paul.

Other Sites

These churches, museums, and other points of interest are not necessarily listed in the order in which one would encounter them while traveling about the city. Those the tourist wishes to visit, however, can be incorporated into the other tours of Rome at his convenience.

67. CHURCH OF SANTA MARIA SOPRA MINERVA. (See church no. 6, below.)

68. CHURCH OF SANTA CROCE IN GERUSALEMME. (See church no. 8, below.)

69. CHURCH OF SAN SEBASTIANO. (See church no. 10, below.)

70. CHURCH OF SANTI QUATTRO CORONATI. (See church no. 11, below.)

71. CHURCH OF SANTA PUDENZIANA. (See church no. 13, below.)

72. CHURCH OF SANTA MARIA IN TRASTEVERE. (See church no 14, below.)

73. CHURCH OF SANTA FRANCESCA ROMANA. (See church no. 15, below.)

74. CHURCH OF SAN PIETRO IN MONTORIO. (See church no. 16, below.)

75. CHURCH OF SANTA MARIA DEL POPOLO. (See church no. 17, below.)

76. CHURCH OF SANTA PRASSEDE. (See church no. 18, below.)

77. CHURCH OF SANTA MARIA DEGLI ANGELI. (See church no. 19, below.)

78. CHURCH OF SAN GREGORIO MAGNO. (See church no. 20, below.)

79. CHURCH OF SANTA TRINITÀ DEI MONTI. (See church no. 21, below.)

80. CHURCH OF SANT'ANDREA DELLA VALLE. (See church no. 22, below.)

81. CHURCH OF SANTA CECILIA IN TRASTEVERE. (See church no. 23, below.)

82. CHURCH OF SANTA SABINA. (See church no. 24, below.)

83. CHURCH OF SANTA MARIA IN COSMEDIN. (See church no. 25, below.)

84. FARNESINA (Myth of Psyche). (See "Art Galleries and Museums" no. 7, below.)

85. NATIONAL GALLERY OF ANTIQUE ART. (See "Art Galleries and Museums" no. 9, below.)

86. **MUSEUM OF VILLA GIULIA.** (See "Art Galleries and Museums" no. 11, below.)

87. **MUSEUM OF VILLA ALBANI.** (See "Art Galleries and Museums" no. 12, below.)

88. **DORIA GALLERY.** (See "Art Galleries and Museums" no. 13, below.)

89. **COLONNA GALLERY.** (See "Art Galleries and Museums" no. 14, below.)

Twenty-Five Churches of Rome

(1) [Site 52] **BASILICA OF SAINT PETER.** (See site 52, in the northwest Rome section, above.)

(2) [Sites 25–27] **BASILICA OF SAINT JOHN IN LATERAN, SCALA SANTA, PALAZZO DEL LATERANO** (ca. A.D. 325–1600). This basilica is known as the mother and head of all churches. It is *the* church in Rome, taking priority over all other churches in the city, and its canons take precedence over the canons of Saint Peter's. It is the first Catholic church built in Rome and the world. It was founded by Constantine in A.D. 315 in or near the great Lateran Palace, which he had presented to Pope Sylvester I as his episcopal residence and which was occupied by all the popes until their removal to Avignon in 1307. It was at first dedicated to the "Holy Savior," but after its destruction by earthquake in 898 it was erected again and dedicated to John the Baptist. It was destroyed by fire in 1308 and rebuilt over a period of years. Most of it dates from the seventeenth century. Note the original Roman **STATUE OF CONSTANTINE** in the Atrium. Note also the beautiful Romanesque-style **CLOISTERS** that were designed by Vassalletus in 1300. A beautiful sculpture of the PIETÀ by Montanti is located in the basilica.

The interior is 426 feet long. Statues of the apostles came from the school of Bernini. The ceiling is sculptured with the coats of arms of popes and emblems of the passion, designed by della Porta.

The **HIGH ALTAR**, at which only the Pope or a substitute appointed by him may celebrate mass, contains many traditional relics, including the **HEADS OF SAINT PETER AND SAINT PAUL**. It contains also a **TABLE** from the catacombs that is said to have been used as an **ALTAR BY SAINT PETER**.

The mosaics in the apse were made in 1290 by Iacobus Torriti. The apse represents the union of heaven and earth by baptism. Ecclesiastial councils like that held by Pope Innocent III in 1215, were held here.

The **TRANSEPT** (altar of the sacrament), erected under Clement XIII, houses the **CEDAR TABLE** which, according to tradition, served for the Last Supper.

In the Corsini chapel is the PIETÀ, by Montanti.

The **LATERAN BAPTISTRY**, an octagonal building, for a long time the only baptistry in Rome, was the model for all later buildings of the kind. According to Roman legend, Constantine's baptism, near his death in A.D. 337, was performed here. The **PAINTINGS** on the walls, by Carlo Maratti, represent the vision of Constantine, his victory over Maxentius, and his triumphal entry into Rome.

The **SCALA SANTA**, a flight of 28 marble steps which traditionally came from Pilate's Palace and which Jesus was supposed to have ascended, were brought to Rome by the empress Helena, the mother of Constantine. It was once part of the old Lateran Palace, but was later removed to its present site. The stairs may be ascended only on the knees. (There are side stairs for the descent). An indulgence of 9 years is granted for this act of devotion. On these steps Martin Luther concluded that the "just" shall live by "faith." So many worshipers have ascended the steps that three different sets of walnut planks have been used to cover the steps. At the top of the stairs is the old private chapel of the popes, the **SANCTA SANCTORUM** (sixth century). Over the altar is a picture of Jesus that according to tradition was begun by Saint Luke and finished by "invisible hands." This relic was brought from Jerusalem to Rome in the eighth century. An inscription in the chapel states: "There is not in the whole world a place more holy." No woman is allowed in the chapel, and it is only open for a few minutes 6 times a year.

Adjoining the Scala Santa is the **TRIBUNE**, a reconstruction of a part of the old **LATERAN PALACE**, in which the Pope entertained Charlemagne after the coronation of A.D. 800 in Saint Peter's. The coronation gave rise to the Holy Roman Empire. Mosaics portray Christ giving the keys to Pope Sylvester and the labarum to Constantine. In one mosaic, Pope Leo and Charlemagne are distinguished by the square nimbus, or glory, around their heads. (A square nimbus is for the living only.)

The **LATERAN MUSEUM** was once located in the Lateran Palace but was moved to the Vatican Museum. (See "Art Galleries and Museums" no. 5, below.)

(3) [Site 19] **CHURCH OF SAN PIETRO IN VINCOLI** (Saint Peter in Chains). This church, whose construction and ornamentation span the period 442–1503, is also called *Basilica Eudoxiana*. It was built as a shrine for the **CHAINS** with which Saint Peter was bound at Jerusalem and those used during the apostle's captivity in Rome. The chains are now preserved in a bronze tabernacle under the high altar. On the vaulting is a painting by Parodi representing the cure of a demoniac by the touch of the holy chains.

One of Michelangelo's most celebrated sculptures is a mausoleum of Pope Julius II. Michelangelo's **MOSES** is flanked by his figures of **RACHEL** (left) and **LEAH**. Moses is a colossal figure animated by a superhuman power. Some feel they can see in the statue of Moses the representation of three men: the genius Michelangelo, haughty Pope Julius II, and lawgiver-priest Moses. When Moses came down from Mount Sinai after receiving the Ten Commandments, the Bible says, "the skin of his face shone" (Exod. 34:29–30). *Shone* is translated from a rare word which contains the consonants of *horn*, and it was so rendered in the Latin Vulgate version of the Bible. As a result of this translation, Michelangelo sculptured his famous *Moses* with horns.

(4) [Site 40] **BASILICA OF SAINT PAUL OUTSIDE THE WALLS** (A.D. 386 and 1854). Erected on the site of a church built by Constantine over the tomb of Saint Paul, this church was destroyed by fire in 1823 and rebuilt in 1854. The plans and dimensions were the same as the original.

The interior is 394 feet by 197 feet and 75 feet high. The **TRI-UMPHAL ARCH**, adorned with outstanding fifth-century mosaics, was preserved from the fire of 1823. The mosaics show Christ and the 24 elders of the Apocalypse. Fragments of the old bronze gates dating back to 1070 still remain.

(5) [Site 24] **BASILICA OF SANTA MARIA MAGGIORE.** Dating back to A.D. 352 or later, this church is also named *Santa Maria ad Nives* (Latin *nives* = "snow"), because of a fall of snow on Aug. 5, 352, which is said to have determined the exact limits of its site. According to the tradition, the Virgin Mary appeared to Pope Liberius and Johannes, a devout Roman patrician, and told them to build a chapel where the snow would fall the next day. This is shown in mosaic on the inside of the building.

Johannes built the edifice at his own expense. A fine bell tower on the building dates back to the thirteenth century. It is the loftiest and one of the best preserved in Rome. The church's interior is 280 feet in length. The ceiling, dating from 1498, was gilded with the first gold brought by Columbus from America, presented to Alexander VI by Ferdinand and Isabella of Spain. The pavement, of Cosmatesque design, dates from about 1150.

The 31 **MOSAICS** adorning the Arch of Triumph are perhaps the finest examples of early (fifth-century) Christian art. They represent biblical scenes. One shows Melchizedek offering bread to Abraham.

In the confessio of the high altar are preserved **RELICS OF SAINT MATTHEW** and **FIVE BOARDS** said to have come from the **MANGER** at Bethlehem.

(6) [Site 67] **CHURCH OF SANTA MARIA SOPRA MINERVA.** Dating from 1280, this church stands on the site of a temple of Minerva. It is the only ancient Gothic church in Rome. The body of **SAINT CATHERINE OF SIENA** is preserved here, and Michelangelo's famous **CHRIST WITH THE CROSS** (1521) is here. The monastery adjoining the church was the **HEADQUARTERS OF THE INQUISITION.** Giordano Bruno, the philosopher, received his death sentence here in 1600, and here in 1633 Galileo, aged 70, was tried before its tribunal for the "heresy" of saying that the earth revolved around the sun. Galileo was obliged to recant on his knees before receiving absolution; but as he rose he is said to have concluded his recantation with the whisper, "Still it moves."

(7) [Site 65] **CHURCH OF SANTA MARIA CONCEZIONE,** Cemetery of the Capuchins. The cemetery has four grim chambers containing holy earth from Jerusalem in which monks are buried. The decora-

tions of these vaults are made of the bones of departed monks. Bare skulls and bones are piled row upon row, and designs made of bones are on the walls and ceilings.

(8) [Site 68] **CHURCH OF SANTA CROCE IN GERUSALEMME**. This is one of the seven churches of Rome. It supposedly has a **PORTION OF THE CROSS OF JESUS** that Saint Helena, mother of Constantine, brought from Jerusalem. This provided a shrine for those who could not go to the Holy Land. The church was rebuilt in 1114 and modernized in 1743. In addition to a portion of the cross and its inscription, the sacred relics include one of the **NAILS** used to crucify Jesus, **THORNS** from the crown, and the **FINGER** with which Thomas convinced himself of the reality of the wound in the side of Christ. The floor of the tribune is built of soil from Jerusalem.

(9) [Site 5] **CHURCH OF SANTA MARIA D'ARACOELI** (sixth century A.D.). This church was erected on the Capitoline hill and is ascended by a flight of 124 steps built in 1348. In the sacristy is the celebrated miracle-working image of the **SANTISSIMO BAMBINO**. It is a small figure of a baby carved out of olive wood from the Mount of Olives, swathed in gold and silver tissue. According to popular belief, the bambino is invested with extraordinary powers in curing the sick. It is in constant requisition in severe cases, and its practice brings in more fees than any physician in Rome. It is always borne in a private car under the care of two Franciscan monks. As it passes through the streets, devout Catholics kneel and cross themselves.

(10) [Site 69] **CHURCH OF SAN SEBASTIANO** (seventeenth century). This church was built over the catacombs. It contains the remains of the martyred Saint Sebastian and the celebrated stone bearing the **IMPRESSION LEFT BY THE SAVIOR'S FEET** when he met Saint Peter fleeing from Rome at the spot now marked by the chapel of "Domine Quo Vadis?" on the Appian Way.

(11) [Site 70] **CHURCH OF SANTI QUATTRO CORONATI**. This medieval church was dedicated to four painters and five sculptors who were martyred by Diocletian. Eight frescoes detail the legendary history of the conversion of Constantine, of his incurable leprosy, and his renouncing of the remedy (which was to bathe in the warm blood of 3,000 infants). He was baptized, built churches, and gave up the Lateran to the Pope.

(12) [Site 48] **CHURCH OF SAINT AGNES**. Originally built by Constantine in A.D. 324 over the grave of the martyred Saint Agnes, this church is interesting because it has preserved many characteristics of the early Christian basilicas. The best preserved **CATACOMBS** in Rome are here.

On Saint Agnes' day (Jan. 21) two lambs are placed on the altar and blessed. They are then tended by nuns until Easter; then their wool is used to make pallia.

(13) [Site 71] **CHURCH OF SANTA PUDENZIANA**. This is traditionally one of the oldest churches in Rome. It stands on the site of the house

of Senator Pudens, where Saint Peter lodged from A.D. 41 to 50 and made many thousands of converts, including the senator's two daughters. The church has been restored many times.

(14) [Site 72] CHURCH OF SANTA MARIA IN TRASTEVERE (second century). This church was founded in the second century on the site where a spring of oil miraculously welled up on the night of the Nativity. Pope Innocent II is buried here.

(15) [Site 73] CHURCH OF SANTA FRANCESCA ROMANA (ninth century). Built on the site of the temple of Venus and Roma, this church was originally named *Sancta Maria Nova*. Over the high altar is a BYZANTINE MADONNA, traditionally attributed to Saint Luke. Nearby, built into the wall, are two PAVING STONES FROM THE SACRA VIA, which, according to tradition, have the imprint made by the knees of Saint Peter when he knelt to pray for the punishment of Simon Magus, who was displaying his magic by flying across the Forum.

(16) [Site 74] CHURCH OF SAN PIETRO IN MONTORIO (fifteenth century). This church was built by funds from Ferdinand and Isabella of Spain. According to medieval tradition, this was the site of the martyrdom of Saint Peter. In the court on the right is a circular temple called the TEMPIETTO OF BRAMANTE, erected in 1502 on the spot where Peter was martyred. Sebastiano del Piombo's painting of the SCOURGING OF CHRIST is in the church.

(17) [Site 75] The CHURCH OF SANTA MARIA DEL POPOLO (1099) stands near the site where Nero was buried. In the adjoining Augustinian convent, Martin Luther resided while in Rome. Art works of Raphael, Pinturicchio, Sansorino, and others adorn its walls. Sepulchral chapels and monuments of cardinals dating to the Renaissance period are the church's chief attraction.

(18) [Site 76] CHURCH OF SANTA PRASSEDE (A.D. 822). Built on a site dating from A.D. 150, this church contains more mosaics than any other church in Rome. In one of the niches is a portion of the COLUMN AT WHICH THE LORD WAS SCOURGED (according to tradition).

(19) [Site 77] CHURCH OF SANTA MARIA DEGLI ANGELI (1563). This church was built by Michelangelo and formed out of one of the great halls of the Thermae of Diocletian, the largest of all ancient Roman baths. The church is one of the most sacred edifices in Rome.

(20) [Site 78] CHURCH OF SAN GREGORIO MAGNO. This church's construction and ornamentation span the period from 590 to the 1600s. It was built originally by Pope Gregory the Great (590–604). Saint Augustine was a monk in the adjoining monastery, and it was from here he was sent to England on a mission.

(21) [Site 79] CHURCH OF SANTA TRINITÀ DEI MONTI (1492–1816). The interior contains Daniele da Volterra's famous art work titled DESCENT FROM THE CROSS. The church stands at the top of the Spanish Steps.

(22) [Site 80] **CHURCH OF SANT'ANDREA DELLA VALLE** (1591). This church has an ornate facade and the largest dome in Rome, next to Saint Peter's.

(23) [Site 81] **CHURCH OF SANTA CECILIA IN TRASTEVERE** (third century). Beneath the high altar lies the body of Saint Cecilia, who, having converted her husband, was martyred in the second century. In the right aisle is the bathroom where, according to legend, Cecilia was thrust into boiling water and afterwards beheaded.

(24) [Site 82] **CHURCH OF SANTA SABINA.** This church is noted for its sculptured scriptural scenes in cypress wood.

(25) [Site 83] **CHURCH OF SANTA MARIA IN COSMEDIN.** This church was founded in the sixth century on the site of an ancient Roman temple. It has been rebuilt many times. In the portico is the **BOCCA DELLA VERITÀ**, a marble disc representing a human face. In medieval times a suspected person was required, in taking an oath, to place his hand in the mouth of this mask, in the belief that it would close if he swore falsely.

Art Galleries and Museums

(1) [Site 58] **VILLA BORGHESE.** This is a magnificent park laid out in the seventeenth century by Cardinal Scipione Borghese and used by the people of Rome. In 1902 it was purchased by the state and given to the city. The **CASINO** consists of two floors of art work, the lower floor containing ancient and modern sculptures and the upper floor the picture gallery.

The statuary consists of several works of Bernini, such as the **RAPE OF PERSEPHONE, APOLLO AND DAPHNE,** and **DAVID.** Canova's **PRINCESS PAULINA BORGHESE** (sister of Napoleon I and wife of Prince Camillo Borghese) is one of his very best works.

The picture gallery contains pictures by Botticelli, di Credi, Sarto, Barocci, Raphael, Pontormo, and many others. Perhaps the most celebrated of all the pieces is **SACRED AND PROFANE LOVE** (i.e., heavenly and earthly love) by Titian (ca. 1515). (See also site 58, "Villa Borghese," in the northwest Rome section, above.)

(2) [Site 6] **PALAZZO DEI CONSERVATORI.** On the Capitoline hill in front of the senator's palace (city municipality), and approached by a beautiful staircase, are two palaces designed by Michelangelo, the **PALAZZO DEI CONSERVATORI** and the **CAPITOLINE MUSEUM.** The Conservatori houses a collection of ancient sculptures, bronzes, and other works of art. On the first floor are the **HALLS OF THE CONSERVATORI** and the **NEW CAPITOLINE MUSEUM**; on the second floor is the **PICTURE GALLERY** (*Pinacoteca Capitolina*).

Of special interest is the **ETRUSCAN WOLF OF THE CAPITOL** by Pollaiuolo. The wolf is said to have nourished the twins Romulus and Remus. This sculpture dates back to 500 B.C. The **CAVASPINA,** or **THORN PULLER** (extractor), is bronze. The head and body were cast separately. Note the hair. The head was designed for an upright statue in the fifth century B.C. (Roman or Greek?) The ESQUILINE VENUS is also a beautiful work.

(3) [Site 6] The CAPITOLINE MUSEUM was founded by Clement XII and augmented by other popes. It contains many admirable ancient masterpieces and a unique collection of portrait busts of members of the various imperial families and other celebrities. Among the more famous works are the DYING GAUL (third century B.C.), a copy in marble of the bronze statue of the MONUMENT OF PERGAMOS, CUPID (Love) AND PSYCHE, the GREEK PHILOSOPHER, and the SATYR, a copy of an original by Praxiteles (the Marble Faun of Hawthorne's romance).

The HALL OF THE EMPERORS houses a valuable collection of busts. In one salon there are 84 busts of Roman emperors and dignitaries. The other salon has busts of illustrious men, such as philosophers, statesmen, and warriors. Among the most important are HOMER, SOCRATES, SOPHOCLES, EURIPIDES, and PLATO.

The ROOM OF DOVES has a MOSAIC OF DOVES that was found in Hadrian's Villa at Tivoli.

The ROOM OF VENUS has the CAPITOLINE VENUS found at Suburra in the seventeenth century.

(4) [Site 23] The NATIONAL MUSEUM (Museo delle Terme) is located in a part of the BATHS OF DIOCLETIAN and was founded in 1899 to house the ancient remains unearthed in Rome since 1870. It rivals the largest museums in the world. Among the masterpieces are the statue of ATHENA PARTHENOS, a marble statue that is a replica of the Athena that was located in the Parthenon in Athens; the BIRTH OF VENUS (Aphrodite) out of the foam of the sea, a bas-relief in marble on the LUDOVISI THRONE, dating back to the fifth century B.C.; THE GAUL AND HIS WIFE; a third century B.C. marble group, APHRODITE OF CNIDUS; the DISCOLOLUS OF CASTLEPORZIANO; the DAUGHTER OF NIOBE; VENUS GENITRIX; JUNO LUDOVISI (fourth century B.C.); and VENUS OF CYRENE (fourth century B.C.). Altars, bas-reliefs, sarcophagi, inscriptions, and so on are multitudinous.

(5) [Site 26] The LATERAN MUSEUM (Museo Cristiano) is now moved to the Vatican. The Lateran was the residence of the popes from the time of Constantine until the departure to Avignon in 1307. The present buildings were rebuilt in 1308 after a destructive fire. The Lateran Museum once existed here, but the art and artifacts have been incorporated into the Vatican Museum.

(6) [Site 53] CASTLE OF SANT'ANGELO (Castel Sant'Angelo). This ancient castle is connected with the Vatican by a corridor in order that popes may escape to the castle in times of danger. Many a pontiff sought refuge within its walls. Its holdings include ancient weapons of war and the beautiful rooms of the papal apartments. The LIBRARY or RECEPTION ROOM, BATHROOM, BEDROOM, and HALL OF THE COUNCIL are beautifully decorated. (See also site 53, in the section on northwest Rome, above.)

(7) [Site 84] The FARNESINA (Myth of Pysche) was built in 1508-

11 as a gay summer residence of papal banker Agostino Chigi of Siena. Raphael composed, designed, and began fascinating frescoes that portray the fable of Cupid and Psyche. Other beautiful frescoes are by Raphael or other noted artists. Most of the figures are nude.

(8)   [Site 58] **NATIONAL GALLERY OF MODERN ART.** Near the Villa Borghese Museum is this large, beautiful gallery of modern art. It is extremely interesting.

(9)   [Site 85] **NATIONAL GALLERY OF ANTIQUE ART.** This palace was built in the fifteenth century, and in 1729 Clement XII acquired it for his nephew, Neri Corsini. It was the residence at one time of Michelangelo and still later of Erasmus. The paintings in the gallery fill 10 rooms and salons of the Palazzo Corsini. Works of almost every school and period are represented.

(10)   [Site 64] The **BARBERINI GALLERY** is located in the Palazzo Barberini. It contains, among other pictures, the famous portrait of **LA FORNARINA,** by Raphael.

(11)   [Site 86] The **MUSEUM OF VILLA GIULIA** is a museum of pre-Roman antiquities. The objects came from Etruscan tombs. This is one of the most important Etruscan museums in Italy.

(12)   [Site 87] The **MUSEUM OF VILLA ALBANI** was built for Cardinal Albani in 1759. This museum is rich in antiquities.

(13)   [Site 88] The **DORIA GALLERY** is in the Doria-Pamphili Palace, perhaps the most magnificent of the Roman palaces, erected in the end of the fifteenth century. Various painters are represented.

(14)   [Site 89] The **COLONNA GALLERY** was founded in 1572 to consecrate the glory of Marc Antonio Colonna, who commanded the papal fleet against the Turks at the Battle of Lepanto (1571). Many important paintings are housed here.

(15)   [Site 66] **VATICAN MUSEUMS.** (See site 66, "Vatican City," above.)

SOUTH OF ROME

APPII FORUM, *"Three Taverns"*

This is a station on the Appian Way 40 miles from Rome. Here Paul was met by Christians who encouraged him (Acts 28:15).

Anzio

This was a beachhead for Allied soldiers in their conquest of Italy in World War II. Nearby is **NETTUNO,** where an American military cemetery and monument are located.

Monte Cassino

Cassino was one of the key defensive positions of the Germans in World War II. The famous **ABBEY OF MONTE CASSINO,** on the hill, was eventually destroyed, but is now rebuilt. It is the original home of the Benedictine Order of Monks.

Caserta

An elegant 1,200-room royal palace, rivaling Versailles, was built in Caserta in the eighteenth century for Charles III of Spain. World War II Allies used the former palace as headquarters. Here on May 2, 1945, the Germans in Italy surrendered, ending the Italian campaign. The Italians had joined with the Axis in 1936, but had surrendered to the Americans on September 3, 1943.

PUTEOLI, Pozzuoli

This was Italy's first port. It is a city just west of Naples, where a quirk of nature caused the ground to rise 28 inches between September 1969 and March 1970, cracking foundations in dozens of buildings. The rising ground level was caused by heating and resulting expansion of a lava bed beneath Pozzuoli. The Italian government offered free transportation to the inhabitants (35,000) who would move to another home. Some people demonstrated against the government's order to move out of the "slow earthquake" area, but many accepted the order.

It was here that Paul found some Christian brethren and spent a week before proceeding overland to Rome.

The city boasts an ancient Roman 40,000-seat AMPHITHEATER, built like the Colosseum of Rome. In this well-preserved theater, many Christian martyrs met their death. The TEMPLE OF SERAPIDE is also in Pozzuoli.

This is the birthplace of the movie actress Sophia Loren.

■ Paul landed here on his way to Rome (Acts 28:13–14).

Solfatara

This is a volcanic area near Naples, with smoke, jets of hot mud, and boiling water — a Yellowstone Park in Italy.

Naples

Naples is one of the largest ports in the Mediterranean, situated on the Bay of Naples and overshadowed by the great mass of Mount Vesuvius. It is the commercial, cultural, and artistic center of southern Italy. It has a population of 1,050,000.

POINTS OF INTEREST

The NATIONAL ARCHAEOLOGICAL MUSEUM, like the British Museum, is very important. Its treasures are mainly from Pompeii and Herculaneum. The red building was first a cavalry barracks (1585) and then the seat of the university (1612).

Among the masterpieces that are seen here are the FARNESE BULL (taken from the Spa of Caracalla), DIANE OF EPHESUS, CALIGULA ON A HORSE, HERMES RESTING, the TIRANCIDES, FARNESE HERCULES,

NIKE MUTILA, and the VENUS OF CAPUA. There are also portraits, bronzes, mosaics, stuccos, glassware, jewelry, vases, and Egyptian antiquities.

The CAPODIMONTE MUSEUM houses the Farnese Art Collection and other art pieces transferred here to give room for archaeological treasures in the National Museum.

The CHAPEL OF SAN SEVERO is also of interest. Beneath the church are two skeletons completely covered with muscular and veinous systems, a marvel of technical reconstruction by Raimondo di Sangro.

The sculpture of G. Summartino, titled CHRIST VEILED, shows great skill, as do the two eighteenth-century sculpture pieces: UNDECEIVED and CHASTITY (a man freeing himself from a net and a shapely woman covered with a thin veil).

The SAN CARLO THEATER, built in 1737, is the most important of its contemporaries. It has near-perfect acoustics. An opera or musical is very impressive in this gorgeous theater.

The CATHEDRAL OF SAINT JANARIUS has a large baptismal font.

Herculaneum

This "Sister to Pompeii" in the misfortune of A.D. 79 has a character of higher elegance than Pompeii. Besides the beautiful houses, one should visit the great baths and the theater.

Mount Vesuvius

Mount Vesuvius is the only active volcano on the mainland of Europe. It is 3,842 feet high, and the top ranges from 50 to 400 feet across. The last eruption was in 1944, when it destroyed the village of San Sebastiano.

Since its eruption in 1944 it has not smoked. In half an hour one can drive to within a short distance of the crater. There is a chair lift to take the inquisitive to the crater's edge.

Pompeii

Pompeii is an ancient Roman city buried in A.D. 79 during the largest eruption of Vesuvius. It was well preserved by lava for almost nineteen centuries. This city gives us a vivid insight into the Roman world of the days of Jesus and Paul. It was a thriving commercial town and resort playground for the rich. It was the pleasure abode of the Roman aristocracy, who introduced all the luxury, vices, and corruption imaginable. The streets of Pompeii are narrow, and chariot ruts in the cobblestones are visible. Running water was supplied to the rich. A MUSEUM houses various artifacts found on the site.

Sorrento

Sorrento is known for its brilliant landscape, flowering gardens, and mildness of air. The town lies on a stratum 500 meters above sea level, and its beauty has attracted visitors for centuries. Its popula-

Temple of Diana and Apollo, Pompeii, with Mount Vesuvius in the background

tion is 12,000. Among those who have come to enjoy its serenity for their work are Goethe, Byron, Walter Scott, Dumas, Renan, Verdi, Longfellow, Oscar Wilde, Nietzsche, Grieg, and Wagner. Roman emperors, such as Augustus and Marcus Aurelius, had villas here.

Capri

This is a 4-mile-long island of calcareous rock with two towns: Capri in the center and Anacapri on the west. It has been a popular resort for 2,000 years. Caesar Augustus bought the island, and his successor, Tiberius, lived here from A.D. 27 to 37, governing Rome from his Villa Jovis. Other emperors stayed on Capri after Tiberius. A chair lift takes visitors to the top of Monte Solaro for a breathtaking view.

The **BLUE GROTTO** is famous for the tonalities of the blue water due to a phenomenon of light refraction.

Positano

Flights of stone steps serve as streets in this town, which clings to a steep slope by the sea.

Amalfi

Amalfi was one of Italy's first independent city-states. In the Middle Ages it was a maritime republic rivaling Genoa, Venice, and Pisa. It is the birthplace of Flavio Gioia, inventor of the compass. Its population is 7,000. The Amalfi drive is one of the most scenic drives in Europe.

Salerno

Salerno was celebrated in the Middle Ages for its school of medicine. Here the first large-scale landing on the mainland by Allied troops of World War II took place on September 9, 1943.

RHEGIUM, Reggio

This is a town on the east coast of the Sicilian straits, where Paul and his companions spent a day waiting for a wind that would bear them on their way to Puteoli (Acts 28:13).

Herculaneum, Mount Vesuvius in the background

SYRACUSE, Siracusa

Syracuse lies on the east side of the island of Sicily, the most populous and fertile island in the Mediterranean Sea. Syracuse was an important Greek colony in the days of Paul. Cicero described it as "the greatest of Greek cities and the most beautiful of all cities." It was founded in 734 B.C. Its ruins include a GREEK THEATER and the EAR OF DIONYSIUS, an artificial grotto with an exceptional echo.

- *Paul spent three days here as he traveled from Melita to Rome (Acts 28:12).*

MELITA, Malta

The island of Malta, 17½ miles long by 9½ miles wide (95 square miles), lies 56 miles south of Sicily. Valletta is its capital. On this island the vessel on which Paul and 275 other people were being carried to Rome was run aground. Soldiers wanted to kill the prisoners, but the centurion desired to save Paul and convinced them to spare the prisoners. While on the island, Paul had experiences with the barbarians, fire, and the snake (see Scripture references below). They stayed on the estate of Publius, the chief man on the island, where Paul healed Publius's father and many others. They remained on the island three months, then departed in a ship of Alexandria.

- *Paul was shipwrecked on the island of Melita (Acts 27:39–28:1).*
- *A snake came out of the fire and fastened onto Paul's hand without harming him (Acts 28:3–6).*
- *While staying with Publius, the chief man on the island, Paul healed the father of Publius and many others (Acts 28:8–9).*
- *Paul and the others remained on the island for three months and then departed for Rome in a ship of Alexandria (Acts 28:11–14).*

NORTH OF ROME

Tivoli, *Tibur*

This city was built 400 years before the foundation of Rome. When Camillus conquered it in 380 B.C. he built the TEMPLES OF SYBIL, VESTA, and HERCULES. Under Augustus, Tivoli became the pleasure resort of the Romans. Under Hadrian the city enjoyed its greatest prosperity, and the VILLA ADRIANA was his favorite residence. He had exact reproductions made in miniature of the monuments he admired in the world.

The VILLA D'ESTE at Tivoli was built in 1549 and is one of the finest villas of the Renaissance period. The unfinished Casino is decorated with frescoes by the Zuccaro brothers. The park, with its terraces, fountains, and waterfalls, is magnificent.

Orvieto

This city crowns the pedestal of a rock. Ceramics and wine are specialties of Orvieto.

Florence, Firenze

This city's history dates back to 1000 B.C. and the days of the Etruscans. Located in central Italy on the Arno River, Florence is one of the richest centers of Renaissance art in the world. It is called the "City of Flowers" and has a population of 400,000.

POINTS OF INTEREST

Dating from 1345, the **PONTE VECCHIO** ("old bridge"), lined with interesting shops, connects the two parts of the city and the two famous art galleries: **UFFIZI PALACE**; and the **PITTI PALACE**, the Medici family palace, with paintings by Raphael, Titian, Rubens, and others. Art and culture flourished here during the Renaissance, with such illustrious men as Michelangelo, Dante, Leonardo da Vinci, Boccaccio, Petrarch, Donatello, and Amerigo Vespucci.

Other places of interest include the **CATHEDRAL OF SANTA MARIA DEL FIORE**, dating back to the thirteenth and fifteenth centuries, and the **BAPTISTRY**, opposite the cathedral. The baptistry is famous for its bronze doors, by Ghiberti, called the *Gates of Paradise*.

Giotto's **CAMPANILE**, near the cathedral, is the most beautiful bell tower in Italy. It was designed by Giotto and begun in 1334. The **ACADEMY OF FINE ARTS** contains several of Michelangelo's works — notably his **DAVID**. The **SANTA CROCE**, built in 1294, contains the bones of Michelangelo and Galileo. It has beautiful frescoes by Giotto. **PALAZZO VECCHIO**, a thirteenth-century palace housing the city's government offices, towers over the **PIAZZA DELLA SIGNORIA**, which features the statues of **HERCULES** and **CACUS** and a copy of Michelangelo's **DAVID**. The **LOGGIA DEI LANZI**, near the Palazzo, is a graceful arcade with excellent sculpture, including the famous **PERSEUS**, by Benvenuto Cellini; the **CHURCH OF SAN LORENZO** houses

Florence

1. Pitti Palace
2. Ponte Vecchio
3. Uffizi Palace
4. Palazzo Vecchio
5. Piazza della Signoria
6. Loggia dei Lanzi (Orcagna)
7. Dante's house
8. Bargello Palace
9. Michelangelo's home
10. Santa Croce
11. Cathedral of Santa Maria del Fiore
12. Baptistry
13. Giotto's Campanile
14. Church of San Lorenzo
15. Municipal Theater
16. Central Railway Station
17. Academy of Fine Arts

Michelangelo's **TOMBS OF THE MEDICI** and **WORKS BY DONATELLO;** **MICHELANGELO'S HOME** is worth a visit; in the **BARGELLO PALACE** is the **NATIONAL MUSEUM.** The **FIESOLE,** on a nearby hill, provides an excellent view of the city.

Pisa

With a population of 80,000, Pisa is a quiet university town in comparison to its past glories as an independent republic. In the eleventh century it ranked with Genoa, Amalfi, and Venice. The old port now lies 6 miles inland and wears the air of a forsaken capital. It is noted for its **LEANING TOWER** (*Campanile*), a bell tower that is often considered one of the seven wonders of the modern world. It was begun in 1174 and completed in 1350. The ground beneath the tower started to sink after the first three stories were built. It has tipped one foot during the last 100 years and is now 16½ feet out of line. In 1928 the government reinforced it to prevent further leaning. It is said that in 1589 Galileo performed here, before witnesses, experiments showing that weight does not affect the velocity of falling bodies. Scholars now question the story, however.

The tower was built entirely of marble and is a fine example of Romanesque architecture. It is 179 feet tall. The walls are 13 feet thick at the base and 6 feet at the top. An inner staircase of 300 steps leads to the top for a view of the city. The nearby **CATHEDRAL,** begun in 1063, has many beautiful antique columns. The eleventh-century **BAPTISTRY** has interesting echo effects. The **CAMPO SANTO** is a cemetery with superb galleries.

Volterra

This is an Etruscan town, with a museum rich in the pottery of a vanished people. Quarrying and carving alabaster is one of the modern specialties.

Siena

Siena, with a population of 60,000, is a medieval city rich in art treasures. The **CATHEDRAL** is one of the earliest of the great Tuscan Gothic churches. The city is famous for its **PALIO DELLE CONTRODE**, a medieval pageant staged July 2 and August 16. The slender **MANGIA TOWER** is the symbol of the town. The **PALAZZO PIC-COLOMINI** is a fine monument of the Renaissance.

Ghiberti's bronze baptistry doors, Florence

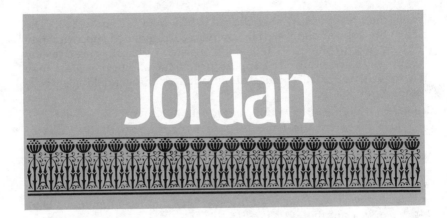

Jordan is about the size of Ohio, with a population of over two million, more than half a million of whom live in Amman, the nation's capital.

HISTORY

BEFORE THE ISRAELITE CONQUEST

Before the conquest of Canaan by the Israelites, the area on the east side of the Jordan River encompassing the present-day Jordan was divided into the following five districts (see map, page 226).

BASHAN

Between the Jabbok and the Yarmuk rivers, North Gilead extends north and south for about 35 miles. The land of Bashan, north of the Yarmuk, reaches to Mount Hermon and eastward to the northern slopes of the Hauran and to the city of Salecah. At the time of the conquest this kingdom was ruled by Og, who was said to have been a giant (Deut. 3:11). Og was defeated by the Israelites at Edrei (in Syria), and his territory of Bashan and North Gilead was assigned to half the tribe of Manasseh (Deut. 1:4; 3:1-14). Og's territory passed from David to Solomon and was lost during the Syrian wars, to be regained by Jeroboam II (2 Kings 14:23, 25). Beginning with the time of Tiglath-pileser III, king of the Assyrians, it passed into foreign control (2 Kings 15:29).

Megalithic graves, or *dolmens*, were once used for burying the dead. These famous great stone graves consisted of tall stones, built in oval formation and every now and then roofed over with a heavy transverse block. They are called locally "giants' beds." In 1918 Gustaf Dalman discovered a dolmen in the neighborhood of Amman, the modern capital of Jordan.

The Bible says about the giant King Og: "Behold, his bedstead was a bedstead of iron; is it not in Rabbath of the children of Ammon [Rabbath-Ammon]? nine cubits was the length thereof, and four cubits the breadth of it, after the cubit of a man" (Deut. 3:11). The size of the dolmen discovered by Dalman corresponded approximately to these measurements. The "bed" consisted of basalt, an extremely hard, gray-black stone. The appearance of such a burying place may have given rise to the biblical description of the giant king's "bedstead of iron."

- Bashan was ruled by Og the giant (Deut. 3:1, 11).
- It was taken by the Israelites and assigned to half the tribe of Manasseh (Deut. 1:4; 3:1-14).
- It was lost during the Syrian wars, but regained by Jeroboam II (2 Kings 14:23, 25).
- From Bashan came the story of Og's giant bed (Deut. 3:11).
- It was taken from Israel by the Assyrians, and the inhabitants were carried into captivity (2 Kings 15:29).
- The Old Testament has several references to the "oaks of Bashan" (Isa. 2:13; Ezek. 27:6; Zech. 11:2).

GILEAD

The term *Gilead* is used loosely in the Old Testament. In Numbers 32:33 the territory assigned to Gad, Reuben, and half the tribe of Manasseh included the kingdoms of Sihon, king of the Amorites, and of Og, king of Bashan, comprising all the territory between the Arnon and the Yarmuk rivers and beyond. The word *Gilead* is employed for the whole of this territory, as well as for part of it (2 Kings 10:33). The Jabbok River divides it in two.

The territory of Sihon, king of the Amorites, extended from the Arnon north to the Jabbok. The Israelites, having been refused permission to pass through Edom and Moab along the King's Highway, went around these two kingdoms as they headed north. When they reached the river Arnon, which was the south border of the Amorites, they again asked permission to use the King's Highway. Sihon refused permission, and the Israelites attacked his kingdom. This marked the beginning of the conquest of Canaan by force of arms.

The original Ammonite kingdom consisted of a small, strongly fortified, fairly fertile strip along the east side of the south-north stretch of the Najal Jabbok (Wadi Zerqa) and reached eastward to the desert. Among the most striking of Ammonite fortifications were strongly built circular towers of megalithic construction, which — sometimes alone, but usually in conjunction with rectangular or square fortifications, also built of large blocks of stone — provided the defenses of the Ammonite kingdom and particularly of the approaches to the capital city of Rabbath-Ammon. Usually the large, rectangular flint (or limestone) blocks were not dressed or smoothed beyond their roughly hewn state. A puzzling question is how the Ammonite builders moved these large, heavy stones into position after the stones had been prepared for use. If earthen ramps were used, no traces of such have ever been reported.

Typical wall construction technique consisted of laying blocks at the corners in headers and stretchers, while between the corners,

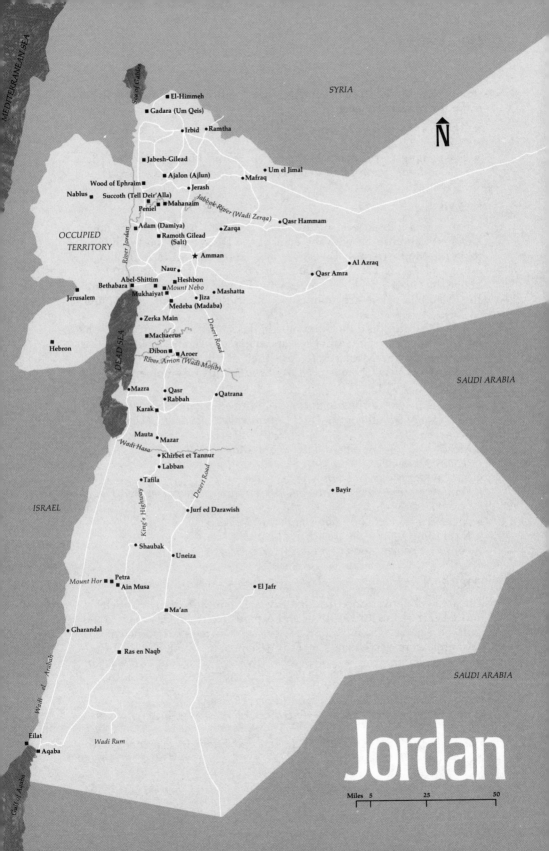

MEDITERRANEAN SEA

SYRIA

Ñ

Sea of Galilee

■ El-Himmeh

● Gadara (Um Qeis)

● Irbid ● Ramtha

■ Jabesh-Gilead

● Um el Jimal

■ Ajalon (Ajlun) ● Mafraq

■ Wood of Ephraim ● Jerash

Nablus ■ ● Succoth (Tell Deir'Alla)

Jabbok River (Wadi Zerqa)

● Peniel ■ Mahanaim

■ Qasr Hammam

OCCUPIED TERRITORY

● Adam (Damiya)

● Zarqa

River Jordan

● Ramoth Gilead (Salt)

★ Amman

● Naur

● Al Azraq

■ Abel-Shittim ● Heshbon

● Qasr Amra

Bethabara ■ Mount Nebo

■ Mukhaiyat ● Mashatta

Jerusalem ■

Medeba (Madaba) ● Jiza

● Zerka Main

DEAD SEA

● Machaerus

Desert Road

Hebron ●

● Dibon ■ Aroer

River Arnon (Wadi Mojib)

● Mazra ● Qasr

● Rabbah ● Qatrana

Karak ■

Mauta ● Mazar

Wadi Hasa

● Khirbet et Tannur

● Labban

● Tafila

Desert Road

● Bayir

ISRAEL

● Jurf ed Darawish

King's Highway

● Shaubak

● Uneiza

Mount Hor ■ ● Petra

■ Ain Musa

● El Jafr

Wadi el- Arabah

■ Ma'an

● Gharandal

● Ras en Naqb

SAUDI ARABIA

SAUDI ARABIA

Gulf of Aqaba

● Eilat

■ Aqaba

Wadi Rum

Jordan

Miles 5   25   50

stones were placed in rude courses, with smaller stones interspersed to make the rows fairly even.

- *Ahab, king of Israel, was mortally wounded at Ramoth Gilead. (1 Kings 22:29–40).*
- *The conquest of Canaan began when Sihon, king of the Amorites, refused Israel permission to cross his territory (Num. 21:21–24).*

MOAB

Moab was a district east of the Dead Sea with its boundaries north and south about even with the ends of the Dead Sea from Wadi Hasa to Wadi Mojib (Arnon River). It was about 35 miles long and 25 miles wide. The area lies 3,000 feet above sea level and 4,300 feet above the Dead Sea. Deep gorges were formed by rivers draining into the Dead Sea. Here are mounts Nebo and Pisgah (Deut. 34:1; Num. 21:20).

The Moabites, like the Ammonites, descended from Lot, the nephew of Abraham. The Amorites and later the Arabs took over this area, causing the Moabites to lose their identity. The chief god of the Moabites was Chemosh, who was worshiped by human sacrifice (2 Kings 3:26–27).

- *Genesis speaks of the Moabites' origin (Gen. 19:30–38).*
- *Israel avoided them as they approached Canaan (Deut. 2:9; 2 Chron. 20:10).*
- *Moses saw the promised land from Mount Nebo, where he died (Deut. 32:48–52; 34:1–8).*
- *Saul smote Moab (1 Sam. 14:47).*
- *David's parents were protected there while Saul persecuted David (1 Sam. 22:3–4).*
- *Moab was defeated by Jehoshaphat (2 Kings 3).*
- *Ruth came from Moab (Ruth 1:4).*
- *Amos reproved Moab (Amos 2:1–3).*

EDOM

The area which was once the territory of Edom (also known as Seir) is located east of the Jordan River and extends from the Dead Sea to the Gulf of Aqaba. Its mountains rise to 5,900 feet. The ancient inhabitants were descendants of Esau (Gen. 14:6; Deut. 2:22). In the Iron Age, Edom was a prosperous, civilized kingdom. It was an enemy to Israel (Num. 20:14–21; 21:4; Deut. 23:7–8).

- *Edom was located near and around Seir (Gen. 32:3).*
- *Edom would not let Moses and the Israelites pass through (Num. 20:14–21).*
- *Saul, David, and Amaziah each defeated Edom in war and David garrisoned the country (1 Sam. 14:47; 2 Sam. 8:13–14; 2 Kings 7–10).*
- *Edom acknowledged the supremacy of Judah (1 Kings 11:14–25; 2 Kings 3:6–26; 2 Kings 14:7).*

■ *Edom was severely criticized by the prophets (Lam. 4:21; Ezek. 25:12–14; 35; Obad.).*

MIDIAN

It appears that this land area, which extends both east and west of the eastern arm of the Red Sea, was inhabited by the Midianites. These people took their name from Midian, one of the sons of Abraham and his wife Keturah (Gen. 25:1–2), who, with his brothers and their families, had gone away from Isaac into the "east country" (Gen. 25:6; 1 Kings 11:18; Judg. 8:11; Num. 32:42; Ex. 3:1). There is a very close relationship between the Midianites and Ishmaelites (descendants of Hagar), to the point that these two names are sometimes used interchangeably (Gen. 37:25, 28, 36; Judg. 8:22, 24).

■ *Moses fled to Midian, where he met Jethro and received a wife from him. From here he was sent to deliver Israel (Exod. 2:15–21; 3:1–10; 4:19).*

■ *Israel wandered in the area (Num. 10:29–36).*

■ *The Midianites joined Balak in seeking a curse on Israel (Num. 22–24).*

■ *Israel sinned by intermarriage with the Midianites (Num. 25; 31: 2–18).*

■ *Gideon overthrew them and saved Israel after seven years' oppression (Judg. 6–8; 9:17; Ps. 83:9; Isa. 9:4; 10:26; Hab. 3:7).*

■ *Hadad and many of Israel dwelt in Midian (1 Kings 11:14–22).*

AFTER THE CONQUEST

After Israel conquered Canaan, the northern districts east of the Jordan River were given to Naphtali. Manasseh was given a district starting north of Lake Hula and ending on the south at the Yarmuk River, just below the Sea of Galilee. Gad had nearly the entire portion immediately on the east of the Jordan River, and Reuben had a district from the north end of the Dead Sea south to about the middle of the Dead Sea. South of that point, the Moabites and Edomites possessed the land.

MODERN TIMES

The Hashemite Kingdom of Jordon became independent as Transjordan in 1946, then as the independent Hashemite Kingdom of Jordan in 1949. King Amir Abdullah reigned over Jordan from 1946 until 1951, when he was assassinated. His son King Talal then ruled, but was not competent. King Hussein, grandson of Abdullah, has ruled since 1953. Young Hussein received his education in Egypt and England. Since ascending the throne in 1953, he has survived many attempts on his life.

RELIGION

The country is predominantly Moslem, but Arab and non-Arab Christians comprise a small percentage of the population and represent a number of Catholic and Protestant denominations, the largest group being Greek Orthodox.

JORDAN TODAY

Jordan is largely an agricultural country, and many of its people are engaged in raising grain and livestock. The country on the whole is fairly dry, with most of its precipitation occurring in the winter season.

Since 1952, primary education has been compulsory in Jordan, but much of the adult population is illiterate. There are few colleges in Jordan.

The government of Jordan is considered a constitutional monarchy, and Jordan's Independence Day is May 25.

The Jordanian unit of currency is the *dinar*, divided into 1,000 *fils*.

CITIES AND SITES

AMMON, RABBAH, RABBATH *("great")*, *Philadelphia*, **Amman**

Amman, the capital city of Jordan, is 25 miles east of the Jordan River and 45 miles northeast of Jerusalem, at an altitude of 3,000 feet. Like Rome, it spreads over seven hills. About 1200 B.C. it was the capital of the Ammonites. The Israelites did not occupy Rabbath (the city's biblical name) after David took the city, but left it in the possession of the Ammonite king, who became David's vassal.

The first dramatic change to affect Amman came with the victorious arrival, in the third century B.C., of Ptolemy II (Philadelphus) of Egypt (265–263 B.C.), who rebuilt Amman and named it Philadelphia. The Seleucids conquered Amman in 218 B.C., and in 30 B.C. Herod the Great took the city for Rome. Herod embarked on an extensive building program, leveling off the Citadel, surrounding it with a wall, and building a massive temple to Hercules.

During the Roman period Amman was a member of the Decapolis. Centuries later, during the Byzantine period, it became the seat of a Christian Bishopric of Petra and Philadelphia. After the Arab conquest of the seventeenth century the city flourished, but gradually it declined in importance until, when Abdullah moved the seat of his newly formed government there in the 1920s, it was only a village.

It is now the seat of the government, however, and the hub of com-

Roman theater, Amman

mercial activity. The population of the city is nearly 600,000, including thousands of Palestinian refugees who have flocked into the city since 1948.

POINTS OF INTEREST

1. A **ROMAN THEATER**, with a seating capacity of 6,000, dates from the second or third century A.D. It is located right behind the Philadelphia Hotel. Outdoor festivals are held in the theater during the summer. Only a few columns remain of the **ROMAN FORUM**, and east of the hotel there is a small theater called the **ODEUM**. On the west was the **NYMPHAEUM**.

2. The **CITADEL** was built on a plateau (Jebel Hussein) where once stood a temple to Hercules (second century A.D.). A **BYZANTINE GATE** still stands, and on the outside of the **ROMAN WALLS** is a rock-carved cistern that supplied the fortress with water when the fortress was under attack. North of the Citadel is **EL-QASR** (the Castle), dating back to the Umayyad period (sixth and seventh centuries).

3. The **AMMAN ARCHAEOLOGICAL MUSEUM** is located on Citadel Hill. Archaeological artifacts include Nabataean pottery and Dead Sea Scrolls.

4. The **BASMAN PALACE** is the "working" palace of King Hussein. It stands on a hilltop facing the Citadel, and Circassian soldiers wearing red and black uniforms guard the king.

Amman

N

4 — To Airport

WADI AL HADADEH STREET

MUSEUM STREET

KING ABDULLAH STREET

SHABSOUGH STREET

MUNICIPALITY STREET

1

2

3

KING FEISAL STREET

SALAH EDDIGE STREET

SALT STREET

JORDAN STREET

OTHMAN STREET

KING TALAL STREET

5

7

KING HUSEIN STREET

MOHAMMAD ABDO

6

KHALID BEN AL WALID STREET

QASSAM STREET

JAREER STREET

ABU BAKER AL SADDEA STREET

OMAR BEN KHATTAB STREET

IMMAM ALI STREET

ASMA STREET

IBRAHIM TOUKAN STREET

AIESHEH EL BAOUNEH STREET

SHAREA COLLEGE STREET

QUEEN ZEIN STREET

SHABAN STREET

BUHTORY STREET

SUKEINA STREET

AL RAZI STREET

MUHAJEREEN STREET

RAS EL AIN STREET

AL RAZI STREET

KING HUSEIN STREET

PRINCE MOHAMMAD STREET

To Jerash and Damascus

ABU OBEIDAH STREET

MAAMOUN STREET

AL HUSEIN BEN ALI STREET

MUTANABI STREET

ABU TAMMAM STREET

ABU FERAS STREET

8

1. Roman theater
2. Citadel
3. Amman Archaeological Museum
4. Basman Palace
5. Refugee camps
6. Shopping center
7. King Hussein Sports City
8. Queen Mother Palace

5. **REFUGEE CAMPS** near the city are the pathetic results of war. Thousands of Palestinian refugees have lived in these camps for nearly 25 years and raised their families in very humble circumstances. The United Nations has been the agent of mercy to these poor Arabs.

The **SHOPPING CENTER, KING HUSSEIN SPORTS CITY,** and **QUEEN MOTHER PALACE** are also of interest.

- *The ancient nation of the Ammonites, with their capital at Amman, were descendants of Lot. They lived on the east of the Jordan and the Dead Sea, between the rivers Arnon and Jabbok. Their chief god was Molech, to whom they offered human sacrifices (2 Kings 3:26–27; Lev. 20:2–5; Deut. 2:19).*
- *Og's bedstead might still be seen here (Deut. 3:11). Some believe this refers to a large dolmen still visible not far from Amman.*
- *The city was mentioned in defining the boundaries of Gad (Josh. 13:24–25).*
- *Amman oppressed Israel and was overthrown by Jephthah (Judg. 11:4–33).*
- *The city was taken by David. In one of the battles Uriah, the husband of Bathsheba, was killed (2 Sam. 11; 12:26–29; 1 Chron. 20:1).*
- *Amman showed mercy to David, a fugitive (2 Sam. 17:27–29).*
- *It was hostile to Israel (2 Chron. 20:1–25; 27:5; 2 Kings 24:2; Neh. 4:1–12; 2 Kings 25:22–26; Jer. 40:13–41:4).*
- *Solomon married an Ammonite woman, whose son succeeded him (1 Kings 14:21, 31; 2 Chron. 12:13).*
- *The cruelty of the Ammonites was denounced by the prophets (Jer. 49:1–6; Ezek. 21:28–32; Amos 1:13–15; Zeph. 2:8–11).*
- *Amman was one of the cities of the Decapolis (Mark 7:31).*

NORTH FROM AMMAN

RAMOTH GILEAD ("heights"), Salt (?)

This is possibly northwest of Amman, on the east side of the Jordan and 12 miles from it. Under Solomon, Ramoth Gilead was the seat of the governor of the province north of the Yarmuk River and may have been the most important Israelite city east of the Jordan.

- *Here Ahab was wounded and died (1 Kings 22:1–35; 2 Chron. 18).*
- *Elisha sent a young prophet here to anoint Jehu king of Israel (2 Kings 9:1–10; 2 Chron. 22:7).*

ADAM ("of the ground"), **Damiya**, Kiriathaim, Tell ed-Damiyeh

This is a place near Zaretan, 25 miles northwest of Amman, beside the Jordan River where the Israelites crossed.

- *The waters were "cut off" so the Israelites could cross the Jordan River (Josh. 3:16).*

JABBOK ("flowing"), **Wadi Zerqa** ("the blue river")

This is a very clear river that crosses the territory of Gilead. It flows at the bottom of a great cleft, cutting the land of Gilead in two.

- *Here Jacob wrestled and was given the name Israel, as he returned from Padan-aram (Gen. 32:22–32).*
- *Sihon ruled to the Jabbok (Josh. 12:2).*
- *The place is mentioned elsewhere in the Old Testament (Num. 21: 24; Deut. 2:37; 3:16; Judg. 11:13; 11:22).*

SUCCOTH ("booths"), **Tell Deir' Alla**

Succoth was a town of Gad, 4 miles east of the Jordan and somewhat over 1 mile north of the brook Jabbok.

- *Jacob built a house for his family and booths for his cattle after separating from Esau (Gen. 33:17; Josh. 13:27).*
- *Gideon and his army punished the people of Succoth after the people refused to give bread to the army (Judg. 8:4–7, 15–17).*
- *Solomon cast bronze vessels for worship in the temple in this area because the rich deposits of clay on the plain of the Jordan River were suitable for casting bronze (1 Kings 7:45–46; 2 Chron. 4: 16–17).*
- *Succoth is referred to in the Psalms (Pss. 60:6; 108:7).*

PENIEL ("face of God"), **PENUEL**, Tubeleth Drahab

Peniel is a place on the east side of the Jordan near the brook Jabbok (Gen. 32:22, 30), possibly near Succoth.

- *Here Jacob wrestled all night with the angel (Gen. 32:22–32).*
- *Peniel was beaten down by Gideon (Judg. 8:4–17).*
- *It was fortified by Jeroboam (1 Kings 12:25).*

MAHANAIM ("two camps")

This was a town east of the Jordan River and south of the Jabbok River. It was a Levitical city of Gad.

- *It was located on the east of the Jordan and on the border between Gad and Manasseh (Josh. 13:24, 26, 29–30).*
- *Jacob came to this place before crossing the Jabbok (Gen. 32:2, 22).*
- *It was the capitol of Ish-bosheth (2 Sam. 2:8, 12, 29).*
- *Here Abner made Ish-bosheth, son of Saul, the king (2 Sam. 2:8–9).*

- *Here David took refuge from his rebel son Absalom (2 Sam. 17:24, 27; 19:32).*
- *Solomon placed Ahinadab in authority over this city (1 Kings 4:7, 14).*

Jerash, *Gerasa, Jarash*

Of the cities east of the Jordan River that were a part of the Decapolis, Damascus was the largest and Jerash was second in size. It is 30 miles north of Amman.

Here is one of the most complete ruins of any Greek-Roman city in the world. It was founded by Alexander the Great about 332 B.C. and continued as an important city until about A.D. 300, when a shift in trade routes helped to cause its decline.

The city as it now stands was chiefly the product of the first and second centuries A.D., but many conquerors had a hand in its making. The city thrived as an important trade route city and had abundant water, with springs running all year round and a river whose banks were green.

But when Rome declined, so did Jerash. It had a Byzantine Christian recovery, but late in the eighth century earthquakes destroyed much of the city and hastened its decline. The Crusaders used the city as a fort, and when they left the city became deserted. In 1878 some Turks — Circassians from the Caucasus — settled the east side of the site.

Jerash has been called the "Pompeii of the East" or "City of a Thousand Pillars." In the 1920s the site was excavated, and since then a rest house has been built.

POINTS OF INTEREST

The ruins include the following:

TRIUMPHAL ARCH. This was built in A.D. 129 to celebrate Hadrian's visit. It is 39 feet high.

HIPPODROME.

TEMPLE OF ZEUS. This temple was built in the second century A.D.

The SOUTH THEATER held 5,000 people (first century A.D.).

The FORUM, with its 56 columns, is the only Roman forum ever discovered that is oval-shaped. It is beautifully reconstructed and very photogenic (first century A.D.).

STREET OF COLUMNS. This is the main street of Jerash, lined with 75 beautiful columns (second century A.D.). It starts at the Forum and runs the entire length of Jerash to the North Gate.

NYMPHAEUM. This is the fountain and temple of the nymphs.

The TEMPLE OF ARTEMIS was built in the second century A.D. for the god Artemis, the local god of Jerash. This is the most impressive ruin of the site, with its 45-foot-tall columns and beautiful Corinthian capitals. The VIADUCT CHURCH is built over the forecourt of the temple.

Ñ

MODERN TOWN
OF JERASH

Jerash

1. North gate
2. Church of the
   Prophets,
   Apostles, and
   Martyrs
3. West baths
4. Propylaea Church
5. East baths
6. Procopius Church
7. Roman bridge
8. Parking
9. Rest house
10. Water gate
11. Old city walls
12. Triumphal arch
13. Hippodrome
14. South gate
15. Forum
16. Temple of Zeus
17. South theater

18. Church of Saints
    Peter and Paul,
    and Mortuary
    Chapel
19. South tetrapylon
20. Nymphaeum
21. Churches of
    Saints Cosmos,
    Damianus, John
    the Baptist, and
    George
22. Saint Genesius'
    Church
23. Synagogue
    Church
24. Temple of
    Artemis
25. North theater
26. North tetrapylon

Miles   1/4

The **ROMAN BATHS** were built in the second century A.D.

The **NORTH THEATER** is a small theater that seats 1,200.

The **NORTH GATE** marks the north end of the city.

The **CEMETERY** is north of the city walls. A small **THEATER** and **SPRING** are located there.

THIRTEEN BYZANTINE CHURCHES have been excavated at Jerash. The fourth-century **CATHEDRAL CHURCH** is probably the oldest.

- *People from Decapolis followed Jesus during his travels in Galilee. He must have been well known in Jerash (Matt. 4:23-25).*
- *Jesus traveled through the midst of the coasts of Decapolis and could have visited Jerash (Mark 7:31).*

AJALON, AIJALON, Ajlun

Located 46 miles north of Amman, and northwest of Jerash about 10 miles, is the town of Aijalon, one of the ancient cities of Dan. Today a **BAPTIST HOSPITAL** is there. A **MOSQUE** has been built on the site of a church, and a **FORTRESS** built by one of Saladin's emirs may be visited. The castle stands on top of a 4,068-foot mountain, the highest in Jordan, and is one of the few Arab castles remaining from Crusader days.

- *Here the moon stood still while the sun stood still in Gibeon, so Israel could avenge herself of the Amorites (Josh. 10:12-13).*
- *The town is mentioned in the Old Testament (Josh. 19:42; Judg. 1:35).*

WOOD OF EPHRAIM *("to be fruitful")*

Northwest from Jerash is a locality called "Wood of Ephraim," where Absalom rebelled against King David, his father, and was killed by Joab (2 Sam. 18).

JABESH-GILEAD

The approximate site of this chief city of Gilead is about 5 miles northwest of Aijalon, on Wadi Yabis, which preserves the name. Several important events of Israelitish history took place there.

- *Israel had vowed at an assembly that they would not give any of their women to the Benjaminites. The men of Jabesh-gilead did not come to the meeting, however, whereupon Israel sent an army to Jabesh-gilead, which slew every living thing in the city except four hundred virgins, whom they brought back as wives for Benjamin (Judg. 21:8-14).*
- *The men of Jabesh-gilead removed the bodies of Saul and his sons from the wall at Beth-shan and burned and buried them in Jabesh. The men were blessed by David (1 Sam. 31:11-13; 2 Sam. 2:4-7; 1 Chron. 10:11-12).*
- *When Saul was king, Israel failed to support him. When the men of Jabesh-gilead asked Saul for aid against the king of Syria, however, Israel rallied behind Saul and he was recognized as king (1 Sam. 11).*

■ *David took the bones of Saul and Jonathan, Saul's son, from the men of Jabesh-gilead (2 Sam. 21:12).*

Irbid (*Arbila*)

Refugees from Palestine have swelled the population of Irbid to approximately 100,000 people. It is located 45 miles north of Amman. The city of BARHA, to the west, is a part of greater Irbid. There are no important archaeological ruins in Irbid.

GADARA, Hammath Geder, El Hamma, El Himmeh, *Gader, Muqes*, Um Qeis

Approximately 5-6 miles southeast of the south end of the Sea of Galilee is Gadara, the area of the Gadarenes. Its territory probably extended to the Sea of Galilee. It has never been excavated to any extent. Its capture by Antiochus III (218 B.C.) is the first mention of it in history. It was taken by the Jews under Alexander Jannaeus (103-76 B.C.) but was liberated by Pompey in 63 B.C. It joined the federation of Greek cities called the Decapolis. It was famous for its hot springs at nearby Hammath Geder (El Hammeth).

■ *Here Jesus cast the evil spirits out of the man (Matt. 8:28–34; Mark 5:1–20; Luke 8:26–39).*

Um el Jimal, *Al Jamal*

Approximately 10 miles east of Al Mafraq are the ruins of this ancient Nabataean city, dating from the first century B.C. It is now a mass of black basalt, but there are towers and houses from a later period that are still in a good state of preservation. Some are inhabited by Arab families.

SOUTH FROM AMMAN

Al Azraq

Sixty-eight miles east of Amman is this desert oasis, with an eighth-century Arab castle, whose walls are covered with frescoes of people, birds, animals, and flowers.

Mashatta, *Qasr el Mushatta*

Eighteen miles southeast of Amman is an eighth-century Arab castle in the desert, probably used as a hunting lodge.

BETHABARA ("*place of passage*"), *Bethabary*, Bet ha'Aravu

This location, 7 miles southeast of Jericho, is the traditional site of Jesus' baptism.

■ *This place is perhaps connected with the Beth-barah of Judges (Judg. 7:24).*
■ *Here John baptized Jesus (John 1:28–34).*
■ *It was accessible to Jerusalem and all Judea (Mark 1:5).*

HESHBON *("stronghold")*, **Hisban**, *Hesban*

Approximately 14 miles southwest of Amman, on the edge of the Eastern Plateau, are these extensive Roman ruins on two connecting hills. This was the capital of Sihon and the Levitical city of Reuben and Gad. It belonged to Moab and then to Amman.

- *Heshbon was the former capital of the Amorite king Sihon (Num. 21:26).*
- *It was taken by the Israelites and assigned to Reuben (Deut. 2:30; Num. 32:27–37; Josh. 13:15–17).*
- *It was supposedly in the hands of Israel for over 300 years (Judg. 11:26; Neh. 9:22).*
- *This is the location of the famous pools described in the Song of Solomon: ". . . thine eyes like the fishpools in Heshbon . . ." (Song of Sol. 7:4). They were perhaps near the spring which rises 600 feet below the city. Nearby are traces of ancient conduits.*

MOUNT NEBO *("height")*, **Syagha**

Directly east of the north end of the Dead Sea, on the edge of the Eastern Plateau, is Mount Nebo. It is the highest point of a ridge called *Pisgah* ("point") in the Abarim range of mountains. It is 27 miles southwest of Amman, 6 miles southwest of Heshbon, and 6 miles northwest of Madeba. Byzantine ruins on Mount Nebo include a sixth-century church and a monastery.

- *The children of Israel pitched their tents before Nebo (Num. 33:47).*
- *It was in this area that the incident involving Balaam and the "talking ass" took place (Num. 22:21–31).*
- *Here Moses first viewed the "Promised Land" (Num. 27:12–14; Deut. 32:49).*
- *Here Moses died (Deut. 34:5–6).*

Zerka Main, *Callirhoe, Zarka Ma'in, Zarqa Main*

From Madeba and Mount Nebo a road runs southwest to the hot mineral springs of Zerka Main, about 14 miles from Madeba and 2½ miles from the Dead Sea. The springs consist of a series of large and small pools that were made famous when used by Herod the Great. In classical times the springs had the name *Callirhoe*.

Mukhaiyat

About 2 miles southeast of Mount Nebo is the site of the largest mosaic floor ever found in Jordan. It dates back to the sixth century. It portrays twisting grapevines and men gathering and treading the grapes. It also has scenes from the sea, mythology, music, bulbs, trees, animals, and a fire altar. A long inscription gives the names of founders and contributors.

ABEL-SHITTIM, SHITTIM ("*meadow of acacias*"),
Tell el-Hamman (*Hamma*), *Abila*

Eighteen miles southwest of Amman and 4 miles northwest of Mount Nebo is Abel-shittim, a site where Israel camped before crossing the Jordan River.

- *Abel-shittim was the last camping site of the Israelites on their journey from Egypt to Canaan (Num. 33:49).*
- *From here Joshua sent spies to Jericho (Josh. 2:1).*
- *Here the Israelites sinned with Moabite women (Num. 25:1).*
- *Here the Lord told Moses that Phinehas, son of Eleazar, was given "the covenant of an everlasting priesthood" (Num. 25:10–13).*
- *The Israelites were numbered here (Num. 26:3–4).*
- *Joshua was set apart to take Moses' place as the prophet. Moses "set him before . . . all the congregation" and "laid his hands upon him, and gave him a charge" (Num 27:18–23).*
- *Prophets spoke of Shittim (Joel 3:18; Mic. 6:5).*

MEDEBA, Madaba, Madeba

Twenty miles south of Amman, on the King's Highway, is the Ammonite, Moabite, Nabataean, Greek, Roman, and Byzantine city of Madeba. The town stands on rising ground in the middle of a plain, which has been the scene of many battles. Its slight eminence is due to its being on a vast mound made up of all the earlier Madebas since the Middle Bronze Age (1580–200 B.C.).

Madeba reached the height of its glory during the Byzantine era (fifth and sixth centuries A.D.), and most of its famous mosaics date from this period. It was destroyed by Persians in 614, then occupied by Arabs. An earthquake in A.D. 747 caused the town to be abandoned until the early nineteenth century, when 2,000 Christians from Kerak settled there. In rebuilding the city the settlers uncovered priceless mosaics that have made Madeba famous. There are houses and churches built over many of the Byzantine church mosaic floors. One floor has a picture of a modern Greek church.

Perhaps the most important and famous mosaic is a map of Egypt and Palestine, with a detailed map of Jerusalem that dates back to the sixth century A.D. It is located in Saint George's Greek Orthodox church. The beautiful map is the only one in the world that shows that area during the early sixth century. The inscriptions are all meant to be read by a person facing east. Its coloring is very vivid: a row of white cubes on black lines depicts a road; roofs are indicated with pink, striped in carmine; church facades are lemon yellow; doors and windows are black outlined with white. Of the principal buildings depicted in this map of Jerusalem, the most interesting is the Church of the Holy Sepulcher. The walls and gates of the city are very clear. Fish in the Nile and Jordan rivers are portrayed like those on Egyptian temple walls.

Saint Catherine's Monastery at Mount Sinai and other monasteries are shown on the map. The church was built over the map in 1896, on the site of another basilica.

Opposite the police station is a small **MUSEUM**. Among other items of interest, it contains a large mosaic showing Achilles, Pan, and Bacchus, of Greek mythology.

Some houses with mosaics are open to the public for a small fee.

There is a rest house in Madeba, where refreshments can be purchased.

- *Madeba was a Moabite city captured by King Sihon and then by Israel (Num. 21:24–30).*
- *It was assigned to Reuben (Josh. 13:7–9, 15–16).*
- *It fell into Ammonite hands during David's time (1 Chron. 19:7).*
- *The Moabite stone (see section on Dhiban, below) says Medeba was held by Omri and Ahab for 40 years.*

MACHAERUS, **Mukawir**, *Mekawer*, *Makhwar*

Eight miles south of Madeba, on the west side of the road, is a high, isolated hill called Libb. At this point, a road goes west 9 miles to Machaerus (Mukawir), a site on the east side of the Dead Sea, on a height about halfway between Wadi Zarka Ma'in and Wadi el Mojib (Arnon River).

This was a fortress built by Alexander Jannaeus and enlarged and strengthened by Herod the Great. According to Josephus, when the wife of Herod Antipas heard of her husband's intention to get rid of her and wed Herodias, she retired to this place and from here escaped to her father, Aretas, King of the Nabataeans. Josephus also reported that it was here that John the Baptist was imprisoned, Salome danced, and John was beheaded.

The fort was one of the last to be taken by the Romans. The site has not been thoroughly excavated. Machaerus offers a magnificent view of the Dead Sea area and even of the city of Jerusalem on a clear day.

- *This is a traditional site of the imprisonment and beheading of John the Baptist (Matt. 14:3–11; Mark 6:17–28); see Josephus, Antiquities of the Jews, XVIII 5:2. (Samaria is also a traditional site of this event.)*

DIBON *("river course")*, **Dhiban**, *Dibon-gad*

This Moabite city was located about 2 miles north of Arair, on the edge of the Arnon valley (Wadi el Mojib), 15 miles south of Madeba and 13 miles east of the Dead Sea. It was apparently the home of King Mesha of Moab, and it also achieved importance in Roman times.

The large mound of Dhiban, north of the modern village, was recently excavated by Nelson Glueck, and it was found that the site dates back to 3000 B.C., and that the ancient Early Iron Age site was northeast of the main area of excavation. The whole surface of the mound is covered with early Arab and Byzantine ruins, immediately below which are remains of the Romans and Nabataeans.

In 1868 a missionary, F. A. Klein, found the *Moabite Stone* (Mesha

Stone) at Dhiban. It is now in the Louvre. The stone is dated at approximately 830 B.C., and its great importance lies in its close correspondence with the Old Testament narrative. The inscription on the stone commemorates victories of Mesha, king of Moab, over Israel (2 Kings 3:4). The revolt took place in the later years of Ahab's reign.

The stone refers to the present-day city of Madeba and Chemosh, the national god of Moab. Mesha tells of the Israelite prisoners and the ditches they dug for him. He fought against Israel to take Nebo and slew 7,000 men, boys, and girls. The inscription reads like a chapter of the Old Testament, and as an external evidence of the Old Testament scriptures the stone is significant.

- *Sihon, king of the Amorites, took Dibon from the Moabites (Num. 21:26, 30).*
- *It was assigned to Reuben and built by Gad (Josh. 13:7-9, 15, 17; Num. 32:1-7, 34).*
- *It was a Moabite town (Isa. 15:1-2; Jer. 48:18, 20-22).*
- *It was taken by Moab under King Mesha, as mentioned in his stela, the Moabite Stone.*

AROER *("juniper")*, **Ara'ir**

This is a town high above the northern bank of the Arnon River, 3½ miles southeast of Dhiban. It belonged to Reuben's tribe.

- *It was a town on the Arnon River (Josh. 12:2; 13:9, 16; Judg. 11:26).*
- *It was taken by the Israelites from King Sihon (Deut. 2:32-34, 36; 4:46-48).*
- *The census of David began here (2 Sam. 24:1, 5).*
- *Hazael occupied Aroer when he overran Transjordan (2 Kings 10: 32-33).*
- *On the Moabite Stone, Mesha records that he fortified Aroer and built a road by the Arnon River.*

RIVER ARNON, **Wadi el Mujib**, *Wadi Mojib, Wadi el Mojib*

This is a valley and stream which gathers water from many tributaries as it flows to the Dead Sea. It was the border between Moab and the land of the Amorites on the north. On the way to Wadi Mojib the traveler will notice two **ROMAN MILESTONES**.

- *It was mentioned as the north border of Moab and the south border of the Amorites (Num. 21:13).*
- *Isaiah referred to it as it flowed between high perpendicular rocks near the Dead Sea. He called it the "fords of Arnon" (Isa. 16:2).*

Qasr, *El Qasr ("the castle")*

Ten miles south of Wadi Mojib are these ruins of a small Nabataean temple, on a plateau near the road. Some pieces of sculpture from the temple have been incorporated into houses in the village.

Rabbah, *Rabba*

Three miles south of Qasr is the site of this ancient Moabite city. In biblical times, *Rabbah* was the name of the present capital city of Amman. Some believe this was also the site of the Roman acropolis. Fine columns and a temple facade are the chief remains. There are also remains of Byzantine houses.

KIR-HARESETH, *Crac de Montreal*, **Karak**, *Al Karak*, *Kerak*

Forty miles south of Madeba, 10 miles east of the Dead Sea, on the Wadi Karak, is the city of Karak. It is situated on a plateau 3,400 feet above sea level, and the "Mountain Road" to Karak follows the crest of the Moabite range. This was a chief city of Moab, dominating the main caravan route linking Syria to Egypt and Arabia.

An ancient citadel, Le Crac de Montreal, dates back to the Crusader period and offers an excellent reconstruction of the life of the Frankish knights, who held it from A.D. 1142 to 1187. This was a part of the Crusader system of fortification by which they dominated the area until Saladin conquered the Citadel in A.D. 1187.

- *It was a strong, important place in Moab (2 Kings 3:24–25).*
- *Isaiah mourned for Kir-hareseth (Isa. 16:7).*

Mauta *and* Mazar

Six miles south of Karak is Mauta, where the first clash between the Islamic and Byzantine forces occurred in A.D. 632. The Arab leaders killed in the battles were buried in the village of Mazar, 2 miles south of Mauta, where a very large mosque has been built over the tomb of Jaafar ibn Abi Taleb.

WADI HASA

Wadi Hasa was the northern limit of Edom (Seir), where Esau wandered after losing his birthright (Gen. 36:6–8).

Khirbet et Tannur

About 15 miles directly south of Karak is Jebel Tannur (mountains of Tannur), on the peak of which there is a temple accessible only on the southeast side by a single steep path. The temple dates from the first century B.C. and is one of the very few Nabataean temples ever to have been excavated. The temple was richly decorated with carving and sculpture, most of which is now housed in the museum at Amman.

KING'S HIGHWAY, Mountain Road

The King's Highway was an old trade route which extended from Syria on the north to Elath on the Gulf of Aqaba. The route existed through the Jordan area which included Edom, Moab, Ammon, and Gilead, and was used through the entire Old Testament period. The modern name for the King's Highway is *Mountain Road*. It runs parallel to and west of the *Desert Road*, with a strip of land about 20 miles wide between them.

- *The Edomites refused Moses and Israel permission to cross Edom via the King's Highway (Num. 20:14–21).*
- *When permission to use the King's Highway to cross Amorite territory was refused, this led to the first battle of the conquest (Num. 21:21–24).*

Shaubak, *Montreal*

Sixteen miles northeast of Petra and 46 miles south of Karak is Shaubak, a fortress built by Baldwin I in A.D. 1115 to control the road from Damascus to Egypt. It was called Montreal because a king founded it. Saladin captured it in 1189, and it was restored by the Mamelukes in the fourteenth century. The circle of walls and the gateway of the castle are complete, but within is only the modern village.

MA'AN

It is believed by some that Ma'an, 20 miles southeast of Petra, was the scene of the healing of the children of Israel by the miracle of the brazen serpent.

- *Moses set a serpent of brass upon a pole (Num. 21:4–9; John 3:14).*

MERIBAH, Ain Musa

A crystal clear cool spring of water gushes forth from the ground in Wadi Musa, about 3 miles east of Petra. Moslems believe this is where Moses struck the rock and water came forth (Num. 20:7–13).

SELA (*"rock"*), SELAH, Petra (*"rock" or "cliff"*), *Joktheel*

The rose-red Nabataean city of Petra is located 169 miles south-southwest of Amman and 50 miles south of the Dead Sea. It is in the canyon of Wadi Musa, surrounded by the rugged mountains of Edom, and was once the capital of Edom. Petra was probably the land of the biblical Horites around 2000 B.C. (Gen. 14:6; 36:20–21, 29–30). Esau, Jacob's brother, migrated to this area and was the ancestor of the Edomites.

The valley is entered by the Siq, a narrow defile in the red sandstone cliffs that rise 200–300 feet. This narrow entrance is only 8 feet wide at some places, and is something less than 2 miles long. Visitors usually ride into Petra on horseback.

About 300 B.C. the Nabataeans from North Africa settled in Petra and carved their homes in the red sandstone. They plundered caravans going between Arabia, Syria, and Egypt, and hid the stolen goods in the caves of Petra. Later they stopped plundering but exacted a high toll for safe passage of the caravans. The Nabataeans prospered and extended their kingdom as far north as Damascus. A Nabataean governor ruled Damascus when Paul was converted.

The Romans under Trajan conquered Petra in A.D. 106 and carved homes, baths, palaces, shops, and an amphitheater that seats 3,000-5,000 persons in the living rose-colored sandstone. During the Roman period there were as many as 7,000 people living in Petra.

The
Treasury,
Petra

The Byzantines lived here in the fourth century, then later the Crusaders, followed by the Moslems. When Petra flourished, there were as many as 6,000 to 7,000 people dwelling in the rock-hewn houses of Petra. It was a wealthy Nabataean city in the days of Jesus. Not only was it the Nabataean capital but it was the center of the caravan trade during the Christian era.

Petra was lost to the world for hundreds of years until 1812, when Johann Burckhardt, posing as a Moslem who had vowed to sacrifice a goat at the altar of Aaron, looked with wonder into the valley. The huge temples and buildings are an artistic and engineering marvel. The city remains a provocative mystery to every visitor.

POINTS OF INTEREST

The SIQ is the narrow winding defile that leads from the east into the area of Petra. It is in Wadi Musa, on the dry riverbed.

The TREASURY (Al Khazneh) is Petra's most exquisite building, ornamented with rock-carved 50-foot Corinthian columns, goddesses in niches, floral pediments, and topped by a rock urn. It is the first large building the visitor sees as he progresses through the Siq.

The ROMAN THEATER was carved into a 300-foot stone, and the facades of ancient tombs were cut away to provide seats high in the cliffs. It seats 3,000 people and dates from the second or third century.

Ornamentation on the
El Deir Monastery,
Petra

The **PALACE TOMB** is one of Petra's largest buildings. It is on the right as you near the **PROCESSION STREET** and **TRIUMPHAL ARCH**. Three stories high, it is believed to be a copy of a Roman palace. Four doors lead into small rooms.

The **URN TOMB** is to the right of the Palace Tomb. It opens onto a paved courtyard with a rock-cut colonnade. A unique feature of this tomb is the extension of the courtyard outward on vaults two stories high. A Greek inscription painted on the walls says that this building was used as a Christian church in A.D. 447.

The **CORINTHIAN TOMB** is between the Palace Tomb and Urn Tomb.

The **TEMPLE**, near the rest house, is the only free-standing building that remains in Petra.

UM EL BIYARA, the Edomite acropolis, is a huge, flat-topped rock rising a thousand feet above the Petra basin. Similar to Masada in Israel, it dominates Petra as it dominated the ancient caravan routes. Biblical scholars believe this was the Selah from which King Amaziah cast down 10,000 Edomites. When Obadiah refers to the Edomites living "in the clefts of the rock" (Obad. 1–4), it is very possible that the "rock" has reference to the **EDOMITE FORTRESS** on top of Um el Biyara, around which the Nabataeans later built their capital city.

The **MONASTERY** (El-Deir) is located northwest of the rest house, at the head of Wadi el Deir. This is Petra's most gigantic building, carved 165 feet wide and 148 feet high into a mountaintop cliff. It is believed to have been a temple, but at one time was used as a Chris-

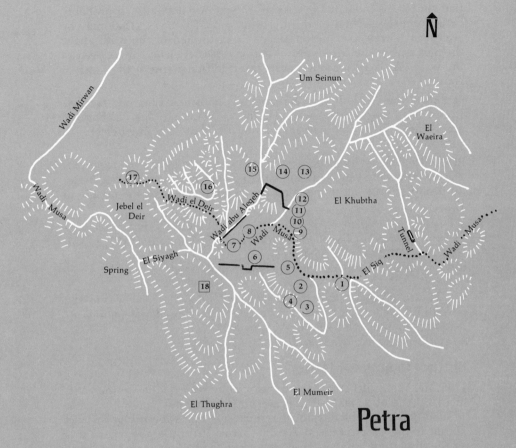

N̂

Um Seinun

El Waeira

Wadi Mirwan

⑰

Wadi Musa

Jebel el Deir

⑯

Wadi el Deir

⑮   ⑭ ⑬

Wadi abu Aleqeh

El Khubtha

⑫
⑪
⑩
⑨

⑧
⑦

Wadi Musa

El Siyagh

⑥

Tunnel

Spring

⑤

El Siq

Wadi Musa

①

⑱

②

④   ③

El Mumeir

El Thughra

Petra

1. Treasury
2. High place
3. Garden tomb
4. Statue tomb
5. Roman theater
6. City wall
7. Temple
8. Triumphal arch
9. Urn tomb
10. Corinthian tomb
11. Palace tomb
12. Florentine tomb
13. Places of the Christians
14. Circular high place
15. Tomb with Nabataean inscription
16. Lion tomb
17. El Deir Monastery
18. Um el Biyara

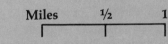

Miles   ½   1

||||| Enclosing hills or plateaus

tian church, as indicated by crosses carved into its walls. It probably dates from the second or third century A.D. The **LION TOMB** may be seen on the way to the monastery. From the top of the wadi above the monastery, the Mountain of Aaron, **MOUNT HOR**, can be seen in the west. A small mosque marks the traditional site of the tomb of Aaron.

EL BARID, the "little Petra," has rock-cut halls and elaborate facades. It also has huge subterranean cisterns for water storage. El Barid is accessible only by two passages so narrow that only one person can pass at a time.

REST HOUSES. At the new rest house just outside the Siq, approximately 60 people can be accommodated with meals and beds. About 70 people can be accommodated at the guest house in the middle of Petra.

- *The Edomites incurred the displeasure of God for refusing passage of the children of Israel through their land (Num. 20:14-21; Obad. 10; Amos 1:11; Ezek. 25:12-14).*
- *Amaziah of Jerusalem, king of Israel, took Selah by war (2 Kings 14:1, 7).*
- *It is very probable that the expression "thou that dwellest in the clefts of the rock" refers to the Edomites who dwelt in ancient Petra (Isa. 42:11; Jer. 49:16-17; Obad. 3).*
- *Isaiah mentioned Sela (Isa. 16:1).*

MOUNT HOR, Jebel Harun

From the peaks of Petra, Mount Hor can be seen 2 miles to the west, at an altitude of 4,780 feet. It is ascended from Petra.

Tradition since the days of Josephus says that Mount Hor in Jebel Harun is the "Mountain of Aaron" above Petra. Arabs regard this as the mountain where Aaron, the brother of Moses, died and was buried, and they have erected a tomb under a small dome on the top of the peak. Modern scholars doubt the tradition and fix other sites, such as Jebel Madra, northwest of Ain Qadeis (Kadesh-Barnea), as the place where Aaron died.

- *Aaron died at Mount Hor (Num. 33:37-39).*

RAS EN NAQB, Ras el Negeb

This was the site of an Edomite fortress that forced the Israelites to go through the wilderness on their journey to Canaan. It is 20 miles southwest of Ma'an.

- *The Israelites had to go around Edom (Num. 21:4).*
- *The road north from Ras en Naqb follows the ancient Roman road built over the King's Highway of the time of Moses (Num. 20:17).*

WADI EL ARABAH

This huge depression, a rift zone, extends from the Dead Sea to the Gulf of Aqaba. In ancient times the wadi was rich in copper and other minerals. The copper mines there furnish an explanation of one of the chief sources of Solomon's wealth. It was exported and used within Israel for such things as the construction of Solomon's temple and palace in Jerusalem.

- *The promised land contained an area full of iron and copper (translated as "brass") (Deut. 8:9).*
- *The harbor at Ezion-geber was a base for Solomon's trading fleet (1 Kings 9:26; 1 Kings 10:11, 22).*
- *Work in the copper mines began after David captured Edom (2 Sam. 8:13).*

AQABA

Located 210 miles south of Ammon, at the southern end of the Arabah and at the northeast corner of the Gulf of Aqaba, is Aqaba, Jordan's only seaport. Aqaba seems to have been founded in the thirteenth century B.C., as the southernmost city in the kingdom of Edom. The Phoenicians converted it into an important seaport under King Hiram of Tyre. During the Roman period (first to fourth century A.D.) Aqaba was an important stop on the great Roman road which ran from Damascus to Egypt. In A.D. 639 the great Arab caliph Omar visited Aqaba on one of his tours and stayed with its bishop. About A.D. 1116, the Crusaders occupied Aqaba under Baldwin I and built a small fortress, whose remains still stand on an island off the coast. Saladin and the Arabs came next, followed by the Mamelukes, who are credited with having built a fort in the fifteenth or sixteenth century A.D. During the First World War, King Faisal made Aqaba his headquarters after the Arabs captured the base from the Turks.

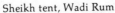
Sheikh tent, Wadi Rum

Like its closest neighbor to the west, Eilat, Aqaba is also a resort city. Fishing, swimming, water-skiing, skin diving, and boating in glass-bottom boats are pastimes in Aqaba. The temperature in winter rarely falls below 68 degrees Fahrenheit; in summer the temperature averages about 95 degrees Fahrenheit and sometimes in late July and August may rise as high as 120.

■ *The Queen of Sheba undoubtedly disembarked in the general area (1 Kings 10:1–13).*

Wadi Rum

Thirty miles east-northeast of Aqaba and 190 miles south of Amman is the spectacular "valley of the moon." This was the desert setting for the film "Lawrence of Arabia." Travelers usually visit this site in jeeps or on camels.

Lebanon

Situated at the strategically important eastern end of the Mediterranean, the "land bridge" of the conquering nations, Lebanon is a historically rich country. But it is very small in size (156 miles long and from 30 to 55 miles wide). Its 4,015-square-mile area is half the size of New Jersey. Of the total two to three million people, the capital city of Beirut has about half a million and Sidon about 50,000. On its southern 45-mile border is the country of Israel, and on the north and east is Syria. Two mountain ranges run north and south through the country: the Anti-Lebanons on the east and the Lebanon mountains on the west. Between these two ranges is the beautiful Bekaa Valley, 10 miles wide and 70 to 80 miles long. *Lebanon* means "white," and the country received its name from the white snow-capped peaks (Jer. 18:14).

HISTORY

The earliest inhabitants of Lebanon were the Semitic Canaanites, later called *Phoenicians* by the Greeks because of a purple dye, called "phoinix," which the Phoenicians manufactured and sold commercially. These early inhabitants were settled in coastal cities as early as 3000 B.C. From them we received an alphabet system that has blessed western civilization. It was the ancient Phoenician mariners that expanded trade, communication, and civilization as they sailed the Mediterranean and even the "unknown" Atlantic.

Being on the "fertile crescent," Lebanon was a natural victim of her conquering neighbors. In 1450 B.C. Pharaoh Thutmose III conquered Lebanon and she became a part of the Egyptian Empire. The Assyrians conquered Lebanon about 875 B.C., Babylonia in turn about 600 B.C., and later, around 525 B.C., Cyrus the Persian controlled the country. Alexander the Great helped to spread the Hellenic civilization to Lebanon when he set out to conquer the world in 334 B.C. When the citizens of Tyre refused him entry to their key naval base, Alexander besieged the city for six months, built a 200-foot-wide

MEDITERRANEAN SEA

To Latakia

Krak des Chevaliers

To Homs and Aleppo

Lake Homs

Tripoli

Zgharta

Hermel

Amioun

Batrun

Becharre

Orontes River

Rachana

Cedars of Lebanon

Anaya

Gebal (Byblos)

Adonis River

Afqa

Faraya

Baalbek

SYRIA

Harissa

Jeita

Inscription Rock

Dog River Valley

Bekaa Valley

Beirut

Beit Mari

Zahleh

Aley

Chtaura

Bhamdoun

Khalde

Anjar

Damour

Litani River

Bekaa Valley

Beiteddine

Sidon (Saida)

Rashaya

Damascus

Zarephath (Sarafand)

Hasbani River

Mount Hermon

Merjayun

Hasbaya

Beaufort Castle

Tyre (Sour)

Cana

Jordan River

N̂

Sea of Galilee

Lebanon

ISRAEL

Miles   10   15   20   25

mole, or causeway, to the island, and left the city in ruins. The Persian fleet, left without a port, became Alexander's. When Alexander died, his general Seleucus I, surnamed Nicator, founded the Seleucid Dynasty in Phoenicia, Turkey, Northern Syria, and Mesopotamia. This rule ended in 64 B.C. when Pompey annexed Lebanon to the Roman Empire. Under Roman rule the inhabitants of Byblos, Tyre, and Sidon were given Roman citizenship. Cedar, perfume, wine, pottery, glass, and purple dye were exported to Rome. A law school was established at Beirut, and this school became an important intellectual center for the Empire. In A.D. 395, when the Roman Empire was divided, Lebanon flourished and continued to do so through the Byzantine period. In the sixth century A.D. an earthquake destroyed the temples at Baalbek and Beirut, and nearly 30,000 people were killed.

The Arabs controlled Lebanon until A.D. 1260 and the area flourished. Castles and towers dot the countryside as reminders of the period of the Crusades in Lebanon (1100–1300), and mosques remind one of the Mamelukes (1252) and the Ottomans (1516–1918), who ruled Lebanon.

The modern state of Lebanon was created in 1920 from five Turkish districts of the Ottoman Empire. Under the League of Nations, Lebanon was assigned as a mandate to France from 1920 to 1943. At the conclusion of World War II French troops withdrew from Lebanon, and on November 26, 1941, she became an independent nation. Political problems continued, however, and it was not until the French withdrew on December 31, 1946, that Lebanon became completely independent.

During the Sinai-Suez crisis of 1956, the Chamber of Deputies announced its support of Egypt. In 1958 government opposition accused President Chamoun of trying to amend the constitution to seek reelection at the end of his six-year term in September, and demanded his immediate resignation. On July 14, the date of the coup d'etat which led to a change of regime in Iraq, President Chamoun requested the United States to send American troops into Lebanon to maintain security. By the first of August 10,000 American marines were in Lebanon. They withdrew three months later under United Nations auspices.

The newly elected president was General Fouad Chehab. In 1964 Charles Helou was elected president, and on September 23, 1970, Suleiman Franjieh, a Maronite Christian, became president of Lebanon for a six-year term.

- God told Moses to go to Lebanon (Deut. 1:7; 3:21–28).
- Lebanon was part of the territory Joshua expected to conquer (Josh. 13:5–6; Judg. 3:1–3).
- In Old Testament times Lebanon was inhabited by the Hivites and Giblites (Josh. 13:5–6; Judg. 3:3).
- The whole mountain range was assigned to the Israelites, but was never conquered by them (Josh. 13:2–6; Judg. 3:1–3).
- Prophets spoke of the fruitfulness, fragrance, and beauty of Lebanon

(Pss. 72:16; 104:16–18; Song of Sol. 4:15; Isa. 2:13; 35:2; 60:13; Hos. 14:5–7; Nah. 1:4).

- *Lebanon was famous for its cedars, which were used in the construction of Solomon's temple (1 Kings 5:8–11; 2 Chron. 2:8, 16; 2 Kings 14:9; Pss. 29:5; 92:12; 104:16; Isa. 2:13; 14:8; Ezek. 27:5; 31:3).*
- *Lebanese cedars were used in the construction of Solomon's palace (1 Kings 7:1–3, 7, 11–12) and also the second temple (Ezra 3:6–8).*
- *Lebanon was called Phoenicia in biblical days (Acts 11:19; 15:3; 21:2).*

RELIGION

Both Jesus and Paul the apostle visited Lebanon, and its valleys and hills have served as places of refuge for many minorities. Christian Anchorites, Moslem Sufis, Druze Ascetics, Maronite Sectarians, Shiites, and Armenians have sought peace in Lebanon. Although her neighbors are predominantly Moslem, mountainous Lebanon has a large Christian population, of whom Roman Catholics represent probably less than 2 percent and other Christians the remainder. The Moslems represent 40 percent and the Druzes about 6 percent of the population.

Parliament members are nominated by the different denominations. For example, a religion having six percent of the population also has 6 percent of the parliament members.

LEBANON TODAY

Since the second half of the nineteenth century, Beirut has been an educational center. The American University was founded in 1866 and the smaller French Saint Joseph's University in 1875. The Lebanese University was founded in 1951 and the Arab University in 1960. There are also 8 other institutions of higher learning. The literacy rate is about 86 percent, the highest in the Arab world. Primary schools are intended for children from 6 to 10 years of age. Youth 10 to 16 attend secondary schools that are almost all private schools.

The monetary unit in Lebanon is the Lebanese *pound (lira)*, divided into 100 *piasters*.

CITIES AND SITES

Beirut, *Berytus*

The capital of Lebanon is a very modern city, with a fifth (about 500,000) of the nation's total population. It boasts a large modern airport and the busiest port in the eastern Mediterranean. Money from Saudi Arabia and from other countries with oil is responsible for many large business and apartment buildings.

Beirut was a Roman colony in the time of Herod the Great and was the seat of a great Roman law school during the time of Justinian. It was destroyed by an earthquake in A.D. 551 and for a time was abandoned, but during the Crusades it once more became an important city.

Under the administration of the United Nations, approximately 350,000 Palestinian refugees live in refugee camps on the outskirts of Beirut. Many have lived there since 1948. Most are Arabs of the Moslem faith, but some are Armenians, Greeks, and Circassians. According to the law, they are not allowed to work in Lebanon, even though 125,000 Syrian laborers are brought into the country to work during labor shortages.

POINTS OF INTEREST

1. **LEBANESE UNIVERSITY.** Housed in the UNESCO palace buildings is a university that has schools of law, political science, pedagogy, literature, humanities, fine arts, sociology, journalism, and other disciplines.

2. **PIGEON ROCK GROTTO.** Near the coast, on the west side of the city, is this white rock rising out of the deep blue waters. It is very picturesque.

3. **LIGHTHOUSE.** Near the seacoast, between the American University of Beirut and Pigeon Rock Grotto, is a lighthouse.

4. **AMERICAN UNIVERSITY OF BEIRUT.** A beautiful hillside campus is the home of the largest American educational school outside the boundaries of the United States. It was founded as a small missionary college by Daniel Bliss, a Congregational minister, in 1866 and now has four faculties: (1) medical sciences (medicine, pharmacy, nursing, and public health); (2) arts and sciences, with 22 departments; and (3) engineering and (4) agricultural sciences. Over 100 different religion classes are taught in Christianity, Islam, and Judaism. The university has trained a great many world leaders. The 75-acre campus is considered to be one of the most beautiful in the world. In 1970 the enrollment was 4,129 students, representing 69 nations and 22 religions. The faculty numbers some 650. Most of them are Lebanese or American, but some are from Egypt, France, and Great Britain. The language of instruction is English.

The university's archaeological museum has an extensive collection of Phoenician artifacts.

5. **NATIONAL LIBRARY.** With 40,000 books and manuscripts, this is one of the best collections of Arabic manuscripts in the world. Many are very rare.

6. **GRAND MOSQUE OF BEIRUT** (El-Umari Mosque). This mosque, originally the Church of Saint John, was built in the twelfth century by the Knights Hospitalers on the site of a Roman temple, at the

1. Lebanese University
2. Pigeon Rock Grotto
3. Lighthouse
4. American University of Beirut
5. National Library
6. Grand Mosque of Beirut
7. Oriental bazaars
8. Sursock Museum
9. Saint Joseph University
10. School of Medicine
11. National Museum
12. Hippodrome
13. Sports City

present Place d'Etoile. It is the only well-preserved historical monument in Beirut.

7. **ORIENTAL BAZAARS.** All of the old bazaars were torn down years ago, but a few newer ones remain near the central section of the city.

8. **SURSOCK MUSEUM.** This is a museum of modern art founded by Nicolas Sursock, and located on Sursock Street. It houses rare books, manuscripts, oriental rugs, paintings, and sculpture.

9. **SAINT JOSEPH UNIVERSITY.** The French Jesuit fathers founded this university in 1875. It has schools of law, engineering, medicine, and oriental studies.

10. **SCHOOL OF MEDICINE.** North of the National Museum on Damascus Street is the School of Medicine.

11. **NATIONAL MUSEUM.** This is located on Damascus Street, at the intersection of Avenue Fouad I. It houses archaeological items that date back to 4000 B.C., and each exhibit is carefully labeled and described. The artifacts from Byblos are especially interesting.

The **MAIN FLOOR** is devoted to outstanding names and dates in the history of Lebanon. The Galleries of the Alphabet and of Colossus, and the Galleries of Ramses II, Echmon, Hygeia, and Jupiter are located on this floor.

The **MIDDLE HALL** has scale models of the reconstructed temple of Baalbek.

In the **BASEMENT** there is a display of tombs, sarcophagi, pieces of furniture, and funeral art, including the 3,000-year-old stone sarcophagus of Ahiram, king of Byblos, with one of the earliest alphabetical inscriptions in Phoenician script.

Other items of interest include a statue of the goddess Hygeia, an Aramaic sundial, the first Phoenician writing after the alphabet was invented (1300 B.C.), marble sarcophagi from Sidon, a private Roman family tomb with painted walls (including a scene from the *Iliad*), a statue of Phoenicia with the first alphabet over her head, skeletons in pottery jars (a very unique burial custom dating back to 3500 B.C.), jewelry, and other exhibits.

12. The HIPPODROME is just west of the National Museum.

13. SPORTS CITY is located in the south end of the city toward the airport, on Camille Chamoun Avenue.

EAST OF BEIRUT

Beit Mari, *Beit Meri, Bayt Miri*

Located at 2,600 feet above sea level, 9 miles east of Beirut, is this small village of 1,500 people. A sixteenth-century church is built on the foundation of a Roman temple to the god Baal Marqod. Other ruins of temples, baths, villas, and mosaics can still be seen.

Chtaura

On the eastern slope of the Lebanon Mountains, 28 miles from Beirut, is a resort town that features cheese, wine, and a favorite eating place, the Akl Restaurant.

Bekaa Valley, *El-Beqa*

This is a beautiful, rich valley about 70 miles long and 10 miles wide. The Lebanon Mountains are on the west side of the valley and the Anti-Lebanons on the east. The valley was known as the "bread basket" of the Roman Empire. MOUNT HERMON (9,055 feet high) is located at the southern end of the valley. The LITANI RIVER starts in the north end of the valley and drains into the Mediterranean north of Tyre.

■ *The Sidonian name for Mount Hermon is* Sirion (Sion) (*Deut. 3:9; 4:48; Ps. 29:6*).

Anjar

Near Anjar are the ruins of a seventh-century Umayyad city, comprising palaces, towers, and arcades. It is 35 miles from Beirut.

Baalbek, *Baalbeck, Heliopolis*

Baalbek is one of the most impressive monuments of the Roman period of history and the most important tourist attraction in Lebanon. It is near the northern end of the Bekaa Valley, close to the western slope of the Anti-Lebanon Mountains, 53 miles northeast of Beirut. History is silent as to its origin, but it is known to be one of the oldest cities in the world. Ruins show that at one time it was a great city, reaching across the entire valley. Baalbek is Lebanon's only inland city to achieve prominence. The present structures were begun under the emperor Augustus and continued to be built for 250 years. It was a project that needed funding from the whole empire.

The first temple of Baalbek was built to honor the Syrophoenician god Baal. The city was called *Baal-Bouqas,* or "City of Baal," but in the days of the Greeks and Romans it was called *Heliopolis,* the "City of the Sun." The temple remains are classical Roman ruins, unexcelled anywhere.

Baalbek has the most gigantic complex of Roman temples ever built, and the harmony of the proportions at a first glance disguises the massive scale of its dimensions. The visitor is not immediately aware that the columns he sees are among the tallest ever erected, the stones the largest ever used, and the whole group of edifices the biggest of its kind ever built. And all of this in the name of pagan religion. Perhaps this was an attempt by the Romans to stabilize their empire against the advances of Christianity.

When Constantine was converted to Christianity, a Christian church was built in the middle of the Court of the Altar, and in 634 a mosque was built. The minaret of the mosque, with a square base and octagonal top, still stands.

The world-famous Saladin, whose father was governor of Baalbek in the early twelfth century, spent his boyhood here.

Although a series of earthquakes destroyed a great deal of the temple complex, a restoration has preserved much of the original. The dining room of the Palmyra Hotel in Baalbek has a painting of the temples of Baalbek as they looked at the height of their glory.

Baalbek has become famous for its annual summer International Festival of Baalbek (July 15–August 31), which includes dancing, musicals, opera, choirs, orchestras, and concerts of various kinds, with the temples of Baalbek as a beautiful backdrop. This festival is the main cultural event of the year in Lebanon. There is also a "sound and light" production on Saturday and Sunday evenings (English at 7:00 P.M.) during the months of April through October.

POINTS OF INTEREST

The **PROPYLAEA** (ca. A.D. 225) is a rectangular colonnade with twelve Corinthian columns and measures about 150 feet wide and 30

Temple of
Bacchus,
Baalbek

Above: Temple of
Jupiter, Baalbek
Below: Altar of
Sacrifices, Baalbek

feet deep. It is approached by a majestic stairway. This is the entrance to what is called the **ACROPOLIS**.

The **HEXAGONAL COURT** (A.D. 249) is a colonnaded forecourt, the second area of importance. It measures 212 feet in diameter. It was

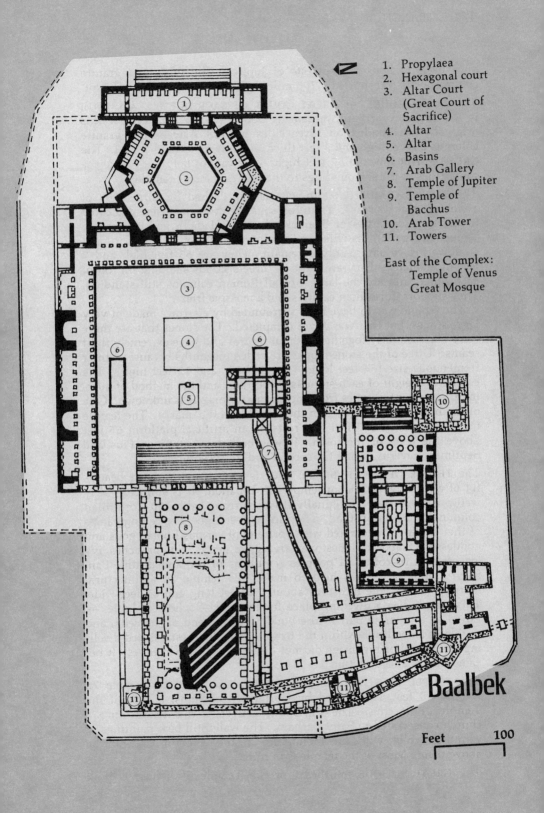

1. Propylaea
2. Hexagonal court
3. Altar Court
   (Great Court of
   Sacrifice)
4. Altar
5. Altar
6. Basins
7. Arab Gallery
8. Temple of Jupiter
9. Temple of
   Bacchus
10. Arab Tower
11. Towers

East of the Complex:
Temple of Venus
Great Mosque

Baalbek

Feet 100

once used to house the priests of Jupiter. The thirty red granite columns were transported 1,200 miles from Aswan quarries, in Egypt.

The **ALTAR COURT**, or **GREAT COURT OF SACRIFICE** (ca. A.D. 150), is the largest courtyard, measuring about 400 by 385 feet. It was originally surrounded on three sides by 128 Aswan rose granite columns 25 feet high and 3 feet thick, supporting a wooden roof. The **GREAT ALTAR** towered 57 feet high. One cannot help but notice the similarities of the surroundings to those of Solomon's temple.

The **TEMPLE OF JUPITER** (A.D. 60) is approached by three tiers of a monumental staircase. Tradition says the three tiers were dedicated to the triad divinities of Baalbek: Jupiter (Hadad), god of heaven; Venus (Atargatis), his wife; and Mercury, their son. Of the original 54 towering columns, only 6 remain. They are 65 feet high and 7 feet in diameter. They are built in three sections standing on top of each other, and are the largest of all Roman columns still standing. They support Corinthian capitals and a massive frieze.

The temple was to have been surrounded by a terrace made of very large stones, but that was never completed. The stones that are there were placed tightly together without mortar and have extremely tight seams. Three of the stone blocks are called megaliths because of their tremendous size (64 feet long, 15 feet thick, and 12 feet high). The estimated weight of each stone is 1,000 tons, and the method of moving these gigantic stones from the quarry to this site is unknown. One of the blocks even larger than these is still in the quarry. The temple measures 290 by 160 feet and rests on an artificial platform 65 feet above the level of the town. It was built by Antoninus Pius and Septimius Severus during the second and third centuries.

The **TEMPLE OF BACCHUS** (A.D. 150) is known as the most beautiful of all surviving Roman temples in Lebanon. It is still in a fairly well-preserved state. Originally it was surrounded by 50 Corinthian columns, and 24 still stand. They are 57 feet high. The ceiling panels of the temple are decorated with portraits of various Roman gods and goddesses. Elaborate limestone carvings of pearls, vine branches, ivy leaves, ears of corn and poppies (emblems of life and death), Pan, Satyrs, and Bacchantes help to make this temple an architectural marvel. The temple measures about 115 feet long and 65 feet wide. This temple has a dwelling place for the god — a holy of holies — raised as a separate part of the building at the end of the cella, and visible as an aedicula within the temple. This long-established dwelling of the god or his image did not disappear in Roman times. It became the Lebanese adytum.

The **TEMPLE OF VENUS** (ca. A.D. 225), a small circular temple 75 feet by 50 feet, surrounded by Corinthian columns, is east of the Temple of Bacchus. The Christians converted this temple into a church consecrated to Saint Barbara. The walls still bear paintings in vermilion color with the monogram of the emperor Constantine above them. Most of the temple is in ruins.

The **GREAT MOSQUE**, northeast of the Temple of Venus, is built of stones and columns from the temples. The minaret may still be seen.

■ *Some believe that the biblical town of Baalath ("belonging to Baal"), an inheritance of Dan, was located at the present-day Baalbek. Some believe this is the Baalath that was built and enlarged for a trade emporium by Solomon. There is no conclusive evidence to confirm either of these two claims, however (Josh. 19:40, 44; 1 Kings 9:17-19; 2 Chron. 8:6).*

SOUTH OF BEIRUT
Beiteddine Palace and Folklore Museum
Twenty-nine miles south-southeast of Beirut is one of the finest examples of classic Lebanese architecture. This palace was built by Emir Beshir-Chehab (1788–1840) and was later used as the residence of Lebanese governors until 1914. The president of the republic sometimes spends parts of the summer here. It has beautiful mosaic floors, arcades, Turkish baths, formal gardens, and a folklore museum.

Khalde
Located 3 miles south of Choueifat, this is where, according to tradition, Jonah was disgorged by the big fish (Jon. 2:10).

SIDON *("fortified")*, ZIDON, Saida
This city, founded by Sidon, firstborn of Canaan, about 2750 B.C., is 28 miles south of Beirut and 25 miles north of Tyre, on the Mediterranean seacoast. It was the ancient capital of the Phoenicians. Its present population is 40,000 and it is one of the oldest Phoenician cities. It was a famous maritime center before Tyre was even built. Like the other cities on the "fertile crescent," it was conquered by the various world powers. At one time, when Ochus, king of Persia, besieged it with 300,000 men, the citizens shut themselves up in the city, burned their fleet, and then burned their homes and perished with their wives and children rather than fall into his hand. About 40,000 died in the flames. In A.D. 1111 it was captured by the Crusaders, who held it until Saladin took it for the Arabs in 1187. The Crusaders regained the town twice after that, but finally abandoned it in the thirteenth century.

The beauty of Sidon's metalwork in silver and bronze and her textile fabrics, embroidered and dyed in the famous Tyrian purple dye, were known everywhere and often mentioned by Greek writers such as Homer. During the time of Augustus and Tiberius, Sidon was noted for its school of philosophy and the great law school that was moved there in 551 B.C.

Sidon was the home of Boethius, the Stoic philosopher (second century B.C.). He rejected pantheism and divided the universe into two parts, one of which was divine and comprised the fixed stars.

Zeno, also of Sidon, was born about 150 B.C. He headed the

Sidon

Epicurean school at Athens, where Cicero audited his lectures. In addition to philosophy, Zeno labored on the fundamentals of geometry.

Today Saida is an important administrative center of South Lebanon and shipping center for the Trans-Arabian Oil pipeline.

POINTS OF INTEREST

The **CASTLE OF THE SEA** is a thirteenth-century Crusader fortress built on an isle in the north harbor. Roman pillars may be seen as a part of the walls.

The **KHAN-EL-FRANJ**, a seventeenth-century fortified warehouse in the old city, was once the residence of the French Consul. Today it is a girls' orphanage.

The **GREAT MOSQUE**, *Jami' al-Kebir*, was previously a church fortress of the Knights of Saint John (Hospitalers).

The ruins of the **CASTLE OF SAINT LOUIS**, where Louis IX of France stayed during his brief reign over Jerusalem (1250–54), are in Sidon. It is also called the "Castle of the Land."

The **HILL OF MUREX**, near the castle, is named after the small shell, murex, from which the Phoenicians extracted their famous purple dye.

The **TABLUN CAVES** are located in the Ain al-Hilweh area, south of the city of Sidon. Near the caves, excavations have unearthed an ancient

Phoenician city. A grave dating back to 400 B.C. had a skeleton of a woman wearing a golden crown, and her body was covered with jewelry. A small statue of Astarte (Ashtoreth), the Phoenician goddess of love, was also found there. This was the first Phoenician grave ever found intact and untouched by robbers. In the same area was found a sarcophagus of King Ashmon Azr II (Eshmunazar) (280 B.C.), now located in the Louvre, in Paris. It has the longest Phoenician inscription ever found. The "ship sarcophagus" in the Beirut Museum was also found there.

Many anthropoidal coffins of Greek marble were found at Ain al-Hilweh. They are in the Beirut Museum. The design for these coffins undoubtedly originated in Egypt.

At Sidon have also been found SCULPTURES REPRESENTING THE CULT OF MITHRAS, a god of Persian origin and a rival of early Christianity. No other Mithraic monuments have been found in Lebanon.

The PHOENICIAN TEMPLE OF ESHMUN, north of Sidon, dates from the fifth century B.C. The temple, called also the *Asklepeion,* is located on a farm called *Bostan al-Sheikh,* near the old bridge built over the River Nahr al-Awali. To the ancients this was the River Asklepios, or Bostrenus. The god Eshmun was the god of healing, like Asklepios (Asclepias).

AYAA is a hamlet east of the city, where the coffin of King Tabnith, father of Eshmunazar, and four magnificent sarcophagi enriched with sculptures were found. These were known as (1) the *Tomb of Alexander the Great,* who died in 323 B.C. in Babylon but was apparently buried in the nearest royal tomb at Sidon; (2) the *Weeping Women's Tomb;* (3) the *Lycian Tomb,* and (4) the *Satrap Tomb.* The first two of these four are now in the Archaeological Museum at Istanbul. Also east of the city in the foothills is the so-called Tomb of Zebulon.

The OLD QUARTERS of the city are worth visiting. Tiny streets with odd and unexpected passages seem to be a resurrection of the Middle Ages.

On the land side of Sidon are GROVES OF TREES: lemon, almond, apricot, orange, banana, and palm.

- *Sidon was founded by Sidon, grandson of Ham, and was the northernmost Canaanite city (Gen. 10:15-20; 1 Chron. 1:13).*
- *It was mentioned in Jacob's prophecy (Gen. 49:13).*
- *Joshua chased the kings of Zidon (Josh. 11:1-8).*
- *The area was allotted to Asher but never occupied (Josh. 13:2, 6; Judg. 1:31; 3:1-3).*
- *Sidon oppressed Israel (Judg. 10:12).*
- *Israel sinned in worshiping the goddess of the Zidonians (Judg. 10:6; 1 Kings 11:5, 33).*
- *This was the home of Jezebel, daughter of Ethbaal, king of Zidon, and the wicked wife of King Ahab. Baal worship was introduced to Israel through her (1 Kings 16:31-33).*
- *It was renowned for its seaborne trade (Isa. 23:2, 4).*

Above: Weeping Women's Tomb, Sidon

Right: Musician playing a rababah, Sidon

- *Ezekiel uttered prophecies against the wicked city of Zidon (Ezek. 28:21–23).*
- *Prophecies stand against it (Jer. 25:18, 22; Ezek. 28:21–23; Zech. 9:1–2).*

■ *Men from Sidon heard Jesus (Mark 3:8; Luke 6:17).*
■ *Jesus pronounced a woe upon it (Matt. 11:21–22; Luke 10:13–14).*
■ *Jesus healed the daughter of a Syrophoenician woman near here (Matt. 15:21–28; Mark 7:24–30).*
■ *Herod was displeased with the Sidonians (Acts 12:20).*
■ *Paul landed here on his way to Rome (Acts 27:3).*

ZAREPHATH, Sarafand, *Sarepta*

This was a Sidonian town about 13 miles north of Tyre, or midway between Tyre and Sidon.

■ *Zarephath belonged to Zidon (1 Kings 17:9; Luke 4:26).*
■ *Here Elijah, after leaving the brook Cherith, was entertained by the widow whose barrel of meal wasted not and whose son Elijah raised from the dead (1 Kings 17:8–24; Luke 4:25–26).*
■ *Some believe that the Syrophoenician whose daughter Jesus healed was from Zarephath (Matt. 15:21–28; Mark 7:24–30).*

TYRE ("rock"), Sour ("fortress wall")

Tyre, 52 miles south of Beirut, was a sister city of Sidon and was the most important city of Phoenicia. It was from Tyre that the famous Phoenician seamen set out to establish the first commercial system in the ancient world. By 1100 B.C. they had sailed beyond the Straits of Gibraltar, and by 900 B.C. they had founded Carthage. Their mariners founded colonies in Spain and north and west Africa, and they sailed as far as Britain, the Red Sea, and the Indian Ocean. The date of the first inhabitants of Tyre is unknown, but its temple of Hercules is said to have been built in 2300 B.C., which probably means there were people in the city at least by 2700 B.C.

The city was originally built partly on the mainland and partly on an island. It had two harbors, one on the north and one on the south, connected by a canal. The island was protected on the land side by a wall 150 feet high, and the population on the island is said to have numbered 40,000. Tyre was subordinate to Sidon until about the twelfth century B.C., when the Philistines subdued Sidon. Tyre then became the leading city. Its great strength is shown by the fact that it withstood the power of such great kings as Tiglath-pileser, Shalmaneser, and Nebuchadnezzar, who besieged the city for 13 years without taking the island part of it. It was overcome by Alexander the Great in 332 B.C., after he built a causeway and blockaded the island for 7 months. He killed 10,000 and took 30,000 captive as slaves. In 40 B.C. Tyre could not be taken by the Parthians, who conquered Syria.

The Epicurean philosopher and poet Antipater (95–46 B.C.) was born in Tyre. He is known especially for his epigrams and epitaphs. It is from Antipater that we have the earliest extant listing of the so-called Seven Wonders of the Ancient World.

Diodorus, the philosopher, was also from Tyre. He headed the Peripatetic school at Athens about 110 B.C. He taught that the greatest good consisted of virtue with absence of pain — a viewpoint that attempted to be a reconciliation between Stoic and Epicurean viewpoints.

The city of Tyre accepted Christianity by the end of the second century A.D. It became the seat of a bishopric and was the scene of a number of councils, such as the one which considered charges against Athanasius in the fourth century. Later on, however, because of an anti-Christian philosophy in Tyre, the city became obnoxious to Christians.

Today the ancient island city is connected to the mainland by a ½-mile causeway created from silting around the mole built by Alexander the Great. Much archaeological excavation is being done there now. Because of an earthquake, the **ROMAN RUINS** are to be found both on land and under the sea. The **ROMAN CEMETERY** is especially fascinating. There are also Greek and Arab ruins.

About 5 miles southeast of Tyre is a traditional monolithic **SARCOPHAGUS**. Some believe it to be the burial tomb of King Hiram of Tyre, but some believe the tomb postdates Hiram by 4 centuries.

Eight miles south of Tyre are reservoirs and aqueducts at **RAS EL-AIN**. According to tradition, they were built by Solomon in payment for cedar wood, brass, and workmen supplied by Hiram for building Solomon's temple.

- *Tyre was assigned to the tribe of Asher but never occupied (Josh. 19:24, 29).*
- *Joshua referred to the "strong city Tyre" (Josh. 19:29).*
- *Hiram, king of Tyre, built David a house (2 Sam. 5:11; 1 Chron. 14:1).*

Temple of Jupiter, Tyre

St. Peter's Square, Rome

- *Hiram was a "lover of David" (1 Kings 5:1).*
- *Hiram furnished materials (cedar and brass) and workmen to aid Solomon in building the temple at Jerusalem (1 Kings 7:13–46; 9:11; Ezra 3:7).*
- *Hiram sent cedar wood for the altar in the temple (1 Kings 6:20).*
- *Hiram cast two temple pillars out of brass for Solomon's temple. He also cast out of brass the molten sea on the backs of twelve oxen, as well as lavers, shovels, pots, and other items used in the temple (1 Kings 7:13–47).*
- *Tyrian Sabbath breakers disturbed Nehemiah (Neh. 13:15–16).*
- *The destruction of Tyre was prophesied (Isa. 23; Jer. 25:18, 22; 47:4; Ezek. 26–28; Amos 1:9–10; Zech. 9:1–4; Joel 3:4–8; Hos. 9).*
- *People from Tyre heard Jesus preach (Mark 3:8; Luke 6:17).*
- *Jesus compared Chorazin and Bethsaida to Tyre and Sidon (Matt. 11:21–22; Luke 10:13–14).*
- *Jesus healed the Syrophoenician woman's daughter near here (Matt. 15:21–28; Mark 7:24–30).*
- *Herod had trouble with the Tyrians (Acts 12:20–23).*
- *Paul spent seven days here on his last journey to Jerusalem (Acts 21:2–6).*

Beaufort Castle, *Qalaat esh-Shaqif*

About 60 miles southeast of Beirut at Arnun is a castle on a sheer cliff 1,000 feet above the Litani River. This crusader castle was taken from Emir Shibab el-Din by Foulques of Anjou, king of Jerusalem. It was later occupied by the Lords of Sayette, Saladin, and the Knights Templars. The Mameluke Sultan Baybars captured it in 1268, and it was last used in the seventeenth century by Fakhr al-Din as a fortress of defense against a Turkish siege.

CANA, Qana

Located southeast of Tyre, this is the site that some believe to be the Cana where Jesus performed his first miracle — that of changing water to wine.

- *Cana was the home of Nathanael (John 1:43–51; 21:2).*
- *It was the scene of Jesus' first miracle (John 2:1–11).*

NORTH OF BEIRUT

Dog River Valley *and* Inscription Rock

At the mouth of the Dog River, 9 miles north of Beirut, is a limestone rock that bears nineteen inscriptions in eight languages commemorating military feats. The languages include Egyptian (Ramses II), Assyrian (Esarhaddon), Babylonian (Nebuchadnezzar), Greek, Latin (Caracalla), French (Napoleon), English (Allenby), and the last one in Arabic by the Republic of Lebanon, commemorating the last troops of the French forces who left Lebanon on December 31, 1946. This location was the point where the natives took a stand against the invaders.

Arch of Titus, Rome

Jeita

A subterranean lake along the gorge of the Dog River is called the GROTTO OF JEITA. This is the source of the Dog River and Beirut's water supply. Explorers have probed the grotto as far as 20,000 feet. A boat takes the visitor on a 45-minute ride through the fairyland of stalagmites and stalactites. The dry upper grotto is reached by cable car.

Harissa

In the mountains 20 miles north of Beirut (altitude 1,700 feet) is Harissa. Here a huge statue and chapel of "Our Lady of Lebanon" may be seen. A cable car ride from Jounie brings the visitor to Harissa, a restaurant, and a captivating view of Jounie Bay in the Mediterranean.

GEBAL, *Gubla, Giblet,* **Byblos,** *Bibylus*

Byblos is the Greek word for "book," from which we get the word *Bible.* The merchants of Byblos supplied the Greeks with most of the Egyptian papyrus which they used for paper. The Greeks called the papyrus *byblos,* after the city of its origin.

According to tradition, Byblos dates its origins back to the dawn of time (5000 B.C. — Neolithic Age). Like Jericho, its ruins cover a historical span of more than 7,000 years. It is the oldest city of the Phoenicians and was a chief center for 1,800 years. The Canaanite god *El,* whom the Greeks identified with Chronos, was worshiped in Byblos. In the early Canaanitish times, Gebal was the scene of much religious activity. The cult of Ishtar, a female fertility goddess, attained prominence. In later time, her worship was assimilated with the worship of Venus or Aphrodite.

The nearby modern town of JEBEIL has a population of 2,000 and is 24 miles north of Beirut.

In 1860 Ernest Renan began archaeological diggings there, followed by the Egyptologist Pierre Montet in 1920–24. Still later, the Lebanese government took over and continued the digging until most of the ancient Phoenician town had been cleared. Over 45,000 objects have been recovered from the ruins. They are now in the Beirut National Museum.

To get the best view of the site, the visitor should climb to the top of the FRANKISH CASTLE in the southeast corner. The site covers about 25 acres and the tell is approximately 30 feet higher than the surrounding area.

At Byblos archaeologists have identified 21 cultures, dating from the Neolithic period (before 3200 B.C.) to the Ottoman period (A.D. 1516–1918). Evidences of international trade are abundant in Byblos. Egypt, Babylonia, Cyprus, Italy, Spain, England, Germany, and Greece traded with Byblos, and from Byblos the cedars of Lebanon were shipped to David and Solomon.

The famous *Tell el 'Amarna Tablets* contain diplomatic correspondence between the Phoenician princes of Byblos and the Pharaohs

Amenhotep III and IV, each prince clearing himself of any disloyalty to Egypt and accusing his neighbors, the Syrians (1580–1200 B.C.). It was at this time that the first documents in alphabetic writing made their appearance. Ugarit used 31 signs of cuneiform aspect, while at Byblos there was a more cursive script, with 22 signs. This could be used to write on papyrus, and it spread over the whole world except China.

By the Roman period (63 B.C.-A.D. 330), Byblos was a minor town compared to Antioch, Tyre, and Sidon. It was a great city, however, because it was the center of the cult of Adonis, who was said to have been born out of a tree and died at Aphca, the source of the Adonis River, after a boar gashed his groin. His blood flowed out and its gift of life passed into the flowers. From its drops sprang the beautiful red anemones (lilies of the field).

The waters of the Adonis River have taken on a red coloring each springtime as a result, supposedly, of the blood of Adonis. At Byblos the feasts commemorating Adonis's death continued for 8 days. The eighth day was a day of rejoicing, commemorating the god's resurrection: "He is risen, Adonis, he is risen!" Even today people still plant quick-growing seeds in "Adonis gardens" at Easter and Christmas time to commemorate the birth and resurrection of Christ. The traditional classical form of the myth of Adonis dates from the fifth century B.C. The "Legend of Osiris" also has a tie with Byblos.

During the Byzantine period (A.D. 330–636) Byblos became densely populated and became the seat of a bishopric of the Greek Orthodox Catholic church.

■ *This was the land of the Giblites (Josh. 13:5).*
■ *It was included in the ideal limits of Israel (Ezek. 27:9; Josh. 13:15).*
■ *Workmen of Gebal helped build ships for mariners from Tyre (Ezek. 27:9).*

Anaya

Thirty-seven miles north of Beirut and east of Byblos are the **ANAYA MONASTERY** and **TOMB OF SHARBEL MAKHLOUF**, the sainted Maronite father.

Rachana

Thirty-five miles from Beirut there is a mountain village called Rachana. On top of a hill there is a permanent outdoor sculpture art exhibit, the work of the Basbous brothers.

Tripoli, *Tripolis, Aradus*

With a population of 90,000, Tripoli is the second largest city in Lebanon. It is 53 miles north of Beirut, and is a shipping center and the terminus of the Iraq Petroleum Company pipeline from Kirkuk, Iraq.

POINTS OF INTEREST

CRUSADER CASTLE OF SAINT GILES (twelfth century).

PORTALS OF THE GRAND MOSQUE.

TAYLAN MOSQUE.

IZZEDINE and other Turkish BATHS.

OTHER BUILDINGS of the Turkish Mameluke period.

The TOWER OF THE LIONS, a small fifteenth-century fortress.

The MONASTERY OF THE DERVISHES, 2 miles east of the city.

The Cedars of Lebanon

Cedars once covered the mountains of Lebanon, and in all ages the cedars of Lebanon have been treasured throughout the Mediterranean world. But now there are very few cedar forests. About 400 old cedars, 200–1500 years of age, are still growing on the slopes of Mount Makhmal, 6,000 feet above sea level, 85 miles north of Beirut. The largest tree is 87 feet high. To reach the cedars from Tripoli, the traveler turns inland through the romantic Qadisha Gorge. On the way one can visit the QADISHA GROTTO, a fairyland of stalactites and stalagmites through which gushes the ice-cold Qadisha River.

As Lebanon's treasured possessions, the cedar trees are the national emblem.

The Egyptians used Lebanon cedar wood as early as the First Dynasty (ca. 3500 B.C.) in making boxes, statues, solar boats, and coffins.

The MOUNTAIN OF THE CEDARS offers excellent skiing from December to May. A modern 7,546-foot ski lift is a part of the skiing facilities.

- *In the temple at Jerusalem Solomon used Lebanese cedar supplied by King Hiram of Tyre (1 Kings 5:1–10, 18; 6:9–10, 15–18; 36).*
- *The altar of Solomon's temple was made of Lebanon cedars (1 Kings 6:20).*

A cedar of Lebanon

Syria

As a large part of the "fertile crescent," Syria has been a meeting place of roads connecting countries and nations who have participated in war, immigration, and trade.

The country has an area of 72,234 square miles — 12 percent smaller than the state of Utah. Its population is over 6,000,000, including about 200,000 Palestinian refugees.

HISTORY

The first to move into the area, between 2800 and 2500 B.C., were the Semitic Amorites who inhabited the Arabian Peninsula. Syria was controlled by each of the various powerful empires from the Assyrian in 733 B.C. to the Roman in the first century B.C., and later by the Arabs and Turks. Its boundaries have changed over the centuries, and in biblical times it extended from the Euphrates to the Mediterranean.

A more recent history would begin at the time of the Arab revival at the turn of the century, which led to the great Arab revolt in 1916. Prince Faisal, son of Husein ibn-Ali, marched with an Arab army against Ottoman rule. The prince joined allied forces to expel the Turks from Syria and entered Damascus at the head of his Arab army on November 1, 1918.

During World War II, British forces entered Syria in 1942. Then the French came in and remained until they evacuated in 1946 under United Nations demands. In 1958 Syria merged with Egypt to form the United Arab Republic, but seceded in 1961 and became known as the Syrian Arab Republic.

- *In the original Hebrew, Syria was also referred to as Aram of Damascus (2 Sam. 8:6).*
- *In the New Testament, Syria means the Roman province, and could be used to refer to the entire area, including Palestine (Luke 2:2; Acts 18:18); or it could refer to the northern area (Acts 15:23, 41; Gal. 1:21) or the region bordering on Galilee (Matt. 4:24).*

RELIGION

Most of the population is Moslem, but there are a few Jews and Christians — the latter mostly Orthodox — comprising less than 10 percent of the population.

SYRIA TODAY

The western part of Syria is mountainous, with desert and steppe-land in the north and west. In much of the country the summers are hot and dry, and, except near the coast, frost and some snow can be expected in winter.

Syria's principal industry is agriculture, and the country produces a great deal of cotton and wheat.

The unit of currency used in Syria is the Syrian *pound*. Coins are in denominations of 50, 25, 10, 5, and 2½ *piasters*.

CITIES AND SITES

DAMASCUS, *Dimashq, Amory*

Syria's capital city of Damascus, with a population of about 650,000, is considered to be the world's oldest continuously inhabited city. It was in existence as early as 2000 B.C., and correspondence between Damascus and Egypt dates from 1600 B.C. Damascus was a garden spot for desert travelers over the fertile crescent — like a harbor for the great Syrian Desert. It is located 69 miles southeast of Beirut and 140 miles northeast of Jerusalem, at the foot of Mount Qassiom (2,275 feet) and on a plain at the edge of the Ghouta Oasis. The plain is 30 miles in diameter and 2,300 feet above sea level. The Barada and Awaj rivers provide water for the agricultural crops in the area, and the Barada River runs through the center of the city.

Some legends have Damascus as the Garden of Eden. By the tenth century B.C., Damascus was the capital of the Aramaic kingdom, and its altar to the Syrian god Hadad was the most sacred of all Syrian sanctuaries. Assyria, Babylon, Persia, and Macedon each in turn controlled Syria from 733 B.C. The Ptolemies and Seleucids fought over Damascus, and by the first century B.C. Syria was a part of the Roman Empire.

Christianity came early to Damascus, and Theodosius I had a church built there about A.D. 375. The Arab Umayyad Empire included Damascus in 635, and in 1516 the Ottoman Turkish Empire ruled over Syria and Damascus.

After World War I Damascus came under the French Mandate, and finally after World War II Damascus, along with Syria, received its independence.

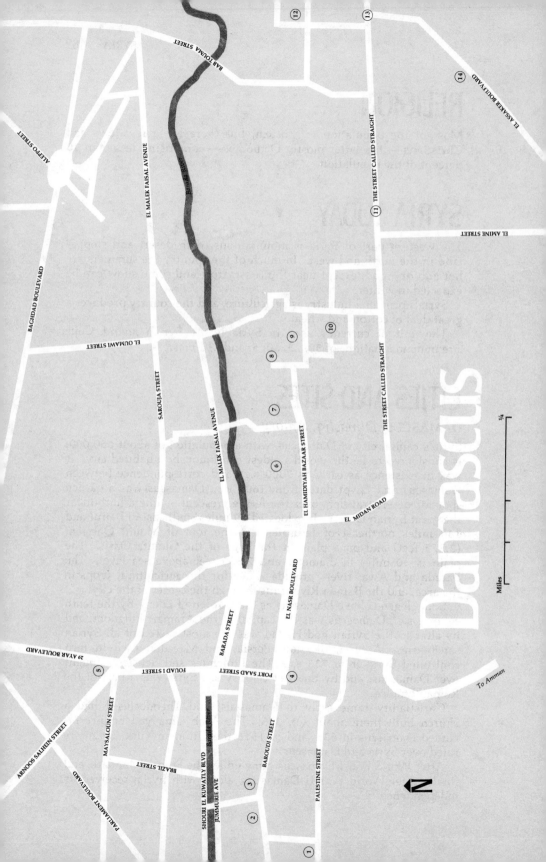

1. Damascus University
2. National Museum
3. Suleiman's Tekkiyeh
4. Railway station
5. Syrian Tourist Office
6. Citadel and bazaars
7. Adlia and Zahirieh schools
8. Mausoleum of Saladin
9. Umayyad Mosque, Temple of Jupiter, and Roman Arch
10. Azem (Azim) Palace
11. Street Called Straight
12. House of Ananias
13. City Walls and East Gate
14. Saint Paul's Window and Cathedral

Damascus has always been a manufacturing city. Our word "damask" bears witness to its fame as a textile center. Weavers and also artisans in mother-of-pearl, brass, leather, and jewelry make shopping a delightful experience in Damascus. The old town still has narrow streets lined with bazaars. Bedouins, donkeys, mosques, and minarets all add to the Oriental flavor of this ancient city.

POINTS OF INTEREST

The **HEDIJAZ SQUARE**, in front of the railway station, is the center of the city. Shoukri el-Kuwatly, the main street in the city, borders the Barada River and leads west to Beirut. On the east the Nasr Boulevard leads to the Souq Hamidiyah. Along this boulevard and north and south of it are the main shopping areas and historical sites. *Abou Roumaneh* is the most modern residential section of Damascus.

The city has many sites of historical and aesthetic interest:

1. **DAMASCUS UNIVERSITY** is located a short distance southwest of the National Museum.

2. **NATIONAL MUSEUM.** This is one of the outstanding museums in the world. Exhibits are beautifully arranged in one of the following four departments: (1) Syro-Oriental antiquities; (2) Syrian antiquities in the Greek, Roman, and Byzantine periods; (3) Arab and Moslem art; (4) modern and contemporary art. In the first department are important objects from Mari (3000–2000 B.C.), Ras Shamra (1500–1300 B.C.), and a stone from Ugarit that has the world's oldest known alphabet inscribed on it. The **SYNAGOGUE OF DURA-EUROPOS**, dating from A.D. 244, was moved to the museum from its location on the Euphrates.

3. **SULEIMAN'S TEKKIYEH** (*El Tekieh Suleimaniah*). This hostelry, near the museum, was built in 1554 by Sultan Suleiman the Magnificent as a shelter for pilgrims en route to Mecca. Its slim minarets and large cupola are very picturesque.

4. The **RAILWAY STATION** is on the south side of Hedijaz Square in the center of the city.

5. **SYRIAN TOURIST OFFICE.** The tourist in Damascus may receive help from the Syrian Tourist Office, directly north of the railway station on the north corner, where Port Said Street and Salhien Street join.

6. **CITADEL** and **BAZAARS.** One of the roofed bazaars is the **SOUQ EL KHOUJA**, and halfway through the bazaar is the thirteenth-century **CITADEL EL QALAA**, built on the site of an earlier Roman and Byzantine fortress. The Syrian mounted police have their headquarters there, and part of it is a state prison. The Souq el Khouja leads to the **SOUQ HAMIDIYEH** (Hamidieh), the most famous bazaar in Damascus. It was built 75 years ago by Sultan Abdul-Hamid II.

7. **ADLIA** and **ZAHIRIEH SCHOOLS.** Northwest of the Umayyad Mosque, on Zahirieh Street, are two schools dating back to the thirteenth century. In the Zahirieh School is the **MAUSOLEUM OF THE MAMELUKE SULTAN BAYBARS.**

8. **MAUSOLEUM OF SALADIN** (Salah ed-Din). This elaborately decorated tomb houses the body of Saladin (A.D. 1138–93). It is located near the Umayyad Mosque. The cupola was donated by the German emperor William II during his visit in the late nineteenth century.

Saladin was the greatest Moslem warrior of the 1100s. In A.D. 1189 he brought about the Third Crusade by capturing Jerusalem for the Moslems. The Moslems regarded Saladin as a saintly hero, and even the Christians honored him for his honesty and bravery. When Saladin aided the Egyptian ruler, who was caliph of the Shiite branch of Islam and a rival of the Sunnite caliph of Baghdad, he became the vizier and later the sultan of Egypt. He then extended his empire to cover Damascus, Aleppo, Mosul, and Edessa, and fought the Christian states along the coast. His troops were besieged by Christians led by Richard the Lion-Hearted at Acre, and after a 2-year battle a truce was made in 1192, giving the coast to the Christians and the interior to the Moslems and allowing Christian pilgrims to enter Jerusalem. Saladin is known for his support of theologians and scholars and his building of schools, dikes, canals, and mosques.

9. **UMAYYAD MOSQUE, TEMPLE OF JUPITER, ROMAN ARCH.** The Umayyad Mosque was the greatest monument of the Arab Umayyad Empire (A.D. 635). It was decorated with fine mosaics of colored glass, gold, and mother-of-pearl, which were formed to make natural scenes, decorative plants, and buildings. It is built on a site where once was a temple dedicated to Hadad, about 1000 B.C., and later the Roman Temple of Jupiter (third century A.D.). The Roman emperor Theodosius (A.D. 379–95) destroyed part of the Temple of Jupiter to build a church dedicated to Saint John the Baptist, because according to tradition John the Baptist's head was buried here. Later the Arabs built the present mosque on the site. The Umayyad Mosque is closed to tourists on Fridays.

The center gates of the Roman temple are the eastern gates of the Umayyad Mosque. The **ROMAN ARCH** (Triumphal Arch) was part of the western propylaea of the Temple of Jupiter. It still stands in front of the Umayyad Mosque. Its pediment stands on six columns, 52 feet high, crowned with Corinthian capitals.

10. **AZEM (AZIM) PALACE.** This palace, built in A.D. 1750 by Asad el Azem, a governor of Damascus under the Turks, is an excellent example of an old Arab palace. The decorations of wood in the walls and ceilings were made by skilled Damascene craftsmen, who developed such a beautiful style of woodcraft that today this type is called *Damascene* all over the world. Marble fountains, courts, trees, and flowers all help make the palace beautiful. The Haramlik (quarters for women and children) houses a **FOLKLORE MUSEUM.**

11. **STREET CALLED STRAIGHT.** It was on the Street Called Straight that Ananias lived and where Paul recovered his sight (Acts 9:10–18). In Roman times it was one of the main thoroughfares of the Empire. It runs east and west and divides the old city into northern and southern sections. Only a monumental arch remains to bear witness of its ancient splendor. The street is still busy, as it was in the days of Paul.

12. **HOUSE OF ANANIAS.** The Church of Saint Ananias marks the traditional site of the house of Ananias (Acts 9:10–18).

Paul being let down over the wall, painting in the Church of Saint Ananias, Damascus

The Street Called
Straight, Damascus

13. **CITY WALLS** and **EAST GATE**. Little remains of the ancient **ROMAN WALL** that encircled the city, but lower levels of large stones date prior to the twelfth century. The **EAST GATE** (Bab Sharqi) is the only one of the seven Roman gates to survive. It dates from the second century A.D. It opened into the Street Called Straight. The **LITTLE GATE** (Gate of Chaqour) on the south side dates from the twelfth century.

14. **SAINT PAUL'S WINDOW** and **CATHEDRAL**. While the Jews sought the life of Paul and watched the gates of the city to destroy him, his disciples took him by night and let him down by the wall in a basket so he could escape (Acts 9:20–25).

A part of the town wall has been restored, a cathedral built, and a window designated as the window of Saint Paul.

- *Damascus was visited by Abraham (Gen. 14:15).*
- *Damascus was the home of Eliezer, Abraham's steward (Gen. 15:2).*
- *Damascus was conquered by David, but remained Israel's enemy (1 Chron. 18:5–8; 2 Sam. 8).*
- *Rezon, opponent of Solomon, was proclaimed king there (1 Kings 11:23–25).*
- *Jeroboam II temporarily recovered control of Damascus (2 Kings 14:28), but a few years later it fell to the Assyrians (2 Kings 16:9).*
- *Damascus joined Asa, king of Judah, in war against Israel (1 Kings 15:16–31; 2 Chron. 16:1–10).*
- *Elijah was told to anoint Hazael to be its king (1 Kings 19:15–17).*
- *Damascus was the capital of Syria (1 Kings 15:18; 19:15; 20:1).*
- *Ahaz met Tiglath-pileser there (2 Kings 16:10).*
- *Elijah returned from Horeb by Damascus (1 Kings 19:8, 15).*
- *Ahab made a foolish vow concerning Damascus, and Benhadad agreed to let Ahab establish bazaars in Damascus (1 Kings 20:34).*

Saint Paul's Window and Cathedral, Damascus

- *Damascus was the home of Naaman, whom Elisha healed of leprosy (2 Kings 5).*
- *When Elisha came to Damascus, Benhadad consulted him about getting well (2 Kings 8:7–15).*
- *Ahaz, king of Judah, made an alliance with the king of Assyria to defeat Damascus, and he copied its altar (2 Kings 16:5–18).*
- *In the reign of Joash the spoil of Jerusalem was carried there (2 Chron. 24:23).*
- *Captives from Judah were taken to Damascus (2 Chron. 28:5).*
- *Prophets referred to Damascus and its destruction (Isa. 8:4; 17:1–3; Jer. 49:23–27; Ezek. 27:18; 47:16).*
- *Paul saw the Lord near Damascus and was struck blind (Acts 9:1–9).*
- *Ananias, who lived in Damascus, saw the Lord in a vision and laid his hands on Paul to bless him with sight again (Acts 9:10–18).*
- *Paul was baptized in Damascus (Acts 9:18). (At that time Damascus was ruled by the Nabataean king Aretas IV, whose governor aided the Jews.)*
- *Paul preached in the synagogues in Damascus (Acts 9:19–22).*
- *When the Jews took counsel to kill Paul, he was let down over the Damascus city wall and he escaped (Acts 9:23–25; 2 Cor. 11:32–33).*
- *Paul went into Arabia, but returned to Damascus (Gal. 1:17).*
- *A document found in Egypt, called the* Damascus Document, *tells of a sect of Jews who migrated to Damascus and were organized into a community like the Qumran community. They were called the sons of Zadok, and the fragment is sometimes referred to as the Zadokite fragment. In Cave 6 of Qumran, more fragments from the Zadokite sect have been found, indicating that the Essenes knew of the Zadokites and their community regulations.*

SOUTH OF DAMASCUS

DERAYA

Deraya is a village 10 miles south-southwest of Damascus where, according to tradition, Paul was struck blind by a vision of the Lord, on his way to Damascus (Acts 9:1-9).

MOUNT HERMON ("prominent," "rugged"), Sirion, Senir, Jebel esh Sheikh

Mount Hermon, 25 miles west-southwest of Damascus, is the highest mountain in Syria. Towering 9,232 feet above sea level, it has snow all year long. It is located in the south end of the Anti-Lebanon mountains and is 16-20 miles long from north to south.

- *Mount Hermon was the northern limit of the kingdom of Og (Deut. 3:8-10; 4:47-48; Josh. 12:1, 4-5; 13:11-12).*
- *The mount was conquered by the Israelites and occupied by them (Josh. 11:3-5, 16-17; 1 Chron. 5:23).*
- *Half of the tribe of Manasseh dwelt there (1 Chron. 5:23).*
- *Mount Hermon is referred to in Hebrew poetry (Pss. 42:6; 89:12; 133:3).*
- *It is called Sirion (Sion) and Senir (Shenir) (Deut. 3:9; 4:48).*
- *It may have been the Mount of Transfiguration (Matt. 17:1-9; Mark 9:2-9; Luke 9:28-36).*

EDREI ("sown land"), Dara'a

In Old Testament times Edrei was a city of Og that was given to Manasseh. The present city of 8,000 is located 60 miles south of Damascus and is the turnoff point for the ancient site of Bosra. The waterfalls of Tell Shehab, from which the Yarmuk Valley can be viewed, are 13 miles northwest of Dara'a.

- *Edrei is mentioned along with Og, king of Bashan, and the giants that dwelt at Edrei (Josh. 12:4).*
- *Here the Israelites slew Og, king of Bashan, his sons, and all his people (Num. 21:33-35).*

Bosra, Busra, Bosra el Shan

The Nabataeans established their capital here in the first century B.C. and embellished their city with palaces and temples. Although its population was 80,000 when it was the capital of the province of Arabia under Rome, its present population is only 3,000. The city was inhabited as early as 4000 B.C., but the ruins are mainly from the Roman era. The second-century ROMAN THEATER held 15,000 spectators, and is the largest and most complete Roman theater. During the Byzantine period Bosra was the seat of a bishopric. The HOUSE OF MONK BOHAIRA is from that period. The Islamic period left the UMAYYAD MOSQUE OF OMAR and the MOSQUE OF FATIMA. A CASTLE and huge ancient columns are also of interest.

Bosra is 85 miles southeast of Damascus and 26 miles east of Dara'a.

Salkhad

Fifteen miles east of Bosra, in the extreme south end of Syria, is a twelfth-century fortress located on the top of a volcanic mountain. It was used in former times as a site for guarding Damascus.

Soueida, *Suweida, Dionisius, Es Suweida, As Suwayda*

Nabataean Arabs inhabited this city in ancient times. It is located 13 miles north of Bosra and is the largest city in the Hauran district. Ruins at the site include the following: a **TEMPLE TO THE GOD DOSARES**; a **BASILICA** with fourth- and fifth-century mosaics; a cistern known as the **ROMAN POOL**; the **SHAHBA CASTLE**; and the **SUWEIDA MUSEUM**, with its rare mosaics.

Kanawat, *Qanawat, Kanatha*

Kanatha was one of the ten cities of the Decapolis as listed by Pliny. It is located 4 miles northeast of Es Suweida. Seven **COLUMNS OF A ROMAN TEMPLE** to the sun-god are still standing, plus a **WALL**, a paved **ROAD**, a **CHURCH**, a **SMALLER TEMPLE**, an **ARCH**, an **AMPHITHEATER**, a **TOWER**, and an **AQUEDUCT**. They were built during the reign of Hadrian.

Shahba, *Philippopolis*

Ten miles north of Es Suweida is the ancient Philippopolis, birthplace of Philip the Arab, the Roman emperor who ruled between A.D. 232 and 237. An **AMPHITHEATER**, **WALLS**, **GATES**, **PAVED ROADS**, **BATHS**, and a **TEMPLE** dedicated to Philip's father are among the ruins.

NORTH OF DAMASCUS

Sednaya, *Seidnaya*

Sednaya is located 23 miles northeast of Damascus at an altitude of 4,640 feet. It has a population of 2,500. According to legend, the emperor Justinian built the village in A.D. 547. It is said that when he aimed to shoot a deer a light appeared and the deer changed into a lady dressed in white. She told Justinian to build a monastery, and she also told him the design. The resulting **MONASTERY OF SEDNAYA** is visited by many pilgrims. The most important treasure is the icon of the Virgin Mary which, according to legend, was painted by Saint Luke. The same legend recalls that during the Crusades oil oozed from the icon's face, and the Knights Templars sent it to churches of Europe as a holy relic. Grottos cut in the rocks in the area were used as tombs.

Maloula

Thirty-seven miles northeast of Damascus, at an altitude of 5,200 feet, is a small village of 1,500 people. Some of the people live in grottos and caves. The **MONASTERY OF SAINT TAKLA**, one of the earliest Orthodox settlements in the world, is here. Saint Takla was traditionally a follower of Saint Paul. Here she is said to have miraculously split a mountain. Near her tomb, miraculous powers are attributed to the water which drips from the ceiling. The CONVENT OF SAINT SARKIS stands near the top of the village.

Of great interest here is the fact that the inhabitants of Maloula speak Aramaic, the language of Jesus. There are only three villages that speak Aramaic; they are all in Syria, and the largest is Maloula.

RIBLAH, Ribleh

On the Orontes River, 22 miles southwest of Homs, was the ancient city of Riblah.

- *Here Pharaoh Necho had his military headquarters (2 Kings 23:33).*
- *Here Nebuchadnezzar established his military headquarters (2 Kings 25:6).*
- *Here Zedekiah's sons were slain before his eyes, his eyes were put out (2 Kings 25:7; Jer. 39:5–7; 52:9–11), and his ministers were also put to death (2 Kings 25:20–21; Jer. 52:26–27).*

Kadesh, Tell Nebi Mind

On the Orontes River 13 miles southwest of Homs is the ancient site of a battle between the Egyptians under Ramses II and the Hittites in 1296 B.C. The Hittites retained control of Syria by routing the Egyptians. The battle is described on the temple walls at Luxor, Abydos, and Abu Simbel in Egypt.

Homs, Hims, Emesa

The third largest city in Syria, with a population of 175,000, Homs is 100 miles north of Damascus in the fertile Orontes Valley.

In ancient times a temple to the sun-god was located there. Septimius Severus married a girl from Homs, and Heliogabalus, high priest of the Temple of Homs, became the Roman emperor in A.D. 218.

The town's GREAT MOSQUE is dedicated to Khalid ibn-el-Walid, a famous Arab leader. There are also underground ruins of a CHAPEL and MONASTERY. The SYRIAN ARAMEAN CHURCH at Homs has a holy relic said to be the sash of the Virgin Mary. It was discovered under the altar in 1953.

Homs has become an important center for industry, including a petroleum refinery and other factories.

HAMATH, Epiphania, Hamah, Hama

Located 125 miles north of Damascus, on the banks of the Orontes River, is the ancient city of Hamath. Allegedly built by Arados, king of the island of Arwad, it was the northern capital of the Aramaic Kingdom about 1100 B.C. Its name was changed by Antiochus IV to Epiphania, but the old name survives in the modern *Hama*.

POINTS OF INTEREST

Interesting places to see include the following: the GREAT MOSQUE; the ARAB FORT OF SHIZAR; the IBN WARDAN PALACE; the thirteenth-century **MAUSOLEUM OF EL MALEK MUZAFFAR**; the eighteenth-century **HOUSE OF AL AZM**, governor of Hama (a miniature of the Azim Palace in Damascus); the **MOSQUE OF EL HAYYAT**; and probably the most interesting of all sites at Hama, the nine 2,000-year-old Roman **WATER WHEELS** (*naoura*), 90 feet in diameter, that lift the water of the Orontes River to irrigate the farms and supply water for the houses and public baths. The wheels produce a melancholy sound that has given Hama the name of "the melodious city." The whole city is very colorful, with local costumes and habits which have been little influenced by the West. The city has a population of 125,000.

- *Hamath was the capital of the region that bore its name (2 Kings 23:33; 25:21).*
- *Hamath was the northern limit of Israel (Num. 13:21; 34:7-8; Josh. 13:5; 1 Chron. 13:5; Ezek. 47:15-17; 48:1).*
- *Toi, the king of Hamath, made peace with David (2 Sam. 8:9-10; 1 Chron. 18:9-10).*
- *Solomon built store cities here (2 Chron. 8:4).*
- *Jeroboam II restored it after Israel had lost it (2 Kings 14:25, 28).*
- *The city was conquered by Assyria, and people from Hamath were transferred to Israel (2 Kings 17:24, 30; 18:34; 19:11-13; Isa. 36:18-19; 37:11-13; Isa. 10:5-9; Jer. 49:23).*
- *Some Israelites were apparently taken to Hamath (Isa. 11:11).*
- *Pharaoh Necho occupied it before the battle of Carchemish and deposed Jehoahaz at Riblah in Hamath (2 Kings 23:33-35).*
- *Amos referred to its greatness (Amos 6:2).*
- *Hamath was classed with Damascus, Tyre, and Sidon by Zechariah (Zech. 9:1-2).*
- *Jonathan advanced to Hamath against Demetrius (1 Macc. 11:25).*

Apamea, *Qalaat el Mudiq*

Ancient **TEMPLES**, **GATES**, **PILLARS**, a **THEATER**, **MOSAICS**, and **WALLS** have been uncovered here. The city walls once covered four miles. The main street, 1,600 yards long and 113 feet wide, crossed the city from north to south and had monumental gates at each end. The city is 40 miles northwest of Hama.

Ma'arat an Nu'man

Here, 32 miles north of Hama, is the **TOMB** of the famous Islam poet and philosopher Abu-al-Ala al-Maarri, who lived in the eleventh century A.D. There are also a twelfth-century **MOSQUE**, a **SCHOOL**, and the remains of a **CITADEL**.

Krak des Chevaliers, *Qalaat el Hosu*

At a point 190 miles north of Damascus, 78 miles north of Beirut, 36 miles west of Homs, and 11 miles north of Tell Kalakh is the best preserved and most magnificent Crusader castle in the world. For almost two centuries the Knights Hospitalers kept the banner of Saint John of Jerusalem flying over its 30 towers. It was built in 1031 as an

Arab fortress. The Crusaders held it from 1110 to 1271, when a four-year siege by the Mamelukes ended the Crusaders' occupation.

At one time the castle held a garrison of 5,000 men. It is surrounded by two great walls, one inside the other, and separated by a moat. Another trench encircled the outside wall. The walls, towers, bastions, arches, cross-vaulting, porches, stables, dining halls, and sleeping quarters are enormous.

From the castle the soldiers could-have a view of the Bekaa Valley in Lebanon and the surrounding country on all sides.

Safita

A Crusader fortress known as CHASTEL BLANC was located just north of the Lebanese border at Safita. It is 22 miles southeast of Tartus. All that is left of the fortress is a tower and church.

Arwad *(Aradus)* Island

This island, about 3 miles off the coast near Tartus, has a population of 3,000. Most of the islanders are fishermen who supply the restaurants of Beirut and Damascus. They also harvest sponges. The streets of the island are narrow alleyways only wide enough for two or three persons. There are no cars on the island. There are ancient Phoenician ruins on the island, fortress walls, and a castle dating back to the thirteenth century. Legend has Saint Paul visiting the island on his way to Rome, but the scriptures are silent on such a visit.

Tartous, *Antaradus, Tortosa, Tartus*

Thirty-seven miles north of Tripoli, Lebanon, is the ancient Tortosa, which was held by the Crusader Knights Templars until 1291. Old parts of the FORTRESS still remain. The CATHEDRAL OF OUR LADY OF TORTOSA serves as a museum. A new $9,000,000 deep-water harbor has been developed to serve central and southern Syria.

Baniyas, *Banias, Balanea, Valenia*

Located 35 miles south of Latakia is the ancient city of Baniyas, which dates back to Phoenician times. The Mansur family deeded the settlement to the Knights Hospitalers in 1186. It was called Balanea in Roman times because of its baths (Latin, *balneum*). The terminus of a 30-inch pipeline from the Kirkuk oil fields in Iraq is located here. A short distance into the mountains southeast of Baniyas is the CASTLE OF MARQAB. It was built in 1062 and was held by the Knights Hospitalers until 1285, when it was captured by the Mamelukes.

Latakia, *Seleucia, La Liche*

This city of 75,000 people is located on the Syrian seacoast 149 miles north of Beirut. It is Syria's major seaport. It is said to have been built by one of Alexander's commanders in the fourth century B.C. It was once a Crusader stronghold and later the seat of a Latin bishopric. A NECROPOLIS is located north of the town. On the south side of the city is a **COLONNADE** with Corinthian capitals, thought to be a part of a temple of Adonis. There are Crusader and Arab fortifications, such as **MARQAB CASTLE**. On a peak east of Latakia is the **CASTLE OF SAYHOUN**.

Ras Shamra, *Ugarit*

Due east of the point of the island of Cyprus nearest to the coast of Syria, 25 miles south of the mouth of the Orontes River on the coast of Syria, and 7 miles north of Latakia is Ugarit (Ras Shamra), one of the oldest sites in the world (6000 B.C.). It was one of the main city-states of the Phoenicians.

Ancient Ugarit first came to light from correspondence on the *Tell el 'Amarna Tablets* (fourteenth century B.C.) of Egypt and from the *Mari Tablets*. Since its discovery in 1928, archaeologists have systematically excavated five levels of civilization. Among the most important finds was a tablet on which was inscribed the oldest alphabet ever discovered (located in the National Museum at Damascus). The language of Ugarit has been very valuable to scholars as they have refined their knowledge of ancient Semitic languages and cultures. Especially important is the clarification of Old Testament passages.

At Ugarit, two **TEMPLES** were discovered, one to Dagon and one to Baal. The homes of the clergy who labored in the temples housed libraries of literary texts called the *Ras Shamra Tablets*, which have shed light on the old Canaanite religions with which Israel was in such contention. They date back to 1500–1400 B.C. It can be seen from these and other tablets that the chief emphasis in Canaanite religion was upon fertility and sex. Sacred prostitution, both male and female, was exceedingly common, practiced in the name of religion at the various centers of worship. The fertility goddess was actually represented by a sacred prostitute, called the *Holy One*. There was a reason for the direct prohibition of sacred prostitution in Deuteronomy 23:17–18.

Although the Bible never mentions Ugarit, this discovery is one of the most important in the field of biblical archaeology. Not only are the tablets contemporary with Moses, but they are written in an archaic Semitic dialect closely related to Hebrew. They contain myth, ritual, and historical traditions of the inhabitants.

The Ras Shamra Tablets reveal a religious system strangely unlike, yet at the same time seemingly related to, what little the Bible allows us to know of Canaanite belief and practice. The chief deity is El, and his power is so supreme as to make the Ras Shamra religion almost monotheistic. The adversary of El is Baal, the son of Dagon. Many scholars of the Ugarit tablets are convinced that the Israelites took over many practices from the Canaanites, although giving them an entirely new and infinitely more spiritual content.

Also in the information supplied by the tablets is the *Keret Legend*, which many scholars see as the only evidence yet discovered for the story of Abraham's journey to the south of Canaan.

The tablets stress that the bull was the symbol of life (God) because of its great strength and virility. They also indicate that snakes as a medical insignia existed long before Moses used them as a sign of "healing."

In describing the fertility goddess, the Ras Shamra Tablets define the relationship of the goddess with the tree of life and explain the significance of the *sērāh*, which might be either a natural or a stylized tree at local Canaanite sanctuaries and which was so abominated in the Old Testament (Exod. 34:13; 2 Kings 18:4).

In the mythology of the tablets are found texts on marriage and fertility rites which provide information on the association of the Hebrew nomads and the Moabite women (Num. 25; Hos. 9:10).

The Ras Shamra Tablets document the Canaanite fertility cult by which the Hebrews were influenced and against the grosser aspects of which their prophets reacted. The legends document the institution of kingship and social practices and shed light on Israel's request for an institution of kingship (1 Sam. 8-10).

These tablets throw light on the contemporary life of the period. At the king's palace were discovered the foreign office archives, which show the city's cosmopolitan aspect and also its foreign contacts. Letters to Egypt, correspondence with the Hittites, bills of shipping to Tyre, Sidon, Cyprus, Crete, the Aegean, Byblos, Accho, Ashdod, and Anatolia — these lend credence to the trade and empire of Solomon and David.

The discoveries of Ras Shamra have added much to the language of the Old Testament. Inscriptions in no less than five scripts and seven languages have been found there. Many lexicons and syllabaries were found, which have aided in understanding these languages. The tablets of Ugarit are of value to the Old Testament because the Ugaritic script is closely related to the biblical Hebrew. It has enabled many of the previously unknown words in the Bible to be identified and the meanings of others made clear. The discovery of the tablets at Ras Shamra is one of the greatest aids yet given to Old Testament study.

Aleppo, *Beroea, Haleb*

This was an ancient caravan center that the Hittites conquered in 1600 B.C. It is located in the northwest corner of Syria, on the route between the Orontes and Euphrates valleys. It is 216 miles north of Damascus and 116 miles northeast of Latakia. The population is about 600,000. It is Syria's major commercial and industrial center and second most important city. Nearly half of the people in Aleppo are Christian, and many are Armenian.

POINTS OF INTEREST

In the old quarters, the khans, bazaars, baths, houses, schools, and mosques maintain the Oriental atmosphere. Some of the sites to visit are as follows: GATE OF ANTIOCH; SOUQ EL ATARIN, MADRESSEH MUKADDAMIYE; BAHRAMIYE MOSQUE; GREAT MOSQUE (eighth century A.D.); **MADRESSEH HALAWIYE** (cathedral); **KHAN AL WAZIR** (caravansary); **BAB QINNESRIN** (gate); **DALLAL HOUSE; CITADEL OF ALEPPO; KHOSRAFIYE MOSQUE; SAINT SAMAAN'S MONASTERY**; and the **ALEPPO MUSEUM** (Mari and Ugarit collections).

Deir Sama'an, *Qalaat Seman, Fortress of Simeon, Monastery of Saint Simeon Stylite*

Forty miles northwest of Aleppo is the Monastery of Simeon Stylite, who was born about A.D. 390 and lived on top of an 88-foot pillar for 27 years. From the pillar he preached to his disciples, who came great distances to hear him. A **CATHEDRAL** has been built over the pillar, some of which remains. The **MONASTERY OF SAINT SIMEON STYLITE** is located about a third of a mile from the cathedral.

NORTHEAST OF DAMASCUS

TADMOR, Palmyra, *Adrianopolis, Bride of the Desert*

This ancient city is no doubt one of the most important of the archaeological sites in Syria. It is 200 miles northeast of Damascus by way of Homs, or 99 miles east of Homs. It was an oasis city on the northern edge of the Syrian Desert. Traditionally it is the site of the biblical Tadmor founded by Solomon, but Assyrian inscriptions show that Tadmor already existed in the time of Tiglath-pileser I (1100 B.C.).

The first mention of Palmyra by a classical writer is by Appian, who tells how the wealth of this caravan city excited the cupidity of Mark Antony (41 B.C.). In the age of Augustus a temple of Bel was built there, and after Trajan wrought destruction there, Hadrian rebuilt the city, calling it *Adrianopolis*. Later, under the rule of Odenathus and his successor, Queen Zenobia, Palmyra became an important power, even conquering Egypt. Zenobia, called the Queen of the Desert, has been described as being "far more beautiful than Cleopatra." In A.D. 271, Zenobia and her son assumed the titles of Augusta and Augustus and had coins made in their image. The Romans called this rebellion and met her in battle. Palmyra surrendered to the Romans. According to the story, the Roman Aurelian placed Zenobia at the head of his triumphal procession to walk with her hands bound in chains of gold. When Palmyra rebelled a year later, Aurelian sacked the town (272), and thereafter it ceased to be important. Diocletian (284–305) turned part of the city into an army camp and Justinian built a city wall in 527–65, but Palmyra never recovered its greatness. The Christian church made some progress in the city, however, and Palmyra sent its bishop to the Council of Nicaea in 325.

Gigantic temples and colonnades in the middle of an enormous desert make a scene of unrivaled beauty at Palmyra. It is traditionally the largest area of ancient ruins in the world. At its height, the city had a population of 30,000 people. About one-half mile from the ruins is the town of Tadmor.

Many Aramaic inscriptions found at Palmyra are important for our knowledge of late phases of Semitic religion.

POINTS OF INTEREST

TEMPLE OF BEL (first or second century A.D.). Of the original 390 columns in the temple, only seven survive. The northern niche of the temple was the Holy of Holies and contained the Palmyrene triad: Bel, Yarihibol, and Aghbol. Its monolithic ceiling is decorated with the seven planets and encircled by the twelve signs of the zodiac. A stairway leads to the top and a view of Palmyra.

The beautiful STREET OF COLUMNS leads from the Triumphal Arch entry. Of the original 375 columns, 31 feet in height, 150 remain.

The AGORA, THEATER, FORUM, SENATE, BATHS, and BANQUET HALL are typical of Roman ruins.

The TEMPLE OF BEL (Baal) SHAMEEN (Shamin), in the northeast corner of the ruins near the hotel, is the most complete temple in Palmyra and dates back to A.D. 130. During the Byzantine period it served as a basilica.

The TOMBS OF THE TOWERS, 150 in number, are peculiar to the Palmyrenes. They are square and built in three or four tiers. The walls of the rooms were designed to hold coffins of the dead. They were built about A.D. 50–150. The JAMBLICHOS TOWER was built in A.D. 83, and archaeologists found mummies there that were wrapped in silk from China.

The UNDERGROUND TOMBS have many statues and decorations. The TOMB OF THE THREE BROTHERS, built in A.D. 140, is the most important. It has 65 bays, each with 6 recesses for the dead, or 390 in all. The reliefs and frescoes are very beautiful and show the Oriental influence in the Greco-Roman art of the period.

A MUSEUM houses many of the finds of Palmyra.

The SULPHUR BATHS are located about a mile from the oasis on the road to Homs.

The FORTRESS OF FAKHR ED-DIN AL MAANI may be seen on the summit of a hill northwest of Palmyra.

■ *Solomon built Tadmor in the wilderness (1 Kings 9:18; 2 Chron. 8:4). (Some believe that the Tadmor that Solomon built "in the wilderness," was not this city but the obscure Tamar in the Judean desert. They believe that a reviser of the scriptures changed the name* Tamar *to* Tadmor *because Palmyra (Tadmor) was such a significant city during the reviser's time that he wanted to attribute the city to Solomon.)*

Mari, *Tell Hariri*

Mari is located on the right bank of the Euphrates River and 10 miles northwest of the Iraq border. It is about 150 miles east of Palmyra.

This was the most westerly of all Sumerian states and an important stop on the trade route between the Persian Gulf and the Mediterranean. Activity seems to have been at a peak in Mari at the beginning of the second millennium B.C. Ishtup II was the founder of

Mari during the same period and was a part of the same racial movement as the dynasties of Isin, Larsa, Assyria, and Babylon. Hammurabi of Babylon destroyed the city about 1700 B.C. (or perhaps two centuries earlier, according to some scholars).

French archaeologists excavated the site between 1933 and 1938 and found sculptures, wall paintings, bronzes, and information on palace and temple architecture. The most important find, however, was a collection of well over 20,000 cuneiform clay tablets, mainly letters and administrative and economic documents. They were found in a 300-room palace in 1935 and dated from 1813 to 1781 B.C. The records of Mari speak of a 10,000-man army in their state.

The translation of the tablets found at Mari is throwing brilliant light on the age of Hammurabi and the patriarchs. They offer parallels to the Old Testament background. Some of the items of interest to a student of the Old Testament follow:

(1) Temples were built in the form of houses. This sheds light on the belief in Solomon's temple as *bet Yahweh* ("house of God") — gods lived in houses as men.

(2) Canaanite cults used *serîm* (wooden poles) and *massēbôt* (stone stelae). A courtyard at Mari shows these serîm on the altar at the foot of the temple of Dagon, and in the courtyard a *massēbāh*, around which the people marched during worship. Gideon cut down the *sērāh* on the altar dedicated to Baal (Judg. 6:25–26).

(3) The construction of the *ziggurat* bears out the Old Testament description almost exactly. The ziggurat was constructed of unbaked bricks with occasional layers of reeds and bitumen. This was faced with baked bricks, cemented together with bitumen to give strength. "They had brick for stone, and slime [bitumen] had they for mortar" (Gen. 11:3).

(4) A mural found here, now in the Louvre, shows many similarities to the Garden of Eden story (Gen. 2–3).

(5) The tablets in the library mention the *Habiru*, who many feel were the Hebrews. They also mention Ur and Haran, as well as a group arriving at Haran. These are called *Bene iamind* (Benjaminites), who, according to the tablets, were plunderers and robbers. This echoes Jacob's blessing to Benjamin: "Benjamin shall ravin as a wolf: in the morning he shall devour the prey, and at night he shall divide the spoil" (Gen. 49:27).

The most notable of all buildings in Mari is the PALACE OF THE KING, where the Mari Tablets were found. The palace covers more than fifteen acres. It was adorned with beautiful mural paintings, portions of which are still preserved. The TEMPLE OF ISHTAR and the ZIGGURAT give us insight into their religious customs.

Dura-Europos, *As Salihiyah*

Located 15 miles northwest of Mari, on the right bank of the Euphrates River, this site marks the remains of a Seleucid fortress that was started about 300 B.C. Architectural remains include

GREEK AND ORIENTAL TEMPLES, a SYNAGOGUE, and the EARLIEST
KNOWN CHRISTIAN CHURCH BUILDING (A.D. 232–33).

GOZAN, Tell Halaf, KHABUR (HABOR) RIVER AREA

On the Khabur River, within a mile of the Turkish border and 58
miles east of Haran, is the ancient site of Gozan. It is 100 miles north
of Salahiyeh, 113 miles north of Mari, and 25 miles south of Al
Hasakah. This is where Sargon II exiled some of the Israelites when
he captured Samaria in 721 B.C.

Some believe that Gozan is the modern Tell Halaf, on the Khabur
River near the Turkish border. Others place it at a point 50–90 miles
down the river from Tell Halaf.

- *Gozan was conquered by the Assyrians (2 Kings 17:6; 19:11–12;
  Isa. 37:11–12).*
- *In the ninth year of Hoshea, king of Israel (721 B.C.), the Assyrians
  under Sargon carried Israel from Samaria into Assyria and placed
  some of them in the Habor (Khabur) River area of Gozan (2 Kings
  17:6; 18:11; 1 Chron. 5:26).*

Turkey

Turkey is a large country between the Black Sea and the Mediterranean, extending over the whole peninsula of Asia Minor and into the easternmost tip of southern Europe. The country is somewhat larger than Texas and has a population of over 30,000,000. The Asiatic side, called Anatolia, has been rocked by many earthquakes. The 1939 quake killed 50,000 persons.

HISTORY

The earliest inhabitants of Turkey came after the Flood, when Noah's ark came to rest on Mount Ararat, in eastern Turkey. The first "historic" peoples of Asia Minor were the Hittites, who rose to power about 1900 B.C. The Persians were probably the first people to rule all Asia Minor; then came Alexander the Great, followed by the Roman general Pompey. When Constantine moved his headquarters from Rome to Byzantium, this city became — and still continues to be — the most important city in Turkey.

The Seljuk Turks were the first Turkish people to invade Turkey. They were a Moslem people, who invaded from the east about 1071. The Ottoman Empire controlled Turkey from about 1200 until the Republic of Turkey was established in 1923.

The United States has been giving millions of dollars in aid to Turkey since the formulation of the Truman Doctrine of 1947. In 1952 Turkey joined the North Atlantic Treaty Organization. In 1959 Turkey and the United States signed a defense agreement and United States missile bases were established in Turkey. The United States has helped Turkey carry on its own atomic research.

RELIGION

Turkey has played an important role in the development of Christianity. Two of Paul's three great missionary journeys concentrated here, and he converted people "almost throughout all Asia" (Acts 19:26), the site of the "seven churches" addressed by John (Rev. 1:11).

Noah and Abraham were also in Turkey during their travels.

The Turks are nearly all Mohammedans (Moslems), that is, adherents of *Islam,* an Arabic term meaning "submission to, or having peace with, God." The Bible of the Moslems is the Koran, and a Moslem has five duties:

(1) Once in his life to say with full understanding and absolute acceptance, "There is no god but God, and Mohammed is his prophet."

(2) To pray five times daily: at dawn, at noon, in the afternoon, at dusk, and after dark. The prayers are set, and traditional postures are preceded by ablutions. Moslems pray facing Mecca.

(3) To give alms.

(4) To keep the fast of Ramadan, which lasts one month.

(5) Once in a lifetime to make the pilgrimage (*Hadj*) to Mecca.

TURKEY TODAY

Almost a third of the Turkish population is employed in agriculture, growing a fair amount of wheat, as well as a number of other crops, such as corn and barley. In the last few decades Turkey has seen a great deal of economic progress, with considerable development of industry. Since World War II the level of literacy has also risen, as a result of the expansion of education, free in government schools.

In 1925 Turks began to wear the European hat in place of the fez, which was originally a Greek headgear adopted by the sultan in the nineteenth century. The international calendar and time system were also adopted. In 1926 polygamy was forbidden, and in 1928 Latin figures and a new alphabet of Latin characters replaced the Arabic. The metric system was adopted in 1934.

The monetary unit in Turkey is the *lira,* containing 100 *kurus.*

CITIES AND SITES

Istanbul

Byzantium, as Istanbul was originally called, was named after the leader, Byzas, who, with some men from Argos and Megara, Greece, founded the city about 685 B.C. Having been given advice by the oracle of Delphi to "settle opposite the Blinds," they first settled at the ancient Chalcedon (Kadikoy); but as they looked west toward a small Greek village called "Ligos," dating from 900 B.C. and located just north of the site of the present Topkapi Palace, they decided to settle there.

The Persians, under Darius, conquered this Greek community in

506 B.C. During the reign of Alexander the Great, Byzantium was under the supremacy of the Macedonians (356–323 B.C.), but then, from the middle of the fourth century B.C. until it merged into the Roman Empire, it enjoyed independence.

In A.D. 196 the Roman emperor Septimius Severus besieged and captured Byzantium, destroying the town and putting the inhabitants to the sword. Severus founded the Hippodrome, the Theater, and a wall enclosing his famous playground. He renamed the city *Augusta Antonia*, in honor of his son, Marcus Aurelius Antoninus, nicknamed Caracalla.

In A.D. 330 the Roman emperor Constantine the Great chose Byzantium to be the new capital of his empire. (It even had seven hills like Rome.) He then changed the name to *Constantinople* (Constantino-polis) and dedicated it to the Virgin Mary. It served as the capital of the Byzantine Empire for almost a thousand years. He then founded Saint Sophia, Forum Augusteum, the Great Palace, and the Senate. He decorated the Hippodrome by bringing the Serpentine Column from Delphi and his own column — now called the *Burnt Column* — from Rome.

Theodosius I (A.D. 390) brought the obelisk from Egypt to adorn the Hippodrome. In 395, Theodosius I died and the Roman Empire was divided between his two sons: Honorius, who went to Rome; and Arcadius, who stayed in Constantinople.

Under Justinian, Constantinople enjoyed a period of prosperity (A.D. 527–65), but when Justinian married a circus dancer from Cyprus, the inhabitants of the city rebelled against him (the Nika Revolt). Justinian quelled the revolt, however, by murdering 30,000 people in the Hippodrome. During the revolt a fire swept the city and burned Saint Sophia, but Justinian rebuilt it along with the city. This is the Saint Sophia that still stands — the greatest masterpiece of Byzantine art. Justinian also codified the laws that form the basis of the present legal systems of Europe.

In A.D. 655 the Arabs besieged Constantinople for the first time. They repeated their sieges in 672, 717, and 733.

In 1204 the city was captured by the Crusade army under the Venetian general Dandolo. Greeks were put to the sword and the city was burned.

In 1299 the Ottoman Empire was established, and in 1392 Sultan Bayazit laid siege on Constantinople, defeated the Crusaders, and built Fort Anadoln Hisar on the Asiatic bank of the Bosporus.

The Turks under Mohammed II laid siege to the city in 1453, and 100,000 men advanced toward the walls while 100 boats approached the harbor. The Byzantines blocked the Golden Horn by a huge iron chain which the Turks could not break, whereupon the latter built sledges and pulled 70 ships overland from Dolmabahçe via Kasimpasa into the Golden Horn. Turkish soldiers forced their way through the walls, and the Christian city Constantinople fell to the Turks and became Istanbul, a Moslem city and capital of Turkey and of the Ottoman Empire until 1923, when Turkey became a republic and Kemal Atatürk became the first president (1923–1938). The capital was moved to Ankara at that time.

Istanbul means the "city of many Islams." The Turkish government did not insist upon using that name until 1930.

Istanbul is located on two different continents, Europe and Asia, along the Bosporus, a narrow strait connecting the Black Sea and the Sea of Marmara. It is separated into three parts: (1) Old Istanbul, called *Stamboul*; (2) the new part, called *Galata* or *Beyoğlu*; and (3) *Üsküdar*, on the Asian side. The old and new parts of Istanbul are separated by a 4½-mile inlet named the *Golden Horn*. Galata is the commercial center of Istanbul, containing most of the banks, stores, and office buildings. It is largely Greek in character. The combined population of Istanbul is approximately 2,000,000.

The geographic importance of this strategic point is realized when one sees that the Bosporus is the only outlet of the Black Sea. Boats must go through the Bosporus, the Sea of Marmara, and the Dardanelles in order to get to the Aegean Sea, an arm of the Mediterranean.

POINTS OF INTEREST

Stamboul (Old Istanbul)

1. **CITY WALLS** (of Theodosius) (*Teodos Karasurlari*). The present walls are 12 miles in length and at one time had 50 gates and 400 towers. The first walls were built by Byzas in the seventh century B.C. The location of the walls has changed from time to time, and new walls were built by Severus in A.D. 196, Constantine in 324–37, Theodosius II in 413, and others. The land-side walls and most of the walls that are viewed today are those built by Theodosius. In addition to the walls, a moat 60–70 feet wide and 30 feet deep could be flooded to make an extra barrier to the city.

The main highway to the airport goes through Topkapi Gate. Between this gate and the Adrianople Gate, one mile to the north, the big Turkish guns destroyed the walls in 1453.

2. **SEVEN TOWERS** (*Yedikule*) and **MARBLE TOWER**. Near the Golden Gate on the south end of the City Walls are seven towers with cone-shaped roofs. The towers are a part of a fortress. Four of them are Byzantine and three are Turkish. The Ottomans used the towers for a treasury, and later the structure was used as a political prison. The cells may be seen upstairs in the Byzantine tower. Today the towers function as a museum. Just before reaching the top, with its striking view, one will notice a room on the left where Osman II was strangled in 1622.

South of the Seven Towers, right on the seacoast, is the Marble Tower.

3. **WELL OF BLOOD** (*Kan Kuyusu*). Through the small door on the left of the Golden Gate, on the first floor, in the center of a wooden platform near a timber support with deep marks of spears and bullets, is the spot of execution. Heads were dropped into the well, which

1. City Walls
2. Seven Towers
3. Well of Blood
4. Golden Gate
5. Mosque of Imrahor
6. Aqueduct of Valens
7. Municipal Museum
8. Column of Marcian
9. Fatih Mosque
10. Bonus Cistern
11. Mosque of Sultan Selim
12. Patriarchal Church
13. Fethiye Mosque
14. Palace of Constantine VII
15. Kaariye Museum
16. Mosque of Mihrimah
17. Aspar's Cistern
18. Prince's Mosque
19. Suleiman Mosque
20. University of Istanbul
21. Bayazit Fire Tower
22. Independence Square
23. Bayazit Mosque
24. Grand Covered Bazaar
25. Osman's Mosque
26. Burnt Column of Constantine
27. Mausoleum of Sultan Mahmud II
28. Binbirdirek Cistern
29. Hippodrome
30. Kaiser's Fountain
31. Obelisk of Theodosius
32. Serpentine Column
33. Walled Pyramid Column
34. Blue Mosque
35. Mosaic Museum
36. Palace of Constantine
37. Bucoleon Palace (Justinian's Palace)
38. Little Saint Sophia Mosque
39. Mosque of Sokollu Mehmet Pasha
40. Saint Sophia
41. Basilican Cistern
42. Fountain of Ahmed III
43. Saint Irene Museum
44. Topkapi (Seraglio Palace)
45. Archaeological Museum
46. Museum of Oriental Arts
47. Egyptian Bazaar (Spice Bazaar)
48. Mosque of Rüstem Pasha
49. Yeni Mosque
50. Galata Bridge
51. Atatürk Bridge
52. Bankalar Caddesi
53. Fountain of Bereketzade
54. Galata Tower
55. Avenue of Independence
56. Monument of the Republic
57. Dolmabahçe Mosque and Naval Museum
58. Dolmabahçe Palace
59. Painting and Sculpture Museum
60. Tchiragan Palace
61. Military Museum
62. Yildiz Palace
63. Atatürk Museum
64. Piyalepasa Mosque
65. Rumeli Hisari

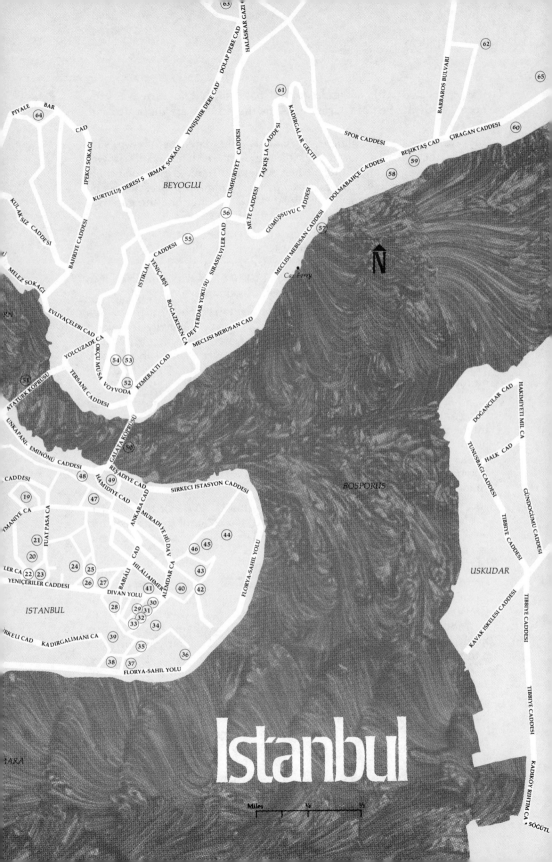

Istanbul

was connected with an underground passage that in turn was connected with the Sea of Marmara. Thus the heads were discarded into the sea.

4. **GOLDEN GATE** (*Yaldizh Kapi*). This gate, dated before A.D. 413, was in the extreme south end of the western land wall. It was originally 60 feet high and 20 feet wide and flanked by Corinthian columns. It was never opened except for triumphal processions, and after the Ottoman victory it was sealed up. At one time the gate was ornamented with gold bas-reliefs and plates.

5. **MOSQUE OF IMRAHOR** (*Imrahor Camii*). About 400 yards east of the Seven Towers is the oldest monastery in the city. It was founded in A.D. 463, and was called the Monastery of Saint John Studios. It was destroyed in the Latin occupation of 1204 and was converted into a mosque. This is one of 450 mosques in Istanbul.

6. **AQUEDUCT OF VALENS** (*Bozdoğan Kemeri*). This aqueduct was built by the Roman emperor Valens in A.D. 368 to convey the water by means of pipes between two hills. The water was brought 20 miles to the city. A most beautiful section crosses over Atatürk Boulevard. The double arches are 32 feet high on the bottom and 27½ feet high on top.

7. **MUNICIPAL MUSEUM** (*Belediye Müzesi*). This museum stands on the Atatürk Boulevard next to the Aqueduct of Valens. It has an interesting collection of the handicrafts of Istanbul: machines, pictures, puppet screens, writing sets, Turkish prints, porcelains, glass, mother-of-pearl, costumes, and so forth. It is especially renowned for its collection of Karagöz characters (figures of the Turkish shadow play).

8. **COLUMN OF MARCIAN** (*Marsiyen Sutunu*). West of the Municipal Museum, in the center of a crossroad, is a 33-foot granite column with a Corinthian capital. The column dates back to A.D. 450–57 and is called *Kiztasi* (the Column of Virginity) in Turkish. A statue of Marcian once stood on top of the column.

9. **FATIH MOSQUE** (Mosque of the Conqueror, *Fatih Mehmet Camii*). Northwest of the Valens Aqueduct, on one of the seven hills of Constantinople, is a mosque with two minarets. It was built in 1470 by Mohammed II, "the Conqueror," who had conquered Constantinople for the Turks in A.D. 1453. Mohammed II's family is buried in a tomb here.

After being destroyed by earthquake the mosque was restored in 1872. Like the Blue Mosque, it has four half domes.

10. **BONUS CISTERN** (*Cukur Bostan*). Directly north of the Conqueror's Mosque is the Bonus Cistern. In Turkish the name means "low field." This is one of three open-air-type cisterns built in the fifth century by Theodosius II. It is 165 yards square and 30 feet deep.

11. **MOSQUE OF SULTAN SELIM** (*Sultanselim Camii*). This mosque is located on the northeast end of the Bonus Cistern, on one of the

muezzins. In a burial ground east of the mosque are the **MAUSO-LEUMS** of Suleiman and his wife Roxelana. The tomb of Suleiman bears an enormous turban. The building also contains a wooden model of the Kaaba at Mecca. A building with small domes on the southwest of the mosque is a **SEMINARY**, containing a library of 100,000 volumes and valuable old illuminated manuscripts.

The **MUSEUM OF TURKISH AND ISLAMIC ART** is a part of the complex, and the **TOMB** of the architect Sinan is a humble one to the northwest of the Mosque.

Suleiman the Magnificent (1490–1566) was the tenth and most celebrated Ottoman sultan. He won his title as a conqueror, lawgiver, administrator, and patron of learning.

20. **UNIVERSITY OF ISTANBUL.** The grand triumphal archway overlooking the Bayazit Square at the south entrance is a remnant of what was the Ministry of War of the Ottoman Empire until 1920. In A.D. 1454 the Conqueror, Mohammed II, built near this area a wooden palace, used until the construction of the Seraglio Palace in 1468.

Istanbul University was established in 1453 following the conquest of the city by Mohammed II. The Conqueror imported the greatest scholars of the time, and the university became the most important center of culture and science in the East. Here law, history, medicine, mathematics, physical sciences, theology, and other courses were taught.

Education at the university is completely free, and students come from all over the Near East.

21. **BAYAZIT FIRE TOWER** (*Bayazit Yangin Kulesi*). This tower on the university campus was built by Mahmud II in 1823 as a fire-watch tower. It is 200 feet high and has 180 wooden steps. A view of the city is a reward of the climb.

22. **INDEPENDENCE SQUARE** (*Hürriyet Meydani*). In front of the entrance to the University of Istanbul, on the third of the seven hills, is an area that was once known as *Forum Thory*. It had an elaborate column dedicated to Theodosius I, which was similar to Trajan's Column in Rome. It was erected in A.D. 393 and had a silver statue of Theodosius I on top. In the early Byzantine period the Column of Virginity stood in the square.

23. **BAYAZIT MOSQUE** (*Bayazit Camii*). Facing Independence Square is a mosque called *Pigeon Mosque*, built in A.D. 1501 in the name of Bayazit II. It has huge gates and side aisles.

24. **GRAND COVERED BAZAAR** (*Buyuk Kapali Carsi*). This large, ancient bazaar was first founded by the Conqueror, Mohammed II, in 1461, and additions were made by Suleiman the Magnificent in the sixteenth century. After being damaged by earthquakes and fires, it was rebuilt of stone in the eighteenth century. Damage from an earthquake was repaired in 1894, and when 1,200 shops were burned in 1954 they were soon rebuilt.

The huge building occupies an area 500 yards square, with 97 vaulted cross streets dimly lit by windows in its walls. It contains

4,000 individually owned shops built very close together. Antiques, silverware, jewelry, shoes and souvenirs of all kinds may be purchased with some "bargaining."

There are ten **GATES** to the bazaar. A walk through the courtyard of Osman's Mosque leads to the popular southeast gate. The west end opens near Freedom Square and the University of Istanbul.

The **SECONDHAND BAZAAR** (Ic Bedestan) is in the center, where over each of its four entrances there was a relief of a Byzantine eagle emblem. This was probably a part of a thirteenth-century library.

25. **OSMAN'S MOSQUE** (Osmaniye Camii). On the southeast corner of the Grand Covered Bazaar is a mosque that was started by Mahmud I in 1749 and completed by Osman III in 1755. This 2-minaret mosque belongs to the single dome mosques of the Turkish Baroque style.

26. **BURNT COLUMN OF CONSTANTINE** (Cemberlitas). Cemberlitas means "hooped stone." This column was in the center of the Forum of Constantine on the second of the seven hills and was erected in A.D. 324–37. It bore the statue of Apollo, which Constantine replaced with his own in A.D. 330. Later on it bore the statues of Julian and then of Theodosius. The column consists of 8 large pieces of Egyptian red porphyry, with a total height of 180 feet. Alexius Comnenus I repaired it and placed a Corinthian capital on it in 1081–1118. After a big fire in 1701 its base was walled and iron hoops were set by Mustafa III to protect it.

27. **MAUSOLEUM OF SULTAN MAHMUD II.** Near the Burnt Column is an octagonal building of pure white marble. It was built first in 1839. It contains the mausoleums of Mahmud II, his wife, and others.

28. **BINBIRDIREK CISTERN**, Cistern of Philoxenus. Philoxenus is the second largest underground cistern in the city and probably the oldest of its kind. It is located on Divan Yolu Street just west of the Hippodrome. The water has been drained. Built by Senator Philoxenus in A.D. 324–37, it is 61 by 70 yards in size and contains 224 columns in 14 rows of 16 columns, 13 feet apart. The capitals are shaped like inverted pyramids, with arches and domes built of bricks.

29. **HIPPODROME** (At Meydani). Just west of the Blue Mosque is the Olympic playground of the Romans, called the Hippodrome. It was founded by Septimius Severus in A.D. 203, after he had burned the city and killed its Greek inhabitants. The Hippodrome runs north and south 1,210 feet and east and west 370 feet. It held 100,000 people and was approximately half as large as the Circus Maximus in Rome.

30. **KAISER'S FOUNTAIN.** This is a German helmet-shaped fountain at the north end of the Hippodrome. It was sent as a gift of Kaiser Wilhelm II in 1898. It marks the site of the Royal Box, which was supported by 24 marble columns. Here also was a platform where the games started. It was here that the Nika Revolt began in A.D. 532. The revolt started with an argument between the emperor Justinian and one of the drivers of the games and ended with the

massacre of 30,000 revolters. Also, 30,000 rebellious Janissaries were killed here by the naval forces of Mahmud II in 1826.

31. **OBELISK OF THEODOSIUS** (*Theodos Dikilitasi*). This is the northernmost of the three columns in the Hippodrome and the oldest historical monument in the city. It was first erected in Heliopolis, Egypt, by Thutmose III in 1471 B.C., and the hieroglyphs record his victories. It was brought to Constantinople by Theodosius I in A.D. 390. It is made of rose granite from the Aswan granite quarries in upper Egypt and measures 64 feet high. The bronze base and its marble pedestal, with its record of ancient scenes of the Hippodrome in marble carving, is beautiful. On the north side is a record of the erection operation of the obelisk. This was done by wetting the ropes and benefiting from their shrinkage. The mate to this obelisk is in Central Park in New York City.

32. **SERPENTINE COLUMN** (*Yilanli Sütun*). This column has three twisted bronze serpents with heads broken off. Two of the heads, however, have been preserved; one is in the Archaeological Museum at Istanbul and the other in London. The column's original height was 26 feet. The three serpent heads originally supported a golden tripod of the oracle at Delphi, Greece. Constantine brought the column to Constantinople in A.D. 329. Apparently the column was originally erected to commemorate the victory of the Plataea and was made of metals captured from the Persians. It was a votive offering to the oracle of Delphi as early as 497 B.C.

33. **WALLED PYRAMID COLUMN** (*Örme Sütun*). This column was made by Constantine VII (called Porphyrogenitus) (A.D. 912–59) to illustrate the victories of his predecessor, Basil I. Its height is 81 feet. Its bronze illustrations were stuck in holes which are still visible on the column. The bronze itself, however, was smelted into coins by the Latins in the thirteenth century. This column is located in the south end of the Hippodrome.

34. **BLUE MOSQUE** (*Sultan Ahmet I Camii*). Immediately east of the Hippodrome is the most beautiful mosque in Istanbul, the Blue Mosque. It is the only mosque in the world with six minarets. After this mosque was constructed, another minaret had to be added to the Mosque of Mecca so it would have seven minarets and thus maintain its superiority in that respect. The Blue Mosque has sixteen balconies, where sixteen muezzins could call the faithful to prayers.

The beautiful Blue Mosque was built in A.D. 1616 by the Turkish architect Sedefkar Mehmet Ağa, who was a pupil of Sinan. The interior is 175 by 170 feet and is lighted by 260 colored glass windows. The central dome is 72 feet in diameter and 141 feet high, with 4 arches that open to 4 half domes and again to 3 semicircular ones. The walls up to the capitals are decorated with beautiful Turkish tiles and the ceiling with delicate frescoes. Because of Mohammedan restrictions against animate designs, there are three motifs: floral, geometric, and calligraphic. The blue color is counted as the color of the sky and hence heaven, red is the Turkish national color, and

Blue Mosque, Istanbul

green is the color of vegetation and therefore was considered religious. The **MIHRAB**, with beeswax candles on either side, is said to have three pieces of sacred stone from the Kaaba (called the "black stone") in the center of it. The **MINBAR** is the special box with stairs, from which the priest's short lecture is given.

35. **MOSAIC MUSEUM** (*Mozayik Müzesi*). Behind the Blue Mosque, at 22 Toun Sokak, is this small collection of mosaics from various periods of Byzantine history, displayed outdoors in the niches of a former bazaar.

A small underground "escape route" walkway recently discovered takes off from the end of the museum's "street." It once led from the Byzantine emperor's palace on the Hippodrome down to a special gate in the waterfront walls of the city. The walkway has some beautiful mosaic work, including hunting scenes, portraits, and mythological episodes.

36. **PALACE OF CONSTANTINE** (the Great Palace, *Buyuk Saray*). Near the Sea of Marmara, southeast of the Blue Mosque (following the first street on the south), is the famous Palace of Constantine the Great. It was found in 1936 by a Mr. Baxter, archaeologist of Saint Andrew's University, Edinburgh. He excavated 15 feet underground and found beautiful colored floor mosaics depicting scenes that dated from the fourth and fifth centuries A.D.

37. **BUCOLEON PALACE (JUSTINIAN'S PALACE**, *Bokoleon veya Justinyen Sarayi*). South of the Blue Mosque, near the shores of the Sea of Marmara, is the Bucoleon Palace. It was built by Theodosius II in A.D. 408–50 and was a place of importance during Byzantine times. From the top, one may have a beautiful view of the Marmara Sea.

38.   **LITTLE SAINT SOPHIA MOSQUE** (Saint Sergius and Bachus Church, *Küçük Ayasofya Camii*). This small church, just west of the Palace of Justinian and 100 yards south of the Pasha Mosque, has a unique dome with eight buttresses. Justinian built the church in A.D. 527–36 and dedicated it to Sergius and Bachus, two saints. It was later converted into a mosque.

39.   **MOSQUE OF SOKOLLU MEHMET PASHA** (*Mehmet Pasha Camii*). This mosque lies on the southwest corner of the Hippodrome on the number 2 hill of the seven hills. It has a single minaret and was built by architect Sinan in 1572 for Sokollu Mehmet Pasha, a noted admiral and prime minister. It has the oldest tiles and stained glass windows.

40.   **SAINT SOPHIA** (Ayasofya Museum, Byzantine Art Museum). A short distance north of the Blue Mosque is the Church or Mosque of Saint Sophia. It was built as a tiny basilical church by Constantine the Great in A.D. 325 over a pagan temple. Theodosius II rebuilt it in 415, and after it was totally destroyed by fire during the Nika Revolt of 532, Justinian rebuilt the present building (532–37). After an earthquake in 557 its dome was rebuilt in the form in which it has been preserved.

This Christian church was converted into a mosque in 1453 by the Conqueror, Mohammed II, who erected a minaret on the southeast side. The other three were added later. Because of Moslem restrictions against animate images in mosques, the glass mosaics were covered.

Constantine's palace, Istanbul

As well as being one of the world's greatest buildings, Saint Sophia forms the supreme achievement of Byzantine (Greco-Roman) architecture and art, which had flourished between A.D. 324 and 1453. In 1932 it was converted into a Museum of Byzantine Art by the Turkish government, and Thomas Whittemore, an American expert from Boston, was appointed to uncover the glass mosaics.

A glass **MOSAIC** over the gate leading to the internal narthex shows the Virgin Mary in the center with Jesus in her arms. Constantine is shown with his walled city on the right, while Justinian with his enlarged Saint Sophia in his hand presents them to the Holy Virgin for protection.

The interior measures 107 by 265 feet, and the dome is 180 feet high and 107 feet in diameter. Forty small windows admit light into the interior.

Contrary to its external appearance, the vast interior has been freed from any heavy loads, conveying a beautiful ancient effect with spaciousness and a miraculously supported great dome. Here the planning idea of the Byzantines has cooperated with the great vaulting skill of the East and has employed the newly developed knowledge of diagonal thrust.

Rich colored glass **MOSAICS** cover the vaulting, and precious stones have been split and put side by side artistically to form a design.

The 107 **COLUMNS** were imported from all over the near east: 8 of the largest green marble columns in the center (4 on each side) were brought from the Temple of Diana in Ephesus; 8 of the red porphyry columns (2 in each bay) were brought from the Temple of the Sun or Jupiter at Baalbek, Lebanon; some of the columns in the second story are from Troy. Of the 107 columns, 40 are on the first floor, 60 are on the second, and 7 are on the top. The capitals are Doric, Ionic, and Corinthian.

The **FLOOR** is covered by white marble with fossils that match and make beautiful designs. The great circular discs on the walls contain the names of the prophet Mohammed and six of his earliest caliphs.

Under the dome, the circular stone mosaic on the floor is the original floor from Justinian's period. This was the **CORONATION SPOT** of the Byzantine emperors.

The two round **MARBLE FOUNTAIN JARS** by the entrances were brought from Pergamum (Bergama).

A **LIBRARY** of 10,000 volumes is located in the mosque.

In the northwest corner there is a finger-pierced column of porous marble. Known as the **WEEPING** or **SWEATING COLUMN**, it keeps moist through absorption of the humidity from the reservoir under the edifice. According to tradition, the hole was the finger mark of Saint George.

The **ABLUTION FOUNTAIN**, with its bronze grilling and hanging roof, is a fine piece of Turkish art of Mahmud I, of the eighteenth century.

The two-storied building on the southwest is an **ORPHANAGE** built by the Conqueror about 1450. The small buildings with the domes are **TOMBS** of past rulers.

Basilican Cistern,
Istanbul

41. BASILICAN CISTERN *(Yerebatan Sarayi).* This cistern is located on the southwest side of Saint Sophia, near the ancient water-balance tower. This cistern still contains water and is illuminated for visitors. Since it supplied water to the Byzantine palaces, it was called *Basilican,* meaning "royal." It covers an area of 230 by 460 feet and contains 336 columns 26 feet high and 13 feet apart. Thirteen rows of 28 columns support Byzantine arches and domes built of flat square Roman bricks about 8 feet below ground level.

The water is supplied by underground pipes and aqueducts from the Belgrade forests outside the city walls. As a precaution in Byzantine days against a sudden enemy attack, these reservoirs were always kept full of water. As the underground reservoirs were cool, the people who lived above them used them as refrigerators, dropping their food in baskets and buckets in the morning and picking it up in the evening cold and fresh — but sampled, perhaps, by cistern guards.

The old water-balance tower nearby is Turkish and is 200 years old. It was used to supply water to higher elevations by means of sucking through pipes from down below.

42. FOUNTAIN OF AHMED III (Ahmed III Cesmesi). This fountain, with its spreading roof, is located on the northeast side of Saint Sophia by the Royal Gate of the Seraglio (Topkapi Palace). It was built by Ahmed III in 1728.

43. SAINT IRENE MUSEUM (Saint Irene Kilisesi). This is the large red-domed building just inside the Topkapi Gate and to the left. It was probably built by Constantine in the fourth century and was dedicated to Saint Irene. It was restored by Justinian after the Nika Revolt in 532 and again in 740. The building was used for storing military captures. It presently serves as a **BYZANTINE ART MUSEUM,** and is second only to Saint Sophia in size.

44. **TOPKAPI (SERAGLIO PALACE,** *Topkapi Sarayi*). A *seraglio* is a palace with a harem, and thus the name. When the Conqueror, Mohammed II, moved his capital to Constantinople, he built a palace near the site of the present university. That one burned down, and the new palace, *Topkapi* (meaning "cannon gate"), was built on one of the seven hills. From one of the gates facing the Bosporus, cannons were fired on occasions of important visits to and from the palace.

The various buildings of the palace were built between A.D. 1468 and 1853. When Abdülmedjid built the Dolmabahçe Palace on the Bosporus, Topkapi was abandoned. In 1923 its treasury and harem quarters were opened to the public. This huge museum is built within three courtyards. The first court includes the **ROSE HOUSE PARK** (Gülhane Park), the largest public park in Istanbul; the **MUSEUM OF ANCIENT ORIENTAL ARTS**, with its valuable collection of Hittite, Egyptian, Chaldean, and Assyrian items; the **MUSEUM OF ARCHAEOLOGY**, with the sarcophagus of Alexander the Great; the **TILE KIOSK** (Çinili Kösk); the **MINT OF SAINT IRENE**; and the **TURKISH MILITARY HOSPITAL**.

The main gate to Topkapi is called *Babihumayun*, meaning the "Royal Gate." Through the gates one enters courtyard number 2, where 5,000 people were entertained on holidays. The courtyard is surrounded by an arcade. The huge **KITCHEN QUARTER** on the right (east) had 1,100 men engaged in cooking. It was built in the sixteenth century and is used now as a **MUSEUM** for 7,000 pieces of select Chinese porcelains — the largest collection in the world. Rooms also contain Venetian glass and porcelain.

Other rooms include the **AUDIENCE ROOM**, the **LIBRARY OF AHMED III** (an old map of America dating back to A.D. 1500 was discovered here), **COSTUME ROOMS**, the **TREASURY** (housing the largest collection of jewels in the world, e.g., an 86-carat diamond on a dagger), the **KIOSK OF BAGHDAD**, the **CIRCUMCISION ROOM**, the **KIOSK OF REVAN**, **RELIGIOUS RELICS ROOMS** (old Koran, relic boxes, bread, seals, and teeth and a foot mark of Mohammed), the **TENT DEPARTMENT**, the **PAINTING DEPARTMENT**, the **SEALS DEPARTMENT**, the **MINIATURE DEPARTMENT**, the **EMBROIDERIES DEPARTMENT**, the **HAREM QUARTERS** (335 rooms), the **ARMORY COLLECTION**, the **COUNCIL**, and others.

45. **ARCHAEOLOGICAL MUSEUM** (*Arkeoloji Müzesi*). The present building located at Topkapi was opened in 1891. It is a marvelous collection of sarcophagi, mosaics, statues, reliefs, arts of various kinds, and other exhibits. Among the more important items are these: the **SILOAM INSCRIPTION** from Hezekiah's Tunnel; the **GEZER CALENDAR**; the **SARCOPHAGUS OF ALEXANDER THE GREAT** (who died in 323 B.C. in Babylon at the age of 33 and was buried at the nearest royal tomb at Sidon); the **WEEPING WOMEN'S TOMB** (350 B.C.); the **ROOM OF PRAXITELES** (salon no. 15), with its head of Alexander the Great from Pergamum (300 B.C.), head of Zeus from Troy (300 B.C.), Apollo (300 B.C.), Hermaphrodites from Pergamum (300 B.C.), and others. Salons 16 through 20 have beautiful statuary.

The second floor has an **INSCRIPTION** dating back to the time of

Christ, forbidding strangers to enter the temple. It also has Turkish tiles and other items of interest.

46. **MUSEUM OF ORIENTAL ARTS** (*Şark Eserleri Müzesi*). This is a small building southwest of the Archaeological Museum. It contains twelve rooms with priceless treasures from the most ancient cultures. It was opened in 1926.

47. **EGYPTIAN BAZAAR** (**SPICE BAZAAR**, Misir Çarşisi). Near the south end of the Galata Bridge and southwest of the Yeni Mosque is the Egyptian Bazaar. It was built in A.D. 1660 and received its name because rare spices of every kind are sold there.

48. **MOSQUE OF RÜSTEM PASHA** (*Rüstempasa Camii*). A hundred yards west of the south end of the Galata Bridge is an elevated mosque with various shops underneath for the purpose of financially supporting the mosque. It was built in 1561 by architect Sinan in the name of the deceased husband (Rüstempasa) of Mihrimah Sultana, the daughter of Suleiman. It is also called the *Tile Mosque*, because of its beautiful tiles.

49. **YENI MOSQUE** (Queen Mother's Mosque, *Yeni Camii*). This two-minaret mosque stands at the south end of the Galata Bridge. It was completed in 1663. It has four half domes, marble carvings, and stained glass tiles.

Galata, Beyoğlu (New Istanbul)

50. **GALATA BRIDGE** (*Kopru*). Galata Bridge was built first in 1845, then again in 1877. The present bridge was built of iron in 1910. Part of it is a drawbridge.

51. **ATATÜRK BRIDGE.** This bridge, west of the Galata Bridge, has a drawbridge that is opened daily between 5:00 and 6:00 A.M.

52. **BANKALAR CADDESI.** The main banks, businesses, and offices are in New Istanbul.

53. **FOUNTAIN OF BEREKETZADE.** Located near the Galata Tower, this fountain, with its reliefs of flowers and fruits in marble, forms a rare specimen of the Tulip Period of Turkish art.

54. **GALATA TOWER** (*Galata Kulesi*). During the reign of Anastasius I (A.D. 491–518) the Galata Tower was built. It is about 160 feet high, and an elevator will take the visitor to the top for a panoramic view or a meal in an attractive restaurant.

55. **AVENUE OF INDEPENDENCE** (*Istiklâl Caddesi*). This is the most crowded street in Istanbul. The best theaters, restaurants, and so forth are here.

56. **MONUMENT OF THE REPUBLIC** at Taksim Square. Erected in 1928 in the shape of an arch, this monument is dedicated to the achievements of Mustafa Kemal Pasha, later called *Atatürk* ("Father of the Turks"). The new republic was born on October 29, 1923.

57. **DOLMABAHÇE MOSQUE** and **NAVAL MUSEUM** (*Deniz Müzesi*).

East of Taksim Square, on the shores of the Bosporus, are the Dolmabahçe Mosque and Naval Museum.

58. **DOLMABAHÇE PALACE** (*Dolmabahçe Sarayi*). Italian Baroque, French style marble carvings, crystals, and silvers make this one of the most beautiful of all palaces. It was built by Medjid in 1853 and was used by the last sultans. Atatürk died here in 1938.

The Turkish hot bath is made of alabaster. The throne room is very elaborate, with an immense 4-ton crystal chandelier — a present of Czar Nicholas the Great of Russia. A harem is also visible. The word *Dolmabahçe* means "filled garden." The palace and grounds stretch a half mile along the Bosporus.

59. **PAINTING AND SCULPTURE MUSEUM** (*Resim ve Hegkel Müzesi*). Near the northwest corner of Dolmabahçe Palace is the Painting and Sculpture Museum.

60. **TCHIRAGAN PALACE** (*Çirağan Sarayi*). This palace is located on the Bosporus about a mile northeast of the Dolmabahçe Palace. It was built by Aziz in 1874 and used as a parliament in 1909. It was destroyed by fire in 1910 and was never restored. Its exterior carving with colored marble columns and lacy gateways are still beautiful.

61. **MILITARY MUSEUM** (*Askeri Müzesi*). The Military Museum contains a collection of very old Turkish captured arms and various military equipment. Wax figures of the Janissaries show their gaily colored costumes. It also has the iron chain which was used by the Byzantines to close the Golden Horn against their enemy, the Turks. It is located by the Winter Sport Palace near the Hilton Hotel. The

New Istanbul and the Galata Tower

Mehter Band of the Janissary soldiers practices at the museum at 3:00 P.M. daily, except Mondays and Tuesdays.

62. YILDIZ PALACE (Yildiz Sarayi) and TANZIMAT MUSEUM. Over the hills from the Tchiragan Palace is a palace that occupies a large land area. It was built by Aziz in 1861–76 and enlarged by Abdül-hamid II. It has a large park area with flowers and trees and buildings. Here the first democrat of Turkey, Midhat Pasha, was imprisoned before he was sent into exile at Tayif, Arabia, by Sultan Abdülhamid II in 1881. There are two imperial kiosks in the huge park, one of which now houses the Tanzimat Museum, with documents and pictures reminiscent of that period. (The Tanzimat was the era of reform under the sultans.)

63. ATATÜRK MUSEUM (Atatürk Müzesi). Directly west of the Yildiz Palace is the Atatürk Museum. It is also directly north of the Hilton Hotel. Atatürk once lived in the old house of the museum, and his possessions, plus other documents related to the revolution of 1923, are housed there.

64. PIYALEPASA MOSQUE. Although this mosque is a little "out of the way" for a visit by most tourists, it is well worth the effort. It is located about a mile directly west of the Hilton Hotel. The mosque was built in the sixteenth century, according to the Ottoman Brusa style.

65. RUMELI HISARI ("European fortress," Castle of Mehmet), on the Bosporus. This is a huge fortress of the Conqueror, the Ottoman sultan Mohammed II, built in 1452. It took 19,000 men three months to build, and consists of three towers enclosed by a wall in the shape of an M, the first letter in Mohammed's name. Mohammed II decided he wanted to enlarge the Ottoman Empire, and in 1452 he built this fortress to launch the conquest of Constantinople. He captured Constantinople in 1453 at the age of 22, changed its name to Istanbul, and earned the title of Fatih Mehmet, or Mohammed the Conqueror. Thus the Byzantine Empire, the last outpost of the Eastern Roman Empire, came to an end. In summer months, the State Theater stages Shakespeare's plays in this unusually dramatic setting.

Üsküdar, Scutari, Chrysopolis

Across the Bosporus from Old Istanbul (in Asia Minor) is the Üsküdar section of Istanbul. It is called the "Golden City," because the sun reflects golden off the windows in the evening. Mosques, tobacco factories, piers, and cemeteries mark the city. The visitor can ascend by auto to the top of CAMLICA HILL (Tchamlijah) at Üsküdar for the finest bird's-eye view of Istanbul. It is 870 feet high.

POINTS OF INTEREST

The KARACA AHMED TURKISH CEMETERY is of interest and also the BARRACKS OF SELIM, where the English lady Florence Nightingale started the nursing profession during the Crimean War, 1854–57.

LEANDER'S TOWER *(Kiz Kulesi)*, offshore from Üsküdar, is said to have been built during the time of Constantine (A.D. 330). It is now used as a lighthouse.

North of Üsküdar, on the Abdullahaga Road next to the Bosporus, is the **BEYLERBEY PALACE**, built in the nineteenth century. The interior of the palace is made entirely of marble.

Kadikoy, *Chalcedon*

On the east side of the Bosporus, directly opposite Istanbul, is the city of ancient Chalcedon.

In the early fifth century the Roman church began emphasizing the primacy of Peter among the apostles, both in faith and government, and claimed that what Peter possessed had passed to Peter's successors. In A.D. 445, Pope Leo I ordered all to obey the Roman bishop as having the "Primacy of Saint Peter." Because of this and other controversies, the Pope called a council to meet in Nicaea in the autumn of 451. The meeting place was changed to Chalcedon, and 600 bishops assembled in the Fourth Ecumenical Council.

Among other things, the Council decided that Constantinople was on a practical equality with Rome (28th canon): "The See of Constantinople shall enjoy equal privileges with the See of Old Rome." Against this action Leo at once protested, and it foreshadowed the ultimate separation between the churches of the East and West in 1054.

Another subject of the Council of Chalcedon was the "Christological Controversy." The *Nicene Creed* had indicated that Christ is fully God, and "was made man." The question arose as to the relationship of the divine and human in Jesus. Out of the council came the *Creed of Chalcedon*, which has ever since been regarded in the Greek, Latin, and most Protestant churches as the "orthodox" solution to the Christological problem. Dioscurus, Nestorius, and others had been deposed because they disagreed, and the powers had their say in the end.

Troy, *Hisarlik, Novum Ilium*

The site of Troy was settled as early as 3000 B.C. Homer's *Iliad* relates the legendary story of the Trojan War, which was fought about 1200 B.C.

For nine years, Homer tells us, Agamemnon ravaged the region around Troy but could not take the city itself. The Trojans drove back the Greeks again and again, and Agamemnon and Odysseus were disabled. When Achilles rejoined the fray, however, the Greeks took courage, and after a bloody battle the Trojans fled behind the city walls. The legend says that the Greeks burned their own houses by the shore near Troy and sailed away, leaving only Odysseus and elite warriors hidden inside a large wooden horse. Trojans breached their walls to drag the wooden horse inside, then celebrated the Greek withdrawal. But as Troy slept, the wooden horse disgorged the Greek warriors and the city was destroyed.

Although strained relations had existed between the Greeks and Trojans before their battle, the immediate cause seems to have been the abduction of Helen from Sparta by Hector's brother Paris.

In 1871, Heinrich Schliemann discovered the rubble of seven cities built on the site of Troy between 3000 B.C. and A.D. 400. Two more have been found subsequently. Ruins of the sixth or seventh layer are probably those of Homer's Troy. Walls still remain on the site. Objects found at Troy are housed in the Museum of Canakkale.

TROAS

This is a city of Mysia, 15 miles south of Troy on the northwest coast of Asia Minor. It was founded by Antigonus and refounded in 300 B.C. by Lysimachus, who named it Alexandria Troas. It was a free city and minted its own coins under the Seleucid kings of Syria. Augustus made it a Roman colony, and it became one of the greatest cities of northwest Asia. The site is in complete ruin. A temple, a theater, a gymnasium, and baths give it the traditional Greek-Roman look. The name *Troas* comes from the Greek *Troad*, meaning the region around Troy.

- While Paul, Silas, and Timothy visited Troas, Paul had a vision in which he was called from Troas to Macedonia (Acts 16:8–13). This was during his second missionary journey.
- Paul spent a week here on his third missionary journey. He preached and brought Eutychus back to life (Acts 20:6–12).
- Paul referred to his first experience here (2 Cor. 2:12–13).
- Paul needed several items he had left here (2 Tim. 4:13).

ASSOS

This is a town over half a mile from the Gulf of Adramyttium (in Mysia, province of Asia) and 30 miles south of Troy. The fortifications are among the most excellent and best preserved of their kind, the greatest part of them dating from the fourth century B.C. It was the birthplace of the Stoic Cleanthes.

- Paul walked 30 miles from Troas to Assos on his third missionary journey and his last visit to Asia (Acts 20:13).

PERGAMUM, Bergama *

The ancient Pergamum is located 15 miles from the sea and 50 miles north of Smyrna, on a mount that rises 1,300 feet above the plain. Evidence shows that it was settled as early as the eighth century B.C. Pergamum became a power in the Hellenistic world. Philetaeros (283–278 B.C.), Eumenes (263–241 B.C.), and Attalus reigned at Pergamum. Attalus became famous when he stopped paying tribute to the Gauls and in battle drove them from the west coast. Later he earned the goodwill of the Romans, and soon Pergamum became the capital of the Roman province of Asia. Eumenes enlarged and beauti-

---

*For much of the material on Pergamum I am indebted to George E. Bean, *Aegean Turkey: An Archaeological Guide* (New York, 1966), pp. 68–94.

fied the city on the hill and surrounded it with a wall. He was like Pericles of Athens. The lower AGORA, the great GYMNASIUM, the famous LIBRARY, and the ALTAR OF ZEUS were built during his day. Art and sculpture were developed in a Pergamene style; the *Dying Gaul* and the friezes of the altar of Zeus are well-known examples. Because of poets, philosophers, scientists, and scholars during the days of Attalus, Pergamum's reputation rivaled that of Athens or Alexandria.

Christianity reached Pergamum very early, and the church here was addressed by John the Revelator (Rev. 2:12–17). In his letter, Pergamum stands as a city of authority. Not only did Roman power exist here, but the power of evil was also centered in this city, and to its victorious church is promised a greater authority, the power of the mighty name of God. The epithet "royal" comes to mind as one views the acropolis rising out of the plain with apparently impregnable strength. The city long remained a religious center, being for a long time the home of a bishop. In 1304 it came into the hands of the Seljuks and in 1336 the Turks.

POINTS OF INTEREST

The GREAT WALL OF EUMENES II may be seen on the extreme summit of the hill.

PERGAMENE LIBRARY. Not far from the top of the hill are the ruins of the famous Pergamene Library, near the temple of Athena. A stone bench in the library rooms kept the public away from the books while the library attendants could reach them. A typical book in the classical period consisted of a long strip of papyrus about a foot wide, rolled around a stick. This was very inconvenient for the finding of a reference, and for the introduction of the paged book — or *codex*, as it was called — we are indebted to the kings of Pergamum. For the Attalids, book collecting was almost a mania. The kingdom was combed, and, with or without payment, the books were taken to the capital. The library collection eventually totaled 200,000 volumes.

The library at Alexandria, Egypt, was the only rival. And since Egypt was the principal, almost the only, source of papyrus, Ptolemy — according to the Roman writer Varro — jealous of the Pergamene collection, prohibited the export of papyrus. Thereupon, the king of Pergamum resorted to the use of skins, as the Ionians had done long before, and from this "Pergamene paper" comes our own word *parchment*. As skins were less suitable for rolling, they were made into paged books. This *codex*-type book led eventually to the abandonment of the papyrus roll.

The library collection was taken to Alexandria and presented as a gift to Cleopatra by Antony. The library survived until the seventh century, when the caliph Omar, or his appropriately named lieutenant, Amribn el-Ass, reasoned that if a book is inconsistent with the Koran it is impious, and ordered the entire library destroyed.

The **ALTAR OF ZEUS**, one of the wonders of the ancient world, consisted of a podium nearly 20 feet high on a foundation of crisscross walls 120 feet by 112 feet in size. The outer wall of the podium was once decorated with the famous frieze representing the battle of the gods and giants (now housed in the Pergamum Museum in Berlin). This frieze was the masterpiece of Pergamum. It has been suggested that this altar of Zeus is the throne of Satan mentioned in the Book of Revelation: "I know . . . where thou dwellest, even where Satan's seat is" (2:13). Satan's throne was probably not this altar but the city of Pergamum itself, the central seat of Roman authority in the area. Some feel the scripture has reference to emperor worship.

The **GREEK THEATER**, the most spectacular thing to see at Pergamum, is built into the steep face of the southwest side of the hill. It is exceptionally high, with 78 rows of seats, divided by two diazomata into three horizontal sections.

The **IONIC TEMPLE** is a rebuilding of Roman date, but the original goes back to the second century B.C. It was probably built to Dionysus and was later dedicated to the Roman emperor Caracalla.

The **PRECINCT OF DEMETER** has a propylon dating back to the time of Eumenes II. The columns have rare leaf capitals, are fluted at the bottom only, and are lacking the usual base mouldings. The **TEMPLE OF DEMETER** is on the west end of the precinct.

The **GYMNASIUM** houses a **LECTURE THEATER** that held 1,000 people.

The **ROMAN BATHS** were supplied with water brought from mountains to the north in pipes on an **AQUEDUCT**, by the siphon principle. To the north of the acropolis, remains of the aqueduct can still be seen. It was built in the second century B.C. and is very impressive.

The **MIDDLE TERRACE** has the foundations of a temple, and the **LOWER TERRACE** has a playground for boys.

RED COURTYARD. Bergama, the modern town, now covers the lower part of the ancient city. In the town itself the most important monument of antiquity is the **KIZIL AVLU**, or **RED COURTYARD**. This Roman courtyard has a three-storied temple and narrow bathing pools fed by hot and cold water pipes. The courtyard is built over the River Selinus, which flows obliquely across it in a double-vaulted tunnel which still serves its purpose. This monument complex dates back to approximately the second century A.D. Some have suggested it was dedicated to three Egyptian deities: Isis, Serapis, and Hermocrates.

The **ASCLEPIEUM**, southwest of the city, is one of the most important ruins at Pergamum. The god Asclepias was the god of healing, and it was here the sick gathered from points far and near to be healed. Asclepias was greatly honored here, and his symbol, the serpent, is often found on coins (not unlike Moses and the serpent of brass representing Christ, or, perhaps, Quetzalcoatl in ancient America). (See Num. 21:6-9; 2 Kings 18:4; John 3:14-15.) This Asclepieum ranked in importance second only to that of Epidaurus. Aristides, a chronic invalid, was a frequent visitor here and wrote about it.

Right: Medical insignia, Pergamum
Below: Asclepieum and amphitheater, Pergamum

Galen, the most famous physician of antiquity after Hippocrates, was
born at Pergamum and practiced in the Asclepieum.

Treatment consisted of three elements: diet, hot and cold baths,
and exercise. Sleeping in the sanctuary and having dreams that

priests interpreted was a part of the cure. Coating oneself with mud and running around the temple was another treatment. Not only was the Asclepieum a place for the sick, but it was also a spa and a religious sanctuary. A theater and library were also a part of the complex. Most of the present Asclepieum was built in the time of Aelius Aristides (second century A.D.). The main temple is dedicated to Zeus and Asclepias. PORTICOS, a small THEATER, a LATRINE, INCUBATION ROOMS, a PROPYLON, a SACRED FOUNTAIN, a LIBRARY, a TUNNEL, a ROUND BUILDING, and the SACRED WAY are all a part of the complex. The process of incubation included the sacred ritual of sacrificing a white sheep.

By the end of the third century, an earthquake, plus the introduction of Christianity, caused the downfall of this sacred site.

AMPHITHEATER. Between the acropolis and the Asclepieum are the scanty remains of the amphitheater — on a small scale, but similar to the Colosseum in Rome. It seems to have served the same purpose. This type of amphitheater is rare in Asia Minor.

MALTEPE AND YIGMA TEPE. Just south of Bergama is a large tumulus, known as *Maltepe*. It is a mound 500 feet in diameter, originally surrounded by a wall. Inside the tumulus are grave-chambers, in which fragments of sarcophagi were found. A half mile southeast is another large tumulus, known as *Yigma Tepe*.

- *In the Book of Revelation, John the Revelator addressed the church at Pergamum as one of the "seven churches" (Rev. 2:12–17).*
- *Here Antipas was put to death — the first Christian to suffer death by the Roman state (Rev. 2:13).*
- *The city's inhabitants were condemned because of their doctrine of Balaam and the doctrine of the Nicolaitanes (Rev. 2:14–15).*
- *A "white stone" and "new name" are promised to those who overcome (Rev. 2:17).*

THYATIRA, Akhisar

This wealthy city of Asia Minor was located on the Lycus River in the northern part of Lydia, about 27 miles northwest of Sardis and 56 miles northeast of Smyrna. The town was refounded by Seleucus Nicator about 300 B.C. It was the trading center for the Lycus valley and center of several cults, such as those of Apollo and Sibyl. Apollo, the sun-god, was the guardian deity here.

Ancient tradesmen dealt in wool, linen, garments, leather, pots, bronze, and dyes. (Lydia from Thyatira was a seller of purple. See Acts 16:14.) The "modern" houses are today built of mud, and the chief industry is rug making. The ruins of an ancient pagan temple may still be seen.

With its low and small acropolis in its beautiful valley, stretching north and south like a long funnel between two gently swelling ridges of hills, the city conveys the impression of mildness, subjection to outward influence, and inability to surmount and dominate external circumstances. This quality is reflected in John the Revelator's letter to Thyatira. The letter is mainly occupied with the church's inability to rise above the associations and habits of contemporary society and its contented voluntary acquiescence in them (called the Nicolaitan heresy). After about A.D. 150 Montanism flourished here. This sect was founded by Montanus, who claimed to be the mouthpiece of the Holy Spirit.

Yet even humble Thyatira will be rewarded with power among the nations. In the remnant of the Thyatiran church, who will have shown the will to resist temptation, weakness will be made strong.

- *Paul may have visited here (Acts 19:10).*
- *Lydia, the seller of purple and first convert from Europe, was from Thyatira (Acts 16:14).*
- *Thyatira was one of the seven churches to which John wrote the Book of Revelation (Rev. 1:11; 2:18-29).*
- *A false prophetess, Jezebel, is condemned (Rev. 2:20-23).*

SARDIS

Sardis is located near Salihli, 35 miles south of Thyatira, in the center of numerous trade routes. In ancient times, until 549 B.C., Sardis was the capital of Lydia. It was at first located on the acropolis, but later spread to the plain. Legend says Candaules was the king about 700 B.C., but Gyges killed Candaules, married his wife, and became the new king. This happened, supposedly, after Gyges saw the wife in the nude.

The Lydians were the first people to make coins of precious metal that were guaranteed in weight by a government stamp. Stamped on the coins was the head of a lion, the royal emblem of Sardis. At first the coins varied in gold content, but Croesus, a resident of Sardis and the last Lydian king, introduced coinage of pure gold and pure silver. This innovation was adopted throughout much of the world.

Wool dying was also supposed to have originated here.

According to Herodotus, the Persians captured the city in 546 B.C., ending the city's monarchy. Later, under Roman rule, Sardis was the capital of a Roman district. The city was destroyed by earthquake in A.D. 17, but was rebuilt about A.D. 120 by the generosity of the emperor Hadrian. After Christianity was established Sardis became known as one of the Seven Churches of Asia. It later had an important bishopric and ranked sixth of all those subject to the Patriarch of Constantinople. After the city was sacked by the cruel Tamerlane in 1401, however, it never recovered. It was gradually covered by the soil that washed down from the acropolis, accumulating to a depth of 30 feet in some areas. The village of Sart is a twentieth-century product.

John's letter to the Sardian church breathes the spirit of death, of appearance without reality, promise without performance. It attributes to the city an outward show of strength, betrayed by want of watchfulness and careless confidence. Such was the city with its history, seen from the north. Sardis held an imposing, impregnable position as it dominated that magnificent broad valley of the Hermus. At close hand, though, the hill is seen to be just mud, slightly compacted, crumbling under the influence of the weather or a blow of a spade. Yet the Sardians always trusted to it; and their careless confidence was often deceived when an adventurous enemy climbed in at some unguarded point where the weathering of the soft rock had opened a way.

POINTS OF INTEREST

Americans have been excavating Sardis since 1958. The most striking monument is the TEMPLE OF ARTEMIS (the patron goddess) in the Pactolus Valley. The temple dates back to 300 B.C. Inscriptions refer to the temple as the sanctuary of Artemis and Zeus, and it is divided into two parts with a wall between them — Artemis on the west and Zeus on the east. It is of interest that the entrances to the Greek temples were normally on the east, and the cult statues inside faced east. This follows the custom of former temples. However, this temple abnormally faced the west. In the second century A.D., the cult statues of Artemis and Zeus were replaced by statues of the emperor Antoninus Pius and his wife Faustina, to whom the temple was presumably dedicated. Some feel that Zeus never did have a part in the temple, and that Antoninus Pius put up the wall and made it the temple of Artemis and Faustina. The building was of the Ionic order, with 8 columns on two ends and 20 on each of the sides.

The hills around Sardis contain hundreds of LYDIAN TOMBS, dating back as far as the seventh century B.C. Tub-shaped sarcophagi of terracotta, painted red, white, and black, are inside some of the tombs. Three of these tombs may be visited by following up the side valley, which opens on the west about a quarter of a mile to the south of the temple. The tombs are on the south side of the hollow in which the valley ends, close above a vineyard.

A GYMNASIUM has been excavated near the road. It dates back to the second century A.D. The marble facing was added under the emperor Caracalla in 212. A Byzantine reconstruction of the fifth to sixth century A.D. is recorded on the walls.

A JEWISH SYNAGOGUE (A.D. 400), BYZANTINE SHOPS, and a marble ROYAL ROAD are clearly visible, but the THEATER and STADIUM are barely recognizable. The BATHING HOUSE is a vast structure, and in 1965 the excavators found an area half an acre in extent occupied by shops and workrooms — like an oriental bazaar. It dates back to the seventh century B.C.

About 6 miles north-northwest of Sardis is BIN TEPE, the great Lydian necropolis called by the Turks the THOUSAND HILLS. These tumuli may be observed from the Sardis road. Three of the burial sites are huge, one with a ¾-mile circumference. They are called the TOMBS OF ALYATTES, GYGES, and TOS.

■ *John wrote to the church at Sardis in his Book of Revelation. It is one of the seven churches to whom the letters are addressed (Rev. 3:1-6).*

- John spoke of the few in Sardis who had not defiled their garments and their future white clothing (Rev. 3:4-5).

PHILADELPHIA, Alaşehir

Philadelphia, the city of "brotherly love," was also one of the seven churches to which John the apostle addressed the Book of Revelation. It was located on the Cogamus River, about 105 miles from Smyrna and 28 miles southeast of Sardis. Former names of the city are *Decapolis* and *Flavia*. It was a center of a wine industry, and its chief deity was Dionysus.

During the reign of Tiberius it was destroyed by an earthquake, but was quickly rebuilt. It remained independent until A.D. 1300, when the Turks and Byzantines captured it. In 1403 Tamerlane captured it and built a wall around the city. Many Jews lived there, but Christianity is the predominant faith today. A Greek bishop resides there.

The present city is noted for its licorice factory, ancient walls, and castle. The foundation of an ancient church may still be seen. Since little has been done by way of excavation, our knowledge rests on literary references, a few inscriptions, and coins.

Philadelphia has had many earthquakes, and the citizens for the most part live outside the town and watch for the next catastrophe. Philadelphia was situated where the road is about to ascend by a difficult pass to the high central plateau of Phrygia, and thus held a key that guarded the door (Rev. 3:7-8).

Of the seven cities, this was the most devoted to the name of the emperors.

The church here had been a missionary church, and Christ himself opened the door for it. John's letter indicates that Jesus would "keep thee from the hour of temptation"— the time when the whole world would face a catastrophe. But for the victor there remains stability— being supported by God until God takes over.

- John's Book of Revelation addresses Philadelphia as one of the seven churches (Rev. 3:7-13).
- To Philadelphia the Lord addressed the promise that a new Jerusalem is to come down from heaven, and to "him that overcometh . . . I will write upon him my new name" (Rev. 3:12).

HEIRAPOLIS

A city in the Lycus River Valley in Phrygia, Heirapolis is located on the north side of the river, 6 miles from Laodicea and 12 miles from Colossae. It derived its name from the medicinal hot springs here which revealed plainly to the ancient mind the presence of divinity. The water is strongly impregnated by alum. Another sacred place nearby is a grotto, called the *Plutonium*, with an opening the size of a man's body, from which noxious vapors issued. Any animal entering it fell dead.

Christianity came to Heirapolis through the influence of Paul (Acts 19:10; Colossians), and traditions of the early centuries declare that the apostles Philip and John preached here. The former allegedly was martyred here.

Epictetus, the Stoic, was born here in A.D. 50. He was a slave under Nero; then after being freed he became a student of Stoicism. By the time he was 40 years old he was exiled, along with other Stoics, by Domitian. The Stoics felt that to woo pleasure was to woo pain. They believed they should face difficulties in order to develop self-mastery, and the secret of their independence lay in their absolute indifference to external things of the world. They believed in being happy regardless of circumstances. They felt that the good and evil were only in the will and not in the circumstance. It was not what happened but how one reacted to what happened that determined the man.

Epictetus was known for his moral philosophy. He believed that a philosopher was a healer of souls. To him morals were more important than intellect, for morals caused man to *do* and not just *think*. Two of his main teachings were the fatherhood of God and the brotherhood of man, also taught by Marcus Aurelius.

By A.D. 50 Stoicism was the philosophy of the masses. It was even taught in the schools. Nero, however, persecuted both Stoics and Christians, as the independence of mind of these two groups would not allow them to bow down to his edicts. By A.D. 138 Stoicism was popular again. The emperor Hadrian was a Stoic, as also were Horace, Vergil, Cicero, and Seneca.

Because of its high morality, Stoicism helped to pave the way for Christianity. Although they did not believe in life after death, the Stoics did believe that God was the father of all men and that freedom consisted in making our own will conform with that of God.

The **ROMAN RUINS** in Heirapolis are among the best preserved in Asia Minor.

■ *Paul referred to Heirapolis (Col. 4:13).*

LAODICEA, **Denizli**

This city of Asia Minor is located in the Lycus Valley, in the province of Phrygia, 43 miles southeast of Philadelphia. It was founded in 261–247 B.C. by Antiochus II of Syria, who named it after his wife, Laodice, and populated it with Syrians and Jews from Babylon. It was a junction of several points, but did not gain prominence until the Roman province of Asia was formed in 190 B.C. It then became prominent because of its fine black wool and Phrygian powder for the eyes (Rev. 3:18). A heathen temple and a school of medicine were located here.

In A.D. 60 the city was destroyed by an earthquake. The citizens rejected proffered aid and rebuilt the city themselves (Rev. 3:17). It was a city of great wealth and extensive banking operations (verse 18). It was the seat of a bishopric, and the bishop Sagaris was murdered here in A.D. 166. In 1071 the city was taken by the Seljuks.

It was recovered for the Christians in A.D. 1119 and fell to the Turks in the thirteenth century.

John's letter marks the Laodicean church as the irresolute one, unable to make up its mind. It wanted to be enriched, clothed in righteousness, and made to see the truth; but it trusted in itself— in its own gold to find wealth, in its own manufactures to make its garments, and in its own famous medical school to seek its cure. It did not feel its need, but was content with what it had. It was neither truly Christian, nor frankly pagan. This letter, alone among the seven, seems not to bring the character of the church into close relation to the great natural features amid which the city stood; but on the other hand, it shows an intimate connection between the character attributed to the church and the commerce by which the city had grown great.

The second half of this letter turns to the epilogue of the whole— to all seven churches.

The ruins, now called *Eski-Hissar,* or "old castle," lie near the modern Gonjelli on the railroad, and have long served as a quarry for building material. Ruins cover many acres, but little excavation has taken place. One Roman **THEATER** is well preserved, and, in addition, the following may be seen: a **STADIUM**, a **COLONNADE**, an **AQUEDUCT** employing stone pipes and the siphon principle, a large **NECROPOLIS**, and the ruins of three **CHRISTIAN CHURCHES**.

- *Laodicea was one of the seven churches written to by John the Revelator (Rev. 3:14–22).*
- *The church here was probably established by Epaphras, along with Mark and Timothy (Col. 1:7; 4:12–13).*
- *The Colossian letter was to be read here (Col. 4:16).*
- *The Savior condemned the Laodiceans because of their lukewarmness, self-sufficiency, and conceit (Rev. 3:14–22): "I would thou wert cold or hot" (Rev. 3:15).*
- *Jesus said to them: "Behold, I stand at the door and knock . . ." (Rev. 3:20–21).*

Aphrodisias

Approximately 8 miles southwest of Denizli (Philadelphia) is Aphrodisias, a city of marble. It thrived until the fifth century A.D. as a major center for the worship of Aphrodite. It is being excavated with the help of the National Geographic Society.

COLOSSAE, Honaz

The ancient Colossae is 10 miles east of Denizli (Philadelphia), in the Lycus valley, near where the Lycus River flows into the Maeander River. It is nearly 100 miles east of Ephesus, on the great highway leading from Ephesus to the Euphrates valley.

In the time of Paul the city was of small consequence. Many Jews lived there, and the place was renowned for a peculiar wool article, probably of a purple color.

During the seventh and eighth centuries, the Saracens invaded. Later, in the twelfth century, the Turks destroyed the city and it disappeared. The ruins of the **CHURCH**, a stone foundation of a **THEATER**, and a **NECROPOLIS** may still be seen.

Paul considered the church established here as his, even though he had never been here. He had sent Epaphras to preach to the Colossians, and he was greatly concerned about the saints at Colossae and also at Laodicea — for whom the epistle to the Colossians was intended (Col. 2:1; 4:16).

The saints here, however, became very lax. They felt little restraint from the lusts of the body. They practiced ascetic customs because they hoped to save the body, which they regarded as evil. Their worship of angels, with Michael as the chief protecting deity of the city, brought condemnation from Paul (Col. 2:18).

■ *Paul wrote an epistle to the Colossians.*
■ *The Colossian church, founded by Epaphras, worked under Paul's direction (Col. 1:5–7; 4:12–13).*
■ *It seems that Paul never visited here (Col. 1:7; 2:1).*
■ *Paul kept himself informed as to the condition of the church here (Col. 1:3–4, 9; 2:1).*
■ *Paul approved the work and discipline of the church here (Col. 1:5–6, 23; 2:5–7; 4:12–13).*

SMYRNA, Izmir, *Eurydiceia*

Izmir, the ancient Smyrna, was also one of the seven churches to whom the apostle John addressed the Book of Revelation (Rev. 2:8–11). It is also known as the birthplace of Homer.

The city has had a flourishing port from antiquity because it is located at the head of a 30-mile-long gulf. Its natural beauty, fertile soil, and excellent climate have attracted settlers since prehistoric times. Strabo calls Smyrna the most beautiful of all cities.

Very little is known of the early history of Smyrna. Although it had been founded by Theseus about 1312 B.C., it was politically non-existent during the Greek classical period. During the Middle Ages Smyrna was the scene of many struggles, the most fierce of which was directed against the Christians by Timur, who built a tower out of a thousand heads of his victims. Smyrna was the last of the Christian cities to hold out against the Mohammedan Turks, but it finally fell in A.D. 1424.

According to the story told by Pausanias, Alexander visited Smyrna in 334 B.C. and went hunting on Mount Pagus, which lies immediately back of the city. While he rested beside the temple of Nemeseis, the goddess Nemeseis appeared to him and bade him found a city on the spot. Alexander initiated the work; then Antigonus and Lysimachus followed. The latter named the city *Eurydiceia* after his daughter Eurydice, but after a few years this name was abandoned.

When Smyrna was nearly destroyed by earthquakes in A.D. 178–80, the city was part of the Roman Empire. It was rebuilt with the help of the emperor and became a very brilliant city, with wide, paved streets, schools of science and medicine, handsome buildings, and a theater that seated 20,000. The year A.D. 155 saw the martyrdom of Polycarp, the bishop of Smyrna, and the year 250 that of Pionius, both in the stadium of Smyrna. A long hollow marks the site of the stadium today — ¼ mile west of the castle.

The theme of the letter from John to the church at Smyrna was faithfulness to the end, even through tribulation. The church was to suffer for a period, but suffering would come to an end. Such has been the case. It gloried in its title of the faithful friend of Rome, true to its great ally in danger and prosperity. The letter is full of joy, life, and brightness, beyond all others of the seven — and such is the impression the city makes on the traveler.

POINTS OF INTEREST

The center of the modern city is about 2½ miles from the ancient site. Traces of the ROMAN THEATER may still be seen by following street number 985 from the principal road up the hill. The AGORA has been cleared, and many columns are still standing. The GRAVE OF POLYCARP is located in the city. The old CARAVANSARY is a historical site, for Izmir was a stop on the Asian caravan routes.

Other sites of interest include the following: the ARCHAEOLOGICAL MUSEUM, the ATATÜRK MONUMENT, KONAK SQUARE, PAGUS HILL, the ARTEMIS BATHS, MOSQUES, the CLOCK TOWER (Saat Kules), CULTURE PARK, the ATATÜRK MUSEUM, and the MARKETPLACE.

In the area near Smyrna may be seen the following monuments from antiquity: TAŞ SURET, a stone Hittite figure of the second century B.C.; ETI BABA, the Hittite "father," in the Karabel Pass (a Karabel warrior mentioned by Herodotus); the TOMB OF TANTALUS, near the village of Bayrakli; and the TOMB OF CHARALAMBOS and the THRONE OF PELOPS, both on Mount Sipylus.

- John the Revelator addressed his letter to Smyrna as one of the seven churches (Rev. 2:8–11).
- "Be thou faithful unto death" (Rev. 2:10).

Colophon, Notium, and Claros

Three archaeological sites are located just northwest of Ephesus. Colophon and Notium were Greek cities, but Claros was the site of the temple and oracle of Apollo, dating back to the seventh century B.C.

Colophon is where the philosopher and poet Xenophanes, founder of the Eleatic school, was born in 570 B.C. He was a religious and social reformer, and opposed the use of cosmetics and the cult of athletic hero worship. He was a "monist" and as such maintained that God was "one" — with no eyes, ears, or parts. He was highly critical of anthropomorphism. To Xenophanes, only mortals thought of God as being born, wearing clothing, and having a human voice and body. Man, he said, designed God after himself. Xenophanes suggested that if horses and lions had hands to paint with, they would paint their gods as horses and lions.

Belevi

Ten miles north of Ephesus is the village of Belevi. Two miles from this village on the road leading to Tire are two monuments worth visiting. One is a MAUSOLEUM, 80 feet square and 50 feet high. Its colonnade, urns, Doric frieze, and other features are very beautiful. Inside a nearby chamber is an elegantly carved sarcophagus. On the lid of the sarcophagus the dead man is represented reclining on his elbow. It is not known who he was. It is believed to date back to the fourth century B.C. The winged lions suggest Persian influence.

The second monument is also a TOMB, but of a different character. It stands on a hill just west of the mausoleum. The wall around the tomb has stones grooved so they will not fall, and a tunnel 20 yards long runs into a hill. At the end of the tunnel are two grave chambers. No sarcophagi remain there. It also dates back to the fourth century B.C.

EPHESUS, *near Selçuk**

Forty-five miles south of Izmir, near the mouth of the Caÿster River and about 3 miles from the coast, is the city of Ephesus, the most famous ancient metropolis of Asia Minor. It lies opposite the island of Samos and near the village of Aya Soluk.

Ephesus was colonized by Greeks approximately 1000 B.C. The oldest settlement (Ephesus I), an Ionian town, flourished in the sixth and seventh centuries B.C. as a member of a league of twelve Ionian cities. It was located on the northern slope of the theater hill—

---

*For much of the material on Ephesus I am indebted to George E. Bean, *Aegean Turkey: An Archaeological Guide* (New York, 1966), pp. 160–79.

Great amphitheater and Arcadiane Street, Ephesus

Right: Great theater, with Arcadiane Street leading to the location of the ancient harbor, Ephesus

Below: Agora, Ephesus

anciently Mount Pion, now Panayir Dagi. Just below it was the coast. The only thing remaining of this first city is a small piece of polygonal wall high up on the north slope of the hill. Here the city remained during the first 400 years of its existence; then Croesus destroyed it.

In 560 B.C. the Lydians possessed it and were forced to move to the

Temple of Hadrian, Ephesus

area of the old temple of Artemis (Ephesus II), and three years later the Persians were in control.

During the sixth century B.C. the famous philosopher Heraclitus lived in Ephesus (540–475 B.C.), spreading his teachings about the eternal flow of all things. He was known as the "weeping philosopher." He hated the masses (he was of royal descent); he ridiculed Greek rites, such as "purifying themselves with blood"; he believed in constant change; he chose fire as the "world stuff" — the ultimate; like the Hindus, he believed that death was not the end but that man would have a sort of cosmic salvation; he believed that "wisdom is at once the unity of all things, the measure and the harmony, but it is pure fire as well; with reservations, it is Zeus."

Alexander and Rome both took the city as a matter of course. Alexander offered to rebuild the Temple of Artemis, which the mad Herostratus had destroyed in 365 B.C., but the Ephesians declined and built the temple themselves with the assistance of the most famous artists of the time: Skopas and Praxiteles.

About 325 B.C. Lysimachus, one of the successors of Alexander the Great, again moved the city, to the area where the main excavations are now found. This metropolis soon flourished and was called the "Bank of Asia." This Ephesus III was the city of Paul's day. It was surrounded by a circuit wall nearly 6 miles in length, and the old harbor was abandoned for a new one below Mount Pion on the west.

Ephesus was the home of the nature goddess Diana (Artemis) and was a very wealthy commercial center. The Temple of Diana, one of the Seven Wonders of the Ancient World, had been destroyed seven times, and seven times it was rebuilt — each time a little larger. It was 425 by 220 feet in size (four times as large as the Parthenon). The marble roof was supported by 127 pillars 60 feet high. The temple took 220 years to build. Here was the statue of Diana or Efes, the body of which was covered with rows of many breasts (or eggs, perhaps, as some believe), indicating that she gave fertility to the soil and sustained all life. The temple was the host of priests and others, such as the artisans who manufactured images of the goddess Diana for the visitors to the temple. In A.D. 263 the Goths destroyed the temple, and it was only hastily rebuilt. By the end of the fourth century most pagan temples were either torn down or converted into Christian churches.

By the time of the early empire of Rome, Ephesus boasted a quarter of a million people. In its inscriptions the city calls itself the "first and greatest metropolis in Asia."

Constant silting up of the harbor by the River Caÿster was a problem from the beginning, however, and in A.D. 61 the proconsul of Asia under Nero had the whole harbor dredged.

The enemy that finally did away with the worship of Diana was Christianity. Ephesus was a fertile mission field and very early became an important center of Christianity. John the apostle, accompanied or not by the Virgin Mother, was in Ephesus by A.D. 67 and perhaps earlier. He may have founded the churches that Paul later visited. Paul arrived here in A.D. 53 and found a small nucleus of converts. He himself lived in the city for three years. Next to Rome, this was the most important city Paul visited. Tradition says that Timothy was the first bishop of the city.

After Domitian had reigned 15 years, Nerva succeeded him (Sept. 18, A.D. 96). The sentences of Domitian were annulled, and the Roman senate decreed the return of those who had been unjustly banished and the restoration of their property. It was at this time that the apostle John left the island of Patmos and took up his abode at Ephesus. Tradition says John died here, and the **CHURCH OF SAINT JOHN** is built over his traditional burial spot in Ephesus IV.

Catholic fathers Irenaeus of Asia Minor and Clement of Alexandria both bear witness of John's having abode at Ephesus. Irenaeus (A.D. 140–202) wrote in the second of his books *Against the Heresies* as follows: "And all the presbyters who had been associated in Asia with John, the disciple of the Lord, bear witness to his tradition, for he remained with them until the times of Trajan" (Jan. 27, A.D. 98). In the third book of the same work, Irenaeus said: "Now the Church at Ephesus was founded by Paul, but John stayed there until the time of Trajan, and it is a true witness of the tradition of the Apostles." Clement wrote of John's overseeing the churches in the area.

When John the apostle received on the island of Patmos the revelations recorded in the Book of Revelation (Apocalypse), he addressed letters (Rev. 2–3) to the Church in general and specifically to seven churches. Ephesus was one of them. The seven letters'were evidently all written together, in the inspiration of one occasion and purpose; yet each is different from all the rest. Each church had a character of its own. John assumed that the church was, in a sense, the city.

The one word describing John's letter to the Ephesians is *change*. The church had been enthusiastic, but it had been cooling and had fallen from its high plane of conduct and spirit. The penalty pronounced against it was that it would be moved out of its place unless it re-created its old spirit and enthusiasm. This has happened. What was water has become land; what was city has ceased to be inhabited. The harbor is now a mere inland sea of reeds.

Deterioration came with the decline of the Roman Empire in the third century A.D., and after the church council of A.D. 431 the city gradually lost its importance. The silting of the harbor was unmanageable. When Justinian founded the great Church of Saint John in the sixth century A.D., he changed the location of the city to a hill on the northeast, above the present town of Selçuk, which thenceforth became the center of habitation (Ephesus IV). The connection with the sea, however, was broken, and the great days of Ephesus were over.

In A.D. 1308 the Turks took it and deported or killed its inhabitants.

An English engineer, J. T. Wood, spent a fortune and eleven years of his life seeking the location of the Temple of Diana, finding it at last, in 1863, under 15 feet of soil at Ephesus II, near the present site of Selçuk.

Excavations at Ephesus have continued since that time. It is estimated that about one-twentieth of the city is uncovered. The work is under the direction of the Austrian Archaeological Institute.

POINTS OF INTEREST

On the site of Ephesus III, the city Paul visited, the following should be observed (starting from the Kuşadasi highway):

GATE OF CORESSUS.

GYMNASIUM OF VEDIUS (second century A.D.).

STADIUM (first century B.C.).

A structure which seems to have been a TEMPLE.

DOUBLE CHURCH, or CHURCH OF THE VIRGIN MARY. It was in this church that the stormy third Ecumenical Council of 280 bishops was held in A.D. 431, where the Nestorian heresy was condemned. On the north side of the courtyard, in the floor of the central room, there is a baptismal font for immersion. Originally this church was the Hall of Muses, used for lectures and other such purposes.

ARCADIANE STREET was a marble paved street that ran 600 yards to the harbor and which even had street lights.

GREAT THEATER (A.D. 41–98). This was a theater of Greek form reconstructed in a Roman fashion. Note that it gets steeper at each

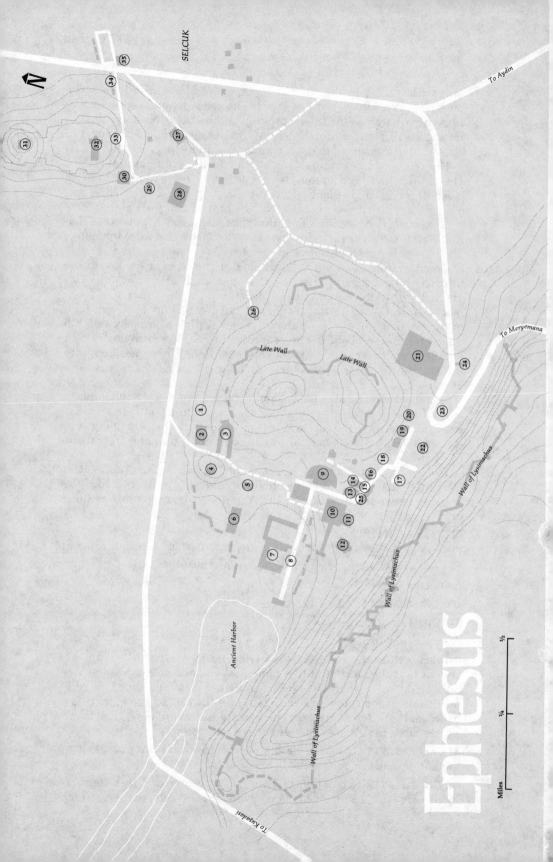

Ephesus

1. Gate of Coressus
2. Gymnasium of Vedius
3. Stadium
4. Temple?
5. Byzantine bath
6. Double Church (Church of the Virgin Mary)
7. Harbor baths
8. Arcadiane Street
9. Great Theater
10. Agora
11. Library of Celsus
12. Temple of Serapis
13. Brothel
14. Baths of Scholasticia
15. Temple of Hadrian
16. Fountain of Trajan
17. Terrace of Domitian
18. Temple of Hestia Boulaea
19. Odeum
20. Bath
21. Girls' Gymnasium
22. Nymphaeum
23. Alleged tomb of Saint Luke
24. Magnesian Gate
25. Statue base
26. Seven Sleepers of Ephesus
27. Museum
28. Temple of Diana (Artemis)
29. Selçuk bath
30. Great Mosque of Isa Bey
31. Castle
32. Church of Saint John
33. Byzantine gateway
34. Aqueducts
35. Mosque

level for better viewing. The theater held 24,500 people. This is where Paul was about to meet the riotous assembly.

AGORA (third century A.D.).

LIBRARY OF CELSUS. This is the finest surviving specimen of its kind. It has three stories, large windows facing east, and so forth, similar to Pergamum's library. (Note the niches in the walls for the scrolls.) It dates back to about A.D. 100. A passage on the north side leads to the **GRAVE OF GAIUS JULIUS CELSUS**, the proconsul of Asia in A.D. 106-7, to whom the library was dedicated. The chamber is kept locked — the guardian holds the key — and contains the actual coffin of lead, still unopened. The privilege of being buried *in* the city was a considerable distinction. The library was built by Celsus' son, Gaius Julius Aquila.

TEMPLE OF SERAPIS (second century A.D.). Although Serapis, the sacred bull Apis, was an Egyptian deity, Ptolemy I built a temple in his honor at Alexandria, giving the god's statue features resembling those of Pluto, the Greek god of the underworld. In this way Ptolemy attempted to establish a cult both Egyptians and Greeks could worship. The Egyptians dropped bull worship, but the Greeks and Romans kept it, and under the Roman Empire almost every city of note in the eastern provinces had a cult of the composite Serapis, frequently associated with Isis and other Egyptian deities. The Serapeum at Ephesus was noted for its massive architecture. Eight columns in front were formed of single blocks of stone, 5 feet in diameter and 46 feet high, weighing 60 tons. The columns were originally painted red, as can still be seen.

BROTHEL. This room adjoining the baths is identified by inscriptions and erotic figurines found there.

The **BATHS OF SCHOLASTICIA** are located behind the **TEMPLE OF HADRIAN**. Both date back to the second century A.D. The original stones are in a museum; the ones seen are casts. The reliefs in the porch, or *pronaos*, show a group of 13 figures, with Athena on the left bearing her round shield. After her on the left come 6 other Greek deities, then a family of 5, representing the emperor Theodosius and his family on either side of a figure of Artemis. We should remember that Theodosius was a bitter opponent of paganism. This acceptance of a pagan goddess, as it were, into the bosom of the royal family is remarkable and shows the strong hold Artemis still had upon the minds of men even at this late date.

FOUNTAIN OF TRAJAN.

TEMPLE OF HESTIA BOULAEA. Here burned the eternal fire, which was never permitted to go out.

ODEUM (second century A.D.).

GIRLS' GYMNASIUM (second century A.D.). This was so called because of the female statues found there.

NYMPHAEUM. This was a large fountain which served for the distribution of water in the city. It was fed by an aqueduct.

The **MAGNESIAN GATE** was the southern gate to Ephesus III.

MUSEUM AND STATUE BASE. Among the inscribed stones lining the street, about 30 yards below the Temple of Hadrian, lying flat behind the upright row, is a statue base erected by the Sacred College of Silversmiths — the same to which Demetrius belonged. A museum at Ephesus has a statue of Artemis with gold leaves, a statue of Apollo, and other artifacts.

NECROPOLIS. Around the east foot of Mount Pion, in a gully of the hillside, is the necropolis. It has single graves and large vaulted halls of brickwork with sepulchral niches and chambers. This was the burial place of the famous **SEVEN SLEEPERS OF EPHESUS**, Christians about A.D. 250 who left the city to escape the obligation of performing sacrifice in the temple.   According to the account, they lay down to sleep in a cave, and when they awoke and went into the city to buy bread they found they had slept not for one night but close to 200 years and that Christianity was the accepted religion.   The emperor Theodosius II was informed of this miracle and recognized a proof of bodily resurrection.   When the young men eventually died, their bodies purportedly were miraculously preserved from decay.   They were given a splendid burial and a church was built over their resting place.   The old church has been found, and graves surround the church in all directions.

- *Paul wrote a profound letter to the saints at Ephesus. It is called* Ephesians.
- *Paul visited here on his second missionary journey (Acts 18:19–21).*
- *Apollos preached here (Acts 18:24–19:1).*
- *Paul spent 3 years in Ephesus on his third missionary journey (Acts 19–20; note 20:31).*
- *Paul struggled with "beasts at Ephesus" (1 Cor. 15:32).*
- *Paul left Timothy here (1 Tim. 1:3–4).*
- *Paul mentioned the kindness of Onesiphorus (2 Tim. 1:16).*
- *Ephesus was the first of the seven churches to which John the Revelator wrote in the Book of Revelation (Rev. 1:11; 2:1–7).*

Panaya Kapulu *(Meryem Ana, House of the Virgin Mary)**

On top of a mountain south of Ephesus is a small building used as a chapel.   One tradition says Mary lived here and died near here.   This is a hotly debated question, however, for canonical tradition says that Mary died in Jerusalem at the age of 63.   The Scriptures are silent on the matter.

The principal evidence of the latter tradition is a passage by Saint John of Damascus, written in the eighth century.   He tells of a letter from the empress Pulcheria, written in A.D. 458 to the bishop of Jerusalem asking him to send the body of the Virgin to Constantinople.   The bishop replied that he was unable to do so, however, because tradition said she was buried at Gethsemane and the apostles found the tomb empty three days later.   Eusebius and Jerome make no mention of that tomb at Jerusalem.

The rival tradition, which goes back at least to the Council of Ephesus in 431, maintains that Mary came with John to Ephesus between A.D. 37 and 48, lived there, and died there.   As he was hanging on the cross, Jesus had entrusted his mother to John, "and from that hour that disciple took her unto his own home" (John 19:27).   Between the years A.D. 37 and 48, there is no record of John's whereabouts, but it is possible that he was in Ephesus and perhaps that Mary was with him.

---

*For much of the material on Panaya Kapulu I am indebted to George E. Bean, *Aegean Turkey: An Archaeological Guide* (New York, 1966), pp. 179–82.

Mary's house and tomb, of course, are unknown. The house that is shown goes back to the sixth century, but the foundations might be older. On August 15 the Orthodox Greeks gather here to celebrate the Dormition of the Virgin. This may be a very ancient custom. The discovery of the building came after an invalid German lady, Catherine Emmerich, saw the building in a vision — she had never been near Ephesus — and described the Virgin's house in detail. In 1891 a search was organized by M. Poulin, Superior of the Lazarists, and the house was found that answered the description exactly. (Or was it laid out according to her description?) In 1892, the archbishop of Smyrna authorized the celebration of mass in the building and pronounced it a place of pilgrimage. Many cures have taken place there. In the chapel may be seen fragments of cloth hung by visitors in gratitude for a cure or hope of a cure to come. The Virgin's tomb was declared by Catherine to be something over a mile from the house, but it has never been found.

TROGYLLIUM

Trogyllium is a promontory which projects from the mainland and overlaps the eastern part of Samos, so as to form a strait less than a mile wide. There is an anchorage nearby, called "Saint Paul's port."

■ *After touching at Samos and before putting in at Miletus, Paul "tarried at Trogyllium" (Acts 20:15).*

MILETUS, *"Birthplace of Greek Philosophy"* *

The earliest pre-Greek settlement at Miletus dates back to Mycenaean and Minoan times (1600 B.C.). Founders apparently came there from Crete. A 14-foot-thick wall was built about 1600 B.C., and a Greek temple to Athena was built directly over its ruins. Homer mentioned the city as the home of "Carians of uncouth speech" who fought against the Greeks at Troy.

About 800 B.C. a fortified city was built on a hill now called *Kalabaktepe*, some 2 miles to the southwest of the present ruins. The excavators are not now disposed to regard this hill as the acropolis of the early Greek Miletus; in fact, it is not determined exactly where the archaic city was.

Under Darius, the Persians sacked and burned Miletus as a chastisement for a revolt against the Persians in 499 B.C., and some of the city's inhabitants were transplanted to the mouth of the Tigris River, on the Persian Gulf, 1,000 miles away.

The ancient site of Miletus was formerly occupied in part by the village of Balat (Palatia). This village was destroyed by an earthquake in 1955, and a new one was built a mile to the south on the road to Didyma.

Miletus was the most important city of Ionia and at one time the

---

*For much of the material on Miletus I am indebted to George E. Bean, *Aegean Turkey: An Archaeological Guide* (New York, 1966), pp. 219–30.

most important city of the Greek world. It was a port city on the Aegean Sea, at the mouth of the Maeander (now Menderes) River. It was famous as a trading and manufacturing center.

The Lydians, Persians, and Greeks ruled Miletus in turn. Alexander took the city in 334 B.C. Under the Roman Empire it was one of the largest cities in Asia Minor.

In classical times the city was right on the sea, but today, because of the silting Maeander River, the ruins are nearly 5 miles from the sea. The Island of Lade stands high and dry as a city on the plain, while the Latmian gulf has become the freshwater lake of Bafa. It takes a strong imagination to picture Miletus as it once was.

Because of the wealth in Miletus, there was leisure time for thinking, which in turn gave birth to Greek philosophy.

The first "school of philosophy" was that of the *Milesians*. (A "school" would be defined as a group of men thinking on the same line.) The first philosophical problems dealt with nature, and the Milesians sought to explain the universe by postulating one principle, or "world stuff," that maintains its identity through change, and by discovering how it changes.

The "father of Western philosophy" was Thales, a resident of Miletus (640-546 B.C.) and the first of the famous Greek philosophers. In determining the "primal substance," or the "nature of reality," he believed that water is the ultimate "stuff." He was the first to explain the universe by one principle, or "world stuff," that maintains its identity throughout change. As the first astronomer, he predicted the solar eclipse of 585 B.C. As a mathematician, he introduced Egyptian geometry to the Greeks. He is credited with diverting the course of the River Halys to allow Croesus' army to cross. He calculated the heights of the pyramids of Egypt by measuring their shadows at the time of day when a man's shadow is equal to his height. He was a civil engineer and had business acumen. His wise sayings included the following: "Swiftest is mind, for it speeds everywhere." "What is divine? That which has neither beginning nor end." Thales thanked the gods that (1) he was human rather than animal, (2) he was a man rather than a woman, and (3) he was a Greek and not a barbarian. He believed Zeus was the chief god of the Greeks and that other gods were local.

Two other philosophers were also famous citizens of Miletus: Anaximander (611-547 B.C.) and Anaximenes (550-500 B.C.). Along with Thales, they comprise the group of philosophers known as the Milesians. Anaximander, a friend of Thales, believed the basic principle was the "infinite" or "unlimited" — that is, it was capable of breaking down into the various material substances of the world we see. He said the "ultimate" is the "infinite" and not "stuff." He taught that motion is eternal — that the elements are in eternal motion — and that there are innumerable worlds, that they came into being and passed away ad infinitum. One of his strongest beliefs was that the earth is a cylinder with flat ends, one of which is our habitat. He had some idea of evolution when he said that animals came from beings raised by the sun, and man from fish or animals. Life began, he said, in moisture.

Anaximander was also the father of geography. He produced the first map of the world, based on principles of symmetry in the disposition of the continents, seas, and rivers. It was very inaccurate, but the geographer Hecataeus, also of Miletus, through his own travels produced a better map.

Anaximenes, the third and last member of the Milesian school, selected air as the fundamental substance of the universe, and by the process of condensation and rarefaction this produces, he felt, all other forms of matter. According to Anaximenes, as air is condensed more and more, it is, in order, wind, water, earth, and stones. Fire is the most purified and the highest level — "a celestial burning of glory." The earth is a disc floating on air, and the stars move like a cap on the head. There are innumerable worlds, and motion is eternal.

In summarizing the opinions of the Milesians, Aristotle said that they were of the opinion that nothing is either generated or annihilated, since this primary entity always persists.

The apostle Paul visited Miletus on his third missionary journey. Because he was in a hurry to get to Jerusalem for the Day of Pentecost, however, he did not want to spend time in Ephesus. Therefore, he invited the elders from Ephesus to come to Miletus, where he gave them a touching farewell message.

POINTS OF INTEREST

Among the ruins of the later city, all else is overshadowed by the THEATER. It was built about A.D. 100 on the ruins of another theater and is the finest of the Greco-Roman theaters. The royal box seats are marked by two pillars. Inscriptions appear on the third to sixth rows of seats, reserving them for certain persons or groups of persons: fifth row — "place of the Jews, also called the Godfearing"; third row — "place of the goldsmiths of the Blues." On a block of the wall at the top of the stairway, at the west end of the upper diazoma, is an inscription that tells of a labor dispute and a near strike.

The CENTER OF THE CITY is east of the theater on the low ground, where the ruins are flooded every winter.

The DELPHINIUM, or precinct of Apollo Delphinius, was the principal temple at Miletus. It dates back to the sixth century B.C.

The BOULEUTERION, or council chamber, dates back to 175–164 B.C. It is one of the oldest surviving buildings at Miletus. Opposite the council chamber stood the NYMPHAEUM, from which water was distributed to the city. Little of the Nymphaeum remains today.

The BATHS OF FAUSTINA are the best preserved buildings at Miletus. (Faustina was the wife of the emperor Marcus Aurelius.) The complex has a gymnasium and stadium attached. The baths had the usual Roman apodyterium, frigidarium, trepidarium, caldarium, and sudatorium (sweating room).

- *Here Paul delivered a farewell testimonial to the Ephesian elders (Acts 20:16–38).*
- *Here Paul predicted his bonds, afflictions, and death (Acts 20:22–23, 25).*

Didyma*

The **TEMPLE OF APOLLO** at Didyma, 11 miles south of Miletus, is probably the most impressive single ancient monument on the west coast of Turkey. It is huge, has a unique plan, and is well preserved. Didyma was never a city, but belonged to the territory of Miletus.

The oracle at Didyma functioned like the oracle at Delphi, except that she received her "inspiration" from a spring of water. The fabulously wealthy Lydian king Croesus tested the soothsaying of the oracles by sending messengers to several oracles at once. Each was asked concerning a prearranged day and time, what Croesus was doing. The Greek oracle at Delphi gave the right answer: the king was boiling a tortoise and a lamb in a bronze cauldron. Didyma's oracle failed utterly and fell out of royal favor.

The first temple was built as early as 600 B.C. The present Temple of Apollo was built by Seleucus about 300 B.C. The order was Ionic, and it had a double row of columns and walls over 70 feet high. It was so large it was never roofed. When Theodosius forbade oracles in the empire in A.D. 385, the decline came. A Christian church was built in the holiest part of the temple.

On the south side of the temple is the **STADIUM**. Names on the lower seats reserve them for particular people.

Bodrum, *Halicarnassus*

Mausolus died here in the fourth century B.C. He had built a vice-royalty on the Carian coast early in the fourth century B.C. When he died, his grieving wife, Artemesia, commissioned five sculptors to decorate his memorial, the *Mausoleum*, a 135-foot-high tomb (in a courtyard 346 by 796 feet) so famous that its name became general for burial tombs thereafter. This tomb was one of the Seven Wonders of the Ancient World. Earthquakes destroyed the Mausoleum and the Knights of Rhodes later used the stones to build their castle, which still stands. The British Museum houses some of the remains of the Mausoleum. The white marble was quarried on the Island of Marmara.

Herodotus, the first Greek historian, was born here in the fifth century B.C. He wrote a history of the world up to his time, and his nine-volume history of the wars between Greece and Persia is unsurpassed. The Roman orator Cicero called him the "father of history."

---

*For much of the material on Didyma I am indebted to George E. Bean, *Aegean Turkey: An Archaeological Guide* (New York, 1966), pp. 231–43.

CNIDUS, *Cape Krio*

Sparta's navy was defeated here in 394 B.C. by the Persian fleet under the command of the Athenian admiral Conon.

■ *As Paul was being transported from Jerusalem to Rome as a prisoner, his boat came "over against Cnidus" (Acts 27:7).*

PATARA, *Gelemish*

Only the ruins remain of this ancient seacoast town on the southwest tip of Turkey.

■ *The apostle Paul embarked here for his last voyage to Palestine while on his third missionary journey (Acts 21:1-2).*

MYRA, Kale, *Gokyazi*

Myra was a city of Lycia in the days of Paul the apostle. It was a seaport town in the southwest part of present-day Turkey.

At Myra an old Byzantine church is named after Saint Nicholas, the fourth-century bishop of Myra. Nicholas was the patron of Russia and of virgins, children, sailors, and pawnbrokers. The pawnbrokers' three-ball sign memorializes three purses of gold Saint Nicholas gave as dowries to three poor virgins of Patara to save them from a life of prostitution. Saint Nicholas is the original Santa Claus.

Nearby are the LYCIAN TOMBS, carved into a cliff 2,000 years ago — like the facade of a temple.

■ *Here Paul was transferred to a ship from Alexandria as he was going to Italy as a prisoner in* A.D. *60-61 (Acts 27:5-6).*

ATTALIA, Antalya

This city, founded in the second century B.C. by the king of Pergamum, Attalus II, is on the southern coast of Asia Minor in ancient Pamphylia, on a flat limestone terrace 120 feet above the seashore. It was the port of entrance from Egypt and Syria to the interior of Asia Minor. Portions of the ancient walls and towers may still be seen. The modern town is built over part of the ancient city. An arched gateway and aqueduct of antiquity are visible, and many ancient monuments exist in the area.

■ *Paul and Barnabas stopped here on their first missionary journey (Acts 14:25).*

PERGA, *Murtana*

Twelve miles northeast of Attalia is the site of Perga. Ruins of a large THEATER, a STADIUM, BATHS, and TOMBS give ample evidence of its former greatness.

The River Kestros flowed through the city and was navigable during the days of Paul. Small boats from the sea could reach the city.

Some of the walls of the city date back to the third century B.C. It had its own coinage, and as a metropolis it continued from the second century B.C. to A.D. 286. Two broad streets intersect each other and divide the city into quarters.

■ *Paul and Barnabas visited here on their first journey (Acts 13:13).*
■ *Paul probably preached here two years later (Acts 14:25).*

LYSTRA, *Zoldera*

Lystra is 20 miles south of Konya (Iconium), in southwest Turkey. It was made a Roman colony by Augustus and became a center of education. Its population in the days of Paul included Lycaonians, Greeks, Jews, and Roman soldiers. They worshiped many gods and nature.

■ *Paul visited Lystra on three — perhaps four — different occasions while on his first three missionary journeys (Acts 14:6, 21; 16:1).*
■ *Lystra was the home of Timothy, who was circumcised by Paul because of the Jews in the city and then joined Paul on his second mission (Acts 16:1–3).*
■ *Paul healed a man who had been born a cripple. The people likened Barnabas to Jupiter (Zeus) and Paul to Mercury (Hermes) (Acts 14:8–18).*
■ *Paul ordained elders in Lystra (Acts 14:21, 23).*
■ *Paul was stoned here and left for dead (Acts 14:19–20).*
■ *Paul mentioned his suffering here (2 Tim. 3:10–11).*

DERBE, *Kerti Huyuk*

Derbe was a city in the southeast corner of the Lycaonian plain. It is first mentioned in Roman times as the seat of Antipater, who entertained Cicero, the Roman orator and governor of Cilicia. As it was the last city in distinctively Roman territory on the road to the east, customs duties were collected here.

This was an important city in early Christianity, and the remains of antiquity date back to the late Roman and Byzantine periods.

■ *Paul and Barnabas visited here on their first missionary journey (Acts 14:20–21).*
■ *Paul visited Derbe on his second missionary journey (Acts 16:1).*

ICONIUM, **Konya**, *Yconium, Conium*

This large city of over 122,000 people makes it the eighth largest in Turkey. It is 170 miles south of Ankara.

The origin of this ancient city goes back to 3,000 B.C., the time of the Hittites. According to Greek legend, Perseus, son of Jupiter and Danaë, came to this region and cut off the head of Medusa and hung it on top of a pillar. Hence the city's ancient name, *Iconium*, meaning "city with an image."

After the apostle Paul's visits to Iconium, the town became an important religious center and men of learning flocked to Konya.

Konya is the home of Melvâna Celaleddin Rumi (1207–73), Turkish poet, scholar, philosopher, founder of the order of whirling dervishes (*mevlevi*), and one of Islam's greatest mystics. Each December from about the seventh to the seventeenth the "Rites of the Whirling Dervishes" are celebrated in Konya.

Historical monuments would include SELÇUK PALACE, MOSQUES, and MUSEUMS.

About 25 miles southeast of Konya is CATAL HÜYÜK, an archaeological dig where artifacts have been found that are 8,500 years old.

At ALANYA, on the coast south of Konya, it is a custom to place two bottles on the top of the chimney if the owner of the home has two daughters ready for marriage. A broken bottle means there has been a divorce there or that the woman is a widow.

- *Iconium was visited by Paul on his first and second missionary journeys (Acts 14:1–6, 21) and probably on his third (Acts 18:23).*
- *Paul's persecutions here are mentioned (2 Tim. 3:11).*
- *Some from Iconium followed Paul to Lystra (Acts 14:19).*

ANTIOCH OF PISIDIA, Yalvac

This city was founded by Seleucus Nicator (301–280 B.C.) and named after his father, Antiochus. Standing on a plateau near the Anthios River, it commanded one of the great highways from the East.

Seleucid colonists were Greeks, Jews, and Phrygians (Acts 13:14, 50). The city became a part of Galatia in 39 B.C. and a Roman colony in 6 B.C. It soon became the capital of southern Galatia. It was a Latin city until the third century, when it became Greek, then later Roman. Ruins of the city lie within a mile of the present village.

- *Paul preached here on his first mission (Acts 13:14–52).*
- *Opposition stirred up by Jews from Lystra caused Paul and Barnabas to shake off the dust of their feet and leave (Acts 13:50–51).*
- *Paul may have visited here on his second and third journeys (Acts 16:6; 18:23).*
- *Paul's persecutions here are mentioned (2 Tim. 3:11).*

PESSINUS

The ruins of this ancient city lie 7 miles south of the present-day Sivrihisar and 80 miles southwest of Ankara. It was in the region of Galatia during the time of Paul. From Galatians 4:19 it is evident that Paul was the founder of the churches in Galatia. The question is — when? The traditional view is that he organized the churches during his second missionary journey, as mentioned in Acts 16:5. This is made more plausible by Acts 18:23, where mention is made of the apostles' finding disciples there, the fruits, evidently, of a previous visit.

- *The apostle Paul probably visited this city of Galatia on his second and third missionary journeys (Acts 16:6; 18:23).*

ANKARA, *Ancyra, Angora, Enguru, Ancora*

From Ankara, Kemal Atatürk planned and directed the Turkish War of Independence in the early 1920s, and in 1923 this shining new city became the capital of the Republic of Turkey, which succeeded the Ottoman Empire. It has a population of nearly a million.

According to legend, Ankara is said to have been founded by Phrygians in the eighth century B.C. It was subsequently captured by the Galatians and then by the Romans. There are also signs of a Hittite empire that ruled here even before the Phrygians.

Because the Romans gave the Galatians semi-independence, in return the Galatians built a TEMPLE to the Roman emperor Augustus, the *Augusteum,* which still stands.

In the Middle Ages Ankara was one of the main centers of Christianity. By 1073 the Turks ruled, but the Crusaders captured it in 1101. The Seljuk Turks recaptured it in 1227. By 1354, it was a part of the Ottoman Empire.

POINTS OF INTEREST

Historical monuments and places include the following: the ANKARA CITADEL with its 20 towers, the TEMPLE OF AUGUSTUS (second century B.C.), the COLUMN OF JULIAN, ROMAN BATHS, MOSQUES, the MAUSOLEUM OF ATATÜRK, the ATATÜRK MUSEUM, the HITTITE ARCHAEOLOGICAL MUSEUM, and ATATÜRK'S HOUSE.

■ *The apostle Paul probably visited this city of Galatia on his second and third missionary journeys (Acts 16:6; 18:23).*

TAVIUM

Tavium is 90 miles east of Ankara and 15 miles west of the nearest city, Yozgat. At Bogazkale (Boghazkoy, Hattushash), 14 miles north of Tavium, thousands of clay tablets were unearthed in the Hittite capital of 1300 B.C. Written in eight languages, they revealed relations with Egypt, Babylonia, and other countries. At Alaca Hüyük (Alaja), 30 miles north of Yozgat, pre-Hittite graves of 2500 B.C. yielded gold ornaments of great artistry.

■ *The apostle Paul probably visited this ancient city of Tavium in Galatia on his second and third missionary journeys (Acts 16:6; 18:23).*

CAESAREA MAZACA, Kayseri; *and Kanish (Kultepe)*

Situated on a large plain in central Anatolia, at the foot of the towering Mount Erciyas, is the key commercial center of Kayseri. It is noted for its production of textiles, smoked meat, and sugar.

Kayseri was a part of the Hittite Empire and dates back to the twenty-fifth century B.C. From the Babylonians it fell into the hands of the Persians in the sixth century B.C. During the days of the Roman Empire it became an important center of Christianity, and because there were many towns called Caesarea, Kayseri was called Caesarea Mazaca at that time.

POINTS OF INTEREST

Sites of historical interest would include the CITY WALL and INNER CITADEL. The walls were constructed by the Byzantine emperor

Justinian. Many beautiful **MOSQUES** grace the city. Also of interest are the **HONAT HATUN TOMB**, **KUMBETS** (funeral vaults), **MONUMENTS**, and the **KAYSERI MUSEUM**, which houses, among other things, approximately 15,000 tablets, seals, idols, and ceramics from nearby Kanish (Kultepe).

■ *Paul the apostle probably visited Caesarea Mazaca on his third missionary journey (Acts 18:23).*

Goreme

Ten miles east of Nevsehir on the road to Kayseri are the strange, eerie, moonshaped volcanic pinnacles that were honeycombed 1200 years ago with 365 churches, chapels, and tombs. Christians from Cappadocia fled invading Turks and settled there. Very well preserved wall paintings depict the life of Christ and the saints in the troglodyte churches. Byzantine fresco art in the rock churches constitutes a matchless gallery, and visitors come from all over the world to see this marvel.

Urgup

Four miles east of Goreme is Urgup, another marvel of nature not unlike Goreme. This is a town where erosion, acting on piles of tufa rock deposited by the lava from Mount Erciyas nearby, has produced pillars, cones, and fairy chimneys, all honeycombed with hermitlike cells and monasteries. Food is stored in these rooms now. Other cones of tufa rock can be seen in nearby Orta Hisar, Uchisar, and Avcilar (Macan).

TARSUS, *Tersous*

Tarsus was the capital of the Roman province of Cilicia (Acts 22:3), in the southeast of Asia Minor, and the birthplace of Paul. It is about 75 feet above sea level and 10 miles from the coast. The river Cydnus ran through the city. The present population is 65,000.

Shalmaneser III, king of Assyria, captured Tarsus about the middle of the ninth century B.C., as did Sennacherib in 696 B.C. The area was taken by Alexander, then by Rome under Pompey about 65 B.C. Cassius forced the people, in 43 B.C., to take his and Brutus's side against Octavian and Antony, but they returned to their former loyalty at the earliest opportunity. Tarsus was made a free city by Antony, who met Cleopatra here for the first time in 41 B.C. Plutarch described this meeting. Cleopatra came in a barge with gilded stern, purple sails, and silver oars. Under a canopy of cloth and gold was Cleopatra, dressed as Venus. The air was filled with the music of flutes and harps and scented with perfume, and in the marketplace the hard-drinking Mark Antony waited. The word spread: "Venus was come to feast with Bacchus for the common good of Asia." Today there is a *Cleopatra Gate* in the city.

The Stoic philosopher Athenodorus (74 B.C.–A.D. 7) lived here. He was distinguished for his lectures and writings. Athenodorus moved to Rome and Augustus was his pupil. In later years he retired to

Tarsus. He was succeeded by Nestor, an academic philosopher. Tarsus was noted for its concern about university life and learning, ranking alongside Alexandria and Athens.

Few traces of its ancient greatness remain. One is the GRECO-ROMAN TEMPLE, known locally as the TOMB OF SARDANAPALUS.

■ *Paul was born at Tarsus (Acts 22:3) and was a citizen thereof (Acts 9:11; 21:39).*

■ *Paul's father was a citizen before him (Acts 22:28).*

■ *Paul probably visited Tarsus on both his second and third missionary journeys (Acts 15:41; 18:22).*

ANTIOCH *(Syrian)*, **Antakya**; *and Seleucia (Samandaq)*

The most famous of sixteen Antiochs which Seleucus Nicator (305–280 B.C.) built and named after his father, Antiochus, was Antioch on the Orontes River in Syria (present-day Turkey).

By his victory in the battle of Ipsus (301 B.C.), Nicator secured the rule over most of Alexander the Great's Asiatic empire, which stretched from the Hellespont and the Mediterranean on one side to the Jaxartes and Indus on the other. The Seleucid dynasty, which he formed, lasted for 247 years. Nicator founded at least 37 cities, of which four are mentioned in the New Testament: (1) Antioch of Syria (Acts 11:19), (2) Seleucia (Acts 13:4), (3) Antioch of Pisidia (Acts 13:14; 14:21, 26; 2 Tim. 3:11), and (4) Laodicea (Col. 4:13–16, Rev. 1:11; 3:14).

Antioch of Syria was 300 miles north of Jerusalem. Although Antioch was 14 miles from the sea, the Orontes River was navigable, and the city was a focal point for sea trade and the caravan roads to Babylon, Persia, and India. Its seaport, Seleucia (Samandaq), although now filled with silt and tilled by farmers, was once a great fortress like Gibraltar. From this port Paul left to go on his missions.

Antiochus I (Soter, "Savior") (280–261 B.C.), who succeeded after the murder of Seleucus, introduced an abundant supply of water to the city, and every private house had its own pipe and running water. He strove to make Antioch the intellectual rival of Alexandria by inviting to his court scholars such as Aratus, the astronomer. The city was later adorned with costly temples, porticos, and statues.

The most remarkable engineering feat was the excavation of the dock at Seleucia, along with the building of the protecting moles and the cutting of a canal inland through high masses of solid rock — 1,869 feet long and, in some places, 120 feet deep.

Antiochus III ("the Great") (223–187 B.C.) captured the city, and later his son Antiochus IV, Epiphanes (175–163 B.C.), succeeded his father to the throne. Epiphanes promoted Greek architecture and culture. He erected a senate house, a temple to Jupiter Capitolinus, and a strong citadel on the mountains that surrounded the city. He laid out a splendid 5-mile street lined with double colonnades in a straight line.

Epiphanes' policy of Hellenizing Judea evoked the determined opposition of the Maccabees. It was Epiphanes who killed 40,000 Jews in Jerusalem, sold an equal number of slaves, and defiled the temple by placing an altar to Zeus (Jupiter) in it (168–164 B.C.).

The Roman general Pompey put an end to the Seleucid dynasty, and the Romans reigned in 64 B.C. Antioch became the capital of the Roman province of Syria. Mark Antony ordered the release of all the Jews Epiphanes had put in slavery and restored their property. As a reward to Antioch's fidelity to him, Julius Caesar built a splendid basilica (the *Caesareum*), a new aqueduct, a theater, and public baths. The ancient walls, 7 miles in circuit, were rebuilt to a height of 50–60 feet, with a thickness of 8 feet, and surmounted by gigantic towers. Earthquakes have demolished the walls, but some castles still stand.

When Christianity came to Antioch, the city had a population of over 500,000 people. It was the "Queen of the East" — "Antioch the Beautiful," but not in morals. Ancient writers agree that licentiousness, superstition, quackery, indecency, and sin made Antioch a very wicked city.

After the death of Stephen, Christian fugitives fled as far north as Antioch, and through their preaching a great number believed. Barnabas was sent to help the church there, but he sought out Paul to help him. Paul and Barnabas stayed there a year and built up a strong church. Antioch is the birthplace of the name *Christian*. It was the second capital of the Christian principality.

It was from Antioch that Ignatius set out on his journey to martyrdom at Rome. The city claimed as its natives John Chrysostom (329–89), a patriarch of Constantinople; Marcellinus; Evagrins; and Libanius. From A.D. 252 to 380, Antioch was the scene of ten church councils, and the patriarch of Antioch took precedence over those of Rome, Constantinople, Jerusalem, and Alexandria.

In A.D. 260 the Persians captured the city. It was burned in 538 by Chosroes and rebuilt by Justinian. The Turks took the city in 1084. The Crusaders retook it in 1098, but the Turks took it back in 1268.

Many earthquakes have destroyed the city. In A.D. 526 200,000 persons were killed by an earthquake. Today the city has around 40,000 inhabitants. It has a very fine **MUSEUM** with rich mosaics.

Jerome, the scholar of the western Catholic Church, believed he saw Christ while on a visit to Antioch, and he turned to a study of Hebrew and lived as a hermit not far from Antioch (373–79). He was ordained a presbyter in Antioch in 379. He lived in Bethlehem from 386 to 420, where he translated the Old Testament — the New Testament already having been completed — into the Latin Vulgate.

- *Nicolas was a proselyte of Antioch (Acts 6:5).*
- *Christians fled from Jerusalem and established Christianity here (Acts 11:19–27).*
- *The Antioch church sent an offering to Jerusalem by Paul and Barnabas and Mark (Acts 11:27–30; 12:25).*
- *Antioch was the birthplace of the name* Christian *(Acts 11:26) and of foreign missions.*
- *It was the center from which Paul performed his missionary labors (Acts 13:2; 14:26; 15:25–41; 18:22–23).*

- *From Antioch Paul and Barnabas went to Jerusalem and secured endorsement of Christian work among the Gentiles (Acts 15:2–31).*
- *Paul and Peter had a discussion on doctrine (Acts 15:1–21; Gal. 2:11–21).*

CARCHEMISH, *Kargamis, Barak, Jerablus*

This was a city 37 miles southeast of Gaziantep on the west bank of the Euphrates River and just inside the Turkish border from Syria. It was an important city because it commanded the principal ford of the Euphrates on the right bank and was therefore indispensable to travel and commerce in northern Syria. Mentioned from the beginning of the second millennium B.C., it came under Hittite influence in the fourteenth century B.C. The Assyrians regarded the city as the Hittite capital. It paid tribute to Ashurnasirpal II and to Shalmaneser III in the ninth century B.C. and was frequently involved in wars until Sargon conquered it in 717 B.C., after which it became the capital of an Assyrian province.

Here Nebuchadnezzar defeated Pharaoh Necho in 605 B.C. and thus ended the latest native Egyptian regime in Asia. After this victory, Nebuchadnezzar extended his borders to include Jerusalem and Tyre, and the most prosperous period of the Babylonian Empire began. The site is marked by a mound called *Jerablus.* Excavations were carried out here for the British Museum from 1876 to 1879 and from 1912 to 1941, and many Hittite hieroglyphic inscriptions came to light.

- *The battle is mentioned (Jer. 46:2; 2 Chron. 35:20; 2 Kings 23:29).*
- *The city was mentioned by Isaiah (Isa. 10:9).*

HARAN, **Harran;** *and* PADAN-ARAM

Haran is the name of a place where Abraham took his family after he left Ur of the Chaldees. It was named after Abraham's brother who died before Abraham left Ur.

Padan-aram is the Old Testament name for Syria and Mesopotamia. It means "acre," "field," or "tableland" of Abram.

After Abraham left Haran it became a site of the temple and worship of the moon god, Sin. Shalmaneser II built a temple here, which was later destroyed and then rebuilt by Ashurbanipal. In the fourth century A.D. it was the seat of a bishopric, but it remained a center of heathen worship until the eleventh century and was finally destroyed in the thirteenth century.

Today the modern city of Harran is located on the Balikh River, southeast of Edessa. This locale was celebrated among the Romans under the name of Charran, as the scene of the defeat of Crassus. The ruins lie on both sides of the river and include those of an ancient CASTLE, a CATHEDRAL, and a well, identified as the WELL OF ELIEZER AND REBEKAH.

- *Haran was Abraham's youngest brother, who died before the family left Ur (Gen. 11:26–28).*
- *At Haran the Lord told Abraham to go to the promised land of*

Canaan and promised him and his descendants certain glorious blessings (Gen. 12:1–3).

- *According to Genesis, Abraham left Haran at the age of 75 (Gen. 12:4).*
- *The city Nahor is where Abraham secured a wife for Isaac (Gen. 24:10).*
- *Here Jacob married Leah, Rachel, Zilpah, and Bilhah (Gen. 29).*
- *All twelve sons of Jacob were born here except Benjamin (Gen. 35:16–19).*
- *Haran was a great trade center (Ezek. 27:23).*
- *Jacob's experience here was referred to by Hosea (Hos. 12:12).*
- *The area was mentioned by Stephen (Acts 7:2–4).*

MOUNT ARARAT ("creation," "holy land"), Buyuk Agri Dagi

Ararat is a mountain peak 16,946 feet above sea level, in the extreme eastern part of Turkey within 25 miles of the Russian and Iranian borders. It is 20 miles south of Igdir, Turkey, and 25 miles west of Ararat, Russia.

The word *Ararat* originally designated a kingdom in the north of what was later Armenia. The name has been transferred from the surrounding district to the two peaks of the Taurus range of mountains: *Great Ararat* and *Little Ararat.*

Josephus wrote (ca. A.D. 70) about the ark that "its remains are shown there by the inhabitants to this day." About A.D. 1300, Marco Polo, who traveled through the area, mentioned the existence of an ark near the summit of Ararat. Frederic Parot, a Russian physician, in 1829 climbed Mount Ararat with Armenians and claimed to have found wood.

For many years airplane pilots and members of various expeditions have laid claim to sighting the "remains" of the ark on Mount Ararat. A recent organization entitled *Search Foundation, Inc.* (Scientific Exploration and Archeological Research of Washington, D.C.) reported in 1969 that it has pieces of wood that were cut in 1955 and 1969 from hand-hewn wooden beams 150 feet long. These were found at the 13,000–14,000-foot level of Mount Ararat. The pieces of wood were dug out of an ice pack nestled against a granite cliff on a shoulder of the mountain. The wood has been estimated by the experts to be approximately 4,000 years old. The leaders of Search Foundation, Inc., say that positive identification cannot be made until 900,000 cubic meters of ice and moraine are removed from a frozen lake between their two discoveries. This is a million-dollar proposed project.

- *Noah was commanded to build an ark (Gen. 6:14–22).*
- *Genesis tells of the Flood (Gen. 6–9).*
- *The ark landed on Mount Ararat (Gen. 8:4).*
- *A rainbow was set in the heavens (Gen. 9:11–13).*
- *The kingdom of Ararat was an ally and neighbor of Minni and Ashchenaz (Jer. 51:27).*

Appendix
and
Index

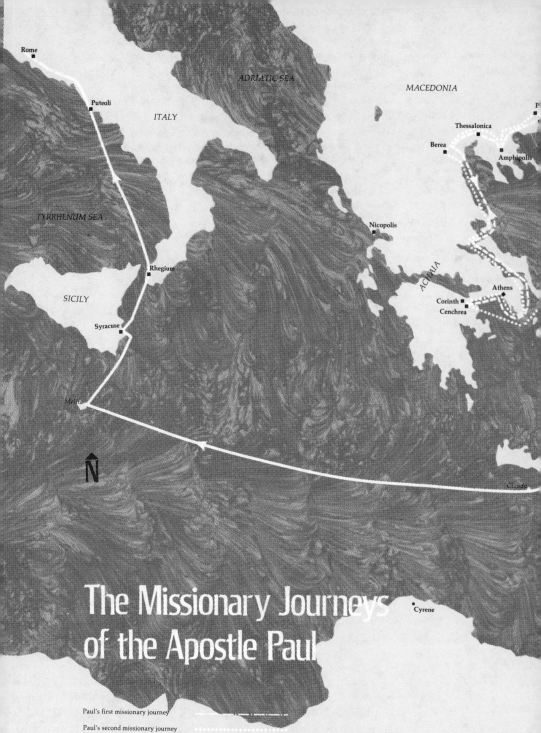

Rome

ADRIATIC SEA

MACEDONIA

Puteoli

ITALY

Thessalonica

P

Berea

Amphipolis

TYRRHENUM SEA

Nicopolis

Rhegium

ACHAIA

Athens

SICILY

Corinth
Cenchrea

Syracuse

Melita

N̂

Claudia

The Missionary Journeys
of the Apostle Paul

Cyrene

Paul's first missionary journey

Paul's second missionary journey

Paul's third missionary journey

Paul's last missionary journey

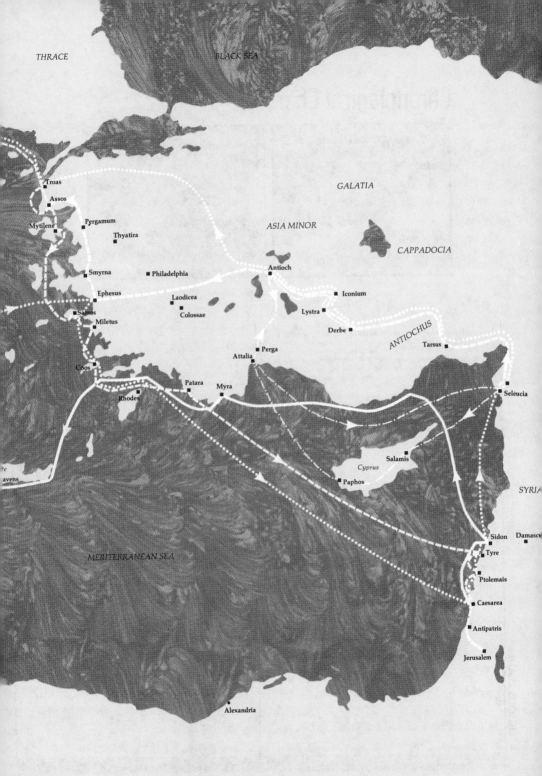

THRACE

BLACK SEA

GALATIA

ASIA MINOR

CAPPADOCIA

Troas

Assos

Mytilene

Pergamum

Thyatira

Smyrna

Philadelphia

Antioch

Iconium

Ephesus

Laodicea

Lystra

Samos

Colossae

Derbe

Miletus

ANTIOCHUS

Tarsus

Coos

Attalia

Perga

Patara

Myra

Seleucia

Rhodes

Salamis

Cyprus

Paphos

SYRIA

ravens

Sidon

Damasc

Tyre

MEDITERRANEAN SEA

Ptolemais

Caesarea

Antipatris

Jerusalem

Alexandria

EGYPT

Chronological Chart

HAMMURABI'S EMPIRE
ca. 1760 B.C.

EGYPTIAN EMPIRE
ca. 1450 B.C.

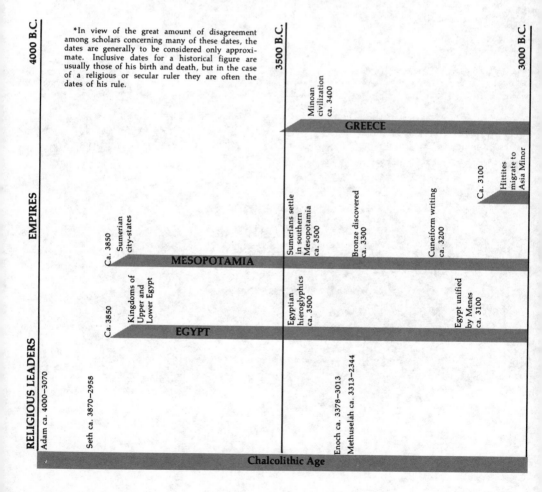

4000 B.C.

*In view of the great amount of disagreement among scholars concerning many of these dates, the dates are generally to be considered only approximate. Inclusive dates for a historical figure are usually those of his birth and death, but in the case of a religious or secular ruler they are often the dates of his rule.

3500 B.C.

3000 B.C.

EMPIRES

RELIGIOUS LEADERS

Adam ca. 4000–3070

Seth ca. 3870–2958

Enoch ca. 3378–3013

Methuselah ca. 3313–2344

Ca. 3850
Sumerian city-states

Ca. 3850
Kingdoms of Upper and Lower Egypt

Minoan civilization ca. 3400

GREECE

Sumerians settle in southern Mesopotamia ca. 3500

Bronze discovered ca. 3300

Cuneiform writing ca. 3200

Ca. 3100
Hittites migrate to Asia Minor

MESOPOTAMIA

Egyptian hieroglyphics ca. 3500

Egypt unified by Menes ca. 3100

EGYPT

Chalcolithic Age

HITTITE EMPIRE
ca. 1300 B.C.

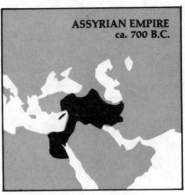

ASSYRIAN EMPIRE
ca. 700 B.C.

2500 B.C.

2000 B.C.

HITTITES

1st DYNASTY OF UR

Ca. 2800

Royal burials
at Ur ca. 2500

Ziggurat of Ur

Ca. 2400
Akkadian
Dynasty
founded by
Sargon I
ca. 2360

3rd Dynasty
of Ur

King of Ur:
Ur-Nammu

Dynasties I
and II
ca. 3100–2686

Memphis
the capital

Dynasty III
ca. 2686–2565

Dynasty IV
ca. 2565–2440

Dynasty V
ca. 2440–2315

Dynasty VI
ca. 2315–2181

Dynasty VII
ca. 2181–2175
Dynasty VIII
ca. 2175–2160
Dynasties IX
and X
ca. 2160–2060
Dynasty XI
ca. 2060–1992

OLD KINGDOM   PYRAMIDS

Noah ca. 2944–1994

Shem ca. 2450–1850

Flood ca. 2352

Peleg ca. 2251–2012

Early Bronze Age

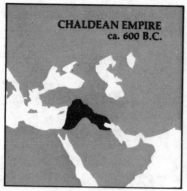

CHALDEAN EMPIRE
ca. 600 B.C.

PERSIAN EMPIRE
ca. 500 B.C.

2000 B.C.

1500 B.C.

1000 B.C.

RELIGIOUS LEADERS   EMPIRES

Knossos palace destroyed and rebuilt

Ca. 1580

MIDDLE MINOAN PERIOD

Fall of Crete ca. 1400

MYCENAEAN CIVILIZATION

Trojan War ca. 1194–1184

Isaac

Jacob

Joseph

ISRAEL

Egyptian captives
Moses

Exodus ca. 1290
Desert travels ca. 1290–1250
Conquest of Canaan ca. 1240

Judges

Saul

Early Hittite kingdoms

Mursilis ca. 1600

HITTITE   EMPIRE

Battle at Kadesh ca. 1296

Hittites driven from Asia Minor ca. 1100

Assyrian independence

Hammurabi ca. 1900 or 1750
1st Dynasty of Babylon
Ashur the capital 1800

Abi-eshu ca. 1647–1620

Hittites conquer Babylon

BABYLONIA
ASSYRIA

OLD BABYLONIAN
EMPIRE

Hurrian kingdom

Kassite rule over Babylon

Shalmaneser I ca. 1300

Assyrian supremacy ca.1300–612

BABYLONIA
ASSYRIA

Tiglath-pileser I ca. 1115–1077

ASSYRIA

Dynasty XII ca. 1992–1786
Sesostris I ca. 1971–1928

Sesostris III 1878–1843

Thebes the capital ca. 1786

Dynasties XIII thru XVI ca. 1786–1570

Dynasty XVII ca. 1600–1567

Ahmose I ca. 1567

Thutmose III ca. 1490–1435
Megiddo captured
Amenhotep III ca. 1411–1375
Akhenaten ca. 1375–1358

Ramses II ca. 1290–1224

Ramses III ca. 1175–1144

Ca. 1085

Dynasty XXI ca. 1085–935

MIDDLE KINGDOM

HYKSOS RULE

NEW   KINGDOM

PRIEST

Abraham ca. 1996–1822

Isaac ca. 1897–1715

Jacob ca. 1760–1613

Joseph ca. 1660–1550

Moses ca. 1370–1250

Saul ca. 1025–1004

Middle Bronze Age   Late Bronze Age

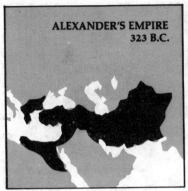

ALEXANDER'S EMPIRE
323 B.C.

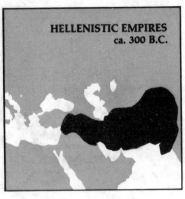

HELLENISTIC EMPIRES
ca. 300 B.C.

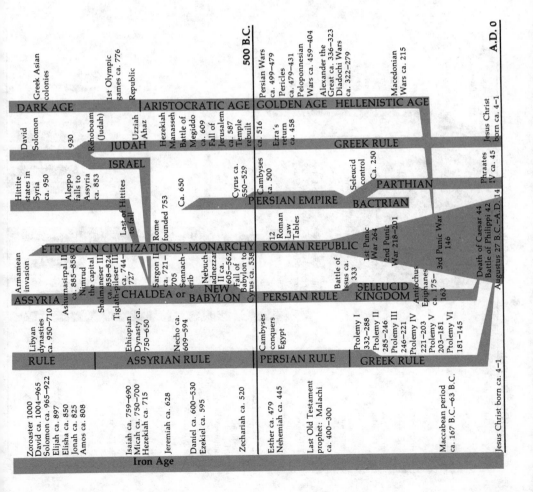

500 B.C.

A.D. 0

Greek Asian colonies

1st Olympic games ca. 776
Republic

Persian Wars ca. 499–479
Pericles ca. 479–431
Peloponnesian Wars ca. 459–404
Alexander the Great ca. 336–323
Diadochi Wars ca. 322–279

Macedonian Wars ca. 215

DARK AGE   **ARISTOCRATIC AGE**   **GOLDEN AGE**   **HELLENISTIC AGE**

David Solomon

Rehoboam (Judah)

Uzziah Ahaz

Hezekiah Manasseh Battle of Megiddo ca. 609 Fall of Jerusalem ca. 587 Temple rebuilt ca. 516

Ezra's return ca. 458

GREEK RULE

Jesus Christ born ca. 4–1

930

JUDAH

ISRAEL

Hittite states in Syria ca. 950

Aleppo falls to Assyria ca. 853

Last of Hittites to fall

Ca. 650

Cyrus ca. 550–529

Cambyses ca. 500

Ca. 250

Seleucid control

PARTHIAN

Phraates IV ca. 45

Armaean invasion

ETRUSCAN CIVILIZATIONS - MONARCHY

Ashurnasirpal II ca. 885–858 Nimrud the capital Shalmaneser III ca. 858–824 Tiglath-pileser III ca. 744–727

Sargon II ca. 721–705 Sennach-erib

Nebuch-adnezzar II ca. 605–562 Fall of Babylon to Cyrus ca. 538

Rome founded 753

PERSIAN EMPIRE

BACTRIAN

12 Roman Law Tables

ROMAN REPUBLIC

Battle of Issus ca. 333

1st Punic War 264 2nd Punic War 218–201

3rd Punic War 146

Death of Caesar 44 Battle of Philippi 42 Augustus 27 B.C.–A.D. 14

ASSYRIA   **CHALDEA or** **NEW BABYLON** **PERSIAN RULE** **SELEUCID KINGDOM**

Antiochus Epiphanes ca. 175–163

Libyan dynasties ca. 950–710

RULE

ASSYRIAN RULE

Ethiopian Dynasty ca. 750–650

Necho ca. 609–594

Cambyses conquers Egypt

PERSIAN RULE

GREEK RULE

Ptolemy I 332–288 Ptolemy II 285–246 Ptolemy III 246–221 Ptolemy IV 221–203 Ptolemy V 203–181 Ptolemy VI 181–145

Zoroaster 1000
David ca. 1004–965
Solomon ca. 965–922
Elijah ca. 897
Elisha ca. 850
Jonah ca. 825
Amos ca. 808

Isaiah ca. 759–690
Micah ca. 750–700
Hezekiah ca. 715

Jeremiah ca. 628

Daniel ca. 600–530
Ezekiel ca. 595

Zechariah ca. 520

Esther ca. 479
Nehemiah ca. 445

Last Old Testament prophet: Malachi ca. 400–300

Maccabean period ca. 167 B.C.–63 B.C.

Jesus Christ born ca. 4–1

Iron Age

ROMAN EMPIRE A.D. 96

EASTERN AND WESTERN CHURCHES

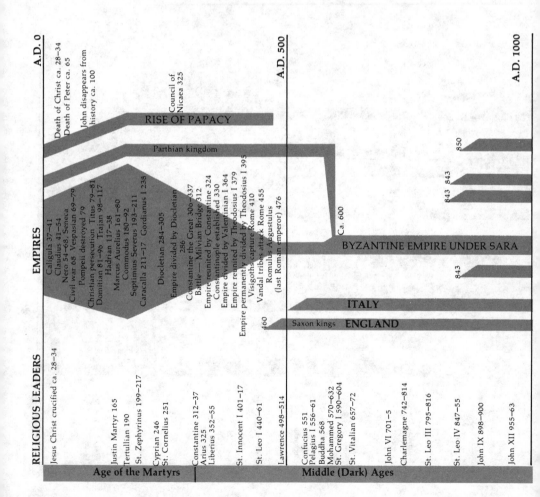

A.D. 0

A.D. 500

A.D. 1000

EMPIRES

Death of Christ ca. 28–34
Death of Peter ca. 65
John disappears from history ca. 100

Council of Nicaea 325

RISE OF PAPACY

Parthian kingdom

Caligula 37–41
Claudius 41–54
Nero 54–68, Seneca
Civil war 68 Vespasian 69–79
Pompeii destroyed 79
Christian persecution Titus 79–81
Domitian 81–96 Trajan 98–117
Hadrian 117–38
Marcus Aurelius 161–80
Commodus 180–92
Septimius Severus 193–211
Caracalla 211–17 Gordianus I 238
Diocletian 284–305
Empire divided by Diocletian
286
Constantine the Great 306–337
Battle — Milvian Bridge 312
Empire reunited by Constantine 324
Constantinople established 330
Empire divided by Valentinian I 364
Empire reunited by Theodosius I 379
Empire permanently divided by Theodosius I 395
Visigoths capture Rome 410
Vandal tribes attack Rome 455
Romulus Augustulus
(last Roman emperor) 476

Ca. 600

850

843 843

843

BYZANTINE EMPIRE UNDER SARA

460

ITALY

Saxon kings **ENGLAND**

RELIGIOUS LEADERS

Jesus Christ crucified ca. 28–34

Justin Martyr 165
Tertullian 190
St. Zephyrinus 199–217

Cyprian 246
St. Cornelius 251

Constantine 312–37
Arius 325
Liberius 352–55

St. Innocent I 401–17

St. Leo I 440–61

Lawrence 498–514

Confucius 551
Pelagius I 556–61
Buddha 568
Mohammed 570–632
St. Gregory I 590–604
St. Vitalian 657–72

John VI 701–5
Charlemagne 742–814

St. Leo III 795–816

St. Leo IV 847–55

John IX 898–900

John XII 955–63

Age of the Martyrs   **Middle (Dark) Ages**

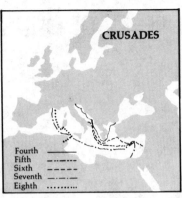

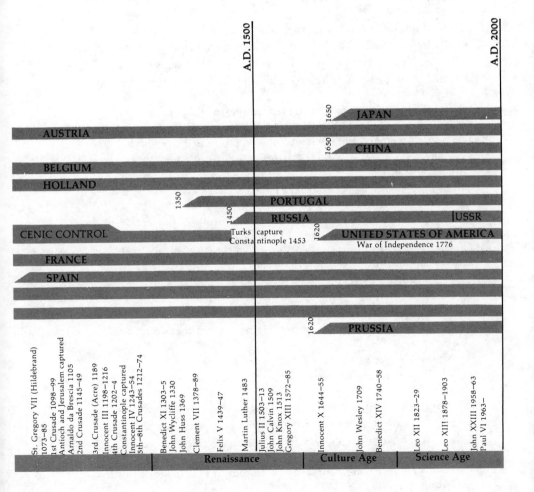

Glossary of Unusual Terms

Adytum (pl. *adyta*)   The innermost sanctuary or shrine in an ancient temple

Aedicula   See *edicule*, below

Apodyterium (pl. *apodyteria*)   A dressing room in an ancient Greek or Roman bath or gymnasium

Baldachin (or *baldacchino*)   A canopy over an altar or other sacred object or seat of honor

Caldarium (pl. *caldaria*)   In ancient Rome, a room for a hot bath

Capital (architecture)   The head or uppermost member of a column

Cartouche   An oval or oblong figure enclosing a sovereign's name

Caryatid   A draped female figure supporting the horizontal, continuous part of a building

Cella (pl. *cellae*)   In a Greek or Roman temple, the inner part (often hidden) which housed the image of the deity

Cenotaph   An empty tomb in honor of a person buried elsewhere

Columbarium (pl. *columbaria*)   A structure of vaults lined with recesses for cinerary urns

Cyclopean (walls, etc.)   Constructed of large, irregular blocks, without mortar

Diazoma (pl. *diazomata*)   In an ancient Greek theater, a passage dividing the lower from the upper rows for convenient access

Dolmen   A prehistoric monument consisting of two or more upright stones supporting a horizontal stone slab

Edicule (or *aedicula*)   A small structure used as a shrine; a niche for a statue

Faience   Earthenware decorated with opaque colored glazes

Frigidarium (pl. *frigidaria*)   In ancient Rome, a room containing a cold bath

Hypostyle   Having a roof resting on rows of columns

Kaffiyeh   An Arab headdress consisting of a square of cloth folded to form a triangle and bound on the head with a cord

Lapis lazuli   A semiprecious stone, usually of a rich azure blue color

Menorah   A candelabrum used primarily in Jewish religious services

Metope   The space between two ornaments on a Doric frieze, often decorated with carved work

Mihrab   A niche, chamber, or slab in a mosque, indicating the direction of Mecca

Minaret   A slender, lofty tower attached to a mosque and surrounded by one or more projecting balconies, from which the summons to prayer is cried

Moshav (pl. *moshavim*)   A cooperative group of farms in Israel

Muezzin   A Moslem crier who calls the hour of daily prayers

Narthex   In early Christian and Byzantine churches, a porch or vestibule just inside the main entrance and at the opposite end from the altar

Nemset   An Egyptian burial headdress

Ostracon (pl. *ostraca*)   In ancient Greece, a potsherd used as a ballot

Pallium (pl. *pallia*)   A cloak worn by men in ancient Greece and Rome; a band of white wool worn by the Pope and confirmed on archbishops

Pronaos (pl. *pronaoi*)   The outer part, or portico, of an ancient Greek temple

Propylaeum (often used in pl., *propylaea*)   A vestibule or entrance of architectural importance before a building or enclosure

Propylon (pl. *propyla*)   An outer monumental gateway standing before a main gateway

Sarcophagus (pl. *sarcophagi*)   A coffin of stone, marble, concrete, or other such material, often ornamented

Shokel   To sway back and forth in conjunction with prayer (a Jewish custom)

Stanza (pl. *stanze*)   Italian for "room"

Stoa   An ancient Greek portico, usually walled at the back, with a front colonnade opening on a public place

Sudatorium (pl. *sudatoria*)   A sweat room in a bath

Tekke   A dervish monastery or shrine

Tell, tel   An ancient mound composed of remains of successive settlements

Temenos (pl. *temene*)   A temple enclosure or court; a sacred precinct

Tepidarium (pl. *tepidaria*)   A warm room of an ancient Roman bath, used to sit in

Troglodyte   A cave dweller

Tumulus (pl. *tumuli*)   An artificial mound, especially over a grave of someone buried in ancient times

Velarium (pl. *velaria*)   An awning over an ancient Roman theater

Wadi   The bed or valley of a stream

Yeshiva   A Hebrew school providing religious and sometimes secular instruction

Selected Readings

Agard, Walter R. *The Greek Mind.* Princeton: D. Van Nostrand, 1957.

Aharoni, Yohanan. *The Land of the Bible: A Historical Geography.* Philadelphia: The Westminster Press, 1967.

Badi, Joseph. *Religion in Israel Today.* New York: Bookman Associates, 1959.

Bassili, William Farid. *Sinai and the Monastery of St. Catherine.* Cairo: Costa Tsoumas, 1962.

Bean, George E. *Aegean Turkey: An Archaeological Guide.* New York: Frederick A. Draeger, 1966.

Bishko, Herbert. *This is Jerusalem.* Israeli United Artists, 1971.

Blau, Joseph L. *Modern Varieties of Judaism.* New York and London: Columbia University Press, 1966.

Bowra, C. M. *Classical Greece.* Great Ages of Man Series. New York: Time Incorporated, 1965.

Breasted, James H. *Development of Religion and Thought in Ancient Egypt.* New York: Harper and Brothers, 1959.

Brosnahan, Tom. *Turkey on 5 Dollars a Day.* New York: Arthur Frommer, 1971.

Burrows, Millar. *The Dead Sea Scrolls.* New York: The Viking Press, 1955.

Casson, Lionel. *Ancient Egypt.* Great Ages of Man Series. New York: Time Incorporated, 1965.

Champdor, Albert. *Babylon.* New York: G. P. Putnam's Sons, 1958.

Comay, Joan. *Everyone's Guide to Israel.* Garden City, N.Y.: Doubleday and Co., 1966.

Craven, Thomas. *Greek Art.* New York: Pocket Books, 1950.

Cross, Frank M., Jr. *The Ancient Library of Qumran.* Garden City, N.Y.: Doubleday and Co., 1958.

Del Turco, Lorenzo. *The Sistine Chapel.* Rome: Lorenzo Del Turco, 1969.

Desroches-Noblecourt, Christiane. *Tutankhamon.* Garden City, N.Y.: Doubleday and Co., 1965.

Duffield, Guy P. *Tourists' Handbook of Bible Lands.* Glendale, Calif.: Regal Division G/L Publications, 1969.

Dunand, Maurice. *Byblos: Its History, Ruins and Legends.* Paris: Librairie Adrien-Maissoneuve, 1964.

Emery, Walter B. *Lost Land Emerging.* New York: Charles Scribner's Sons, 1967.

Fattorusso, Joseph. *Wonders of Rome.* Florence: "Impronta" Press, 1964.

Gandelman, Claude. *Israel.* Tel Aviv: Massada, Ltd., 1968.

Gaster, Theodor H. *The Dead Sea Scriptures.* New York: Doubleday and Co., 1956.

Goodwin, Frank J. *A Harmony of the Life of St. Paul.* Grand Rapids: Baker Book House, 1964.

Grant, Michael. *The World of Rome.* New York: New York Library, 1961.

Hadas, Moses. *Imperial Rome.* Great Ages of Man Series. New York: Time Incorporated, 1965.

Hale, William Harian. *The Horizon Book of Ancient Rome.* New York: American Heritage Publishing Co., 1966.

Hammond, C. S. *Atlas of the Bible Lands.* New York: C. S. Hammond and Co., 1950.

Hastings, James. *Dictionary of the Bible.* New York: Charles Scribner's Sons, 1963.

Hitti, Philip K. *Lebanon in History.* New York: Macmillan Co., 1967.

Hoade, Fr. Eugene. *Guide to the Holy Land.* Jerusalem: Franciscan Press, 1962.

Home, Gordon. *Cyprus Then and Now.* London: J. M. Dent and Sons, 1960.

Kaloyeropoulou, Athena G. *Old Corinth.* Athens: M. Pechlivanides and Co.

Keller, Werner. *The Bible as History.* New York: William Morrow and Co., 1964.

Keshishian, Kevork K. *Everybody's Guide to Romantic Cyprus.* Nicosia: Kevork K. Keshishian, 1967.

Lange, Kurt, and Hirmer, Max. *Egypt: Architecture, Sculpture, Painting, in Three Thousand Years.* Hirmer Verlag München, 1968.

Levi, Abraham. *Bazak Israel Guide.* New York: Harper and Row, 1971.

Lieber, Joel. *Israel and the Holy Land on $5 and $10 a Day.* New York: Arthur Frommer, 1968.

Louvish, Misha. *Facts About Israel, 1970.* Jerusalem: Keter Books, 1970.

MacKendrick, Paul L. *The Greek Stones Speak.* New York: St. Martin's Press, 1962.

Mattingly, Harold. *Roman Imperial Civilization.* New York: Doubleday, 1959.

Mayne, Peter. *Istanbul.* New York: A. S. Barnes and Co., 1967.

Meade, N. F. Mansfield. *Luxor.* Luxor: Gaddis Photo Stores, 1967.

Meletzis, Spyros, and Papadakis, Helen. *Delphi.* Munich: Schnell and Steiner, 1964.

Ministry of Tourism. *Egyptian Museum.* Cairo: Al Akhbar Press, 1969.

Ministry of Tourism. *Tourist Information.* Cairo: Middle East Public Relations, 1969.

Munimeser, M., ed. *Istanbul: Encyclopedic Guide.* Istanbul: Yenilik Basimevi, 1967.

National Tourist Organization. *Syria Tourist Guide.* Damascus: National Tourist Organization, 1969.

Nims, Charles F. *Thebes of the Pharaohs.* New York: Stein and Day, 1965.

Oppenheim, A. Leo. *Ancient Mesopotamia.* Chicago: University of Chicago Press, 1968.

Otto, Eberhard, and Desroches-Noblecourt, Christiane. *Egypt.* London and New York: Phaidon, 1968.

Otto, Eberhard, and Hirmer, Max. *Ancient Egyptian Art.* New York: Harry N. Abrams, n.d.

Panhellenic Committee for Cyprus Self-Determination. *Some Facts About Cyprus.* Athens: M. Pechlivanides and Co., [1956?].

Parrot, André. *Babylon and the Old Testament.* London: SCM Press, 1958.

Penteas, Ev. *What to See in Greece.* Athens: Patris, n.d.

Porter, Berta, and Moss, Rosalind L. B. *Topographical Bibliography of Ancient Egyptian Hieroglyphic Texts, Reliefs and Paintings.* Oxford: Clarendon Press, 1960.

Purcell, H. D. *Cyprus.* New York and Washington: Frederick A. Praeger, 1969.

Ramsay, W. M. *The Letters to the Seven Churches of Asia.* Grand Rapids: Baker Book House, 1963.

Richter, Gisela. *A Handbook of Greek Art.* New York and London: Phaidon Press, 1969.

Roux, Georges. *Ancient Iraq.* Baltimore: Penguin Books, 1966.

Saggs, H. W. F. *Everyday Life in Babylonia and Assyria.* New York: G. P. Putnam's Sons, 1965.

————. *The Greatness That Was Babylon.* New York: Frederick A. Praeger, 1962.

Showker, Kay. *The Arab Middle East.* New York: Pan American World Airways, 1967.

Shulamit, Schwartz Nardi. *The Shrine of the Book and Its Scrolls.* Jerusalem: The Jerusalem Post Press, 1966.

Sinnigen, William G. *Rome.* New York: Macmillan Co., 1965.

Smith, Wilbur M. *Israeli/Arab Conflict and the Bible.* Glendale, Calif.: G/L Publications, 1967.

Steindorff, George. *Egypt.* New York: J. J. Augustin, 1943.

Strommenger, Eva, and Hirmer, Max. *5000 Years of the Art of Mesopotamia.* New York: Harry N. Abrams, n.d.

Suetonius. *The Twelve Caesars,* tr. Robert Graves. Baltimore: Penguin Books, 1957.

Thiessen, H. C. *Introduction to the New Testament.* Grand Rapids: William B. Eerdmans Publishing Co., 1958.

Thomas, D. Winton. *Documents from Old Testament Times.* London and New York: Thomas Nelson and Sons, 1958.

Thompson, J. A. *The Bible and Archaeology.* Grand Rapids: William B. Eerdmans Publishing Co., 1962.

Tidwell, Josiah Blake. "Bible Lands and Places with Their Biblical Connections." *The Baylor Bulletin,* 45 (July 1942).

Trever, John C. *The Untold Story of Qumran.* Old Tappan, N.J.: Fleming H. Revell Co., 1965.

Venturini, E. *Rome and The Vatican.* Rome: Casa Editrice Lozzi.

Vilnay, Zev. *The Guide to Israel.* Jerusalem: Da'at Press, 1969.

Weiner, Herbert. *The Wild Goats of Ein Gedi.* Garden City, N.Y.: Doubleday, 1961.

Wheeler, Robert Erle Mortimer. *Roman Art and Architecture.* New York: Praeger, 1964.

Wilson, John A. *The Culture of Ancient Egypt.* Chicago: University of Chicago Press, 1956.

Woolley, C. Leonard. *Ur of the Chaldees: A Record of Seven Years of Excavation.* New York: Norton and Co., 1965.

Wright, Ernest G. *Biblical Archaeology.* Philadelphia: The Westminster Press, 1960.

Yadin, Yigael. *The Message of the Scrolls.* New York: Grossett and Dunlap, 1957.

Young, Robert. *Analytical Concordance to the Bible.* 22d ed. Grand Rapids: William B. Eerdmans Publishing Co., n.d.

Ziock, Hermann. *Guide to Egypt.* Cairo: Lehnert and Landrock, 1965.

Index

This index consists mainly of names of places and points of interest to visit. Documents, works of literature, and art works (painting, sculpture, etc.) are shown in **bold type**. A few other subject references, such as noteworthy persons and events, are included where they seem to be especially useful for the reader. These are in *italics*.

The listing is word by word, short before long, as in most library card catalogs. Thus *Beit Ur et Tahta*, for example, precedes *Beitin*. Articles, prepositions, and titles (*Saint, Sultan*, etc.) are usually ignored and an entry is alphabetized under the following word. In main entries these are inverted: *Sophia, Saint*; in subentries they are not: *Saint Sophia* (alphabetized by *Sophia*). As a convenience for the reader, some sites are listed under both the title and the name. For instance, this subentry under *Churches* appears in two places: *Mary, Armenian Church of the Blessed Virgin* (listed under *M*); the Blessed Virgin Mary, Armenian Church of (listed under *B*).

Aaron 460
Abbeys. *See* Monasteries
Abda 368-369
Abel, Abel-Maim 321
Abel-Meholah 292-293
Abel-Shittim 452
Abila 452
Abou Habba 185
Abraham, house of 199
Abraham's Well 361
Abraham Wax Collection 259
Abu Ghosh, Abu Gosh 337
Abu Rodeis 113
Abu Zeneima, Abu Zenima 113
Abydos 75
Acacia tree 377
Academy of Sciences 133
Accho, Acre, Acco 334-335
Aceldama 248-249
Achmetha 203
Achor, el-Buquei'ah 275
Achzib 336
Acro-Corinthus 153
Acropolis, Athens 130
Acropolis of Corinth 153
Adam 446
Adam, altar of 228
Adam, tree of 202
Adora 365
Adoraim 365
Adrianopolis 501-502
Adullam 344
Adummim 269-271

Aelia Capitolina 215
Afula 302
Agergoof, Aqarquf 172-173
Agora, Argos 148
Agora, Athens 138-141
Agora, Corinth 153
Agri Dagi 560
Ahmed III, fountain of, Ahmed III
    Cesmesi 521
Ai 269, 284
Aid Jalud 304
Aijalon 449
Ain el Qudeirat 120-122
Ain Musa 456
Ain Qadeis 120-122
Ain Shems 343
Airport, Lod 342
Aiyun Musa 112
Ajalon, Aijalon 339
Ajalon, Ajlun 449
Ajalon, Valley of 339
Akhisar 531-532
Akir 340-341
Akkad, Agade, Akkud 172
Akko 334-335
Al Basrah 202
Al-Fustât 52
Al Hadhr 175-176
Al Hillah 185
Al Kifl 194
Al Kufah 194
Al Mawsil 183
Al Qurna 202

Alaca Hüyük (Alaja)   555
Alanya   554
Alaşehir   534
Alasia   19
Albright Institute of Archaeological
    Research   257
Aleppo   500-501
Alexander the Great, Tomb of
    477
Alexander Zeia, statue of   298
Alexandria   70-73
Alexandria lighthouse   72
Alfasi Cave   259
Allenby Bridge   274-275
Allonim, Kibbutz   298
Alma   320
Altar, Canaanite   256-257
Altar of the Twelve Gods   138
Altar with horns, from Megiddo
    256-257, 295
Amalfi   428
Amarna letters   72-75, 318, 339,
    346, 351, 482-483, 499
Amathus   27
Amazia   347
American Embassy, Cairo   54
American Institute of Holy Land
    Studies   249
Amenhotep III, court of   78
Amenhotep III, scarab of (granite)
    84
Amman, Ammon   442-445
Amman, North from   445-450
Amman, South from   450-462
Ammaous   339
Ammochostos   23-24
Ammon, Amman   442-445
Amory   487
Amos, home of (Tekoa)   359-360
Amphipolis   159
Amwas   339
An Najaf   194
An Nasiriyah   195
Ananias, house of   491
Anata   279
Anathoth   279
Anaximander   549-550
Anaximenes   549-550
Anaya   483
Andronicus, Clock of   138-140
Anjar   470
Ankara, Ancyra, Angora, Ancora
    554-555
Annals,
    First Hall of   84
    Second Hall of   84
Annas, house of   235
Anne, Saint, Seminary   226
Ant   75-76

Antakya   557-559
Antalya   552
Antaradus   498
Antioch of Pisidia   554
Antioch (Syrian)   557-559
Antipatris   327-328
Antonia   228
Anzio   425
Apamea   497
Aphek   325, 327
Aphrodisias   536
Aphrodite, birthplace of (Paphos)
    28
Aphrodite of Cnidus   424
Apollo and Daphne   410, 423
Apollonia   329
Appian Way, Old   397
Appii Forum   397-398, 425
Aqaba   461-462
Aqaba, Gulf of   110, 461-462
Aqarquf, Agergoof   172-174
Aqua-Bella   337
Aquarium   49, 72
Aqueduct, Caesarea   330
Aqueduct of Pasha Ahmad Jezaar
    335
Aqueduct, Pergamum   529
Aqueduct, Secret, Mycenae   153
Aqueduct of Valens   512
Aquila and Priscilla   381
Arab Development Society   274
Arabah, Arava   369-370
Arad   373
Aradus   483
Ara'ir   454
Aravu, Bet ha'   450
Arbel, Valley of   310
Arbela, Arbailu   184
Arbila   450
Arcades   219
Arcadiane Street   543
Arch of the Goldsmiths   390
Areopagus, Areios Pagos   135
Argos   148
Arid Zone Research Center   366
Arimathea   282
El Arish   123
Ark of the Covenant   312
Armageddon   295-297
Armenian mosaic   254
Armenian Quarter   235
Arnon Valley   453
Aroer   454
Around the Sea of Galilee and
    North   306-325
Arshaf   329
Arsur   329
Art Galleries and Museums, Rome
    423-425

Artist's Quarter   411
As Samawah   195
Asasif, El   90
Asclepieum, Pergamum   529-531
Ashdod   352
Ashkelon   351-352
Ashtoreth, Stela of the Goddess
   305
Ashur, Assur, Ash Shargat   175
Ashurnasirpal II, Annals of   176
Askar   286
Asklepeion, Athens   135
Asklepeion, Coos   161
Aspar's Cistern   514
Assos   527
Assyria   166-168
Assyrian "king list"   183
Astartu, The Capture of   179
Aswan   103-105
Aswan area   103-109
Aswan Dam, Old   103-105
Aswan High Dam   103
Asyut (Assiout)   75
Atarot Jerusalem Airport   283
Atatürk, Kemal   509, 523, 524,
   525, 555
Atatürk Bridge   523
Atatürk Monument   538
Atatürk's house   555
Athena Parthenos   424
Athena Promachos   131
Athena, statue of   131
Athens   130-141
Atlit, Athlit   332
Atreus, Treasury of   151
Attalia   552
Augusto, Piazza   411
Aurelius, Marcus, column of
   399
Aurelius, Marcus, statue of   387
Avaris   32
Avdat   368-369
Aven   62
Avenue of Independence   523
Avenue of the Righteous   265
Ayaa   477-479
Aya Soluk   539
Ayelet-Hashahar, kibbutz   320
Azekah   343
Azereyeh, el-Azariye   269
Al Azm, house of   497
Azotus   352
Al Azraq   450
Azzah   350-351

Baalbek, Baalbeck   470-475
Baba Gurgur   184
Babel, Tower of   192-194, 197
Babylon   185-193

Babylon, Temple Tower (ziggurat)
   of   191-192
Babylonia   168-171
Babylonian Chronicle   168, 181,
   187, 214
Babylonian Talmud   309
Baghdad   171-172
Baghdad, North of   172-184
Baghdad, South of   184-202
Baha'i Archives Building   333
Baha'i Gardens   333
Baha'i House   335
Baha'i Shrine   333
Baha'ullah, first prophet of the
   Baha'i faith   334
Bahriat   195
Bahurim, Ras et-Tmim   279
Balata, Balatah   286
Banias (Baniyas, Balanea), Syria
   184, 498
Banias (Baniyas, Caesarea
   Philippi), Israel   322
Baptismal fonts, Masada   374
Baptistry, Florence   431
Baptistry, Pisa   433
Baptistry, Shivta   369
Barak   559
Baram   317
Barberini, Piazza   411
Barcaccia Fountain   411
Barnabas, native of Cyprus
   15-16
Bashan   437-438
Basilican Cistern   521
Basilicas. *See* Churches
Basra, Al Basrah   202
Bayazit Fire Tower   515
Bayazit Yangin Kulesi   515
Bayt Layy   347-348
Bayt Miri   470
Bazaars. *See* Markets
Beach of Natanya   329
Ic Bedestan   516
Beer-Menuha   370
Beeroth   283
Beersheba, Beer-sheva   365-367
Behistun Inscriptions   163
Beirut   466-470
Beirut, East of   470-475
Beirut, North of   481-484
Beirut, South of   475-481
Beisan   305
Beit Alpha   304
Beit Guvrin   344
Beit Hanassi   259
Beit Jibril   344
Beit Lahm   354-358
Beit Mari, Beit Meri   470
Beit Netofa, Valley of   300, 311

Beit Shearim 298
Beit-Shemesh 343
Beit Ur el-Foqa 337
Beit ur et Tahta 337
Beitin 283
Bekaa Valley 470
Belevi 539
Bell Caves 344
Bema (Tribune) 155
Ben-Gurion, David 367-368
Ben-Gurion, David, home of
    (Degania) 308
Berachah, Berakha, Valley of 360
Berea, Beroea 159
Bereketzade, Fountain of 523
Berekhat Ha Meshushim 316
Berenice 370-372
Bergama 527-531
Beqa, El- 470
Beroea, Aleppo 500
Berytus 466-470
Bet Yerah 308
Beth Horon 337
Beth-maacha 321
Beth-Phelet 349
Beth-Shean, Beit-Shean 305
Beth-Shemesh 343
Beth-Zur, Beit Zur 360
Bethabara, Bethabary 450
Bethany 269
Bethaven 283
Bethel 283
Bethesda, Beth-Zatha, Pool of
    226
Bethlehem 354-358
Bethphage, Keft et-Tur 269
Bethsaida 313-314
Beyoğlu 523-525
Biban el-Harim 89
Biblical Zoo 267
Bibylus 482-483
Bileam 293
Billy Rose Art Garden 260
Binbirdirek Cistern 516
Bir Hasana 120
Bira 283
Birch, el- 283
Birket Ram 323
Birs Nimroud 194
Bisharin Village 107
Biyehuda 365
Blue Grotto 428
Boats, glass-bottomed 370
Bocca della Verità 390-423
Bodrum 551
Bogazkale (Boghazkoy) 555
Bonus Cistern 512
Bohaira, Monk, house of 494
Borghese, Paulina 410-423

Borsippa 194
Bosh-Ha-Ayin 327
Bosra, Bosra el Shan 494
Botanical Gardens 49-51
Bouleuterion 138, 550
Bozdoğan Kemeri 512
Bride of the Desert 501-502
Broken Prism 175
Brothel, Ephesus 546
Bukharian Quarter 258
Bur Said 109
Burj, el- 332
Busra 494
Buyuk 560
Byblos 482-483
Byzantium 506-525

Cabala 316
Cabul 334
Caesarea 329
Caesarea Mazaca 555-556
Caesarea Philippi 322
Caiaphas, cell dungeon of 252
Caiaphas, house of 249
Cairo 49-61
Cairo, Old 52
Cairo, Tower of 49
Calah 176-179
Callirhoe 451
Calvary 231, 256
Campidoglio 387
Cana 300-301
Cana, Lebanon 481
Cape of the Grotto 336
Cape Krio 552
Capernaum 311-313
Capitol, Rome 387
Capitoline Venus 424
Capri 428
Caracalla, Baths of 397
Carchemish 559
Carmel Caves 332
Carmelit Subway 333
Carved ivory panels, Nimrud 179
Castles
    Al Azraq 450
    Beaufort 481
    Buffavento 30
    Chastel Blanc 498
    Chevaliers, Krak des 497-498
    Frankish 482-483
    Giles, Crusader Castle of Saint
        483
    Haran, Castle 559
    Saint Hilarion 30
    Justinian 288
    Kalaat Namrud, Kalat Nimrud
        322
    Kantara 30

Castles, *continued*
  Kolossi   27
  Krak des Chevaliers   497-498
  Kyrenia   30
  of Saint Louis   476
  of Marqab   498-499
  Mashatta   450
  of Mehmet   525
  Montfort   336-337
  Nimrod   322
  Old Castle, Laodicea   536
  Paphos   28
  Qalaat el Hosu   497-498
  Qalaat esh-Shaqif   481
  Qalaat Nemrod   322
  El-Qasr, Amman   443
  Qasr, El Qasr   454
  Qasr el Mushatta   450
  Rumeli Hisari   525
  Sant'Angelo   408-409, 424
  Sayhoun   499
  Sea, Castle of the   476
  Shahba   495
Catacombs. *See* Tombs
Catal Hüyük   554
Cathedrals. *See* Churches
Cavaspina   423
Cave of Machpelah   361
Cave of the Innocent Children   243
Cave of the Revelation, Patmos   160
Cavern of Agony   243
Cecropia   130
Cedars of Lebanon   484
Cellar of the Holocaust   252
Cemberlitas   516
Cemeteries. *See* Tombs
Cenacle   251
Cenchrea   158
Chagall windows   266
Chalcedon   506-509, 526
Chalcedon, Creed of   526
Chaldea   186
Chalice   233
Chamber of Martyrs   252
Chapels. *See* Churches
Charioteer   145
Charnel House   116
Charran   559-560
Cheese Maker's Valley   246
Chittim   15-30
Chora   160
Chorazin   314-315
Christian (origin of term)   558
Christian Quarter   233-234
Chrysopolis   525-526
Chtaura   470
Churches, Basilicas, Chapels,
    Cathedrals
  Abu Serga   52

Adam, Chapel of   231-233
Aemilia, Basilica   394
of Saint Agnes   421
of Saint Agnes in Agone   401
the Agony, Basilica of   240, 242
of All Nations   240-242
of Saint Ananias   491
of Sant'Andrea della Valle
    417, 423
the Angel, Chapel of   233
of Saint Anne   226
the Annunciation, Greek
    Orthodox Church of   299
the Annunciation, Latin Church
    of   299
the Apparition, Chapel of   233
Archbishopric and Saint John's
    19
of the Ascension   237, 240
of the Assumption of Mary
    243
Ayia Phaneromeni   26
Ayia Solomoni   29
Ayios Georghios Xorinos, Greek
    Orthodox Church of   24
of Saint Bartholomew   390
the Blessed Virgin Mary,
    Armenian Church of   18
the Burning Bush, Chapel of
    116
Byzantine, Masada   374
Byzantine, Tell Bet Yerah   308
Cathedral, Pisa   433
Cathedral Church   449
of Saint Catherine   356
Catholic Franciscan   300-301
of Santa Cecilia in Trastevere
    417, 423
Christian Church Building
    504
of Chrysopolitissa   28-29
of Condemnation   228
Coptic Church El-Moallaka   52
Santa Croce   431
of Santa Croce in Gerusalemme
    417, 421
Crusader, Abu Ghosh   337
of Domine, Quo Vadis?   398
Dominus Flevit   242
the Dormition, Basilica of   249
Dura-Europos   504
Ecce Homo Basilica   229
Saint Elias (Elijah), Greek Church
    of   301
of Elijah   354
Elijah's Chapel   117
El-Moallaka, Coptic Church
    (Holy Virgin's Church)   52
Saint Epiphanius, Basilica of   23

Churches, *etc., continued*
Eudoxiana, Basilica   419
of Evil Counsel   259
the Finding of the Cross,
    Chapel of   233
of the Flagellation   228
of Santa Francesca Romana
    417, 422
Gabriel's   299
Saint George, Lod   342
Saint George, Navplion   148
Saint George's Greek Orthodox
    452
Saint George's (Mary Gurguis)
    52
Granite Chapel   84
Greek Orthodox, Bethany   269
Greek Orthodox, Cana   301
Greek Orthodox Catholic
    Patriarchal   513
Greek Patriarchate   234, 252
of San Gregorio Magno
    417, 422
Saint Helena, Chapel of
    230, 233
of the Holy Sepulcher   230-233
Holy Virgin's   52
House of Caiaphas, chapel   249
Saint James Cathedral   235
Saint Janarius, Cathedral of
    427
of Saint John, Ein Karem   266
of Saint John, Ephesus   542
Saint John in Lateran, Basilica
    of   397, 418-419
of Saint John the Baptist,
    Jerusalem   234
of Saint John the Baptist,
    Samaria   291
of Saint Joseph   299
Julia, Basilica   392-394
Kapnikarea, Byzantine Church
    of   141
of Saint Lazarus, Bethany   269
of Saint Lazarus, Larnaca
    25-26
of San Lorenzo   394, 431-433
Madresseh Halawiye Cathedral
    501
the Manger, Chapel of   356
of Santa Maria ad Nives   420
of Santa Maria Concezione
    411, 420
of Santa Maria d'Aracoeli
    387, 421
of Santa Maria degli Angeli
    417, 422
of Santa Maria dei Miracoli
    410

Santa Maria del Fiore, Cathedral
    of   431
of Santa Maria del Popolo
    410, 417, 422
of Santa Maria in Cosmedin
    390, 417, 423
of Santa Maria in Monte Santo
    410
of Santa Maria in Trastevere
    417, 422
Santa Maria Maggiore, Basilica
    of   397, 420
of Santa Maria sopra Minerva
    417, 420
Saint Mary, Armenian Church
    of   24
Mary, Armenian Church of the
    Blessed Virgin   18
Mary Gurguis   52
Saint Mary Latina, Crusader
    Church of   234
Mary Magdalene, Russian
    Orthodox Church of   242
Mary Major, Basilica of   397
Mary, Church of the
    Assumption of   243
Mary, Church of the Virgin
    543
Maxentius, Basilica of   394
Mensa Christi   299
of the Milk Grotto   356
of the Multiplication   311
Saint Nathanael   301
of the Nativity   354-356
Saint Nicholas   552
Notre Dame de Sion Convent de
    l'Ecce Homo (Church of the
    Sisters of Zion)   228
Our Lady of Lebanon, Chapel of
    482
Our Lady of the Spasm   229
Our Lady of Tortosa, Cathedral
    of   498
of Our Lady the Angel Built   26
of the Pater Noster   241
Patriarchal, Patrikhane Kilisesi
    513
Saint Paul Outside the Walls,
    Basilica of   399, 420
Saint Paul's Window and
    Cathedral   492-493
Saint Peter, Basilica of
    401-408, 418
of Saints Peter and Paul   24
Saint Peter in Chains   396-397,
    419
Saint Peter's Church (Chapel of
    the Primacy)   311
Saint Peter's in Gallicantu   252

Churches, *etc., continued*
  of San Pietro in Montorio 417, 422
  of San Pietro in Vincoli, 396-397, 419
  of Santa Prassede 417, 422
  the Primacy, Chapel of 311
  of Santa Pudenziana, 417, 421-422
  of Santi Quattro Coronati 417, 421
  Redeemer's Church, Lutheran 234
  of the Rock 311
  Rome, Churches of 418-423
  of Santa Sabina 417, 423
  the Sacred Heart, Basilica of 241
  Sancta Sanctorum 419
  Scala Santa 397, 418-419
  Saint Sebastian, Basilica of 398
  of San Sebastiano 417, 421
  Saint Sergius and Bachus Church 519
  Saint Sergius's Coptic Church (Abu Serga) 52
  San Severo, Chapel of 427
  Siena Cathedral 435
  Saint Simeon Stylite, Cathedral of 501
  of the Sisters of Zion 228-229
  Sistine Chapel 414-417
  Saint Sophia 229, 519-520
  Saint Spyridon 148
  Stella Maris, Carmelite Church of 334
  of Saint Stephen 243
  Stylite, Saint Simeon, Cathedral of 501
  Syrian Aramean 496
  Saint Theodore, Byzantine Church of 141
  Saint Theodorius's 369
  Tortosa, Cathedral of Our Lady of 498
  the Transfiguration, Basilica of 301
  the Transfiguration, Byzantine Church of 116
  of Santa Trinità dei Monti 411, 417, 422
  Tsipori Basilica 300
  Viaduct Church 447
  of the Virgin Mary 543
  the Virgin of the Cave, Chapel of 135
  the Visitation, Church of 266
Churches of Rome 418-423
Çinili Kösk 522

Circus Maximus 390
Citadels. *See* Forts
Citium 25-26
City Hall, Tel Aviv 326
City of David 214-268
City of Peace 214-268
Claros 538
Claudian Aqueduct 399
Cleobis and Biton 145
Cnidus 552
Cnossos (Knossos) 162
Codex Hammurabi 202-203
Codex Sinaiticus 116
Codex Vaticanus 412
Coenaculum 251
Colleges. *See* Universities
Colophon 558
Colossae 556
Colosseum 391
Colossians 381
Colossus 161
Column of Gabriel 299
Column of the Flagellation 233
Command Square 257
Conium 553-554
Constantia 381, 390
Constantine 381, 390-391
Constantine, Arch of 390-391
Constantine, Baptism of 413
Constantine, Burnt Column of 516
Constantine, Statue of 418
Constantine, Victory of 412
Constantine's Donation of Rome to Pope Sylvester 412
Constantinople 508-525
Constitution Square 141
Convents. *See* Monasteries
Copts' Quarter 52
Corinth 153-155
Corinth Canal 155-158
Cornelius, baptized in Caesarea 332
Crenides 159
Cross of Jesus 230-231
Cross of Jesus, portion of 421
Crypts. *See* Tombs
Ctesiphon 185
Cukur Bostan 512, 514
Cupid (Love) and Psyche 424
Curia 392
Curium 27
Cuth, Cuthah 185
Cyprus 15-30
Cyrus Cylinder 186, 214

Daburiyya 301
Dafni 158
Dagon Grain Silo 333

Dahshur 69-70
Dalmanutha 310
Damascus 487-493
Damascus Document 493
Damascus, North of 495-501
Damascus, Northeast of 501-504
Damascus, South of 494-495
Damiya 446
Dan 321
Dara'a 494
David 423-431
David and His Sling 410
David, City of 214-268
David's Tower 234
Dead Sea 277
Dead Sea Scrolls 277-279
Degania 308
Deir el-Bahri 92-94
Deir Mawas 73-75
della Signoria, Piazza 431
delle Terme 397
Delphi, Delfi 141-147
Demeter, Precinct of 529
Dendera 75
Denizli 535-536
Deraya 494
Derbe 553
Derekh Hayam 295
Desert Road 455
Dhahab 119
Dhiban, Dibon, Dibon-gad
    453-454
Didyma 551
Dimashq 487-493
Dimonah, Dimona 367
Diocaesarea 300
Diocletian, Baths of 397, 424
Diolkos 157-158
Dionisius 495
Dionysius, Ear of 430
Dioramas in the Hechal Shlomo
    259
Diospolis 341-342
Diwaniyah 194-195
Dog River Valley 481
Dolmabahçe 523
Dome of Ascension 219
Dome of the Chain 222
Dome of the Rock 218-222
Dor, Dora 332
Dothan, Dothian 293
Dovrat 301
Drusus, Arch of 397
Dur-Kurigalzu 172-173
Dur-Sharrukin 183-184
Dura 365
Dura-Europos 503-504
Dwelling Quarters, Ur 199
Dying Gaul 424, 528

East of Beirut 470-475
East of the Mount of Olives
    269-289
East of the Old City (Jerusalem)
    236-249
Ecbatana 203
Ecce Homo Arch 228
Eden, Garden of 202
Edfu 102
Edict of Milan 409
Edom 440-441
Edomite acropolis 458
Edrei 494
Eglon 348-349
Egypt 31-123
Egypt, Upper 73-101
Egyptian Stela, Megiddo 295
Eilat 119, 370-372
Ein-Boker 373
Ein-Dirwa 360
Ein-Dor 302
Ein Fashkha 279
Ein Gedi 374-377
Ein Gev 325
Ein Karem 265-266
Ein Sukhna 110
Ein-Zevan 324
Ein Zohar 373
Ekdippa 336
Ekron, Eqron 340
El Bab (Mirza Ali Muhammed)
    334
El Barid 460
El-Deir 458-459
El Kahera 49-61
El Kas Fountain 223
El Matariya 61-62
El Muweilah 120-122
El Shatt 112
El Thamad 119
El Qusaima 120-122
Elah, Valley of 344
Elam 202-203
Elath, Elat 370-372
Elephantine Papyri 105-106
Eleusinian Mysteries 158
Eleusis 158
Eleutheropolis 344
Elim 113
Elijah, Cave of 297, 334
Elijah, Statue of 297
Elisha, birthplace of
    (Abel-Meholah) 292-293
Elisha's Fountain 273
Elon-beth-hanam 339
Emek, the 295
Emek Hefer 329
Emeq Ayyalen 339
Emeq Refaim 353

Emesa   496
Emmaus   337, 339
En Eglaim   279
En-Gannim   293
En-Gedi   374-377
Endor   302
Engomi, Enkomi   19
E-Nun-Mah   197
Ephraim   284
Ephrathah, Ephrath   354-358
Ephesians   381
Ephesus   539-547
Ephron   284
Epic of the Creation   180
Epic of the Flood   180
Epictetus   535
Epidaurus   148-150
Epiphania   496
Er Ram   282
Erech, Erekh   195
Eridu   200-202
Esagila Tablet   192
Esdud   352
Eshcol, Valley of   361
Eshed Kinnrot   311
Eshkol   361
Eshnunna, code of   172
Eshtaol   342
Eshtemoa, Eshtamoah   365
Eshwa   342
Eski-Hissar, Laodicea   536
Esna   102
Esquiline Venus   424
Eti Baba   538
Etruscan Wolf   423
Eurydiceia   537-538
Eutychus   527
Exhibition Grounds   49
Expedition Gardens, Tel Aviv   327
Ezion-Geber   119, 370-372
Ez-Zib   336

Famagusta   23-24
Fara   195
Farnese Bull   426
Faustina, Baths of   550
Feiran Oasis   114
Field of Blood   248
Field of the Shepherds   356
Fiesole   433
Fiq   325
Florence, Firenze   431-433
Flour Cave   372
Fontana del Tritone   411
Fornarina   411-425
Foro Italico   409
Foro Mussolini   409
Forts, Fortresses, Citadels
   Accho, Citadel of   335

Acronauplia   148
of Ajalon   449
Aleppo, Citadel of   501
Amman Citadel   443
Ankara Citadel   555
of Argos   148
of Babylon   52
Belvoir   305
Bokek   373
Bourtzi   148
Burj es-Sultan Crusader fortress   335
Caesarea Mazaca Citadel   555
of Cecilia Metella   398
Chateau de Pelerin   332
Central Fortress (Ancient Museum), Babylon   191
Citadel, Cairo   52
Citadel, Old Jerusalem   234
Crac de Montreal Citadel   455
Crusader and Turkish fortress, Tiberias   309
Crusader fortress, Caesarea   330
of Dura-Europos   503-504
Edomite   458
El Nakhl   120
European   525
of Fakhr ed-Din al Maani   502
Forty Columns   28
Herodion   358-359
Herod's great fortress   228
Judin, Crusader fort   336
Kait Bey   72
Kassile, Tell   327
Kochav Hayarden   305
of Larnaca   26
Latrun   339-340
Machaerus   453
Masada   373-374
Northern   191
Palamidi   148
Qal'at el Nakhl   119-120
El Qalaa, Citadel   490
Qasila, Tell   327
Ras el Gindi   120
Salkhad   495
Sant'Angelo   408-409, 424
Sea, Castle of the   476
Seven Towers   509
Shaubak   456
Shizar, Arab fort of   496
of Simeon   501
of Tartous   498
Tower of Lions   484
Yedikule   509
Zohar, Citadel of   373
Forums
   of Augustus, Rome   387

Forums, *continued*
  of Caesar, Julius, Rome 387
  Granite, Salamis 23
  at Jerash 447
  Marble, Salamis 23
  of Nerva, Rome 387
  Palmyra 502
  Roman, Amman 443
  Roman, Rome 391-395
  Roman, Samaria 291
  Stone 23
  of Trajan, Rome 386
Fountain of Naiads 397
Fountain of Neptune 401
Fountain of the Moor 401
Fountain of the Rivers 400-401
Fountain of the Virgin 245
Fustât, Al- 52

Gadara, Gader 325, 450
Gadarenes, country of the 325
Gader 325
Galata 523-525
Galata Bridge (Kopru) 523
Galata Tower, Galata Kulesi 523
Galilee 293-294
Galilee Man 315
Galileo 420, 431, 433
Galleries. *See* Museums
Gan Ha Shelosha 304-305
Garibaldi, Giuseppe, monument of
    401
Gasur 184
Gates
  Al Wastani 172
  Bab el Amoud 254
  Bab el Khalil 234
  Bab el Maghariba 225
  Bab el Nasr 254
  Bab en Nabi Daoud 249
  Bab Sittna Miriam 226
  Cleopatra 556
  Damascus 254
  of David the prophet 249
  Dung 225
  Eastern 224
  of Flowers 256
  Gates of Paradise 431
  Golden, Istanbul 512
  Golden, Jerusalem 224
  Herod's 256
  Hulda 225
  Ishtar 189-191
  Ishtar Gate Reconstruction 189
  Jaffa 234-235
  Jericho 218
  Lion, Mycenae 151
  Lion's, Jerusalem 225-226
  of the Maghrebians 225

  Mandelbaum 257
  Saint Mary's 226
  of Mercy 224
  Moors 225
  Nablus 254
  New 254
  of Paradise, Gates 431
  Saint Paul's 399
  Saint Sebastian 397
  San Sebastiano, Porta 397
  Shechem 254
  Sheep 218
  South Gate, Baghdad 171
  Saint Stephen's 226
  of the Sultan 254
  of the Tribes 218, 226
  Yaldizh Kapi 512
  Zion 249
Gath, Gat 348
Gath-Hepher 300
Gaugamela 184
Gaza 350-351
Geba 283
Gebal 482-483
Gederah, Gedera 352
Gehenna 248
Gelemish 552
Gennesaret, Plain of 311
Georgeospolis 342
Gerar 350
Gerasa 447-449
Gergesa 325
Gethsemane 243
Gezer 340
Gezer Calendar 340, 522
Ghezzeh 350-351
Ghouta Oasis 487
Gianicolo, Piazzale del 401
Gibbethon 341
Gibeah, Gibeath 279-281
Gibelin 344
Gibeon 281-282
Giblet 482-483
Gidona 304
Gihon Spring 245-246
Gilead 438-440
Gilgal 275, 285
**Gilgamesh Epic of the Creation
    and the Flood** 180
Ginnosar 311
Giotto's Campanile 431
Giuseppe Mazzini, Piazza 409
Giza 51, 63-65
Gokyazi 552
Golan 324
Golan Heights 324
Golden Helmet 199
Golden Horn 509

Golgotha, Catholic version 230-233
Golgotha, Protestant version 256
Goliath 344
Gomorrah 372
Good Samaritan Inn 269-271
Gordon's Calvary 256
Goreme 556
Goshen 62
Gournah, Sheikh Abd el- 90-92
Government Offices, Nicosia 19
Gozan 504
Grain Silos, Megiddo 295
Grand Staircase 225
Granite quarries, Aswan 105
Graves. *See* Tombs
Great Court of Sacrifice 474
Greece 124-162
Greece, Northern 159-160
Greek Islands of the Aegean 160-162
Greek Patriarchate 234, 252
Grotto of the Annunciation 299
Grotto Garden 49
Grotto of Gethsemane 243
Grotto of Saint James 244
Grotto of the Nativity 356
Grotto of the Shepherds 356
Grotto of the Virgin's Birth 226
Gubla 482-483
Gülhane Park 522
Gush Halav 317
Gymnasium, Salamis 23

Ha Gosherim Kibbutz 321
Há Ogen Kibbutz 329
Ha Tannur Waterfall 321
Habiru 503
Hadera 330
Hadhr, Al 175-176
Hadrian's Arch 140
Haifa 332-333
Hala Sultan, Tekke (shrine of) 26
Haleb 500
Halhul 360
Halicarnassus 551
Hama, Hamah, Hamath 496
Hamadan 203
Hamma 452
Hamma, El, El Himmeh 450
Hammam Faruon 113
Hammam Musa 118
Hammath, Hammat, Hammata 308
Hammath Geder, Jordan 450
Hammet Geder, Israel 325
Hammurabi, Code of 185, 202-203
Handle of a Mirror or Scepter, Hazor 318

Hanging Gardens 190
Hanging Room, English 335
Haram es-Sharif 217-218
Haran, Harran 559-560
Harissa 481
Harmhab, Colonnade of 78
Hatra 175-176
Hattushash 555
Hawara 113
Hazazon-tamar 374-377
Hazor Hamatara 256
Hazor, Hatzor 317-320
Hebrews 381
Hebron 361-363
Hechal Shlomo 259
Hedijaz Square 489
Heirapolis 534-535
Helena, Pool of Saint 341
Heletz oil field 351
Heliopolis, Egypt 61-62
Heliopolis, Lebanon 470-475
Heptapegon 311
Hera, Sanctuary of 160
Heraclitus 541
Herculaneum 427
Hermes 147
Herod Agrippa I, died in Caesarea 330
Herod the Great
    born in Ashkelon 351
    had home in Caesarea 330
    lived at Masada 373
Herodotus 551
Herzliya 329
Heshbon, Hesban 451
Hessy el Khattatin 114
Hexagonal Court 472
Hexagonal Pools 316
Hezekiah, Pool of 234
Hezekiah's Tunnel 246-248
Hilla 193
Hillah, Al 185
Hillah Rest House 189
Hills. *See* Mountains
Hims 496
Hinnom, Valley of 246-248
Hippodrome, Beirut 470
Hippodrome, Istanbul 516
Hippos 325
Hisarlik 526-527
Hisban 451
Holon 352
Holy City 214-268
Holy Grail 331
Homer 424, 537
Homs 496
Honaz 536-537
Horns of Hittin 310
Hospitals
    Augusta Victoria 236-237

Hospitals, *continued*
  Baptist   449
  General, Nicosia   19
  Hadassah   266
  Hadassah, former   236
  Turkish Military   522
Hula (Hulah) area   320
Hürriyet Meydani   515
Hurshat Tal   321

Ibleam   293
Iconium   553-554
Iliad   526
Immaculate Conception, Column
  of the   411
Imwas   339
Independence Park, Jerusalem
  259
Independence Square, Istanbul
  515
Inscription Rock   481
Iran   202-204
Iraq   163-204
Irbid   450
Irene, Mint of Saint   522
Isin (Ishan)   195
Islands
  the Aegean, Greek Islands of
    16, 160-162
  Arwad (Aradus)   498
  Botanical   107
  Clauda (Cauda)   162
  Coos, Cos   161
  of the Coral   119
  Crete   162
  Dilos, Delos   161
  El Gezira   105-106
  Elephantine   105-106
  Gavdos   162
  Gezira   49
  Kitchener's   107
  Kos   161
  Mitylene, Mytilini, Mytilene,
    Mitilini   160
  Palmosa   160
  Patmos   160
  of Philae   105
  Rhodes, Rodos   161-162
  Roda   51
  Samos   160
  Tiran   118-119
  Yi Haalmogim   119
Ismailia, Ismaileya   110
Israel   205-377
Israel Stela of Merneptah   58, 89
Istakhar   203-204
Istanbul   506-525
Istanbul, New   523-525
Istanbul, Old   509-523

Isthmia   158
Istiklâl Caddesi   523
Italy   378-435
Izmir   537-538

Jaba   283
Jabesh-Gilead   449-450
Jabneh   352-353
Jaffa   325-326
Al Jamal   450
Jamnia   353
Jarash   447-449
Jason's Cave   259
Jebeil   482
Jebus   214-268
Jedur   325
Jehoiakin Tablets   214
Jehoshaphat, Valley of   243-244
Jehu Stela   176
Jeita, Grotto of   482
Jenin   293
Jerablus   559
Jerash   447-449
Jeremiah, birthplace of (Anata)
  279
Jeremiah's Grotto   256
Jericho   271-273
Jerome   356, 416, 558
Jerusalem   214-268
Jerusalem Cave   260, 347-348
Jerusalem, model of ancient   267
Jerusalem, Near the Center of the
  New City   258-259
Jerusalem, New   258-268
Jerusalem, New, Outlying Areas
  259-268
Jerusalem, Old   217-236
Jerusalem, South of   353-377
Jerusalem Talmud   309
Jerusalem to Nablus (Shechem),
  North from   279-289
Jerusalem, West and Southwest of
  337-353
Jerwan   183-184
Jewish Quarter   225
Jewish synagogues, Masada   374
Jezreel   302
Jib, el-   281-282
Jiljiliya   285
Jimal, Um el   450
Jish   317
Job, Cave of   311
John the Baptist, birthplace of (Ein
  Karem)   266
John the Baptist's head   239, 291
Joktheel   456-460
Jolan   324
Jonah, birthplace of (Gath-Hepher)
  300

Joppa 325-326
Jordan 436-462
Joseph's Workshop 299
Josephus, Flavius, home of (Kafr Yasif) 335
Jotapata 334
Julian, Column of 555

Kabul 334
Kadesh 320, 496
Kadesh Naphtali 320
Kadikoy 506-509, 526
Kafr Yasif 335
Kaiser's Fountain 516-517
Kale 552
Kalhu 176-179
Kanawat, Kanatha 495
Kanish 555-556
Karak, Al Karak 455
Karamless 184
Karbala 185
Kargamis 559
Karnak 78-86
Kato-Paphos (Lower Paphos) 28
Kavalla 159-160
Kayseri 555-556
Keats 411
Kebres 22-23
Kedesh 320
Kefar-Kana, Kafr Kannā 300-301
Kefar Nahum 311-312
Kefar Vitkin 329
Kefar-Zekharia 343
Kennedy Memorial 266-267
Kerak 455
Kerem Yavne 352-353
Keret Legend 499
Kerti Huyuk 553
Khabur (Habor) River Area 504
Khalde 475
El Khalil 361-364
Khan-el-Franj 476
Khan el Umdan caravansary 335
Khan Hathrour 269-271
Khan Yunis 350
Al Khazneh 457
Khirbet Asqalan 351-352
Khirbet Beit Lei 347-348
Khirbet Belame 293
Khirbet Egla 348-349
Khirbet el-Mefjer 275
Khirbet el-Muqanna 340
Khirbet et Tannur 455
Khirbet et-Tubeiqah 360
Khirbet Qana 300-301
Khirbet Timna, Khirbet Tibneh 343
Khirbet Zuheilikah 349
Khirokitia 26-27

Khnum (sacred ram), mummy of 105
Khorsabad 183-184
Khorsabad Annals 183-184
Khorsabad Pavement Inscription 183-184
Kibbutz (defined) 308
Kibbutz Allonim 298
Kibbutz Degania 308
Kibbutz Ha Gosherim 321
Kidron Valley 243-244, 246
Kidron Valley Area 243-249
Kifl, Al 193
Kikar, Dizengoff 326
King Hussein Sports City 445
Kings' Garden 245
Kings' Highway 455-456
Kings, Valley of the, Jerusalem 244
Kings, Valley of the, Luxor 94-101
Kinneret Pumping Station 311
Kir-Haresseth 455
Kiriathaim 446
Kiriya 263
Kirjath-Arba, Kiriath-Arba 361-364
Kirjath-Jearim, Kiriyat-Yearim 337
Kirkuk 184
Kiryat-Natsrat 298-300
Kiryat Shmona 320
Kish 194
Kiti 26
Kition 25-26
Kittim (Cyprus) 15-30
Kittim (Larnaca) 25-26
Kiz Kulesi 526
Kizil Avlu 529
Kiztasi 512
Knesset 260
Kom Ombo 102
Konya 553-554
Korazin, Khorazin, Kerazeh 314-315
Kotel Hama'aravi 224-225
Kouklia 28-29
Kouros 140
Krak des Chevaliers 497-498
Ktima 28-29
Kuds esh-Sherif, el- 214-268
Kufah, Al 194
Kulonieh 337
Kultepe 555-556
Kuneitra, El Kuneitra 324
Kypros 15-30
Kyrenia 30

La Fornarina 411
La Liche 498-499

Lachish, Lakhish 181, 346-347
Lachish Letters 343, 346-347
Laish 321
Lakes
of Bafa 549
Hula 320
Larnaca Salt 26
of Lot 277
Laodicea 535-536
Larnaca 25-26
Last Judgment 414-416
Latakia 498-499
Lateran Baptistry 418-419
Latin Vulgate Bible 356
Latrun 339
Leander's Tower 526
Leaning Tower, Mosul 183
Leaning Tower of Pisa 433
Lebanon 463-484
Ledra 18-19
Lehi 349
Leshem 321
Libraries
Ashurbanipal, Royal Library of 179-180
at Saint Catherine's Monastery 116-117
of Celsus 545
Hadrian's 138-140
National, Athens 141
National, Beirut 467
National, Cairo 54
Pergamene 528
Sultan's 18
Vatican 412
Wix Central 353
Lighthouse, Beirut 467
Limassol 27
Lion of Babylon 191
Lithostrotos 228
Lod 341-342
Loggia dei Lanzi 431
Lohamei-Hagetaot Kibbutz 335-336
Lot's Wife 372
Lotus-Capital Column 79
Lubban Shargiya 285
Luxor 76
Luxor, Modern 76-78
Luxor to Aswan 102
Luz 283
Lycopolis 75
Lydda 341-342
Lydia 532-534
Lystra 553

Maale Adummim 269-271
Ma'an 456
Ma'arat an Nu'man 497

Maccabees 341
Machaerus 453
Machpelah, Cave of 361
Madaba, Madeba 452-453
Magdala, Magadan 310
Mary Magdalene, home of (Magdala) 310
Magharah 113
Mahanaim 446-447
Maimonides 309
Makaria 15-30
Makhtesh-Ramon 369
Makhwar 453
Maloula 495-496
Malta 430
Mambre 361
Mamertine Prison 396
Mamilla Pool 259
Mamre, Oak of 361
Manger at Bethlehem, boards from 420
Mangia Tower 435
Maon 365
Maon, Wilderness of 365
Marah 112
Marble Tower 509
Marcian, Column of 512
Mareshah 344-346
Mari 502-503
Mari Tablets 499, 502-503
Mari Ziggurat 503
Marissa, Marasha 344-346
Marj Elid 284-285
Markets, Bazaars, Souks (Souqs)
Agora (marketplace), Athens 138
Aladdin Cave Market 172
Bedestan 18
at Beersheba 366
Bethlehem Market 356
Buyuk Kapali Carsi Bazaar 515
Carmel Market 326
Copper Bazaar 172
Egyptian Bazaar 523
Flea Market, Rome 390
Flea Market, Tel Aviv 327
Grand Covered Bazaar 515
Jerusalem Bazaars 235
Khan Khalily Bazaar 53
Mahane Yehuda 259
Marketplace, Izmir 538
Misir Çarşisi Bazaar 523
Oriental bazaars, Beirut 469
Secondhand Bazaar 516
Souq el Atarin 500
Souq el Khouja 490
Souq Hamidiyeh 490
Spice Bazaar 523
Women's Market 18

Marmaria, Sanctuary of 147
Marsiyen Sutunu 512
Martef Hashoa 252
Mary, Column of 299
Mary Gurguis, church 52
Mary, House of the Virgin
    547-548
Mary, Martha, and Lazarus, home
    of (Bethany) 269
Mary's Fountain, Ein Karem 266
Masaada, Golan Heights 322
Masada 373-374
Mashhad 300
Masr 49-61
Mastabas. *See* Tombs
Mausoleums. *See* Tombs
Mausolus 551
Mauta 455
Mawsil, Al 183
Maxentius, Circus of 398
Mayosa 23-24
Mazar 455
Mazor 342
Mea Shearim 257-258
Medeba 452-453
Megara 158
Megiddo 295-297
Mei-merom 320
Meiron, Meron 317
**Mekal, Lord of Beth-Shean, stela
    to** 305
Mekawer 453
Melchizedek, Cave of 302
Melita 430
Memnon, Colossi of 87
Memphis 66
Menesterli Garden 51
Menorah 260
Merathaim 202
Meribah 456
Merj es-Sunbul 301
Merj Ibn Amir 295
Merkes, Mound of 191
Merkhah Port 113
Merneptah, Israel Stela of 58, 59
Merom-Golan 324
Meryem Ana 547-548
Mesha Stone 453-454
Mesopotamia 166
Messiah's Chair 317
Metsada 373-374
Metulla 321
Mevlevi Dervishes, Tekke of the
    18
Mevo Hamma 325
At Meydani 516
Michelangelo 414, 431
Michelangelo's Home 433
Michmash, Mukhmas 283

Midian 441
Mifale Sdom Salt Works 372
Migdal 310
Migdal Shalom 326
Milesians 549
Miletus 548-551
Milvian Bridge 409
Minaret in Spiral 175
Minerva, Obelisk of 400
Minya 311
Mishna 298, 309, 353
Mistra 147
Mit-Rahina 66
Mitla Pass 120
Mitroon 138
Mitspé-Ramon 369
Mizpah, Mizpeh 281
Mizraim (Egypt) 31-123
Moab 440
Moabite Stone 453
Modin, Modim 341
Monasteries, Abbeys, Convents
    Anaya Monastery 483
    Saint Anthony's Monastery 110
    Aqua-Bella Monastery 337
    the Ark, Monastery of 337
    the Apostle Barnabas,
        Monastery of 21-22
    Bektashi Monastery 53
    Bellapais Abbey 30
    Benedictine Monastery, Tabgha
        311
    Byzantine Monastery, Avdat
        369
    Carmelite Convent, Jerusalem
        241
    Carmelite Monastery, Haifa
        297, 333-334
    Saint Catherine's Monastery,
        Sinai 115-117
    Saint Charalambos, Monastery
        of 230
    Conclusus, Hortus, Monastery
        of 360
    Coptic Monastery, Jerusalem
        230
    the Cross, Monastery of 259
    El Deir, Monastery of 458-460
    Deir el Shayeb, Coptic
        Monastery of 85
    Deir Sama'an Monastery 501
    the Dervishes, Monastery of
        484
    Saint Elijah, Carmelite
        Monastery of 297
    the Forty Days, Greek
        Monastery of 273
    Franciscan Monastery,
        Capernaum 312

Monasteries, *etc., continued*
Saint George, Greek Monastery
of 271
Greek Orthodox Monastery,
Jerusalem 229
Saint John, Monastery of 160
Kykko Monastery 29-30
Mar Elias Monastery 354
Mar Saba Monastery 358
Monte Cassino, Abbey of
425-426
Mountain of the Cross,
monastery 26
Notre Dame de France
Monastery 254
Saint Oniprius, Greek Convent
of 248
Our Lady of the Ark of the
Covenant, monastery 337
Saint Paul's Monastery 110
Saint Peter, Monastery of 326
Qalaat Seman Monastery 501
Russian Monastery 361
Saint Samaan's Monastery 501
Saint Sarkis, Convent of 496
Sednaya, Monastery of 495
Saint Simeon, Coptic Monastery
of 107
Saint Simeon Stylite, Monastery
of 501
Stavrovouni, Monastery of 26
Saint Takla, Monastery of
495-496
Terra Sancta Convent 299-300
Monte Cassino 425
Montfort 336
Montreal 455-456
Monument of the Republic 523
Mosaics at Kato-Paphos 29
Moses 419
Moshav, Nahalal 298
Moslem Quarter 236
Mosques
of Abraham 361-363
of Sultan Ahmet I 517-518
Aksa 222-223
Al-Azhar 53
Al Hussein 53
of Sultan Al-Nasir 52
Alabaster 52, 53
of Almahidi 175
of Amr 52
Bahramiye 500
Bayazit 515
Blue 517-518
of the Conqueror 512
Djami Mosque 183
Dome of the Rock 218-222,
237

Fatih Mehmet (Fatih) 512
of Fatima 494
Fethiye 513
Friday's 175
Grand, Beirut 467-469
Grand, Tripoli 484
Great, Aleppo 500-501
Great, Baalbek 474-475
Great, Hamath 496
Great, Homs 496
Great, Mosul 183
Great, Ramla 341
Great, Sidon 476
Guyushi 53
Sultan Hassan 52
of El Hayyat 497
Ibn Tulun 52
of Imrahor 512
of Sultan Inal 53
of El Jezaar 335
Kaariye 514
Kadhimain 172
of Khanqa 234
Khora, Mosaic Mosque of 514
Khosrafiye 501
Kücük Ayasofya 519
of Lala Mustafa Pasha 24
Leaning Tower, Mosul 183
Mehmet Pasha 519
of Mihrimah 514
Minaret in Spiral 175
Mohammed Ali 53
Municipal, Beersheba 366
of Omar 234
Omar, Umayyad Mosque of
494
Osman's, Osmaniye Camii 516
Pigeon 515
Piyalepasa 525
Prince's 514
Queen Mother's 523
Rowdha al Askaria 175
of Rüstem Pasha, Rüstempasa
523
Sehzade 514
of Sultan Selim 512
Selimiye 18
of Sokollu Mehmet Pasha 519
of Saint Sophia 519
of Little Saint Sophia 519
Spring of the Vineyard (Ein
Karem) 266
of Suleiman 514-515
Taylan 484
Tile 523
El-Umari 467-469
Umayyad 490-491
Women's 361
Yeni 523

Mosul   183
Motsa   337
Mountain Road   455-456
Mountains, Mounts, Hills
    of Aaron   460
    Ammunition Hill   267
    Ararat   560
    of Beatitudes   314
    Camlica Hill   525
    Carmel   297
    Cassino, Monte   425-426
    of Corruption   241
    Ebal   289
    Eslamiyeh, Jebel   289
    of Evil Counsel   245-246,
        248-249
    Fakua, Jebel   304
    Gerizim   287-289
    Gilboa   304
    el Halal, Jebel   118
    Harun, Jebel   460
    Hatsofim, Har   236
    Hermon   324, 470, 494
    Herzl   265
    Hor   121, 370, 460, 470
    Horeb   117-118
    Hussein, Jebel   443
    Janiculum Hill   401
    Katherina, Jebel   117-118
    Little Hermon   302
    Lycabettus   141
    Mageddon, Har   297
    Makhmal   484
    Mar Elyas, Jebel   297
    Mars' Hill   135
    Memorial   265
    Moreh, Hill of   302
    Moriah   217-218
    of Moses   117
    Murex, Hill of   476
    Musa, Jebel   117
    the Muses, Hill of   137
    Nebo   451
    of Offense   241, 245-246
    of Olives   237-243, 246
    Ophel, Hill   246-248
    Pagus Hill   538
    Panayir Dagi   540
    Parnassus   141
    Philopappus Hill   137
    Pincio   410
    Pion   540
    Pisgah   451
    Pnyx Hill   135-136
    of Precipitation   299
    Qassiom   487
    Ras Sufsafeh   117
    of Scandal   245-246
    Scopus   236

    Senir   324, 494
    Serbal   114
    esh-Sheikh, Jebel-   324, 470,
        494
    Sinai   117-118, 121
    Sirion   324, 470, 494
    Tabor   301-302
    Tahuna, Jebel el   114
    Tannur, Jebel   455
    Tchamlijah Hill   525
    Temple Hill   249
    of Temptation   273
    Tor, Jebel et   288-289
    of Transfiguration   301-302,
        322, 324, 494
    et Tur   301-302
    Um el Biyara   458
    Vesuvius   427
    Zion   249
Mozah, Moza   337
Muhraka   297
Mukawir   453
Mukhaiyat   451
Muqattam Hills   53
Muqes   450
Murtana   552-553
Muristan   234
Musa al-Alami   274
Museums, Galleries
    Abin Palace Museum, Cairo   54
    Academy of Fine Arts, gallery,
        Florence   431
    Acropolis Museum, Athens
        135
    Agricultural Museum, Cairo
        49
    Agricultural Museum, Jerusalem
        263
    Aleppo Museum   501
    Alphabet Museum, Tel Aviv
        327
    Al Wastani Gate, museum,
        Baghdad   172
    Anderson Museum, Cairo   52
    Antiquities, Collections of,
        Vatican Museum   412
    Antiquities, Museum of, Tel
        Aviv   327
    Antiquities, Museum of,
        Tiberias   309
    Antioch Museum   558
    Archaeological Museum,
        Amman   443
    Archaeological Museum,
        Istanbul   522
    Archaeological Museum, Izmir
        523
    Archaeological Museum, Mosul
        183

Museums, *etc., continued*
Armenian Museum, Jerusalem
235
Askeri Müzesi, Istanbul
524-525
Atatürk Museum, Ankara   555
Atatürk Museum, Istanbul   525
Atatürk Museum, Izmir   538
Ayasofya Museum, Istanbul
519
Azem Palace, Folklore Museum,
Damascus   491
Babylon Museum   189
Barberini Gallery, Rome   411,
425
Beersheba Museum   366
Beit el Kretelia, Cairo   52
Beit Gordon Museum, Israel
308
Beit Shearim Museum, Israel
298
Beiteddine Palace and Folklore
Museum, Lebanon   475
Belediye Müzesi, Istanbul   512
Benaki Museum, Athens   140
Bet Hagana Museum, Tel Aviv
327
Beth-Shean Museum   305
Betzelel Museum of Art and
Folklore, Jerusalem   260
Biblical Museum, Jerusalem
226
Biga, Sala della, Rome   416
Borghese Museum and Gallery,
Rome   410
Borgia Apartment, gallery,
Rome   412
Bronfman Archaeological and
Antiquities Museum,
Jerusalem   260
Byzantine Art Museum, Istanbul
519, 521
Byzantine Icon Museum, Cairo
52
Byzantine Museum, Athens   140
Byzantine Museum, Nicosia   19
Canakkale, Museum of   527
Candelabri, Galleria dei, Rome
416
Capitoline Museum, Rome
387, 423-424
Capodimonte Museum, Naples
427
Castel Sant' Angelo Museum,
Rome   408-409, 424
Central Fortress (Ancient
Museum), Babylon   191
Central Museum for Fine Arts,
Alexandria   73

Chagall Artists' House, Haifa
333
Chiaramonte Museum, Rome
412
Christian Antiquities, Museum
of Rome   412
Christiano Museo, Rome   424
Citadel Museum of Heroism,
Accho   334
Clementine, Pius, Museum of,
Rome   412
Colonna Gallery, Rome   418,
425
Constantino, Sala di, Rome
412
Coptic Museum, Cairo   52
Corinth Museum   155
Cotton Museum, Cairo   49
Crete Museums   162
Cyprus Museum   19
Dagon Archaeological Museum,
Haifa   333
Delphi Museum   145
Deniz Müzesi, Istanbul
523-524
Dolmabahçe Museum, Istanbul
523-524
Doria Gallery, Rome   418, 425
Egyptian Museum, Cairo   54
Egyptian Museum, Rome   412
Elephantine Museum, Egypt
105
Eleusis, Museum of   158
Epidaurus Museum   150
Ethnological Museum, Haifa
333
Etruscan Museum, Rome   412
Farnesina Gallery, Rome   417,
424-425
Folk Art Museum, Nicosia   19
Folkloric Museum, Baghdad
172
Galleria Geografica, Rome
416
El Gawhara Palace Museum,
Cairo   53
Geological Museum, Cairo   54
Greco-Roman Museum,
Alexandria   73
Greek Handicrafts, Museum of,
Athens   140
Gulbenkian Museum, Baghdad
172
the Hagana Underground
Movement, Museum of, Tel
Hai   320
Hall of Heroism, Jerusalem
258
Hazor Museum, Israel   318

Museums, *etc., continued*
Hechal Shlomo, Jerusalem   259
Herzl Museum, Jerusalem   265
the History of Tel Aviv,
  Museum of   326
Hittite Archaeological Museum,
  Ankara   555
the Holocaust, Museum of,
  Lohamei-Hagetaot   335-336
Illegal Immigration and Naval
  Museum, Haifa   333
Immacolata, Sala dell', Rome
  416
Iraqi National Gallery, Baghdad
  172
Iraqi National Museum,
  Baghdad   171
Saint Irene Museum, Istanbul
  521
Islamic Art Museum, Jerusalem
  263
Islamic Art, Museum of, Cairo
  52-54
Islamic Museum, Baghdad   172
Islamic Museum, Jerusalem
  222
Israel Company for Fairs and
  Exhibitions, museum, Tel
  Aviv   327
Israel Export Institute, museum,
  Tel Aviv   327
Jabotinsky Museum, Tel Aviv
  327
Japanese Art Museum, Haifa
  333
Saint John Museum, Accho
  335
Joppa Museum   326
Kaariye Museum, Istanbul   514
Kailani Museum, Baghdad   172
Kayseri Museum, Caesarea
  Mazaca   556
Keats and Shelley Museum,
  Rome   411
Keramikos, Museum of, Athens
  140
Khan Mirjan, Baghdad   172
Konya, Museums of   554
Lapidaire, Musée, Nicosia   18
Lateran Museum, Rome   419,
  424
Madeba Museum, Jordan   452
Man and His Work Museum,
  Tel Aviv   327
Maritime Museum, Eilat   371
Maritime Museum, Haifa   333
Military Museum, Cairo   53
Military Museum, Istanbul
  524-525

Mosaic Museum, Mozayik
  Müzesi, Istanbul   518
Mukhtar Museum, Cairo   49
Municipal Museum, Istanbul
  512
Municipal Museum of Ancient
  and Modern Art, Haifa   333
Museum Center, Tel Aviv   327
Musical Instruments Museum,
  Jerusalem   263
Mustafa Kamel Museum, Cairo
  53
National Archaeological
  Museum, Athens   140
National Archaeological
  Museum, Naples   426
National Gallery of Antique
  Art, Rome   417, 425
National Gallery of Modern Art,
  Rome   425
National Historical Museum,
  Athens   140
National Museum, Beirut   469
National Museum, Damascus
  489
National Museum, Florence   433
National Museum, Jerusalem
  260-263
National Museum, Rome   424
National Museum of Modern
  Art, Rome   410
National Museum of the
  Thermae, Rome   397
National Picture Gallery,
  Athens   140
National Struggle Museum,
  Nicosia   19
Natural History Museum,
  Jerusalem   263
Naval Museum, Istanbul
  523-524
Niccolo V, Chapel of, Rome
  413
Oriental Arts, Museum of,
  Istanbul   522-523
Painting and Sculpture Museum,
  Istanbul   524
Palazzo dei Conservatori,
  Rome   386, 423-424
Palazzo Venezia Museum, Rome
  386
Palestine Archaeological
  Museum, Jerusalem   256
Palmyra Museum   502
Permanent Industrial Exhibition,
  Tel Aviv   327
Persepolis Museum   203
Pierides Private Museum,
  Larnaca   26

Museums, etc., continued
Pinacoteca (Gallery of Pictures), Rome 416, 423
Pitti Palace Gallery, Florence 431
Pius Clementine, Museum of, Rome 412
Polish Roman Catholic Biblical-Archaeological Museum, Jerusalem 229
Pompeii Museum 427
Porcelain Museum, Istanbul 522
Prehistory, Museum of, Haifa 333
Railway Museum, Cairo 49
Raphael, Loggias of, Rome 414
Raphael, Stanze of, gallery, Rome 412
Resim ve Hegkel Müzesi, Istanbul 524
the Risorgimento, Museum of, Rome 386
Rockefeller Museum, Jerusalem 256-257, 296
Russian Archaeological Museum, Jerusalem 242
Safed Museum 316
Sala della Biga, Rome 416
Sala dell'Immacolata, Rome 416
Sala Regia, Rome 416
Samos Museum 160
Sant'Angelo Castle, Rome 409
Saqqara, Museum at 68
Sark Eserleri Müzesi, Istanbul 523
Seven Towers Museum, Istanbul 509
Shalom Aleichem House, Tel Aviv 327
Shrine of the Book, Jerusalem 260-263, 277
the Sisters of Zion, Museum of, Jerusalem 229
Sistine Chapel, Rome 414-417
Saint Sophia Museum, Istanbul 519-520
Sparta Museum 147
Sursock Museum, Beirut 469
Suweida Museum 495
Tanzimat Museum, Istanbul 525
Tartous Museum 498
Taxation Museum, Jerusalem 263
Tchernichovsky Museum, Tel Aviv 327
Tel Aviv Museum 327
Terme, Museo delle, Rome 424
Terra Sancta Convent, museum, Nazareth 299-300
Topkapi Museum, Istanbul 522
Tortosa, Cathedral of Our Lady of, museum, Tartous 498
Turkish and Islamic Art Museum, Istanbul 514-515
Uffizi Palace, Florence 431
Vatican Museums 411-412, 425
Villa Albani, Museum of, Rome 418, 425
Villa Borghese Gallery, Rome 423
Villa Giulia, Museum of, Rome 418, 425
at Volterra 501
War Museum, Baghdad 172
Yad Mordechai Museum 351
Yad Veshem Memorial, Jerusalem 265
Yedikule Museum, Istanbul 509
Zappeion (Exhibition Hall), Athens 141
Museums and Art Galleries, Rome 423-425
Mycenae 150-153
Mycenaean exhibits 140
Myra 552

Nabk, Oasis of 119
Nablus 254, 286-288
Nabi Musa, Nebi Moussa 271
Nabonidus Chronicle 186
Nahal Kesloh 342
Nahalal 295, 298
Nahariya 336
Nain, Na'im Nēn 302
Nanna
court of 197
shrine of 197
Naples 426
Narmer, Palette of King 60
Natanya 329
Nathanael, home of (Cana) 301, 481
National Gardens 141
Navplion, Nauplia 148
Naxos (Naxia), Sphinx of 145
Nazareth 298-300
Nazirah, el- 298-300
Neapolis, Greece 159-160
Neapolis, Israel 286-288
Nebi Moussa 271
Nebi Samwil 281
Nebi Shu'eib 310

Necropolises. *See* Tombs
Nefertiti, bust of 74
Negba 352
Negev, Negeb 364
Nein 302
Nero's Aqueduct 390
Neronica, Neroneus 322
Nestor 557
Nettuno 425
Neve'-Ur 305
Neve'-Zohar 373
Nicene Creed 526
Nicholas, Saint 552
Nicodemus and Joseph of
    Arimathea, Saints, Hospice of
    341
Nicopolis 339
Nicosia 18-19
Nightingale, Florence 525
Nilometers, Elephantine Island
    105-106
Nilometers, Roda Island 51
Nimrud 176-179
Nimrud Prism IV 183
Nineveh, Ninua 179-183
Ningal Shrine Egipar (Gig-Par-Ku)
    of Bursin 197
Nippur, Nibru 194-195
Nitsana 689
No 76
Noah, altar of 288
Nob 279
Noph 66
North from Amman 445-450
North of Beirut 481-484
North of Damascus 495-501
North from Jerusalem to Nablus
    (Shechem) 279-289
North from Nablus (Shechem) to
    the Sea of Galilee 289-305
North of Rome 430-435
Northeast of Damascus 501-504
Northwest Rome, the Pantheon,
    Saint Peter's 399-411
Notium 538
Novum Ilium 526-527
Nuweiba 119
Nuzi 184
Nymphaeum, Amman 443
Nymphaeum, Ephesus 546
Nymphaeum, Jerash 447
Nymphaeum, Miletus 550
Nyssa 305

Oak of Mamre 361
Obelisks
    at Heliopolis 61
    at Luxor 78
    at El Matariya 61, 62
of Minerva 400
at On 61
Pharaoh's Needle 61
at the Piazza del Popolo
    410
of Queen Hatshepsut 84
of Sesostris 61
of Theodos Dikilitasi 517
of Theodosius 517
of Thutmose I 79
Odeums. *See* Theaters
Ohel Vizkor 265
Oil Press, Beit Shearim 298
Olivet 237-243, 246
Olympia 147
Omariye, El 228
Omphalos (navel) 145-147
On 61-62
Ono 342
Ophrah 286
Örme Sütun 517
Orvieto 430
Othello, Tower of 24

Padan-aram 559-560
Palaces
    Abbasid 172
    Abin 54
    of Ahab 291
    Al Qubba 49
    Archiepiscopal 19
    of Ashurnasirpal II 176-179
    Azem (Azim) 491
    Babel Mound and Summer
        Palace 191
    of Badr ud-Din Lulu (Qara
        Serai) 183-184
    Barberini 411, 425
    Bargello 433
    Basman 443
    Beiteddine Palace and Folklore
        Museum 475
    Bel-Shalti-Nanna, the high
        priestess, palace of 200
    Beylerbey 526
    of Blachernae 514
    Bokoleon veya Justinyen Sarayi,
        Bucoleon 518
    Buyuk Saray 518
    of Caiaphas 252
    Caliph Hisham's 274
    Caserta 426
    Çiraḡan Sarayi 524
    dei Conservatori 423
    of Constantine 518
    of Constantine VII 514
    Corsini 425
    of Cyrus the Great 203-204
    of Darius 203

Palaces, *continued*
  Dolmabahçe 524
  Doria-Pamphili 425
  El Gawhara 53
  Episcopal, Paphos 29
  Farnese 401
  di Giustizia 409
  Great 518
  Guards, Royal Palace and 141
  Hanging Gardens 190
  Herodion 358-359
  Herod's, Jerusalem 234
  Herod's, Masada 373-374
  Herod's Winter Palace 271
  Ibn Wardan 496
  of Justice 409
  Justinian's 518
  of the King 503
  Lateran, del Laterano 397,
    418-419
  Madama 400
  Montaza 73
  Mycenae 153
  Nebuchadnezzar, Southern
    Palace of 190
  of Omri 291
  Piccolomini 435
  Pitti 431
  Presidential 19
  Queen Mother 445
  del Quirnale 399
  Ras el Tin 72
  Royal 399
  Royal Palace and Guards 141
  Sargon's 183-184
  Selçuk 554
  Seraglio 522-523
  Senatorial 387
  Severus, Septimius 390
  Spada 401
  Sumerian palace, Kish 194
  Tchiragan 524
  of Tekfur 514
  Tiryns 148
  Uffizi 431
  of Ur-Nammu and Dungi
    (E-Hursag) 197
  Vatican 411
  Vecchio 431
  Venetian 24
  Venezia, Venice 386
  the Vestal Virgins, House of
    394
  of Xerxes 203
  Yildiz 525
Palatine 394-396
Palio delle Controde 435
Palmyra 501-502
Panathenaea 131, 138

Panaya Kapula 547-548
Paneas 322
Pantheon 399-400
Paphos 28-29
Paphos, Kato (Lower Paphos) 28
Paphos, New 28-30
Paran 114
Paran, Brook of 369
Parchment 528
Parliament Building, Jerusalem
  260
Parliament Building, Old, Greece
  141
Parsa 203-204
Pasargadae 204
Pasha Ahmad Jezaar Aqueduct
  335
Passageway, E-Dub-Lal-Mah 197
Passover Papyrus 106
Patara 552
Paternoster Row 199
Patriarchs, Bath of the 234
Paul 556
Paul's Pillar, Saint 28-29
Paul's Window, Saint 492-493
Pavement 228-229
Pavement Inscription, Khorsabad
  183-184
Pelops, Throne of 538
Peniel, Penuel 446
People, Square of the 410-411
Peratsim Canyon 372
Perga 552-553
Pergamum 527-531
Persai 203-204
Persephone, Rape of 410, 423
Persepolis 203-204
Perseus 431
Persia 202-204
Pessinus 554
Petah-Tikva, Petah Tiqwa 327
1 Peter 381
Peter in Chains Church, Saint
  396-397
Peter, home of (Capernaum) 354
Petra 370, 456-460
Petra tou Romiou 27-28
Pharaoh's Needle 61
Pharos (lighthouse) 72
Phasaelis, El Fasayil 274
Philadelphia, Jordan 442-445
Philadelphia, Turkey 534
Philemon 381
Philip, Spring of 360
Philippi 159
Philippians 381
Philippopolis 495
Philistia 350
Philoxenus, Cistern of 516

Phocas, Column of 392
Phoenicians 463
Piazza Navona 400-401
Pietà 404, 418
Pigeon Rock Grotto 467
Pinnacle of the Temple 224
Piraeus 141
Pisa 433
Pithom 63
Plain of Esdraelon 295
Plain of Jezreel 295
Pompeii 427
Pompey's Pillar 71
Ponte Cestio 390
Ponte Fabricio 390
Ponte Milvio 409
Ponte Umberto 409
Ponte Vecchio 431
Pontius Pilate, home of (Caesarea)
   330
Popolo, Piazza del 410
Port Said 109
Porta Ostia 399
Porta San Paolo 399
Portico Octavia 390
Poseidon 140
Poseidon, Sanctuary of 158
Positano 428
Potter's Field 248-249
Pottery Factory 86
Pozzuoli 426
Praetorium 228
President's Residence, Jerusalem
   259
Procession Street (Ai-ibur-shabu),
   Babylon 189-190
Procession Street, Petra 458
Propylaea, Athenian Acropolis
   130
Propylaea, Baalbek 471-475
Propylaea, Eleusis 158
Ptolemais 334
Puteoli 426
Pylons, Karnak 79
Pyramids
   Ammenemes III, Black Pyramid
      of 70
   Ammenemes II, White Pyramid
      of 70
   Bent Pyramid of King Snefru
      70
   Black Pyramid of Sesostris III
      70
   of Cestius, Gaius 399
   of Cheops (Khufu) 64
   of Chephren (Khafre) 64
   of Djoser (Zoser) 66
   of Giza 63-65, 103
   of Khafre (Chephren) 64

   of Khufu (Cheops) 64
   Meidum 70
   of Menkure (Mycerinus) 64
   Red 70
   Sesostris III, Black Pyramid of
      70
   Snefru, Bent Pyramid of 70
   Step Pyramid of Zoser 66
   of Unis (Onnos) 68
   of Zoser (Djoser) 66

Qadisha Gorge and Grotto 484
Qalaat el Mudiq 497
Qal'at Shergat 175
Qana, Lebanon 481
Qanawat 495
Qasr 172-174
Qiryat Shemona 320
Quarantana 273
Quarries, Limestone, Cairo 53
Queens, Valley of the 89
Qumran 277-279
Quneitra, Qnaitra 324
Qurna, Al 202

Rabbah, Rabba 455
Rabbah, Rabbath 442-445
Rachana 483
Rafa, Rafah 349
Rahah, Plain of 117
Railroad Terminal, Rome 397
Ram Caught in a Thicket 199
Ramad el-Khalin 361-364
Ramah, Arimathea 282
Ramah, Rama 317
Ramah, Ramathaim Zophim,
   Rentis 281
Ramallah 283
Ramat Rachel, Ramat-Rahel 267,
   353-354
Ramath-Lehi 349
Ramathaim Zophim, Ramah,
   Rentis 281
Ramban 309
Rameseum 89-90
Ramla 341
Ramot Naftali 320
Ramoth Gilead 445-446
Ramses 62
Ramses II
   Court of, Luxor 78
   Mortuary temple of 89-90
   Square of, Cairo 49
   Statues of, Luxor 78
   Statues of, Memphis 66
   Statue of, West Bank 89-90
Ramses III, Pavilion of 87
Ras el-Ain 480
Ras el-Kharrubeh 279

Ras en Naqb, Ras el Negeb   460
Ras Shamra   499-500
Ras Shamra Tablets   499-500
Ras Sudr   112
Ras Umm et-Tala   279
Rashid   73
Red Courtyard   529
Red Sea Area (West Side)
   109-110
Red Wall   408
Red Ziggurat of Ur   196-197
Refugee Camps, Amman   445
Refugee Camps, Jericho   271
Reggio   428
Regine Viarum   397-398
Rehovot   353
Rephaim, Valley of   353
Rephidim   114
Rest houses, Petra   460
Rhegium   428
Riba   275
Riblah, Ribleh   496
Rishpon   329
Rivers
   Adonis   483
   Arnon   454
   Awaj   487
   Barada   487
   Cherith, Brook   275
   Euphrates (Shatt el-Furat)   166
   Hiddekel   164-166
   Jabbok   446
   Jordan   275-277
   Litani   470
   Paran, Brook of   369
   Tiber (Tevere)   409
   Tigris   164-166
Robinson's Arch   225
Rock of Agony   242
Rock of Dighenis   29
Roman Agora, Athens   138-140
Rome   379-425
Rome, Ancient Central, and the
   Forum   386-387
Rome, North of   430-435
Rome, Northwest, the Pantheon,
   Saint Peter's   399-411
Rome, South of   425-430
Rome, Southeast, the Catacombs,
   Saint Paul's   397-399
Romulus and Remus   380
Rose granite shafts   84
Rose House Park   522
Rosetta   73
Rosh Haniqra   336
Rostra   392
Royal Annals   181, 291
Rumi, Melvâna Celaleddin
   553-554

Russian Compound   239, 259

Sa'ad, Kibbutz   350
Sabastiya   289-292
Sabil Quait Bey   222
Sacred and Profane Love   410,
   423
Safed, Safad   316
Saffuriya   300
Safita   498
Safsafot, H.   302
Saida   475-479
Saint, Sant', San, Santa, Santo.
   See also listing under
   following word
Saint Anne Seminary   226
Sakhne, el-   304
Saladin   471, 490
Salamis   22-23
Salem   214-268
Salerno   428
Salihiyah, As   503-504
Salonika   159-160
Salt   445-446
Samaria   289-292
Samaritans   287, 291
Samaritan Pentateuch   287
Samarra   175
Sammui, Es   365
Samson, birthplace of (Zorah)   343
Samu, Samua   365
Samuel, birthplace of (Ramah)
   281
San Pietro in Carcere   396
Sanatorium   148
Sant'Angelo, Bridge of   409
Santa Maria Antiqua   394
Santissimo Bambino   421
Sanur   292
Saqqara   66-68
Sarabiel Khadim, Sarabit el
   Khadim   113
Sarah, Bath of   361
Sarafand   479
Sarcophagi. *See* Tombs
Sargon II, city of (Khorsabad)
   183-184
Sardis   532
Sarepta   479
Saruhen   349
Sassanian Arch   185
Saturnalia   392
Scala Santa   228, 397, 418-419
Schools. *See* Universities
Scutari   525-526
Scythopolis   305
Sde Boker   367-368
Seal of Sheva   295-296
Search Foundation, Inc.   560

Seas
  of Behr Tabariyeh, Galilee
    306-308
  Dead 277
  of Galilee, Gennesar,
    Gennesaret, Kinneret,
    Chinnereth 306-308
  of the Plain 277
  Salt 277
  of Tiberias 306-308
Sebaste, Sebastia 289-292
Sede Boqer 367-368
Sednaya, Seidnaya 495
Sedom, Sedem, Sdom 372
Seilun 285
Seir 361
Sela, Selah, Petra 370, 456-460
Selçuk 539-547
Seleucia, Iraq 184
Seleucia, Syria 498-499
Seleucia (Samandaq), Turkey
    557-559
Selim, Barracks of 525
Senate House 392
Sennacherib before Lachish
    181-183
Sepphoris 300
Sermon on the Mount 310
Serpentine Column 517
Seti I, Stela of 305
Seven Sleepers of Ephesus 547
Severus, Septimius, Arch of 392
Shahba 495
Shalmaneser, Black Obelisk of
    167, 179, 291
Sharm el Sheikh 118
Sharon, Plain of 329
Shaubak 456
Shavei Zion 336
Shechem, Sechem 286-288
Shefaram 334
Sheikh Abd el-Gournah 90-92
Shelley 411
Shibah 365-367
Shiloh, Shilon 285
Shinar 168, 186
Shiqmona, Tell 332
Shittim 452
Shivta 369
Shu'fat 279-281
Shunem 302
Shuruppak 195
Shushan 202-203
Sidon 475-479
Sidr 112
Siena 435
Siir, Siair 361
Siloam Inscription 246, 522
Siloam, Pool of 246-248

Siloam Tunnel 246-248
Silwan 245
Simon the Tanner, House of 326
Sinai Peninsula 110-123
Sinjil 285
Sion of God 214-268
Sippar 185
Siq 457
Siracusa 430
Skala 160
Slaughter, Valley of 246-248
Smyrna 537-538
Socrates, Prison of 137
Sodom 372
Solem 304
Solfatara 426
Solomon, Pool of 361
Solomon's Pillars 370
Solomon's Pools 360
Solomon's Stables, Jerusalem
    223-224
Solomon's Stables, Megiddo 295
Solomon's Temple Stone Quarries
    254-256
Somaan, Anba 107
Sophia, Saint 519-520
Sorek 342
Sorrento 427-428
Soueida 495
Souks. See Markets
Sounion 158
Sounion Kouros 158
Sour 479-481
South from Amman 450-462
South of Beirut 475-481
South of Damascus 494-495
South of Jerusalem 353-377
South of Rome 425-430
South Stoa, Corinth 155
South, West, and North of the
    Old City (Jerusalem) 249-258
Southeast Rome, the Catacombs,
    Saint Paul's 397-399
Spafford Children's Center
    235-236
Spagna, Piazza di, Spanish Steps
    411
Spanish Square 411
Sparta 147
Sphinx, Alabaster 66
Sphinx, Great 65
Sphinxes, Avenue of Ram-Headed
    78, 79
Sports City, Beirut 470
S.P.Q.R. (Senatus Populusque
    Romanus) 383
Spring of the Sultan 273
Stadium, Athens 140
Stadium, Delphi 145

Stadium, Epidaurus 150
Stamboul 509-523
Standard of the Snake Goddess 318
Starting Gate 158
Stations of the Cross 228-231
  1. Pilate's Judgment Hall 228
  2. Where Jesus received the cross 228-229
  3. Where Jesus fell for the first time 229
  4. Where Jesus met his mother 229
  5. Where Simon the Cyrenian was compelled to bear the cross of Jesus 229
  6. Where Saint Veronica wiped Jesus' face 229
  7. Where Jesus fell the second time 229-230
  8. Where Jesus consoled the women of Jerusalem 230
  9. Where Jesus fell for the third time 230
  10-14. Church of the Holy Sepulcher 230
  10. Where Jesus was stripped of his garments 230-231
  11. Where Jesus was nailed to the cross (Golgotha) 230-231
  12. Where Jesus was crucified and died on the cross 231-233
  13. Where Jesus was taken down from the cross 231-233
  14. Where Jesus was laid in the chamber of the sepulcher and from there resurrected 231-233
Stephanos, Skeleton of Saint 116
Stoa of Attalus 138
Stoa of Eumenes 135
Stone in David's Tower, A 234
Stone of Unction 233
Stone upon which angels sat 233
Street Called Straight 491
Street of Columns, Jerash 447
Street of Columns, Palmyra 502
Street of Columns, Samaria 291
Subeita 369
Succoth 446
Suez, El Suweis 110
Sulam 302
Suleiman the Magnificent 514-515
Suleiman's Tekkiyeh 489
Sulphur Baths 502

Sumer 186, 195-196
Summer Pulpit 222
Susa, Susan, Susiana 202-203
Susita, Sussita 325
Suweida, As Suwayda, Es Suweida 495
Syagha 450
Sycaminium 332
Sychar 286
Syene 103-105
Synagogues
  Ancient Synagogue, Jericho 274
  Baba Tama 258
  of Baram 317
  Bet Yerah 308
  Bukharian 258
  Cairo, Old 52
  Capernaum 312
  at Dura-Europos 503
  of Dura-Europos, Damascus 489
  Hammath 308
  Hechal Shlomo 259
  Johanan ben Zakkai 226
  El Kursio 325
  Old Synagogue, Nazareth 299
  of Ramban 226
  Rome 390
  Samaritan 287
  Sardis 533
Syracuse 430
Syria 485-504

Taanach, Ta'annek 294
Taba 119
Tabariyeh 308-310
Tabgha, Tabigha 311
Tablun Caves 476-477
Tabularium 387, 392
Tadmor 501-502
Tahpanhes 64
Taiyibeh, et- 286
Tal at ed-Damm 269-271
Tanis 62
Tantura 332
Taq-Kisru 185
Tarichaea 310
Tarpeian Rock 387
Tarsus 556-557
Tartous, Tartus 498
Taş Suret 538
Tavium 555
Taylor Prism 167, 181-183, 214, 247-248, 346
Tekfur Sarayi 514
Tekoa 359-360
Tel Aviv 326-327
Telesterion 158

Tell 317
**Tell el 'Amarna Tablets and
    Letters** 72-75, 318, 339, 346,
    351, 482-483, 499
Tells
  Abil 321
  Abu Shahrain 200-202
  Abu Sifri 292-293
  Achzib 336
  el 'Amarna 73-75
  Arad 373
  Arshaf 329
  Avdat 368
  Balatah 286-288
  Beit-Shemesh 343
  Beit Zaida 314
  Belameh 293
  Bet-Shean 305
  Bet Yerah 308
  ed-Damiyeh 446
  Defneh 64
  Deir' Alla 446
  Dotha 293
  ed-Duweir 346-347
  Fara 349
  el Farah 289
  el Fukhkhar 334
  el-Ful 279-281
  Gamma 350
  Gat Hefer 300
  Gezer 340
  Hai 320
  Halaf 504
  el-Hamman 452
  Hariri 502-503
  Harmal 172
  Hazor 317-320
  Hessi (Hasi) 348-349
  Hum 311-312
  el-Husn 305
  Ibrahim 185
  el-Jemmel 350
  el-Jurn 374-377
  Kassile (Qasila) 327
  el-Kheleifeh 370-372
  Kouyoundjik 179-183
  Lakhish 346-347
  Main 365
  Malot, el-Melat 341
  Maresha 344
  el-Maqlub 292-293
  el-Muqayyar 195-200
  el-Mutesellim 295
  en-Nasbeh 281
  Nebi Mind 496
  Nebi Yunus 179-183
  el-Obeid 200
  el-Ohaimer 194
  el-Qadi 321

  el-Qedah 317-320
  Quades 320
  er-Retabeh 64
  es Safret 348
  es-Sandahannah 344-346
  es Seba 365-367
  Sharuhen 349
  esh-Sheikh-Madhkur 344
  Sheva 366
  Shiqmona 332
  es-Sultan 271-273
  Tequ'a 359
  Tsiglag 349
  al-Ubaid 200
  Zakariyeh 343
Temple Square on Mount Moriah
    217-218
Temple Tower, Borsippa 194
Temples
  Abu Simbel, Rock-Temple of
    108-109
  of Adad 193
  of Adonis 499
  of El-Amada 108
  of Amen 79
  of Amenertais 87
  of Antoninus and Faustina 394
  of Aphrodite, Corinth 153
  of Aphrodite, Paphos 28
  of Apollo, Corinth 153
  of Apollo, Delphi 145
  of Apollo, Didyma 551
  of Apollo Hylates, Curium 27
  of Apollo, Rhodes 162
  of Ares 138
  of Artemis, Eleusis 158
  of Artemis, Jerash 447
  of Artemis, Sardis 533
  of Artemis Orthia 147
  of Asclepias, Epidaurus 150
  of Asclepias, Pergamum
    529-531
  of Asclepias, Rome 390
  of Ashurnasirpal II 176-179
  to Aten 74
  to Athena, Miletus 548
  of Athena, Rhodes 162
  Augusteum 555
  of Augustus, Ankara 555
  of Augustus, Caesarea 331
  of Augustus, Rome 394
  of Augustus, Samaria 291
  of Baal, Ras Shamra 499
  of El Bab (Mirza Ali
    Muhammed) 334
  of Bacchus, Baalbek 474
  of Beit-el-Wali 108
  of Bel 502
  of Bel (Baal) Shameen 502

Temples, *continued*
of Belit Nin 193
of Caesar, Julius 394
Canaanite, Nahariya 336
of Castor and Pollux 394
Chalkioikos, Temple of Athena
147
of Dagon, Ras Shamra 499
of Dakka 108
of Debrid 108
of El Deir 458
of Deir el-Medina 89
Delphinium 550
of Demeter 529
of Dendur 108
of El-Derr 108
of Diana 542-543
to Dosares (god) 495
of Ekur 194
of Ellesiya 108
of Enki 199
Erechtheum 134-135
Esagila 192
of Eshmun 477
Etemenanki 191-192
of Fortuna Virile 390
Great Hypostyle Hall (Hall of
Columns) 79
Greco-Roman, Tarsus 557
of Gula (temple Z) 193
of Hadrian 546
of Haruar and Sebek 102
of Hathor 110-112
Hathor, Rock-Temple of 109,
113
at Hatra 176
of Hatshepsut 92-94
of Hephaestus 137-138
of Hera 148
of Hercules 430
of Herod 217
of Hestia Boulaea 546
of Homs 496
of Horus 102
Illumine 192
Ionic 529
of Ishtar 503
of Ishtar of Akkad (Agade,
Emeshdari) 191
of Jupiter, Baalbek 474
of Jupiter Capitolinus, Rome 387
of Jupiter, Damascus 490-491
to Jupiter, Jerusalem 231
of Kalabsha 108
of Kertassi 108
Khafre, Valley Temple of 65
of Khnum, Esna 102
of Khnum, Elephantine Island
105

of Khons 84
of Lake Nasser 107-109
of Luxor 76-78
of Marduk 192
of Santa Maria del Sole 390
of Mars Ultor 387
of Medinet Habu 87
Mentuhotep, Mortuary Temple
of 94
Merneptah, Mortuary Temple
of 89
of Minerva 387
of Mut 84
Nabataean 455
Nebuchadnezzar II and
Nabonidus, Harbor Temple
of 200
the New Year Festival, Temple
of 191
of Ninmakh (Ninmah, E-Makh)
190
of Ninurta (Temple of Ninib or
E-Patutila) 193
of Olympian Zeus, Athens 140
Orthia, Temple of Artemis 157
Pantheon 399-400
Parthenon, Temple of the
Virgins 131-134
at Petra 458
of Philae 105
of Poseidon, Isthmia 158
of Poseidon, Sounion 158
of Ptah, Karnak 84
of Ptah, Memphis 66
of Ramses II, Abydos 75
of Ramses III, Karnak 84
of Ramses III, Luxor 87
Rameseum 89-90
Red 195
Roman, Kanawat 495
of Romulus 394
Round 390
of Saturn 392
Second 217-218
of Serapide 426
of Serapis 546
of Seti I, Abydos 75
Seti I and Ramses III, Mortuary
Temple of 87, 89, 100
of Seti II, Karnak 79
at Shahba 495
of Shamash 193
Solomon's 217-218
of Sounion Athena 158
of Sybil 430
of Tafa 108
Theseum 137-138
Thutmose III, Mortuary Temple
of 89

Temples, *continued*
  of Trajan   387
  Trajan, built by   105
  of Venus, Baalbek   474
  of Venus Genitrix, Rome   387
  of Venus and Roma, Rome   394
  of Vespasian   392
  of Vesta, Rome   390, 394, 430
  of Wadi of Sebua   108
  White   195
  of the Wingless Victory (Athena
    Nike)   131
  of Yahweh   105-106
  of Zerubbabel   217
  of Zeus, Jerash   447
  of Zeus, Olympia   147
  of Zeus, Pergamum   531
  of Zeus, Rhodes   162
Tersous   556-557
Teveriya   308-310
Thales   549
Theaters, Amphitheaters, Odeums
  Agora Odeum, Athens   138
  Amman, amphitheater at   443
  Amman, odeum at   443
  at Apamea   497
  Argos, odeum of   148
  at Argos   148
  at Babylon   187
  at Beth-Shean   305
  at Bosra   494
  at Caesarea   330, 331
  Corinth, odeum of   153
  at Corinth   153
  at Curium   27
  at Delphi   145
  of Dionysus   135
  at Ein Gev   325
  at Ephesus   543-546
  at Epidaurus   150
  Flavian   391
  Herod Atticus, Odeum of   135
  at Jerash, north theater   449
  at Jerash, small theater   449
  at Jerash, south theater   447
  at Kanawat   495
  at Laodicea   536
  of Marcellus   390
  at Miletus   550
  at Mount Scopus   236
  National Theater, Athens   141
  at Palmyra   502
  at Perga   552
  Pergamum, amphitheater at
    529
  Pergamum, Greek theater at
    529
  Pericles, Odeum of   135
  at Petra (Selah)   457

  at Pozzuoli   426
  at Puteoli   426
  at Rhodes   162
  at Salamis   23
  at Samaria   291
  San Carlo, Naples   427
  at Shahba   495
  at Smyrna   538
  at Sparta   147
  at Syracuse   430
  at Tsipori   300
Thebes   76
Thebes, Necropolis of   87-101
Thebez   292
Thessalonica, Thessalonike   159
Thieves' crosses   233
Thinis   75
This   75
Tholos, Athens   138
Thorn Puller   423
Thrace   159
Three Taverns   425
Threshing Floor   218
Thutmose III, Festival Hall of   84
Thyatira   531-532
Tiberias   308-310
Tibur   430
Tiglath-pileser III, Tablets of   181
Tikrit   175
Tile Kiosk   522
Timn'a   370
Timnath, Khirbet Timna   343
Timnath, Timnath-Serah   286
Timothy, home of (Lystra)   553
2 Timothy   381
Tiryns   148
Tirzah   289
Titus, Arch of   394-396
Tivoli   430
Tombs, Catacombs, Cemeteries,
    Crypts, Graves, Mastabas,
    Mausoleums, Necropolises,
    Sarcophagi, Sepulchers
  of Aaron   370
  Absalom's Pillar, or Tomb   244
  of Abu-al-Ala al-Maarri   497
  of Agamemnon   151
  Agha Khan III, Mausoleum of
    107
  Saint Agnes, catacombs of
    398, 421
  of Rabbi Akiva   310
  Alexander the Great,
    sarcophagus of   477, 522
  of Alyattes   533
  of Amenemhab (no. 85)   90
  of Amenhotep II (no. 35)
    98-101
  of Amenhotep III (no. 23)   100

Tombs, *continued*
of Amran ibn-Ali 192-193
of Prince Amunkhopeshfu 89
Anfoushy (Anfushi) Necropolis
  72
of Artaxerxes I 203
Atatürk, mausoleum of 555
Augustus, mausoleum of 411
of Baal-haness, Meir, Rabbi 309
Baybars, Mameluke Sultan,
  Mausoleum of 308
Beehive Tomb 151
at Belevi, mausoleum and tomb
  539
Bin Tepe, necropolis 533
British War Cemetery 236
of the Caliphs and Mamelukes
  53
Saint Calixtus, catacombs of
  398
Campo Santo 433
Capuchins, cemetery of the 420
Castel Sant'Angelo 408-409
Catacombs 398
of Cecilia Metella 398
of Celsus, Gaius Julius 545
of Charalambos 538
Columbaria in the Vigna Codini
  398-399
Corinthian Tomb 458
of Cyrus the Great 204
of Daniel 203
of Darius I 203
of Darius II 203
of David 251-252
Domitilla Catacombs 398
of Enne (no. 81) 90
Ephesus, necropolis of 546-547
of Ezekiel 194
of Gaius Julius Celsus 545-546
of Gamaliel 353
Garden Tomb (Protestant
  Version) 254
Grotto of Saint James 244
of Gyges 533
Hadrian's Mausoleum 408
of Haggai, Malachi, and
  Zechariah 241
of Hatshepsut (no. 20) 100
of Harmhab (no. 57) 100
of Harmhab (no. 78) 90
Herod's family tomb 252
of Hillel the Elder 317
Holy Sepulcher 233-236
Honat Hatun Tomb 556
Jamblichos Tower 502
of Jehoshaphat 244
Jesus, sepulcher of 231-233
of Jethro (Shu'eib) 310

Jewish Cemetery 242
Saint John, Crypt of 335
of Joseph 286
of Joseph of Arimathea 231,
  233, 257, 282
of the Judges 267
of Khaemhat (no. 57) 90
of Prince Khaemwas 89
of the Kings, Jerusalem 257
of the Kings, Paphos 29
Kom el Shuqafa, Catacombs of
  71
Kumbets 556
Lion 460
Lycian, Myra 552
Lycian, Sidon 477
Sultan Mahmud II, Mausoleum
  of 516
of Maimonides 309
of Makhlouf, Sharbel 483
El Malek Muzaffar, Mausoleum
  of 497
Maltepe 531
the Mameluke Sultan Baybars,
  Mausoleum of 308
of Sheikh Ma'ruf 171
Mausoleum of Mausolus,
  Bodrum 551
of Mary (the Virgin) 243
Mazor, Roman mausoleum
  342
of the Medici 433
of Rabbi Meir Baal-haness
  308-309
of Menna (no. 69) 90
Mereruka, Mastaba of 68
of Merneptah (no. 8) 100
Military Cemetery, Jerusalem
  265
of Mohammed Ali 53
of Nakht (no. 52) 90
of Neferhotep (no. 50) 90
of Nefertari 89
of the Nobles, Aswan 107
of the Nobles, Luxor 90-92
Palace Tomb, Petra 458
of Pancratti and Valerii 399
of the Patriarchs 361
of Pentamenopet (no. 33)
  90-92
Pharaohs, tombs of the first 75
of Polycarp 538
of the priestly house of Hezir
  244
of Priscilla 398
Priscilla Catacombs 398
Protestant Cemetery, Rome
  399
Ptah-Hotep, Mastaba of 68

Tombs, *continued*
of Rachel   354
of Ramose (no. 55)   90
of Ramses I (no. 16)   100
of Ramses III (no. 11)   100
of Ramses IV (no. 2)   100
of Ramses V and VI (no. 9)   100
of Ramses IX (no. 6)   100
of Rekh-mere (no. 100)   90
Roxelana, mausoleum of   515
Royal Cemetery, Ur   199
Royal Tombs, Ur   196-197
of the Sages   309-310
Saladin, Mausoleum of   490
of Saleh, Sheikh Nebi   115
Sanhedrin Tombs   267
of Sardanapalus   557
Satrap Tomb   477
Scipio's family tomb   397
Saint Sebastian Catacombs   398
of Sennufer (no. 96)   90
Serapeum, burial site for Apis
    bulls   68
of Seti I (no. 17)   98-99
of Seti II (no. 15)   100
of Setnakht (no. 14)   100
Shebna, Royal Tomb of   245
of Sheikh Avrekh   298
of Simon the Just   258
Suleiman, Mausoleum of   515
of Tantalus   538
at Tell el'Amarna   74
Thebes, Necropolis of   87-101
Thousand Hills   533
of the Three Brothers   502
Ti, Mastaba of   68
of Titi   89
Tomb 33: Pentamenopet   90-92
of Tos   533
of the Towers   502
of Tutankhamen (no. 62)   95-98
of the Unknown Soldier, Athens
    141
of the Unknown Soldier,
    Baghdad   172
of the Unknown Soldier, Rome
    386
Unknown Soldier Monument,
    Jerusalem   254
Ur, Royal Tombs of   197-199
Urn Tomb   458
of Userhat (no. 56)   90
Weeping Women's Tomb   477,
    522
of Xerxes I   203
Yahia, Mausoleum of   183-184
Yigma Tepe Tomb   531
of Zebulon   477
of Zechariah   244-245

of Zobeidah   171
Topkapi, Topkapi Sarayi
    522-523
Tor, el Tur   118
Tortosa   498
Tower of Ascension   239
Tower of the Winds   138-140
Trajan
    Column of   386-387
    Forum of   386-387
    Fountain of   546
    Trajan's Baths   396
Transfiguration   302, 322, 416
Treasure houses, Delphi   145
Treasury, Persepolis   203
Treasury, Petra   457
Trevi Fountain   399
Tribune   419
Tribune (Bema)   155
Tripoli, Tripolis   483-484
Triumphal Arch, Damascus
    490-491
Triumphal Arch, Jerash   447
Triumphal Arch, Petra   458
Trogyllium   548
Troy   526
Truman Research Center   236
Tsefat   316
Tsipori   300
Tubas   292
Tubeleth Drahab   446
Turan   301
Turkey   505-560
Turmus-Aya   285
Tveriah   308-310
Twelve Stones   288
Tyre   479-481
Tyre, Ladder of   336
Tyropoeon Valley   246

Ubaid, al-   200
Ugarit   499-500
Um el Biyara, Petra   458
Umm-Jerar   350
Um Qeis   450
United States Embassy, Cairo   52
United States Embassy, Nicosia
    19
Universities, Colleges, Schools
    Adlia School   490
    Ain Shams University   49
    American University, Beirut
        467
    American University, Cairo   54
    Athens, University of   141
    Cairo University   49
    City University, Rome   397
    Damascus University   489
    Hebrew University   264

Universities, *etc., continued*
  Hebrew University on Mount
    Scopus 236
  Institute for Desert Research,
    Sde Boker 367-368
  Islamic University 53
  Istanbul, University of 515
  Lebanese University 467
  Al Mustansiria, College of 171
  Saint Joseph University 469
  School of Medicine, Beirut 469
  Technion, Haifa 333
  Tel Aviv University 326
  Zahirieh School 490
Upper Room of the Last Supper 251
Urasalimu 214-268
Urgup 556
Ur of the Chaldees 195-200
Urim 349
Ur-Nammu, courtyard area of
  (E-Yemen-Ni-Gur) 197
Ur-Nammu, Temple Tower of
  196-197
Uruk, Unug 195
Üsküdar 525-526

Valenia 498
Valens, Aqueduct of 512
Valleys
  of Armageddon 295
  of the Dancers 285
  of Hinnom 246-248
  of Inscriptions 119
  of Jezreel 295
  of Kings, Jerusalem 244
  of the Kings, Luxor 94-101
  of the Queens 89
  of Salt 277
  of Slaughter 246-248
  of Sorek 342
  of the Thieves 284
  of the Tombs 203
Varosha 25
Vatican City 411-417
Vatican Grottos 408
Venetian Column 18
Venezia Square 386
Venus (Aphrodite), Birth of 424
Venus, birthplace of (Paphos) 28
Venus, birthplace of (Petra tou
  Romiou) 27-28
Venus of Capua 427
Venus of Cyrene 424
Veroia, Verroia, Veria 159
Vesuvius 427
Via Dolorosa 226-227
Via Sacra 392
Victor Emmanuel II, monument
  to 386

Villa Adriana 430
Villa Borghese 410
Villa d'Este 430
Viri Galilaei 237
Virgin, Fountain of the, Jerusalem
  245-246
Virgin Fountain, Nazareth 299
Virginity, Column of 512
Virgin's Tree 62
Volterra 435

Wadis
  Amud 314-315
  el Arabah 460-461
  el Deir 458-460
  Ein Avdat 368-369
  Feiran 114
  Gharandal 113
  Hasa 455
  Hinnom 248
  Jirafi 369
  Karak 455
  Kelt 271
  el-Maktab 113
  el Mojib 453
  Musa 456
  Qilt 271
  er-Rababi 248
  Rum 462
  Ruman 369
  es-Sant 344
  es-Sarar 342
  el Sheikh 115
  of Writings 113
  Yabis (Brook Cherith), Israel 275
  Yabis, Jordan 449-450
  Zerqa 446
  Zohar 373
Wailing Wall 224-225
Walled Pyramid Column 517
War Memorials in the Jerusalem
  Corridor 339
Warka 195
Watchtowers 285
Waterfall, Ha Tannur 320
Water System, Gibeon 282
Water System, Hazor 318
Water System, Masada 374
Water System, Megiddo 295
Water System, Taanach 294
Water Tank, Salamis 23
Water Tunnel, Gezer 340
Water Wheels, Roman, Hamath
  497
Weeping Women's Tomb 477
Weizmann Institute of Science
  353
Wells
  of Abraham, Beersheba 365

Wells, *continued*
  of Abraham, Hebron   361
  of Blood   509-512
  King David's   356
  of Eliezer and Rebekah   559-560
  of Harod   304
  Hot Wells, Tiberias   309
  Jacob's   286
  of Joseph   52
  Mary's, Nazareth   299
  of Moses, Aiyun Musa, Egypt
    112
  of Pirene   155
  Sacred, Corinth   155
Weset   76
West Bank, Luxor   87-101
West Coast from Joppa to
    Lebanon   325-337
West and Southwest of Jerusalem
    337-353
Western Wall   224-225
Whirling Dervishes   554
White Tower   341
Wilson's Arch   225
Window of Saint Paul   492-493
Winged bull   178-179
Wood of Ephraim   449

Xenophanes   538

Yad Mordechai   351
Yad Vashem Memorial   265
Yadin, Yigael   374, 377
Yafo   325-326
Yalo   339
Yalvac   554
Yamnia   353
Yavne, Yabneel, Yavniel, Yavneh
    352-353
Yavne Yam   353

Yconium   553-554
Yehiam, Kibbutz   336
Yemin Moshe   216, 252
Yerebatan Sarayi   512
Yeshiva of the Diaspora   252
Yilanli Sütun   517
Yizre'el   302
YMCA Building, New Jerusalem
    259
Yodefat   334
Yorghan Tepe   184
Yotapata   334

Zaafarana   110
Zadokite fragment   493
Zamalik   49
Zarephath   479
Zarin   302
Zarka Ma'in, Zarqa Main   451
Zedekiah, Cave of   254-256
Zefat   316
Zeno, birthplace of (Larnaca)
    25-26
Zeno, bust of   26
Zerka Main   450
Zeus, Altar of   529
Zeus of the Agora, altar to   138
Zidon   475-479
Ziggurat, Mari   503
Ziggurat, Shushan   203
Ziglag (Ziklag)   349
Zion   214-268
Ziph   365
Zohar, "Book of Splendor"   317
Zoldera   553
Zoo, Biblical, Jerusalem   267
Zoo, Rome   410
Zoo, Tel Aviv   327
Zoological Gardens, Cairo   49-51
Zorah   342-343